An Agrarian History of South Asia

David Ludden's book offers a comprehensive historical framework for understanding the regional diversity of agrarian South Asia. Adopting a long-term view of history, it treats South Asia not as a single civilisation territory, but rather as a patchwork of agrarian regions, each with its own social, cultural, and political histories. The discussion begins during the first millennium, when institutions of ritual, conquest, and patriarchy formed an archipelago of farming regimes that steadily displaced and assimilated pastoral and tribal communities. It goes on to consider how, from the sixteenth to the nineteenth century, the concept of modern territoriality evolved as farmers pushed agriculture to its physical limits and states created permanent rights to all the land. Subsequent chapters focus on the development of agrarian capitalism in village societies, which emerged under the British and which formed the bedrock of the modern political economy. In contemporary South Asia, the book argues, economic development and social movements continue to reflect the influence of agrarian localism and the shifting fortunes of agrarian regions with histories which can be traced back to medieval times.

As a comparative synthesis of the literature on agrarian regimes in South Asia, the book promises to be a valuable resource for students of agrarian and regional history, as well as of comparative world history.

DAVID LUDDEN teaches South Asian and world history at the University of Pennsylvania. His publications include *Making India Hindu: Community, Conflict, and the Politics of Democracy* (1996) and *Peasant History in South India* (1985).

THE NEW CAMBRIDGE HISTORY OF INDIA

General editor GORDON JOHNSON

President of Wolfson College, and Director, Centre of South Asian Studies,
University of Cambridge

Associate editors C. A. BAYLY

Vere Harmsworth Professor of Imperial and Naval History, University of Cambridge,
and Fellow of St Catharine's College

and JOHN F. RICHARDS

Professor of History, Duke University

Although the original **Cambridge History of India**, published between 1922 and 1937, did much to formulate a chronology for Indian history and describe the administrative structures of government in India, it has inevitably been overtaken by the mass of new research over the last sixty years.

Designed to take full account of recent scholarship and changing conceptions of South Asia's historical development, **The New Cambridge History of India** is published as a series of short, self-contained volumes, each dealing with a separate theme and written by one or two authors. Within an overall four-part structure, thirty-one complementary volumes in uniform format will be published. Each will conclude with a substantial bibliographical essay designed to lead non-specialists further into the literature.

The four parts planned are as follows:

I   The Mughals and Their Contemporaries

II   Indian States and the Transition to Colonialism

III   The Indian Empire and the Beginnings of Modern Society

IV   The Evolution of Contemporary South Asia

A list of individual titles in preparation will
be found at the end of the volume.

THE NEW CAMBRIDGE HISTORY OF INDIA

IV · 4

An Agrarian History of South Asia

DAVID LUDDEN
University of Pennsylvania

CAMBRIDGE
UNIVERSITY PRESS

PUBLISHED BY THE PRESS SYNDICATE OF THE UNIVERSITY OF CAMBRIDGE
The Pitt Building, Trumpington Street, Cambridge CB2 1RP

CAMBRIDGE UNIVERSITY PRESS
The Edinburgh Building, Cambridge CB2 2RU, United Kingdom
http://www.cup.cam.ac.uk
40 West 20th Street, New York, NY 10011–4211, USA   http://www.cup.org
10 Stamford Road, Oakleigh, Melbourne 3166, Australia

First published 1999

Printed in the United Kingdom at the University Press, Cambridge

Typeset in Garamond 10.5/13pt [CE]

A catalogue record for this book is available from the British Library

Library of Congress cataloguing in publication data
Ludden, David E.
An agrarian history of South Asia / David Ludden.
p. cm. – (The new Cambridge history of India)
Includes bibliographical references (p.   ).
ISBN 0-521-36424-8 hb
1. Agriculture – Economic aspects – India.
2. Agriculture – India – History.
I. Title. II. Series.
DS436.N47 1999
630′.954–dc21   98-43856 CIP

ISBN 0 521 36424 8 hardback

FOR ROCHONA

CONTENTS

GENERAL EDITOR'S PREFACE

The New Cambridge History of India covers the period from the beginning of the sixteenth century. In some respects it marks a radical change in the style of Cambridge Histories, but in others the editors feel that they are working firmly within an established academic tradition.

During the summer of 1896, F. W. Maitland and Lord Acton between them evolved the idea for a comprehensive modern history. By the end of the year the Syndics of the University Press had committed themselves to the *Cambridge Modern History*, and Lord Acton had been put in charge of it. It was hoped that publication would begin in 1899 and be completed by 1904, but the first volume in fact came out in 1902 and the last in 1910, with additional volumes of tables and maps in 1911 and 1912.

The *History* was a great success, and it was followed by a whole series of distinctive Cambridge Histories covering English Literature, the Ancient World, India, British Foreign Policy, Economic History, Medieval History, the British Empire, Africa, China and Latin America; and even now other new series are being prepared. Indeed, the various Histories have given the Press notable strength in the publication of general reference books in the arts and social sciences.

What has made the Cambridge Histories so distinctive is that they have never been simply dictionaries or encyclopaedias. The Histories have, in H. A. L. Fisher's words, always been 'written by an army of specialists concentrating the latest results of special study'. Yet as Acton agreed with the Syndics in 1896, they have not been mere compilations of existing material but original works. Undoubtedly many of the Histories are uneven in quality, some have become out of date very rapidly, but their virtue has been that they have consistently done more than simply record an existing state of knowledge: they have tended to focus interest on research and they have provided a massive stimulus to further work. This has made their publication doubly worthwhile and has distinguished them intellectually from other sorts of reference book. The editors of *The New Cambridge History of India* have acknowledged this in their work.

The original *Cambridge History of India* was published between 1922 and 1937. It was planned in six volumes, but of these, volume 2 dealing with the period between the first century AD and the Muslim invasion of India never appeared. Some of the material is still of value, but in many respects it is now out of date. The last fifty years have seen a great deal of new research on India, and a striking feature of recent work has been to cast doubt on the validity of the quite arbitrary chronological and categorical way in which Indian history has been conventionally divided.

The editors decided that it would not be academically desirable to prepare a new *History of India* using the traditional format. The selective nature of research on Indian history over the past half-century would doom such a project from the start and the whole of Indian history could not be covered in an even or comprehensive manner. They concluded that the best scheme would be to have a *History* divided into four overlapping chronological volumes, each containing short books on individual themes or subjects. Although in extent the work will therefore be equivalent to a dozen massive tomes of the traditional sort, in form *The New Cambridge History of India* will appear as a shelf full of separate but complementary parts. Accordingly, the main divisions are between I. *The Mughals and their Contemporaries*, II. *Indian States and the Transition to Colonialism*, III. *The Indian Empire and the Beginnings of Modern Society*, and IV. *The Evolution of Contemporary South Asia.*

Just as the books within these volumes are complementary so too do they intersect with each other, both thematically and chronologically. As the books appear they are intended to give a view of the subject as it now stands and to act as a stimulus to further research. We do expect the *New Cambridge History of India* to be not the last word on the subject but an essential voice in the continuing discussion about it.

ACKNOWLEDGEMENTS

This book has taken a long time to finish. I thank everyone connected with *the New Cambridge History of India* for their patience, especially Chris Bayly and Marigold Acland. Along the way, my thinking has been improved by Romila Thapar, Muzaffar Alam, Neeladri Bhattacharya, Sugata Bose, Ayesha Jalal, Sanjay Subrahmanyam, Tosun Aricanli, Rosalind O'Hanlon, Burton Stein, Nick Dirks, Sheldon Pollock, James Boyce, Gyan Prakash, Dina Siddiqi, Ahmed Kamal, Michelle Maskiell, David Rudner, Binayak Sen, Zillur Rahman, Arun Bandopadhyay, M. M. Islam, and David Washbrook. Cynthia Talbot, Ahmed Kamal, Robert Nichols, James R. Hagen, David Gilmartin, M. M. Islam, Minoti Chakravarty-Kaul, R. Vasavi, and K. Sivaramakrishnan gave me unpublished manuscripts that were vitally important. I benefited from seminars at the Yale Center for Agrarian Studies, University of Calcutta, the University of Melbourne, the University of New South Wales, Curtin University, the University of Chicago, Jawaharlal Nehru University, Columbia University, the Indian Institute of Technology (Madras), The Power and Participation Research Centre (Dhaka), and the University of Pennsylvania. I have used research funding from the National Endowment for the Humanities, the American Philosophical Society, the American Institute for Indian Studies, the University of Pennsylvania, and Fulbright-Hays. I thank the professional staff at the National Archives of India, the Library of Congress, the Tamil Nadu Archives, the National Archives of Bangladesh, the National Library of India, the India Office Library and Records, and the Madras Institute for Development Studies. The library staff at the University of Pennsylvania are a constant help, and I especially thank Kanta Bhatia and David Nelson. Thanks to Robert Nichols, Supti Bhattacharya, Amy Iwata, Vivek Bhandari, Sarah Diamond, Jeremie Dufault, and Teresa Watts for their able research assistance.

xiii

INTRODUCTION

This book is about history's attachment to land. It considers the present day in the context of the past two millennia, because a wide historical view is needed to appreciate the ideas that shape contemporary mentalities, and because earthly environments today are being shaped by long-term historical forces. As the book goes on, I consider some elements of Eurasian history and introduce some ideas about geography, technology, patriarchy, ritual, ecology, and other subjects that situate South Asian farmers in their wider world. I also indicate that more research into the historical dynamics of territoriality is needed to improve our knowledge of culture and political economy. But, like other volumes in *The New Cambridge History of India*, the main goal of this book is to draw together research by many scholars on a coherent set of historical themes without rehearsing academic debates or piling up citations. The bibliographical essay is a guide to relevant literature that sprawls across the disciplines of history, anthropology, economics, geography, political science, and rural sociology. I apologise for not covering many regions well enough and particularly for slighting Assam, Baluchistan, Chhattisgarh, Kerala, Nepal, Orissa, and Sri Lanka. This failure results partly from the state of research but mostly from my own inability to compile appropriate data in the time and space allotted. For these reasons, territories in Bangladesh, India, and Pakistan form my central subject matter.

The marginality of agrarian history demands attention. It is not unique to South Asia, but proportionately more books do seem to treat the agrarian past in Europe, the Americas, Russia, China, and Japan. Though culture and political economy are not more detached from the land in South Asia than elsewhere, scholars would seem to think so. This may reflect a more general alienation. As the urban middle-class intelligentsia came into being in the modern world economy, they wove the countryside into their epics of nationality, and, to this day, agrarian history evokes interest to the extent that country folk represent national identity. Everywhere, agrarian history is submerged in the historiography of nations and states. We need to keep this in mind because historical knowing is a force in modern transformations of the world and a tool for making the country in the image of the nation. National histories have formed territoriality and incorporated rustic folk into the project of modernity, so the past of its peasantry maps the rise of national power on the land. Modernity's general alienation from its agrarian environment pervades agrarian studies, and when combined with orientalist stereotypes, it simply pushed peasants more deeply into the margins of history in South Asia than elsewhere. Because villages there seemed totally traditional, lacking any inherent drive to modernity, they were assumed to have no actual history, only timeless permanence. Studies of the rural past thus recounted the incorporation and subordination of villagers by city folk. Urban elites made nations, and they made the history that brought South Asia from ancient times to the present. The village past seemed to be a permanent affliction.

There is much to learn on the margins of history. Most evidence on the agrarian past continues to be unused today, not because it is inaccessible but because it has seemed uninteresting and unimportant for the history of modernity; and we can use this neglect to measure the blinkers of modern minds. If we want to understand modernity as a moment of human history, agrarian history is a good place to look and South Asia is a good place to work, because here modern machineries of knowing have mangled less of the original data. In Europe, the Americas, and East Asia, scholars have constructed rural history as the legacy and memory of modernity and they have built national identity on a solid agrarian footing. In South Asia, domineering epistemologies of nationality have not paved over so much of the landscape or cemented together the past of nations and of peasants so comprehensively. Villages fit much more firmly and neatly into national histories in France, England, the United States, China, and Japan than they do in Sri Lanka, Nepal, Pakistan, India, and Bangladesh. The lasting force of regional diversity in South Asia derives from the fact that, historically, its agrarian territories have marched to different drummers, and even in different directions. Scholars have repeatedly argued that agrarian South Asia evades the discipline of progress. All the histories of all the empires and nations in South Asia could never capture the history of all its peoples.

With this in view, I want to explore agrarian history outside modernity's construction of the past. Life on the land seems to entangle, confront, and suffuse modernity without being overwhelmed or absorbed by it; and, when urban middle-class scholars write agrarian history, we stumble repeatedly and awkwardly upon this stubborn, enticing otherness. The misty longevity and persistent localism of agrarian history resist narration and escape the grids of time and space that define national history. Narratives cannot untangle all the rhythms of agrarian change or trace all the lines of movement in apparently stable rustic routines. Agrarian South Asia thus provides a historical vantage point from which to reconsider modernity and nationality. For this purpose, we need an extended chronology for tracing the rise of contemporary conditions. In this book, history's trajectory is not moving toward national independence or national development but rather into the trends that influence agrarian environments today. These trends represent other histories that are still unfolding inside national states but outside their control, in small-scale agrarian territories which have never been fully defined by modern nationality. These territories have their own histories in which local struggles are tangled up with national and international institutions and also with global networks of power, mobility, and communication.

In studies that cover long periods of time, semantic problems abound. I employ place names from different epochs – calling ancient Kosala 'the region of Lucknow' or 'Central Uttar Pradesh', for instance – to enable the reader to keep track of various terms that attach to places over millennia. This anachronism also encourages a reader to imagine a distant past alive in the present; and, indeed, people build a future on a past that never really disappears. Common terms that I use for regions (Awadh, Deccan, Bengal, Punjab, Assam, Uttarakhand, Gujarat, Telangana, and such) refer broadly to old regions rather than to the strictly bounded territories of today. Modern cities and towns are useful landmarks, and contemporary political and administrative territories are convenient markers for large regions in all times. Modern district names help to identify small regions, but we need to keep in mind that district names and boundaries change, as do their identities within states and nations, especially after 1947. I use the district names for these geographical areas found in Joseph E. Schwartzberg, *A Historical Atlas of South Asia* (second impression, Oxford University Press, New Delhi, 1992, p. 79).[1] Many district names continued to be used after

---

[1] For regional names during the historical periods before and after 1200, see Joseph E. Schwartzberg, *A Historical Atlas of South Asia*, New Delhi, 1992, p. 137.

3

1947 – though they have been changed with increasing frequency in the past twenty years – and whenever possible I refer to districts without naming the national state within which they lie. This helps to avoid the impression that the boundaries of contemporary states were inscribed on the agrarian landscape before 1947. The relationship between national territories and agrarian territory is a subject for discussion in chapters 1 and 4. When I use states within the Republic of India to discuss times before they were formed, I do so only for the purpose of location; and this does not imply that these political boundaries had some incipient historical reality in the distant past. The historical formation of modern political regions is discussed in chapters 3 and 4.

Many terms need to be handled carefully because they resonate with contemporary politics. When I refer to the Tamil, Telugu, or Kannada country, or to 'the Marathi-speaking region', I am simply referring to a widely recognised linguistic region, rather than to a linguistic state or cultural territory. The Tamil country, for instance, has always included many non-Tamil speakers, and much of its important literature is composed in languages other than Tamil. Referring to the south-eastern part of the coastal plain as 'the Tamil coast' does not mean that this is the only way or the best way to refer to this region; it is merely the most convenient for me here; and it also serves to remind us that agriculture occurs within culture. Similar caveats pertain to all sites with new meanings in cultural politics: I use 'Bombay' rather than 'Mumbai' because it is more recognisable. I use 'Madras' rather than 'Chennai', 'Uttarakhand' rather than 'the Himalayan districts of Uttar Pradesh'. Terms for agricultural landscapes that pertain across the whole period of my discussion are defined in the last section of chapter 1. These landscapes are not meant to displace other regional terminologies; they simply help to organise regional complexity for an agrarian historical geography.

Personal names do not pose serious problems and their most commonly used forms are employed here. The names of groups, dynasties, and some events (such as the wars of 1857) are more troublesome. Group names often appear in personal names and they are almost always necessary for locating people in society. But in long stretches of historical time, groups move in and out of existence and group names change meaning very drastically. For instance, the term 'Rajput' acquired its modern meaning from the sixteenth century (chapter 3), but with suitable caveats, and despite the controversial character of origin stories, I use this terms to indicate group character-istics, if not subjective identity, over a longer period of time. Other group names – such as Vellala, Jat, Kunbi, Maratha, and Marava – have also changed meanings but they can be used in a similar way. When I refer to the distant past of social groups whose present identities are marked by such terms, and when I speculate as to their social composition or activities before modern times, I often discuss the past in terms that people in these groups will not endorse today. The creators of social identities recount collective experience in terms that become part of human experience, but historians can tell other tales to indicate other aspects of the past. This difference is not just one of perspective, or a feature of insider and outsider subject positions. Because history reshuffles and redefines perspectives, we need to trace the emergence of subject positions historically, and this is most difficult when they are in the making, which many are today. Quickly changing, hotly contested social identities pose the most serious problem, for instance with groups identified as Untouchables, Har-ijans, and Dalits. I use the term 'untouchable' here to refer to the caste condition of this lowest-ranked group in the *varna* scheme, and 'harijan' and 'dalit' to refer to their representation and identity within modern political movements. Though the term 'adivasi' is preferable in our contemporary political context, the terminology of 'tribes' and 'tribal peoples' is much more common in the literature; it captures a critical feature of the cultural distinctiveness of these groups, and it attaches to the official census and legal category of 'scheduled tribe'. I use 'adivasi', therefore, to refer to tribal peoples in their contemporary condition of political activity; and these tribal mobilizations form a theme in agrarian history that is central for understanding long-term change. Using any term to refer to a social group or population has the additional pitfall of implying that everyone in a group is the same, that collective identities are built into individuals, and that terms which have by convention come to identify a group are used by people in the group to represent themselves. Group names are deployed for various political, cultural, and rhetorical ends and terms that are used here have various connotations which cannot be con-trolled by any tricks of phrasing. Similarly, terms for religious group-ings are quite contentious today, and I try to avoid using them except as general labels of cultural location.

CHAPTER 1

AGRICULTURE

Most of human history in South Asia is a feature of life on the land, but most documents that we use to write agrarian history concern the state. Kautilya's *Arthasastra* set the tone by putting farming and herding under the heading of state revenue. Hundreds of thousands of stone and copper inscriptions appear in the first millennium of the Common Era (CE). Scattered across the land from Nepal to Sri Lanka, they documented agrarian conditions, but their purpose was rather to constitute medieval dynasties. After 1300, official documents narrate more and more powerful states. In the sixteenth century, Mughal sultans built South Asia's first empire of agrarian taxation, and their revenue assessments, collections, and entitlements produced more data on agrarian conditions than any previous regime. In 1595, Abu-l Fazl's *Ai'n-i Akbari* depicted agriculture in accounts of imperial finance. After 1760, English officials did the same. After 1870, nationalists rendered the country as part of the nation, and since 1947 agriculture has been a measure of national development. For two millennia, elites have recorded agrarian facts to bolster regimes and to mobilise the opposition, so we inherit a huge archive documenting agrarian aspects of historical states.

Over the centuries, however, agrarian history has also moved along in farming environments, outside the institutional structure of states, almost always connected in one way or another to state authority, but embedded basically in the everyday life of agricultural communities. Dynasties expand into agrarian space. Empires incorporate farm and forest, using various degrees and types of power, gaining here, losing there, adapting to local circumstances and modifying state institutions to embrace new regions of cultivation. Modern nations appropriate agrarian identity and territory. But polities condition agriculture without determining the logic of farming or the character of agrarian life; and country folk always seem to elude state control, even as some locals are sinews of state power in the village. Rulers and farmers – state power and agrarian social forces – interact historically and shape one another and, in this context, states tell only part of the story of the agrarian past. Scholars need documentation produced outside the state and a critical perspective on official records to situate the historical imagination at the slippery articulation of state institutions and agrarian communities.

HISTORICITY

Maintaining this kind of perspective – seeing agrarian history askew of state power and reading official sources against the grain – becomes more difficult for the period after 1870, when documentation also becomes most plentiful. A respected modern scholarly canon and a vast modern official archive have colluded to make it difficult for scholars to imagine that agrarian *history* – as distinct from timeless, age-old, village tradition and peasant culture – has any real autonomy from the power of the state. Villagers, farmers, agricultural workers, forest cultivators, and pastoral peoples often appear in the dramas of history, but they most often appear to be moving on history's stage in reaction to state activity or in response to elite initiative, obeying or resisting controls imposed upon them by state institutions and by powerful, autonomous elites. The rustic world – both in itself and for itself – appears in such accounts to be an ancient repetition. Agrarian folk appear as a negative mirror image of all that is urban, industrial, and modern; not as makers of history, but rather as inhabitants of history, endowed with mentalities and memories which can be recovered, but not with creative powers to transform their world. Such an appearance took hold in the nineteenth century, as a very long trend of increasing state power in South Asia accelerated dramatically under British rule. A turning point occurred around 1870, by which time the institutions of imperial bureaucracy, ideologies of development, and analytical sciences of management had been combined with industrial technology to form the material and cultural context for agrarian life that we call modernity. Until then, official documents still recorded aspects of agrarian societies that eluded state control and official understanding, but, from this point onward, texts render the country-side through the lens of the modern state's minute and comprehensive managerial empiricism. Agrarian sites now appear as standardised objects of administration, policy debate, and political struggle. Idiosyncratic local histories and old agrarian territories were in effect buried by imperial modernity under mountains of homogeneous, official data, as villages, towns, districts, and provinces became standard units for conventional studies of politics, economics, culture, and society. The non-modern quality of the agrarian past became quaint stuff for gazetteers and folklore, irrelevant for history except as a reflection of archaic peasant memory and tradition – marginalia – cut off from the modern historical mainstream.

Modernity's understanding of the 'agrarian' focused first and foremost on matters of state policy, agricultural production, law and order, and resistance and rebellion. Agrarian history appeared first as a chronicle of state policy, whose impact was measured in the endless dance of numbers on agrarian taxation, rent, debt, cropping, output, living standards, technology, demography, land holding, contracts, marketing, and other money matters. For the city folk who worked in government and in the urban public sphere – the brains of modernity – rustic localities became alien, peripheral, and abstract. All the places, experiences, and circumstances 'out there' in the country became significant primarily as indicators of conditions and trends in modern state territory. To comprehend the country, modernity invented statistics and theories to capture the basic principles of agricultural production and rural society in parsimonious assumptions, models, and ideal types. Compact and comprehensive data informed theories of caste society, village tradition, capitalist transformations, agricultural improvement, and the market economy; these were formalised and packed into portable textbooks and handbooks. Farm statistics rolled off government presses. Official manuals codified agrarian administration. All things agrarian entered the book of the modern state. Agrarian facts entered modern minds through policy debates, statistical studies, guide books, travel maps, law reports, ethnography, news, and theories of modernity and tradition.

In this context, the urban middle classes invented an agrarian discourse that was preoccupied with matters of public policy. By 1870, agrarian conditions appeared most influentially in statistics that measured economic progress and government efforts to develop agriculture. By then, policy debates about rural India excited Indian middle-class intellectuals for whom modernity involved a cultural opposition between their own urbanity and the rural, rustic, tradition of the village. Already in the 1850s, when Karl Marx sat in London using East India Company dispatches to write about India for readers of the *New York Tribune*, a modern world information network was beginning to span urban sites of English literacy running from East Asia to Europe and the Americas; and all the English-speaking middle classes had soon formed a broadly similar sensibility toward agrarian issues, which emphasised the state's responsibility to facilitate the expansion of private production and wealth. Thus a book like Robert Mulhall's *The Progress of the World in Arts, Agriculture, Commerce, Manufacture, Instruction, Railways, and Public Wealth*, published in London (in 1880) came rapidly to Philadelphia and New York; and it described economic progress in terms that typified public discourse in British India. Though many urban intellectuals in South Asia knew the countryside personally – as landowners, merchants, bankers, and lawyers, and by their own family experience – their public discussions and formulations of agrarian knowledge did not highlight their own direct, intimate knowledge. Their sense of agrarian territory rested firmly on official knowledge. By 1880, competing interest groups were vocal in national policy debates concerning agriculture in Europe, America, and territories of the British empire spilling over into Africa, Australia, and the Caribbean,[1] and agrarian issues made a good public showing in British India during policy debates about taxation, land law, money lending, tenancy reform, tariffs and trade, irrigation expenditure, commodity crops (sugar, tobacco, indigo, cotton, tea, and opium), bonded labour, indenture, famines, land alienation, cooperative credit, survey and settlement, agricultural sciences, and forestry. More than any direct experience of village life, these debates informed the evolution of national ideas about the historical substance of agrarian South Asia.

The modern intelligentsia found their countryside in the interwoven discourses of empire and nationality. In the major urban centres of British India, national leaders among the Indian middle classes shared with Europeans an urban identity, alienated from the countryside. But at the same time, imperial ideology lumped all the natives together as native subjects, so India's political nationality evolved as intellectuals brought town and country together in the abstract opposition of 'Indian' and 'British'. This enabled Indian nationalists to produce a distinctively *national* sense of agrarian territory inside the British empire. Nationalism protected the cultural status of the urban middle

---

[1] Niek Koning, *The Failure of Agrarian Capitalism: Agrarian Politics in the UK, Germany, the Netherlands and the USA, 1846–1919*, London, 1994, pp. 167–9.

classes as it united peoples of India against the oppressions of colonialism. By promulgating modern ideas about religious community, racial identity, linguistic identity, national development, and political progress, middle-class leaders made the foreign character of British rule the central issue in agrarian history. They subsumed the history of all the national land and all the people of the nation into a unitary history of the Indian nation. Modern nationality made the Indian middle classes both equal to and superior to, both like and not like, their country cousins; equally native but more knowledgeable, articulate, international, and modern – ready for leadership. Educated leaders of the nation could speak for the country, on behalf of country folk. As a literate voice for illiterate people, a national intelligentsia could present agricultural problems to the public and represent the inarticulate 'rural masses'. National voices expressed a distinctively middle-class middleness by translating (vernacular) village tradition into the (English) language of modernity. They made the problems of the country into a critique of colonial policy so as to make agrarian South Asia a colonial problem, calling out for national attention. By the 1850s, texts written along these lines appear in Calcutta, Bombay, and Madras; and from the 1870s, a national agrarian imagination formed among authors such as Dadabhai Naoroji, Bankim Chandra Chattopadhyay, Romesh Chandra Dutt, and M. G. Ranade. After 1870, novels, short stories, plays, poetry, and academic studies depicted the national countryside more and more frequently in a set of iconic images. By the 1920s, national agrarian studies were institutionalised in universities. National culture had subsumed agrarian territories.

Between 1870 and 1930, agrarian South Asia assumed its modern intellectual appearance and acquired its own history. Old orientalist and official knowledge – from the days of Company Raj – were still basic. But the conjuncture of famines (and, in Bengal, devastating cyclones) with the rise of the national intelligentsia in the 1870s, 1880s, and 1890s made a deep, lasting impression. Agrarian localism and diversity dissolved into a national history of endemic village distress, calamity, and poverty that demanded urgent attention from progressive agents of development. After 1877, stereotypes of famine spread widely and quickly. To raise funds for his relief organisation in India, George Lambert rushed to America in 1898 to publish a book entitled *India, Horror-Stricken Empire (containing a full Account of the*

Famine, Plague, and Earthquake of 1896–7. Including a complete narration of Relief Work through the Home and Foreign Relief Commission). In 1913, a student, Alexander Loveday, wrote a prize-winning essay at Peterhouse, Cambridge, declaring sophomorically: 'Poverty in England, or America, or Germany is a question of the distribution of wealth . . . [whereas in] India, it is a question of production.' Loveday went on to explain India's woes by citing the quality of soil, weather, technology, and agricultural practices; and, like Lambert, he opined that only massive state investment and relief, supported by enlightened, generous, public contributions, could reduce the suffering of the poor in British India.[2] By 1900, it was firmly planted in the mind of modernity that South Asian villagers live perpetually at the edge of death and starvation, on the brink of catastrophe.

In the 1840s, we can see the early beginnings of a modern development discourse (which would provide a strong narrative centre for agrarian historical studies) in petitions by critics of the East India Company against excessive, coercive taxation, and in petitions by Arthur Cotton for increased government irrigation expenditure. In 1869, Lord Mayo argued for the foundation of an imperial department of agriculture in terms that indicate the tone of public discussion:

For generations to come the progress of India . . . must be directly dependent on her progress in agriculture . . . There is perhaps no country in the world in which the State has so immediate and direct an interest in such questions . . . Throughout the greater part of India, every measure for the improvement of the land enhances the value of the property of the State. The duties which in England are performed by a good landlord fall in India, in a great measure, upon the government. Speaking generally, the only Indian landlord who can command the requisite knowledge is the state.[3]

Nationalists used Mayo's argument against his government. They argued that Indian prosperity had become poverty under the British. Famine deaths had increased. Excess taxation had ruined agriculture. Land settlements had punished investors. Deindustrialisation had forced workers onto the land. State expenditure for improvement was

[2] Lambert's book was published by the Mennonite Publishing Company, Elkhart, India. A. Lovejoy, B.A., *The History and Economics of Indian Famines* (Le Baz Prize Essay, 1913), first published, 1914; reprinted by Usha Publishing, Delhi, 1985, pp. 5–8.
[3] Elizabeth Manak, 'Formulation of Agricultural Policy in Imperial India, 1872–1920: A Case Study of Madras Presidency', Ph.D. dissertation, University of Hawaii, 1979, p. 27.

paltry and the government's claim to be working in the interest of the people was at best hypocritical.

The national agrarian scene became a ground for debate, research, and political action; and in these formative decades, state institutions and urban intellectuals invented the modern sciences of development. Engineers had already captured the field of irrigation. Soil scientists, chemists, biologists, and botanists did research that would be organised under the Imperial Council for Agricultural Research and catalogued extensively in 1929 by the Royal Commission on Agriculture. State scientists made British India into a laboratory for breeding new crop varieties fifty years before the green revolution. Economists studied mountains of official statistics on food supplies, prices, commodity crops (indigo, opium, sugarcane, tea, coffee, jute, tobacco, groundnuts, wheat, and rice), farm incomes, investment, and productivity; and they also developed an original theory of Indian economics, which stimulated the first round of village studies in the 1920s. The science of Indian economics was described authoritatively by Radhakamal Mukerjee, in 1916, in a textbook that began with a model of a traditional village economy disrupted by heavy tax demands, private property laws, voracious money lending, and capitalist commercialism, all imposed by the British.[4] Commercialisation loomed large for the early economists and, drawing on data going back to the 1840s, their studies often focused on problems of coercion. This focus was logical because their model of a traditional village economy did not include any indigenous commercial impulse or history, so that coercion would seem necessary to initiate agrarian commodity production and taxation. Forced sales, bonded labour, coerced revenue collections, and excess land alienation were seen as colonial pathologies, producing poverty and needing to be studied and remedied. Freedom from colonialism became widely identified with freedom from all the coercion and disruption of capitalism. Basic elements of the national model of village India were not unique to India, and Gandhian ideas of village self-sufficiency, solidarity, and harmony were also found in pre-modern Britain, for instance by Gilbert Slater, the first professor of Indian Economics at the University of Madras. Like his contemporaries, H. H. Mann and Radhakamal Mukerjee, Slater saw the village economy in Europe and Asia as traditionally stable and coherent; this

---

[4] *The Foundation of Indian Economics*, Bombay, 1916.

provided what Mann would call the 'social framework of agriculture' – what Karl Polanyi would later describe as the 'embeddedness' of the economy in traditional society. Using this broadly accepted theory of indigenous, village India, many economists sought to bolster village tradition while making villagers richer at the same time, to make modernisation and development more authentically and effectively Indian. Gandhian and Nehruvian ideas about Indian modernity had the same scientific roots.

By 1930, historians had also nationalised agrarian India. But they took a different path. A century before the convocation of the Indian National Congress, Indologists and orientalists – Indians and Europeans – were composing texts that would inspire the national imagination. In the middle-class college curriculum, history informed nationality. R. C. Dutt was a towering figure. He responded to W. W. Hunter's (1868) call for 'rural history' with his own study of Bengal peasant conditions (1874); he wrote a serious study of ancient India (1896); and then he wrote the first nationalist history of colonial agrarian policy (1908). With Dutt, history joined the national movement, and in the 1920s it became a national ground for debate and exhortation. History books discussed all types of national issues and formed a repository for competing accounts of national character.[5] In this context, in 1929, William Moreland published the first academic monograph on agrarian history, *The Agrarian System of Moslem India*.[6] Dutt and Naoroji had set the stage by recounting the greatness of classical India and the depredations of British rule, and Moreland confronted the nationalist critique of British land policies with a study of pre-British north India, going back to the fourteenth century, to argue that old elements from India's past explained its agricultural backwardness, not British rule. He countered the national glorification of Indian tradition with an account of pre-colonial oppression, which put Muslim rulers specifically in a bad light. The 'idea of agricultural

[5] See David Ludden, 'History (Pre-Colonial)', in Joseph W. Elder, Ainslee T. Embree, and Edward C. Dimock, eds., *India's Worlds and U.S. Scholars: 1947–1997*, Delhi, 1998, pp. 265–82.

[6] Intellectual connections across the wider world of historical thinking are indicated by the fact that disruptions of modernity and 'the long-term evolution of rural society from the Middle Ages to the present' were also the foundational themes in rural history in England and France. The public presentation of Marc Bloch's long-term study of French rural society began with a series of lectures in Oslo in 1929. See Richard Kerr, 'The Nature of Rural History', in Richard Kerr, ed., *Themes in Rural History of the Western World*, Ames, 1993, pp. 4–5.

development', he said, 'was already present in the fourteenth century, but the political and social environment was unusually unfavourable to its fruition'. Specifically, he said, from the Delhi sultanates (1206–1526) through the Mughal empire (1556–1707), 'two figures stand out as normally masters of the peasants' fate . . . the [revenue] farmer and the assignee' who together waged 'a barren struggle to divide, rather than . . . to increase, the annual produce of the country', a 'legacy of loss, which Moslem administrators left to their successors and which is still so far from final liquidation'.[7]

By 1930, agrarian history entered national policy debates and, ever since then, the writing of agrarian history has meshed with political disputation. Moreland pushed a line of argument against landlordism that was just gaining momentum when Jawaharlal Nehru became President of the All-India Congress Committee in 1930. He announced a radical turn in politics by writing this:

the great poverty and misery of the Indian People are due, *not only to foreign exploitation in India but also to the economic structure of society, which the alien rulers support so that their exploitation may continue.* In order therefore to remove this poverty and misery and to ameliorate the condition of the masses, it is essential to make revolutionary changes in the present economic and social structure of society and to remove the gross inequalities.[8]

Nehru married history and politics; he used history politically the way Gandhi used philosophy. When he wrote *The Discovery of India*, in 1944, he found many lessons for the nation and its leaders in Indian history, going back to ancient times, and by 1947 Nehru's official version of agrarian history was etched into the Congress party platform:

Though poverty is widespread in India, it is essentially a rural problem, caused chiefly by overpressure on land and a lack of other wealth-producing occupations. India, under British rule, has been progressively ruralised, many of her avenues of work and employment closed, a vast mass of the population thrown on the land, which has undergone continuous fragmentation, till a very large number of holdings have become uneconomic. It is essential, therefore, that the problem of the land should be dealt with in all its aspects. Agriculture has to be improved on scientific lines and industry has to be developed rapidly in its various forms . . . so as not only to produce wealth but also to absorb people from the land . . .

---

[7] William Moreland, *The Agrarian System of Moslem India*, Cambridge, 1929; reprinted Delhi, 1968, pp. 205–6.

[8] A. Moin Zaidi, ed., *A Tryst with Destiny: A Study of Economic Policy Resolutions of the Indian National Congress Passed During the last 100 years*, New Delhi, 1985, p. 54, italics added.

Planning must lead to maximum employment, indeed to the employment of every able-bodied person.[9]

During the half-century after 1947, agrarian South Asia changed dramatically. I discuss this in chapter 4, but, to explain my approach in this book, I need to note that, during the 1950s and 1960s, state institutions charged with national development dominated politics and thinking about agrarian history. In these decades, historians focused primarily on state policy. Ranajit Guha's *A Rule of Property for Bengal* and Irfan Habib's *The Agrarian System of Mughal India* both appeared in 1963, and they represent a historical perspective from which official statements of state ideology seem to determine state policy and to generate logical effects everywhere that policy reigns. The nationality of the countryside under British rule – its national unity as agrarian territory – seemed to be self-evident in these decades; and it was described beautifully in A. R. Desai's *The Social Background of Indian Nationalism* (1948), and many other books. But during the 1960s – the decade of Nehru's death, of the early green revolution, and of continuing struggles for land reform – arguments began to gain ground among historians to the effect that dominant state ideologies do not necessarily determine the content or conduct of state policy; and, in addition, that states do not dictate the course of history. How ideas about history changed so radically in the 1960s and 1970s remains to be studied. Certainly historians of South Asia expanded their appreciation of the diversity of the subcontinent and of the longevity of its disparate agrarian regions. The national unity of colonial experience came unravelled with empirical work that challenged the arguments put forth in the 1947 Congress platform. Historians began to emphasise the local diversity of social forces and political alliances in British India. Regional diversity became more politically prominent after the 1956 states' reorganisation, the rise of non-Congress state governments, and the independence of Bangladesh in 1971. An intellectual rupture also occurred in the paradigm of national development, which polarised agrarian studies. The theory and practice enshrined in the green revolution – based on state-sponsored science and technology – faced opposition from theorists and movements promoting revolutionary transformations based on worker and peasant mobilisation, a red revolution. During the last

[9] A. Moin Zaidi, *A Tryst with Destiny*, p. 72.

decade of anti-imperialist war in Vietnam, historians discovered a long history of agrarian radicalism in South Asia, and more evidence appeared to substantiate diverse, contrary theories of agrarian history.

By 1980, agrarian history had moved away from the state toward society. Though modern history remained officially confined to the colonial period, agrarian history continued to reach back into the medieval period and to extend to the present day; and it continued to reach beyond the limits of South Asia in its concern with poverty, revolution, imperialism, and other Third World issues. By 1985, some writing in agrarian history was still concerned primarily with national history, but more and more work focused on local, subaltern, peasant, pastoral, and tribal experience. When Ranajit Guha's first volume of *Subaltern Studies* appeared in 1981 and his *Elementary Aspects of Peasant Insurgency in Colonial India* arrived in 1983, it was clear that a major shift in historical thinking had occurred since 1963. In the 1980s and 1990s, the study of the state was further displaced by studies of social power. This trend was not confined to South Asia. The historical profession in general turned away from politics and economics toward society and culture. In these decades, national states also lost power in their own national territories as structural adjustment and economic liberalisation changed the role of the state in development. Nationalism became an object of academic and cultural criticism. State-centred development strategies came under attack; people-centred, grassroots development became prominent. Environmentalism, feminism, and indigenous people's movements challenged old development agendas. Again, South Asia was not alone. A modern world regime of economic development which began to emerge in the 1920s – centred on the complementary opposition of capitalism and socialism – crumbled in the 1980s (though some of its old players – the World Bank, the IMF, huge foundations, multinational corporations, and big capitalist countries – are still thriving today). In South Asia, new social movements arose as the Congress Party declined. Battles in Punjab, Jharkhand, Telangana, Bihar, Jaffna, Kashmir, Assam, the Chittagong Hill Tracts, and elsewhere turned attention toward regional and local issues. Many scholars who would have been looking for the roots of revolution during the 1970s turned instead in the 1990s to localised, often doggedly individualistic resistance among subaltern peoples. Historians began to look at both capitalist and socialist states with a new critical eye, 'from the bottom up', which gave the state a new kind of theoretical meaning. The state now came to be studied not so much from the inside – from the centre of state policy thinking – as from the margin, from points of critical perspective outside the state and its policy consciousness.

These intellectual trends have left scholars in a better position to explore social power in state territories and everyday life. We can now use history to illuminate contemporary conditions and bring history down to the present, rather than stopping history in 1947. This book considers a long history of social power in many agrarian environments rather than treating agrarian history as a feature of nationality, nationalism, or nationhood. It combines research in a number of different theoretical paradigms to form a comparative history of regions and localities. It does not attempt to represent authentic local voices in agrarian societies, subaltern or otherwise. Recent efforts to capture subaltern voices are salutary, but they pinpoint historical situations rather than describing agrarian change, and they have little to say about patterns of diversity. Everyday life obscures patterns of change across generations and across landscapes of disparate local circumstances. As we accumulate more accounts of local experience, we need to step back periodically to assess patterns and trends, and that is my intention here. Moreover, studies of existing consciousness do not confront the veracity of ideas about the agrarian past, and old ideas tend to survive in popular discourse long after scholars have shown them to be untrue. For instance, a fallacious assumption still remains that basic stability characterised the agrarian world before colonialism. This sturdy idea leads many authors, even today, to imagine the nineteenth century as it was theorised by Karl Marx, R. C. Dutt, and Radhakamal Mukerjee, as a time of radical disjuncture and discontinuity imposed on stable village society, culture, and economy by European conquest and colonial domination. Agrarian history has other stories to tell.

SEASONS

South Asia includes well over a billion people (a quarter of the world's population), and eight of ten live in places classified officially as 'rural', surrounded by agriculture. A much smaller proportion work on the land and non-agricultural employment is growing rapidly, but a substantial majority still depend on agriculture for their livelihood.

Agrarian history is not just a local matter, therefore, even though farming is always local in its everyday conduct: the agrarian past has conditioned states as well as most other social institutions. For historical study, we can define agriculture as the social organisation of physical powers to produce organic material for human use. Animal and forest products fall within this definition, so agriculture includes not only farming but also animal husbandry, pastoralism, fishing, and harvesting the forest (though not mining, manufacturing, trade, transportation, banking, ritual activity, writing history, and other related occupations). This broad definition is useful because many specialised types of production are tightly intertwined in agrarian environments and we need one term to embrace many specialists even as we consider their situations separately. To historicise agriculture, we need to map its complexity as a social phenomenon involving the daily exertion of energy and intelligence by many individuals. Agrarian space is at once political, social, and cultural. It is political because power and resistance constitute work on the land, effect control over assets, and distribute products. Farms are also sites of culture. As the words 'culture' and 'cultivation' indicate, farming is embedded within powers to 'civilise' land, and agriculture entails symbolic and dramatic activity that might seem to have little to do with farming – including religious rituals, urban spectacles, and even history writing. Agriculture is obviously economic in the original household sense, but also in the modern sense that farms represent individual rationality and sustain national wealth. Farming is full of input–output rationality and calculations that do not necessarily obey the economists. Farms are physically built into specific bits of land to create landscapes that farmers change over time, so farming falls into the realm of natural and physical science in addition to social science. No one academic discipline controls the study of agriculture.

We can bring together all the various dimensions of agriculture by focusing on landscapes of social power. Farming is the point of contact between the human powers that organise agriculture and the changing natural environment. No other occupation changes the land so much as farming. It is the major engine of ecological change in human history. State institutions enclose and influence social power in agricultural territory, and, though historians often appreciate the changes wrought by states on human living conditions, the powers of transformation in agriculture come primarily from the activity of farming itself. Farms change the land and produce new possibilities for the future. Agriculture articulates broadly with nature and civilisation, but its specificity as a historical phenomenon comes from the character of farming as a social activity. Other kinds of social action occur on the land, so decisions about their conduct are often located consciously within a specific physical setting, but none more than farming. And none is more dedicated to its time and place in the seasons of the year. In many other types of social activity, the land provides symbolism, context. But every act in farming directly implicates the soil, so that nature is an active participant – in a particular place – from which farming cannot be detached, and local conditions shape the conduct and outcome of human activity in farming, in two senses: nature is perceived as an agent in farming by farmers themselves, within culture; and nature also works outside culture – behind its back – because seeds, rain, and soil, like human bodies, have logics to which people must simply adjust. Agrarian cultures accept and rationalise this behind-the-back quality of nature in their famous pragmatism, experimentalism, fatalism, and common sense.

Farming mingles social labour with nature, like the rain with the soil, and, in the process, physical and cognitive aspects of agriculture give the land cultural meaning, conditioning how people think about landscapes. *Agricultural* landscapes emerge over long periods of time from farming activity that conditions the natural world of human aesthetics. Agriculture creates thereby a cultural text for the human experience of nature. Farming defines nature, how it feels and looks in practice. Agriculture is civilisation at work on the land, humanising nature and naturalising the powers that human societies exert upon nature. Territorial concepts, powers, and social forms are built into landscapes to define the land as an agricultural aspect of nature. But agriculture also changes nature to create the physical characteristics of spaces in which people carry on social life, changing over time how people think about their world. Agriculture is humanity sculpting the earth, designing habitats, making a landscape as a kind of architecture, and producing symbolic domains that form the spatial attributes of civilisation.

Farms mark time at the point of contact between human powers and natural forces outside human control. Agrarian history unfolds in the seasons of everyday life in agricultural societies. Farming moves to the rhythm of holiday seasons, wedding seasons, rainy seasons, and seasons of fruits, vegetables, and grains; seasons of war, famine, and state pageants; and seasons of opportunity and hunger, which embrace whole territories of civilisation. Seasonal time seems to be cyclical, because ideas about seasons are modelled on patterns of natural repetition. But seasonality is also historical, because its cultural construction moves back to the future, as people predict and gamble based on their remembered experience. The understanding of seasonal patterns comes from observation and past predictions, apprehensions of the future; it encodes memory and evidence from past events. The regularity of seasonal rhythms – which define the calendar of human activities in each farm setting – allows investment to occur in one season with the hope and probabilistic expectation that dividends will accrue in the next. Correct action today creates future dearth or prosperity, depending on what the future brings. Lost opportunities and bad times can hurt for years. Understanding today's condition always requires dredging up the past, to see what went right or wrong. Any loss or accumulation represents the yield of the past. The cyclical quality of seasons thus encourages thinking about the future and the past, together, and calculations of past yield for making future-oriented decisions. Family incomes, state revenues, and capitalist profit depend on the predictability and the unpredictability of price movements across the seasons.

Agrarian time has physical substance and human emotion. Its content arises in part from the influence of seasons on the timing and the outcome of decision-making and in part from cultural experience. We know when we have entered a new kind of territory when the season has a different character, when local wisdom treats the same time of year very differently. The synchronisation of social life with nature means that big decisions must take the season into account; and decisions can affect the future drastically. War, migration, industrialisation, state building, irrigation building, urbanisation, and rebellion represent decisions by many individuals in seasons of their own agrarian space; and decisions accumulate to alter the experience and reality of seasonality. The flood, the famine, the drought, the plague, and all the big events in agrarian life are always connected culturally and experientially to the nature of the harvest and to human entitlements to the fruit of the land. Every year, a harvest consists of perishable produce with a limited, predictable life span, which not only feeds people in the present but also influences the future size, health, and activity of a population; and the harvest also determines prices for a period of time. Harvests affect prices very widely even in industrial economies and thus influence social experience and exchange relations throughout society; so that harvests influence the building and repair of cities and also the conduct of war, rituals, weddings, manufacturing, and commerce. Predictions and plans for future production on the farm are tied up tightly with seasonal planning for marriages and other events in the production of kinship and community. Plans for new planting and farm investments are tied up not only with predictions about rain but also with political gossip and economic prognostication. Daily decisions on the farm are inflected by big decisions in capital cities, where rulers need funds and support from the countryside. Historically, therefore, a great many elements influence the size, character, and feeling of agricultural space, in addition to the influence of states, empires, and nations.

Seasons connect farming time to natural time and divinity. Agriculture coordinates heaven and earth. Repetitive seasons – readable in the skies – display signs that forecast and stimulate the conduct and outcome of many kinds of social activity which intersect in farming. Agriculture's seasonality provides a temporal pattern of predictability, calculation, expectation, and planning for agrarian society as a whole. Seasonal uncertainty likewise provides a temporal framework in which to calculate risk and provisioning: it provides a temporal logic for social exertions of control, cooperation, solidarity, and initiatives against catastrophe. Agriculture constitutes a history of experience that informs thinking about survival and prosperity, investment and success. Each season is a day in the life of all the many social institutions that intermingle with farming in agricultural territories.

The physical quality of seasons in South Asia forms a huge transition zone between the aridity of Southwest Asia and the humidity of Southeast Asia. As we travel east from the high, dry Sulaiman slopes, across the arid Peshawar valley, the Salt Range, the Punjab and the Indus valley, and then down the increasingly humid Gangetic plain to the double delta of the Ganga and Brahmaputra rivers, we move from arid lands dotted by fields of wheat and millet to a vast flatland of watery paddy and fish farms. Looking outward from South Asia to the west and east, we see its distinctive pattern of monsoons giving way in Afghanistan to a temperate zone pattern of hot summers and cold winters, with less rain all year, and giving way in Myanmar to the humid tropics' cycle of long, heavy rainy seasons with high average temperature and humidity. Chittagong is ecologically on the borderland of Southeast Asia; Kabul lies at the border of Central Asia. The sun moves the months of humidity and aridity that define agricultural time in South Asia. Winter cold and summer heat are more pronounced in the north, where they influence the extent of wheat cultivation, but otherwise do not have major implications for the activity of farming, except at high altitudes. The same crops can be grown in all the plains and valleys of South Asia with suitable inputs of water. Temperature regimes differ somewhat but we find the same seasonal pattern in Kashmir, Assam, the Konkan Coast, and Sri Lanka – all rice-growing regions. North–south differences are less pronounced in South Asia than across comparable distances between Scotland and Italy, Beijing and Hong Kong, or New England and Florida. Everywhere (except at very high altitudes), the calendar and historic rhythms of farming in South Asia are pegged not to temperature but rather to moisture. In general terms that apply to the long expanse of agrarian history, the seasonal pattern can be described as a cyclical narrative, roughly as follows. The physical substance of the seasons organises a vast range of variation in South Asia and sets it apart from other agricultural environments in Eurasia.

In January, the sun heads north across the sky from its winter home south of the equator, as the air dries out and heats up. Days lengthen and winter rains dissipate. April and May are the hottest months when it almost never rains. In June, Himalayan snow-melt gorges the rivers in the north and the summer monsoon begins. The leading edge of the monsoon moves north-west from May through July, from Myanmar into Afghanistan. By late May, the monsoon has hit the Andaman Islands and Sri Lanka, and then it hits Kerala and Chittagong at about the same time. The earliest, heaviest, and longest monsoon season engulfs the far south (Sri Lanka and Kerala), the north-east (from Bihar to Assam and Chittagong), and the central-eastern regions of Orissa, Chhattisgarh, and Jharkhand. These are the most tropical regions with the most densely tangled natural forest cover and the most extensive jungles. At the summer solstice, when the sun begins to move south again, the summer monsoon will have touched all of South Asia. But it provides the least rain to the arid western plains and the north-west, which have the shortest, driest rainy season; and it brings very little rain to the interior of the central peninsula, which lies in the rain shadow of the Western Ghats. These are dry regions of savannah, scrub, and desert. As the days begin to shorten, from July onward, the rains continue but scatter more and more, week by week, though it can still be raining periodically in October, when a second season of rain begins, called the winter monsoon, which pours unpredictably on the south-east and north-east and often brings cyclones off the Bay of Bengal to attack Andhra and Bangladesh.[10] This fickle second monsoon lasts into January, when five months of dry days begin again.

The seasonal calendar is marked by festivals, astrological signs, and natural phenomena which articulate agriculture with a vast array of social activities. People enjoy the cool of December and January. As the sun moves north and the summer sets in, the sun becomes harsh, hot days accumulate, water bodies evaporate, the earth hardens, and farm work slackens. It is time for travel, migration, and moving herds to water and pasture in the hills; time for hunger, cholera and smallpox, skin and eye infections, malnutrition, dehydration, crying babies, and scavenging; time for trading and transporting, stealing, guarding, and fighting; time for rituals of honour and spectacle, and for building, repair, loans, and debt, sometimes desperate commitments that will influence social relations of agriculture for seasons to come. The dry months of the year are full of preparations for the next rainy season, sustained by the immediate yield of the harvest.

Crops move off the land at different times of the year, but most profusely during the second and third months after the start of each monsoon, and the biggest harvest period is September–December. For example, in the north-east, with its high rainfall running from June into January, there are three major harvest seasons. *Rabi* crops are mostly rice but include wheat, barley, and pulses in Bihar, and the rabi season covers March, April, and May. *Bhadoi* crops, which include millets in Bihar and Chota Nagpur in addition to rice, arrive in August–September. The *aghani* season – called *kharif* in north India – covers November, December, and part of January and brings the great harvest of the year. Winter rice, called *aman*, 'was incomparably the

---

[10] Damaging cyclones were recorded in Bengal in 1831, 1832, 1833, 1840, 1848, 1850, 1851, 1864, 1867, 1874, 1876, 1885, and 1942. The worst by far were in 1864, 1867, 1874, and 1942. See Arabinda Samanta, 'Cyclone Hazards and Community Response', *Economic and Political Weekly*, 20 September 1997, p. 2425.

most important and often the sole crop grown in the districts of Bengal, Bihar and Orissa' at the end of the nineteenth century, covering almost half the total land under cultivation.[11] By contrast, in the dry hills of western India, for the Bhils in the Narmada River basin, at the western tip of the Vindhya mountains, the agricultural year begins abruptly in May, after long, hot months without rain or local work, and now 'people cannot sleep in the afternoon' because it would 'appear indolent, and nature bestows her bounty only on those who bring it their industry as tribute'. Anticipating rain, 'people who had migrated to the plains return home for the start of work' and harrowing and planting start with the rain in June. Harvesting maize and *bajra* millets begins in August, and harvesting *jowar* millets and groundnuts continues through October. In November and December, 'people sell chula, groundnuts, and other cash crops, carrying them to the traders'.[12] After every harvest, crops take new life in the realm of circulation. They assume new material forms as movable measures and as piled-up stores of grain, fruit, pulses, and vegetables, in stocks, carts, trucks, bags, head loads, and shops. Crops become food, cuisine, feasts, stocks, clothing, and adornments; they realise their symbolic potential as gifts, offerings, tribute, largess, shares, alms, commodities, and credit advances. In this realm, in the season of circulation, investments by the buyers of farm produce, made in anticipation of the harvest, when crops were in the ground, seek dividends – because prices drop at harvest time and then rise predictably as the heat prolongs, and, by June, predictions about the coming monsoon also begin to affect prices. Speculators seek returns accordingly. Agrarian wealth arises from the social powers that articulate these two great seasons – of cultivation and circulation – in the life of agricultural produce. The calendar differs for animal and vegetable products, for fish, fruit, and forest products, and for different grains in every region; but everywhere, it moves to the rhythm of the sun, the rain, and the harvest cycle. Commodity prices and markets – and thus profits and revenues for business and government – move along the temporal path of agricultural seasonality; and, today, farm seasons influence the

---

[11] Malabika Chakravarti, 'The Lethal Connection: Winter Rice, Poverty and Famine in Late Nineteenth Century Bengal', *Calcutta Historical Journal*, 18, 1, 1996, 66–95.

[12] Amita Baviskar, 'Displacement and the Bhilala Tribals of the Narmada Valley', in Jean Dreze, Meera Samson, and Satyajit Singh, eds., *The Dam and the Nation: Displacement and Resettlement in the Narmada Valley*, Delhi, 1997, pp. 119–120.

timing and outcome of elections and set the stage for most major political decisions in South Asia.

In the hottest months, in the season of circulation, as crops move off the land, people also move out in search of work. Families that do not grow enough food on their own land to support their diets for the whole year have always constituted a large proportion of the farm population; and, when farming is done and the heat is intense, many go out in search of sustenance. Their numbers and trajectories vary with the season. In years of plenty, they can find food close to home, and during droughts they go farther afield. But, with predictable regularity, food becomes more costly as labour is let loose from the farm in the hot season. For those who must work for others, this is a time of distress. For those who have powers to employ, it is a time to acquire workers for seasonal off-farm labour; and people with stores of food and money do just that. Today, landowners with year-round supplies of irrigation water from mechanical pumps, wells, and canals in Punjab bring workers all the way from Bihar, and, as we will see, such inequalities in the distribution of capital and labour have had a major influence on patterns of social power and economic development over the centuries.[13] Historically, seasonal workers have moved in large numbers into warfare, manufacturing, building, and hauling, all perennial options. They transport and process crops in the season of circulation. The expansion and contraction of opportunities for such non-farm work in the hot season is a major determinant of workers' annual income. Dirt roads trampled hard and riverbeds dried up in the hot sun make this a good time to transport workers, grain, animals, and building materials. Haulers, herders, carters, and grazing land are badly needed during the season of circulation. Water and fodder for animals are a problem. Transhumant animal keepers take their flocks to the hills for grazing, and herds moving up and down the slopes for grazing are major elements in mountain ecology, where farming and grazing often compete for land, as they do today in the Siwalik hills and higher ranges above Punjab.[14]

Supply, demand, people, goods, and news on the move travel through towns and cities, where social needs, social accumulation, and

[13] Manjit Singh, 'Bonded Migrant Labour in Punjab Agriculture', *Economic and Political Weekly*, 15 March 1997, 518–19.

[14] Richard P. Tucker, 'The Evolution of Transhumant Grazing in the Punjab Himalaya', *Mountain Research and Development*, 6, 1, 1986, 17–28.

social power mingle in markets, on the streets, and under the eye of the ruler, engendering conflict and competition as well as negotiation and exchange. Markets and urban centres are places where all the various people of the countryside mingle with one another – causing endless problems – under an umbrella of power held by the people who order the world and receive the riches of the land in return. Holding that power is a magical dream. In the *mangala kavya*s of eighteenth-century Bengal, for instance, the poets 'sing ecstatically of *vakula* trees in blossom, and cows grazing on the river-banks and water-birds and lotuses and peacocks', but rustic heroes go to town in search of wealth and crave to be king.[15] In the eighteenth century, when Bijayram Sen travelled from Bengal to Benares, he described each town as a place of temporal authority and also of homage and piety; and in his travelogue, the *Tirthamangala*, divinity and authority dissolve into one another.

He describes, for instance, how the whole contingent stops to pay obeisance to the patron Krishnachandra's family deity at Gokulganj and [at] the marketplace established by his brother, Gokul Ghoshal, agent to Verelst, president of the Board of Revenue of the East India Company:

> One by one we prostrated before all the gods
> And came back after offering expenses of worship.[16]

The season of circulation is also a time to raise armies and to mobilise demonstrations in towns and cities. The land is free of crops, so gang labour can be organised for clearing jungle, digging wells and canals, and building dams, temples, mosques, monuments, palaces, and forts. When the sun is most unrelenting, bandits are desperate and feed off travellers on the road – this is a popular theme from ancient Tamil literature that rings true today in the tales of Chambal valley gangs who rob passing trains, and in the tales of Phoolan Devi. The hot season is belligerent. Benevolent rulers need force to keep the peace and ambitious rulers can use hungry soldiers to increase their territory.

In late May, all eyes turn to the skies and labour moves back to the land. This time is for preparation and expectation. Cultivation begins with the promise of rain. Work preparing fields for the crops varies in

[15] Edward C. Dimock and Ronald B. Inden, 'The City in Pre-British Bengal, according to the *mangala-kavyas*', in Richard Park, ed., *Urban Bengal*, East Lansing, 1969, p. 15.

[16] Sudipta Sen, *Empire of Free Trade: The East India Company and the Making of the Colonial Marketplace*, Philadelphia, 1998, pp. 33–4.

its timing, complexity and demand for workers, animals, and equipment, depending on the crops to be sown, soil to be planted, rainfall timing and quantity, and water supplies from other sources, such as wells, tanks, or streams; and it also depends on the kind of assets that can be invested in anticipation of the harvest in specific places, because rich farmers can afford to make more elaborate preparations, and new technologies allow for new investments before planting begins. Calculating all of these variables, their interaction, and their risks and benefits consumes massive intellectual energy, endless hours of debate, argument, and negotiation during the season of cultivation. Expertise and experience are crucially important and highly valued. The accumulated wisdom of farmers, patriarchs, astrologers, almanacs, scientists, old sayings, magicians, holy men, textbooks, extension officers, radio, and TV pundits all come into play. Prediction and calculation continue each day based on the rains that come and the level of water in rivers, streams, and reservoirs, for it is not only the total amount of rain that will determine the harvest but also the timing of rain and water supply as they affect each type of seed and soil on each bit of ground. Bad signs dictate conservative strategies for farmers living close to the margin. For farmers with extra assets, however, rumours or signs of an impending bad monsoon or war might indicate potential profit during a subsequent season of scarcity and high prices; and this might stimulate a calculated gamble, extra planting. Such gambles often fail. Whatever the expectation of rain, any extra planting or investments in potentially more profitable crops – such as cotton, jute, rice, wheat, vegetables, sugarcane, tobacco, and plantain – often require a loan. As we will see, historically, the expansion of farms into forests and scrublands has typically involved credit extended in the expectation of future yields; and increasing the capital intensity of farming – by the addition of irrigation, fertilisers, machinery, processing equipment, animals, or labour – usually depends upon credit.[17] For farmers living close to the margin, debt may finance the next meal, and poor workers often enter the planting season already in debt because of food loans during the dry months.

[17] With the increasing intensity of cultivation in India since 1970, credit has risen as a percentage of total capital formation in agriculture and allied sectors from 19 per cent to 33 per cent; and compound growth rates rose from 20 per cent during the 1970s to 35 per cent after 1980. K. P. Agrawal, V. Puhazhendhi, and K. J. S. Satyasani, 'Gearing Rural Credit for the Twenty-First Century', *Economic and Political Weekly*, 18 October 1997, 2717–28, and table 8.

At planting time, old sayings and common sense generally dictate that farmers must follow conservative strategies, and it is typically seen as being better to secure some returns at harvest time than to lose everything with a bad bet. But old sayings on this subject are so prominent because they are so often disobeyed, and a great many conflicts arise from gambles that go bad – especially, perhaps, in the home – and the ruination of the improvident farmer and his family is a poignant theme in literature.

At the time of urgent investments when summer crops must be sown, gains from the past go to work, and the price of food is high when people are hungry for work. Past losses now hurt the most and farmers who have gambled and failed or lost labour in their households owing to death or migration feel the pain of being unable to carry on without help, which can be humiliating. Conflicts over resources rage at this time of year, especially over water and good land. Fights that stew for years erupt as the time approaches to plough, plant, fertilise, and apply irrigation. Newly acquired assets go to work: cattle purchased at summer fairs; land bought, leased, or conquered; new fields cleared from forest; dams built and channels dug; wealth secured by marriage; the labour of growing children; and a good reputation that builds credit-worthiness on solid standing in the community. Many farmers need advances of seed, food, and cash to accomplish the planting, and advances may or may not enrich creditors, but the commitments they involve do create social bonds that are critical, and often lasting, for both sides. Social commitments within families, communities, sects, castes, and other groups – cemented during ritual events that punctuate the calendar – enable farmers to acquire what they need to plough and plant. Reciprocity and redistribution enter a productive phase: horizontal solidarities and vertical bonds of loyalty and command facilitate planting, and seek returns. Gods also play their part. Supernatural beings take ritual offerings and hear lots of promises. In sacred sites, human fear and hope meet the natural powers that fix the fate of the crop. Omens are discussed. Many interactions that animate the heady season of ploughing and planting bring villagers into town and city folk into villages. In cities and towns, past returns from trade, taxes, and sacred donations seek their productivity on the land. Creditors, tax collectors, landlords, merchants, and lawyers come from town to invest in the crop and to make sure they will get their due.

Too many rainless days bring despair and high prices. Scarcities that become famines set in after July when past seasons have been bad and food stocks are low. The poorest people must do whatever they can for food, which often means committing themselves or their children in desperate ways – in this context, what we call 'bonded labour' can be seen as exploitation and also as protection against starvation. The scattered, unpredictable nature of monsoons in many places, and the possibility of flood or devastating storms in others, make the maintenance of subsistence options in times of dire distress a critical life-strategy for many people.

Rains bring hope, mosquitoes, malaria, flooding, and waterborne disease. As the crops sprout and mature, so do estimates of their yield and the calculation of payments to be made for obligations incurred to do the planting. Farmers, creditors, landlords, and state officials evaluate their potential returns. Speculation and negotiation proceed along with uncertainty about the outcome of the season. The connection is again being forged between the wet and dry months, between seasons of cultivation and circulation, between times of investment and reward.

Crops must be protected as they ripen, and predators take many forms. Conflicting interests – among landlords, farmers, labourers, creditors, and tax collectors – mature with the crop. The immediate labour of village people on the farm itself – required to bring the crop to fruition – becomes most critical as the harvest approaches. Farm labour is needed at just the right time for timely watering, weeding, cutting, hauling, winnowing, drying, and storing the crop. Disruptions to the work at hand during this climactic phase of cultivation can ruin the crop and spoil the future that is planned on predictions of yield. As a result, enmity can take a nasty turn. The reliable commitment of labour to the farm becomes most valuable now; and the real market value of labour increases as the harvest begins. At harvest time, prices fall as labour demand is peaking, and labour demand is particularly high when another crop will be immediately sown, which is often the case in regions that benefit from the winter monsoon; and irrigation often allows a second or third crop to be planted. The most hectic work time hits all the farmers at once in each locality, and, at this time, stability and harmony in social relations – so prized in agricultural communities around the world – become critical for determining dividends for everyone who has invested in the crop. This is also a time when conflicts intensify over the division of the crop and over the fulfilment of past promises.

Festivals, rituals, and weddings follow the harvest and bring relief from work and tension. But struggles over the division of the produce follow it into its season of circulation, especially when the yield is worse than predicted and expectations are frustrated. This is a time when tax collectors, creditors, in-laws, and landlords can become nasty. The big harvest festivals mark the completion of the agricultural year and forge the social bonds for another cycle of seasons. Each year influences the next by providing the material and social assets with which all the many participants in agriculture face one another in the negotiations of everyday life. Among these assets, divine blessing is basic, and gods get lots of attention when the harvest is done.

Because the sun controls the seasons, it exerts general control over agricultural time. In popular mythology, Surya drives a chariot pulled by seven white horses, and turns around among the stars to head north in January, moving into the celestial house of Makara (Capricorn). The turn of the solar year occurs during the overlapping months of the summer and winter harvests (between November and February) and is celebrated everywhere in South Asia. But the start of the cultivation year actually falls at the end of the hot season, in June.[18] For all the agrarian states which have pinned their well-being and revenue on seasons of agriculture, financial transactions with the farmers continue throughout the solar cycle and the revenue year has conventionally started with the summer monsoon. The fiscal year – or *fasli* (revenue settlement) year, which is derived from Mughal practice and retained by modern states – runs from the middle of one solar year (July) to the next. In India today, the summer session of Parliament also starts in July, and elections are timed to precede the monsoon, which makes the planting season a time of political promises as well. In the drier parts of South Asia, the harvest from the summer crop is much more prominent than the winter harvest and thus, for the agricultural population, the farming year in effect ends in December, a popular time for marriages. October and November also witness major festivals: Dassara, Durga Puja, and Navaratri. The winter crop

---

[18] The monsoon's starting date is officially announced in the media and awaited publicly with eager anticipation. Its onset is more predictable than its benevolence: in twenty-five years from 1972 until 1996, it began more than five days before or after 1 June only seven times, though starting dates ranged from 24 May to 18 June.

season is most prominent in wetter regions and wherever irrigation is abundant, and here there is greater emphasis on festivities in January–February, as in Tamil Nadu, where Pongal marks the new year and also celebrates the harvest. Everywhere, the solar cycle is the basis for calendrical timings for festivals of many kinds which punctuate the social life of agriculture.

The more we investigate agriculture, the harder it is to draw definite boundaries around it. In seasons of farming, farm families and others involved in farming do essential work on and off the land, and what they do in the mosque, in the bank, or at court may be as important as work in the field to their survival and to the harvest. If we define 'farming' to include every activity that directly determines what is accomplished on a bit of farmland, then it must include off-farm and non-farm work by farm family members (including all the work inside the household); and it must also include activity by non-farmers that immediately affects farming – such as irrigation-building, negotiating rental arrangements, collecting taxes, making loans, repaying debts, settling property disputes, and mobilising labour. *Farming* thus involves a wide range of social activities, but even defined in this broad way it still constitutes only a small proportion of *agricultural* activity, which is more widely dispersed among many social settings. It is little wonder that vernacular texts in South Asia from ancient times to the present describe 'agriculture' very vaguely and broadly, treating ritual and astrology, for instance, as critical features of agricultural knowledge. Modern mentalities may assign prayer, worship, myth, marriage, and pilgrimage to the realm of religion; genetics, hydrology, engineering, medicine, meteorology, astrology, and alchemy to the realm of science; metal working, carpentry, spinning, weaving, and pot making to the realm of manufacturing; and trade, banking, war, herding, migration, politics, poetry, drama, adjudication, administration, and policing each to their separate realms of social activity. But all these are part of agriculture. They contain essential agricultural activity.

Historically, a majority of social activities and institutions in South Asia have had some agricultural aspect or dimension. This is what makes a social space and cultural environment *agrarian*. A region or social space is agrarian not because farming forms the material basis for other activities, but rather because a preponderance of social activity engages agriculture in some way or another during seasons of cultivation and circulation. In this respect, industrialism has overtaken agriculture very slowly and partially around the world. Industry and urbanism may be identified with modernity, but vast areas inside industrial, urban countries remain agrarian today; and most of the modern world is in fact agrarian as measured by the use of its land, the work of its populations, and the origins of gross domestic product. Agrarian histories intersect the history of modernity everywhere. South Asian history involves a broad mix of agricultural and industrial activities and a constant mingling of rural and urban environments. But modernity's urban middle classes around the world detached themselves from agrarian life and took history with them, so that agrarian history now seems smaller – more compact, specialised, and marginal – than the political, cultural, and social history within which the urban middle classes find their own past.

To analyse the history of social power in agriculture and its articulation with states and environments, we can look for dispersed activities that constitute agriculture and are scattered across *agrarian space*. For long periods and in large territories of agrarian history, there was little if any organisational power to coordinate agricultural activity in much of agrarian space. Nowhere in the world do we ever find one overarching systemic intelligence holding together all the physical elements and forms of social power that constitute agriculture, even today, even in the most centrally controlled agricultural regimes. Nature's variability discourages any overbearing, non-local control over the intimate, everyday conduct of farming. A single farm – or a slave plantation, or a commune – might be tightly organised, but controlling farming activity minutely in a large territory is impossible. As we will see, the organised effort to establish large-scale institutional mechanisms to control farming locally is a basic project of modernity, and it dominates the process of agricultural development. From this perspective, Moreland was quite wrong, for what he called 'development' in the Delhi Sultanates and Mughal empire was a very different kind of project from the modernisation that he had promulgated as an agricultural officer in the 1920s. Pre-modern projects of development deployed no state power worth mentioning inside the operation of the farm itself. State powers mobilised under British rule were of a much greater magnitude, they had deeper local penetration, and they were designed to influence the operation of individual farms. They had some success. After 1947, national states extended their local powers considerably. Since the 1970s, international financial institutions, most notably the World Bank and the International Monetary Fund, have sought to supersede the powers of national states in South Asia and elsewhere, by using their financial leverage to open farms everywhere to the discipline of global markets. Institutions of control over production form a large part of agrarian history.

Cultivation and circulation are never haphazard in agrarian space, even in the absence of centralised controls. Regularities form within natural landscapes and interconnected agrarian activities articulate variously self-conscious social powers that organise agriculture in the circumscribed spaces that we can call *agrarian territory*. A single logic or dominant form of social power may not control agriculture in such territory, but the markings of agrarian territorialism can be mapped, and the changing formations of social power can be charted chronologically. Mapping patterns of control and order, including internal resistance and external disruptions, defines the historical geography of agriculture. States help to organise agriculture by forming zones of power that co-ordinate many kinds of social activity that intersect on the farm. But many types of circulating elements inhabit agrarian space. Farms are only the most immediate point of contact between land and labour – the most tangible site of production – and most of what constitutes agriculture circulates far beyond the boundaries of the farm and well beyond boundaries of cultivation. Institutions of many kinds – including those that form the state – organise the movement of materials and activities into and out of farming and thus agriculture.

States exert their powers by defining, enclosing, and regulating territorial units of agricultural organisation. Describing territory and legitimating state authority in agrarian space constitute essential work for state elites and affect the character of social power in farming. We can see documentary traces of this activity from the time of the Mauryas onwards, but the ideas about territory which modern historians routinely impose on the land in South Asia derive from colonial times. As the East India Company drew state boundaries for the Raj, it also 'settled' farming regions with laws of landed property and policies of revenue collection that regulated agrarian territory. By 1815, the Raj had settled upon the village as the basic unit of agrarian administration. Within the boundaries of British India, authors enshrined the village community as the core political, economic, and social unit. Initially, this accompanied blatant efforts to discredit previous rulers and to eliminate their territorial traces. But, as modern ideas developed about civilisations of the Orient, evidence accumulated that the peasant village community had survived through all the ages of empire and calamity before British rule. Ideologically, the village came to represent a survival of agrarian tradition and the administrative foundation of agrarian modernity. Modern authors then constructed a civilisation territory within the territory of British India, and this defined the national heritage for the peoples of modern South Asia. Nepal, for instance, would not be the territory it is today without a specific set of victories in wars with the East India Company, but today this nation state marks a civilisation territory with an ancient heritage. Modernity invented traditions of civilisation and, within them, village territories, where individual peasant families farmed their own land with their own self-possessed resources. The territory called 'India' became traditional and the village and family farm became its elemental units. The cultural construct called 'India' came to rest on the idea that one basic cultural logic did in fact organise agriculture in all its constituent (village) territories from ancient to modern times. Debates have raged as to whether this unitary logic should be understood in terms of exploitation or consensus, but, within all the national territories of modernity in South Asia, stable, traditional village societies were taken to be territories of ancient agrarian civilisation which had survived basically unchanged over the millennia before colonialism.

The modern invention of civilisation territories continues a very old elite project of using narration to organise agrarian territories. Modern imperialists projected the map of British India back into histories of ancient times to legitimate their authority over all the villages in this agrarian territory and to authorise their own ability to speak for the poor, downtrodden, country folk. Nehru's *Discovery of India*, like the *Akbarnama*, narrates geography and genealogy to inscribe territorial order and authority. The modern master narrative of Indian civilisation thus bestows upon leaders of the modern state the charisma of epic heroes and classical emperors. This narrative begins with Aryans and Vedas and moves on to a 'classical age' led by the Mauryas and Guptas, so that a linear evolution of civilisation defines the land of *Bharat*. In the ancient past, classical traditions came into place which are presumed to have filled out the civilisational space of *Bharat*, so that later migrations into this territory can be seen as 'foreign invasions'. After 'foreign conquests' by the Hunas, our civilisation narrative recounts the fall of the Guptas and the onset of a medieval period of political fragmentation and regionalisation, which spans about 1,200 years. Before 1290, we learn, Hindu kings established vibrant regional cultures, but then once again foreign conquerors came from Central Asia and began the epoch of Muslim rule. Still another political fragmentation followed the end of the Mughal imperium, which led to another foreign invasion and conquest – by the British – and thus to all the transformations and disruptions of modernity. In the modern period, the master narrative concludes, the natives in this civilisation territory drove out the British, and, by 1971, popular national movements had created the independent states of Bangladesh, India, Nepal, Pakistan, and Sri Lanka. Notwithstanding differences among these states, their official histories agree that their boundaries are inscribed on the land from ancient times. They also agree that basic traditional forms of village society remained intact from ancient to modern times.

The core continuity in this official narrative – that the village represents a constant unit of agrarian order from ancient times to the present – indicates how ideologically important village tradition is for modern states. The scale of conceptual control over agrarian territory exercised in this linear narrative by the people who claim to represent the true legacy of this civilisation also indicates the importance of old empires for modern states. Though this master narrative pertains to the legacy of nations, and describes neither the chronology nor the geography of agrarian history, its rendition of civilising power does indicate some contours of the institutional environment within which social powers have sought to organise agriculture over the centuries. Elites who define civilisation in their own image are also designing agrarian territories in moral, political, and mythological terms. Mythology helps to sustain institutions of social power on the land. Civilising power is controlling, imaginative, mythical, and magical. We can jettison ideas about there being one (or any fixed number of) civilisation(s) in South Asia, and view South Asia instead as a geographical space in which many elements of civilising power have been combined historically, including cities, states, high culture, organised religion, elites, manufacturing, merchants, science, and philosophical reflections on the nature of the universe. Such powers do exert control over agricultural activities and define agrarian space, giving agrarian territory subtle substance, because culture instigates powers of control over nature and over work on the farm.

MAPS

Physically, work on the farm is mostly lifting, pushing, pulling, cutting, pouring, hauling, pumping, chopping, digging, and otherwise moving things around. Farms seem to be fixed in space, but even the plants in the ground turn into crops only when they move into the realm of circulation. Historical geography needs to consider not only changing farm areas over time but also the moving elements that must converge at moments-in-space to make farming happen. The powers that people exert to confine these elements spatially and temporally mark agricultural territories; but confinements that form boundaries and borderlands are always porous and partial. Think about water. It defines farm environments of South Asia more than any other physical element. Nature distributes water but does not determine its agricultural geography. Water moving in the sky, on the ground, and under the ground creates the timing and location of aridity and humidity. Farms control water. Farming in South Asia means putting elements in place that will make the most of water when it arrives. Water never stops moving and changing form: it percolates, evaporates, falls, runs, freezes, and melts. Its local supply and its local effects on farms might seem to be simply the product of rain falling on the ground – as the old saying would have it, 'Farming is a gamble on the monsoon' – but agriculture is not simply a series of bets about chance occurrences. Irrigated agriculture is a massive social project, in which people in South Asia have engaged since ancient times. Today, the expansion of irrigation by pumping water from deeper and deeper levels and by extending controls over the length of every river is a prime strategy to increase farm productivity. Irrigation defines agrarian space not only by its landscape architecture and physical powers over water above and below the ground, but also by its institutions and social formations. The social institutions that bring drainage and subsoil water onto farmland always implicate elite non-farmers in cities and towns across regions that stretch miles away from the site of irrigation itself. The historical geography of irrigated agriculture includes the physical distribution of surface and sub-surface water, the territorial configuration of institutions that bring that water onto farms, and the movement of ideas about technology, power, and justice that make those institutions work.

So-called dry farms have no irrigation, but they also depend on complex social institutions that control agricultural elements circulating in territories that surround dry fields and villages. Getting seeds into the ground in time for the rain requires labour, equipment for ploughing, and materials such as seeds and manure which need to be applied in a timely fashion – timing is critical – even if the farmer does not have the necessary resources immediately at hand and nothing is left in store from the previous season to supply these inputs. Seasonal circumstances or chronic shortages often require external finance before ploughing can begin; financing must somehow move into the farm nexus and facilitate the movement of necessary goods and services onto a farmer's land. All farms, moreover, depend on seeds bred over centuries to catch the moisture and make the most of the rain as it moves from the sky down into the ground and evaporates back into the atmosphere. Seeds and seed breeding represent technology for controlling the local effects of water mingled with nurturing elements in the soil. Farmers seek seeds that yield more with less water, grow faster to make the most of scarce water supplies, or, like the primeval arid-zone crop (pearl millet) produce something with almost no rain. The green revolution is based on seeds that can be made to yield much more than older varieties with additional inputs of water and fertiliser; it is an old strategy that is being bent toward increasing productivity with the assumption of higher inputs of moisture and plant nutrition. Seed selection and breeding activities must occur in wide agricultural spaces before they are applied on specific bits of land. Though, in the short run, seeds that a farmer plants might come from the yield of the previous season, promiscuity makes pollination creative and adaptive. Over the years, the selection and breeding of crops must occur within wide zones of pollination in order to be effective for any individual farmer, even as farmers restrict the breeds and breeding in their own fields. Adding organic material to the soil makes the most of water at hand, whether by adding silt and minerals with irrigation water, grazing animals to make grass and stubble into manure, ploughing in organic matter brought from forests, or applying chemicals. These materials come to the farm from outside, and institutional arrangements for their movement are critical in farming. Wooded lands for green manure have very often been controlled by communities, rulers, and landlords, rather than by individual farmers. Nomads or transhumant shepherds often bring animals to graze on the fields. Chemical fertilisers come from petro-chemical plants, state industries, and multinational corporations. The origin, control, and terms of trade that bring added fertility to the land make a big difference in everyday farm life.

Knowledge is a critical element in farming and brings all the elements together. Many texts therefore implicitly describe territories of social power in agriculture. Ideas moving among farmers create territories of knowledge. An elusive geography of ideas surrounds farmers who need to know how to make the best (or even safest and simplest) gamble with the rains. Each farmer needs to know about soil preparation, seed selection, planting, watering, manuring, and weeding for the specific combination of water, crops, soil, and labour condi-tions on each farm. Ways of knowing come from generations of learning in wide regions. Every individual calculation and decision on each farm is the result of conversations among many farmers and other people, which accumulate over generations. Textual representa-tions of old forms of agricultural knowledge can be found in Sanskrit texts from the first millennium CE, such as *Varahamihira's Brhat Samhita*, which give astrologers and people who control powerful mantras and rituals key roles in agriculture. *Brhat Samhita* verses say that all astrologers must know 'indications of the approach of the monsoon . . . signs of immediate rainfall, prognostication through the growth of flowers and creepers . . . [celestial influences on the] fluctuation in the prices of commodities [and] growth of crops . . . treatment and fertilising of trees, water-divination [etc.]' [no. 16]. Because deities enjoy trees and water [no. 537], the astrologer needs to know signs on the earth that indicate water sources below [nos. 499–561]. He needs to know portents of famine: sunspots are a dire signal, but so too are certain rainbows [no. 29], shapes on the moon's face [nos. 36–8], eclipses [no. 58], dust storms [no. 67], appearances of Venus [no. 105], and comets [nos. 146–51]. The *Brhat Samhita* introduces its treatment of portents of rain with phrasing that we often find in old texts: 'As food forms the very life of living beings, and as food is dependent on the monsoon, [the monsoon] should be investi-gated carefully' [no. 230]. Seven chapters consider rain signs, and, just like Tamil proverbs recorded in the 1890s, focus on configurations of the planets and signs such as rainbows, cloud shapes, insect and animal behaviour, the sounds and shapes of thunder and lightning, and rainfall during each division of the solar *and* the lunar calendar. Many agricultural proverbs recorded in modern times refer to the wisdom of astrologers, who provided guidance for farmers. In 1802, Benjamin Heyne found a set of instruments in Mysore for measuring rain that were used to compile almanacs and to presage 'the quantity of rain allotted to each country'; and the *Brhat Samhita* shows astrologers how to make such rainfall measurements accurately [nos. 245–6].[19] The *Krishiparasa* gives mantras to ward off insect and animal pests from the field, while the *Sarangadharapadhati* describes effective natural pesticides. In the 1870s, Lal Behari Day recorded a range of local curses, omens, and magical powers at work on Bengal farms.[20]

Geographies of labour mobility also define agrarian territory. For most farmers, most of the time, moving labour onto the land at the right time to do the right thing is no mean feat. Effective control over material and labour matched to specific bits of farmland is never merely a gamble, nor is it determined on a single farm. Patriarchy, labour markets, and other elements in the micro-politics of labour control link together many farms and sites of power in agrarian territories.[21] Historically, moreover, a vast amount of agricultural production in South Asia has involved moving labour over the land in patterns that are not typical of what we think of as sedentary agriculture. Slash-and-burn farming, long- and short-fallow farming (in which fields are planted over a range of fallowing intervals), and alternating field use for different crops, grasses, and animals have been prominent for centuries. Many farming communities have moved as whole communities around an agricultural territory to define its shifting boundaries and to relocate their farms over seasons and generations. And over the long term, as we will see, migrations of labour and capital have changed the landscape by creating farms where there were none before, and by replacing one type of farm with another. Moving labour onto a particular bit of farmland in each

[19] All references to *Varahamihira's Brhat Samhita* are to the edition by M. Ramakrishna Bhat, Delhi, 1981.

[20] Mazharul Islam, 'Folkore as a Vehicle of Ethnological Study in Bangladesh', in Shamsuzzaman Khan, ed., *Folklore of Bangladesh*, Dhaka, 1987, p. 21.

[21] See Jens Lerche, 'Is Bonded Labour a Bound Category? – Reconceptualizing Agrarian Conflict in India', *Journal of Peasant Studies*, 22, 3, 1995, 484–515; Ashok Rudra, 'Local Power and Farm-Level Decision Making', in M. Desai, S. H. Rudolph, and A. Rudra, (eds.), *Agrarian Power and Agricultural Productivity in South Asia*, Berkeley, 1984, pp. 251–80; and chapter 4 below.

season is an activity that occurs within wide movements of labour, and all these nested geographies of labour mobility are not necessarily confined by the village or by political boundaries that appear on ordinary maps. Very often, labour moves away from farming activity altogether – into manufacturing, transportation, military, and other occupations – and needs to be brought back to the farm in time for the planting; or, if it moves away permanently, it needs to be replaced, perhaps by using cash remittances sent by children from far away places. Turning income derived from non-farm work and from other investments into assets which can be deployed effectively on the farm has long been a key to prosperity in farming.

Prices define another moving, elusive geography. The cost of farm inputs, the exchange value of outputs, and the quantity of produce that remains in the hands of a farmer at year's end, to be applied the next year – all these are in part determined in wider spatial domains than are defined by the farm, village, cultural region, state, or empire. Farm families are almost never content to consume only what grows on the farm and they are often unable to sustain themselves with their own farm products or income, so that off-farm labour and non-farm products are important for the reproduction of the most self-sufficient farm families, whose local entitlements typically depend upon prices.

Finally, mythologies and sacred geographies define agrarian space, because no farming population has ever believed that activity on the farm itself is sufficient for success in farming. Propitiating deities, paying homage to holy persona, visiting sacred places, and gathering with one's own people to create ritual conditions for success on the farm are essential in agriculture.

Agriculture thus involves the exertion of powers of control over many moving elements – including esoteric knowledge, supernatural beings, human migrations, prices, commodities, and elements of nature – within which farmers apply labour onto the land. Control over the means of production is thus no simple function of property rights, social status, or class structure. Agriculture is an aspect of social institutions and power relations within which farms and farmers work. It is an aspect of civilisation which generates, combines, and focuses physical powers over naturally moving and socially movable objects in production. The historical geography of agriculture is there-fore not simply described by the extent of fields and farms, or by the boundaries of states, or by cultural regions, although fields, farm territory, and political and cultural powers do mark territorial boundaries in agrarian space.

Agrarian territory is the part of agrarian space that can be effectively bounded, physically and culturally, and marked as a spatial domain for organised social power and activity. Agrarian territory is reproduced over time by the reproduction of social power within *social institutions*. The *state* is a collection of institutions which have central points and figures of authority. *State institutions* are those most directly under the control of people in official hierarchies of authority. There are many kinds of state institutions – military, fiscal, legal, and managerial – and they vary in their ability to organise social power in agriculture. *Social power* in agriculture is by definition distributed unequally, not only in amount but in quality, because it is constituted by effective decisions which direct the movement of the elements that are combined productively in farming. Power meets resistance. Physical power meets physical resistance. Forest growth resists the expansion of farmland. Animals fought back in the Sunderbans and became the scourge of Bengal settlers there. Water constantly resists control and seems at times to want to flood the land and to hide in the earth. Physical force can also be used to overcome resistance from people. But coercion is not the only kind of interaction between *social power* and *social resistance*. The various qualities of social power interact in various combinations, negotiations, alliances, exchanges, accommodations, and forms of conflict. These interactions form patterns within the *institutions of agrarian territoriality*. Because all the moving elements in agriculture resist control, agrarian territoriality – like nationality – is always an on-going project, and movements into and out of institutional territories are constantly problematic. Within agrarian territory, control is always relative. At one end of the spectrum, natural phenomena – such as monsoons, topography, evaporation, photosynthesis, and soil types – resist human control absolutely. Prices, knowledge, beliefs, and migration are nearly as hard to control as the wind, but efforts to control them have long been objects of territorial ambition. At the other end of the spectrum, humans do control things such as cropping patterns, wage rates, marriage choices, occupational options, state institutions, and the like. Such controllable items form the visible landmarks of territoriality in agrarian space.

Institutions define agrarian territory with social routines of control over dispersed, moving elements in agricultural production. As we will see, violence is prominent in agrarian South Asia and it is critical in Ranajit Guha's brief treatment of territoriality, which can serve as a benchmark. Guha defines a peasant in British India as a subaltern subject of a semi-feudal regime controlled by landlords, money-lenders, bankers, high castes, and colonial officials. These elites form a 'composite apparatus of dominance over the peasant'. He argues that peasant consciousness appears in 'the general form of peasant resistance', and that territoriality is an elementary aspect (a basic component) of peasant insurgency, expressing resistance and consciousness. Inscribed in peasant thought and action, peasant territoriality facilitates and circumscribes insurgency. It is distinctly subaltern, wholly outside the state, analytically and politically opposed to elite identity and control. Relatively small in extent, peasant territoriality is fluid, anti-geometrical, and logically opposed to modern boundary definitions. Formed in natural landscapes by social networks, sacred places, myths, and personal alliances, territoriality is inscribed in peasant consciousness by social and cultural history, and by old logics of social action that Guha finds manifest in violent uprisings in colonial times. Guha indicates that insurgency is one fleeting rendition of a cultural map that is drawn by many means over centuries of life on the land. He does not, however, explore the history of peasant territoriality. Is it historical, that is, produced by conscious human agency over time, changing, mutable, and recorded in evidence from the past? Guha says that the 'dye of a traditional culture was yet to wash off the peasant's consciousness',[22] so it would seem that peasants inherit territory as tradition. But we could propose that histories of various kinds – involving kinship, religion, trade, migration, and states – constructed old territories in the peasant world. Peasant territorialism had utility and meaning in activities other than insurgency, for instance in farming, trade, marriage, war, pilgrimage, and diplomacy. These uprisings were actually part of a long history of territorial conflict on frontiers of intensive agriculture as it pushed into more extensive tribal regimes of cultivation. Peasant insurgencies were violent formations of social power that the mostly tribal insurgents produced to conquer people who were taking away their land. From a

---

[22] Ranajit Guha, *Elementary Aspects of Peasant Insurgency in Colonial India*, Delhi, 1983, pp. 6–8, 12–13, 170–1, 333–4.

long-term perspective within agrarian history, such insurgency under colonialism represents a moment of territorialisation. In the late twentieth century, descendants of the insurgents fight for their land in elections, courts, and international agencies.

Territorial institutions – including caste groups, lineages, clans, tribal groups, village communities, armies, sects, businesses, states, and war – inscribe their identity on agrarian space and constitute social power in agrarian territory. The nation is one such institution. Agrarian history is informed most copiously by the records and other traces (including the sculpting of the land itself) that territorial institutions leave behind. Social institutions may not be able to control monsoons, but they can (1) control elements such as water, finances, and commodities, (2) determine rules for entitlements to means of production, (3) accumulate wealth and finance technologies that increase the total pool of farm assets, and (4) organise power for the benefit of specific groups in agrarian society. Agrarian institutions leave texts behind which indicate that they have changed radically over millennia, in part because of the fluidity, permeability, and reconfiguration of their territories. Mobility across territories seems to be a major threat when seen from inside territorial institutions; from the outside, however, we can see that such mobility provides the very reason for the existence of boundaries between territories and of the powers that define them. The extent of mobility influencing agrarian South Asia has never been confined to the subcontinent, conventional images of Indian civilisation notwithstanding. Interlaced trajectories, networks, circuits, zones, and regions of mobility connect western, eastern, and southern Eurasia from prehistoric to modern times. All agrarian territories in South Asia have distinctive features which have been imparted by their location within zones of mobility that define southern Eurasia by land and sea.

One zone of mobility defines South Asia overland inside inland southern Asia. This zone includes two broad corridors: one connects the Ganga–Brahmaputra delta in the east with Iran and Palestine in the west; the other runs north–south from central Asia into central India and the southern peninsula. These corridors intersect in two strategic regions: Kabul, Herat, and Mashad lie astride corridors that connect south, central, and west Asia; Delhi, Ajmer, and Bhopal lie astride the intersecting corridors that connect Kabul, Bengal, and Gujarat with the Deccan and southern peninsula. Though mountains are often seen as natural boundaries to mobility – most prominently, the Himalayas and Vindhyas – they do not so much obstruct as channel the movement of elements that influence agrarian history. Travels across Nepal to and from the Gangetic plain have always been less prominent than along routes running through Kashmir; and overland treks from Assam into China are fewer still. But, to the west and north-west, barriers to mobility across the Hindu Kush, Iran, Central Asia, and China have been erected mostly by military force – by Mauryas against Indo-Greeks, Turks and Afghans against the Mongols, and by the British against the Russians. In the east, dense tropical jungles have restricted transportation over the high mountains, but, in the west, battle lines have more effectively determined transport costs along the inland corridors of southern Asia.

A second zone of mobility defines South Asia by sea. Crossing some rivers may be arduous but substantial bodies of water in general represent low transportation costs on routes of gravity and wind. The historical geography of South Asia by sea extends along coastlines from East Africa and the Red Sea across Southeast Asia into China. In each few centuries, technological change has lowered transport costs below their former level, with the most dramatic changes during the latter half of the second millennium. Long-distance and bulk transportation were always cheaper, safer, and quicker along water routes until the advent of the railway. From Roman times onward, waterways connected South Asia with the Mediterranean and South China. In the day of the Delhi Sultans, sea routes spanned Eurasia; by Akbar's time, they crossed the Atlantic and Pacific to connect coastal regions around the world. The coast extended in effect along deltaic waterways north into Bengal past Dhaka and then west up the Ganga as far as Patna. The Ganga also formed a highway up to Agra, along which flowed the Mughal revenue. Along the coast, boats land almost anywhere, moving with monsoon wind. Waterways form open zones of interaction, but some inland areas are much better connected than others to sea routes. From the mouth of the Indus to the Konkan coast, and from Kanya Kumari to Chittagong, inland areas are very accessible to the sea. Afghanistan, Kashmir, and Nepal are isolated from the Indian Ocean. In Myanmar and Malaysia, mountain forests and jungle cut off inland corridors from the sea. Likewise, coastal Orissa and Kerala are relatively isolated from inland corridors.

These connected zones of extensive mobility – rather than any fixed territorial expanse of Indic civilisation – have defined a world which has continuously shaped agrarian institutions in South Asia. Harappa and Mohenjo-daro are at the eastern edge of an urban region that was strung along land and sea routes running from the Mediterranean to the Indus. During the millennium before the Mauryas, archaeological and linguistic data describe an extensive zone of settlement and cultural movement running from the Mediterranean to the eastern Ganga basin; and new regions of material culture are indicated by distributions of painted grey ware, black and polished ware, cists, urns, and cairns in the Indo-Gangetic plains and the southern peninsula. Under the Mauryas, data from literature, archaeology, travellers' accounts, and other sources describe networks and centres of mobility running from Iran to Bengal and from the Oxus to the Narmada; and in this inland zone, a political boundary was drawn west of the Indus, dividing Maurya domains from those of the Achaemenids and Indo-Greeks. This boundary – pivoting in the north-west around Taxila and Gandhara, where Panini was born – divided eastern and western regions of southern Eurasia; but mobility across this boundary made it so important politically, and Panini's *Astadhyayi* indicates increasing commercial connections across the inland routes of southern Eurasia under the Mauryas. Mobility across this political divide would shape agrarian history on both sides without interruption from Mauryan times onward.

At the start of the first millennium CE – when Sangam literature was being composed in the southern peninsula – texts to inform history multiplied rapidly east of the Sulaiman Range. This resulted from new powers in agrarian states over the movement of people, goods and ideas. A proliferation of texts resulted particularly from the activity of Brahman literati who moved among and settled in regions of intensive agriculture. Agricultural intensification, state expansion, and cultural production accelerated together under the Guptas, who put an imperial model of civilisation, first invented by the Mauryas, firmly in place. Imperial Gangetic dynasties sanctified the Ganga and made their own core political territory into a heartland of universal authority. In the second half of the first millennium, many dynasties used technologies of power produced by the Guptas to create boundaries in the agrarian lowlands. But inland corridors of mobility across Eurasia remain visible under the Mauryas and Kusanas, under Guptas and Hunas, and they appear again in the tenth and eleventh centuries in data that mark the overlapping ambitions of Ghaznavids, Hindu Shahis, Candellas, Later Kalacuris, Paramaras, and Ghorids. Inter-regional political competition to control inland corridors made Kabul and Delhi strategic places around which military competition would revolve from then on. Beginning with the Ghaznavids – then with Ghorids, Mamluks, Khaljis, Tughluqs, Lodis, and Mughals – people who came from west of the Indus increasingly controlled the inland corridors; and, for the Brahman literati in medieval agrarian states, this fact took on the appearance of foreign invasion and rising Muslim power. From an agrarian perspective, however, the transformation of southern Asia during first half of the second millennium looks rather different.

In centuries just before 1300, agrarian territories were expanding in size all across Eurasia, from western Europe to China. Networks of trade connected territories from England to Shanghai, by land across the Silk Road and by sea across the Indian Ocean. Strong, compact, expansive regional states all across southern Asia generated and drew upon assets that moved along the inland corridors and in the maritime zone of the Indian Ocean. For the Paramaras in Malwa (tenth to thirteenth century), Hoysalas in Mysore (eleventh to fourteenth century), Caulukyas in Gujarat (tenth to thirteenth century), Warangal Kakatiyas in Andhra (twelfth to fourteenth century), Devagiri Yadavas in Maharashtra (thirteenth century), Gahadavalas in Kasi (twelfth century), Cahamanas in Rajasthan (tenth to twelfth century), Gangas in Orissa (eleventh to fifteenth century), Kalyani Calukyas in the Deccan (eleventh to twelfth century), Cholas in Tamil country (tenth to thirteenth century), and Senas in Bengal (twelfth to thirteenth century), dynastic wealth expanded along routes that ran north and south overland, to the coast, and overseas. Later medieval rulers, based at the cross-roads of the inland zone, around Delhi, rose to power within the interactive history of regions along the inland corridors. The Delhi sultans facilitated and depended upon widening movements of people and goods by land and sea, which brought travellers, settlers, warriors, and sufis into the subcontinent. All competing states in southern Asia expanded in size and power amidst expanding mobility after 1100. Old agrarian territories continued to grow under the impress of new military and organisational powers brought to bear by late medieval rulers. The Ghorids (twelfth century), Mamluks (thir-teenth century), Khaljis and Tughluqs (fourteenth century) worked within a vast political region which the Gurjara-Pratiharas had previously built, running south beyond Malwa into the peninsula; and north-south mobility along the inland corridors became even more important for all states south of the Narmada after 1300. The old regional boundaries drawn by Cholas and Calukyas were drawn again by more powerful Vijayanagar, Bijapur, and Bahmani states in the fifteenth century. Territories of agricultural expansion developed continuously in Rajasthan, Bengal, Punjab, Malwa, Orissa, and the Ganga plain as they were incorporated into later medieval states. Babur lived in this world of state power. The powers that built the Mughal empire ran along the full expanse of southern Eurasia.

Many texts indicate that old agrarian elites experienced their changing medieval context as an age of foreign invasion and conquest. Along the Ganga plain, in Malwa and the Deccan, and south to Kanya Kumari, the end of the thirteenth century marked the end of an age dominated by ruling elites whose institutional powers had descended from the Guptas. Historians have many documents from temples, bards, pundits, and artists that describe invasions of their sacred space and violations of their sacred order. In the view of literary elites, the earlier medieval conquests which had produced their own social power represented morality and cultural florescence; and the new warriors and intellectuals who came from afar – whose networks and identities covered great distances – brought the end of their golden age. But, as we will see, agrarian history is marked by striking continuities in the dynamics of power from the last of the Guptas to the rise of the Mughals. Continuities remain after 1550, but Mughal conquest and administration put in place new territorial institutions. The inland zone of southern Asia was integrated as never before by the Mughal, Safavid, and Ottoman empires in the sixteenth and seventeenth centuries, which dramatically increased mobility, east and west. The Mughal, Ottoman, and Safavid empires depended for their wealth on networks of trade that linked them to one another by land and sea. Records at Bursa reveal that the bulk of its sixteenth-century eastern imports came from India, including spices but predominantly textiles. Across southern Eurasia, the net flow of manufactured goods and spices moved from the east to the west; and the net flow of precious metals moved in the opposite direction, a reciprocal movement which connected London, Istanbul, Bursa, Cairo, Damascus, Baghdad, Isfahan, Multan, Dhaka, Surat, Hyderabad, and Madurai, as well as all the ports of the Indian Ocean and South China Sea. As early as the 1470s, the Bahmani sultans organised a trade initiative at Bursa, and Bahmani correspondence with Malwa sultans proposed joint control over sea trade to the west. Inland trade to the west justified great Mughal expense to keep the mountain passes to Kabul open for safe travel. At the same time, the Portuguese brought new crops – among them chillies, tomatoes, potatoes, tobacco, and coffee.

It is most appropriate, therefore, to study agrarian South Asia in the context of an historical geography that is formed not by a closed civilisation territory but rather by extensive, shifting, open corridors of mobility stretching overland to Syria and China and overseas to Europe and the Americas. It is quite inappropriate to imagine agrarian South Asia as being demarcated by boundaries fixed during Maurya, Gupta, and medieval times, and violated thereafter by invading Muslims and Europeans.[23] By 1750, people from western parts of Eurasia had participated in cultures along the coast for more than a millennium; culturally, the South Asian coast, particularly its urban centres, resembled other coastal regions around the Indian Ocean more than it did the Mughal heartland, which was influenced prominently by inland flows across Iran and Uzbekistan. From the start of the Common Era, agrarian elites in South Asia have exercised power and gained wealth within corridors of mobility that criss-cross southern Eurasia, by land and sea, and agrarian history needs to be understood in that light.

LANDSCAPES

Agrarian territories took distinctive forms in six kinds of environments, which we can divide into forty geographical units. All have ancient traces of agrarian activity. They housed medieval agrarian territories of various types, discussed in chapter 2. In chapter 3, we see how in the early-modern period, *circa* 1500–1850, farming territories

---

[23] Parallels between Muslim and British conquests are very widespread in the historical literature. See, for instance, Herman Kulke and Dietmar Rothermund, *A History of India*, London, 1990, p. 162, which says that, in the thirteenth century, 'having developed relatively undisturbed by outside influences in the Early Middle Ages, India was now subjected once more to the impact of Central Asian forces . . . [which] new impact can only be compared to that made by the British from the eighteenth to the twentieth century'. The opening lines of J. L. Brockington, *The Sacred Thread: A Short History of Hinduism*, Edinburgh, 1981 (reprinted Delhi, 1992), assert that 'the Mughal period (1525–1761) . . . was basically as much of a foreign domination as the British Raj which followed it' (p. 1).

were brought together to form agrarian regions – culturally coherent, spatially organised territories of social power – and in chapter 4, we see how these regions were institutionalised, integrated, and differentiated by modernity. Farming landscapes are therefore defined primarily not by their physical or environmental qualities, but rather by the long-term interaction of geography, culture, technology, and social power. Environmentally, landscapes can be divided rather simply between two sets of binary oppositions, according to elevation and humidity, whose combination and transitions define much of the physical setting: mountains versus plains, and semi-arid versus humid tropics. Most farmland lies in the semi-arid plains, including river valleys and plateaux; and almost all of the remainder is in the humid lowlands, which have a higher proportion of population than of farmland. But all the divisions, interactions, and intersections of uplands and lowlands and dry and wet lands occur in historical space and amidst changing conditions of social power which alter the land over time. Rivers change course, deserts expand and contract, dry lands receive irrigation, forests grow and disappear, cropping patterns change, human settlements alter nature, and farms give way to city streets. We need to describe the land in ways that allow us to track changes in ecology and in the human content of agrarian territory. This outline of agrarian landscapes endeavours to combine all the various elements of agrarian territory to define spatial units for the long-term historical geography of agriculture in South Asia. Historically, Gujarat, Malwa, Bengal, Assam, Khandesh, and Berar are at the intersection of landscapes, and they are thus repeated in the list of landscape subdivisions.

Northern river basins

The basins of the upper Indus and its tributaries, the Yamuna, Ganga, and Brahmaputra, form one of the largest expanses of riverine farmland in the world. Soils are mostly alluvium. Farming is challenged and enriched by river drainage from mountains all around. Rivers bring moisture and nutrients, but floods wreak havoc with frightening regularity. In 1784, the whole of Sylhet was under flood water and animal carcasses were floating like boats on the sea as the population fled to the hills.[24] In 1875, the notorious Kosi river destroyed all the

---

[24] *Sylhet District Records*, Bangladesh National Archives, vol. 293, pp. 131–57.

Geographical subdivisions of agrarian South Asia

I.   Northern river basins
1. Punjab
2. Western Ganga-Yamuna Plain (Delhi-Agra-Mathura)
3. Central plain and doab (Lucknow-Allahabad)
4. Eastern Ganga basin (Gorakhpur, Benares, Bihar)
5. Bengal, Ganga-Brahmaputra Deltas (West Bengal, Bangladesh)
6. Assam (Brahmaputra Basin)

II.   High mountains
7. Kashmir
8. Western Mountain Regions (Punjab, Himachal, Uttar Pradesh)
9. Nepal
10. Bhutan
11. Eastern Mountains, (from Assam into Myanmar)

III.   Western plains
12. Indus Valley
13. Sindh
14. Rajasthan
15. Northern Gujarat and Saurashtra
16. Malwa

IV.   Central mountains
17. Malwa
18. Bundelkhand
19. Baghelkhand
20. Chota Nagpur and Jharkhand
21. Chhattisgarh
22. Orissa Interior
23. Bastar
24. Khandesh (Tapti Basin)
25. Berar (Waiganga Basin)

V.   The interior peninsula
24. Khandesh (Tapti Basin)
25. Berar (Waiganga Basin)
26. North (Maharashtra) Deccan (Maharashtra; Godavari and Bhima Basin)
27. South (Karnataka) Deccan (Karnataka; Krisha-Tungabadra Basin)
28. Mysore Plateau (Palar– Ponnaiyar–Kaveri Basin, above the Ghats)
29. Telangana (Krishna-Godavari Interfluve)
30. Rayalaseema (Krishna-Pennar Interfluve and Pennar Basin)
31. Tamil uplands (Vaigai, Kaveri, Ponnaiyar, Palar Basins, below the Ghats)

VI.   Coastal plains
32. Gujarat
33. Konkan
34. Karnataka

35. Kerala
36. Sri Lanka
37. Tamil Nadu
38. Andhra
39. Orissa
40. Bengal

farmland in its path; an indigo planter wrote that 'miles of rich land, once clothed with luxuriant crops of rice, indigo, and waving grain, are now barren reaches of burning sand'.[25] The Ganga provided natural routes for transit and shipping to the Bay of Bengal and Arabian Sea. Bounded by desert and mountains, the climate in the riverine flatlands changes gradually from aridity in the west to humidity in the east. Along this gradient, monsoon rainfall and drainage from the hills increase and the dominant food grain shifts from wheat to rice. Since 1960, wheat and rice cropping has overlapped because quick-growing varieties have allowed farmers with adequate irrigation to grow both in rotation, and today almost a quarter of the net sown area in Bihar, West Bengal, UP, Haryana, and Punjab grows wheat-and-rice, which is very rare outside the Indo-Gangetic basins.[26]

In the north-west, separated by a low watershed from the Ganga basin (in Haryana), the Punjab is a triangular territory formed by the Indus and its tributaries (Jhelum, Chenab, Ravi, Beas, and Sutlej), and rimmed by mountains in the west and north (Sulaiman Range, Salt Range, Panjal Range and Lesser Himalayas). Rainfall increases with proximity to the northern hills from the Jhelum eastward, and aridity increases to the west and south. Groundwater recharge is most fulsome near the riverbeds and closer to the mountains, and the up-river Punjab also has more alluvial soil. Moving downstream toward the base of the Punjab at the confluence of tributaries with the Indus, rain and groundwater diminish, and soils become brown and then sandy, as the Punjab shades into the arid western plains in Rajasthan and the lower Indus basin. In Punjab, as in general throughout the northern basins, the long-term geographical spread of intensive agriculture

---

[25] Christopher V. Hill, *River of Sorrow: Environment and Social Control in Riparian North India, 1770–1994*, Ann Arbor, 1997, p. 11.

[26] Ramesh Chand and T. Haque, 'Sustainability of Rice–Wheat Crop System in Indo-Gangetic Basin', *Economic and Political Weekly*, 32, 13, 29 March 1997, Review of Agriculture, A-27.

moved outward from places where drainage is simpler to harness for farming to places where more strenuous controls are necessary. In drier regions like Punjab, this means that intensification expanded from naturally wetter into drier areas; whereas in the flood plains and humid tropics farmers expanded initially from higher and drier parts of the lowlands into the more water-logged areas at the river's edge. Everywhere, agriculture also moved up river valleys into the highlands. In the Yamuna–Ganga basin, the general trend of expansion of intensive agriculture has been from east to west and upland from the lowlands; and, in the Punjab, from north-east to south-west. A major modern stage in this long process of expansion began with the construction of a vast canal network during the nineteenth century; the most recent stage is the spread of motorised pumps and tubewells since the 1960s. The wet lands of riverine Bihar were ancient sites of intensive cultivation; and, since 1880, naturally arid lands in Rajasthan have had the highest rate of increase in cultivated area of any lowland region in South Asia because of new irrigation.

In the eastern regions of the northern basins, Bengal and Assam have the highest rainfall regime; and the great volume of river water and the density of tropical jungles have historically presented the major challenges to expanding paddy cultivation. Today, the density of the human population is often seen as an obstacle to prosperity, but historically it has been more commonly a sign of the great fertility of the land. The Ganga delta shifted eastward over the centuries and in the eighteenth century joined the Brahmaputra in what is now Bangladesh. Agricultural frontiers in Bengal have moved east with the river, south into the Sunderbans, and also, as throughout the northern basin landscape, up from the lowlands into the high mountains. High tropical mountains have always had their distinctive, tribal farming societies, whose interaction with farmers in the lowlands is one of the most complex, difficult subjects in agrarian history, for there is a broad, shifting historical and geographical borderland between hills and plains. Our documentation comes primarily from the plains and indicates constant interaction with upland peoples and constant integration of uplands into agrarian regions centred in the lowlands.

The northern basins are bordered by mountains on all sides, except in Rajasthan. Down the mountains their rivers flow. In the mountains lie reservoirs of timber and grazing land; and the mountains are the homeland for many tribal societies. As we will see, lowland people have historically extended their power up-river into their surrounding mountains to colonise, conquer, and annex territory. Rajputs conquered up into Uttarakhand and the mountains above Punjab. From ancient times, upper reaches of the Chambal and Parbati (tributaries of the Yamuna running down the craggy ravines of the Malwa Plateau) were attached to the agrarian economies of the Gangetic plain, though they belong physically to the central mountains and they shade off in the west into the western plains.

High mountains

From the Makran Range in the west, running north across the Sulaimans and Hindu Kush, and curving east across the Karakoram Range and Himalayas to the Naga and Manipur Hills and then Myanmar, a vast high-altitude landscape connects South Asia with Central Asia, Tibet, China, and Myanmar. It is steeply sloping mountain terrain, with sharp valleys and countless rivers, which mark natural routes of transportation and drainage, rushing down into the plains below and leading upward to the high plateaux of inner Asia. Winters are much colder than below in the plains, and summers are much cooler, creating different, complementary ecologies for animals, vegetation, forests, farmers, and markets. As in the lowlands, the climate changes from extreme aridity in the west to heavy rains and humidity in the east, with attendant changes in natural vegetation and agricultural options. Run-off is rapid, snow-melt gorges the rivers in the spring, and erosion is severe. Geologists have found huge boulders from the prehistoric Himalayas as far south as Jaipur, and satellite photos show Himalayan silt spilling from the Ganga under the Bay of Bengal almost as far as Sri Lanka. Forests have always defined a basic natural resource for human settlements in the high mountains. Agricultural territories formed in valleys have extended up the slopes, growing wheat and millets in the west and paddy in the east. Agricultural spaces are connected by valleys and passes and separated by high ridges and peaks, along routes of trade and migration. Large agricultural territories have formed in the Vale of Kashmir, Kathmandu valley, and upper Brahmaputra basin; and in all three, rice is the dominant food grain among a great variety of crops. Great distances and obstacles to travel separate agrarian territories in the high mountains from one another, and these territories are connected more effectively to proximate lowland regions than to one another. In the west, Baluch and Pashtu mountain societies live in the corridors between Iran, Afghanistan, the Indus basin, and Punjab. The Brahmaputra upland is so intensely engaged in the history of the northern basins as to form a semi-detached part of that landscape; though it also participates in the history of Southeast Asia and China. Various forms and qualities of attachment to adjacent lowlands define agrarian regions in high mountain valleys. Except for Nepal and Bhutan, all are today political parts of lowland states, but a long period of rebellion in Nagaland and Mizoram indicates a continuous struggle for political autonomy, which is also visible in Baluchistan, Kashmir, and the Chittagong Hill Tracts. The Kathmandu basin has always maintained a separate political identity. Though separated from the Indo-Gangetic lowlands, its institutions of agrarian power still derive from the history of migration and settlement that it shares with the rest of South Asia. All across the high mountains, from the Yusufzai borderlands with Afghanistan to the Chittagong Hill Tracts between Bangladesh and Myanmar, cultural oppositions and separations between peoples of the hills and of the lowlands are typically stark. The term 'tribe' is most often applied in modern times to the smaller-scale social formations that thrive in the small, relatively isolated agrarian spaces of the high mountains.

Western plains

The semi-arid western plains abut the high mountains in the west and they merge so gradually with the northern river basins in the Indo-Gangetic watershed (Haryana) and with the central mountains (in Malwa and Gujarat) that we can see them as a set of expansive, connective zones for the long-term historical movement of people in every direction. Rainfall is very low and spatially the plains are dominated by the aridity of the Thar Desert. In prehistoric times, the river Saraswati ran deep into western Rajasthan before it ran west into its inland delta near the Indus; and Rajasthan, the Indus basin, and Sindh seem to have become increasingly dry over millennia. There is indirect evidence, as we will see, that Rajasthan dried up noticeably during medieval centuries. The scrub-covered, rocky, and scattered Aravalli Hills rise abruptly from the flatlands in the east, providing fortress material and drainage for adjacent valleys. Irrigation, mostly from wells, and good monsoons are more common in the east, where they create good rich farmland for *bajra*, maize, wheat, *jowar* and cotton. Soil becomes increasingly sandy to the west; and in the south, grey-brown sandy soil becomes good red loam, creating a naturally favoured zone for farming that runs along a corridor from Haryana through Jaipur and Ajmer into Gujarat. As in all arid regions, people and animals travel often in search of water and wealth, and agrarian life here has always featured nomadism, pastoralism, stock rearing, and migration for trade and conquest. Medieval warriors and merchants – most famously, Rajputs and Marwaris – moved from old centres to acquire more wealth in regions of better farming in the east, north, and south. Dense population centres in the western plains are based on locally irrigated farms, strategic locations on trade routes, and extensions of political power embracing numerous similar centres across expanses of sparsely populated land. Trade connections to bordering regions on all sides and to the sea lanes are critical for the vitality of population centres. Like the camel – its characteristic pack animal – this land has always had a tendency to wander uncontrollably into its surroundings, making its boundaries vague.

Central mountains

This landscape of interlacing mountains, valleys, rivers, plateaux, and plains extends from Gujarat in the west, along the rim of the Gangetic plain in the north, to Chota Nagpur in the north-east, to the Deccan plateau in the south, and to the edges of the Godavari river basin in the south-east. Today it includes all of Madhya Pradesh, most of Bihar south of the Ganga, and all of Orissa outside the coastal plain. Its agrarian regions have formed amidst an interlaced complex of river basins that run in every direction to feed all rivers north of the Krishna and east of the Indus. The Chambal, Parvati, Betwa, and Ken rivers run north from the Malwa Plateau and Bundelkhand into the Yamuna; their valleys form historic highways into the Gangetic plain. The Vindhya and Satpura ranges form the valley of the Narmada river, which, like the Tapti to the south of the Satpuras, drains west into the Gulf of Cambay. The Mahi also drains Malwa into the Gulf, by arching north and then running south. East of Malwa and Bundelkhand, in Baghelkhand, waters from the Maikala, Mahadeo, and Ramgarh mountains send the river Son north-east into the Ganga; they send the Narmada west, the Mahanadi east through Chhattisgarh into Orissa and the Bay of Bengal, and the Waiganga south into the Godavari. East of Baghelkhand, the Ranchi and Hazaribagh plateaux dump the Damodar river into the Hooghly and send the Subarnarekha straight into the Bay of Bengal. Ringed by mountains, Chhattisgarh forms a bowl-shaped radial drainage basin, into which streams enter from all sides before joining the Mahanadi and running east into the Bay of Bengal. South of Chhattisgarh lie the dense hills of Bastar and inland Orissa, from which the Indravati drains into the Godavari.

Like the climate in the high mountains and the northern basins, which it parallels geographically, the central mountain climate is dry in the west and wet in the east. In the west, the barren scrublands of the Chambal ravines – on the edge of Rajasthan – run with torrents of mud in the monsoon only to bake into red brick in the summer heat. In the east and south, tropical forests cover Jharkhand, Orissa, and Bastar. As in the high mountains, agrarian history in this landscape is dominated by interactions between mountains and valleys, forests and lowlands, and their respective farming communities. Farms have been cut historically into the forest – dry scrub in the west and tropical jungle in the east – fomenting interactive struggles within and among farmers, hunters, and pastoralists. This is a landscape in which shifting cultivation and tribal populations have been most prominent; and the largest tribal groups live here – the Bhils in the west, the Gonds in the central regions, and the Santals in the east.[27] More than in the high mountains – because of better soils, wider valleys, longer summers, and constant invasions by agrarian powers on all sides – the trend in land use and social power here has strongly favoured the hegemony of lowland farming communities and the expansion of more intensive farming regimes among hill people. Farms today show great variety in techniques and options, ranging from irrigated wheat farms in the Narmada and upper Chambal valleys to vast rice mono-cropping in Chhattisgarh, to shifting cultivation in Bastar, and to mixed forestry and millet farming in Baghelkhand. This variety parallels the great variety of social formations, which combine tribal and caste elements more widely and intensely than anywhere in South Asia. Intensive farming is most dominant where soil, water, and states have favoured the formation of a few extensively controlled, homogenised tracts – in

---

[27] K. S. Singh, *People of India, National Series, Volume III, The Scheduled Tribes*, Delhi, 1994, cites 1981 census figures as follows: all the groups of Bhils totalled 7,367,973 in southern Rajasthan, western Madhya Pradesh, Gujarat, and northern Maharashtra (p. 118); the many Gond groups added up to 7,388,463, spread over seven states but with 5,349,883 in Madhya Pradesh (p. 294); and Santal groups comprised 4,260,842 people in Bihar, West Bengal, Orissa, and Tripura (p. 1041).

the Narmada valley (which benefits from deposits of black cotton soil), the upper Chambal valley, the Waiganga valley (Gondwana), and Chhattisgarh. Khandesh and Berar participate in the history of the central mountains, but also in that of the interior peninsula.

The interior peninsula

This semi-arid landscape consists of river basins and interfluvial plains, and its agricultural character derives from lines of drainage, seams of good soil, and underground water tucked away in the rocky substrate of the Deccan Trap. Geologically, these features come from the volcanoes which left behind caverns of underground rock, boulders on the land, and black soil under foot. The Deccan Trap holds water to facilitate labour-intense but rich cultivation under well irrigation. The peninsula is cross-cut by the Ajanta and Balaghat mountains in the north, and its surface is strewn with sometimes dramatic rock outcrops and disconnected mountains. In the south-east, the outcrops become the Nallamalais, Eastern Ghats, Javadi Hills, Shevaroy Hills, and Pachaimalai Hills, which punctuate the descent of the peninsula into the eastern coastal plain. Framed by the Eastern Ghats, south of the Godavari, by the Western Ghats in the west, and by central mountains in north-east, the interior peninsula landscape touches the western plains in Gujarat, where Saurashtra forms the north-western corner of the Deccan Trap.

South of the Tapti and Narmada, all the big rivers of the peninsula drain the Western Ghats and run for most of their distance across predominantly dry, flat plateaux, which slope from west to east behind the Western Ghats, on the north-west–south-east bias of the Krishna–Godavari system. Fertile black soils run in wide seams along the Narmada basin, the upper Godavari river in Maharashtra, and all along the Krishna river and its tributaries in Karnataka, the Bhima, and Tungabhadra. Outside the black soil tracts, the northern Deccan soil is predominantly medium black; and the southern soils in Karnataka and upland Tamil Nadu are mixtures of red with patches of black. All these soils are quite fertile when water is sufficient – which it usually is not – and the blacker the soil is, the better it can produce good crops with meagre moisture.

Getting enough water is the main problem for farmers, because most of this land is in the rain shadow of the western Ghats; and everywhere, monsoons are fickle. Historically, intensive agriculture has expanded outward from places that are favoured by rivers and good soils. As in other landscapes, a rainfall gradient runs from west to east, and a north-west–south-east gradient is also inscribed across the peninsula by drainage water which can be used for irrigation. In the Maharashtra Deccan, wells provide most irrigation from underground supplies, even today, after the spread of large river dams and canals. But on the Karnataka plateau and north-east to Hyderabad and Warangal, irrigation from tanks formed by walls built across routes of drainage becomes more important. Tanks multiply further to the south-east. The gradual increase in drainage from north-west to south-east has allowed parallel increases in irrigated acreage, multiple cropping, and population density; but a major hole in this gradation lies in the very dry north Deccan interior and in the Pennar–Krishna interfluve (Anantapur, Bellary, Kurnool, Adoni, Raichur, Bijapur), where numerous tanks have long supported meagre irrigation and sparse population. As we will see, there is some evidence of desiccation in the driest parts of the interior peninsula since the early nineteenth century.

Agriculture has expanded over centuries into three forest types that distinguish the peninsula from the natural steppe land of thorny shrubs in Punjab, Rajasthan, and Gujarat. Originally, dry tropical forest of deciduous trees covered the flatlands. By 1900, it was reduced to more or less tree-covered savannah. Monsoon forests that lost their leaves in the dry season (providing natural manure) once covered the slopes of the high plateaux and eastern Ghats; and they were also once full of teak, most of which is now gone. Rain forest, evergreen, covered the western Ghats historically, and much of it remains. Into each forest type, farms pushed over the centuries, and, overall, the peninsula's north-west–south-east gradient organised the geographical diversity of agro-technological milieus. Pastoralism and long-fallow millet cultivation dominated the driest parts, especially north and west, into the nineteenth century. Shortening fallow and well irrigation enabled more intense dry farming to take over where rainfall, technology, and water table allow. Rainfall and drainage have long made wet paddy cultivation more prominent in the south. Variegated soil and water conditions create various cropping regions, in which millets, cotton, and oilseeds predominate, with patches of intensive well cultivation and irrigated paddy (especially in the south) and also expanses of animal raising and pastoralism, especially in the north.

Coastal plains

This composite landscape along the sea coast is formed of river valleys, plains, and deltas and their adjacent interfluvial flatlands; everywhere it includes the immediately adjacent uplands and mountain sides, and it is dominated agriculturally by the riverine plains, alluvial soils, and paddy fields. Its mountain border on the west coast and its proximity in the east to the tropical depressions that form the winter monsoon in the Bay of Bengal bring this landscape much more rain than the interior peninsula. On the whole, it is more tropical in appearance, even its driest parts along the Tamil and Andhra coast in the southeast. It is a borderland with the ocean, and this creates a fishery ecology and social life along the beach that is an integral part of its agrarian history, as are the coastal sea trade and connections to sea coasts everywhere in the Indian Ocean, Bay of Bengal, and Arabian Sea. Some of its constituent territories are also relatively isolated from inland corridors – Chittagong, Orissa, parts of Kerala, and, above all, Sri Lanka – and coastal regions communicate most intensively by sea, often more so with one another than by land with adjacent inland territories. The Tamil and Kerala coasts are thus part of a cultural space that also embraces coastal Sri Lanka, and the cultural traffic between the South Asian littoral and Southeast Asia has been constantly influential over the centuries. Bengal's most prominent historical connections have run along water ways to Orissa, Assam, and Bihar. Migrations are common among these coastal regions, which logically have similarities in diet (featuring more fish) and in occupations, with more fishing communities and water transportation. Rice is the dominant food grain everywhere in this watery landscape.

CHAPTER 2

TERRITORY

The long history of agriculture is of countless ecological interventions that have given nature its civility, and imparted personality to the land, as people have cut down forests, diverted rivers, built lakes, killed predators, tamed, bred, and slaughtered animals, and burnt, dug, and axed natural growth to replace it with things that people desire. Farming occurs in a land of emotion, and agrarian territories need gods, poetry, ritual, architecture, outsiders, frontiers, myths, borderlands, landmarks, and families, which give farms meaning and purpose. Together, brute power and refined aesthetics culture the land, and war is so prominent in old poetry because making a homeland is violent business. In the long span of agrarian history, therefore, a great variety of skills have combined to make nature a natural environment, and agrarian territories have emerged historically much like cuisine. Clearing the land and sculpting the fields create a place for the nurture and collection of ingredients. Skilled labour selects, cultivates, kills, dresses, chops, and grinds. Fuels, pots, knives, axes, hoes, mortar and pestle, and many other implements are involved in making all the daily meals and special feasts that sustain work, family, and community. Like a farmer's home territory, a cuisine's complexity and refinement always develop within networks of exchange and specialisation, because materials, ideas, techniques, and tastes come from many sources; but each cuisine also emerges inside spaces of cultured accumulation and experimentation, in which people experience their place in the world, territorially, as they make their very own set of special ingredients into appropriate foods for appropriate occasions.

Radiocarbon dates indicate that people were inventing agriculture in various parts of South Asia 7500 years before the Common Era (BCE).[1]

---

[1] Carbon-14 dates indicate the indigenous, multiple origins for agrarian communities in the valleys of the Ganga and Belan rivers (in the Vindhyas) over the millennia before 7000 BCE, which included plant and animal domestication, changing food habits, seed selection, population growth, and the cultivation of rice (*oryza sativa*). See G. R. Sharma, V. D. Misra, D. Mandal, B. B. Misra, and J. N. Pal, *Beginnings of Agriculture: From Hunting and Food Gathering to Domestication of Plants and Animals. Studies in History, Culture, and Archaeology, Volume IV*, Allahabad, 1980, pp. 30–1.

Indus Valley cities appear abruptly in the third millennium BCE at intersections of huge zones of farming and pastoralism which left behind archaeological remains over a million square miles running from Iran to Awadh and Afghanistan to Gujarat. The oldest ploughed field yet to be excavated dates to the early Harappan period, *circa* 2600 BCE, and at this time, pastoral peoples also moved routinely in the summer from the high mountains in Baluchistan west into Iran and east into the valley of the Indus. Pastoral encampments dominate early archaeological records in the western plains and mountains. Evidence of permanent farming increases during the Harappan period and clusters along the lower Indus and the old Saraswati river. Painted grey ware sites indicate that the Saraswati retreated steadily and disappeared during the first millennium BCE. Mohenjo-daro was surrounded by small settlements of farmers and herders along networks of trade and migration; and, in post-Harappa centuries, agro-pastoral societies expanded their reach and impact. Today, in Saurashtra, earthen mounds rise up on the land in open spaces between wealthy Gujarati farming villages and contain evidence of agro-pastoral settlement and circulation. Prehistoric herders moved their animals among watery places as some dug in to farm the land and produced variously stable farming communities here and there.

The regulation, extension, and elaboration of social power to organise the interaction of farming and herding formed ancient agrarian territories that come into better view in the last millennium BCE. Ritual was critical; we can see this at Harappa. Vedic hymns indicate that, around 1500 BCE, agro-pastoral people who performed Vedic rituals were moving south from Haryana and east down the Gangetic basin. We can imagine this movement as an extensive pursuit of water and new farmland, but the hymns also record the spread of Vedic rituals among different societies of herders and farmers during an eastward expansion of agro-pastoralism, which eventually moved into the eastern jungles, where it met other farming societies. The hymns tell of the fire god Agni burning his way eastward under the patronage of a human lord of the sacrifice, the *jajman*, who ruled and protected his people. Forty or so generations of farmers must have burned and cut their away into Gangetic forests, carving the rim land and the lowlands of the basin, learning to use iron tools, and inventing a new cuisine full of meat, rice, spices, and vegetables, before documented agrarian history begins in the middle of the first millennium

BCE, in the region of Magadha, around the sites of Rajagrha and Pataliputra, in Bihar. It is most probable that a spread of Vedic rituals among ancient peoples occurred alongside migrations by Indo-Aryan language speakers moving down the Ganga basin; but the ritual nexus would certainly have embraced ever more diverse populations as the old rice-growing cultures of the humid tropics in the east made their independent contributions to the rise of agrarian culture in ancient Bihar. As agro-pastoralism and warrior migrations connected the eastern Ganga basin to Iran, Afghanistan, and the Indus–Saraswati cultural complex, the people living in the eastern rain forests and the riverine travellers among littoral sites around the Ganga delta and Bay of Bengal must have contributed to the rise of rice-growing farm societies in Magadha. By the end of the first millennium BCE, Indo-Aryan linguistic evidence mingled with Dravidian and other cultural forms in agrarian sites scattered from the Indus to the Brahmaputra and south of the Vindhyas to Kanya Kumari. A number of distinctive ritual and social complexes emerged, marked by many regionally specific artefacts, such as megaliths and burial urns in the southern-most peninsula. The absorption of tribal peoples into the ritual complex that slowly evolved from Vedic rites gave rise to numerous animal deities and blood sacrifices missing in early Vedic texts.

When imagining the oldest periods of the agrarian past – for which empirical evidence is steadily increasing, forming a vast puzzle with an unknown number of missing pieces – we must contend with the old view that ancient states evolved with the progress of Aryan conquest, during Aryan elite differentiation, and with the incorporation of native peoples into an Aryan political and social order, described in Sanskrit texts. Most scholars have discarded this narrative but it still appears in many textbooks. There were actually no Aryan *people* as such (defined either as a race or as a linguistic or ethnic group). Rather, what we have is a number of texts that reflect the linguistic elements that scholars classify as 'Indo-Aryan'; and these texts, spread over many centuries and locations, convey a number of ritual, prescriptive, descriptive, and narrative messages, whose authorship, audience, influence, and cultural coherence remain debatable. Archaeological evidence constitutes an increasing proportion of our evidence on ancient sites, and indicates that a number of connected cultures were developing separately in many parts of South Asia. Various trajectories of historical change can be proposed using available evidence; and various indigenous peoples with their own histories in the eastern Gangetic basin, adjacent hills, nearby coastal areas, and across the Bay of Bengal must have played a significant part in the rise of ancient Magadha. Ancient India's many histories intersected, diverged, and travelled independently, so that instead of a linear trend connecting the RgVeda and the Mauryas, we can generate many open-ended hypotheses to account for shifts among various forms of socio-political order. Increasingly complex forms of social organisation – state institutions and imperial dynasties – did evolve in the last half of the first millennium BCE, but the shift that Romila Thapar has described as a general movement from lineage polities to full-fledged states did not constitute a comprehensive evolutionary shift *toward* state formation and *away* from older forms of lineage society. Very old and very new forms of social, political, and economic organisation coexisted and interacted, as they would continue to do for many centuries. Ancient South Asia was a universe of small societies in which some of the more powerful groups left us records to indicate some of their most prominent features. Famous ancient states arose in the eastern flood plain at the intersection of trade routes, and territorial markers in ancient texts indicate sites and peoples around them. One striking continuity between the days of Harappa and of the Mauryan empire is the importance of trade and migration among sites in South Asia, Central Asia, and the Indian Ocean basin.

In this context, agriculture expanded within individually named territories that were called *janapadas* and *mahajanapadas*, The proper names for these kinds of territories appear in epigraphy throughout much of the first millennium. In Magadha and the Maurya heartland, ancient agriculture seems to have been more intensive – combining more labour and supporting more non-farming elites per unit of land – over a larger territory than anywhere else in the subcontinent. Two lines of development converged here. Technological change in metallurgy, irrigation, plant breeding, and farming techniques facilitated more intensive farming; in this, the old rice cultures around the Bay of Bengal and minerals from Chota Nagpur and Jharkhand would have been significant. Alliances among warriors, traders, ritualists, and farmers formed the state institutions that connected settlements to one another, connected farms to sources of iron ore, and disciplined labour (for farming, fighting, building, hauling, mining, smelting, forest clearing, and other work) to produce an expanding agrarian territory around the central urban sites of dynastic authority in the eastern Ganga basin. Ancient material and social technologies of agrarian power spread together. State authority and intensive agricultural production moved together and depended upon one another. Dynastic capitals rose along routes of trade and migration across landscapes filled with many types of farming settlements. Kautilya's *Arthasastra* reflects a compilation of elements that pertain to the Maurya core zone over a period of about seven hundred years, down to the time of the Guptas, and indicates that here state institutions did exert direct power in agriculture. But not so much elsewhere. Most agrarian territories that felt the fleeting impact of Maurya power were inhabited predominantly by pastoralists, shifting cultivators, and small settled farming communities. Agro-pastoral societies along the model of the post-Harappa sites in Gujarat must have remained a typical form throughout dry landscapes of the north, west, and central peninsula well into the first millennium. In most *janapadas*, the Mauryan empire seems to have consisted of strategic urban sites on routes of trade and conquest, connected loosely to vast hinterlands.

Independent but connected agrarian histories were under way in many areas during Mauryan times; this is indicated by the many new centres of power that enter the historical record in the first centuries of the Common Era. In Maurya times, Sri Lanka and Cambodia would have formed an outer rim of interconnected, rice-growing territories. Puskalavati, Taxila, and Gandhara arose along the upper Indus and Kabul rivers, along overland trade routes in the north-west. Satavahana inscriptions show new state authorities rising in the peninsula, around Pratisthana in Berar, Girinagara in Saurashtra, Amaravati in the Krishna–Godavari delta, and Vanavasi in the southern Deccan. In the far south, Sangam literature reflects another emerging agrarian culture. Buddhist and Jain texts depict many pre-Gupta urban sites along old trade routes from north to south, which like Kanchipuram thrived in agricultural settings; and, by the second century, we can see Buddhist sites in most riverine and coastal areas in which medieval dynasties would later thrive. In the fourth century, when the Guptas sought to extend their own empire, they faced stiff opposition, and they never did conquer the Vakatakas, who succeeded the Satavahanas in the north Deccan.

The Gupta empire produced a new kind of articulation between state institutions and social power in agriculture. The Mauryas had thrown impressive land bridges across many *janapadas*, among islands of farming in the sea of pastoralism, and they concentrated their power in urban sites along extensive routes of trade and transport. The Gupta imperium launched a conquest of the *janapadas* by farming. Mauryas travelled a more extensive empire. Guptas were more down to earth. A Gupta core zone of intensive agriculture expanded westward to include not only Magadha and adjacent Vaisali and Videha but also *janapadas* around ancient Allahabad (Prayaga) and Ayodhya (at Kasi and Kosala). Gupta agrarian power also expanded north and south toward the hills on both sides of the Ganga basin as it embraced a larger number and diversity of farming peoples. Gupta rituals sanctified agrarian kingship. State-sponsored religious institutions (temples), elites (Brahmans), and sacred texts sanctified land as they incorporated local community leaders. Historians have shown how the Gupta system empowered rising elites outside the imperial court in a ritualised state which had expansive capacities for political inclusion. Gupta ritual techniques for alliance-building were adopted widely and adapted to many local conditions from the third century onward. Saiva, Vaishnava, and Buddhist cult institutions combined with state authority to create powerful but flexible agrarian alliances among farmers, warriors, merchants, ritualists, kings, and literati.

Sanctification constituted real social power with tangible benefits for its participants, and its social production and meaning changed over the centuries as sanctity attached to more and more land in culturally distinct, interconnected territories. With scattered evidence from literary sources, we can dimly see how Vedic rituals had helped to organise agrarian power in a world of agro-pastoralism. Vedic ritual pacified conflict between nomadic pastoralists and sedentary farmers and formed stable structures of alliance by sanctifying the performance of ritual and the composition of community. Ancient myths depict battles between herders and farmers as supernatural struggles between *devas* and *asuras*; and ritualistic gambling – performed with the injunction, 'Play the cow for rice!' – may represent 'a sacrificial contest [that] could also be put to work to regulate and sanction conquest, tribute levying, overlordship and generally, state formation'.[2] Expanding the scope of agrarian territoriality involved the elaboration

[2] J. C. Heesterman, 'Warrior, Peasant and Brahmin', *Modern Asian Studies*, 29, 3, 1995, 645, 649.

and adaptation of ritual negotiations in countless new competitive settings in each agrarian landscape. Rituals spread and changed form as they proved effective in creating stable alliances in a world in which communities of settled farmers were certainly a minority.

Pastoralism occupied much of the subcontinent until later medieval times. When Indus Valley urbanism disappeared, its culture dispersed into mostly pastoral surroundings. Rgvedic society was pastoral. The *Mahabharata* depicts a society full of pastoralism. Krishna was born among Yadava cattle herders and many gods have similar origins among hunters and pastoral people. Sangam poetry describes five ecological regions and only one is sedentary. The ancient Tamil mountain, forest, wasteland, and seashore regions were the home of tribes, hunters, gatherers, nomads, and travellers. Hero stones across the peninsula record the pre-eminence of cattle raiding as a political activity in the first millennium. Old Tamil society was probably conquered from the peninsular steppe by nomads called Kalabhras in the fourth century. South Asia is in fact part of a vast historical space in which pastoralism is very prominent, stretching from Mongolia across Central Asia, Syria, and Egypt to the Maghreb and Sahel. In this wider world of arid climates, pastoralism has historically surrounded and permeated agrarian landscapes in which farms cluster around water sources along trade routes. South Asia is a borderland between this world of pastoralism and humid Southeast Asia, where dense forest and intensive agriculture exclude nomads herding large flocks. In the eastern wet lands, rice typifies agriculture, natural forest is very dense, domestic animals breeding was challenged until quite recently by tiger populations, and nomadic pastoralism is quite foreign. But in the west and the peninsular interior of South Asia, dry agrarian space is more like south-west and central Asia, where millets and wheat dominate field crops, thirst and drought preoccupy society, lowland forests are predominantly scrub, herds abound, and nomads pervade agrarian history. Ancient states in South Asia arose at the intersection of these two very different worlds of agrarian ecology.

In the first millennium, the creation of landscapes of settled agriculture moved ahead more rapidly, as agrarian institutions promoted ritual negotiations to solve conflicts among farmers, pastoralists, warriors, merchants, forest dwellers, and many others. Agrarian territories expanded when conflicts could be resolved routinely by stable institutions of social power and authority. War could destroy social routines that stabilised territory and routinely allowed the jungle and wild animals to invade farmland that had previously nurtured piety and nobility. Farming communities became increasingly populous and complex as agrarian territories evolved to embrace larger and larger populations of people on the move. War became a cultural institution for negotiating competing interests and preventing war from destroying structures of agrarian stability was a critical secret of agrarian success. In the sixteenth century, the *A'in-i Akbari* and other sources support speculation that nearly 20 per cent of the population depended on fighting for their livelihood, which of course meant travelling much of the time. Armies would pillage some farms to provision warriors who returned with their loot to their own farms when battles were done. The dry season was always a time for fighting; drought sent villages out to fight for food; and armies subsisted in turn on pillaging drought-stricken villages, causing communities to flee to fortress towns or to go out in search of new land. Migrations by whole communities were common and many agricultural sites have thus been settled and resettled, historically, over and over again. Herders heading to the hills in the summer and back down to the lowlands with the monsoon, seasonal worker migrations, people fleeing war and drought, army suppliers and camp followers, artisans moving from town to town, farmers moving into new settlements looking for new land, traders, nomads, shifting cultivators, hunters, pilgrims, and transporters would have added up to perhaps half the total population at almost any point in most regions during centuries before 1800. What we call 'sedentary agriculture', therefore, was not really sedentary. Reigning social powers settled, inhabited, identified with, and controlled territories of agricultural investment and political order, but farmers worked within institutions that embraced many conflicting social forces, many of which were constantly on the move.

Gupta-era institutions developed new capacities to control territory by sanctifying the land and by establishing rules of *dharma* (religious duty) that disciplined labour for the co-ordinated performance of all the activities of agriculture. In Sri Lanka, Anuradhapura was the centre of a Buddhist empire of irrigated agriculture that expanded across the dry north of the island in the first millennium, at the same time as the Guptas began seriously to sedentarise *Bharat*. Maurya conquest had first defined the territory of *Bharat* as a triangle with its apex in the eastern Ganga, in the sacred precincts of Magahda, Kasi, and Kosala, and with its base in the fertile parts of Rajasthan. The northern leg of the triangle ran west-north-west up across submontane Punjab and the Khyber pass; and its southern leg ran west-south-west down the Narmada into Gujarat. The western frontiers of ancient *Bharat* thus ran north–south; and at the base of the triangle lay Gandhara in the north and Nasika in the south. The Gupta's version of *Bharat* was concentrated in the agrarian lowlands. Samudragupta's fourth-century Allahabad inscription divides Gupta conquests into four categories, which correspond roughly with the literary geography found in the Puranas. In the territory called *Aryavarta*, the inscription says, rulers were subdued and territories brought under Gupta administration – in the Ganga plain, Naga domains (Bundelkhand and Malwa), Kota territory (around Delhi and Bulandshahr), and Pundravardhana and Vanga (in Bengal). These became Puranic home territories, called *desa*. Here, Gupta cities – Prayaga (Allahabad), Benares, and Pataliputra (Patna) – provided ideological reference points for the sacred geography of *Bharat*. The sanctity of *Bharat* would bolster agrarian power in many medieval territories. But Puranic *desa* did not explicitly include the highlands around the Ganga basin, nor the Indus valley, Punjab, and western Rajasthan. Puranas describe the *desa* of *Bharat* as *Purva-desa*, *Madhya-desa*, and *Aparanta desa*, which embraced the Ganga lowlands, north Bengal, the Brahmaputra valley, Avanti (Malwa), Gujarat, Konkan, and the Deccan around Nasik. Old *janapadas* which lay outside the land of the *desa* would have been frontiers and peripheries of the Gupta regime. The western plains, Punjab, high mountains, central mountains, and coast and interior peninsula outside *Nasika-Konkana* are not called *desa* in Puranas, but rather *asreya, patha,* and *pristha*.[3]

The Gupta imperium fell apart in the late fifth century as new dynasties detached Saurashtra, Malwa, Bundelkhand, and Baghelkhand; as Vakatakas expanded from the northern Deccan into Dakshina

[3] In the other three areas of Gupta conquest, the regime seems to have been indirect at best. The Allahabad inscription says that in Dakshinapatha (south of the central mountains), Dakshina Kosala (Chhattisgarh), Mahakantara (inland Orissa), and the lands of the Kalingas (on the Andhra-Orissa coast) and Pallavas (on the Tamil coast) rulers were conquered and restored to their thrones as tributaries. Rulers scattered in the mountains and plains frontiers – who numbered five in the east and north and nine in the west – were forced to pay tribute. In the far periphery, Kusanas, Murundas, and Sakas in the north-west and peoples of Simhala (Sri Lanka) were also said to have paid tribute. See Joseph E. Schwartzberg, *Historical Atlas of South Asia*, Chicago, 1978, pp. 27, 179, 182–3.

Kosala, Baghelkhand, and Malwa; and as Hunas conquered the low-lands along routes running south and east from the north-western highlands. Puranic authors called this *Kali Yuga*, but the idea that a classical age collapsed with the fall of the Guptas pertains at best to Gupta core regions and their ruling elites. Many historians describe the second half of the first millennium as an age of political fragmentation and regionalisation, but this imagery fits only *janapadas* in *Bharat* and Puranic *desa* in *Aryavarta*. Gupta centres may have been the wealthiest in the subcontinent but most people lived outside Gupta territory. In fact, agrarian history outside *Bharat* comes into much better focus *after* the Guptas, as social powers which had been nurtured in the Gupta realm disperse and develop. Many new regimes now took up the project of protecting *dharma* and formed a cultural basis for medieval dynasties. As regimes of royalty and ritual multiplied after the fall of the Guptas, they produced new historical documentation. Inscriptions on stone and copper provide raw material for medieval historiography and their interpretation continues to be filled with unresolved debates. Two debates are most important here. One concerns 'the Indian state' in medieval centuries. Should it be understood as bureaucratic, feudal, segmentary, patrimonial, or something else? The other concerns the mode of production, and specifically whether European models of feudalism or Marx's model of the Asiatic mode of production apply in South Asia. Both debates hinge on the effort to reconstruct typical or characteristic institutional forms in medieval South Asia. But instead of looking for 'the medieval state', we can examine the range of institutions that organised social power during the expansion and intensification of agriculture. Instead of describing 'the mode of production', we can try to outline the working of social power in agriculture, keeping in view the great diversity of agrarian conditions.

PEASANTRY

Most information for medieval history comes from inscriptions that record donations of land, animals, and other assets to Brahmans and to temples to support Vedic knowledge, *dharma*, and rituals for Puranic deities. Donations typically come from named, titled individuals, acting under dynastic authority; and they typically name donors, recipients, protectors, and asset holders, who are often members of

farming communities. Donative inscriptions often depict the transfer of land entitlements to Brahmans in the name of – or at the behest of – a king. They represent a transactional nexus that involves dynastic royalty (warrior-kings and their families, officials, and retainers), Brahmans (individually and in groups, Vedic scholars, ritualists, and temple administrators), and agricultural communities (farmers, herders, artisans, and merchants). Brahmans are pivotal figures and the most obvious beneficiaries, and in other ways, too, the agrarian power of Brahmans is quite apparent in the second half of the first millennium. As farm territory multiplied and expanded, Brahmans produced more agricultural literature. One elusive persona, Kasyapa (perhaps a mythical authority rather than a single author), wrote that 'for pleasing the gods and protecting the people, the king should take keen interest in agriculture', and further he said, 'Agriculture should be practised by priests, Brahmanas and ministers particularly.' He tells the king to mine 'iron, copper, gold, [and] silver', to have agricultural implements made by 'expert iron smiths, cutters, and goldsmiths in villages and cities', and to 'distribute these among the village people'.[4] The role of the good king in linking together various agricultural activities is clear in these injunctions, and kings in Sri Lanka, Nepal, and many places in medieval South Asia seem to have followed this advice. Dozens of dynasties emerged from the sixth century onward, complete with centres of production and rising aggregate farm yields where Brahmans recorded, created, and propagated agricultural knowledge.

The *Kamba Ramayana*, *Krsisukti*, *Vrksa Ayurveda*, and *Paryayamuktavali* are among the texts that describe irrigated tracts in the south, east, and north. The distribution of inscriptions also leads to the conclusion that, in the early-medieval period, the organised social effort to build agrarian territories was concentrated spatially in irrigated tracts in the lowlands, near riverbeds throughout the northern basins, the coastal plains, and the Deccan, Maharashtra, Gujarat, Malwa, and Rajasthan. Inscriptions record investments in fixed assets – irrigation tanks, dams, wells, channels, paddy fields, temples, towns, markets, and cities – and transactions in networks of exchange, marriage, ritual, and dynastic authority, which connected settlements to one another. Inscriptions describe a world of kings, Brahmans, and temple deities that constituted medieval agrarian

---

[4] M. S. Randhawa, *A History of Agriculture in India*, Delhi, 1986, vol. I, p. 484.

territory physically, socially, morally, and mythologically. Inscriptional *prasasti*s (preambles) narrate dynastic genealogies (*vamsavali*) and map royalty into social territory, and devotional poetry and temples likewise brought the gods into the farming landscape. Medieval Tamil poems such as the *Tevaram* depict a sacred geography of Shiva temples that sanctified the land much more extensively and intensively than did the Sangam poetic accounts of Murugan cult sites in the *Tirumurugattruppadai* or post-Sangam accounts of Buddhist centres in the *Manimekalai* (in the Gupta age). Territorial power and symbolism are more definitely documented in early-medieval literature and inscriptions; and intensive, sedentary farming – particularly using irrigation – required more control over land and labour, as farms advanced forcefully into space inhabited by pastoralists, nomads, forest people, hunters, wild animals, and malevolent spirits. Building agrarian territory was difficult and contested. It was not peaceful. Farms carved up nature, enclosed open land, and commandeered the physical world to constitute civilisation on the frontiers of farming. Taming the landscape meant displacing forms of land use and social life other than those represented by kings and gods, who spread the rule of *dharma*. Expanding intensive agriculture involved disciplining workers, coordinating their activities, and reorganising the allocation of resources. Medieval inscriptions recorded events in this process – as a technology-of-record – in compact agrarian territories.

Many types of agrarian societies came into being. A general contrast emerged between the wetter eastern landscapes and the coastal plains, on the one hand, and the drier west and interior peninsula, on the other, which was based on broad differences between wet and dry cultivation. In the humid wetlands, wild animals, disease, dense jungle, forest people, and floods posed the roughest obstacles to the expansion of permanent field cultivation. In semi-arid regions, by contrast, the worst battles were waged against pastoral people and warrior nomads, whose income was readily enhanced by raids on farming villages, whose grazing lands were being converted into farmland, and whose herds were being captured and domesticated. In the drier landscapes, settlements were more scattered and pastoral nomad warriors more prominent. Walled towns were more common, and long-distance trade was more visible in dynastic core settlements where military activity was a permanent adjunct to farming. In the wetter landscapes, farmers needed more labour to carve out fields from jungle; the higher

nutritional output of paddy fields also sustained denser populations and a higher proportion of non-cultivating elites. Dry regions grew millets and, in the north, wheat; their population was thinner and elites depended on trade and wide systems of exchange and expropriation. Wet, dry, agro-pastoral, forest, fishing, and other kinds of settlements were generally mixed together in agrarian territories, which would have at their centre a central place of power and authority. Inscriptions often reflect a cultural hierarchy that distinguished the more cultivated central settlements from surrounding hamlets that were part of the territory but less cultured and privileged.

The medieval states that produced inscriptions had a basic commitment to the expansion of permanent field cultivation as the foundation of their power, and *dharma* was the moral code that stabilised their territory. The weakness of agrarian territorialism and thus of the rule of *dharma* is apparent throughout the first millennium, when many wars recorded in inscriptions no doubt reflect a breakdown of territorial institutions during violent conflicts among sedentary farmers, pastoralists, shifting cultivators, hunters, warriors, and forest dwellers. Pastoral and tribal polities often opposed the rule of *dharma* successfully. But pastoral and tribal peoples also became powerful in lowland territories of settled cultivation and their role was particularly pronounced in the western plains, central mountains, Punjab, western Gangetic basin, and the interior peninsula. Rajput rulers came to recognise Bhil chiefs as allies, for instance, and an 1890 account depicts the central role of Bhil chiefs in Rajput coronation ceremonies.[5] As permanent field cultivation conquered agrarian landscapes, farm by farm, pastoralism, nomadism, and forest cultivators were increasingly pushed to the margins, and many herders, hunters, nomads, and tribal people also entered agrarian society, becoming labourers, farmers, craft producers, animal breeders and keepers, transporters, dairy producers, soldiers, traders, warriors, sorcerers, and kings. This transformation of the land involved very long transitions and subtle changes in social identity, which further differentiated agrarian societies. It also involved a lot of violence, which can be seen refracted in mythical stories about the conquest of demons by gods. Many *vamcavalis* (introductory invocations) depict battles against tribal peoples who are viewed as enemies of civilised society. The *Ramayana*

---

[5] K. S. Singh, *People of India: The Scheduled Tribes*, Delhi, 1994, p. 119.

was reproduced in many forms, attesting to the wide relevance of its central theme: the struggle and triumph of civilisation in a land of demons and *mlecchas* (barbarians). The Mughals would take special precautions to protect farmers against hill tribes as they pushed farming into the higher valleys. As agricultural territories expanded and multiplied, they came to include more diverse populations, not only many different kinds of farmers (including families who worked their own plots and families who used others to cultivate their fields) but also non-farming groups whose work and assets were essential for farming (artisans, cattle herders, hunters, transporters, traders, collectors of forest produce, well-diggers, priests, engineers, architects, healers, astrologers, and mercenaries). Many people who came to work in agricultural sites came from lands that were being newly incorporated into agrarian territory. Without the skills, assets, and labour of erstwhile outsiders, agricultural expansion could not proceed, and their incorporation was a major social project. Open spaces around all farming settlements also provided plenty of opportunity for groups to set out on their own to establish independent communities.

Medieval agrarian space came to consist of (1) hundreds of small agrarian territories with permanent field cultivation, diverse, changing populations, and dynastic core sites, (2) thousands of scattered settlements of farming families in the hills and plains, on the outskirts or margins of dynastic territory, and (3) vast interstitial areas in which farms were absent or temporary, featuring dry scrub-forest or dense tropical jungle and filled with tribal societies and polities. Almost all of our documentation pertains to the dynastic territories of agrarian expansion. This land was endowed with the best supplies of everything needed for agriculture. It was prize territory and required the most intense internal controls and protection. Medieval kings concentrated on controlling this land, to protect their people and prosperity, which involved coercion as well as cultural powers to inculcate deep beliefs in principles and values that sustained agrarian order. Around core dynastic sites swirled all the activity of territorial expansion; and, as populations in core sites increased in number, some of their number would strike out to expand agrarian power. They formed scattered settlements that became new dynastic centres, conquered other farming communities, and fought for land and labour with pastoral and forest peoples. Non-farming populations in the hills and plains often settled down to farming in the lowlands, forming their own distinctive communities. A separate agrarian history unfolded in the high mountains, of which we have little record.

In this diversity of agrarian social forms, a 'peasantry' is hard to define. Unlike Europe, South Asia contained tropical conditions suitable for intensive paddy cultivation, expanses of arid and semi-arid plains, high-quality soils that could produce nutritious millets with relatively small labour inputs, vast tropical mountains and jungles, and large areas dominated by pastoralism – all of which sustained very different types of agricultural expansion and intensification, leading to various configurations of agrarian society. In South Asia, there was no analogue to the Roman empire or Catholic Church under which a feudal nobility could establish itself and define the peasantry as a category of subordinate subject. Unlike China, agrarian states in South Asia evolved significantly within, among, and out of pastoral cultures and they integrated pastoral and forest people into forms of agrarian society that were not embraced by the classificatory system of a single imperial (and ethnic, Han) heritage. Modern images of the peasant that come from western and eastern Eurasia – which describe a rude rustic living under the jurisdiction of urban elites who embody high culture and civilisation – do not fit medieval South Asia.

The term 'peasant' can be useful to refer in a general sense to family farmers, and in doing so I do not mean to endorse the theory of peasant family farming – developed by A. V. Chayanov to counter V. I. Lenin's account of peasant differentiation during capitalist development in Russia. Rather, I intend to highlight the role of kinship and farm families in agriculture; and we will see later in this chapter that the elaboration of kinship organised much of medieval agrarian space in lineages, clans, castes (*jati*), sects, and the four ritual ranks (*varna*) of Brahmans, Kshatriyas, Vaisyas, and Sudras, which embraced farmers and kings. The peasant as a family farmer has no fixed class status. Class divisions between peasants and lords took many forms and medieval farmers were encumbered by many types and degrees of subordination, ranging from mere tax or rent obligations for land entitlements to intimate personal servitude. Institutions of control and subordination are the subject of the remainder of this chapter. The most intense subordination of farm families appears to have arisen where very low Sudra and untouchable caste (*jati*) groups worked under Brahman and Kshatriya domination in the rice-growing Gupta core territories and in early-medieval lowlands along the coastal plains. But this is not a general pattern. Farm families entered the ranks of local ruling elites in many regions of militant peasant colonisation. In agro-pastoral and tribal settings, family farming was a communal enterprise which included military control over mobile resources and shifting farm territories.

The term 'peasant' makes the most sense when agrarian social strata are clearly defined by states and when status depends upon strictly ranked entitlements to land. This situation became more common in the second millennium. It began earlier in territories of warrior colonisation, for example, by Gurjara-Pratiharas, when conquest formalised the ranks of lord and peasant. After 1500, social ranks in some parts of South Asia came increasingly to resemble Europe, and after 1820, European categories came into vogue under British rule. In the twentieth century, many political activists call themselves 'peasants', modelling their usage on revolutionary Russia and China. As we see in chapter 4, this usage appears primarily in tenant struggles against landlordism, where ranked entitlements to land are at issue. In that context the term is ideological and normative, rather than being accurately descriptive. As a translation of *kisan*, 'peasant' has been deployed where 'landholder', 'farmer', 'village petite bourgeoisie', or even 'tribal' could also apply; and it is usually more accurate to refer to so-called peasant groups by the ethnic or *jati* terms that they use to refer to themselves. *Rai'yat* (or ryot), which might also translate as 'peasant', attaches to people with various types of entitlements and class positions, as we will see. No term translates strictly as 'peasant', carrying precisely the same cultural connotations, in any South Asian language. As a result, we can aptly consider the rise of the *utility* of the category of 'peasant' in South Asia as a product and component of modernity and use this term to discuss the power position of small farmers and tenants in opposition to landlords and states.

The term 'gentry' is not widely used in South Asia but it does have utility. Multi-caste agrarian farming elites were formed by the interaction of state elites with local patriarchies and by expanding family alliances, upward mobility, and the imposition of state-enforced, ranked entitlements to land. The term 'gentry' has had no place in official terminology in South Asia, as it has had in China, but an important sector of the village farming population in South Asia more resembles Chinese gentry than European peasants. I consider the gentry to consist of relatively high-status local land-owning groups that marry their own kind and form alliances with other high-status families to expand their horizons as they redefine their ties to the land. Gentry families are privileged as mediators with state authorities; and, because of their land holding, education, and urban connections, they are active in commercial networks. This agrarian status elite is always open to new recruits. It is rural and urban, economic and cultural, social and political. A gentry first arose in the context of Gupta state rituals, which produced dominant caste alliances that came to control agrarian assets of all sorts, including the labour of subordinate *jatis*. The idea of a locally dominant caste cluster maps with rough equivalence onto my sense of what a gentry is; though a gentry does not need caste ideology, because other modes of status marketing can serve the same purposes.

DHARMA

Inscriptions indicate that, in the sixth century, royal Gupta lineages had settled down in all the regions of the Gupta realm and may have been settling the frontiers of *Aryavarta*. Ambitious lineage leaders may have loosened their ties to the capital as they moved further afield, carrying with them the apparatus of Gupta power. In frontier regions, they would have needed local allies, who may have undermined their attachment to the Gupta dynasty. Gifts of land by kings and their officers to temples and Brahmans – to sustain classical learning, the rule of *dharma*, and the worship of Puranic deities – became a hallmark of new dynasties at the end of Gupta hegemony, from the sixth century onward. The Maukharis appear in the western reaches of the Gupta heartland, around Kanyakubja (Kanauj), in what would later become Awadh, and Pusyabutis emerged in the western Yamuna basin and Haryana. Dynastic core sites thus moved still further west from the ancient heartland of *Bharat* and so did land grants to Brahmans, which multiplied with the founding of new regimes and capital cities. In the seventh century, it is said, Harsha moved the Pusyabuti capital to Kanyakubja to better defend the plains against the Hunas, but his move also signalled the rise of the western parts of the Ganga basin as a new agrarian core for his dynasty. This event was marked by a land grant to two Brahmans. The grant was made by a soldier serving Harsha and protected by the *janapadas* in

Harsha's realm, to represent the support of local community leaders. New dynasties and donative inscriptions also multiplied in territories very far from Gupta lands. On the northern Tamil coast, the Pallavas of Kanchipuram stepped up their donations during the Gupta decline. Many new dynasties marked territories in sites of intensive cultivation: in Kashmir, the Karkotas of Srinagar; in Bengal, Later Guptas, Sasankas of Karnasuvarana, and Palas of Gauda (at the top of the delta); in Malwa, the Paramaras of Ujjain; in Malwa and adjacent Deccan and Gujarat, the Kalacuris of Mahismati; in Berar (Vidarbha), the Rashtrakutas of Acalapura; in the Krishna-Tungabadra doab in the south Deccan, the Calukyas of Vatapi; and on the south Tamil coast, the Pandyas of Madurai and Cholas of Tanjavur.

At least forty new dynastic lineages were proclaimed during and soon after the sixth century, and from the seventh century on they typically construct elaborate genealogies for themselves to trace their origins to mythical progenitors. Migrations of Brahmans, Gupta princes, and Gupta generals may have influenced these early-medieval trends, but most new dynasties sprang up outside *Aryavarta*, and even peoples who had repulsed the Guptas later adapted technologies of power which Guptas had developed. Between 550 and 1250, the interactive expansion of agricultural and dynastic territories produced the basis for all the major agrarian regions of modern South Asia. This is the crucial formative period for agrarian history in the subcontinent. Though agricultural conditions, techniques, and social relations varied across regions, and though trends in the high mountains, western plains, and central mountains are not well documented, some basic elements which pertain to many if not most agrarian territories in this period appear in data from places where major dynasties were firmly established. We know most about elements that form the explicit subject matter of the inscriptions: kingship, Brahman settlements, and temples.

The ritual and architectural complex now called 'the Hindu temple' emerged in full form in the later Gupta period and its elaboration and spread from the sixth to the fourteenth century provide us with dramatic medieval remains, from Mahabalipuram to Khajuraho. Medieval inscriptional records appear predominantly in temple precincts, which were central nodes for the accumulation of power in early-medieval kingdoms. By the tenth century, old theories and practices of kingship had been widely adapted in many new medieval territories.

As in Rama's mythical realm in the epic *Ramayana*, protection and prosperity were signs of a good king; and piety, chastity, and wealth all came together under kings who nurtured *dharma*. This theme forms a continuity with very old ideas about kingship, as Kasyapa's advice that 'the king should take keen interest in agriculture' resonates with a Tamil poet's advice to a Pandya king, probably in the first centuries CE. Many medieval kings followed this advice, most spectacularly in Sri Lanka.

> Oh great king, if you crave wealth in the next world
> and yearn to vanquish other kings who protect this world
> and thus to become the greatest among them
> hearing songs of praise to your glory,
> listen to me to learn what deeds guarantee these rewards.
> Those who give food give life to living beings
> who cannot live without water.
> Food is first for all living things, made of food,
> and because food is but soil and water mingled together,
> those who bring water into fields
> create living beings and life in this world.
> Even kings with vast domains strive in vain, when their land is dry
> and fields sown with seeds look only to the sky for rain.
> So Pandya king who makes dreadful war, do not mistake my words:
> quickly expand watery places that are built to bring streams to your land!
> For those who control water reap rewards
> and those who fail cannot endure. [6]

Water and ritual were critical for medieval kingship. So were innovation and adaptation. The kings who built medieval temples nurtured forms of *dharma* with distinctively medieval substance. In contrast to ancient prescriptions, medieval texts do not insist that a king be a kshatriya and, in much of the subcontinent, medieval caste (*jati*) ranking developed without the presence of all four *varnas*. *Rajadharma* still meant protecting *dharma*, but *sastras* (sacred texts) now prescribed that kings protect local customs, so that kings could enshrine as *dharma* virtually any form of social power and style of social ranking. Land grants to temples and Brahmans confirm the adaptation of cosmic law for local purposes, by bringing Brahman powers of ritual sanction to bear in new agrarian territories to sanctify patterns of social power in Puranic temple worship. Temples were ritual and also political institutions. They incorporated many different

---

[6] *Purananuru*, No.18, lines 13–30.

groups who were clearing and planting the land, building towns, and contracting transactional alliances, which are recorded in the inscriptions.

The *Manusmriti* says that *dharma* includes a sacred right of first possession for the people who clear the land, even if they have taken use of the land away from others – for example, hunters and pastoralists – which would often have been the case. Protecting this right was a bedrock of royal authority. But beyond this, a king's ambition extended over his neighbours (*samantas*), as the Pandyan poet indicated. Homage, tribute, and services from subordinate rulers (*rajas*) were prizes for kings who took titles like *Maharajadhiraja* (Great King of Kings) and *Paramesvara* (Supreme Lord). In the methodology of medieval kingship, gifts to Brahmans and temples measured and dramatised royal power. In Sri Lanka, the same method channelled massive patronage to Buddhist monks and monasteries from the second century BCE; and irrigation, paddy cultivation, and monastic property expanded together until the fourteenth century. Like monasteries, temples managed by Brahmans often owned tracts of irrigated land, and individual Brahmans and Brahman settlements (*brahmadeyas*) often received grants that comprised royal investments in irrigation. Like monks, Brahmans meant prosperity. They attracted people to agrarian sites who had skills and assets needed for expansion. A proliferation of texts on agriculture, astrology, medicine, and related sciences and on temples and irrigation in the lowland areas that were most favoured for Brahman settlement indicate that a Brahman intelligentsia was busily working in many fields other than ritual and Vedic studies. Even esoteric learning could be useful in constructing an agrarian order. Shankaracharya's philosophy, for instance, concerns the disputation of sacred authority. Intellectual innovations in doctrine and ritual enabled local cults to be woven together into expanding Puranic traditions. Great temples multiplied with royal patronage. So did their poetic publicity. The greatness of the gods enhanced the glamour of royal patrons. Rich centres of temple worship combined in their precincts many of the technical skills – controlled by Brahmans – that were needed to develop agrarian territories, from architecture and engineering to law and financial management. Building a great temple or monastery attracted Brahmans and monks and provided a theatre of royal grandeur; here a king could make alliances and enjoy dramatic

displays of submission. Great kings built great temples and commanded the services of the most learned Brahmans.

A donation to Brahmans, monasteries, monks, or temples represented an investment in agrarian territoriality. Inscriptions, typically
carved on a temple wall, served as contracts and advertisements. The
more popular a place of worship became – the more praised in song,
and the more attractive for pilgrims – the greater became the value of
its patronage. The rise of *bhakti* (devotional) movements enhanced the
virtue of pilgrimage, increased the number of worshippers, and raised
the value of temple donations. Making donations became increasingly
popular among aspiring groups as a means of social mobility, as
temples became commercial centres, landowners, employers, and
investors. The rising value of temple assets increased the value of
membership in communities of worship. Increasing participation in
temple rituals made them more effective sites for social ranking:
temple honours were distributed according to rank, and all worshippers were positioned in ranked proximity to the deity. Rulers came
first. Popular *bhakti* devotional movements generated more popular
religious participation, more ritual power for dominant local groups,
and more glory for kings (even when temples were not centres for
royal cults, which they sometimes were). Devotionalism produced a
populist ideology for alliances among dominant agricultural lineages
and warrior-kings, and formed communities of sentiment among
disparate groups involved in agricultural expansion.

Temples were divine sites for enacting social rank among devotees
who protected *dharma* and sustained ritual; and, like kingship, rituals
changed as people brought gods into changing agrarian contexts. A
wide diversity of rituals brought rain, secured crops, drove away
disease, delivered healthy babies,, and bolstered dynasties; but among
all the rituals – by all kinds of spiritualists and officiates, from all
kinds of social backgrounds, in all manner of locations – those by
Brahman priests for Shiva, Vishnu, and their relatives produced most
surviving documentation, because of their lasting, widespread influence. Impressive temples came to mark agricultural territory, towering over the land as sacred landmarks. For many centuries,
Brahmanic rituals had evolved as a potent force in social ranking and
alliance-building, and specifically for ranking dominant groups in
relation to royalty; and it appears that, with the expansion of temple
worship and popular devotionalism, the principles and practices of

ritual inclusion and participation provided a template and methodology for the construction of social power in agrarian territories where the most powerful people traced their sacred genealogies to the gods of the Vedas.

Ritual powers which had been confined to Vedic ritual space were generalised within farming households, communities, and kingdoms. Brahman communities spread and Brahman models of social order spread with the influence of temples and temple patrons. In communities of temple worship, the roles and terms of Vedic ritual assumed new, mundane meanings. It seems, for instance, that the Vedic *jajman* was transformed into a person who controls the resources needed for temple ritual, which came to include not only food and animals but also the services of workers. Hence a *jajman* would be the pivot of power in circuits of redistribution and in what would be called 'the *jajman*i system', in which village land-owning elite families receive labour and assets from subordinates throughout the agricultural year and distribute produce from their land to workers at harvest time. Inscriptions also support the inference that agrarian territory became bounded by *dharma* as ritually ranked circles of marriage and kinship evolved into ranked caste groups (*jati*s). Coercion was certainly involved in the creation of these caste societies, but the practice of ranking *jati* groups according to the principles of *varna* would also have been attractive for many groups. The adoption and enforcement of caste norms consolidated and expanded caste social space as it organised agriculture and sustained agrarian states.

Religious rituals of social ranking enabled families to form political alliances by providing measures of their respective status within agrarian territory. The labour, land, and assets of low-ranking *jati*s were organised for production by being subordinated to the power of dominant caste families, who carved out territories in strategic transactions with Brahmans, gods, and kings. Dominant caste alliances thus formed medieval agrarian territories at the intersection of kingship and local communities. The expansion of caste society appears to have been a top–down process, which included but did not necessarily depend upon everyday coercion. It might be best characterised as an evolving caste hegemony, in which the coercive features of social power were hidden by an ideology of *dharma* that became widely accepted as it provided everyone with a place in the ranks of agrarian entitlement. Inscriptions further support the proposition that *jati* ranking was propelled by strategies of alliance among rising powers in agrarian society. New dynastic realms and agrarian territories were places for social mobility where the building of ranking systems made good sense. Dynastic lineage leaders and Brahmans were critical actors in creating these systems of social difference, status, rank, and power, which enabled powerful non-Brahman families to become gentry.

Temples and Brahman settlements were sites of honour around which to form ranks of privilege. Like kings, Brahmans acquired their social rank historically. Building dynastic territory was a complicated process that involved innovation, risk, improvisation, and experiment; and the wide open spaces of medieval times enabled people to become Brahmans as well as Rajputs, Kshatriyas, Marathas, and Sat-sudra gentry. To become Brahman meant to be accepted as Brahman, patronised as Brahman, respected as Brahman; thus one came to command the skills, social status, and kinship of Brahmans, according to scriptures that allow people to become Brahmans through their deeds. Controls over access to Brahman status were strict, so that entering Brahman ranks would have been difficult. But the widespread establishment of new Brahman settlements – duly recorded in the inscriptions – provided many opportunities for new Brahman lineages and clans to be formed. Founders and protectors of Brahman settlements, builders of temples, and donors who financed temple rituals were the moving force behind the Brahmanisation of agrarian territories. Land grants to temples and Brahmans are there-fore less an indication of traditional Brahman power or peasant subordination than a reflection of alliance-building by aspiring agrarian elites who used ritual ranking to lift themselves over competitors and institutionalised their status by patronising gods and Brahmans.

Giving land increased the status of a donor and allied 'protectors' of the grant, who are also often named in inscriptions; by extension, these donations elevated all their kin. As kinship circles formed around the lineages that fed gods and Brahmans, whole sets of kin groups, forming as high-status, non-Brahman *jati*s, elevated them-selves above others in temple ritual and agrarian society. This may explain why leaders of *janapada*s in Harsha's realm protected a gift of land to Brahmans, and why one of his generals made the gift under Harsha's authority. In the open spaces of Rashtrakuta power, one inscription records a gift of 8,000 measures of land to 1,000 Brahmans, and 4,000 measures to a single Brahman. Similar generosity is evident in many places in the medieval period. In each specific context, a donative inscription appears to mark an effort by a non-Brahman power block to enhance its own status and that of its local allies. Such gambits were not without risk and opposition. Raising the status of some groups lowered others, and Brahman settlements created ranked entitlements in everyday social transactions. Brahmans did not usually farm land themselves and they were entitled by grants to receive the produce of farms, including taxes; so they became a significant social force, protected by royal power, and also a landed elite whose well-being depended upon the control of other people's land and labour. Brahman lords of land became a model for other elites. Brahmanisation sustained the rise of landed elites and aspiring royalty, whose superior claims to land and labour were legitimated by their patronage and protection of Brahmans.

A small but significant set of inscriptions records opposition to Brahman settlements, to their collection of taxes, and to their claims on local resources such as pastures, often contained in grants. Most opposition seems to come from leading members of local farming communities. The authority of kings who patronised Brahmans was clearly not accepted by everyone in medieval societies; and the authority of Brahmanical kingship spread slowly – often violently – into the vast spaces that lay outside its reach in early-medieval centuries. In many instances, land grants appear to mark frontiers of royal power, and here the most resistance might be expected. Even where local society did accept the ritual and social status of Brahmans, fierce competitive struggles might flare up over land grants. Some opposition to Brahman settlements certainly came from local competitors who were fighting against the families who sought to elevate themselves by patronising Brahmans with land grants. In the ninth century, local conflicts of this kind accompanied new Brahman settlements on the Tamil coast, where they were an old and widely accepted feature of agrarian territoriality. The open spaces of Rashtrakuta ambition were another matter. Inscriptions from the northern peninsula warn that violence and curses will be heaped upon opponents of Brahman land grants, and texts proclaim that people who murder Brahmans will be punished harshly, which implies that such murders did in fact occur. But striving lineages also had options other than revolt, for, as Bhisma says in the *Mahabharata*, 'If the king disregards agriculturists, they become lost to him, and abandoning his dominions, [they] betake themselves to the woods.'[7]

Territories of permanent cultivation, irrigation, worship, pilgrimage, dynastic authority, temple wealth, *jati* ranking, caste dominance, and Brahman influence grew together. Inscriptions depict idioms of territoriality as they pinpoint the location of a royal donor, the ranks of officials involved in a grant, the status of local protectors, and the names of religious personnel and institutions. Power relations in agricultural expansion were thus more complex than we can see using a simple division of the agrarian world between the state and society. There was more at work in the medieval political economy than interaction between kings and peasants or dynasties and villages. The most important social forces within medieval states worked the middle ground between rulers and farmers, where leaders of locally prominent families made strategic alliances that constituted dynastic territory. An agrarian gentry thus emerged as a constituent of royal authority. The constant rhetorical and ritual elevation of the king above all others mirrored and mobilised social ranking; it served the cause of gentry mobility. The superiority of rulers served all subordinates by elevating them above lower orders in their relative proximity to the king. When an aspiring warrior family elevated itself by declaring a new dynasty, it benefited the whole clan and their home locality. Inviting Brahmans to live in its territory, generating for itself a cosmic lineage, building temples, and adopting royal titles and rituals, the new king would pursue allies. In this pursuit, recognition by an established, superior king could be a boon. Kings would thus extend their domains by forming unequal alliances with *samanta*s, whose subordination would raise their local status. Subordinate rulers could then support or protect a grant in the great king's name, to enhance their status further. A rising dynasty would then accumulate its own subordinate *samanta*s on the periphery of its core territory, while subordinate rulers on the frontier would improve their position at the same time. Core regions of agrarian expansion would expand as emerging leaders allied with regional dynasties, and leaders on the frontiers of several royal territories shifted loyalties or combined them. A successful *samanta* might seek to overturn his master, so the

---

[7] Harbans Mukhia, 'Was There Feudalism in Indian History?' in Herman Kulke, ed., *The State in India, 1000–1700*, Delhi, 1995, p. 128.

advice of King Lalitadiya of Kashmir (in the eighth century) makes good sense: 'Do not allow the villagers to accumulate more than they need for bare subsistence, lest they revolt.'

The early-medieval period – from the sixth to thirteenth century – laid the foundations for later agrarian history in many ways. New forms of social life emerged in many places at the same time. What M. N. Srinivas called 'Sanskritisation' evokes part of the process, because social groups and institutions were being formed around models of behaviour, identity, aesthetics, and patronage codified in Sanskrit texts. Brahmans were key people because they sanctified social rank and political alliance. Rising families wanted to hire Brahman genealogists and court poets, patronise Brahman and temples, endow feeding places for mendicants and pilgrimages, stage festivals, feed saints, and join the activities that united gods, priests, kings, and farmers. All this occurred as farmland was expanding and as peasant farmers, nomads, pastoralists, hunters, and forest tribes were slowly changing the substance of their social identity, over many generations, as people became high-caste landowners, kings, protectors of *dharma*, Kshatriyas, Vaisyas, superior Sudras, inferior Sudras, Untouchables, and aliens beyond the pale. Such transformations obscure the ancient identity of the people who propelled medieval agrarian history, but the result was that gentry castes filled the ranks of landowners and ruling lineages. Many of these groups remain powerful in their regions in modern times. They became Kunbi, Vellala, Velama, Reddy, Kapu, Kamma, Nayar, and other landed castes. The ancient social background of some dynasties can also be dimly perceived. Hoysalas came from Melapas, hill chiefs in the Soseyur forests. Udaiyar and Yadava dynasties descended from herders. Tevar kings descended from Marava and Kallar hunters. Marathas had ancestors in the hills. Gurjaras certainly had a pastoral past. Rajputs did not have one original identity but emerged from histories of warrior ranking and mythology, and many had ancient pastoral and tribal roots. All these transformations are entangled in the politics of religious leadership, devotion, and loyalty; and every state in the history of South Asia has afforded special privileges – including tax exemptions – to religious institutions and religious leaders. Many social movements that moderns might call 'religious' might be better understood as formations of agrarian territorialism, as we will see in chapter 4.

Geographically, early-medieval territories seem to have concentrated in the riverine lowlands. Here the influence of Brahmans and medieval Sanskritisation was most compelling. In scattered rice-growing and irrigated lowlands, aspiring elite families patronised Brahmans and Puranic deities as they fought to control prime farmland and to create their own sacred rights of first possession. Mapping agrarian territories which are documented by inscriptions is not easy because transactions recorded epigraphically occurred within a moving constellation of dynastic donations that has not been mapped comprehensively. This medieval territoriality was defined not by fixed boundaries but rather by its individual transactions, and such transactional territory can remain firmly in place only as long as the transactional system that defines it. But the agrarian elites that came into being within medieval polities – through their participation in this transactional system – remained in power in many locations of intensive medieval agriculture for centuries to come. In the nineteenth century, for instance, a local official reported from the old Gupta core region in Saran District, Bihar, that 'Brahmans, Rajputs, and Bhumihars were the only castes that figured in the "actual life" of the district'.[8] In early-medieval times, such groups were coming into existence, their social identities were being produced transactionally, and the inscriptions perpetuate their reputation.

Medieval kingdoms were composed of networks of transactions rather than bureaucratic institutions of a kind that would define later agrarian territories of revenue and judicial administration. In the 1950s, K. A. Nilakanta Shastri argued that the Cholas had built an '*almost* Byzantine royalty', and since the 1960s, R. S. Sharma has argued that post-Gupta states in general represent a form of feudalism. Historians have developed alternatives to these models, but they have not replaced them, and today there is no consensus concerning the nature of medieval states. But inside dynastic domains, inscriptions indicate that agrarian territories were small, consisting of settlements linked together by locally dominant caste power. Inscriptional terms mark transactional space by using titles for individuals and groups and by using place names attached to the people in transactions – terms such as *nadu* or *padi*. The *nadu* in modern 'Tamil Nadu' is a territorial marker from medieval inscrip-

---

[8] Anand Yang, *The Limited Raj: Agrarian Relations in Colonial India, Saran District, 1793–1920*, Berkeley, 1989, p. 44.

tions which designated a tiny region that was defined by its ritual, land, water, kinship, and royal transactions. The term appears most often in references to leaders of the *nadu* who engaged in donative transactions with temples and Brahmans. In later centuries, it acquired more expansive meanings; but medieval *nadu*s along the Tamil coast were composed of core settlements along routes of drainage, where Brahmans and temples received land grants, and they were connected to one another by donative transactions and surrounded by vast tracts of land which was not controlled by dominant groups in core *nadu* sites.

Where inscriptional sites of agrarian power have been mapped, they cluster along rivers, so it appears that the nexus of power that they reflect concentrated on the control of riverine farmland. Over time, Brahman influence spread widely, and Brahmans and allied gentry and service castes became mobile state elites. Locally, gentry caste power dug in and expanded steadily. Based in prime locations along rivers and trade routes with clusters of temple towns and old dynastic capitals, caste communities incorporated tribal, hunting, pastoral, and nomadic groups into the lower echelons of society, where the new entrants retained much of their character, redefined in caste terms. Tribal deities entered the Puranic pantheon, adding cultural complexity and expressing the richness of agrarian territories. The social and cultural character of agrarian regions emerged in later centuries, but medieval territoriality left its traces and imparted distinctive qualities to localities by giving special importance to Brahmans, temples, and high-caste gentry. Where we do not find medieval donative inscriptions – as in Punjab, in Jat territories in the western Ganga plains, and in the mountains – the population and cultural importance of Brahmans remains comparatively small in agrarian societies today. Inscriptional territories concentrate in eastern and central Uttar Pradesh, West Bengal, Gujarat, western Maharashtra, and along the coastal plains. Brahmanism seems less deeply rooted in other areas, where other types of social power were more prominent in the later formation of agrarian territories.

CONQUEST

One Candella inscription announces that Anand, brother of Trailo-kyavarman, reduced to submission 'wild tribes of Bhillas, Sabaras and

Pulindas'.[9] Conquering tribes and expelling them from the land is a major theme in genealogy and epigraphy. Warrior lineages expanded in number and influence after the Guptas, creating and conquering agricultural territories, and preserving their victories in inscriptions, epic poetry, folklore, and hagiography. From the eighth to the eleventh century, Gurjara-Pratiharas conquered along western plains and northern basins, moving into the central mountains and high mountain valleys. Along the coast of the southern peninsula, Pandya, Chera, and Chola lineages repeatedly conquered each others' territory. Many warriors planted settlements of warrior-farmers along routes of conquest. From the eighth to tenth century, Rashtrakutas migrated and conquered territories all across the north Deccan, Gujarat, and Orissa. The Vakatakas emulated earlier Satavahanas and expanded outward from Vidarbha (Berar); they split into four branches, with shifting capitals spread from Chhattisgarh across the Deccan to the upper reaches of the Bhima river basin. In the sixth century, Kalacuris appeared in the north Deccan territories of the Vakatakas; in the eighth, inscriptions show them in Tripura, near the head of the Narmada river; and as late as the thirteenth century they appear in Bengal. Chola armies conquered northern Sri Lanka, leaving a population of colonists behind. Calukya lineages had bases in Vatapi along the upper Tungabhadra river in the seventh and eighth century, and in Kalyani, well to the north, in the eleventh and twelfth. From the fourteenth to the sixteenth century, Vijayanagar dynasties expanded from the vicinity of old Vatapi across the southern Deccan and eastern plains; and they shifted their capitals into coastal lowlands as they broke up into smaller dynasties in the sixteenth and seventeenth centuries. Under Vijayanagar, Telugu warrior clans conquered territory all along the south-eastern coastal plain.

This is only the start of a list of medieval conquests that barely begins to indicate how widely they influenced agrarian territoriality. Conquest colonisation exerted its influence quite separately from territorial *dharma*, but together they produced agrarian territories that expanded to become agrarian regions. Conquering colonists knitted together many small-scale domains of localised, dominant caste power; they connected new frontiers and old dynastic sites. Activities

---

[9] Brajadulal Chattopadhyay, 'Political Processes and the Structure of Polity in Early Medieval India', in Kulke, *The State*, p. 219.

depicted in Harsha's seventh-century inscription are typical of many events in this process. Many donative inscriptions reflect similar activity by subordinate officers and local leaders, for whom gifts to Brahmans and temples represent incorporation into conquest territories. Conquest created ranks of warriors above the locally dominant castes; and superior entitlements created by conquest moved agricultural wealth along trade routes of warrior power in the form of tribute and temple endowment. Warriors used agrarian wealth from one location to support conquest in others; and traders, pastoralists, and warrior-farmers moved agrarian wealth among sites. These transfers of wealth employed monetary instruments and commercial intermediation, which are most visible in the inscriptional evidence as they pertain to temple endowments. Conquest and trade went hand-in-hand with religious endowments and investments in farming.

Warriors created territories of authority in which their officers could establish local roots within communities, where they distributed local entitlements to kin, allies, and subordinates. Distant localities were connected to one another by the social networks that formed along routes of conquest and extended the reach of conquering clans. Local caste elites were assimilated into extensive realms of clan power as subordinates, dependants, and rising stars. Some warrior clans created a non-farming nobility living high in fortress towns, looking down on farm communities; these became landmarks on agricultural landscapes, as prominent as temples and other sacred places. Warrior competition among siblings in each successive generation would send another wave of fighters out to conquer new territory; in this enterprise, these clans faced one another on the battlefield, so that battles among warriors became a dominant motif in hagiographies, genealogies, and local lore about the land. The exploits of great men became material for epics, rumours, gossip, and popular songs, landmarks in local history.

Two broad geographical zones of warrior influence can be roughly discerned. One was formed by clans that became Rajputs – Gurjaras, Cahamanas (Chauhans), Paramaras (Pawars), Guhilas (Sisodias), and Caulukyas (Solankis) – who conquered from the eighth century onward across the western plains, northern basins, adjacent high mountain valleys, and central mountains. Local leaders rose up to ally with and to join the ranks of conquering clans, by imitation, alliance, genealogical invention, inter-marriage, and combinations of these strategies. Rajput rulers protected *dharma* and became ideal Kshatriyas. Brahman settlements and temple rituals were not as important for Rajput royalty as warfare, genealogies, hagiographies, and court ceremonies. Their lineages measured their status in victories, alliances, marriages, and accumulations of tribute in their palaces, forts, and market towns – including Brahmans and temples. Nobles endowed temples and employed Brahmans as ritualists and servants, but it was more their devotion to battle, to their own clan, and to the rules of martial kingship that measured their devotion to *dharma*. In warrior territory, the ritual ranking of agrarian society followed the logic of warrior lineages, stressing military alliance, victory, service, and publicly demonstrated powers of physical command and subjugation. Agrarian social power concentrated much less in a local landed gentry and much more in warrior lineages. Genealogies became records of rank and they proliferated across the entire span of the medieval epoch to mark the expanding area of Rajput influence. Surajit Sinha has shown that 'state formation in the tribal belt of Central India is very largely a story of the Rajputisation of the tribes'.[10] The interaction of expansive Rajput lineages with locally powerful Jat clans produced a militarist pattern of agrarian development in the western frontiers of old *Bharat*, where agrarian power focused on fortified villages and strategic hill towns.

A second warrior zone lay south of the Vindhyas in Khandesh, Berar, Maharashtra, central mountain valleys, and the interior peninsula, where warriors were attached to agricultural communities and concentrated power in their own hands but followed no single dominant model such as that of the Rajputs. Instead – from the time of the Satavahanas, Vakatakas, and Rashtrakutas, to that of the Yadavas, Calukyas, Hoysalas, Kakatiyas of Warangal, Sultans of Ahmadnagar and Bijapur, Udaiyars and Sultans of Mysore, and the Marathas – dominant social powers in agriculture arose from and mingled with the evolution of peoples living in and drawn from pastoral, hunting, and mountain populations. Standing to fight became part of farming. Running off to war became part of the agricultural routine. In the

---

[10] Surajit Sinha, 'State Formation and Rajput Myth in Tribal Central India', Presidential Address, Section on Anthropology and Archaeology, Forty-ninth Indian Science Congress, 1962, reprinted in Kulke, ed., *The State*, p. 305. See also Surajit Sinha, 'Bhumij-Kshatriya Social Movements in South Manbhum', *Bulletin of the Department of Anthropology* (University of Calcutta), 8, 2, 1959, 9–32.

interior peninsula, extensive tracts of dry land were open for cultivation for the people who could fight to keep it; and throughout medieval centuries, cattle, manpower, centres of trade, strategic positions, and places with good water and access to valuable forests were more valuable assets for aspiring warrior lineages than most farmland, except in the stretches of deep black soil along the big rivers that were perpetual sites of warrior-peasant competition. The dominant agrarian castes were both warriors and cultivators. In the Maratha Deccan, for instance, expanses of open land that were available in the sixteenth and seventeenth century allowed many warrior-farming lineages to carve out local territory for themselves. A lineage leader would become a *patel* (village headman); and then, by combining his military power with strategic alliances, he could become a *deshmukh* (headman) for a circle of villages, a serious player in regional politics. In the context of constant local military competition and shifting alliances, there was little scope for the rise of an agrarian gentry until warrior-farmers could control an area long enough to institutionalize their elite status, which eventually did occur later in the medieval period in Maratha core areas, as well as among Vokkaligas and Boyas in Karnataka, and among Reddy and other locally dominant Telugu castes in Telangana.

In the eleventh century, warriors came on horseback from Afghanistan and Central Asia to engage warriors in the lowlands and they swept across the subcontinent to connect the zones of warrior colonisation north and south of the Vindhyas, which had been until then quite separate. They pushed into historical spaces of conquest colonisation that were many centuries old. The military competition that ensued increased the influence of conquest colonisation on agriculture as a whole by increasing the number and force of warriors. Because temples, cities, and irrigation represented authority and prosperity, they were natural targets in war.[11] Warriors often dislocated farming communities when they attacked their enemies. The great eleventh-century irrigation builder, the Paramara Raja Bhoj, had built a wall to form a huge irrigation reservoir at Bhojpur, near Bhopal, and armies of the Sultan of Mandi, Hoshang Shah, later cut the dam to destroy the lake, killing the irrigation. This kind of warfare discouraged heavy investments by farmers in fixed agricultural assets

---

[11] Richard H. Davis, 'Indian Art Objects as Loot', *Journal of Asian Studies*, 52, 1, 1993, 22–48, and 'Three Styles in Looting India', *History and Anthropology*, 6, 4, 1994, 293–317.

such as irrigation works, unless they could be protected by local arms, as wells could be, which helps to explain their popularity in all the regions of conquest colonisation. A militarisation of farming occurred in all the dry regions where wells are most important. By the fifteenth century, professional armies had established their military superiority over the local hordes of warrior-peasants, but no state could destroy the independent warrior lineages which had fought successfully to control local territories. In wide fields of warrior-farming, lineages expanded their cultivation and coercive power at the same time under medieval dynasties. Warrior Jats colonised Punjab and the western Ganga basin and formed agrarian mini-polities which became regional states in the eighteenth century. Stable centres of professional military power emerged in many territories in the interior peninsula, some, as on the Mysore plateau, with old formations of caste dominance endowed with all the institutional traditions of royalty and Brahman patronage.

Conquest colonisation made much of agrarian space a constant battleground, and the careers of the Vijayanagar and Maratha empires reflect important features of this aspect of agarian history. In a region of Telugu conquest, Vijayanagar, 'the city of victory', was built in the fourteenth century in old agricultural territory near the old Calukya centre of Vatapi, along the upper Tungabhadra river. Endowed with magnificent irrigation, the city accumulated so much warrior wealth that Portuguese visitors took it to be richer than Paris, with its great temples, royal cult, and vassals arriving at festival time with mountains of tribute. Fighters led by *nayakas* (commanders) spread Vijayanagar's dominion outward in waves of conquest colonisation, creating the first empire to embrace all the land south of the Krishna. Telugu warrior-peasants opened up new land for dry farming along the eastern coast – in dry stretches filled with deep black cotton soil between old riverine clusters – and these colonies would sustain a vast expansion of cloth manufacture for world markets in the seventeenth and eighteenth century, when Nayakas became kings. Vijayanagar itself was destroyed, however, by sultans at Bijapur, another old site in the former Calukya realm. The city of victory had disappeared completely by the end of the seventeenth century.

In 1640, Shivaji was married in Bangalore at the court of the Bijapur sultan, whom his father, Shahji, served as a general. Shahji's *jagir* (assigned revenue territory) near Pune became Shivaji's patrimony and a base for his later military expansion. In his day, good rainy seasons and peaceful times saw farmers expanding cultivation, though even in good years they would go off to war during dry months. Building in one place accompanied destruction elsewhere. Droughts would routinely drive more farmers out to fight, loot, and colonise. The great fortresses that became great cities – like Vijayanagar – could disappear without a trace, because their ruling lineages and urban populations would move overnight to other sites. New cities and towns rose on ruins everyday in the world of warrior-peasants and military entrepreneurs. One story goes that in the seventeenth century, on the fringes of Maratha power, in the southern Deccan,

Doda Mastee and Chikka Mastee, two brothers with their families and cattle, came from the north and built two houses. They cleared the jungle around and maintained themselves by cultivating the soil. They invited inhabitants from other parts, advancing them money to increase the cultivation. The brothers next built a fort and gave their village the name Halla Goudennahally . . . In time the brothers quarrelled because the younger brother Chikka Mastee made a tank which endangered the village. Doda Mastee being displeased with his brother's folly removed and built north of the first village another village called Goudennahally and all the inhabitants moved to the new village . . . Halla Goudennahally was in the meantime inundated by the water of the tank.

Building and breaking, moving and settling – these are old themes, but the story elides a suspicion that Doda Mastee broke the tank of his younger brother to force the villagers into his new settlement. Building a new settlement often entailed violence, much like planting new fields meant cutting down the jungle. In 1630, when villages in his revenue territory (*jagir*) lay waste from famine, Shivaji's guardian, Dadaji Kondev, 'set about repopulating and developing the jagir', for which purpose 'Deshpandes were seized and taken in hand, [and] the refractory among them were put to death'.[12]

From the eighth century onward, conquest colonisation is well enough documented to allow us to distinguish different types, which can be identified by their association with specific groups. (1) Some professional warrior lineages emerged from ancient roots at the margins of old agricultural societies, from pastoral and hunter peoples for whom extensive mobility and killing were ancient skills. These warrior specialists conquered agricultural communities and formed a nobility. For simplicity, we can call this the Rajput pattern, with its

---

[12] Stewart Gordon, *The Marathas 1600–1818*, Cambridge, 1994, p. 60.

various spin-offs and variants that arose with emulation and alliance-building among other warrior groups. (2) Some warrior lineages came from the ranks of dominant caste farmers who had formed a military force and allied with professional warriors, often serving under them. Conquering widely, these fighting peasants would retain their local agrarian base. If successful, they could spread their power by alliance and conquest across territories dominated by allies in similar warrior-peasant castes. This is the outline of the Maratha pattern, which had a long history in the Deccan before the rise of Shivaji. (3) A warrior lineage could split off from a dynastic authority, using symbols and alliances derived from that dynasty to lead fighting colonists into new territories, to conquer, displace, and/or assimilate local tribes and others, and thus to form new agricultural communities and new agrarian territories. This pattern, exemplified by the Mastee brothers, also typified Telugu colonists in the black soil tracts of the Tamil country. (4) Warrior-farmers could simply conquer and settle new territory, dividing the land among the lineages. The conquering group itself would form the bulk of the agrarian population in this territory. Kings would rise within it and clans would differentiate over time into many ranks. Groups would splinter off for new colonisation. This pattern – typified by the Jats – may be the most common of all and probably dominated the hills and valleys of the central mountains, for instance in Gondwana, Chhattisgarh, and other areas of tribal Rajpu-tisation. It also typifies lowland warrior-farming groups such as the Maravas and Kallars, in southern Tamil country, including the Pir-amalai Kallar studied by Louis Dumont.

Late-medieval warrior lineages – from the Ghorids to the Mughals – followed the Rajput model, which was also prevalent in various forms in Central and West Asia. As they subsumed other warriors under their authority, they increased the power of subordinates such as Shivaji who could form local alliances with warrior-peasant lineages. Sultans had less interest even than Rajputs in farming themselves, living among farmers, or tinkering with production locally. They conquered warriors who already ruled over agrarian territories. They lived in fortress towns and their movements connected all the old fort-centres of warrior colonisation not only to one another but also to urban centres across inland corridors of southern Asia from Dhaka to Istanbul. Like their predecessors, the sultans brought retinues from their homelands and new technologies of power, and they encouraged migrants from their home territories to settle in their new dominions, primarily in the established urban centres but also on agricultural frontiers, where, like the Brahman settlements of the early-medieval period, *ulema* (learned men) and Sufis provided erudition and leadership for agricultural expansion in the Indus Valley, Punjab, the western Gangetic plain, the Deccan, and eastern Bengal. Again, new skills and productive powers came into agrarian territories with new ruling elites. This was like the dispersion of productive powers that followed the end of the Gupta empire, but on a much greater scale, with more dramatic consequences, and with more detailed documentation. With warrior-sultans from the western reaches of southern Asia came architects, accountants, scholars, genealogists, bureaucrats, poets, scientists, merchants, bankers, musicians, and the entire cultural heritage of Persia. The centre of gravity in Persian cultural history moved into South Asia, where a Persian lexicon and technologies of power organised a widespread reintegration of agrarian territories. New strata of non-farming elites were formed by sultans who granted their subordinates entitlements to revenue from the land. Again, royal patronage fed the rise of new agrarian elites.

Sultanic regimes continued and reinforced long historical trends in conquest colonisation. Muslim rulers did not dramatise political alliances in temple ritual, but they sustained temple authority in agrarian territory. Old land grants to temples remained in place. New royal donations were added in the form of the tax remissions. Victorious sultans defeated old defenders of *dharma*, and this again brought Kali Yuga to mind for some Brahmans; some fled into mountain valleys and into rapidly expanding agrarian territories around Kathmandu. Sultans brought superior military technology into the field, which altered the competitive environment of conquest colonisation. Defeated warriors launched new waves of conquest, extending warrior power from the Deccan and the Ganga basin into deltaic and coastal regions. But imperial expansion still depended upon unequal alliances with subordinate rulers, who increased their own status by hitching their fortune to victorious sultans. Sultanic regimes developed institutions of military bureaucracy that focused authority on the emperor's family, relatives, and his highest ranking allies, who formed the imperial nobility; and, from the time of Akbar's marriage alliance with Rajputs, the imperial wedding became a ritual of the highest statecraft. Rajput, Maratha, and other protectors of *dharma* formed a new nobility under the umbrella of sultanic regimes and increased their investments in temples; so that temple ritual and Hindu court culture flourished under the sultans. Akbar's and Dara Shuko's experiments in religion reflect a continuing effort to articulate political alliance-building with philosophical speculation; and rituals of theological disputation at Akbar's court remind us of the medieval innovations in religious thought and performance which accompanied the incorporation of new groups into agrarian regimes. Outside the court, eclectic mysticism and devotionalism expanded their reach. Brahmans were in high demand in the apparatus of imperial taxation and law, and their occupational horizons expanded. More than ever, building accompanied destruction under the sultans, in the expansion of urbanism and in the expansion of agriculture. When Akbar's troops marched into Bengal, they brought in train tools and men to clear the jungles to expand cultivation. Sufis came into the eastern delta to open the jungles to farming. To protect strategic mountain routes of trade, Mughal armies conquered and settled many sites of agrarian expansion, including Kashmir. Aurangzeb began his famous 1665 *farman* (edict) on administration with words that echo Kasyapa and the Pandyan poet: 'the entire elevated attention and desires of the Emperor are devoted to the increase in the population and cultivation of the Empire and the welfare of the whole peasantry and the entire people.' Aurangzeb reiterated the *Manusmriti* on the sacred right of first possession when he declared that, 'whoever turns (wasteland) into cultivable land should be recognised as the (owner) malik and should not be deprived (of land)'.[13]

PATRIARCHY

Families passed the right of first possession from one generation to the next. At the base of medieval states and at the apex of early-modern empires, family formed a core of social power and experience. In agrarian territory, kinship formed basic entitlements to means of production. Kin groups joined together to clear land, build fields, dig wells, and cultivate. Settlements and communities formed around collections of kin. Marriage networks connected villages. Families

---

[13] Mukhia, 'Was There Feudalism?', pp. 127, 201.

pushed the frontiers of farming and fought for control of agrarian space within realms of ritual and conquest. Kinship underlay class and caste; and, in state institutions, market networks, and community organisation, kin formed the most powerful bonds of alliance, allegiance, loyalty, and solidarity. The *Ramayana* and *Mahabharata* are fundamentally family dramas and the *Manusmriti* is obsessed with the implications of marriage for caste ranking. During medieval centuries, family histories, emotions, rituals, intrigues, conflicts, and loyalties permeated agrarian life and territoriality, from family farm to imperial court. Family suffused all the institutions of entitlement. On the Tamil coast, for instance, the word *pangu*, meaning 'share', came to refer both to an individual's share in family property and to a family's share of village assets, so that *pangali* referred to relatives and also to shareholding landed gentry families in a farming community. The term *kulam* likewise referred to a household, lineage, clan, and local caste group (*jati*); and *nadu* meant an agrarian space (as opposed to *kadu*, forest) defined as the domain of authority of its most prominent family leaders *(nattar)*. The inscriptional corpus is substantially the record of transactions among the heads of families who built agrarian territory, built dynasties, and travelled in search of new land to conquer and farm.

Kin followed the lead of earlier generations to create expansive domains of kinship which became localities, kingdoms, and empires. Along riverine tracts of irrigated agriculture where medieval inscriptions were most densely distributed, families sought control over expanses of farmland, grazing land, forest, and water supplies. Succeeding generations spread their power from one bit of cultivated ground to the next and prominent gentry families and an expanding set of kinfolk produced small, compact domains of dominance. Marriages formed dense links among dominant families in adjacent settlements, which became related to one another in patterns that resembled the patchwork of paddy fields. In such settings, the norms and practices of kinship strongly stressed local alliances among families and they formed intricately graded ranks within gentry strata of society. Marriage also marked divisions between local elites and groups who were barred from owning land, who served the gentry as dependent servants and farm workers. These distinctions took many forms within the idioms of caste society. But in general the formation of solid traditions of local gentry and rural elite dominance entailed

97

the reproduction of a genealogical connection to celestial and royal authorities who legitimated their patrimony.

In this context, agriculture became a deeply patriarchal enterprise. Senior men ruled junior men and senior women lorded over their inferiors. Family ranking elevated all members of higher families, men and women, according to their lineage, clan, *jati*, *varna*, wealth, sect, office, or other mark of status rank. Patriarchy is a kind of power – never absolute, uncontested, or unaffected by other kinds of power – wielded by men by virtue of their rank in society, and agrarian patriarchy defined agricultural territory as a domain of ranks, entitlements, leading families, and family heads. In the ancient text *Milinda-panho*, Nagasena explains to King Menander that the people he calls 'villagers' (*gamika*) are in fact the patriarchs who head the village families:

Now when the lord, oh king, is thus summoning all the heads of houses (*kutipurush*), he issues his order to all the villagers but it is not they who assemble in obedience to the order; it is the heads of the houses. There are many who do not come: women and men, slave girls and slaves, hired workmen, servants, peasants (*gamika*), sick people, oxen, buffaloes, sheep and goats and dogs – but all those do not count.[14]

Many men and women did not come – only the 'heads' or the leaders of families came. Such scenes have been re-enacted millions of times. Of course, the lord, the king, and the sultan are also heads of families, men of superior rank among kinsfolk and subordinates. Many medieval inscriptions depict the ranks of patriarchs being formed and reformed among men who head families at various levels of power. Family rank came to entail entitlements, which became glossed as 'property rights', but property in practice amounted to power over assets substantiated by and reflected in family rank. Property was also parcelled out within families to members according to rank. Agrarian territory came to be composed of proprietary units formed among families led by their senior men. From early-medieval times, inscriptions indicate that property entitlements were often individualised and transferred in market and political transactions; but property was also defined and protected by social powers in communities and territories. The inscriptional authority of the local protectors of grants to Brah-

---

[14] Quoted in Irfan Habib, 'The Peasant in Indian History', in Irfan Habib, *Essays in Indian History, Towards a Marxist Perspective*, New Delhi, 1995, p. 134.

mans and temples indicates that powers of entitlement depended upon recognised leadership in *janapada*, *nadu*, *padi*, *desa*, *grama* (village), *ur* (village), and other kinds of named territories. Dynasties were established as patriarchies at the apex of territorial ranking systems; and states were thus composed of nested, ranked sets of family entitlements, defined by transactions among patriarchs in systems of ranking which are depicted in the inscriptions.

Patriarchy formed a dynamic, productive power which connected intimate family life with wide historical trends. Family is most often assumed to be a cultural constant within the realm of tradition. Scholars tend to think of kinship as a durable structure that is reproduced innocuously in private life. But family is an engine of change in politics and in struggles over resource control at every level of society. Marriage decisions, rituals, and alliances became politically important in ancient times as lineage leaders began building early state institutions. Elite matrimony became a political event of the first order. Competition among sons generated expansive political domains as younger sons went out in search of new territories, and, in early-medieval centuries, dispersions of ranked lineages created wide nets of alliance and competition. Medieval inscriptions record transactions among patriarchs, articulate ranks among them, and thus encode episodes in family history that formed agrarian territory and dynastic genealogies. Temple rituals articulate alliance, loyalty, devotion, and competition among units of patriarchal power and kinship. Many if not most groups with collective identities in South Asia use some form of genealogical reckoning to express family feelings and histories. Ancestral patriarchs and mythical progenitors populate origin stories. In the dense forest of north Bihar, in the eighteenth century, a Kayasth named Dullah Ram founded the village of Changel, and local lore preserves the story that he obeyed a dream and found a horde of gold coins near the temple to the mother goddess, which he duly dug up 'and his descendants lived happily ever after'; whereas the more prosaic truth is that Dullah Ram and his kinsfolk founded the village by usurping the land and subjugating the labour of the local tribal population that worshipped the mother goddess there.[15] Landless Buinhya workers in south Bihar recount the victories of their heroic

[15] Arvind N. Das, 'Changel: Three Centuries of an Indian Village', *Journal of Peasant Studies*, 15, 1, 1987, 4–5.

progenitor, whose valiant exertions clearing and turning the jungle into farmland dignify their subservient labour today.[16] Vellala gentry on the north Tamil coast trace their origins to a royal Chola ancestor who migrated north with 48,000 Vellala families, conquering Kurumba hunters. Genealogies from Mysore and Andhra begin with great patriarchs. So do family histories among Rajputs and other royal families across the northern basins. A group that calls itself 'rulers of the hills' (Malaiyalis) traces its descent from ancestors who migrated up from the Tamil lowlands with their gods in hand at the sharp end of enemy spears. Countless genealogies depict patriarchs as founding fathers who begin the chain of succession and entitlement that runs down over generations. Ancestral personalities become icons of group identity. Their exploits become collective accomplishments. 'Our history' for many groups became a story of family feelings forged by lore and worship, beginning with great patriarchs whose offspring populated the land. As if to replicate earth in heaven, the Puranic pantheon filled up with marriages and families of gods. Earthly kings became descendants of Vedic divinities. Cosmic and mundane genealogies together defined social identities around powers and sentiments that linked families to one another in territories of divinity and heritage. Temples embodied the cosmic power of gods in the territory of patriarchs.

Caste – *jati* – defined units and idioms of family alliance and ranking within *varna* ideologies, but patriarchy also transcended caste and escaped the rule of *dharma*. Warrior-kings connected disparate, distant territories to one another, and the rule of *dharma* could organise only parts of these expansive territories. In the sixth century, groups outside the ranks of caste society comprised the bulk of the population and, though *dharma* did subsequently expand its reach by various means, people outside caste society – whether beneath the lowest of the low or outside the pale altogether – remained numerous. Though excluded from temples and other rituals in respectable gentry communities, low castes and non-castes lived in agricultural territory. Because the power of caste society expanded downward from the top ranks and outward from centres of ritual and conquest, groups at the lowest ranks and on the margins of dominant caste control comprised

---

[16] Gyan Prakash, *Bonded Histories: Genealogies of Labour Servitude in Colonial India*, Cambridge, 1990.

a moving borderland between caste society and its surroundings. Outsiders in and around localities of high-caste control were critically important for the vitality of every agrarian locality, and many did enter into the rituals of *dharma* in various ways, but many also remained outsiders. Such people continued to arrive in every agrarian territory with new waves of migration and conquest colonisation throughout the first and second millennia. Idioms and practices of patriarchal alliance allowed for the loose inclusion of countless groups within transactional territories formed by systems of market exchange and political ranking. Lineage and clan leaders among tribal groups, merchant patriarchs from distant places, travelling artisan headmen, nomadic chiefs, and military commanders from virtually any background could form alliances with locally dominant caste patriarchs based not on their caste ritual rank but rather on the mutual recognition of their respective patriarchal powers. Heads of households and heads of state could negotiate as patriarchs because they could rely on one another to command the labour and allegiance, assets and loyalty of their kinfolk. This produced trust, confidence, and stability in transactions that relied upon payments in the future for promises in the present, whether loans, contracts, or agreements to pay taxes in return for entitlements to land.

Patrimonial entitlements thus defined property rights and powers over labour independently of the rituals of caste and temple worship; and transactions that formed proprietary entitlements also produced state revenues as well as profits and capital for the market economy. Medieval inscriptions depict very complex market transactions, and in many cases temple donations also represent tribute. In payments of tribute, conquerors, kings, and financiers took payments from local patriarchs in transactions that constituted ranks of patriarchal entitlement. Routines of tribute collection became systems of taxation as they became routinised and acquired ideological legitimacy in agrarian cultures as instruments for transactional ranking and entitlement. Within the rituals of taxation, *dharma*, markets, and conquest, patrimonial property became securely established as a foundation for agrarian authority.

As disparate groups with different backgrounds settled in agrarian territory and worked with one another over generations, they developed complex etiquettes of rank, deference, and residential segregation, expressed in housing, personal habits, marriage, clothing, language, ritual, literature, and cuisine. Agrarian societies were not conceptualised by their participants as being composed of *jatis* working within a unified ritual order of caste ranking or *dharma*; so there is no 'caste system' described in the records of medieval agrarian communities. Creating a system of ranks to include all participants in any local society was actually beyond the scope of *dharma*. The adaptive and inclusive capacities of temple and caste ritual could not keep pace with the expansive diversity of agrarian social space. Local societies came to include not only Buddhists, Jains, Parsis, Muslims, Christians, and tribals, but also many groups who did puja but were excluded from temples, who observed ritual ranks among themselves but were excluded from the territories controlled by dominant agrarian castes. Vast open space and towns sprouting up here and there allowed many groups to establish settlements with their own local rules of ranking and alliance, within which they lived and from which they engaged in social relations of great importance to their livelihoods with groups elsewhere who followed different rules of ranking. Settlements of people who followed mutually incompatible systems of ranking could not relate to one another on the basis of either ranking system; and transactions among such groups included barter, exchange, employment, patronage, alliance, conquest, and subordination. *Dharma* could not define this kind of transactional territory, but patriarchs could always represent their own people in relations with others. Genealogies that begin with founding patriarchs produced legitimate authority for the headmen of prominent families, for community leaders, for village elders, and for the family heads who were members of village councils called *panchayat* or *shalish*. Thousands of little social groups occupied and partitioned agrarian space and acquired names and genealogical histories as they interacted with one another. Some became part of a caste structure in agricultural settlements, but many stood apart. Many hunters, tree cultivators, herders, fisher folk, harvesters of the forest, merchants, artisans, miners, diggers of tanks and wells, tribal groups, and peasants formed their own little ethnic communities outside territories of dominant caste authority. Their headman patriarchs represented these groups in their relations with one another and received recognition and entitlements as the natural leaders of their communities.

The politics of patriarchy also propelled a medieval transition that came with the second millennium. From the eighth to the thirteenth

century, patrilineal warrior clans with backgrounds in pastoral nomadism conquered farming communities all across south, central, and
south-west Asia. In the vast territories of the warrior clans, competition by junior members and collateral branches propelled expansion
and conflict. Marriage formed ranks and alliances among all the
warrior lineages, and when warriors did marry into agrarian communities they formed new ranks in which the sons of kings remained
superior to the sons of the soil. In the early centuries of the second
millennium, Ghaznavids, Ghorids, Khaljis, and Tughluqs expanded
into lowland territories of military competition among Yadavas,
Calukyas, Paramaras, Sisodias, and others. These specialised, warrior
groups had much in common. They unified their own forces by
kinship and ritual practices that formed extensive family ties. They
made alliances by marriage. They conquered farming groups to rule
and protect them. They lived in fortress towns and formed an elite
stratum ranked above the kin networks of farmers. They formed
hierarchical alliances among superior and inferior families, lineages,
and clans. Their family ranks within military hierarchies allowed for
strategic calculations in political hypergamy. They gave 'subaltern' a
distinctive meaning: subalterns among warrior clans were junior
patriarchs in the ranks of lineages and dynasties. A son born to a
ranking lineage member inherited a family position that provided a
specific set of options for the ranking of his own family as the son
became a patriarch himself. Alliances gave subaltern families leverage
in their struggles to maintain and to improve their position. Becoming
a subordinate ruler raised the subordinate family's rank in relation to
peers and competitors. Accumulating subordinate patriarchs (*samantas*) under one's own authority was the very definition of a king.
Among the warrior clans, daughters married up – to express the
subordination of a patriarch and to seek upward mobility for the
family – and sons married down, to express the superiority of a
patriarch by the stature of his allied subalterns. Patriarchal polygamy
expanded the possibilities of subordinate alliance-building, as women
became hostages to fortune and some became the mothers of kings. In
these settings, *purdah* (female seclusion) and *sati* (widow immolation)
became auspicious expressions of female purity, piety, devotion, and
heroism. Strength and sacrifice sustained one another. In the political
institutions formed by competitive alliances among warrior patriarchs,
subordination was a moment of power in which all alliances were built

upon measurable inequalities of rank. Dominance rested upon extensive alliances with subalterns whose movement up in ranks often meant challenging superiors in war. War and marriage, militarism and family ties, rank and alliance, negotiation and resistance – all together formed patriarchal power in the warrior clans.

Dharma could not produce stable alliances among these groups, because warring medieval patriarchs invoked the names of many different gods in prayer, and the rituals of war gave losers the option of moving out to look for other farmers and warriors to conquer. Moving out from Central Asia, Turk and Afghan warrior clans pushed Rajputs down the Ganga basin, into high mountain valleys and into the central mountains; and they pushed Telugus up the Tungabhadra basin toward Vijayanagar, and Telugu Nayakas into the Tamil country. In all the regions of later medieval warrior competition, marital and martial techniques of social ranking provided a cultural basis for new, sultanic regimes. Rathore Rajputs married daughters to sultans before Akbar's time, and almost all the great Rajput patriarchs would marry into the Mughal nobility, strengthening Mughal power and opening wide avenues for mobility and advancement for Rajput clans, and at the same time opening a status division between rising Rajput nobility and lesser Rajput and Thakur lineages. One Rathore princess married Prince Salim. He became Jahangir and she bore a son who became Shah Jahan, as lesser Rajputs lineages declined. In the eighteenth century, Qazi Muhammad Ala said that ordinary chiefs (*rausa*) 'are now called *zamindars*'.[17]

In late-medieval times, from the thirteenth to the sixteenth century, new institutions of patriarchal ranking evolved; they formed a cultural context of sultanic secularism, which contained many kinds of canon, idioms of ritual, and moral systems under the umbrella of sultanic authority. Sultans rose above all patriarchs. Their regimes compiled the small agrarian territories of the early-medieval period into regional forms with distinctively early-modern characteristics. By the seventeenth century – most dramatically in Maharashtra and Punjab – alliances among imperial, military, fiscal, and agrarian patriarchs produced regional patriarchies. Great patriarchs like Shivaji and Guru Nanak formed the basis for regional identities of a new kind. Rights of first possession expanded metaphorically to include collective rights

---

[17] Habib, *Essays in Indian History*, p. 149.

for all the people of the dominant castes assembled under a great patriarch to rule their homeland. This early formation of territorial and ethnic nationality emerged from the expansive powers of patriarchal authority produced under sultanic regimes as it absorbed intense attachments to the land among dominant caste farm families and local conquest regimes.

When Rajputs and Mughals married, they tied together two traditions of patriarchal power which, though expressed in different spiritual idioms, had basic commonalities that formed a coherent logic of ranking, competition, and alliance. Mughal sultans became apical agents and icons of ranking for all patriarchs below. In the Mughal regime, mosque, temple, or church could mark communities of sentiment; sacred genealogies could be reckoned from Rome, Palestine, Arabia, or *Aryavarta*, because the Mughal institutions of patriarchal power – within which patriarchs ranked one another and held patrimonial entitlements – superseded and encompassed the ideology of *dharma*. No religion constrained a sultan's power to confer rank on subordinates. A sultan's status arose from rituals of conquest and entitlement whose authority went back to the days of the Gurjara-Pratiharas. Sultanic power reached its height under the Mughal, Safavid, and Ottoman dynasties, but its logic was not contained by Islam. Hindu practitioners included not only the Rajputs but also the Rayas of Vijayanagar, who were in effect sultans of the south. The English East India Company used sultanic authority for its own Christian imperialism. Thus the expansion of Muslim dynastic power in South Asia should not be conflated with the expansion of Islam: the Mughal imperial system set itself apart from all its predecessors by making the rituals and conditions of patriarchal entitlement more agnostic than ever before.

Social ranks defined by Mughal imperial titles inflected the idioms of social rank almost everywhere in South Asia, influencing group identity subtly and pervasively. From village and caste headmen to hill chiefs, to merchants and bankers and artisans; and from Rajputs, and titled officers called *zamindar*, *nayaka*, *chaudhuri*, *ray chaudhuri*, *jagirdar*, *palaiyakkarar* (Poligars), and raja to all kinds of tax farmers – positions of leadership, authority, and political mediation in state institutions became focal points of social identity formation. Mughal entitlements and modes of patriarchal ranking entered family strategies of marriage alliance and thus influenced kin-group formation at many levels of society. In the Mughal system, patrimonial entitlements depended upon personal recognition by a superior patriarch under the authority of the sultan. In families, occupational groups, sectarian organisations, and caste and tribal societies, an officially recognised headman had to attain his status – at a price – in rituals of state. The darbar (sultan's court) became a centre of transactions that defined agrarian territories, locally and regionally, in the ranks of all the patriarchs. Moving down the ranks, superiors granted honours, titles, and entitlements to those below. Moving up the ranks, inferiors paid tribute, service, and allegiance to those above. State revenues were collected in return for honours and titles conferred by state authorities; and the increasing value of these revenues accumulated at the higher ranks as they fed the evolution of early-modern states. At the lowest echelons, peasant patriarchs paid for titles to land.

From 1500 onward, the agrarian utility and spread of money also increased along with supplies of precious metals and sultanic currencies. Money could buy a wider variety of entitlements to resources within disparate agrarian territories connected by systems of sultanic ranking that were open to participants of all sorts. Aggressive patriarchs bought and fought their way into positions of power in agrarian territories; they became military officers and revenue intermediaries entitled to collect local revenues from local headmen. A diffusion of imperial titles and ranks facilitated a broader commercialisation of the agrarian economy that was also propelled by the military integration of ecologically diverse agricultural territories and by increasing state demand for cash payments, as we will see in the next chapter. Buying titles and official positions of rank became a basic patriarchal strategy. This further accelerated a broad shift away from *dharma*, caste, and Brahman ritualism as the most prominent means to secure assets in agrarian territories, though technologies of temple ritual also expanded their territorial reach under sultanic regimes. The pace of temple building and temple endowment accelerated steadily after 1500, as patriarchs with state entitlements and commercial assets sought additional resources through investments in temples.

Politically and socially, any group could be defined by its representation at court (darbar). Though temple and caste rituals extended their reach, darbari (courtly) dramas had wider powers of incorporation and entitlement. Transactions that defined agrarian territory came increasingly to focus on key people who provided states with revenue.

Mughal revenues fattened the nobility and fuelled the war machinery, and, like other acts of submission, paying revenue constituted entitlements for patriarchs who paid to secure positions of power. Because revenue payments secured patrimonial property at every rank – right down to the lowest levels of the peasantry – it is understandable that a myth emerged among Europeans that the sultan owned all the land in India: who would counter this claim when all patriarchs held their property rights by submission to the Emperor? In this political culture, acts of resistance and rebellion were also acts of negotiation and strategic positioning. Patriarchs faced opposition all around – in the land, unruly nature; in the home, unruly women; in the fields, unruly workers; in the villages, unruly peasants; in the forests, unruly tribes; in the provinces, unruly *zamindars* and rajas – and negotiations among patriarchs always had to take into account resistance from below and demands from above. Patriarchal expectations for obedience and loyalty often met frustration. Many new, assertive identities formed around rebellious patriarchs who, like Shivaji, had official entitlements to represent 'their people' in transactions with higher authorities.

The Mughal regime brought more kinship groups under one system of ranking and military alliance than any before. All its constituent groups became designated by terminologies that in effect formed an ethnic typology. Ethnic identities, based on combinations of language, religion, and region, emerged dramatically among Rajputs, Marathas, and Sikhs, but also in many other places at lower registers. Competitive alliance formation raised the most powerful agrarian patriarchs up into the status of regional leaders. Shivaji inherited a *jagir* that his father obtained under Ahmadnagar and he continued the project of constructing a multi-*jati* Maratha warrior-farming elite by acquiring titles from other sultans in the Deccan. Over several generations, in a long process of competitive alliance-building, conquest, and institutional formation, Marathas built a state that became deeply involved in the enforcement of family ranking and in regulating female behaviour, as warrior patriarchs set about defining Maratha territory and identity. The subsequent preoccupation of Maratha hagiographers with Shivaji as the ideal ruler not only reflects the capacity of Muslim states to nurture Hindu leadership, but, more importantly, it represents the creation of a semi-deified patriarchal icon around which new collective identities were formed, combining ethnicity, language, and religion.

The long-term interaction of family and statecraft produced geographical patterns in regional styles of kinship within agrarian territories. Irawati Karve once argued that more extensive and intensive kinship territories typified the northern plains and southern peninsula, respectively, with Maharashtra being a bridge between the two,[18] but Bina Agarwal's more detailed analysis of kinship practices and women's land rights reveals three broad zones of kinship in South Asia. In each zone, kin groups form distinctive types of territory and regions are characterised by the prevalence of the kinship strategies pursued by prominent land-owning groups, most importantly dominant castes. The position of women is a critical feature of these kinship and territorial regimes.

(1) The north-east high mountains, the southern peninsula, Sri Lanka, and Nepal.
'In all of these, women marry either in their natal villages or in nearby ones, and close-kin marriages are preferred. There is no adherence to purdah, and the overall control of female sexuality is less than in other parts of the subcontinent. Women's labour force participation varies between medium and very high.'

(2) The western plains and northern basins.
In Punjab, Haryana, Uttar Pradesh, and Rajasthan, 'village endogamy is typically forbidden, marriages are often at some distance from the natal village (especially among the upper-caste land owning communities), close-kin marriages are usually taboo, purdah is practised, control over female sexuality is strict, and women's labour force participation rates are low'. Though in Pakistan and Bangladesh, 'village endogamy and close-kin marriages are permitted, and women's inheritance rights are endorsed by Islam . . . female seclusion practices negate these advantages to a significant degree'.

(3) The central mountains, Maharashtra, and West Bengal.
'Village endogamy is not common but neither is it usually forbidden, and women in many communities do marry within the village or nearby villages. Some communities do allow close-kin marriages. Purdah is practised in some communities and not others.' [19]

---

[18] Irawati Karve, *Kinship Organisation in India*, Poona, 1953.
[19] Bina Agarwal, *A Field of One's Own: Gender and Land Rights in South Asia*, Cambridge, 1994, pp. 368–9.

Agarwal stresses that tribal kinship patterns, most prevalent today in the mountains, differ significantly from those in the agrarian lowlands, especially in the amount of sexual activity allowed for women outside marriage. Historically, groups called 'tribes' are *by definition* those that have been relatively isolated from lowland agrarian states in modern times and therefore distant from the enforcers of *dharma*. Tribal groups interact with caste societies and economies but they have also been kept apart, especially in the tropical high mountains in the north-east. Agarwal notes that the prevalence of tribal communities in the central mountains and their territorial admixture with non-tribal communities creates the mixed character of her third kinship zone.

The broad division portrayed by Karve and Agarwal is between extensive and intensive strategies of kinship alliance, which appear to predominate according to the respective influence of warrior colonisation and territorial *dharma* in pre-modern centuries. There is also an overlap between forms of kinship territoriality and the prominence of irrigated agriculture, rice cultivation, medieval inscriptions, and pastoral nomadism. In general, when we move from low-lying riverine tracts of the early-medieval gentry, where older inscriptions cluster, into drier areas dominated by warrior-farmers, we see a transition from more intensive to more extensive kinship practices. In this same transition, we see a shift in the gendered substance of patriarchal power. Matrilineal descent was prevalent only in Agarwal's first zone, which also contains territories of intensive kinship where women live within a small circle of kin for their whole lives. By contrast, in extensive kinship regimes, women pass between distant kin groups as icons of family honour and agents in marital alliances. Maharashtra contains both kinds of kinship territory, and also transitions not only between tribal hills and caste lowlands but between coastal regions of more intensive medieval wet farming and interior regions of more extensive dry farming. So Maharashtra is not so much a transition zone between cultures of the north and south, described by Karve, as a mix of practices that characterise different types of agrarian territory. A separation of irrigated lowlands from dry uplands also divides coastal Andhra from its interior and the Kaveri basin in southern Karnataka from the Deccan; and more intensive kinship patterns usually pertain in the wetter regions. In general, the distribution of more intensive forms of kinship even today coincides with that of more intensive farming in pre-modern centuries. Extensive regimes, like warrior power, spread widely over time. Extensive kinship strategies concentrate today in territories which have more pastoral nomadism and warrior colonisation in their agrarian history. In Maharashtra, Bihar, Bengal, Bangladesh, and elsewhere, extensive warrior patterns of kinship were imposed upon more intensive local strategies, creating elite alliances and models of status which diffused downward like the powers of *dharma*. Extensive kinship patterns would have helped to extend the agricultural frontier in the east, and more intensive kinship forms perhaps developed in old pastoral areas that became characterised in modern times by more intensive irrigated farming, especially in Punjab. A mixing of kinship forms occurred everywhere with the rampant migratory resettlements of the early-modern period. In the Tamil country, Telugu warriors settled tracts between river valleys and some have retained extensive kinship strategies and even observed *purdah* until recently.

Despite all the imperfections in the fit between old farming regimes and kinship, we can see that intensive kinship alliance-building is a good strategy for protecting family property in local communities and territories. Family alliances that formed the local gentry also produced the funds and controlled the labour which built up early-medieval irrigation and paddy cultivation. Patriarchs sought to control contiguous territories for the expansion of succeeding generations. Marriages formed dense links among dominant families, who became related to one another like their paddy fields, as sustenance flowed from one family to another and from one generation to the next. Families partitioned social space into contiguous kinship territories, which became more diverse by the inclusion of new groups into *jatis* and by the fissioning of lineages, but retained an intricately kin flavour. In riverine lowlands, kinship stressed local alliances among families and formed intricately graded ranks within gentry strata. Families maintained a genealogical sense of descent from medieval kings, but domestic patriarchy concentrated on markers of status within local communities. The marriage of sons and daughters was normatively contrived within finely graded social strata, within close proximity to the natal village, and within an existing nexus of family ties. Agricultural communities and regions were organised around webs of intensive, intersecting family alliances. On the Tamil coast, it would not be uncommon for people to be related to one another in several ways at once, as a result of cross-cousin marriages over generations. The language of family permeated all the institutions of agrarian patrimony, as the meanings of *pangu*, *pangali*, *kulam*, *nadu*, and *nattar* attest. Institutionalised among dominant castes, the intensive pattern of kinship and its idioms of village share-holding also became typical among agricultural workers and other groups in irrigated regions of the medieval era. In this setting, appropriate female decorum is a community as well as a family concern. Husband and wife are most often reckoned as kin from birth, sharing the same agrarian homespace. A wife's devotion to her husband does not need to conflict with loyalty to her father; and, though she leaves her father's house at marriage, she in effect never leaves home. Migration brought similar types of family networks into being in nested agglomerations of family ties that came to characterise the paddy-growing lowlands.

In the dry territories of nomadism and in domains of conquest colonisation, by contrast, and particularly among warrior colonisers such as the Rajputs and Jats, a woman's transition from daughter to wife came to mean moving into the household of a stranger whose superiority to her father was dramatised in the marriage itself. Patriarchal strategies of marriage alliance designed for upward mobility put women in a difficult, intermediary position, as marriage helped to extend lineage power out over territory in a pattern like that of the banyan tree. Expressions of family power focused on the wife as the icon of her family's honour and rank. Multiple marriages expanded the power of a great patriarch, his wives being ranked as representatives of their fathers. A woman's devotion to her in-laws always conflicted in principle with loyalty to her parents and siblings. Personal, intimate, ritualised expressions of devotion to her husband as opposed to her father were built into the disciplinary activities particularly of her mother-in-law, who had survived this same transition. But the status of wife and mother in a superior family could also open up new opportunities for her natal kin and their offspring; so that serving her husband would most likely be her father's most fervent desire, because pleasing her husband would be the best way to improve her natal family's prospects. *Purdah* and *sati* became particularly widespread as auspicious expressions of female purity, sacrificial devotion, sacred heroism, and divine power. Extreme controls over female sexuality enhanced family honour in a culture of heroic sacrifice and harsh discipline. *Sati* became divine at landmarks of heroism which marked warrior territory. Forts and palaces enshrine the valour of great men. Perched high above Ajmer on a rocky mountain ledge, Prithvi Raj Chauhan's fort has today become an icon of militant Hindu nationalism. At Mandu, it is said, hundreds of palace women became *sati* as the sultan marched his troops to death in battle. At Mandore, in 1459, Rao Jodha 'took an extreme step to ensure that the new site proved auspicious' by burying alive one Rajiya Bambi in the foundations of the new fort, promising that 'his family and descendants would be looked after by the Rathores'.[20]

[20] Dhananajaya Singh, *The House of Marwar*, New Delhi, 1994, p. 33.

CHAPTER 3

REGIONS

In the fourteenth century, South Asia became a region of travel and transport connecting Central Asia and the Indian Ocean. This redefined the location of all its agrarian territories. In the wake of the Mongols, overland corridors of routine communication extended from the Silk Road to Kanya Kumari and branched out to seaports along the way. Connections among distant parts of Eurasia became numerous and routine. New technology, ideas, habits, languages, people and needs came into farming communities. New elements entered local cuisine. People produced new powers of command, accumulation, and control, focused on strategic urban sites in agrarian space. By 1600, ships sailed between China, Gujarat, Europe, and America. Horses trotted across the land between Tajikistan and Egypt, Moscow and Madurai. Camels caravaned between Syria and Tibet, Ajmer, and Agra. A long expansion in world connections occurred during centuries when a visible increase in farming intensity was also reshaping agrarian South Asia. In the dry, interior uplands, warriors built late-medieval dynasties, on land formerly held by pastoralists and nomads; and sultans established a new political culture, whose hegemony would last to the nineteenth century. Slow but decisive change during late-medieval centuries laid the basis for more dramatic trends after 1500, when agricultural expansion accelerated along with the mobility and the local agrarian power of warriors and merchants. Regional formations of agrarian territory came into being, sewn together by urban networks, during a distinctively early-modern period of agrarian history, whose patterns of social power, agricultural expansion, and cultural change embrace the empires of Akbar and the East India Company.

FRONTIERS

As we have seen, early-medieval farming concentrated production, population, and political power in lowland riverine sites where perennial drainage and predictable rains supported intensive land use, stable food supplies, Brahmans, temples, and kings. From Mauryan times onward, wells, dams, channels, and tanks (walls of earth and stone built across routes of drainage to irrigate the land below) marked sites across the northern basins, the eastern coastal plains, and northern Sri Lanka. After the Guptas, inscriptions indicate that irrigation building accelerated in all these areas and that it reached a crescendo in the thirteenth century, which corresponds with the rise and peak of medieval dynasties, temple building, and epigraphy. By 1100, inscriptions indicate that wet and dry cultivation were expanding into new areas. This did not involve major technological change but did alter the geography of agriculture significantly. On the whole, it seems, sedentary farmers preferred to clear drier land – which could be irrigated by various means, most prominently by wells – rather than pioneering in densely forested tropical foothills and high valleys. Intensive agriculture expanded into the drier up-river and interfluvial lands much more rapidly than into heavily wooded hills and tropical jungles. In the process, pastoral nomadism was displaced and its human and animal resources steadily absorbed into agrarian societies, which thereby enhanced their abilities to engage in long-distance trade, use dry land productively, and make war. The proportionately greater influence of formerly pastoral peoples in agrarian societies in the dry interior – from Kabul and Punjab down to the southern Deccan – became a major mark of their cultural distinctiveness.

Tribal communities had a huge world mostly to themselves in tropical and subtropical jungles full of wild animals, wood, fruits, herbs, spices, and many other items for local use and trade in the high mountains, central mountains, and Western Ghats. We have no statistics, but the population and land area committed to shifting, swidden plots – 'slash-and-burn' cultivation, called *jhum* in many areas, but also *bewar*, *marhan*, etc., and practised in a great variety of ways – surely must have increased over the centuries. *Jhum* was the first kind of cultivation to influence forest growth in the eastern Ganga basin, Bengal, and the central mountains, and in many places, the only kind until the nineteenth century. *Jhum* sites formed territories of rotating cultivation over expanding stretches of forest and they supported complex systems of exchange and interaction among different kinds of agrarian societies. The social formation of *jhum* and of permanent field cultivation, respectively, came to be characterised by the contrast between caste and tribal societies and, eventually, between hills and plains; the two systems maintained their social distance and otherness, even as they interacted and overlapped. Sedentary farmers tended, in the long run, to usurp tribal territories, however, and in a broad sense these two forms of agrarian society were in competition for land, labour, and natural resources. Well into the nineteenth century, this competition was usually invisible, because *jhum* cultivators could move further afield as farmers encroached upon the forest, moving onto land already clear for *jhum*. In 1885, when W. W. Hunter, as Director-General of Statistics in British India, sent a circular to district officers to ascertain techniques of 'land reclamation', he received responses that describe the interaction of peasant and tribal cultivators in Maldah, Gonda, and Nimar, which lie on the eastern, northern, and western rim lands of the central mountains. Typically, the Maldah collector said of Santals: 'Their habit is to clear the jungle and then make the land fit for cultivation. As soon as they have done this they sell their holdings to Muhammadan cultivators and spend the price of it in feasting and drinking and move to clear new pieces of land.'[1]

Sedentary agrarian society – especially landlords, overlords, and financiers – did not always pay for the land, of course, and encroachments into tribal land did cause conflict in medieval times. As we have seen, many inscriptions depict the conquest and absorption of tribal cultivators by sedentary communities. But, as long as forest lands remained in abundance, *jhum* cultivators could move away, deeper into the jungle. In general, this involved relocations at higher elevations, up the slopes away from advancing lowlanders; and eventually tribal societies were confined predominantly to mountain forests.

In 1798, Francis Buchanan described *jhum* cultivation near Chittagong, and its moving borderland with rice farming on the coastal plain:

During the dry season, the natives of these places cut down to the root all the bushes growing on a hilly tract. After drying for some time the bush wood is set on fire, and . . . as much of the large timber as possible is destroyed . . . The whole surface of the ground is now covered with ashes, which soak with the first rain, and serve as manure. No sooner has the ground been softened by the first showers of the season than the cultivator begins to plant. To his girdle he fixes a small basket containing a promiscuous mixture of seeds of all the different plants raised

---

[1] Dietmar Rothermund, 'A Survey of Rural Migration and Land Reclamation in India, 1885', *Journal of Peasant Studies*, 4, 3, 1977, 233.

in Jooms. These plants are chiefly rice, cotton, Capsicum, indigo, and . . . fruits. In one hand the cultivator then takes an iron pointed dibble with which he strikes the ground, making small holes . . . Into these holes he with his other hand drops a few seeds . . . as chance directs, and leaves the further rearing of the crop to nature.[2]

Buchanan goes on to say that perennial farming along the Chittagong lowlands had not supplanted *jhum*, and that some paddy fields were so new that they were still pocked with huge tree stumps. In the mountains, he reported *jhum* to be the only cultivation. The cultural contrast between hills and plains people emerged for him starkly in the fact that highland farmers were not Muslims; they worshipped what Buchanan called a form of Shiva. This indicates a more general pattern: hill peoples developed sophisticated agrarian territories in highland forests and jungles where they remained culturally independent of the agrarian lowlands. This was true in the mountain borderlands of the Deccan as well, where forest rajas ruled the land until they were uprooted by warriors and farmers under the Maratha regime.[3]

In the 1880s, *jhum* land was still being steadily converted into permanent cultivation all around the vast expanse of the central mountains. All along the northern basins, permanent farming communities seem to have moved much more slowly into the tropical forests than into the drier plains and high valleys. The *A'in-i Akbari* indicates that, in 1595, high-quality rice was being grown on the banks of the Ghagar and Sarju rivers up to Dugaon and Bahraich, when wild elephants filled the land north of the Sarju, along the Rapti and Gandak, and around Gorakhpur. Paying bounty for wild elephants was still a significant item of state expenditure in Sylhet in the 1770s, and the village of Changel, in northern Bihar, was typical of that region in being 'settled' by permanent cultivation only in the eighteenth century. Farmers expanded wheat, pulse, and millet cultivation into the lightly wooded land in the western basin around Agra centuries before they cut down forests south of the Yamuna and in the uplands of the Gomati, which remained jungle in 1800. The drier west of the Ganga basin had many advantages. Not only was it easier to

[2] Francis Buchanan, 'An Account of a Journey Undertaken by Order of the Board of Trade through the Provinces of Chittagong and Tipperah in Order to Look Out for the Places Most Proper for the Cultivation of Spices, March–May, 1798', quoted in Richard M. Eaton, *The Rise of Islam and the Bengal Frontier, 1204–1760*, Berkeley, 1994, pp. 236–37.

[3] Sumit Guha, 'Forest Politics and Agrarian Empires: The Khandesh Bhils, c1700–1850', *Indian Economic and Social History Review*, 33, 2, 1996, 133–55.

clear and plough, but plenty of land lay all around for animal grazing, and trade routes extended in every direction. Uplands were more attractive when they were more temperate, suitable for seasonal grazing, free of malaria, and strategically situated. Valleys into the high mountains of the Indus basin were prominent agrarian sites in ancient and early-medieval times. Taxila and Gandhara were core sites under the Mauryas. Kashmir, Kangra, and Champa have many medieval inscriptions. When the Chinese traveller Hsuan Tsang visited Punjab in the seventh century, he did notice fertile land around towns in the upper doabs, but he described in more detail the splendid orchards and fields in submontane tracts and all along water courses in the hill valleys. The flatlands in the upper Punjab doabs do not seem to have been heavily farmed in the first millennium. The absence of inscriptions in what would later become the heartland of agrarian Punjab may explain its relatively low Brahman population and lack of Brahmanical cultural influence, as compared with Kangra and Champa. Early-medieval dry farming developed in Sindh, around Multan, and in Rajasthan, where the Persian wheel and step wells are attested by Kasyapa's *Krsisukti*. From here, Jat farmers seem to have moved into the upper Punjab doabs and into the western Ganga basin in the first half of the second millennium. We have noticed previously that the prehistoric Saraswati once ran into Rajasthan, and the surface desiccation and deepening of groundwater that are indicated by its disappearance seem to have continued to make the lower Indus basin and western plains increasingly drought prone across the first millennium. This would have encouraged Jats to move with their herds toward the hills, into western Uttar Pradesh and Punjab, to farm land where more water was within reach of their wells. Jat migrations would have accompanied a slow conversion of lineages from pastoralism to farming and the extension of Rajput conquest colonisation. All these trends combined to open new agricultural territories from Panipat to Sialkot along very old trade routes running from Kabul to Agra. By the sixteenth century, Jalandhar and Lahore were thriving towns surrounded by lush farmland. By this time also, behind the Salt Range, Paxtun clans had moved down along the Kabul river to build farming communities around irrigation in the Peshawar valley.[4]

[4] See Romila Thapar, 'The Scope and Significance of Regional History', in Romila Thapar, *Ancient Indian Social History: Some Interpretations*, Hyderabad, 1978, pp. 361–77; and Robert Nichols, 'Settling the Frontier: Land, Law, and Society in the Peshawar Valley,

Wheat lands expanded west of the Ganga and in Punjab doabs astride trade routes and around old trading towns where distinctively urban commercial and administrative groups were already prominent, above all Khatris. As farmland expanded in spaces between the plains and high mountains, new opportunities for trade arose at ecological boundaries, and this stimulated more commercially oriented production and processing. By the sixteenth century, tobacco, sugarcane, honey, fruits, vegetables, and melons fed Punjab commercial life, along with profits from sericulture, indigo, and all the elements of cloth manufacturing. Down river, Multan featured cotton, opium, and sugarcane. Similarly in Gujarat, where early-medieval farming seems to have clustered along rivers and trade routes that connected the Maurya heartland with the Persian Gulf, mixed irrigated and dry cultivation expanded into forests and plains, toward the mountains, again producing more ecologically diverse farm territories that stimulated more commodity production. In the sixteenth century, ship builders worked in Broach, Surat, Navsari, Gogha, and Daman; on the plains running up to the Vindhyas, Satpuras, and Aravallis, farmers grew sugarcane, fruits, and melons; and farms produced all the elements of cotton and silk cloth manufacture. As in Punjab, trade routes in Gujarat also ran across various territories endowed with complementary natural resources. More ecological diversity in farm territories encouraged commodity crop specialisation and a combination of agrarian activities developed that formed the basis for textile industries.

Along the coast from Gujarat south to Kanya Kumari and northeast to Bengal, the expansion of farm territories connected the sea and mountains, and sites along the coast were also connected to one another by water routes. Coastal territories collected commodities from forests, fisheries, and wet and dry farming, as intensive agriculture expanded inland. Ship building depended upon tall timbers from the uplands, and mountain products such as pepper and other spices were prime commodities for the overseas trade. From the twelfth century onward, farmers were also moving upland to clear dry lands and build new irrigation along the Kaveri, Krishna, and Godavari rivers. Like the Kongu region in the Kaveri basin – around Coimba-

1500–1900', Ph.D. dissertation, University of Pennsylvania, 1997. This and the paragraphs below draw heavily on Irfan Habib, *An Atlas of Mughal Empire: Political and Economic Maps with Notes, Bibliography and Index*, Delhi, 1982.

tore – the up-river tracts in Andhra, Maharashtra, and Berar were rich with black cotton soil. Dry farms in the interior combined with old farm societies along the irrigated coast to produce all the raw materials for the textile industry and to provide profitable sites for weaving. One community of weavers migrated from Saurashtra to set up operations in Madurai, and the mobility and versatility of many professional weaving communities in the peninsula came from their experience in the dry zones of military competition, trade, and agricultural expansion which tied together the black cotton soil of the upland interior and the corridors of the sea trade during late medieval centuries.[5]

In Bengal, dense tropical forests posed a formidable obstacle for farmers, and farming frontiers moved steadily south and east, deeper into the delta, as they also moved north-west into Chota Nagpur and north-east into the Brahmaputra basin. Gupta-era inscriptions appear at the top of the old delta in West Bengal. Pala and Sena epigraphy has a somewhat wider distribution in the lower delta. But before the fourteenth century, land grant inscriptions still concentrated on the relatively high ground to the north, east, and west of the low, deltaic flood lands. In the fourteenth century, the shift of the Ganga delta to the east encouraged farmers to move in that direction, but, in 1605, sites of Mughal documentation still clustered in the north and west, though they also extended to the Meghna river and clustered again around Dhaka. The expansion of cultivation from the fourteenth to the eighteenth century moved farming closer to the sea and into the mountains. It created a rich, expanding zone of interaction between sea lanes, mountains, and the northern basins, along the riverine highways.[6]

Everywhere, conquest colonisation added muscle to agrarian expansion. Pastoral and hunting peoples were conquered. Raja Bhoj built his massive tank near Bhopal in the eleventh century. The Kakatiyas made Telangana into land of tank irrigation in the thirteenth century; and one of their tanks, near Warangal, drains 80 square miles.[7] In the fourteenth century, warriors from Afghanistan and Turkestan fought

[5] Mattison Mines, *The Warrior Merchants: Textiles, Trade and Territory in Southern India*, Cambridge, 1984; Prasannan Parthasarathi, 'Weavers, Merchants and States: The South Indian Textile Industry, 1680–1800', Harvard University dissertation, 1992.

[6] B. M. Morrison, *Political Centers and Cultural Regions in Early Bengal*, Tucson, 1970; Eaton, *The Rise of Islam and the Bengal Frontier*, pp. 17–27; Habib, *Atlas*, Map 11.

[7] Cynthia Talbot, manuscript of chapter 4 of forthcoming book on medieval Andhra and

their way into rapidly expanding agrarian territories and built rocky fortress towns in the uplands and dry plains which became new centres of coercive power along trade routes. Fort-cities arose at Kota (1264), Bijapur (1325), Vijayanagar (1336), Gulbarga (1347), Jaunpur (1359), Hisar (1361), Ahmedabad (1413), Jodhpur (1465), Ludhiana (1481), Ahmadnagar (1494), Udaipur (1500), and Agra (1506). Delhi began its long career. Accounts of famine, plague, and food scarcity also begin to multiply, clustered around new warrior capitals. Reports of death and distress indicate that disease also migrated across Eurasia and that hard human costs were paid for war. New dynasties increased population density in fortress and town in dry landscapes with erratic seasons and precarious water supplies; and deadly sieges, droughts, and disease led to the abandonment and destruction of numerous centres, grand examples being Vijayanagar and Fatehpur Sikri. Nonetheless, after 1300, major new urban sites became permanent and they marked a new kind of territoriality, which focused on the sultan's darbar. Regions of warrior power formed around capitals that became sites for the articulation of commerce, war, industry, and farming, and also of regional identities and *dharma*. Warrior states built roads and carried their demands for revenue across old divisions among agrarian territories; and they founded and protected sites of trade at ecological boundaries and along old trade routes. Most importantly, their conquests and demands for tribute connected the dry interior regions, coastal plains, and ocean ports; so they integrated agrarian spaces that ran up to the mountains and down to the sea, and these connections made agrarian territory more commercially active. Sultans also invested in the fertility of the land. When Firoz Tughluq built the Western Jamuna Canal along old riverbeds north of Delhi, he began a tradition of large-scale state investments in irrigation that would make his capital a model for a new kind of agrarian urbanism – a site for intersecting, often conflicting interests among warriors, farmers, and financiers, who all invested in agriculture on an increasingly commercial basis within the framework of institutions of state revenue collection.

'The Making of Andhradesh', South Asia Seminar presentation at the University of Pennsylvania, 29 October 1997.

SULTANS

From the fourteenth century onward, it becomes increasingly relevant for historians to ask if state power was being used to coerce commercial cropping and if warriors were impoverishing peasants with increasing (and often violent) demands for revenue. Many historians have answered 'yes' to both questions, but some qualifications and further research are necessary. Certainly, subsistence-first farming strategies would have prevailed in peasant societies, but the idea was also prominent that agriculture can be profitable and provide state revenue at the same time. When peasants paid warriors, they certainly incurred a loss, but did they gain anything? There is a tendency to see late-medieval history in terms of war and conquest, but Ibn Battuta was perhaps as typical of the age as Khaljis and Tughluqs; and in the fourteenth century, though warriors did use force to collect taxes, there was also commercial revenue in farming communities over and above what would have been necessary to pay taxes. Ibn Battuta – like Abu-l Fazl and Hamilton Buchanan – viewed his world in commercial terms and, standing outside the state, he does not indicate that coercion was needed to generate commodities. At each stop in his journey, he observed everyday commercialism. 'Bangala is a vast country, abounding in rice,' he wrote, 'and nowhere in the world have I seen any land where prices are lower than there.' In Turkestan, 'the horses . . . are very numerous and the price of them is negligible'. He was pleased to see commercial security, as he did during eight months trekking from Goa to Quilon. 'I have never seen a safer road than this,' he reported, 'for they put to death anyone who steals a single nut, and if any fruit falls no one picks it up but the owner.' He also noted that 'most of the merchants from Fars and Yemen disembark' at Mangalore, where 'pepper and ginger are exceedingly abundant'. In 1357, John of Marignola, an emissary to China from Pope Benedict XII, also stopped at Quilon, which he described as 'the most famous city in the whole of India, where all the pepper in the world grows'.[8] Though we inherit most commercial evidence from coastal sites, similar observations could have been made along trade routes that connected inland ecological zones where exchange economies thrived. In the more sparsely populated open spaces of the interior – away

[8] M. S. Randhawa, *A History of Agriculture in India*, Delhi, 1986, vol. II, pp. 68–9.

from the sea – forced revenue collections were part of war for participants on all sides, including peasants, who fled, fought, and farmed for subsistence or profit, as the season allowed. Inscriptions from the Tamil coast indicate that monetary instruments were being used to establish entitlements to agrarian assets by the ninth century; and over the centuries, as more families bought the materials for their own subsistence by exchanging goods and services, farmers sold more and more. Coercion did abound in agriculture, to be sure, but by the sixteenth century the militant Mughal tax machine forced its way into agrarian territories which already had active money economies and substantial commercial farming. The cotton textile economy gave even rugged warrior-peasants in black soil tracts an abiding interest in commodity production. Patriarchs in farming communities could secure their entitlements to land and labour by paying tribute, and under the Mughals, if not before, the revenue system itself had become a major source of agrarian profit. Commerce and taxation evolved together and supported one another in violent territories of agricultural expansion.

Trends that begin to assemble the elements of modern agrarian environments are sufficiently visible in the sixteenth century to justify using the phrase 'early-modern' for the period *circa* 1550–1850. Doing this simply highlights some particular features of historical change during this period, which are better documented from Akbar's time onward, though some began much earlier, most importantly urbanisation. Abu-l Fazl mentions 180 large cities and 2,837 towns, and bigger cities embellished more powerful states. Urban sites had always accumulated various kinds of powers within agrarian landscapes but, after 1550, transactions that harnessed moving elements in agriculture were tied more extensively to darbars and markets. Hierarchies of central places also emerge more clearly from Mughal times onward. Cities that defined early-modern territories include Dhaka, Calcutta, Lucknow, Delhi, Agra, Lahore, Multan, Surat, Ahmedabad, Bombay, Pune, Bangalore, Hyderabad, Madras, Cochin, and Trivandrum. Some elements that define modern cultural regions – linguistic, literary, ethnic, and religious – were already in place in 1500, but regions become more clearly institutionalised in the following centuries. Forts and armies created strategically dominant sites for stabilising regional cultures. First Devagiri and then Ahmadnagar, Aurangabad, Junnar, and Pune defined an emerging Marathi linguistic and cultural area within regional networks of peasant-warrior alliance and religious pilgrimage; and Marathas refer to *maharashtradharma*, 'the *dharma* specific to Maharashtra'.[9] By the seventeenth century, Warangal, Golkonda, and Vijayanagar redefined 'Andhra *desa*' as a land that included both the coast and the dry interior, which was called 'Telugu country' for the first time in the fourteenth century. The Hoysalas built a new, lasting centre of power in a new Kannada heartland at Dvarasamudra, named for its irrigation tank (Sanskrit = *samudra*) and poised above the Mysore plateau and the upper Kaveri basin.[10] There is a telling eighteenth-century map in the British Museum that depicts Mughal territory as strings of urban sites connected by routes of transportation, running from Kabul to Bengal and Berar. In each central place, a Mughal official would have drawn a similar map in his mind to connect his own headquarters to all the towns subordinate to his authority . . . and so on down the line . . . down to little villages. Around these sites of accumulation and mobility, regional networks of agrarian territory took physical and institutional form in hierarchies of power, authority, and influence.

In 1790, East India Company officers drew identical maps of their own territories. This kind of linear, transactional, urban territoriality had an increasing impact on agrarian space from Akbar's time onward, and it provoked new forms of documentation to suit environments of inter-city mobility and communication. Inscriptions declined in number and significance. Portable paper documents dominate the historical record after 1550. The new records come not only from ritual sites but also from specialist accountants, surveyors, preachers, travellers, merchants, and tax collectors; and they are composed in many languages. These records touch upon agriculture over much wider spaces in more standard terms than did their medieval predecessors. They are concerned above all with trade and revenue. Though localised in detail, early-modern agricultural data can be compiled to form general impressions. The old inscriptional corpus represented an agricultural archipelago of core sites separated by empirically empty space; its transactions were disconnected from one another. Thus there is no compendium of inscriptional data that covers even a fraction of the area covered by Abu-l Fasl's *A'in-i-Akbari*. Early-modern states

[9] Sumit Guha, 'An Indian Penal Regime: Maharashtra in the Eighteenth Century', *Past & Present*, 147, 1995, 101–27.

[10] Cynthia Talbot, 'The Making of Andhradesh'.

produced increasingly detailed, comprehensive data on the conduct of farming, during more widespread, regular, and financially complex state revenue transactions; and not only in Mughal domains. In Karnataka, 'black books' came into vogue for accounts in monastic and landlord estates. Local chronicles in Assam record the first manpower census in 1510, and Ahoms started a land survey in 1681.[11] In the seventeenth century, a number of different institutions – states, temples, monasteries, *waqf* endowments, businesses, and landed estates – generated texts to indicate that statistical accounts were becoming more popular in asset management. Mughal revenue and monetary records reflect a general rise of statistical accounting. The *A'in-i-Akbari* measured agricultural production, manufacturing output, and trade by the value of state revenues; it converts territory into exchange value. These accounts were disciplinary devices to track people and their obligations. Institutional accounts had been produced earlier, for specific transactions and endowments, as in the twelfth-century accounts of the Chola emperors who recorded all the costs and rights involved in royal temple construction. Vijayanagar inscriptions use tabular statistics in the fourteenth century and later separate numbers from text in tabular accounts using standardised units of measure. By the sixteenth century, accounting, coinage, cash calculations, commercial entitlements, and tax discipline all travelled together among urban centres of state power. They produced new landscapes of knowledge and agrarian textuality as they organised territory into regions of value and hierarchy.

The *A'in-i Akbari* stands alone, however. It did not become a template for imperial accounts and seems never to have been up-dated or replicated. Personal devotion to Akbar motivated Abu-l Fazl, and Akbar ruled a personal empire as he moved among its urban centres. His domain was transactional, built upon personal alliances, and, however wide spreading, it never produced a revenue bureaucracy. Our documentation concerning seventeenth- and eighteenth-century revenue conditions actually improves in the late eighteenth century when the English East India Company did retrospective assessments. It seems that Mughal tax demands peaked under Aurangzeb but Company officials could not reconstruct a good record of taxation

---

[11] Amalendu Guha, 'The Medieval Economy of Assam', in Tapan Raychaudhuri and Irfan Habib, ed., *The Cambridge Economic History of India*, vol. 1, Cambridge, 1982, p. 485.

before 1700. It is reasonable to conclude that recorded rates of taxation which we find dating back to the *Arthasastra* and running down to 1700 – including the *A'in-i-Akbari* – represent normative guidelines for official activity more than accounts of regularised assessments and collections. This is not to say that taxes were not collected or assessed with any regularity – medieval inscriptions are replete with tax accounts – but rather that there was an empirical gap between *local* tax practices and *regional* documentation, which continued through the eighteenth century and which early-modern state officials worked hard to eliminate, including, no doubt, Abu-l Fazl. Eighteenth-century states produced substantial evidence to indicate that they were systematising agrarian taxation, and extending and regularising procedures which had been instituted under the Mughals. The *Risala-i Zira't* ['Treatise on Agriculture'], commissioned by the Company in 1785, describes a process of standardisation in regional revenue practice in Bengal which had been going on for perhaps fifty years; though state taxation and accounting were much older than this and though even this standardisation was probably more normative than regulatory.[12] The Company continued to standardise a revenue system, and its territories were defined as regions of official knowledge, regulated state income, and government authority. Maratha, Mysore, Sikh, and other regimes did the same.[13] As the Company built its tax routines, it utilised ideas and techniques which had been practised and circulated among state intellectuals across Eurasia for several centuries, and Company intellectuals added some new ideas from England. Persian techniques for assessment, accounting, and granting entitlements moved through Mughal domains into Bengal and thus into Company blueprints for *zamindari* revenue settlements there. Mughal and European practices mingled in eighteenth-century Maratha territories, where they produced detailed village accounts, and Maratha practices travelled with Brahman accountants via Mysore and Hyderabad into Company survey and revenue offices in Madras.

[12] See Harbans Mukhia, *Perspectives on Medieval History*, New Delhi, 1933, pp. 259–94.

[13] This trend is not confined to South Asia. From about 1450 to 1830, Myanmar, Thailand, Vietnam, France, Russia, and Japan 'all exhibit tendencies ... toward political consolidation, administrative centralization, cultural integration, and social regulation. The dynamics underlying these developments are related to economic growth, military competition, accumulation of institutional expertise and intellectual support for political order.' Victor Lieberman, 'Transcending East–West dichotomies: State and Culture Formation in Six Ostensibly Disparate Areas' (The Eurasian Context of the Early Modern History of Mainland South East Asia, 1400–1800), *Modern Asian Studies*, 31, 3, 1997, 463–507.

English debates about land revenue and land rights adapted old ideas from many sources to build colonial understandings of agriculture. Company intellectual practices drew upon many other regimes and its agrarian discourse was thus more distinctively early-modern and broadly Eurasian than narrowly British or even European.

Early-modern texts focus their attention on the power of absolute rulers and on the rights, titles, and obligations of ranked individuals in revenue transactions that delivered agrarian wealth into the treasury. Early-modern *imperial* taxation, as it affected most villages, seems in general to have been more in the nature of tribute, being coerced, irregular, and arbitrary. *Taxation* itself was ancient, going back to the Mauryas. But imperial taxation had never been widely routinised, legitimised, and integrated within *local institutions* that contained most tax transactions until the late eighteenth century. Inscriptions indicate that early-medieval agrarian territories were defined transactionally by various transfers of wealth among farming localities through state officials, merchants, and temples. Transactions between villages and kings secured local entitlements, and these are the main business for many inscriptions. Payments for local goods and services and the transfer of local entitlements generated income for local gentry; and they in turn paid *samanta*s and rajas to maintain their own local authority. Such payments by local leaders to secure local entitlements increased steadily after 1300. The Mughal imperial system collected wealth from a great many localities through powerful intermediaries – *zamindar*s and rajas – as Mughal *jagirdar*s inserted themselves militarily into existing territories of payment-for-entitlement. Empire evolved as a many-layered cake of authority and entitlement.[14] The people at the top did not have much to say about what went on at the bottom. They focused rather on funnelling more wealth to the top and on regulating transactions above the ranks of raja and *zamindar*. Mughal records never did dig below the level of *zamindar*s or keep track of payments moving up the hierarchy from villages and towns, to regional centres, to the imperial capital. Eighteenth-century states developed this capacity. Records from Maratha, Sikh, and Company capitals enumerate local payments-for-entitlement and could track payments to regional authorities; and some regional authorities could

---

[14] This phrase comes from Richard Danzig, 'The Many Layered Cake: A Case Study of Reform of the Indian Empire', *Modern Asian Studies*, 3,1, 1969, 57–96.

even regulate local systems. But such local administrative powers in wide-spreading revenue transactions were tenuous and eighteenth-century wars made them more costly to maintain. Before 1800, it seems, Marathas did the most local administrative regulation. The Company's Native State treaties and early *zamindari* settlements continued the conventional practice of collecting revenue through intermediaries who were granted open-ended local authority in return. This kept down central costs of imperial administration and it also had the advantage of rewarding subordinate allies with the incentive to raise the value of their own territories, and thus to expand the extent of their own revenue collections. It was only after 1800 that Sikh and Company regimes developed the power to regulate the activity of subordinate authorities in local systems of payment-for-entitlement.

The Mughals provided a basic vocabulary for this early-modern state project. Mughal terminology spread widely to designate ranks and terms of revenue payment. That regional norms for taxation and entitlement were coming into vogue during the eighteenth century is suggested by the frequency with which ideas such as 'illegal exactions' appear in revenue disputes. This idea reflects a discourse of disputation, resistance, and critique concerning contested rights and entitlements in the revenue ranks. The various regional systems display similarities that derive from pervasive Mughal influence. What the Company called a revenue 'farm' was a contract to collect taxes from a specific territory in return for a share of collections; and this was considered an irregular if not immoral arrangement almost everywhere. It was considered to be a degraded practice because Mughal rules stipulated that taxes be fixed and collected not by speculators but rather by ranked officers at official rates. Taxes were to be collected within a *fasli* year. From a Persian term for 'crop' and 'cropping year' the Mughal *fasli* year ended with the last tax payment from the last winter crop (however small), in mid-April. Other important terms in the revenue lexicon – *jagir, zamin, rai'yat, inam, watan,* and *miras* – were attached to official revenue roles and personalities. The holder of a *jagir* (*jagirdar*) was a state official who collected revenue from a large territory to pay the emperor. This role defined the Mughal nobility and provided leadership for regional successor states. A *zamindar* paid revenue to a *jagirdar* and received revenue in turn from *rai'yats*. When Anglicised in the Company's revenue discourse, 'zamindar' and 'ryot' were understood to represent not only roles in the revenue system but also types of property rights in land; and they were translated as 'landlord' and 'peasant', respectively.

The Company's big agrarian debate concerned the practice of collecting revenue from zamindars and thus confirming their entitlements. Company officers found an alternative procedure only after 1792, when they broke into dry territories which had been pioneered by warrior-peasants in the late medieval period. Here, in Kongu and Rayalaseema, the Company acquired territory in which Mysore sultans had broken into the local nexus of payment-for-entitlement and thinned the ranks of zamindars. Maratha and Sikh regimes did much the same, but in most of the Ganga basin and Bengal, along the coast, and in the hills, the title 'zamindar' had been attached to rajas, lineage leaders, and tribal chiefs who were deeply entrenched locally; or it had been acquired by financial middlemen, revenue farmers, and warrior entrepreneurs. Because Company officers believed that the Mughals had managed an imperial bureaucracy, they looked for one traditional, authentic 'native' practice which assigned specific entitlements to each peasant or tenant, but they found many instead. Over time, other terms for 'farmer' or 'peasant' – such as *kisan* (Hindi) and *krishak* (Bengali) – entered the Company's lexicon by identification with *rai'yat* and also came to be translated as 'tenant' in *zamindar*i areas. This set of terms has caused endless confusion ever since, because Company officials defined each rank in the revenue hierarchy as a kind of property right and failed to situate each term in its local context, where it had meaning in practice. British officers did not know that they were dealing with an agrarian world bigger and more varied than Europe; their analysis was geared rather to the scale of England or France. But, as empire builders, they were determined to create firm bureaucratic, legal definitions for these terms; and to this end they made their official definitions and projected them back into history to fabricate authentic native practices, based on classical tradition. In actual agrarian societies, a *rai'yat* (ryot) could be a gentry high-caste landowner who used servile labour to cultivate his fields or a landlord, or a tenant, or a self-cultivating, independent warrior-peasant. Similar variations in social content obtained for all the official revenue roles which were codified bureaucratically in the regions of Company administration.

The terms *inam*, *watan*, and *miras* represent important features of early-modern systems of payment-for-entitlement. These were hereditary rights to resources held by people of stature within local society; and they were bought, sold, accumulated, and otherwise deployed to build local (and sometimes wider) estates. Gifts of lands to temples and Brahmans became *inam* and *miras*, and often took the form of tax exceptions or privileged, low-tax, land rights. In Maratha regions, a *watan* was a bundle of rights to land, services, and tax payments, which defined agrarian nobility and gentry families in agrarian communities. These terms represent transactional entitlements in the complex of payments and obligations which formed alliances among elites at the local, regional, and imperial levels of authority. Company officials who were seeking to build an impersonal bureaucracy could see this kind of personal right to revenue only as a nuisance and as a violation of the principle that, in India, the emperor owned the land. But now we can see that early-modern states were composed of small agrarian territories whose old, local entitlements were being redefined as they were being incorporated into imperial hierarchies. These revenue systems entailed public, symbolic enactments of political ranking. State rituals at critical moments in the *fasli* year constituted authority, locally and regionally; and these rituals included payments that moved up the ranks to accumulate in capital cities. Subalterns in the revenue ranks paid superiors for entitlements in acts of ritual deference that formed power positions in agrarian territory; and some of the cash that travelled up the ranks came to be counted as state revenue.

Historians have focused attention on the wealth that accrued to the Mughal nobility and to the British Raj, but, as tokens of value travelled up the ranks, tokens of value also travelled down: money went up, entitlements came down. Transactions at low levels controlled most of the moving elements that mingled on the farm. Payments by family patriarchs confirmed their status in communities. Payments by the headmen of villages, *muhallas* (urban neighbourhoods), castes, and sectarian and occupational groups confirmed community identity and leadership. Payments to temples, dynasts, Brahmans, and community leaders confirmed farmers' rights to land, labour, water, and credit. In early-modern times, payments that came to be called 'taxation' or 'rent' (depending upon who received them) became increasingly complex, numerous, and necessary in farming communities. These transactional markers of subaltern status did not always involve paying cash – they could mean payments of goods and services – but, from Mughal times onward, local entitlements came to rest increasingly upon payments of cash that moved out of localities to join streams of revenue flowing into regional capitals. The *rai'yat* subaltern paid for powers over land and over people of lesser rank. The *rai'yat* – whether he farmed the land with his own hands or not – paid revenue which confirmed his status as a local patriarch in a local population of rate payers. In the rituals of revenue, states did not suppress or even undermine other kinds of power; indeed, the *sarkar* (ruler) depended upon the local powers of subalterns in the revenue ranks to realise the revenue. *Inam, miras*, and *watan* were some of the terms that marked local sites of transactional power. Personalities of influence and honour acquired these titles to build the local revenue foundations of early-modern states. This form of property eventually became archaic in modern bureaucratic regions of agrarian administration.

LAND

In the early-modern period, as more wealth became revenue, a distinctive political economy emerged at the articulation of state institutions and farming communities, during a gradual shift in material conditions and agrarian cultures. The land itself took on new meanings. The value of farmland became the measure of agrarian territory. Land taxation increased sharply under the Mughals, again in the eighteenth century, and again under the Company. The British increase was most dramatic if not the most violent or disruptive. After 1857, however, land revenue declined in real terms and also as a proportion of state revenue, though state power continued to increase. The Indian National Congress demanded an absolute reduction of the land tax, and after 1947 it fell below zero. State power still increased, but states now turned revenue back to farmers and state subsidies had surpassed land revenue by 1970. Uniquely then in the early-modern period, agrarian taxation funded many upward trends – in the power of state institutions, in the size and wealth of state elites, in urban populations, in monumental building, in artistic and ritual patronage, and in the speed and volume of communication and transportation (including the railway) – all of which were sustained by payments to the state from agriculture. At the same time, state institutions defined entitlements on the farm more widely and forcefully. From 1556 to 1860, struggles to collect revenue and to enforce state power over land rights produced rampant warfare; and the rising real value of land revenue financed Mughal imperial grandeur, rebellions against the Mughals, eighteenth-century wars, and British conquest. Historians have explained the rising revenue trend primarily as a consequence of state action, and military coercion, in particular, has been assigned a central role. Agrarian factors need more consideration.

By 1600, the accumulation of wealth on major routes made strategic sites well worth fighting for. Defending, ruling, protecting, and taxing central places became more valuable and contentious as cities and towns came to include a higher proportion of liquid assets generated by trade, manufacturing, and revenue transactions. Taxes collected in town, like the food and cloth in the market, reflected the character of agrarian territory. Urban officials and merchants drew upon the wealth of the land, and what the East India Company would call 'land revenue' actually included taxes on a variety of assets. As we have seen, rights to land were not just powers over dirt; they formed membership and rank in farming communities and represented a family's entitlement to community resources. Payments-for-entitlement were thus constituents of agrarian society and tools of territoriality. The meaning of 'taxation' changed radically in the nineteenth century but, before 1850, the land whose tax value increased so sharply certainly did include its old community constituents. In retrospect, it was quite sensible then for the British to think of payments that marked *agrarian territoriality* as being a state charge for rights of *land ownership*, because the people who had titles in territory made payments-for-entitlement to state officials. Weavers, merchants, ironsmiths, bankers, herders, and many others also paid taxes. But, except in larger urban settings, non-farmers seem to have paid for entitlements mostly through patriarchs at the apex of local society who were also official mediators in state revenue transactions – rajas, *zamindars*, *deshmukhs*, *patels*, village headmen, and the like. As agrarian sites became more valuable, the value of this role increased along with the price to be paid for performing it.

In the territories in which state taxation increased most dramatically – and left the best records – trade and urbanism were also enhancing the commercial value of land by stimulating demand for agricultural commodities. Indigo and other dyes, animal products, ginger, turmeric, tobacco, toddy and arrack, silk, grapes and melons, fruits and vegetables of all kinds, saffron, sugarcane, oilseeds and oils, peppers and spices, chillies, opium, pulses, rice, wheat, cotton, and palm and other tree products head the list of commercial crops that pushed up land values. Commodity production depended on farm assets that needed protection, not only irrigation works and wells but also trees, terraced fields, and processing equipment such as oil presses, Persian wheels, looms, and forges. Manufacturing increased at the same time, most prominently in textiles, and it is important to keep in mind that all the elements in textiles were agricultural products, so that all the labour that cleaned, spun, wove, dyed, washed, and carried the input and output of the textile trades also added value to farms. Expanding agricultural production increased demand for manufactures, from cooking pots and ploughs to houses, jewellery, and armaments. Direct and indirect commercial investments in agriculture – in manufacturing, irrigation, and commodity markets – increased along with investments in revenue finance, as military competition for taxation drove up the revenue value of farms in financial markets. Much of the liquid capital for agricultural expansion moved through the very same transactions that provided revenue. Temples invested in irrigation. Warriors and financiers advanced loans and granted revenue reductions to increase the stability, intensity, and market value of production. Advances to farmers came increasingly from state authorities who thereby sought to secure their own share of the crop. (These advances were called by various names, such as *taccavi* in Madras.) Remember the Mastee brothers. Their tale includes the assertion that they advanced cash to farmers to lure them to the new village. We will see that *zamindar*s in Chittagong also advanced cash to expand farming. Urbanisation circulated capital from trade and manufacturing through various circuits of investment in farming. Investing in irrigation paid solid dividends, whatever the source of the capital, and we can see from medieval inscriptions and nineteenth-century British sources alike that the building and repairing of irrigation tanks relied on capital raised in a host of ways, including the use of temple funds. As the money supply increased after 1600, it pushed up the cash value of farm assets and taxes at the same time in communities endowed with commercial connections, commodity crops, irrigation, and investors. Land in these places became well worth protecting and paying to keep in the family.

Coercion and violence increased land revenue, but not only for state officials. Mughals fought for revenue, tax collectors fought for it, and the East India Company fought for it; but, as more people paid more for land, more people also fought back to resist claims from above and to expand local claims. Physical fighting distinguished the etiquette of early-modern payments-for-entitlement. Revenue transactions combined negotiation, ritual, status marking, gambling, entrepreneurship, and brute struggles. Fighting and paying for land became inescapable as agrarian space filled up, and subaltern resistance became more common as standing to fight and paying for rights became unavoidable. The option of flight into the forest became less and less attractive as open land for new settlement disappeared. By 1850, Bhisma's old adage had become archaic, because even wooded lands were no longer open space for escape and colonisation: states taxed them and communities controlled them. Creating such domains of local control involved a lot of fighting and paying for entitlements, as the vast, open frontiers of agrarian expansion which had characterised the medieval period closed down. Early-modern imperialism enabled agrarian communities to redefine local territoriality. Wide-spreading transactional hierarchies marked empires in which every level in the ranks took payments from below and all the ranks spread out to control more and more land. The many-layered cake of imperial revenue increased the total value of state income, funnelled more wealth to the higher levels, and also expanded the agrarian base. Land values rose with more competition. State officials added force to the extension of cultivation and to the appropriation of open land by local subordinates. Agricultural communities defined territory by enclosing the land, carving it up, fighting, and paying. Empty land vanished as landscapes filled up completely with territories of entitlement. Agricultural land came to include all the land for which communities made claims with taxes, rituals, battles, and lore.

Using *A'in-i-Akbari* statistics, Shireen Moosvi estimates that the gross cropped area in the Mughal heartland in the northern basins and western plains covered 61 per cent of the total land area that would be covered with farms in 1910.[15] This temporal comparison is not exact because Mughal data – like all such data before 1870 – do not measure *cropped area* but rather *land in the revenue category* of 'cropped land'. Early-modern assessments measure not cultivation, crops, or yields, but rather a kind of land value in systems of payment-for-entitlement.

---

[15] Shireen Moosvi, *The Economy of the Mughal Empire c.1595: A Statistical Study*, Delhi, 1987, pp. 39–73.

With this in mind, it is still useful to note that Moosvi's ratios comparing figures for 1595 and 1910 run from an average of 85 per cent for Agra, Bet Jalandhar, Baroda, and Surat, to 29 per cent in Champaner and Rohilkhand, and down to 8 per cent in Sindh Sagar, indicating that much more of the land was being farmed in politically central, commercially well-connected parts of the Mughal domain, and that relatively *less* subsequent expansion of farmland was possible in core Mughal areas. Such core areas, pulsing with trade and manufacturing, provided most Mughal revenues. James R. Hagen argues that, in the lowlands and adjacent hills of the Gangetic basin and Bengal, roughly 30 per cent of the *total area* was occupied by farms in 1600. He estimates that this figure increased to 50 per cent in 1700, remained at 50 per cent in 1800, and rose to 65 per cent in 1910 and to 70 per cent in 1980. These estimates suggest that farm acreage expanded over 40 per cent of the total land area between 1600 and 1980, with half the increase occurring by 1700, another huge increase in the nineteenth century, and very little in the twentieth century.[16] Much *more* expansion was possible after 1600 in naturally well-endowed areas that were *less* developed in Akbar's time. Outside Bet Jalandhar, for instance, the Punjab lowlands were barely cultivated in 1600, and in 1800 most land south of the hills remained open for grazing. Between 1850 and 1939, the government built 20,886 miles of canals in Punjab, and by 1945 canals irrigated 15,688,000 acres, much of it for more than one crop each year. Regional disparities in the pace and timing of agricultural expansion typify agrarian history and are critical for an accurate understanding of the agrarian content of modernity. As Punjab was booming, some old areas of agricultural prosperity were hitting a resource limit.

In 1595, outside Mughal territory, higher proportions of farmland to total arable would certainly have pertained in old core areas of riverine cultivation along the coast and in the Ganga basin. Moosvi's figures for Baroda and Surat probably reflect conditions in many parts of the coastal plains, especially along riverbeds and in the deltas, except in Bengal. As Hagen's estimate suggests, the overall increase in farmland would have been smaller in the eighteenth century, during wars, plagues, and famines that were particularly bad in the later

---

[16] James R. Hagen, 'Gangetic Fields: An Approach to Agrarian History Through Agriculture and the Natural Environment, 1600–1970', Paper delivered at the annual meeting of the Association for Asian Studies, 1988.

decades. Bengal took decades to recover from the 1770 famine. W. W. Hunter reported that 35 per cent of the total population and 50 per cent of the farmers died in that year, and that depopulation continued in later years amidst *zamindar* feuds to attract tenants to their estates. Decades of strong expansion seem to have preceded the famine, however, as indicated by a surge in temple building after 1730 by *zamindar*s and businessmen.[17] In the Krishna–Godavari and Kaveri deltas, late-eighteenth-century wars broke irrigation works, deprived tanks of repairs, and displaced communities, which took a lot of land out of cultivation; and all along the eastern coast the expansion of rice farming in the decades 1800–1850 involved the reclamation of old fields. In 1850, wide areas open for new cultivation did remain in Bangladesh, Assam, Punjab, Haryana, Gujarat, Rajasthan, Sindh, and the western Ganga basin. New large-scale irrigation then produced new farmland in the Indo-Gangetic plains and in the deltas of the Kaveri, Krishna, and Godavari rivers. But, in territories that were heavily farmed in 1850, there was very little expansion thereafter, although even this incremental change would have further displaced hill peoples and forest ecologies in the central mountains, the high mountains, and the Western Ghats.

A rough summary of the overall trend begins with the impression that less than half of all the farmland in 1900 had been farmed in 1600. Though the oldest fields were ancient, most of the land being farmed in 1600 had come into cultivation during *eleven* centuries after 500. Over half of the farmland in 1910 was thus created during just *three* centuries after 1600. This implies a substantial increase in the pace of new cultivation. In 1800, dry and upland tropical areas were still sparsely farmed and held substantial populations of pastoralists and shifting cultivators. In the nineteenth century, dramatic increases occurred in dry cultivation, irrigation building, and forest clearance; and modes of resource scarcity and competition came into being which have continued to the present day. After 1850, agrarian unrest increased with competition over land, water, and rights amidst the final enclosure of farming frontiers. After 1880, ecological change and human dislocation caused by the expansion of farming concentrated in the higher altitudes and in the dry western plains. From 1880 to 1980,

---

[17] Hiteshranjan Sanyal, 'Social Aspects of Temple Building in Bengal: 1600 to 1900 AD', *Man in India*, 48, 1968, 201–24.

the highest rates of increase in the ratio of total farmland to total land area appear in Tripura (9.03), Sikkim (6.98), Nagaland (4.05), Assam (3.33), Rajasthan (3.26), Mizoram (2.88), Arunachal Pradesh (2.71), and Orissa (2.06). Low figures running from 1.03 to 1.22 appear in Tamil Nadu, West Bengal, Uttar Pradesh, Maharashtra, and Kerala.[18] After 1880, agricultural expansion was very substantial (with new irrigation) in dry regions of Rajasthan, Haryana, Punjab, Gujarat, Karnataka, northern Sri Lanka, and Sindh, and (with forest clearance) in all tropical uplands, including Orissa and Madhya Pradesh. But the most dramatic change in modern times has been on the farthest frontiers of medieval and early-modern agrarian territories, in the tropical high mountains and Assam. The colonisation and clearing of forests in these areas by people and states moving up from the lowlands accelerated under the Mughals and again under the British. Rapid acceleration began with the expansion of the railway, but it peaked only after 1950. The percentage of land under cultivation in the high mountains remains low even today, so that agricultural expansion at high altitude still has a long way to go. But the rapid proportional increase of farm acreage in the uplands, along with forest cutting for other purposes, helps to explain the rapid increase in conflict over mountain land in the twentieth century. A dramatic reduction of the high forest cover has produced a sense of crisis over the sustainability of mountain ecologies.

Demography and technology do not account for the upward pace of agricultural expansion after 1600. Population increase may have moved in harmony with trends in total farm *output*, but farm *acreage* moved ahead more rapidly than population. Rates of population growth rose after 1800 but jumped to their current pace only in the 1920s. Technologies did change in the late nineteenth century, when large irrigation works, railways, and road building opened up new areas to cultivation. But irrigation building moved along throughout the medieval and early-modern period, and irrigation tank and well digging led the expansion of farming in the peninsula after 1500, as recounted in the story of the Mastee brothers. Few new tanks were

---

[18] This paragraph is based on calculations from district data compiled by John F. Richards and his colleagues for the period 1880–1980. See J. F. Richards and E. P. Flint (R. C. Daniels, ed.), *Historic Land Use and Carbon Estimates for South and Southeast Asia, 1880–1980*, Carbon Dioxide Information Analysis Center, Oak Ridge National Laboratory, Experimental Sciences Division, Publication No. 4174. Data are available on the internet.

built after 1800, and a good proportion of the new irrigation in the nineteenth century put new water into old canals. Wells continued to be dug at a steady pace and remained the major source of new irrigation in dry regions, right down to the present day. Like demography, technological change became a driving force in agricultural expansion only at the end; and new kinds of irrigation, seeds, and chemicals have been most important in productivity increases *per acre* since 1950. The long expansion after 1600 came primarily from the transformation of agrarian territoriality. States fought to enclose territory to extract more wealth as revenue; in this effort, innovations in military technology did affect agricultural trends. At the same time, local farming communities enclosed land around their settlements to secure entitlements in the face of commercial opportunities, state demands, competition from other communities, and declining land availability. In the local context, demography would have had an influence on the rate of expansion. Agrarian struggles of the early-modern period were not so much about revenue as about territory. They brought all the farming landscapes under the control of states and local communities during centuries that span Mughal and Company rule.

A modern state environment for agrarian history thus began to emerge from the sixteenth century onward. At the highest level, an imperial state extended its authority over a vast terrain that was defined by a network of urban centres, inter-city routes, and state elites. At a second level, elites in regional capitals and local men of substance formed networks of alliance within regional state institutions. Elites at these two levels confront one another continuously. Today, they articulate regional politics and nationality. In the seventeenth century, Mughals brought the Punjab and Deccan into the imperial fold and Sikh and Maratha warriors defined regional movements, representing alliances among warrior-farmers in dispersed territories of conquest colonisation. Here and elsewhere, early-modern farming communities fought to control land and labour in the framework of regional networks and alliances, and agrarian regions emerged in territories defined by dominant social powers in agriculture. The cultural setting of farming also became more regionally defined by the homogenising power of early-modern states.

Violence punctuated the early-modern evolution of agrarian regions. State violence helped to advance agricultural expansion, as when Mughals armies cleared jungles and subdued hill tribes. All agrarian states conquered nomads and pastoralists, hastening their integration into the urban economy and agricultural communities. With Rajput, Mughal, Maratha, Sikh, and Company conquest, the sedentarisation of hunting, herding, and tribal populations continued, along with the expansion of farming into forests. In the central mountains, for instance, from the rim of the northern basins to the Satpuras and Orissa, tribal groups in the uplands were increasingly brought into state systems that included lowland peasant farmers in caste societies. Dominant groups extended idioms of caste and applied institutions of ranked entitlements to create official community leaders and to form transactional hierarchies that would connect ethnically diverse local communities in regional revenue systems. New agrarian territories were thus formed of diverse, endogamous, ethnic groups, living and working separately in their own ecological settings, spreading across the hills and valleys. Formerly independent Bhils, Gonds, and others were subsumed within an overarching military power structure erected by Marathas and expanded by the British. Formerly independent rulers of the hills entered agrarian states and farming communities. Violence occurred at many moments in such transformations of social identity and power. Efforts to enclose territory triggered militant migrations that made it more difficult to enclose territory without violence. The rapid expansion of agriculture and state power in the seventeenth and eighteenth centuries produced new agrarian territories and changed the composition of many more, provoking violence along the way. Mobility increased to such an extent that state elites sometimes coerced workers and farmers to keep up the cultivation. Migrants came from south-west and central Asia into Kashmir, the northern basins, and Bengal, where they pushed farming into the jungles and the hills. Warriors and farmers cleared Rohilkhand, Gorakhpur, Gaya, and other forested upland tracts along the Ganga basin. They expanded into the high mountains and Nepal; while in Nepal, states pushed from Kathmandu westward, creating a new region of farming and of military conflict at high altitude. Colonists moved across Myanmar and into the Brahmaputra basin. Cooch Behar became a borderland between Ahoms up-river and new settlers from the west and south; farmers high in the adjacent mountains kept their autonomy. Assam has been a zone of conflict among agrarian groups ever since. Jat lineages conquered and settled across Punjab. Bhojpuri peasant soldiers fought in armies across the northern plains and the Deccan. Lodis migrated from the north into the Narmada valley. Farming expanded with conquests in Khandesh, Berar, the upper Godavari basin, Telangana, and the realms of Golkonda and Hyderabad. The upper Kaveri basin became a rich agricultural territory under the Udaiyar Rajas, Hyder Ali, and Tipu Sultan. The southern band of dry lands of Rayalaseema running across the peninsula from Bijapur to Chandragiri seems to have witnessed an exceptionally rapid growth of tank-fed millet and cotton farming under the rule of Bijapur sultans and the later Nayakas.

Considerable violence accompanied the creation of new intermediary positions in the ranks of state institutional authority. *Jagirdar*s had to secure their own powers to collect revenue, as did *zamindar*s and lesser authorities. The cash value of a territory would increase when subordinate and intermediary positions in the revenue ranks were filled by wealthy, well-connected people who could collect and transmit revenue effectively. These intermediary positions became more valuable as territories developed economically; and such development also stimulated and financed defections and rebellions. Subordinates would fight to deepen their control over local resources to support a drive for political independence, as best exemplified by Murshid Quli Khan, who pressed heavily on his *zamindar*s between his appointment as Subahdar of Bengal in 1705 and his death in 1727. Local and regional struggles for independence from higher authorities were at the same time struggles for territorial control at lower levels. This basic feature of modern nationalism can be seen in the regional states of the eighteenth century. If successful, strategic manoeuvres in the regions of imperial states produced an independent ruler whose capital city grew in wealth and status, as did that of Murshid Quli Khan. His regime fostered 'a sharp rise in the number of temples built by businessmen . . . [who] came to constitute 32 per cent of the total number of temples, while the contribution of the zemindars fell from 87 to 60 per cent'.[19] This chain of events was repeated many times in the eighteenth century. Subaltern insurgency and secessionist struggles – though anathema to empire – could actually improve local agrarian conditions and work to the benefit of local elites, despite the cost of war. Imperial fragmentation thus did not contradict economic growth

---

[19] Sanyal, 'Social Aspects of Temple Building', p. 207.

in the eighteenth century any more than it did in the twentieth century.

Battles for autonomy and supremacy waged by sultans, *jagirdars*, *zamindars*, rajas, *nawab*s (Mughal governors), and the English East India Company could engage peasant and warrior allies by contributing force to local struggles for control over the land around farming villages. Regional struggles for autonomy and imperial struggles for supremacy both needed local allies in agricultural communities and added muscle to local fights for village land. In Mysore, Maharashtra, Malwa, Punjab, Rajasthan, Kashmir, and the central mountains, Mughal successor states arose from alliances between former imperial nobility and rising warrior-peasant elites who exercised a powerful hold over state revenues locally. In the wet lowlands, along the coast from Gujarat to Bengal, and in Bihar, the eighteenth-century imperial nobility allied instead with medieval gentry, rajas and merchant financiers who capitalised their position in the ranks within expanding networks of trade, revenue, and manufacturing. In the 1740s, the Company's pursuit of agrarian wealth began along the coast around Calcutta and Madras, where it confronted a confusing set of claims to revenue and proprietary authority that derived from medieval land grants, Mughal authorities, and regional states. In this context, the official status and wealth of the entrepreneurial revenue intermediary (the revenue farmer), who came equipped with his own military power, rose with his ability to deliver the revenue, by whatever means necessary. Company *sarkar* arose in this competitive climate of agrarian struggles and revenue finance.

CULTURE

In the evidence from early-modern centuries, we can see substantial shifts in the discourse of agrarian identity and territoriality. As more local wealth became state revenue, local leaders entered the ranks of empire, and farming communities became institutions of entitlement within regional systems of imperial power. New positions at the low end of the revenue ranks defined power over property that was becoming more commercially valuable under the twin disciplines of market exchange and state authority. Terminologies indicate the change in the nature of territoriality. The term *zamindar* came to have widespread utility for local leaders and for revenue intermediaries of various kinds, and, in contrast to the term *raja*, it denoted a person whose authority depended upon payments-for-entitlement. But a raja also had to pay for his independence and this status also came to be fixed as a rank within a region of state authority rather than being a claim within medieval ritual networks of *samanta*s and *maha-adi-raja*s. At lower levels, similar changes occurred. In medieval Tamil parlance, *kaniyatchi* denoted a village sharehold, most basically, in land (*kani*); and its holder, a *kaniyatchikarar*, was a patriarch among the local gentry. This inscriptional term was displaced in eighteenth-century documents by *zamindar* and then by another Persian term to denote hereditary rights – *mirasidar* – before being displaced after 1800 by 'ryot', taken from the Mughal lexicon to denote an individual tax-paying property owner who had a receipt for revenue payments that constitutes an official title to land, a *pattah*. These displacements indicate a shift from early-medieval forms of collective community entitlements, to a ranking system of entitlement and inheritance under the Mughals, and to a private property system under the Company. Through all these displacements, the Brahman and Vellala gentry retained control in farming communities as they climbed the official ranks, like the Medai Delavoy Mudaliar, who became the Nayaka governor in Tirunelveli, and expanded their commercial horizons, like Ananda Ranga Pillai, who became Dupleix's *dubash* (bilingual agent) at Pondichery.

Articulations of social power and state authority created regions of community. In Bundelkhand, senior Rajput lineage leaders became rajas under the Mughals as lesser lineage brethren (*thakur*s) formed the regional ranks of zamindars. Each lineage ruled over a local community of farmers in subordinate castes of Lodis, Kurmis, Kachhis, Ahirs, and Gujars. Among these latter groups, Kurmis seem to have been most prosperous in the nineteenth century, and they included families with *zamindari* entitlements; but, at the same time, some Ahir families formed special family ties with Rajputs and consequently enjoyed special patronage. In this complex of ranked communities, individual villages were composed of several settlement clusters linked across Bundelkhand by inter-marriage, land owning, and labour movements. A region of community sentiment thus formed as Bundela Rajputs colonised from west to east. In the process, Thakur power increased in the older regions of colonisation; so that during the 1857 rebellion even the most prestigious Rajputs lineages in the east had little influence on events in the western districts adjacent to Malwa.[20]

In Bengal, Francis Buchanan witnessed one phase in the regional formation of Chittagong. It began with Mughal conquest, in 1666, when Mughal troops cut jungles to promote farming, and one *sanad* (grant) gave a single grantee 166.4 acres of jungle to be cultivated for the support of a mosque, ordering that he 'must assiduously pray for the survival of the powerful state'. By 1780, Mughal authorities had made 288 grants of tax-free land in the Chittagong region to support mosques and shrines, in the same vein as temple grants in medieval inscriptions. The titles of the men who were endowed with such grants indicate that 28 per cent (*chaudhuris*, *ta'alluqdars*, and *khan*s) were men of substance in Chittagong when they received the grants; other endowments went to religious leaders and holy men, the largest category being *shaikh* (31 per cent). These recipients were land clearance entrepreneurs. They contracted with *zamindars* to finance cultivation; and *zamindars* then advanced funds to peasant farmers, receiving crops and labour in return. Here we see the beginnings of the intricately ranked entitlements to the land that typify the agrarian frontiers of Bengal. By 1798, regional agrarian society in Chittagong had three distinctive types of community.[21] Elite *zamindars*, mostly Hindus, lived in the city, along with a large population of urban port workers and merchants. In the flatlands, up to the base of the hills, rice paddy fields were cut from jungle, dotted with mosques and shrines, and worked by Muslim peasants under Muslim men of substance who descended from the original contractors. Non-Muslim *jhum* cultivators had their own communities in the hills, in the path of lowland expansion. Today, descendants of these people living in the Chittagong Hill Tracts are embroiled in conflict with the government of Bangladesh from a position that is strictly defined as culturally distinct from the national community of Bengalis.

In Maratha and Sikh territories, militant agrarian patriarchs fought to enhance their local claims and to enclose open space in the lowlands and adjacent mountain valleys. At the same time, urban elites accumulated assets in centres of state power and long-distance trade. Status ranks came to be pegged to the titles that formed regional alliances

---

[20] Tapti Roy, *The Politics of a Popular Uprising: Bundelkhand in 1857*, New Delhi, 1994, pp. 199–233.
[21] Eaton, *The Rise of Islam*, pp. 243–51.

among locally dominant warrior-farmers. Beginning with Shivaji, warrior-peasant alliances displaced Mughal imperial elites but used Mughal-derived ranks to organise competition and collaboration. Conflicting demands on local land and revenues generated minute record-keeping and adjudication that elevated the status of Brahmans within the Maratha state. Dominant warrior-peasants became the local protectors of a Maharashtra-*dharma* that blessed dominant caste control in villages under the Maratha military. In Punjab, Sikh religious law enshrined the rule of *misls* (military bands) in local domains of Jat control. In both regions, an increasing proportion of entitlements were being held by the allies and superiors of the village patriarchs, in towns where forts, godowns, bankers, cantonments, scholars, and courts defined regional dominions. Villages became sites of agrarian expansion, nested within regions of military alliance; religion and language became tokens of regional identity. In these territories, we find the most extensive development of village-level record-keeping and administrative institutions. Maratha records were adapted locally all across the dry interior from Pune to Rayalaseema to Mysore and Coimbatore, in other areas of warrior-peasant colonisation.

In Bundelkhand, Chittagong, Punjab, Maharashtra, and elsewhere, we can see regional ethnicities forming inside early-modern territoriality. Jat, Sikh, Maratha, Muslim, Bengali, Rajput, Thakur, Ahir, Ahom, and other identities formed within ideologies of alliance; and they became more territorialised within the ranks of early-modern states, as farmers, warriors, merchants, and revenue intermediaries allied within networks of urban influence to form agrarian regions of community sentiment. In some cases, a dominant ethnic stratum emerged above ethnically diverse localities, such as the Bundela Rajputs. Hindu zamindars spread across Muslim peasant villages in eastern Bengal. In the old Gupta homeland, Brahmans, Bhumihars, Rajputs, Kayasthas, and Baniyas comprised a powerful zamindar class, while the more substantial cultivators were Ahirs, Kurmis, and Koeris, who in turn employed lower-caste groups. Elsewhere, dominant caste groups formed ethnic mini-polities. Rajputisation among tribal groups produced ethnic kingdoms in the central mountains. Kallars, Nayakas, and Maravas formed compact territories of early-modern kingship, dominated by their lineages and clans in the Tamil country. Early-modern states confirmed and enhanced the power of local ethnic configurations, encouraging their control of territory for the expansion of farming and state revenue. The ethnicity of power thus informed state discourse and strategy. Abu-l Fasl listed zamindars by ethnicity, showing that the parganas of Delhi subah were divided territorially among Brahmans, Tyagis (cultivating Brahmans), Rajputs, Jats, Gujars, Ahirs, and Muslims. The British continued this practice, as indicated by Francis Buchanan's stress upon the religious affiliation of the groups in Chittagong. Localities became politically identified with dominant groups at the base of early-modern states.

Patterns of agrarian culture were formed in regions of state authority. Folklore surrounding dominant groups like the Rajputs inscribed their supremacy on the land. Identities became entrenched in regions of community. In common parlance, cultivating groups would often assert that only they know how to farm the soil of their home territory correctly, or how to raise a symbolic crop such as rice, millet, or cotton properly. Social identity, expertise, and control were packed into territoriality; and regions of popular culture were formed by the circulation and experience of myth and memory in drama, poetry, and song. Popular sayings collected in Tamil and Telugu at the end of the nineteenth century often assert that only the dominant farming castes know how to farm properly and that both Brahmans and low castes make bad farmers. Farming is in the blood, as Vellala farmers reported to the officials who were collecting popular ideas about farming. The power to farm (*velanmai*) is in farmers' nature (*kunam*). In this view, the land does not so much belong to its owner as constitute a farmer's being and community. Composite formations of agricultural knowledge, identity, ritual, honour, and authority composed ethnic territories that became ecological, ideological, emotional, poetic, and sacred, all at once. Local dominance by politically well-connected families and castes defined the cultural identity of land. This is another precursor of modern nationality.

As groups of various kinds preferred, gravitated to, and concentrated in specific types of location, some groups – such as *jhum* cultivators in the tropical highlands and pastoral nomads in the arid plains – were also pushed into circumscribed territories. Exclusion, marginality, dependency, and poverty thus attached to people and places that were identified with each other. Places with specific natural qualities became associated with specialist inhabitants. Forest dwellers, fisher folk, even rice and wheat farmers were attached physically and culturally to natural settings, with their own cuisine, rituals, folklore, and aesthetics. Near Kanya Kumari, a group called Shanars specialised in palmyra tree cultivation and settled in sandy tracts that were not good for farming but were excellent for growing palmyras. In Bundelkhand, the Ahirs lived in villages along rivers and in ravines where forests gave them access to farm and grazing land. A geographical concentration of groups that specialise in specific types of work using specialised skills and knowledge became typical in many localities and regions. Such spatial concentration of groups on the land resulted not only from group preferences but also from battles that partitioned the landscape to form social and territorial boundaries at the same time. The Shanars and Ahirs were not allowed to own the best agricultural land, which was controlled by Thakurs and Vellalas, whose superiority was also expressed in the richness of their farms. Low-caste and tribal farmers were pushed to ecological margins by more powerful groups, and violence quite often marked borderlands between forest and farm. Battles over territory marked the moving frontier of cultivation. Forms of territoriality that Ranajit Guha sees in peasant insurgencies took shape at this borderland where fighting farmers fought for territories of collective identity.

Urban centres had their own kind of people, although urbanism did not always include sharp distinctions between city and country. Abu-l Fasl did not see Mughal territory as being clearly divided among villages, towns, and cities – and neither did early East India Company officials – because the stature of a place depended on who lived there, and major sites of revenue collection, state authority, and economic importance had a decidedly rural appearance. As a result, it is difficult to measure exactly how urban – or rural – South Asia really was. Indeed, this dichotomy is actually misleading. The British practice of dubbing virtually any site outside a capital city a 'village' or at best a 'town' obscures the composition of agrarian landscapes, as does the modern habit of associating ruralism with illiteracy and subsistence farming, in contrast to elite, industrial, cosmopolitan cities. Manufacturing and commercial assets, educated elites, and political power often concentrated in settings that British observers called 'rural' and labelled 'villages'. Perhaps the absence of fortifications and monumental architecture led Company officials to assume that a place was rural. Monumental, fortified centres marked the western plains, Gujarat, the Mughal heartland, and the peninsular interior; and they were common among ports along the coast, but not so much in other regions. Urbanism often blended aspects of city and country. Manufacturing and commercial activities were usually spread out among a number of nearby residential settlements. Production was most often organised in clusters of centres at walking distance from one another, rather than being stuffed into fortifications and city walls. Economic specialisation was organised largely within endogamous identity groups (defined by *jati*, sect, and ethnicity), each living in their own separate neighbourhood, so that complex economic interdependence – such as in the textile industry – involved extensive commercial interactions among many settlements, which clustered together along routes of trade. In 1805, in Rayalaseema, one of the driest and by its appearance most 'rural' of regions, about a third of the population was engaged in mercantile, manufacturing, transportation, and related occupations. State revenue was routinely collected in cash, and most farming households depended on loans and non-agricultural income from various sources. Dozens of places have such a predominance of non-agricultural occupations that they look distinctively 'urban'. In all the regions that produced cotton cloth for the overseas trade – Punjab, Gujarat, Bengal, and the south-eastern plains, including Rayalaseema – exports emerged from a widespread manufacturing network in which cotton farming, cleaning, spinning, weaving, bleaching, dyeing, packing, and shipping were each typically done in different places where families could readily move among various activities, in and out of agriculture, in regular adaptations to seasons of rain, war, and price fluctuations. These were among the great industrial regions of the early-modern world, and they produced the bulk of cotton cloth in world markets in 1750.

Urbanism was spread out, dispersed, and embedded in agriculture. Bulls could plough the land and pull carts when the land was dry and hard. Seasonal migrations to work, trade, and fight were very common, so the physical and occupational mobility that we identify with urbanism in modern times typified large parts of the early-modern countryside. Concentrations of urban activity clustered along river routes and at river crossings, but then they also spread out over adjacent land. An urban location in the central place hierarchy of an early-modern region was defined not so much by its physical appearance as by the rank of the officials in it and by the character of the elites who gave it distinction. A state revenue headquarters could include a large population that was spread among many settlements, and small centres could become important sites of revenue collection. Central sites such as temples, shrines, and monasteries were often set apart and situated among the fields that supported them. Many important places had a rustic appearance.

Detailed data from the Tamil country show that, in 1770, the great urban centre of Kanchipuram was actually a constellation of settlements, temples, and monasteries, supported by hundreds of land grants spread all over the southern coastal plains. The urbanism of Kanchipuram came from its symbolic and economic centrality, not from its enclosure of a large population within a dense city space. Near Kanya Kumari, along the Tambraparni river, many sites of revenue collection that the Company called 'villages' in a census of 1823 had small populations but substantial concentrations of manufacturing, processing, and commercial activity as well as very high population densities. After all, when a small place became sufficiently wealthy, its leaders would want to make it a separate revenue jurisdiction – to declare their local independence – so that small territorial units of social power proliferated in fertile lands and in booming commercial and manufacturing regions. Ambasamudram, a centre on the Tambraparni river, had sixteen subordinate villages in its jurisdiction in 1477 but only three in 1823, by which time it had a population of only 3,952, because in the interim it had spawned more and more independent sites of local political authority. Some of the smallest 1823 census sites in Tirunelveli had high concentrations of looms, mat frames, gunny frames, toddy shops, arrack shops, and other commercial assets, in addition to artisan and merchant castes. The urban centre of the Tirunelveli region consisted of three close-by urban centres, each with its own identity, a temple town (Tirunelveli), a fortress town (Palayamkottai), and manufacturing centre (Melapalayan). These three centres were not administered together until 1993. This sprawling composite urban site was broken up in all the census operations before 1991 and thus it was empirically hidden as an urban feature of the landscape. This Tirunelveli urban complex included about 25 per cent of the population in the central river valley in 1823, but was buried under the quaint category of 'mofussil town'.

Agrarian South Asia seems not to have been nearly as rural as British observers led us to believe; and early-modern urbanity was more rural than we might imagine. The economic simplicity of the pre-modern countryside is largely a fiction of modern urbanites. We get a more accurate picture if we imagine many localities with urban economic, social, and cultural characteristics strung together by networks of mobility to form urban agglomerations of various sizes. Urbanism lay inside agriculture rather than being set apart and its internal transport system moved at a walk or a boat's pace. It did not confine labour in tightly bounded city spaces, separating workers from everyday farming activities. It relied on the proximity of non-agricultural workers to local supplies of food and raw materials. Its manufacturing was closely connected with agriculture, not only economically by exchange relations, but spatially by locational decisions that formed localised proximity among specialised producers, resources, and markets. Then as now, the movement of labour among economic activities animated urbanism. But then, the locational advantages of specific urban sites were formed socially by residential decisions among groups who partitioned the landscape into what we can call ethnic territories, each composed of specific combinations of social groups. The availability of open land for new settlements and the mobility of the population discouraged concentrations of capital and labour inside city walls, so that efforts to attract and hold labour and capital in particular places were very prominent political activities; the accumulating attractions of a place constituted its urbanity.

Regions of urbanism, ethnicity, empire, literature, and territoriality made the land look very different in 1800 than it had looked in 1200. We have some evidence to suggest the quality of the change in the way that people thought about the land; for example, the history of the Tamil term for 'forest' – *kadu* – indicates something about cultural change in agrarian societies in the peninsula. In Old Tamil poetry, composed around the turn of the Common Era, *kadu* meant 'burning ground', and the land was so full of forest that the poets needed many words to capture its meanings. Three of their five poetic milieus were forest: *kurinji* was tropical mountain forest; *mullai* was deciduous woods along hillsides, where animals threaten travellers; and *palai* was dry flatlands, thick with prickly scrub and robbers (that is, hunter-pastoralists). Only one milieu had comfortable domesticity: the irrigated villages (*marutam*), watery lowlands like those along the Tambraparni or in the Kaveri delta. By early-medieval times, the Tamil landscape had been simplified textually into a stark dichotomy between *nadu* and *kadu*, where *kadu* meant the untamed, rugged, forest without cultivation or civility, while *nadu* denoted agrarian territory, which dotted the coast. A series of cultural identifications were thus established. The *kadu* was wild, inhabited by unruly folk who needed to be brought into the orbit of royal authority. The *nadu* was civilised, controlled by Brahmans and Vellalas; it had trading towns, irrigation, temples, gods, and ceremonial order. The agricultural borders of wet lands, dry tracts, or small settlements (in the dry tract) could also be referred to as *kadu*, which term became a part of many place names to indicate original settlement in the forest. Kings and chiefs sought to incorporate the land and people of the *kadu* into their domains. Wars of conquest and incorporation brought labourers from the *kadu* into the ambit of the *nadu*, people of the *kadu* being hunters, pastoralists, and long-fallow farmers. Many medieval Tamil chiefdoms depended on pastoral people, whose names and settlements populate the inscriptions. But such political settings and their ecologies were wiped out by agricultural expansion, causing striking discontinuities between the composition of medieval and early-modern territory. By 1700, the political power of pastoralists had diminished to nothing. By 1800, Tamil language formulations of agricultural knowledge differed both from their medieval antecedents and from their Malayali, Telugu, Kannada, and Marathi contemporaries, not only because of linguistic change, but also because Tamil farmers ignored the tropics to the west, destroyed pastoralism which survived in the northern peninsula, and were bent on destroying the long-fallow dry regime that still survived on the Tamil plain and dominated much of the Tamil uplands. Linguistic cultures made sense of particular types of agrarian space.

After 1300, probably after 1500, *kadu* took on the meaning of 'dry land', whether cultivated, fallow, or waste, and by 1800 this meaning was prominent. Dry farming – using strong bulls to plough deeply and to lift deep well water to nourish garden crops – increased the relative value of dryland. In addition, many of the best dry land farmers in the Tamil country were immigrant Telugus, allied with Nayakas from Vijayanagar, who typified the political landscape of the eastern coast after 1500, ruling the country from their rustic forts. *Nadu* lost its specific territorial meaning to become merely a term for 'country', like *desh* or *desa*, a usage that is now enshrined in Tamil Nadu. By 1800, the Tamil vocabulary had formed a basic contrast between dry farmland (*kadarambam* = kadu {dry land} + *arambam* {tract}) and wet land (*nirarambam* = *nir* {water} + *arambam*), and thus between dry cultivation (*punsey*) and irrigated agriculture (*nansey*). The superiority of irrigated land is clear because *punsey* connotes meagreness and *nansey*, goodness. But the forest – *kadu* – had by now changed its cultural form and moved from the exterior, to the periphery, and to the centre of the Tamil agrarian lexicon. As it became more central, its meaning became more varied. In proverbs collected in the 1890s, it refers to forest, waste, open pasture, closed pasture, dry farmland, or dry field. Subba Rao, the editor of a collection of agricultural sayings, avers that *kadu*, 'translated as "forests" must also be taken to include pastures', and he continues, 'in these days, *as the country is filling up*, these should no longer be the wild common-grazing grounds on which hitherto dependence has been placed, but also *enclosed and cultivated pasture fields*' (emphasis added).[22]

In the land of *kadu*, the animal economy had been domesticated within the confines of farming villages, and the separate cultural space of pastoralists had totally disappeared by the end of the nineteenth century. On the saying, 'To ruin a *kadu*, let loose goats,' Subba Rao comments: 'the destructive results of grazing sheep and goats are alluded to, though here again the word *kadu* may either be the jungle or the field with a crop on it', because goats eat the field stubble that could fertilise the next crop as surely as they destroy open pasture or wild scrubland. Subba Rao's mention of 'enclosed and cultivated pasture fields' indicates a feature of *kadu* that also appears in eighteenth-century revenue surveys, which show enclosed pasture as being included in taxpayers' land. A number of proverbs from the 1890s prescribe 'fencing in' land, and, where these do not refer to fencing small garden plots watered by wells (normal practice today), they clearly advise the enclosure of land that had previously been open for common access. One saying can be rendered, 'Look at the *kadu* of a man who has closed it off (from use by others) and you will see the cattle of a man who knows how to graze livestock properly.' Likewise, another reads, 'Sow your seeds and shut the door.' People should not be allowed to use dry land as common land. In the 1800s, dry land,

[22] Tamil sayings come from C. K. Subba Rao, *Tamil Sayings and Proverbs on Agriculture*, Madras, Madras Government Agriculture Department Bulletin No. 34, 1896. Telugu sayings come from C. Benson, *A Collection of Telugu Sayings and Proverbs Bearing on Agriculture*, Madras, Government Press, 1897.

forest, and livestock became sufficiently valuable and private property rights well enough established that forceful enclosure became desirable for dominant caste farmers to keep the neighbours' animals off their fields, to keep their own grazing land for themselves, and to make proprietary claims on village commons.

The property value of *kadu* came from two main sources. As pasture, its value derived from livestock. One old saying reads: 'Rich *kadu* make strong cattle; strong cattle make prosperous people; prosperous people make rich temples; rich temples make rich kings.' In 1802, Benjamin Heyne reported that, in upland Karnataka, cattle were the farmer's most valuable asset, without which he was ruined: 'it is the last of his property arrested by his creditors and if he owes anything to the *sarkar* they will be seized but never actually taken from him.'[23] Sayings in Tamil and Telugu villages indicate the second major source of *kadu* value. A Telugu saying reports, 'there is no want in a house where the spinning wheel and churn are at work'; and the Tamil saying argues, 'there is no famine (*panjam*) for a man with milk and cotton plants.' Cotton is an archetypal dry land (*kadu*) cash crop. Rivalled after 1880 by oilseeds and groundnuts, cotton was never surpassed as the prime crop for the best black soil. Among dry crops, cotton is the one that Tamil sayings have yielding 'potfulls [of money]' and cash (*panam*). It is labour intensive and thrives with the deep ploughing of rich black soil (*karisal*). It wants strong bulls, well fed. Closely associated with the rearing, buying, and grazing of bulls and cows throughout the peninsula, cotton farmers provided the raw material for cloth exports, and then for raw cotton exports which doubled every few decades after 1840. Cotton cultivation underlay the expansion of cotton manufacturing in the seventeenth and eighteenth century. Dry land used for commercial production encouraged the privatisation of dryland property rights, so that *kadu* became entangled in the politics of agricultural commodity production.

The prominence of commercialism in agrarian life produced a body of everyday wisdom concerning the role of markets and moneyed men in farming. In general it seems that kinship, religious rituals, alliances among dominant families, ethnic or caste identities, and royal authority were valued as intrinsic to agriculture, so that commercial

[23] Benjamin Heyne, 'Correspondence to Captain Mackenzie, Superintendent of the Mysore Survey', National Archives of India, Foreign Miscellaneous Series, No. 94, 1802, p. 78.

exchange and calculations within this set of social relations seemed quite natural; but, at the same time, professional money lending and financial speculation seemed exogenous if not anathema inside farming communities. A cultural opposition between landed and commercial groups is reflected in the division between 'left hand' and 'right hand' castes in the Tamil country, and it pops up repeatedly in Tamil proverbs, which posit a natural enmity (*jenmapakai*) between *velanmai* (the power of farming) and parsimony, cost accounting (*settu*) as well as merchants (*setti*). The cultural power of the farmer (*velanmai*) is said to be lost when he adopts the merchant's habits or succumbs to merchant control: 'The man who takes a loan to farm is like a tree climber who lets go with his hands.' The conflict here is between farmers and merchants – two sets of prominent caste groups in agriculture – not between farmers and the profit-making, for profits had long been part of *velanmai*. These sayings represent the pride and fear of dominant caste landowners who are already enmeshed in commodity production.

Commercialism was deeply entrenched in agricultural discourse in many regions during the early-modern period. In the Tamil country, all varieties of land and capital assets became known in local parlance for their commercial value. In the Tirunelveli region, revenue records show a series of equations among types of land, their produce, their market value, and their revenue assessment. Dry land (*punsey*) typically produced millets, oilseeds, pulses, and cotton; and it varied in value according to its soil type. The best black soils were controlled by the most powerful warrior-farming castes, Nayakas and other Telugus, who had the strongest bulls and the richest granaries. The middling red soil territories were held predominantly by Maravas, the second tier in the hierarchy of warrior-farmers. Tracts full of the worst sandy soils were held by lower castes, mostly Shanars. Dry lands had their own modalities of revenue assessment and market evaluation. Officials measured the area of cultivation with a *sangili* (chain) or in rods. The length of the measuring device differed from place to place, but everywhere in the peninsula people seem to have talked about dry land in terms of its linear area – a practice that may have come from estimates of land area by the number of rows a team of bulls could plough in a day, a method reported by Heyne in Mysore. Everywhere in the south, dry land also appears to have been assessed for revenue purposes according to cultivated area (not by the crop) and by soil type, in cash. Tax-related agricultural knowledge preserved by Company records indicates that Tamils systematically distinguished wet and dry land as objects of commercial evaluation and taxation. Dryland taxes were collected in cash, in the manner of customs duties. Wet fields (*nansey*), were taxed predominantly in kind, on the assumption that they produced rice. Wet land gained in value from irrigation, not soil type, which was not recorded. Culti-vated area was not so important as grain output, so that land was measured for assessment by the volume of seed sown upon it, not by its linear area. The term for 'land tax on wet land' was, appropriately, *varam* (share), and social power in the wet lands derived from shares of the paddy crop.

Like the state's share in the crop, shares in village land (*pangu*) that measured stature in the community had acquired market value long before 1800. Garden cultivation, tree crops, houses, shops, and a long list of commercial as well as artisan assets were counted, taxed, and described in commodity terms in the eighteenth century. As *kadu* travelled from the periphery to the centre of farming, the landscape as a whole was commodified. By 1800, markets permeated agrarian life.

ADMINISTRATION

The centralisation of state power increased under early-modern regimes. But even powerful rulers like Murshid Quli Khan or Tipu Sultan did not control the everyday activity of all their local officers, and neither did the East India Company. These regimes focused on standardising the institutional transactions that brought revenue from villages to the capital and sent orders back out into the country. States became more bureaucratic and centralised as transactions became more rule driven, less personal. By 1700, rulers in distant parts of the world used very similar administrative technologies, so that agrarian societies experienced empires similarly in the Americas, Europe, and Asia. Local officials would be well known to farmers. In regular contact with village leaders, they exerted influence in local affairs. Regional royalty lived in town. They would discipline the local officers now and then, either personally or through intermediaries, and they could be appealed to occasionally. Imperial potentates lived at a great distance. Their identity, composed substantially of rumour, ritual, and myth, was abstract. In such political settings, empires increased their power by standardising state operations and cultivating loyalty. The general strategy was to use one's own men to discipline all those who carried state authority, so officials would carry out instructions from above and transmit revenue from below without being closely monitored. Rulers improved transportation to speed the flow of information and troops, as standardisation spread cultural commonalities among the men who organised the state. Centralising states thus defined territories in which administrative elites acquired common languages and identities. A status culture of elite sentiment formed among intermediary groups in regional states, rooted locally and also connected to the capital.

State discipline and ritual conditioned the identities, interests, and sentiments of key people in the countryside and produced regions of agrarian politics. But agrarian conditions limited what states could accomplish. Early-medieval dynasties had spawned local gentry who were similar in outlook and loyalties, and late-medieval conquerors had spread their influence far and wide, but, under medieval conditions, no ruler could contain agrarian forces of political dispersion. The Mughals increased the density and reach of agrarian territories under their standard; and, amidst increasing competition for land, successor states did the same, deepening the discipline of revenue institutions and broadcasting the Mughal vocabulary from places such as Arcot, where Mughals had never trod. When the Nawab of Arcot allied with the East India Company to bring revenue from as far afield as Kanya Kumari, Kurnool, Vizagapatnam, and Malabar, an administrative elite of Marathi and Tamil Brahmans fanned out in a new administrative territory, which soon became Madras Presidency. Likewise in Bengal, Punjab, Awadh, Maharashtra, Mysore, and Kerala, eighteenth-century states built regions of ritual, intrigue, and alliance. But farming communities also fought for the land as regional states cast their net, and the interaction of local and imperial power became a central theme in the agrarian history of modernity.

Today, local territorialism is still intense in South Asia and, in part, it reflects a local resistance to the centralising state. But it also reflects a legacy of empires which have fostered local power to secure local loyalty, producing nested layers of territoriality. Imperial strategies of this kind flourished in the transactional environment of early-modernity and shaped British rule. In Eurasia, they have long facilitated rough-and-tumble imperial expansion and stability – even as they limit a state's ability to centralise – amidst countless, particularistic identities, loyalties, and attachments to land. In South Asia, as in Central Asia and the Middle East, lineage and clan organise many localising loyalties. As in Southeast Asia and China, tribal societies formed separate territories in tropical forests and mountains. Sectarian, ethnic, and caste solidarities added to the intricacy of localism over centuries of migration and resettlement, as different groups concentrated in their own particular places. Micro-ethnicities developed strong local attachments to landscapes that were carved into homelands for hundreds of thousands of groups that clustered together on the land. Urbanisation generated new kinds of localities. As a result, differently composed agrarian societies developed in differently endowed agrarian territories. By 1700, for instance, agrarian urbanism along the coast had developed strong attachments to the Indian Ocean world of commercial activity, whereas in the interior regions, from Kabul to Mysore, urban society was much more attached to the authority of warrior-sultans. Imperial incorporation became more difficult for the Mughals as they pushed away from their own homeland into their southern periphery, where the military culture of the Mughal–Rajput nobility could not generate firm loyalties among Marathas. In Bengal, business interests entangled with European companies around Calcutta and Murshidabad became the financial basis for a post-Mughal regime. In all the eighteenth-century states, commercial networks sustained the rising power of men whose shared sentiments, mentalities, interests, and identities were based on the urban, mercantile, political economy of their own local home territories. From the 1740s, when the Company began fighting its way into regional revenue systems around Calcutta and Madras, its most critical allies were elites who combined commercial wealth and state authority in settings of agrarian urbanism. The Company used its own men to discipline its subordinates but, like the Mughals, it also had to incorporate a great diversity of localities to build an imperial polity.

By 1820, the Company had replaced the Mughals, but even the modernisation of British India after 1860 did not erase the localism which the Company had built into its empire. It began in the 1740s, when the Company forced itself into revenue transactions around Madras and Calcutta, receiving revenue from local contractors who also conducted trade, finance, and military business on its behalf. These men had independent power. Some were Company merchants acting as free agents. Some were businessmen and bankers with investments in trade and revenue (portfolio capitalists) – entrepreneurs working at the broad intersection of states and markets.[24] But at lower levels, people who paid revenue worked in the ranks of local officials and community leaders. Many revenue interests focused on the land, and many people sought to entrench their own position by paying for entitlements. Decisions by men of rank at all levels influenced the formation of modern agrarian polities, even as the British imagined their Indian empire to be purely the product of their own power. Tipu Sultan, Poligars, Marathas, Pindaris, Sikhs, Afghans, Gurkhas, and rebels in 1857 fought hard for territory; they formed a zone of high military resistance to the Company that stretched from the tip of the peninsula up through the Deccan, Malwa, Bundelkhand, Awadh, Rajasthan, Punjab, and Nepal and into the high mountains bordering Afghanistan. Warriors against the British were also involved in local military struggles when the British arrived demanding tribute and subordination. They saw the British as a part of their own political environment, in which warriors were most concerned with their own position. Forming unequal alliances to secure subordinate rank in a new imperial system could improve one's position, and many warriors, kings, local officials, and community leaders took this option rather than fighting to the end. Many had done the same before. Rulers of Native States mostly followed this path of strategic alliance. Some, like the Nizam of Hyderabad, became crucial military allies for the Company. Scholars have not yet paid much attention to the reasoning behind these fateful decisions, or to their political context or historical implications.

When the Company captured territory, it moved immediately to settling the revenue and to writing legal codes and administrative policies to standardise revenue transactions. Local men of rank were forced to come to terms with the new *sarkar*. Taxes ascended the official ranks and entitlements descended from the *sarkar* to the village. The results varied wildly from one part of the new empire to another, in part because British India took more than a century to complete. Imperial expansion began in 1757 (with the acquisition of Bengal and Bihar), rushed ahead from 1790 to 1820 (Madras Presi-

---

[24] Sanjay Subrahmanyam and C. A. Bayly, 'Portfolio Capitalists and the Political Economy of Early Modern India', *Indian Economic and Social History Review*, 25, 4, 1988, 401–24.

dency, Northwestern Provinces, Bombay Presidency), added more territory before 1857 (Punjab, Awadh, Sindh, Central India, Lower Burma), and finally subdued Awadh and other sites of rebellion (including Bundelkhand) after 1857. Old regimes left many different kinds of entitlement behind; administrative politics varied within British regions; and policies changed with Company charter renewals in 1793, 1813, 1833, and 1853. The process of settling the revenue changed in character with change at the top and the bottom of the imperial hierarchy; after 1870, major differences in agrarian policy and law remained, among and within regions. The Native States and Nepal had their own rulers, who inherited eighteenth-century territories. Though the British intervened regularly in the Native States, their official autonomy prevented deep British meddling in the organisation of agrarian administration. Hyderabad, the largest Native State, is a case in point. Its nobility was confirmed in control of the countryside by the Nawabs, despite pressure to raise more state income and to recognise tenant rights; and the ossification of this landed aristocracy became the context for the Telangana peasant revolution in the 1940s. Even the dozens of tiny states in Gujarat and Rajasthan retained their own property systems down to the 1950s.

Inside British India, local influence on the agrarian system came from several directions. Most basically, local personnel entered the administration, bringing with them old identities, roles, and skills. Key people in the country became influential, especially men of rank. These were patriarchs with entitlements confirmed by official honours and by past revenue payments. They had serious local problems that needed tending to. Many were involved in conflicts over entitlements when the British arrived. Armies and gangs were loose and demanding tribute. Competitors were fighting for pasture, forest, and open land around farming settlements. Dams, channels, tanks, and fields were broken. Farm workers were being scattered by local distress and running off with the season, which made farm labour unpredictable and costly. Local men of substance wanted the new government to settle such matters in their favour. Revenue settlements became political negotiations with the people deemed by the British to be most legitimately entitled to pay for revenue in return for titles to land.

Land settlements comprised a formal code of unequal alliance between the new *sarkar* and local leaders, a legally binding template for subsequent transactions, not only for tax payments but also for dispute resolution, reassessment, and policy reform. Land settlements formed a legal constitution for an agrarian Raj. The *sarkar* became part of the local agrarian order. Like their predecessors, the British defined an agrarian citizenry by their official transactions with household headmen, whose proprietary entitlements the state would define, document, legitimate, regulate, protect, and, of course, tax.

Between the 1780s and 1820, working in London and with urban intellectuals in Calcutta and Madras, Company officers developed the ideas that would create a unified theory of British rule and help the administration adapt to regional and local circumstances. Orientalist scholars saw Europe and India as comparable, related civilisations; so, as in Europe, also in India, classical texts held the key to basic cultural principles. William Jones and his contemporaries dismissed Muslim rulers as invaders and tyrants; when the Company was fighting Tipu Sultan, the Company erased the legitimacy of Muslim authority in its theory of agrarian governance. The Company established itself as the protective ruler of a land of Hindu tradition. This was in some sense a recuperation of the idea that the righteous ruler is a protector of *dharma*, and, like medieval kings and Marathas, the Company defined *dharma* in its own terms. Jones found the essence of India in Sanskrit texts, especially in texts on *dharma*. The principle was quickly established that diligent investigations could reveal all the salient facts about the real India to inform British governance, and it was determined that agrarian India was everywhere organised by the rules of caste society and by principles of *varnashramadharma* that represented traditional norms and a spiritually sanctioned social order. Around 1810, we can see a shift in the organisation of Company accounts of the rural population: they were subsequently compiled according to the rank order of castes (*jati*) within the *varna* scheme (Brahman, Kshatriya, Vaisya, and Sudra), even where this set of categories had not been applied in earlier English accounts and was not in vogue in local society. In the Company scheme, Hindu and Muslim law codes needed to be kept separate, and Muslims treated separately. Family law and proprietary institutions needed to be adjusted by the Raj to suit the traditions of the people, whose literary elites, mostly Brahmans, were the experts on tradition. Orientalism provided a flexible tool for weaving together revenue settlements and for adjusting colonial *dharma* to local conditions.

In 1793, the Act of Permanent Settlement granted a new kind of entitlement to zamindars in Bengal, in return for high, fixed cash payments, collected strictly on schedule. Defaults would trigger the transfer of zamindar titles at auction. These men were thus made legally into landlords with ownership rights over and above the tenants who paid rent to cultivate zamindari property. As we will see, more ranks were formed within this two-tiered zamindari scheme, but, from the state's point of view, zamindars were the legal owners of land and all subsidiary rights accrued to people living on their estates. Some estates were large, territorially compact, and stable, sometimes based upon old royal lineages; and others were small, fragmented, and spread over many scattered plots and villages, cobbled together from the bits and pieces of revenue farms or lineage holdings. In 1801, some zamindars were also anointed in Madras Presidency under the authority of the 1793 Act, and here they had virtually all been rulers of large, compact territories of conquest colonisation. Such men became the agrarian foundation for the new regime in Bengal, Bihar, and the central Ganga basin, where they used their existing powers and Company authority to claim all the land within British territory. The character of their social power and the fate of their family fortunes were quite diverse. They included old rajas, former state officials, bankers, and revenue contractors. Some ruled their estates as real lords of the land and others merely had their men visit the villages now and then to collect the rent. Some held onto zamindar titles for many generations; some lost them by default within a few years; and, everywhere, the turnover of zamindar landownership in decades after 1793 moved property rights around quite considerably. But all these were men of high social status and rank; and in the regions that came to be defined by zamindar institutions, they formed a class that was capable of sustaining the Company's revenue. When one defaulted, another zamindar could always be found to pay the revenue. In the Madras and Bombay Presidencies, however, though warrior rajas in territories of conquest colonisation did come forward to become zamindars, they controlled but a fraction of the total revenue. The term 'zamindar' had been used in the eighteenth century to designate virtually any person who paid revenue for land, but the 1793 Act stipulated that ranks must exist to separate landlords and tenants, and they often could not be found. Some influential Company officers also craved to enhance the revenue, eliminate revenue intermediaries, and extend state power into the villages beyond what was possible under Permanent Settlement and zamindari property law. With such motives, Thomas Munro and his allies resisted the broad application of the 1793 Act in Madras. Munro fought for twenty-five years against the imposition of the Calcutta system; and, at the same time, Utilitarians and Evangelicals savaged the Orientalists. New renditions of ancient tradition were thus contrived to justify new revenue policies.

To liberate Madras Presidency from Calcutta's Permanent Settlement, Munro argued that collecting taxes directly from ryots in their villages would lower tax rates for farmers and also increase government revenue. But, to legitimate his land settlements, he had to show that they also served the principles of native tradition, that they followed indigenous precedents. He compiled evidence for *The Fifth Report on East India Company Affairs* to prove that ryotwari, not zamindari, better suited British India. To win his case, Munro had to discredit officials such as Francis Ellis, who had textual and ethnographic evidence to show that Munro was wrong. Ellis had studied old gentry villages along the coastal plain, whereas Munro had studied warrior-peasant dry villages in Rayalaseema and Kongu. Ellis argued that, yes, the village was the basis for traditional social order, but, no, peasants did not traditionally own their own land individually; rather, they held the land as community property, with each family having a set of shares in all community assets. Munro would have nothing of this. He insisted that ryots were all individual peasants, as much individualists as English farmers; that they had always been family property owners who lived in their own village societies, regulated by caste tradition; and that only extortionate Muslim overlords like Tipu Sultan had forced them to accept revenue intermediaries and zamindars standing between themselves and the ruler. Munro vanquished Ellis, became governor in 1820, and established ryotwari as the definitive legal basis for land settlements in Madras. His formulations became official wisdom, and they radically homogenised the agrarian landscape. His stereotype of the village as 'a little republic' dates from 1806. Published by Mark Wilks, in 1810, during the campaign to write *The Fifth Report*, it would be a pillar of modern administration. Its most famous reformulation came in a minute by Charles Metcalfe for the Select Committee of the House of Commons on the Affairs of the East India Company, in 1830, which had a powerful influence on Karl Marx. It reads in part as follows:

The village communities are little republics, having nearly everything they want within themselves, and almost independent of any foreign relations. They seem to last where nothing else lasts. Dynasty after dynasty tumbles down; revolution succeeds to revolution; Hindoo, Patan, Mogul, Mahratta, Sik, English are all masters in turn; but the village communities remain the same . . . If a country remain for a series of years the scene of continued pillage and massacre, so that villages cannot be inhabited, the scattered villagers nevertheless return whenever the power of peaceable possession revives. A generation may pass away, but the succeeding generation will return. The sons will take the place of their fathers; the same site for the village, the same position for the houses, the same lands, will be occupied by the descendants of those who were driven out when the village was depopulated.

As colonial conquest moved ahead, many bouts of research and debate about tradition and policy moved from villages to capitals, to Parliament, and back again; so that as the *sarkar* pushed up its revenue, year by year, land settlements came to include the ideas and interests of many local men with expert knowledge, authority, and influence, especially Company officers, landowners, and the urban intelligentsia. The empire institutionalised authority at three levels. Local authority lay in the village, the taluk (township), and the district (county). Regional authority accumulated in provincial and Native State capitals. Imperial authority descended from London, Calcutta, and New Delhi. Documents produced by and for the higher levels took pride of place in the colonial archive, and this imperial perspective became most compelling for nationalists and national historians. Documentation at the lower levels pertains more directly to agrarian communities and gathers dust in provincial and district record rooms. The character of all the colonial records changed over the nineteenth century as the railway, steamship, printing industry, science, and imperial bureaucracy developed modern powers over agrarian administration. Agrarian South Asia was steadily homogenised empirically as London sent standard forms to be filled out by bureaucrats in every locality of the realm. Administrative practice and law involved debate at each level. For people in farming communities, the lower levels were most powerful, but these did not get much attention in provincial and imperial capitals, where localities appeared to be identical sites for the implementation of policy. National cultures came into being in big cities and initially connected provincial capitals to one another and to London; this produced a two-tier imperial polity, in imperial and provincial public arenas, from which national movements spread into the countryside. Modern political history has been understood primarily as a process operating at the higher levels of empire and nationality, from which it moved out into the villages.

But power also moved in other directions. The logic of land settlements allowed the majority of early-modern patriarchs to reproduce their own local authority in agrarian territories that were not actually as homogeneous as they appeared to be in Madras, Calcutta, Bombay, and New Delhi. Imperial and national policy makers did not control agrarian governance as much as they imagined, and local struggles often determined the character of local institutions. In the western regions of the northern basins, militant lineages of warrior-peasants, most prominently, Jats, fought to free their entitlements from zamindars. In Punjab, where zamindars had been removed under the Sikh regime, the Company settled quickly with the locally dominant Jat lineages in 1848. The wars in 1857 have been studied primarily as an anti-imperial struggle, but locally they also involved battles for control of agrarian territory across a huge area spanning eastern Punjab, Awadh, Bundelkhand, and Malwa. Here as elsewhere in the zone of high military resistance, warriors fought not only *against* the Company but also *for* control of territory; they fought the Company because it threatened their rank, status, entitlements, and income – their identity and position in agrarian society. These struggles and many more accentuate the political character of land revenue settlements and the imperial importance of stabilising property entitlement by giving it to the strongest local contenders. After 1857, in Awadh, the biggest landed aristocrats were confirmed as the rulers of the countryside. Adjusting policy to garner loyalty among key people in the country stabilised the empire, and the local social forces that spoke to the state most effectively in the nineteenth century have remained prominent ever since.

Agrarian regions took a more definite shape as the empire subsumed every locality within its homogenising intelligence and provincial governments assumed responsibilities not only for collecting revenue and maintaining law and order but also for administering development. A transition is visible in the middle decades of the nineteenth century toward a more modern, bureaucratic, centralised empire, more involved in managing its agrarian resources. By the 1840s, Parliament was gathering information routinely from the provinces for compilation and analysis in London. An imperial picture of agrarian India was taking shape as the Great Trigonometrical Survey was claiming comprehensive accuracy in mapping.[25] Parliament investigated bonded labour and means to make improvements in cotton cultivation. In the 1840s, when prices were low and complaints were increasing against Company officials for coercive tactics in revenue collections, questionnaires considered administrative and legal reform and sought means to expand British investments in India. In Madras, the Torture Commission concluded that native officials needed to be replaced with more obedient, well-trained, British bureaucrats. In Calcutta, officials responded to entreaties from sugar planters in Trinidad by sending shiploads of indentured plantation workers to replace freed slaves. In London, arrangements were made for major capital investments in Indian railways and Arthur Cotton was arguing for big state investments in irrigation. In all this flurry of activity during the 1840s and 1850s, we can see early examples of a modern discourse on agricultural development. It began to project a power to transform agrarian conditions that moved out from London to provincial capitals and into the villages. In the global perspective of empire – which we can see in 1844 Parliamentary hearings that considered what to do to about the threat posed by boll weevils in Georgia, and concluded that increasing cotton supplies from India and Egypt was the only answer – modern science and technology travelled from Europe to the East, as raw materials and workers moved in the opposite direction; and British India became a unified agricultural territory for analysis and improvement, under the gaze of a hierarchically structured, scientific system. As surveyors set out to map every inch of India, detailed lithograph maps appeared in British books with accounts of economic products and business opportunities. During Lord Dalhousie's tenure as Governor-General (1848–1856), 'rural India', 'Indian agriculture', 'peasant India', and 'village India' became objects of discussion, not only in official accounts but also in journalism and social theory, as in the work of Karl Marx.

Provincial governments turned this new information into programmes of improvement, and their political institutions most clearly shaped modern agrarian polities, because provincial capitals constituted the effective apex of authority on most agrarian issues. Provincial

---

[25] Matthew H. Edney, *Mapping an Empire: The Geographical Construction of British India, 1765–1843*, Chicago, 1997, p. 304.

boundaries marked territories of law, transportation, local languages, and irrigation building. Each province had its own terms for entitlements, which defined its agrarian citizenry. In Bengal, Bihar, Awadh, eastern Uttar Pradesh, and the Central Provinces, the men who mattered most for the state in the country were the large landlords: zamindars, talukdars, malguzars. In the Madras and Bombay Presidencies, Sindh, Assam, Arakan, and lower Burma, they were instead substantial ryots and village leaders. In Punjab and western Uttar Pradesh, they were smaller zamindars and leaders of joint proprietary communities, organised around kinship units (*biradari*). All the administrative territories of modern agrarian political history were inscribed on early-modern regions in which the legacy of the Mughals is apparent. Where strong military alliances had succeeded the Mughals in the eighteenth century, Native States appeared (in Rajasthan, Malwa, Bundelkhand, Baghelkhand, Saurashtra, Kashmir). Where successor states maintained Mughal zamindari ranks, zamindar settlements emerged under the British (in northern basins and central mountains – Bengal, the United Provinces, and Central Provinces). Where Mughal successor states broke through the ranks of zamindars to form direct connections between regional rulers and agricultural communities, the Company followed suit: here we find joint property communities (Punjab) and village Ryotwari settlements (Bombay and Madras). Big states on the Mughal periphery became independent states (Nepal) and Native States (Hyderabad, Trivandrum, Mysore).

More than a third of the land area of South Asia came by treaty into Native States and independent dynasties. Though they came under heavy-handed influence and pressure from the British, these rulers had the power to create their own agrarian institutions. Native States concentrated in areas that were distant from the central sites of Company power in the eighteenth century; in these regions, Company authority would have been most expensive to establish and maintain. They were also most prominent in the zone of high military resistance, in the peninsular interior (Hyderabad and Mysore), in Rajasthan and adjacent areas of Saurashtra, in a ring of the central mountain landscape running from Malwa to interior Orissa, and in the high mountains (Kashmir, Nepal, Bhutan, Sikkim). These were also areas that were dominated politically by on-going conquest colonisation at the time of British accession. The archives of Native States are quite unlike those of British India, so the documentary basis for writing the agrarian history of South Asia remains highly fractured and disparate even in modern times. British territory (that is, land outside the Native States in British India) has been the main object of historical studies. A very old historical separation of different kinds of agrarian regions has thus remained even under the homogenising force of modernity; and it was only partially overcome by the profusion of integrating technologies, from the railway and monetary system to English education and electronic media. Regions such as Rajasthan, Kashmir, and Telangana, which have good documentation for agrarian history under the Mughals, virtually drop out of agrarian historical research after 1800. Other areas – like Assam, the Central Provinces, and Uttarakhand – become visible as never before under the British. The high mountains in the north-east and north-west remained under separate administrative agencies, separated from lowland administrations. Sri Lanka and Myanmar came under Colonial Office administration rather than under the India Office in London – and their historical literature has been fully detached from the history of British India. Strategic areas of special administration in the eastern and western high mountains generated records that are also detached physically and thus historiographically from other regions. As a result, it is quite impossible to write a modern agrarian history that is both comprehensive and sensitive to all the regions.

A very sketchy picture of the institutional geography that organises modern agrarian history can be achieved, however, by superimposing colonial settlements on farming landscapes. Native and independent states are prominent in the high mountains (Kashmir, Nepal and Terai, Bhutan), the western plains (Sindh, Rajasthan [Jaisalmere, Marwar, Mewar, and Ajmer], northern Gujarat, Saurashtra, and Malwa), the central mountains (Baghelkhand, Chota Nagpur, Jharkhand, interior Orissa, Bastar), and the peninsula interior (Mysore, Hyderabad). Regions of special administration were established in the high mountains in the west and east (in Baluchistan, Himachal, Kangra, Uttarakhand, along the Karakoram Range, and in Nagaland, Mizoram, Manipur, and Assam). The areas for which the most continuous, accessible historical record is available from medieval to modern times are those that came under direct British administration, and their institutional geography divides roughly into two groups of territories. Zamindari and malguzari regions covered the northern river basins and the valleys and plains in the central mountains. Here, agrarian colonialism meant landlordism (in western Punjab, Ganga basin, Bengal, and Assam, and also in many western mountain regions, in Uttarakhand, the Indus valley, Sindh, and Bundelkhand). The expansion of cultivation and legal struggles produced various admixtures of private farmer and peasant holdings, which became ever more prominent in territories of (later) malguzari settlements in the Central Provinces (Chhattisgarh, Khandesh, and Berar). Regions of ryotwari and mahalwari (village) settlement covered the peninsula, including most of the coast and the interior (Madras and Bombay Presidencies), and also Myanmar, Ceylon, and eastern Punjab. These regions had some zamindars and Native States, but the British regime for the most part enforced individual farm property rights. Here, the land of individual owners – ryots – was assessed individually and revenue was collected in return for a *pattah* that became a title to private property. In Punjab, Uttar Pradesh, and the Nagpur territories (across Chhattisgarh and much of the central mountains), the British applied a motley combination of zamindari and ryotwari modes, depending largely on local circumstances. Like all ryotwari and mahalwari revenue settlements, these were temporary; that is, the amount due to the state would vary according to periodic assessments by state officials.

CHAPTER 4

MODERNITY

In the nineteenth century, industrial empire brought new force into the transformation of agrarian regions. Britain controlled the corridors of mobility in southern Eurasia. English became the imperial language. A new rupee homogenised the money supply.

In 1800, cowry shells from the Andamans were the currency in Sylhet, and dozens of different silver, gold, and copper coins filled markets from Surat to Chittagong. Money changers worked every corner. But in the 1820s, the Company's silver rupee set the monetary standard and market prices began a tumble that lasted thirty years. In these hard decades, markets contracted along routes of imperial expansion, real taxation increased, seasons of scarcity were common, and overseas cloth exports died. The Act of 1793 had established a permanent settlement with no survey, no records of rights, and no definite method of assessment; after 1820, zamindari settlements required the recording of rights, annual assessments of cultivated land, and periodic reassessments. Almost everywhere, routine revenue collections provoked struggles and dislocations. When indigo stocks crashed on the London exchange, Bihari peasants lost their income and tenants lost their land. The Torture Commission in Madras reported routine beatings by revenue officers. Company critics multiplied in London but could not quite topple the old regime before rebellions killed the Company in 1857. Crown rule ended an imperial crisis. Prices had begun moving upward again by 1855, and decades of inflation then steadily lowered the real cash burden of revenue and rent. Land became more attractive for investors as a veneer of modernity covered British India. An imperial system of weights and measures, administration, and law spread along with commodity production in every region, as open land for new farms disappeared. Horrible famines marked the decades from 1860 to 1900, but a long upward price trend stimulated commercial agriculture until the crash in 1929. Then, the great depression introduced two decades of disruption and radicalisation; and it also made the elimination of village poverty and the protection of internal markets a central concern for nationalists. After independence, national governments embraced all regions with projects of national development. Today, we look back over a long modern century in which farming communities have engaged a world of states, capitalism, and nationality.

MOFUSSIL

Mofussil:

'The provinces,' – the country stations and districts, as contra-distinguished from 'the Presidency'; or, relatively, the rural localities of a district as contra-distinguished from the *sudder* or chief station, which is the residence of the district authorities.[1]

The British imperial state defined the agrarian economy for rational, centralised management. In the 1790s, surveyors like Hamilton Buchanan had begun to assess potentials for agricultural exports. The first British missions to the interior of Ceylon went to assess the potential for British investment in exports. From the early 1800s, imperial policies deliberately depressed Indian cloth exports, encouraged British cloth imports into India, and promoted Indian exports of opium, cotton, and indigo, and later tea, coffee, leather, rice, wheat, jute, and rubber. By 1840, the *Parliamentary Papers* published detailed accounts of economic matters in many regions of Asia and the Americas. Of all the national economies of the western world, the British economy depended most on agricultural imports and least on the buying power (thus the income) of its own farmers.[2] Agrarian regions in South Asia acquired export identities. Opium from Bengal and Bihar became the linchpin of the China trade. The City bankers who raised capital for railways in India worked with Parliament to boost cotton exports from Bombay, Madras and Egypt in order to address cotton supply problems at Manchester caused first by boll weevils and then by impending civil war in Alabama and Georgia. Berar became cotton country, alongside Egypt. Assam, Darjeeling, and Sri Lanka became tea country, as British planters took mountain land away from hill farmers by buying it from the government and acquired labour supplies from Bihar and Madras to build their new

---

[1] *Hobson-Jobson: A Glossary of Colloquial Anglo-Indian Words and Phrases*, edited by Henry Yule and A. C. Burnell, first published 1886; new edition 1985, p. 570.

[2] Niek Koning, *The Failure of Agrarian Capitalism: Agrarian Politics in the UK, Germany, the Netherlands and the USA, 1846–1919*, London, 1994, p. 168.

plantations. Mysore coffee was first a peasant crop, but British plantations took over the hills to produce coffee exports. As the Malnad became coffee country, warrior races manned the imperial army. Nepal and Punjab exported Gurkha and Sikh fighters, as Bihar exported landless workers. Bhojpuris came to Calcutta to board ships for Trinidad, as Caribbean sugar planters lobbied in London against loud critics of indentured labour. Workers imported from India came to many sites of British export production in Africa, Fiji, and Malaysia. Agrarian South Asia exported labour, raw materials, and processed goods for world markets, and the list grew longer as time went by to include rice, wheat, jute, hides and skins, pulses, and many other products, as well as workers from virtually every agrarian region.

In this context, a shift occurred in the character of the state's interaction with farming communities and also in the character of social power in agriculture. In 1840, an old kind of territoriality still prevailed, composed of transactions among key people on the land. The Company collected taxes from its local allies and subordinates, and gave entitlements in return. Transactional territories were formed among patriarchs whose names and social identities are prominent in the local records of early British rule, when the internal and external boundaries of empire remained in flux. By 1880, modern, administrative territories had emerged in the pacified lands of British India. Farmland was surveyed and demarcated. Maps recorded the boundaries of plots, estates, villages, roads, forests, and public property. State bureaucracy and law defined entitlements to land, labour, and capital. Industry defined a new kind of territory: railways formed scaffolding for new military, urban, and commercial structures, and the Indian Civil Service was dubbed 'the iron frame' of empire. World markets for Indian commodities expanded and commodity production became much more visibly part of everyday agricultural life, especially along the railway. Urbanism accelerated most rapidly along these same tracks, because all the people and institutions that connected the world economy to farming villages clustered in cities and towns, most of all at terminal points by the sea. In colonial cities that were among the biggest in the world, British and Indian elites defined modernity, each in their own terms.

Village folk also played key roles in making modern institutions. Moving out – like the Mughals – from their fortress towns, the

Company had called suitable men to settle the revenue, and everywhere patriarchs had come forward. For these men, settling with the British never meant voting in favour of colonialism, much less giving up their independence; rather, it meant dealing with the *sarkar* to bolster entitlements. Settling with the Company did not diminish the old potency of ritual, *dharma*, kinship, credit, coercion, and social status; and the *sarkar* actually needed powerful local allies to collect its revenue and maintain law and order locally. Many armed rulers and peasants did fight *against* subordination to the British as they battled *for* local and regional power in agrarian territories, and these struggles continued throughout British rule and beyond. Company settlements and assessments typically met resistance. Yet, in the accumulation of negotiations and struggles, imperial needs for revenue and stability eventually met local needs for entitlements and protection; and, little by little, enough key people in the country aligned their ambition with the Company to establish a new regime.

The new state came to be quite different from its predecessors. The white elite with its peculiar language and dress, detached itself from agrarian society. Its laws were foreign, penned in English, and purported to adapt, even to perfect, ancient principles. The *sarkar* demanded taxes in cash and set tax rates without reference to seasonal variation in the harvest. Government refused to see the local complexity and variability of entitlements. Instead, it enforced crude codes of property ownership that separated individual rights from group claims to the shifting sets of elements that formed bundles of agrarian patrimony. Legally, it even detached land ownership and taxation from family status and community rights, obligations, and membership. This state also claimed to have a supreme right of ownership over all land, so that failure to pay its cash revenue on time justified the official auction of land deeds to other taxpayers. The British were parsimonious rulers, apparently ignorant of the ancient power of royal generosity. They did not like to give out advances to finance farm operations at the start of the season. *Sarkar taccavi* loans did continue – and could be substantial, as we see below – but they became rare and lost the quality of personal honour. British rulers withdrew from patronising temples, mosques, and rituals, and from entertaining local nobles at court. Christian rulers did not respect or patronise *darbari* patriarchy. Religious patronage boomed, but it now assumed a new kind of private status, detached from the official operations of the state. Tax collectors did not respect the social rank of taxpayers or give indefinite extensions or special dispensations in recognition of social status. Government eventually even eliminated tax-free land grants, old symbols of rank and sources of respectable income. Invisible legislators in mythical London dictated rules and procedures that local authorities seemed helpless to change. District Collectors, who had autocratic powers of enforcement, seemed impotent to change the rules to suit local interests. To change government policy, influential men had to present their case in district towns and in provincial capitals, where making personal connections with officials became more complex and costly than ever. Specialists for this purpose became more numerous. Representing landed interests in town became a speciality for the sons and retainers of the gentry and zamindars. Already in 1784, when Sylhet zamindars were still waging wars for land on the battlefield, they retained vakils (pleaders) in Calcutta to argue cases in court against the English Collector. The 1881 census counted 357 vakils in the tiny district town of Tanjore in Madras Presidency. Landowners in all districts made regular representations to Boards of Revenue, and pleading for landowners and publicising their difficulties became a good profession. By the 1840s, landowners' associations were hard at work in the provincial capitals, and in the 1880s, landowners and their representatives filled Local and District Boards in every province. In 1892, the Tax Payers Association became the District Association in the Kistna District of Madras, reorganised along the lines of the Indian National Congress. By 1900, landowner demands for lower taxation had become a permanent agrarian plank for the Congress.

Land ownership became a qualification for a peculiar kind of imperial citizenship whose character derived from the political position of property rights in each region. Property owners participated actively in state institutions. They had official standing – status – in the state. Their disputes filled Company courts, as the cost, conditions, definition, expansion, and protection of landed property rights became the central issue in agrarian politics. English education expanded opportunities for landed families. Family status now depended upon property, wealth, and profession, in addition to other symbolic assets; though family connections remained critical assets, they declined as criteria for status in the state. Fathers passed the village offices of headman and magistrate down to their sons, and, in zamindari estates, relatives of the owner and his minions formed the local elite; but a broader based agrarian citizenry formed politically as the state acquired more power to adjudicate and appoint without reference to heredity. Lawyers and politicians emerged as actors in agrarian politics. Even tenants became people endowed with rights, in legal theory and practice, so that zamindari became one kind of property right among others, sandwiched between the state and peasants. Bureaucracy displaced family ties and old modes of social ranking. Unlike previous rulers, the Anglo *sarkar* would not marry their sons to the daughters of subaltern allies. State transactions were shorn of their family and their commercial elements. State offices ceased to be hereditary property and marketable commodities. Buying offices or state favours became illegal. Old, respected practices for pressing personal influence continued, but their official status changed with the invention of 'corruption'. The portfolio capitalist – part banker, entrepreneur, warrior, tax collector, and nobleman – disappeared. Transactions between the state and landowners shrivelled in their cultural content, along with the substance of entitlements, as locally dominant families became less involved in the overall construction of agrarian authority, now monopolised by a bureaucratic state. Agrarian patriarchs were reduced to dealing with the state on a narrow set of issues concerning taxes, rights, and the value of land. Land had been but one feature of agrarian territory; now it was everything. It became a domineering commodity that defined the nature of social relations in farming communities and power relations between farmers and the state. The power of money also increased dramatically as entitlements to land came to rest solely on the ability to pay taxes and rents – no exceptions. The best a Collector would do in response to personal pleas for tax relief was to grant a remission for reasons of general distress. The power of professional money men increased further because the higher cost of growing commodity crops had to be met before the harvest, which entailed debts, mortgages, and accumulating interest. It became more common for people to lose their land for failure to pay cash on time either to the *sarkar* or to the *sowkar* (banker or moneylender). Finance became more critical as a moving element in agriculture because now it could buy entitlements protected by the state independently of the will of communities or dominant families. Money could buy power independently of family rank.

This new institutional environment evolved and expanded slowly.

Each decade, it encompassed more territory, and on its frontiers the old rules still applied, as old rajas, zamindars, and farming communities brought new land under the plough. Old entitlements were smuggled into new properties and many old modes of power were codified, surveyed, and legalised. The British respected rights of first possession and many grants by previous rulers. Old *mirasidar* rights to tenant land became ryot property in Madras, and, in Maharashtra, rentier *khot* claims were included within ryotwari *pattah*s. B. H. Baden Powell reported that, in 1880, 20 per cent of all ryotwari land in Bombay Presidency included landlord and rent-free *inam* elements.[3] 'The multilayered complexity of hereditary revenue rights was only partially transformed by colonial administration during the 19th century', and many former titled officers called *jagirdar*s, *sardar*s, *inamdar*s, *deshmukh*s, and *deshpande*s kept revenue estates inherited from Maratha days.[4] Old rates of assessment also entered the new tax regime. Favourable rates and concessions continued which had been granted to local elites and officials. Religious institutions of all sorts retained their land, not because the Company was generous, but because local power was most often decisive in shaping the details of revenue practice. Initially, locals even set the rates of assessment and procedures for collection. Company officials did not understand all the factors that impinged upon farm yields and, greedy for revenue, they often assumed high, stable productivity and ignored seasonal fluctuations when assessing the value of land. This produced steep, regressive tax schedules, which assessed poor dry lands and poor peasants at proportionately higher rates than the best irrigated land and rich landowners. The Company thus followed the same logic that pertained within zamindari estates in the northern basins: high-status tenants with better land exerted more influence and paid lower taxes. But the Company never knew exactly what land was being taxed, where it was, and how it was being used; this was not ascertained before the plot-by-plot surveys, after 1870.

Under the Company, the 'revenue village' became the elemental unit of administration, and it became so everywhere in South Asia. But villages were also territories of social power outside the state, and,

---

[3] Neil Charlesworth, 'The Myth of the Deccan Riots of 1875', in David Hardiman, ed., *Peasant Resistance in India, 1858–1914*, Delhi, 1993, p. 216.

[4] Donald W. Attwood, *Raising Cane: The Political Economy of Sugar in Western India*, Boulder, 1992, p. 102.

even today, there is a persistent discrepancy between what the state calls 'a village' and what villagers think.[5] Initially, powerful locals determined where one revenue village ended and another began, and until the 1870s many struggles for land occurred outside official view. Because official status accompanied land rights, people with rights to land had various degrees of power to define those rights in practice, and boundaries remained fuzzy between local politics, society, law, police, and administration. The making of modern institutions that delimit precisely the content of property rights took a long time and entailed a long set of shifts in power relations between localities and the imperial state, which altered modes of power in agrarian territories across the nineteenth century. Like the Mughals, the British initially provided military muscle for prominent local families in competition for resources, and these families in turn stabilised the *sarkar* at its base by forming local proprietary institutions through which the state could realise tax revenues and codify its regime. The property system that emerged has long outlived British rule as the foundation of agrarian politics in modern South Asia. It includes many simmering conflicts that periodically boil up violently during bad seasons, even today. But records of local conflicts over land indicate that, during the settlement process itself, there was a formal regime of proprietary politics at work in each agrarian region. Some rules and rights came from the old regime into British rule but, with the arrival of the British and the disappearance of open land for new colonisation, the rules changed. Money and litigation gave local contenders new leverage. As a result, during revenue settlements, surveys, tax collections, petitions, demonstrations, riots, battles, and policy revisions, claimants to land formed agrarian polities within British India. Lawyers and bureaucrats formed a class of mediators and representatives for conflicting agrarian interests. Little by little, warfare on the land faded away and struggles inside agriculture assumed their modern civility.

By 1900, proprietary institutions enjoyed a substantial hegemony. Since then, agrarian struggles have worked within the framework of individual private property rights, though some tribal movements have asserted collective rights and sought legal protection for tribal territories. Even communists have fought to expand the scope of

---

[5] Shapan Adnan, *Annotation of Village Studies in Bangladesh and West Bengal: A Review of Socio-Economic Trends over 1942–88*, Kotbari Comilla, 1990, p. 35; and E. Valentine Daniel, *Fluid Signs: Being a Person the Tamil Way*, Berkeley, 1984.

private property. The village has also remained the accepted micro-territory of public authority and agrarian politics. Civility in agrarian polities does break down, as we can see today in Kashmir, Bihar, Telangana, Nagaland, and Sri Lanka. Violent struggles continue in village life. State violence always lurks inside civil institutions. But for a century now, property conflicts have had a remarkably civil demeanour in most regions and localities, and the institution of private property has never been the object of sustained political assault. Modern agrarian struggles focus rather on the redistribution of rights, and the normative trend is toward wider, more equitable distribution, toward the creation of more individual holdings and more private rights. A consensus would seem to hold across a wide political spectrum that the ideal agrarian condition is one in which farm families in village societies privately own and work their own land, endowed with all the finance, implements, and inputs necessary to increase productivity, under state protection. This model guides land reform, economic planning, the green revolution, and party politics. On the Left, 'land to the tiller' encodes a struggle to end feudalism and to fulfil Jawaharlal Nehru's promise to 'remove gross inequalities' from Indian society. On the Right, private property is a bedrock of tradition. Public protection for private property is certainly one major pillar of the legitimacy of the modern state in South Asia, including the colonial state; because of this, legitimate political activity inside state institutions has dominated politics rather than struggles to overthrow existing institutions of law and governance.[6] True, state institutions provide a framework for repression and privilege; but they also support striving, patronage, collective mobilisation, and conflict resolution. Peasant struggles have primarily had private property in view. The architect of zamindari abolition in Uttar Pradesh, Charan Singh, understood this well when he said this in 1957:

The political consequences of the land reforms are . . . far reaching. Much thought was given to this matter since the drafters of the legislation were cognisant of the need to ensure political stability in the countryside. By strengthening the principle of private property where it was weakest, i.e. at the base of the social pyramid, the reformers have created a huge class of strong opponents of the class war ideology. By multiplying the number of independent land-owning peasants there came into

---

[6] For national politics, see Shashi Joshi, *Struggle for Hegemony in India, 1920–1947: The Colonial State, the Left and the National Movement. Volume II: 1920–1934*, New Delhi, 1992; and Bhagwan Joshi, *Struggle for Hegemony in India, 1920–1947: The Colonial State, the Left and the National Movement. Volume I: 1934–41*, New Delhi, 1992.

being a middle of the road stable rural society and a barrier against political extremism.[7]

There is still much to learn about the history of this hegemony. Until now, scholars have relied upon theories of colonial encounter, and we can see in the literature two sets of images, whose elements can be combined. One depicts a juggernaut of western modernity rolling over traditional Eastern communities, which were mauled, transformed, modernised, or shocked into rebellion and resistance, though some of their cultural features did manage to survive – and among these survivals, caste, patriarchy, and religious identity are most conspicuous. Another set of images depicts colonial alliances being made between British and Indian elites, which combined old and new forms of power to create a new kind of agrarian environment. The first set of images resonates with cultural ideas like those of Radhakamal Mukerjee and more broadly with theories that render societies in terms of structures and ideal-types. Historians have used it to explain social disruption and peasant upheavals under colonialism.[8] The latter set of images, by contrast, reiterates Nehru's argument that 'the great poverty and misery of the Indian People are due, not only to foreign exploitation in India but also to the economic structure of society, which the alien rulers support so that their exploitation may continue'. This imagery of class alliance and exploitation spawned the idea of a semi-feudal mode of production which cannot move into full-fledged capitalism because it depends on feudal forms of power (caste, patriarchy, and direct coercion) but also cannot remain fully feudal because it needs and feeds the capitalist economy and modern state. Scholars have used this class imagery to explain the rise of political parties, persistent underdevelopment and inequality, and the general condition of subaltern domination.[9] Both kinds of imagery of colonial encounter render the mofussil an abstraction, a place without history, a set of structures and forms of power without internal

[7] Charan Singh, *Agrarian Revolution in Uttar Pradesh*, Allahabad, 1957, p. 41, quoted in Peter Reeves, *Landlords and Government: A Study of Their Relations Until Zamindari Abolition*, Bombay, 1991, p. 295.

[8] See, for example, Ravinder Kumar, *Western India in the Nineteenth Century: A Study of the Social History of Maharashtra*, London, 1968; and Hardiman, ed., *Peasant Resistance*, pp. 1–13.

[9] David A. Washbrook, *The Emergence of Provincial Politics: The Madras Presidency, 1870–1920*, Cambridge, 1976; Amit Bhaduri, *The Economic Structure of Backward Agriculture*, London, 1983; and Ranajit Guha, *Elementary Aspects of Peasant Insurgency, in Colonial India*, Delhi, 1983, pp. 6–8.

conflicts and dynamics that interacted with the moving force of colonialism.[10] But evidence from a century of disparate colonial encounters indicates that agrarian societies were all in flux at the time of their incorporation, quite independently of British intervention. From the beginning of British rule, local struggles – to establish entitlements, expand cultivation, increase commodity production, and intensify land use – shaped the form of the colonial state and influenced its operation in the countryside. At first, property entitlement and revenue collections were the main connection between the empire and its villages, and we have seen how pre-modern territoriality was embedded in ranking and ritual activity that crossed the line between village and state. Local entitlements continued to depend on the conversion of material resources into symbolic forms such as patriarchal rank, money, and temple honours, and this produced many kinds of entitlement to the elements of landed property, which remained as the modern state drew legal and bureaucratic lines between village society and the state. Legally, the state separated property in land from social powers over labour, ritual, water, and forest. It homogenised territory by propagating an abstract appearance of modernity. But country folk brought official abstractions down to the ground, and countless local histories of the emergence of modern institutions still hide in the archives, out of public view. District records maintained in Collectors' offices contain the most detailed information on struggles over land, labour, and capital before 1880; and detailed court, police, and administrative records that form provincial archives are supplemented after 1920 by local academic studies.

Historically, neither imperialism nor agrarian society was a unitary structure, and many features of modernity which appear to be impositions of colonialism or inventions of British India were a much longer time in the making. Certainly, the British did codify private property and induce commodity production, but they did not need to invent

[10] Partha Chatterjee has rearranged the elements and combined these two sets of images by separating a *'feudal* mode of power' that is 'characterized fundamentally by sheer superiority of physical force . . . founded on conquest or some other means of physical subordination of a subject population . . .' from a *'communal* mode of power' that 'exists where individual or sectional rights, entitlements, or obligations are allocated on the authority of the entire social collectivity'. See his 'More on Modes of Power and Peasantry', in Ranajit Guha, ed., *Subaltern Studies II: Writings on South Asian History and Society*, Delhi, 1983, pp. 311–50, reprinted in Ranajit Guha and Gayatri Chakravorty Spivak, eds., *Selected Subaltern Studies*, New York, 1988, pp. 351–90 (quote: p. 358).

either one, because both have longer histories going back to medieval times. Theorists of tradition have long claimed that a lack of private property in South Asia derived from a monopoly of land ownership by the state and from collective social controls in village communities, and that caste, sect, and other forms of cultural collectivity in village society thwarted capitalist individualism and the privatisation of property. A stark theoretical opposition has thus emerged between Europe's competitive, individualist rationalism and Asia's collective, traditional, peasant community consciousness. But early-medieval inscriptions document strong communal, village institutions and *also* individually owned *family* property in farming communities. Early-modern records show many kinds of community arrangements for sharing, dividing, and reallocating land among fiercely independent, possessive families. Such arrangements still remain today. In Andhra Pradesh, villagers distribute risk by sharing costs and responsibilities in agriculture. In the Paxtunistan, land redistribution among clans (*wesh*) continued until 1960. Such local institutions entail conflictual negotiations, agreements, and diplomacy among *families* who have individual entitlements to land, whose self-interested family members depend upon and constitute their family's power and position in the community. Kinship involves constant inter-family negotiations that facilitate competitive enterprise. In Gujarat, village women chat regularly in circles of kin to maintain co-operative alliances among their families. In coastal Andhra, village elders typically attest to and adjudicate rental agreements between private parties, and caste and kinship form bonds of trust in oral contracts that are pegged to market prices. Village community institutions such as the *panchayat* and *shalish* resolve conflicts among families amidst cross-cutting solidarities and in the face of competing, private interests. We thus see in contemporary and historical evidence that agrarian communities are typically held together as their internal diversity and conflict are combined with co-operation and accommodation in social networks of agrarian activity; and that few agrarian communities form solid collective identities with closed, unitary moral economies.

Farming communities did participate in rebellions that erupted from the everyday stresses and strains of oppression, social change, and resource competition. At moments of mass mobilisation, peasants may appear as a collective or a communal mass rising up against their rulers, and self-absorbed British observers certainly thought that peasant upheavals were Indian assaults on the existence of their government. But in South Asia, agriculture is not a collective peasant enterprise, except in some tribal societies, and peasants are not a unitary mass, even during upheavals. Rebellions before 1857 were primarily wars for territory of a sort that had been waged for centuries; after 1857, they became political struggles inside the framework of the state. It is only in tribal societies that old collective identities have been organised routinely as collective political opposition to the modern state itself. Forest, *jhum*, and other modes of tribal cultivation were accomplished by multi-family collectives, and tribal communities were not typically integrated in the ranks of entitlements and revenue transactions that defined the older agrarian states. After 1800, tribal groups retained distinctive farming communities even as they mingled with non-tribal societies and were pushed into the hills. Forest tribes and farmers had always flourished in the mountains, where they came under attack by the state and its associated agrarian interests. To manage conflict in tribal territories, states recognised tribal enclaves like the Daman-i-Koh around the Rajmahal Hills in Jharkhand; and thus *modern* tribal enclaves, created by the state, became territories for the evolution of *modern* tribal identities. Battles over tribal land arose typically from the aggressive extension of property claims by the state, zamindars, farmers, and moneylenders in tribal territories that were defined as such both by tribal communities and the state. Conflict increased with the rapid expansion of cultivation, and, in the nineteenth century, tribal warriors sometimes fought to the death for collective independence.

What we see in all the records of agrarian turmoil is not so much broad popular resistance to the colonial imposition of western-style private property rights and commodity production as a gradual, conflictual invention of new state institutions to enforce private property amidst on-going local struggles for entitlement. The new state now invested rights legally in individuals rather than in families. It defined land as a commodity. This particular form of entitlement was indeed a nineteenth-century invention. It became hegemonic as it was applied in practice at the intersection of empire and farming communities and as state institutions were embedded within agriculture. Across the nineteenth century, rebellions that demonstrate a radically communitarian opposition to private property rights did break out during the subjugation of tribal communities, as the expansion of lowland farming and state power turned tribal land into private property. After 1857, however, agrarian struggles in general ceased to be struggles for political autonomy or territorial supremacy. Instead, they sought private benefits for individuals, families, and kin groups within the framework of state institutions. They focused on everyday issues, above all secure possession of land, labour, and capital. Ever since, members of farming communities have mobilised publicly thousands of times to advance their claims to the many specific elements that comprised legal entitlements, such as fair rates of taxation and rent, better prices for inputs and outputs, occupancy rights, access to roads, forests and temples, and freedom from violence at the hands of landlords, state officials, and village patriarchs.

DEVELOPMENT

Modern institutions took shape at the higher levels of Company authority, in major cities and towns, and gradually worked their way down the hierarchy into small towns and villages, where they met their local fate. Their personnel concentrated in urban centres on routes of trade and administration, and, though historical maps depict blocks of territory being added to British India at each phase of military expansion, this is misleading because, historically, empire had a more linear quality. It spread along routes into the interior, out from imperial centres into remote locations. This had important consequences locally, because earlier sites of Company authority became bases for later expansion and remained higher-order centres in hierarchies of power. Company revenues and profits first concentrated in old centres near the coast. Then the railways connected ports to interior centres along lines of commercial investment and commodity production, so that sites on the railway became nodes for the expansion of modern institutions, including law, bureaucracy, police, schools, the military, science, industrial technologies, and nationalism. The older, bigger colonial centres contained more English people and things and they had closer connections with Britain; this enhanced their prestige and provided privileges for residents of larger centres. A central place hierarchy was built permanently into the geography of modernity. The main corridors of empire ran up and down the coast from Bombay and Madras, and inland along the railway into Berar, Maharashtra, Karnataka, and the Deccan; they ran up from Calcutta across the northern river basins into Punjab and Assam; and they also ran up from Karachi and Surat along the Indus basin into Punjab. Other interior and upland regions became distant hinterlands. The urban corridor from Calcutta to Peshawar held a preponderance of imperial personnel and assets; this became the imperial heartland and the central zone for state-sponsored agricultural development. The imperial scaffold is still visible today in the routes of the main trunk lines, in the location of national capitals, and in the central place hierarchy, as well as in the geographical distribution of wealth and political power. Localities far from the railways are still disadvantaged in the flow of goods and services. Lesser towns and villages still occupy the hinterland, and the high mountain interior regions still remain cultural and political frontiers for the expansion of lowland states. By 1900, modern institutions were established throughout the agrarian lowlands and were moving into the uplands of the central mountains; but their expansion into the higher uplands was slow and spotty, and much of the high mountains away from Kashmir, Darjeeling, Simla, and Kathmandu remain remote even today. Every locality has its own position of rank in modernity's spatial arrangement of inequality, and, most importantly, urban–rural divisions are marked constituents of modern social identity.

An appropriate date for the arrival of modernity among farmers, pastoralists, and forest dwellers might be the day when the land was surveyed, plot-by-plot, drawn into survey maps, and printed in books to regulate the allocation of property rights. This activity began in the 1850s and spread rapidly between 1870 and 1920. The resulting records still exist and in addition to property rights they record agreements between officers and villagers for the maintenance of irrigation works and the protection of local forests. In Punjab, they also record the membership of land-owning lineages, and thus vestiges of old transactional territories. Everywhere, they record the names of landowners and village officers. As these records were being produced, the state was also building a vast new network of new canals in Punjab and western Uttar Pradesh and a massive bureaucracy for census-taking, agricultural surveillance, and other purposes, including the regulation of forests. Though forests were not measured internally until later, their boundaries had been surveyed by 1920, by which time the state had demarcated all the land that it claimed as its own property, all the woods, seashores, and riverbeds, drainage runs for irrigation tanks, other uncultivated land not included in *pattahs*, transport rights-of-way, and public space in cities, towns, and villages. State regulation of public space had begun long before – by 1800, the Company regulated access to land and roads in Madras and Calcutta, and in 1850 it could enforce laws that allowed Untouchables to walk the streets in district towns like Tirunelveli – but in the 1870s government had just begun to enforce its claim to forest land outside the reach of lowland farmers. By 1920, public lands had been demarcated; and every bit of private property had been surveyed, demarcated, and recorded within British India. The state could now register (and tax) all legal transfers of real estate.

After 1870, agrarian citizenship came into being within the agrarian polities of British India, and it entailed much more than holding a pattah and haggling over land rights and revenue. The orderly representation of rural interests became a distinctively modern political power as the state became a managerial institution within agriculture, a source of authority in allocations of labour, technologies, water, and finance. In the 1880s, District and Local Boards institutionalised the role of local notables in the administration and funding of state projects that became *public* activities with a high social profile. By this time, many rural men of means were already involved in privately funding education, publishing, and public works, and the public sphere in the mofussil developed largely with financial support from landed families. Government embraced landed interests instinctively. When agriculture departments invented and propagated new seeds, animal breeds, and farming techniques, they concentrated their efforts on the most profitable commercial crops, especially sugarcane and cotton; and when government built irrigation and promoted co-operative societies, the benefits went primarily to commercial producers. Ideologically, all these efforts served the public good. Then, in the 1870s, murderous cyclones in Bengal (1874) and horrible famines in all the semi-arid regions (1876–8) raised the issue of the state's liability for civilian calamity, and British responsibility for public health and welfare became a hot topic of public discussion, as Indian organisations began to press for official representation in government. The scope of state responsibility expanded very quickly, and in 1888 the *Report on the Conditions of the Lower Classes of the Population in Bengal* (the Dufferin Report) used the first detailed empirical studies of 100 sample villages 'to ascertain whether there is any foundation for the assertion frequently repeated that the greater part of the population of India suffers from a daily insufficiency of food' (p. 12).[11] This was a critical moment for the emergence of modern development discourse: modern institutions began to mobilise public opinion around agrarian issues and urban leaders began to stake their legitimacy on service to a public that was predominantly rural. At this point in history, a new question arises: who are those folks, out there in the country, who shape political discourse and mobilise the public?

Developmentalism attained instant cultural hegemony as local demands for state investment in agriculture became morally and politically compelling in imperial circles. State-sponsored development may perhaps be intrinsic for all modern states, even colonial empires, because modernity demands progress and makes the state the ultimate guarantor of public well-being. Modern political struggles revolve around who will be served by the state, what sectors of society are most important, and which claims on the exchequer are most urgent. By 1880, the spectre of class war had been let loose in Europe and the idea was already established that state investments in public welfare would stabilise national enterprise; this idea would become increasingly prominent in the twentieth century. The critique of the negative impact of British policy on Indian well-being thus became an elementary aspect of Indian nationalism, and the inadequacy of imperial development efforts has received considerable academic attention. Nationalist critics were surely correct to say that, overall, the British drained wealth from India, depressed India's industrial growth, and restricted opportunities for Indian employment and investment outside agriculture. Nationalist critics also chided British rulers for excessive taxation and inadequate attention to agricultural improvement. Since 1970, scholars have expanded this critique to include the negative ecological impact of railways (which blocked drainage to provoke malaria epidemics), canals (which waterlogged the soil to produce poisonous salinity), and deforestation (which induced erosion and displaced forest people). But many continuities are striking from the 1870s to the present day in state efforts to increase aggregate agricultural output, expand commodity crop production, and secure the profitability of agriculture for investors. State development expen-

---

[11] Quoted in Willem van Schendel, 'Economy of the Working Classes', in Sirajul Islam, ed., *History of Bangladesh*, Dhaka, 1992, vol. II. p. 528.

diture increased after 1870, declined after 1920, and rose to new heights after 1947, but all modern states have faced public critics who say the state is not doing enough, and all states have publicised and praised their own development efforts. From the first famine commission report, in 1878, to the latest five-year plan, in 1997, states have sought to improve their own public image as developers and they have conducted regular inquiries on the cause and extent of development problems.

An assessment of the impact of state development activities is well beyond the scope of this book. But some points are relevant. Famine was the first policy issue that separated modern development from the long history of state-supported agricultural expansion. Prominent years of famine mortality clustered in the 1870s, 1880s, and 1890s; then again in 1918–19, and again in 1943–4, 1966–7, and 1973–5. All these famines (like droughts and cyclones) affected some regions more than others and can be considered in the context of other regional disparities (about which more below). Until 1920, famine mortality clustered in dry regions, especially in the Deccan, western plains, and central peninsular. As we will see, these famines must have been aggravated by ecological stress and decay in community-financed irrigation, some of which was mitigated in later decades. After 1870, government invested heavily in irrigation and instituted famine prevention measures, but government irrigation mostly benefited commercial farmers and the impact of government activity on reducing mortality is unclear. Most new irrigation was built by farmers who invested in wells for commercial farming, and, though state famine policies may have helped to reduce peaks in mortality, very high levels of everyday hunger, mortality, and morbidity continue to plague the dry famine zones even today. In the 1940s, 1960s, and 1970s, famine and near-famine scarcities hit Bengal, Bihar, and Bangladesh, regions that have also been seriously deprived relative to others by modern development regimes; here, too, famine struck regions most heavily that were most precariously sustained against the vagaries of the monsoon, depending on unirrigated winter rice.[12] Before 1950, the largest government investments in irrigation came to western Uttar Pradesh and Punjab, where dividends to the state and to commercial

[12] Malabika Chakravarti, 'The Lethal Connection: Winter Rice, Poverty and Famine in Late 19th Century Bengal', *Calcutta Historical Journal*, 18, 1, 1996, 66–95.

interests were high, but there is still an academic debate today as to whether the UP canals were, on the whole, *counter*-productive because, in addition to spreading intensive cultivation, they also spread malaria and waterlogging. After 1950, disproportionate government irrigation benefits also accrued to western regions. Since 1975, there have been no major famines anywhere, and monsoons have been better than average. This does not diminish the continued importance of public investment, however, which has still not eliminated hunger or the threat of mass starvation; and development expenditures have still not benefited poor people and poor lands in proportion to their share of the total population.

Development constitutes a more complex historical subject than any list of costs and benefits could ever indicate, however, because the discourse and practice of development encode a modern state's relationship with its people, and the Dufferin Report suggests imperial anxiety at the height of empire over state responsibility for malnutrition. Though famines can be called natural calamities and poverty can be explained away, everyday starvation threatens the legitimacy of a modern state. Development anxiety suffuses modernity. Tools have been honed to measure the nutritional status, health, wealth, and well-being of every individual and the media have broadcast scathing attacks on the reputation of rulers based on the implications of their policies. As British rule weakened politically after 1920, it became less capable of improving local conditions, which weakened it further, and nationalists increased their own credibility by attacking government. Congress won the loyalty of locally prominent men by convincing them that they had much to gain from a Congress regime, beginning with lower taxes and rents. The Krishak Praja Party stood for lower rents and more secure land tenures in Bengal. No-tax and no-rent agitations attracted agrarian support and sketched a blueprint for the nation's relationship with farmers after independence. In the 1940s, the Congress and Muslim League formulated plans for national development which evolved during depression and war and envisioned an even stronger role for the state, and, since 1947, development projects have expanded the political base for governments.

After 1947, populist discourse and far-reaching government activities to increase agricultural productivity made development increasingly egalitarian and democratic. The colonial government had nothing like the power of national states today to bring tailor-made packages of technology and inputs to farmers in the village. In addition, of course, farmers could not vote before 1947. But continuities since 1870 are impressive and are not confined to the proclivity of states to build large-scale irrigation dams to bring water to vast agricultural tracts from one central source under state control. Development has a firm agrarian base. Under the British, as today, state projects to improve agriculture were designed to benefit landowners on whom their success depended. William Moreland reflected an official agrarian mentality in the British empire when he said that non-productive landlords exploited peasants and undermined agriculture. This sentiment has been reiterated many times, and in 1940 even the Tenancy Committee in Hyderabad argued that giving more land and finance to peasants would serve economic as well as political ends.[13] Thomas Munro and Henry Lawrence had also argued that, to improve agriculture, the state must invest in its farmers.

The discourse and institutions of agricultural development made a place for *farmers* (also called agriculturists) – as distinct from landowners – in the modern state. Because states need to mobilise social power to increase production, they need farmers who can use their own private means to supplement state expenditure effectively. For Munro, mobilising the peasantry simply meant keeping taxes low, eliminating speculative middlemen, and securing private property, all of which, he argued, would encourage investment. By the 1850s, more ambitious arguments for state-sponsored irrigation had taken hold. To increase its revenue, proponents argued, government should build new irrigation to open new, more valuable, secure cultivation. Early state projects in the Kaveri and Krishna–Godavari deltas showed that investments could bring the promised revenues; and later famines gave the state other reasons to invest in irrigation. Huge irrigation works were installed in Maharashtra, Uttar Pradesh, and Punjab, as ancient morals took modern form. The Tamil poet advised the Pandya king to expand irrigation, and the modern state also needs to spread water upon the land. To repay its investments, the state needs revenues; and families who most directly profit from state investments, who combine land, labour, and capital to increase production, are best able to repay the state. These same people are the leaders of their communities. Agrarian patriarchs have authority and political connections. In

[13] Barry Pavier, *The Telengana Movement, 1944–1951*, Delhi, 1981, pp. 11–12.

the nineteenth century, old political imperatives which had long compelled rulers to grant wealth and authority to powerful local men were thus joined with development ideas within a framework of private property to form a new kind of agrarian citizen, the farmer who invests in his land. This new citizen would displace his predecessors, the village landowner and landlord, when the old gentry drifted away from agriculture into urban occupations during the twentieth century.

Local power influenced development policy and its impact. Local resistance made it costly to raise tax rates on old farmland, and even nominal increases were minimal after 1870, as inflation reduced the real value of taxes and new state revenues came primarily from sources other than land, such as stamps, fees, and duties. After the early settlements, new land taxes had come primarily from new cultivation, from formerly 'concealed cultivation', and from increasing assessments on land pegged to its increasing value. Local resistance to any kind of tax increase became more and more public until, by 1920, taxes were the central issue in Congress agitations in prosperous farm regions, most famously, in Gujarat. Demonstrators shouted that the state must hear the farmers' complaints and redress grievances, a demand with a long pedigree, not so much in Delhi and London as in provincial and district headquarters. Provincial regulations concerning inheritance, land alienation, debt recovery, and tenancy multiplied after 1870 to strengthen people who invested *directly* in farming, which benefited the well-endowed farmers in ryotwari tracts and many tenants in zamindari regions.

The impact of state policy on landlordism became more and more ambiguous. The British government remained committed to landlord property to the end, but zamindari estates also obstructed the increase of modern state power and revenue, and peasants became the best investment for government on political and economic grounds. On permanently settled land, state revenue increases were out of the question, and new cultivation was hard to locate and tax on zamindari estates. Legally and politically, therefore, though government supported zamindars, talukdars, and malguzars, tenancy legislation and the expansion of police jurisdictions, forest controls, and other official interventions into zamindari estates undermined zamindari autonomy. Zamindars were among the greatest beneficiaries of irrigation works in the Krishna–Godavari basin, and Ganga canals enriched talukdars in

Awadh. Government had no qualms about investing in zamindari areas to expand new cultivation, even though this had the effect of increasing landlord power, to the chagrin of people like William Moreland, who pointed out that zamindars did not invest very much in farming. Overall, however, government did not invest much in any of the permanently settled regions. The majority of zamindars raised most of their income from rent and money lending, keeping their distance from farming; and by the twentieth century we see a general movement of landlord income away from farming. Zamindars' children moved to the city to pursue education, employment, and professional careers. This trend was most important for Calcutta, where zamindari descendants, heirs, employees, and representatives – many impoverished as the generations passed – filled the ranks of the *bhadralok* (the respectable people of the middle classes). Some of the early nationalists who came from this milieu, like R. C. Dutt, criticised the British for undermining zamindari property rights, while other nationalists pushed for tenant rights. Conflicting interests in the political culture of zamindari thus entered modern politics, and the ambiguity of British policy toward zamindars echoed among nationalists who sought political support from zamindars and tenants at the same time.

State investments nurtured localities of expanding commercial cultivation along routes of imperial expansion. Development became synonymous with empire. Big cities along the railway grew faster than smaller cities and towns, and areas well endowed with huge state irrigation advanced rapidly over others. These two factors combined to increase regional wealth in Punjab and western Uttar Pradesh compared with old imperial territories in Bihar and Bengal. Towns boomed in the cotton-growing and sugar-farming irrigated tracts in Gujarat, Maharashtra, and along the Tamil coast, in contrast to regions of declining tank irrigation in the driest parts of the Deccan, Rayalaseema, Bihar, and Bengal. Ecological distress became most visible in the driest Deccan districts, as lush new irrigated colonies were opening up in Punjab and western UP. In 1911, the shift of the imperial capital from Calcutta to Delhi symbolised a long movement of imperial investment. Modernity's most politically and economically powerful agrarian macro-region in South Asia expanded across Punjab, Haryana, Rajasthan, Gujarat, and western UP; it has been consistently favoured by state investments relative to other regions since 1870.

As agrarian regions acquired economic identities, the mobilisation of power on farms became more intricately entangled with the urban public sphere. Local conflicts involving landlords, tenants, rural financiers, farmers, and government officials moved from village to town as fast as rumour. Debates in London and decisions in capitals travelled to distant villages with a telegram. Regions of agrarian politics centred on district headquarters and provincial capitals. After the Deccan Riots Commission published its report in 1878, laws were passed to protect landowners against foreclosure, and governments used the registration bureaucracy to prevent the transfer of land to non-farming moneylenders. Tenancy laws were passed to regulate the rights of farmers in zamindari estates. State officials sought to protect the property of plantation owners, ryots, tenants, and zamindars, and these property rights often conflicted with one another as well as with the rights of tribal groups and even of the state itself.

There was no single imperial intelligence to guide government activity in all these conflicts, and agrarian polities emerged during the formulation of provincial solutions to local problems. The state drew lines around tribal forests to facilitate direct administration, creating separate political territories, while regional polities developed around the administrative centres in which the middle classes settled and landowners invested. In 1883, for instance, Krishna–Godavari irrigation effectively irrigated 24,592 double-cropped acres, and, by 1897, double-cropping covered 163,481 acres, enriching zamindars, ryots, and bankers and business families, who invested in towns. Territories that benefited most from state investments saw the fastest growth of middle-class activity, and, in 1881, 241 vakils worked in Godavari District, more than in Madras, the provincial capital.[14] As agricultural labourers became urban workers, they often moved back and forth from city to village from season to season; and it seems that smaller towns had an edge in the expansion of non-farm employment, especially along the railway, where towns became entrepôts for the agrarian hinterlands. The circulation of capital between town and villages produced a critical and often conflictual power relationship between finance and farming, which preoccupied the modern state

---

[14] G. A. L. Satyarani, 'Commercialization of Agriculture and its Impact on the Socio-Political Awakening in the Godavari and Krishna Districts of the Madras Presidency, AD 1858–1914', Ph.D. dissertation, Indian Institute of Technology, Madras, 1989, pp. 295–7.

because of its importance for economic development and political stability.

Politically, only the biggest cities were important at the imperial level, but, regionally, every major town had a middle class that performed mediating roles between farmers, the state, and commodity markets, as teachers, lawyers, bankers, brokers, investors, merchants, technical experts, and officers in state agencies dealing with roads, railways, forests, medicine, construction, irrigation, plantations, mining, and eventually hydro-electric power and other projects. The size and influence of the middle class grew with state penetration into agriculture; locally, every state activity generated political feedback into urban centres. The reservation of forests, for instance, produced countless law suits by zamindars who claimed forest lands on the borders of their estates: middle-class bureaucrats, lawyers, and zamindar sons and retainers were involved in these conflicts – on all sides – in towns and cities. Resistance to the plot-by-plot measurement of village lands was localised but widespread, and politically most visible in zamindari estates, where tenant land rights undermined zamindari power. In Bengal, the boundaries of villages had been matters of local custom until the surveys of the 1860s. In Bihar, zamindars blocked state surveys of tenant lands, and in Uttar Pradesh and elsewhere surveys moved along slowly and unevenly, encouraged and stymied according to the relative influence of zamindars and tenants. Every agrarian dispute rippled into town. In the 1840s, the Calcutta intelligentsia debated what to do about distress in the indigo fields. Taxpayers' associations multiplied. In the 1870s, the government created District and Local Boards to advise Collectors on local policies. Regional agrarian polities thus developed as territories of political interaction around agricultural communities, mediating their entanglement with the imperial state.

MOBILISATION

By 1900, agrarian polities had emerged from the combination of modern state institutions and local struggles over land, labour, and finance. These territories of social power and mobilisation have been submerged in historical writing by imperial and national trends, but they form the basic geography of agrarian political economy and culture in the twentieth century. Constituted legally in land settlements and politically by administrative boundaries, they took shape during the long closure of agricultural frontiers, as locally dominant landed groups and their opponents and competitors acquired professional and political support in the public sphere. Expanding urban economies provided new frontiers for rural ambition and for labour mobility as the world economy and the imperial state extended their powers over agrarian resources through urban centres. Social power and strife in the villages travelled to town as urban influence radiated outward into the countryside, creating distinctive political cultures overlaid by imperial and national politics. National politicians needed regional allies who needed local bases of support, and local movements worked their way up the political system. As Charan Singh knew very well, local agitations could become mass movements that could challenge national elites, and, after 1920, loud calls for radical change became frequent and insistent. They came from all levels of society. The British had incorporated influential landowners into their early settlements, but the subsequent expansion of agriculture and commodity production changed power equations dramatically in every locality. By 1920, Congress leaders faced many conflicting interest groups in every region and sought to incorporate them all into a single national project. But each agrarian polity imbued 'the nation' and 'independence' with its own distinctive meanings.

Punjab is the best known agrarian polity because particularly tight connections developed there between the state and farmers. A Punjab school of colonial policy took hold after annexation in 1849 and, during settlements, officials codified local powers vested in the community of village landowners. Officially, the Punjab village became a proprietary body composed of land-owning lineages. Administrators endeavoured to reach agreements about the limits of villages to ascertain the frontiers of agricultural expansion at the time of the settlement, because here, as elsewhere, the state claimed all the land on which taxes were not paid and villagers also claimed the woods, grazing land, and cleared land surrounding their fields, which they gleaned for fuel, fodder, water, and food. By paying taxes on farmland, farmers could avoid state expropriation and use the state to support their own claims to land. By clearing new land for farming, they could establish new rights and perhaps avoid taxes until a new official survey was undertaken. The incentives for expanding cultivation onto new ground produced many local conflicts as the claims of farmers clashed with one another, as farm communities claimed the land of pastoralists and forest cultivators, and as the state, zamindars, tenants, and ryots asserted rights to newly cultivated land. The cultural character of villages in Punjab changed as collective arrangements for local defence became unnecessary and as the joint interests of lineages came to focus instead on privatising family control over land and labour. Weaker families could secure their rights against stronger neighbours by acquiring private property rights, even though collective village resource sharing did benefit weaker community members by spreading the cost of crop failures and protecting the village commons. Stronger landowners also benefited from community resource sharing, but they also had the most to gain by establishing exclusive rights to the most valuable village land. Village headmen and zamindars could use their local authority and official position to increase their private land holdings by hiring labour to bring more land under their personal cultivation. There were thus good reasons for rich and poor landed families alike to value *both* community solidarity *and* individual property, and, in Punjab and elsewhere, solidarities *among* dominant families enforced their *individual* privatisation of landed property.

As Jat lineages expanded family control over agricultural territory, their sons became prime recruits for the imperial army. This made Punjab even more politically important and brought more public investment and military salaries and pensions into the country. Starting in 1887, irrigation along the Chenab river opened new lands to intensive cultivation in state-run canal colonies, and Punjab became the most prolific regional exporter of agricultural produce, which it remains today. Jat farm enterprise supported the power of lineages, and vice versa, in agrarian territories that received more state attention, finance, and intervention than any other. The combination of Jat family farming, lineage political organisation, and state intervention in agriculture produced a booming regional economy and an agrarian polity characterised by militant collective action by land-owning lineages.

Initially, in each village, settlement officers had parcelled out rights to individual farms, collective 'common lands', and external lands used by pastoral peoples; in doing so, Punjab administrators produced new village proprietary groups by lumping together lineages even when they had no previous relations to one another. Early land administration thus encouraged local alliances across lineages, based on village entitlements; and, despite the official collectivity of the Punjab village, Punjab landowners had privatised all the commons by 1900. Government canal colonies became the first modern plan for agricultural expansion that involved the large-scale relocation of farmers and creation of new farm communities. This kind of state-planned agrarian colonisation has been accomplished many times since, in different parts of the world, and it always creates communities that live and work in unusually close quarters with state bureaucracies. In Punjab, canal colony farmers were also beneficiaries of state policies to support dominant caste groups who were critical in the military. Moving loyal, productive families into new frontiers of farming was intended not only to increase agricultural production but to expand the Punjab political system, as the state pushed more deeply into Punjab community life. Individual farm plots granted in the colonies were very large and provided ample scope for investment and family expansion, in return for relatively low rents. By 1897, along the Rakh and Mian branches of the Chenab Canal, the Punjab government had granted 341,998 acres to officially defined 'peasant' families who owned one square of about 27 acres each; 30,473 acres to 'capitalist' farmers holding from five to one hundred squares; 36,630 acres to 'yeomen' farmers with up to three squares; and 6,313 acres to 'military' grantees holding up to three squares.[15] These grants echoed the political logic of old land grants to temples and mosques. They also subsidised a rapid growth in the area of farmland planted with food and fodder crops, which further hastened the disappearance of common lands for grazing. In the Fazilka canal tract, cultivation expanded 48 per cent between 1886 and 1897 and the number of cattle almost doubled. Everywhere in Punjab, commons land (*shamilat*) had gone into private hands even before legal privatisation because powerful families would take possession of valuable portions as the village paid the revenue. As irrigation, cotton, and sugarcane spread over the land, 'the traditional pattern of land-use and institutional order inevitably changed under the impact of increased cultivation'.[16]

[15] N. Gerald Barrier, 'The Punjab Disturbances of 1907: The Response of the British Government of India to Agrarian Unrest', in Hardiman, *Peasant Resistance*, p. 231.

[16] Minoti Chakravarty-Kaul, *Common Lands and Customary Law: Institutional Change in North India over the Past Two Centuries*, Delhi, 1996, p. 120; also pp. 68, 89, 104, 112, and 118.

By 1900, Punjab agriculture had become a serious state concern. More state investments justified more state control, and the Punjab Land Alienation Act prohibited the sale of land or its transfer in foreclosure to anyone who did not belong to an 'agricultural tribe'. The state defined ethnic divisions by religion and caste with its census operations and ethnographic surveys; and now it used these divisions to regulate credit markets. The purpose of this legislation was to keep land in the hands of families who had a racially coded capacity for farming, but it also institutionalised ethnic identities and solidarities among dominant caste lineages. Families passed land from one generation to another, and, likewise, military honour ran in families. Rituals and genealogies recorded at temples, shrines, and *gurudwaras* (Sikh temples) defined lineages. Now descent and ethnicity also became the basis for participation in land and credit markets. Urban groups protested their exclusion and this opened a political split between farming and commercial interests defined officially by caste, tribe, and religion. During the nationalist movement, these divisions were mapped onto political oppositions between Muslim farmers and Hindu merchants in the western districts, as financial wealth accumulated within the Muslim 'agricultural tribes'. Tight connections between farming and state administration, especially in the canal colonies, also made everyday farming more inherently political in Punjab than anywhere else. As the Chenab colonies were filling up, bureaucrats tightened their control over access to land, and, in 1907, protesters confronted the state in demonstrations that attracted the attention of Lajpat Rai, the head of the Arya Samaj. His participation at a Lyallpur meeting punctuated a long modern history of entanglements between urban nationalists, religious reformers, and agrarian interests, which runs down through the rise of the Akali Dal and the Muslim League, the Partition of British India in 1947, and the subsequent demands for a separate Haryana and independent Khalistan. In Punjab, the meaning of the nation was suffused with solidarities among dominant farming castes, above all, Jats, and the cry for independence has been repeatedly raised to carve out territories within which state power and Jat family power might be more effectively combined. Since 1906, the mobilisation of religious identities has endeavoured to harmonise the disparate interests of rustic farmers, urban financiers, and professionals within communal solidarities, as Muslim, Hindu, and Sikh political movements have produced separate state territories in the Indian Punjab, Pakistani Punjab, and Indian state of Haryana.[17]

Farmers in the old Punjab now live in separate polities, carved by state and national boundaries. In each, the politics of lineage power produced an ethnically and religiously defined agrarian citizenry. Title to land is legal but also genealogical, enforced by states but also by the lineages. The green revolution and national planning have accentuated state interests in agriculture and provoked political movements whose strength is augmented by the fact that Punjab produces critical food supplies for India and Pakistan. In 1992, Punjab and Haryana together held 9 per cent of India's population, 8 per cent of its cultivated acreage, and 17 per cent of its food grain. In India, only Punjab and Haryana have large food crop surpluses to export to other states: Punjab has proportionately six times as much food as it has people, and Haryana three times. Their food stores sustain India's food security. Since 1960, Punjab and Haryana have also had the highest growth rate in the value of their overall agricultural produce (at 4.89 per cent and 4.14 per cent, respectively), though recent evidence indicates a relative decline since the 1980s (and serious trouble in parts of Punjab, as a result of waterlogging).[18] In addition, very substantial farmers own this prime farmland. In India as a whole, 73 per cent of all farmers work holdings of less than 1 hectare. In Punjab, this figure is 45 per cent, and in Haryana, 61 per cent.[19] Here we also find an agrarian culture dominated by aggressively capitalist owner-cultivators, the backbone of the green revolution in India and Pakistan, and some of the most successful farmers are now mobilised for globalisation. Gurpeet Khehra is one of these agro-tycoons. Thirty-three years old, with a Ph.D. in tissue culture from Britain, he invested Rs 400,000 in Israeli drip irrigation and received Rs 2 million in 1997 from crop sales and research fees. He grows strawberries on 50 acres, raises vegetables for export and plans to buy a fast-food franchise and build a Rs 7.5 million research laboratory. Other tycoons have bigger farms:

[17] K. L. Tuteja, 'The Punjab Hindu Sabha and Communal Politics', in Indu Banga, ed., *Five Punjabi Centuries: Policy, Economy, Society and Culture, c.1500–1990. Essays for J. S. Grewal*, Delhi, 1997, pp. 126–40.

[18] Statistics from Government of India, *Area and Production of Principal Crops in India* (various years), Ministry of Agriculture, New Delhi. See also Bharat Ahluwalia, 'Land of Five Tears', *Outlook*, 4, 51, 28 December 1998, 47–51.

[19] Amita Shah, 'Food Security and Access to Natural Resources: A Review of Recent Trends', *Economic and Political Weekly*, 32, 26, 28 June 1997, A46–54.

J. B. S. Sangha, for instance, has 6,000 acres under potatoes; and A. S. Dhinda, has 700 acres of flowers, which yield 70 tonnes of seed and half a million dollars in export earnings to the United States.[20]

Poor Biharis work on rich Punjabi farms. As Punjab exports food, Bihar exports hunger. In Ludhiana and Hoshiarpur districts in 1981, researchers counted over 400,000 farm workers who had come from northern Bihar districts, almost all members of low castes. Workers also came from tribal Chota Nagpur, where recruiters had gone to bring them for the employers who bid for them at auction. Though this illegal trade had ceased by 1991, rich Punjabi farmers were still advancing huge sums to bring Biharis to work in their fields; when official investigations found some workers being held in bondage, they were released to local authorities.[21]

In all other regions, too, agrarian ethnicities have been attached to the land, and symbols of class and social status have formed the regional vocabularies of agrarian politics. State-defined property rights are culturally charged, and entitlements to resources adorn individuals and families like regalia. Legal and administrative codes enhanced and institutionalised the social value of symbols of respect and honour by inscribing local ranks of status into the everyday operation of the state. Individuals and families have long gained access to the means of production by social alliances celebrated in rituals – above all, marriage – that reproduce social power in dialects of ethnicity, *jati*, *varna*, and sect. Combining land, labour, and finance in agriculture still depends on the accumulation of symbolic assets. The modern state intervened by legalising customs in civil law; by codifying castes and tribes; by enumerating population according to ethnic categories of race, tribe, caste, and religion; by measuring social conditions and stereotyping groups by ethnic category, so that Jats, for instance, officially became the best farmers in India, and Muslims and Hindus are always opposed to one another in government discourse; and by creating ethnic entitlements within the state itself, sometimes officially, as in the case of Sikh regiments in the army, and sometimes tacitly, as in the case of the vast Brahman corps of bureaucrats and state intellectuals. As employer, patron, and supreme arbiter of social status and entitle-

---

[20] Ramesh Vinayak, 'Futuristic Farmers', *India Today*, 1 June 1998, 39–42.

[21] Manjit Singh, 'Bonded Migrant Labour in Punjab Agriculture', *Economic and Political Weekly*, 32, 11, 1997, 518–19; and see Manjit Singh, *Uneven Development in Agriculture and Labour Migration: A Case of Bihar and Punjab*, Shimla, 1995.

ment, the state became the master institution for the production, regulation, and accumulation of cultural capital as it increased its material power over economic and social mobility. Brahmans became prominent everywhere in higher education, administration, law, engineering, medicine, sciences, and journalism, and also in the Indian National Congress, along with a few other high-caste groups, including Kayasths and Baniyas. In effect, the British became an imperial caste, marrying among themselves, living in their own settlements, dressing alike, and eating together. Brahmans became the national caste in British India.

Every region developed its own particular set of politically important groups; its own cultural profile of social rank, dominance, and conflict; its own ethnic flavour, reflected in its cuisine, crafts, dialects, and voting patterns. Medieval core territories in the northern basins in Uttar Pradesh and Bihar had the highest percentage of Brahmans at every level in agrarian society. Today, Uttar Pradesh contains 40 per cent of all the Brahmans in India. Before 1950, Brahmans, Muslims, and Rajputs were the great zamindars and talukdars of central and eastern UP. Rajputs, Brahmans, and Bhumihars ruled agrarian Bihar. Beneath their dominance, Goala (Ahir), Kurmi, and Lodis were prominent tenants and farmers all along the Ganga basin. In western UP, Rajasthan, Malwa, and the Central Provinces of British India, the Brahman, Jat, Rajput, Maratha, and Muslim rajas and zamindars each had their own tracts. The Bengali *bhadralok* came from the respectable classes of high-caste zamindars and their retainers, from estates where tenants were Muslims and middle-caste farmers, who in turn had lower-status landless workers under them in the villages. Three major tenant castes dominated localities in nineteenth-century West Bengal: Sadgop, Kaibartta, and Aguri. They had colonised their territories before Permanent Settlement, and in the twentieth century their power was challenged by upwardly mobile caste groups (Mayra, Chasadhoba, Jogi, Namasudra, and Pod).[22] The urban homes of the *bhadralok* and the factories in Calcutta obtained low-caste Bihari workers from the countryside. In Assam, the Ahom, Koch, Kalita, and Rajbangshi had their territories and faced waves of immigrant Bengalis. Meanwhile, Gujarati Kunbis, Maratha Kunbis, Malayali Nayars,

---

[22] Sekhar Bandyopadhyay, 'Caste, Class, and Census: Aspects of Social Mobility in Bengal under the Raj, 1872–1931', *Calcutta Historical Journal*, 5, 2, 1981, 93–123.

Telugu Kammas, Kapus, and Reddys; Kannadiga Vokkaligas, Lingayats, and Boyas; and Tamil Vanniyas, Vellalas, Kallars, and Maravas – and all the other dominant farming castes – had their own local territories in regions over which a tiny population of Brahmans held the highest positions in native society under British rule. In Native States, ruling families and allies formed ethnic elites, some very small, like the Muslim dynasty in Hyderabad and Hindu rulers in Kashmir.

The public pronouncement of the name, population, and status of each group became a feature of its social identity within the territory of the modern state, particularly during census operations.[23] From the first imperial census, in 1871, social movements emerged in which culturally subordinate groups made claims to higher social status and *at the same time* to superior entitlements under the protection of the state. Directed particularly against the supremacy of the British, Brahmans, and Rajputs, social movements sought to raise the status of lower-ranked groups and to eliminate disabilities that came with their lower status, such as exclusion from temples, universities, and public office. These movements had much in common with the group pursuit of social mobility in earlier centuries.[24] But commercialisation and urbanisation fuelled many new kinds of mobility and the modern state opened new institutional possibilities. An early example comes from 1850, when low-caste workers moved into Tirunelveli more frequently and their mobility challenged high-caste control over urban space. When battles broke out over Pariah funeral processions, the military stepped in to enforce public access to the streets.[25] The modern state acquired powers to regulate access to land, roads, temples, water, electricity, sanitation, education, and a great many other resources; and to coerce and protect people almost everywhere in society. Modern social movements were thus directed at the state, seeking official recognition, protection, and the improvement of group status

[23] The last official counting of castes was in 1931. See *Census of India, 1931*, vol. I, part 2, Imperial Tables, table XVI, 'Race, Caste, Tribe'. Joseph E. Schwartzberg, *Historical Atlas of South Asia*, Chicago, 1978, p. 108, has excellent maps of 1931 census data; so does S. P. Chatterjee, *Bengal in Maps: A Geographical Analysis of Resource Distribution in West Bengal and Eastern Pakistan*, Bombay, 1959.

[24] Hitesranjan Sanyal, 'Continuities of Social Mobility in Traditional and Modern Society in India: Two Case Studies of Caste Mobility in Bengal', *Journal of Asian Studies*, February, 1971, 315–39.

[25] Robert E. Frykenberg, 'On Roads and Riots in Tinnevelly: Radical Change and Ideology in Madras Presidency during the Nineteenth Century', *South Asia*, 4, 2, 1982, 34–52.

and entitlements. They reflect changing social relations and also the changing character of the state, whose elites can use public force in various ways. These movements have often involved serious social conflict, and, in British India, regional systems of order and conflict created political environments within which various versions of nationalism developed. Some of these local conflicts have received wide attention – for example, the breast cloth controversy in Kerala, the cow protection movement in Uttar Pradesh, Kshatriya movements in Gujarat and Bihar, and temple entry movements in Tamil Nadu – but they all have local idioms and specific ethnic contexts attached to the land. Many revolve around religious institutions and include theology, sectarianism, and mass devotion, which give agrarian polities like Punjab an air of exalted passion. Among low castes and especially Untouchables, conversions to Christianity, Islam, and Buddhism expressed social movements against upper-caste *dharma*. In 1900, a prominent Brahman official in Madras, S. Srivinasa Raghava Aiyangar, reported officially that Pariahs could make no progress without leaving Hinduism,[26] and at the end of his life B. R. Ambedkar came to the same conclusion, launching a Buddhist movement which has remained strong among Dalits in Maharashtra. In Punjab, Mangoo Ram led the Ad Dharm movement to liberate Untouchables within a Hindu sectarian framework.

As in Punjab, elsewhere too, environments and ecologies also changed dramatically as farmers pushed agriculture to the limit. In the Maratha Deccan, registered cultivation increased 67 per cent from the 1840s to the 1870s, with many taluks showing rates of increase over 100 per cent and a few over 200 per cent. Population growth also accelerated after 1820 but registered farmland grew at annual rates running from 2 per cent to 9 per cent, indicating a drive to bring land under the plough and to pay for its ownership. Prices for cotton soared in 1860, which further encouraged ploughing, planting, and property acquisition. This resulted in a substantial increase in loan activity, farm debt, and conflicts over land, both among farmers and between farmers and financiers. Many precarious dry farms came into being as poor farming families ploughed up marginal land with bad soil in areas of low rainfall. In the Deccan, water for new well

---

[26] G. Aloysius, *Religion as Emancipatory Identity: A Buddhist Movement among the Tamils under Colonialism*, New Delhi, 1998, p. 197.

irrigation lay deep in rock and could be tapped only with a considerable investment. Without irrigation, on the old margins of cultivation, land was rapidly desiccated by exhaustive cotton crops and hungry herds, especially goats. As a result, the cotton boom ended abruptly in Khandesh and proved temporary in much of the Deccan. Already in the 1830s, officials had warned that high taxes on poor lands were forcing farmers to assume debts that they would not be able to repay during inevitable bad years of drought and/or depression. After 1850, debt caused many conflicts. In two districts in western Khandesh (Poona and Ahmadnagar) between 1851 and 1865, the annual number of court disputes over land rose from 98 to 689 and from 75 to 632, respectively. In 1875, when a combination of a price slump and drought hit these districts, Maratha farmers attacked Marwari moneylenders, tearing up their debt agreements. (Perhaps they had heard about the Mahadev Kolis who had cut off Marwari noses and burned account books along with moneylender houses in 1872.)[27] After the 1875 riots, the rains failed, and in 1876–7 famine struck. Virtually every Deccan district suffered massive mortality, but the Famine Commission found that landless labourers, artisans, and poor tenant farmers died in the highest proportion. The victims of starvation were thus not the militant Maratha farmers who had attacked Marwari bankers during the Deccan riots, but rather poor people who had been deprived of entitlements during the privatisation of village land as the sorely indebted Maratha farmers expanded their holdings. Similar crop failures had occurred in 1824–5 and 1832–3, when government had provided no relief, but famine came in 1877 because the local safety net had disappeared which had previously been provided by village common lands, by hereditary family rights in villages, and by open lands outside village control. The animal population dropped as open land was lost to grazing. Herders went to the hills and drought killed animals in large numbers. The 1877 famine emerged from a combination of price slump, crop failure, and animal death that killed local demand for labourers and artisans, cutting exchange entitlements to food for people without land to feed their families.[28]

[27] David Hardiman, 'Community, Patriarchy, Honour: Raghu Bhanagre's Revolt', *Journal of Peasant Studies*, 23, 1, 1995, 88–9. For more detail on Deccan riots, see David Hardiman, *Feeding the Baniya: Peasants and Usurers in Western India*, Delhi, 1996, pp. 202–20.

[28] Sumit Guha, *The Agrarian Economy of the Bombay Deccan, 1818–1941*, Delhi, 1985, pp. 56–9, 66, 70–2.

Between 1876 and 1878, one quarter of the population also died in Bellary District. The semi-arid peninsula – from Gujarat across Berar and Khandesh and throughout Telangana, Karnataka, Andhra, and the Tamil coast – had begun to feel the ecological and social costs of the race to privatise land and to expand cash cropping. Farmers continued to cut down trees and scrub, pushing tribal farmers and herders into the hills, privatising control over food, fodder, fuel, and raw materials, as competition for land and struggles for income confronted the limits of the land. In this agrarian landscape, a prosperous farm locality required ample supplies of water to compensate for the meagre, fickle monsoon, and farmers needed financing to bring land, labour, and water together. Stable irrigation represented solid investments, and, in Gujarat, private wells and government dams multiplied along routes of drainage and across the extensive water table, producing a substantial class of Gujarati Kunbi farmers who became the heart of the Congress agitation in the region. Even where water was not available, farms multiplied and landed property increased in social value beyond what might seem rational on economic grounds. In 1926, Harold Mann described 'land hunger' in the Deccan to the Royal Commission on Agriculture by saying, 'The man would rather get Rs. 10/- a month by cultivating his own plot, rather than getting Rs.15/- a month and work for somebody else.'[29] Farming was a matter of honour and power for peasant patriarchs, and even a small bit of land that paid low economic returns could provide more subsistence stability than agricultural labour. Owning some land maintains family status for marriage alliances within the landed castes. Even small amounts of poor land can provide some subsistence and collateral, so that poor peasant families would logically work marginal lands very hard to sustain themselves and to pay off their loans by selling cash crops. In the dry peninsula, the overall expansion of cultivation was driven substantially by such poor peasant families; they provided a huge aggregate demand for rural credit and they produced a large proportion of the cash crops that went to market, particularly cotton, groundnuts, oilseeds, castor, linseed, and sesame.[30]

[29] Sumit Guha, *Agrarian Economy*, p. 155.
[30] David Washbrook, 'The Commercialization of Agriculture in Colonial India: Production, Subsistence and Reproduction in the "Dry South", c. 1870–1930', *Modern Asian Studies*, 28, 1, 1994, 129–64; Sumit Guha, 'Family Structures, Property Relations and the Agrarian Economy of the Bombay Presidency', *Journal of Peasant Studies*, 20, 3, 1993, 151–70.

Today, in the dry peninsula interior – from eastern Maharashtra, Berar, and old Vidarbha in the north, to Rayalaseema in the south – the limitation of the green revolution to irrigated land is most apparent, the contrast with prosperous Punjab could not be greater, and the pride of the peasant patriarch can turn tragic. In 1997–8, 200 poor farmers, burdened with huge debts in order to plant cash crops (mostly cotton, but also pulses), committed suicide when faced with crop failure, foreclosure, and destitution.[31] In the first three months of 1998, twenty farmers killed themselves in the northern Karnataka districts of Bidar, Raichur, Gulbarga, and Dharwad, where tur dal prices had been booming since 1990. Prices crashed in 1997, sending many farmers to the moneylenders, and then heavy commitments of new debt and of leasing in new land for expanded cultivation met drought, floods, and pests, which killed the crop.[32] These farmers and fathers of small children usually kill themselves by drinking pesticide, a symbol of a green revolution that left them behind.

Juxtapositions of growth and decline, wealth and poverty, vigour and sickness, became typical of modern agrarian landscapes. Central sites of agrarian power developed around places of capital accumulation, commercial expansion, and new irrigation. Taking a broad, aggregate perspective, we can see a steady growth of urban sites along railways and at ports; these became the expansive core of agrarian polities and their prominence increased steadily in the twentieth century. Among regions, Punjab is a growth region above all others, from the later decades of the nineteenth century to the present, followed by western Uttar Pradesh, adjacent Rajasthan, and Gujarat, which have caught up with Punjab since the 1970s. Already in the 1920s, observers had noted the contrast of this region's growth with relative decline in Bengal and Bihar; it became a subject of sustained discussion again in the 1970s, when its relevance for development policy added weight to explanatory arguments. Some early analysts thought that population growth dragged the eastern regions down and favoured the west as a place for new investments. Some explained disparities by citing the natural proclivities of the farmers, which seemed to raise productivity wherever Jats were more numerous. Such factors have now been discounted in favour of two others: landlordism

[31] Samar Harlarnkar, 'Harvest of Death', *India Today*, 8 June 1998, 33–37.
[32] Muzaffar Assadi, 'Farmers' Suicides: Signs of Stress in Rural Economy', *Economic and Political Weekly*, 33, 14, 1998, 747–8.

and irrigation. In the east, social structures and land tenures were more prominent that took funds away from farming into urban investment and did not benefit agricultural productivity. Eastern regions of the northern basins thus provided the empirical basis for theories about the causal role of semi-feudalism in economic backwardness. Government expenditure on irrigation was also much more prominent in the west, adding massive new stores of capital assets to farmlands from which landlord classes took a relatively small share of the proceeds for unproductive urban expenditure. The western parts of the northern basins became the land of agrarian capitalism despite the fact that landlordism and Brahman and Rajput feudal power remained strong in its zamindari and talukdari domains.[33]

Regional contrasts are less stark in the peninsula, but the mobilisation of agrarian capital still focused on urban centres and around irrigation, and government investments were always an important variable. In nineteenth-century Khandesh, Berar, and other black soil tracts, substantial landowners went deep into debt but sold enough cotton to finance their own independent operations, as they accumulated cattle, dug wells, hired labour, and expanded investment in agricultural finance and local politics. By contrast, in many places across the dry south of the Maratha Deccan, Karnataka, Rayalaseema, and Telangana, and along the Tamil coast, irrigation tanks declined along with community and state investments in tank repair, and other sources of irrigation did not take their place. Good soil might sustain subsistence during a time of low prices but a good well would be needed even to keep the bulls at work in dry years. In southern Andhra, the gap between the rental value of irrigated and dry land steadily increased from 1850 to 1990, and dry land got progressively poorer by comparison.[34] Everywhere, government investments made a critical impact on patterns of capital accumulation. The Bombay government made *taccavi* advances to enable property owners to dig wells, and in 1877–8 most of the Rs 300,000 in *taccavi* was for digging wells. During famine years in 1899–1902 and 1918–19, about a

[33] Amiya Kumar Bagchi, 'Reflections on Patterns of Regional Growth in India during the Period of British Rule', *Bengal Past and Present*, 95, 180, 1976, 247–89; Eric Stokes, 'Dynamism and Enervation in North Indian Agriculture: The Historical Dimension', reprinted in David Ludden, ed., *Agricultural Production and Indian History*, Delhi, 1994, pp. 36–52.
[34] M. Atchi Reddy, *Lands and Tenants in South India: A Study of Nellore District, 1850–1990*, Delhi, 1996, p. 181.

quarter of the *taccavi* loans, which totalled Rs 35 million, were specifically for digging and repairing wells. In the 1860s, government also began to build canals, and famine rapidly increased their economic and political value. The first big, modern irrigation project in Bombay Presidency began as a work of famine relief in 1876 and went into operation in 1885, with a capacity of 113,000 acres. Much smaller than the Chenab colonies, this and later projects disappointed Bombay government because farmers did not use (or pay for) all the water that canals made available. But those who did use the water became agrarian entrepreneurs in the regional sugar economy, backed up with urban finance capital, which combined private and government funds. By the 1930s, cooperative credit and sugar factories enhanced the position of sugar growers in river-irrigated Maharashtra, where political struggles in the twentieth century have centred squarely on the project of bringing sugar financing, sugar refineries, and cane farming into harmony, and where rich farmers have formed the heart of the agrarian polity.[35]

As in Punjab and Maharashtra, in many other regions agricultural capital accumulated locally among substantial landed families in areas of expansive cash cropping and new irrigation. Urban financiers and foreigners like the Marwaris faced village landowners who had close allies in town and who had ancestors among medieval gentry and conquering warrior clans. The Yusufzai, Gujars, Lodis, Jats, Rajputs, Yadavs, Thakurs, Maratha Kunbis, Maravas, and Nayakas shared a warrior heritage; while the Gujarati Kunbis, Gounders, Vellalas, Brahmans, Kammas, and Reddys shared a gentry past. Families invested in agriculture within circuits of cultural capital. Religious rituals, temple, mosque, and shrine were sites for alliance-building and symbolic capital formation. As the sons of landowners became middle-class educators and political figures, they projected their identities into regional polities. Regional language and cultural identity movements which have been so prominent in the twentieth century owe much of their original strength to the ability of prominent landed families to project their own values and heritage out from farming localities into regions of public representation and state administration. In Tamil Nadu and Maharashtra, this involved a radical displacement of Brahmans from their position of cultural authority in the British adminis-

---

[35] Attwood, *Raising Cane*, pp. 50–1.

tration. Literary erudition in vernacular languages became the mark of a true native, a son of the country, and universities became not only vehicles for upward mobility but also key sites for cultural production. Struggles to elevate the non-Brahman castes produced new cultural capital for landed castes, who thus improved their stature in agrarian politics. Among Marathas, Yadavs, Lodis, and others, becoming Kshatriya improved their social standing, while other groups adopted more Brahmanical modes of ritual, eating, dress, and exclusion. Social mobility and capital accumulation sustained and rewarded movements for caste uplift. In Madras Presidency, non-Brahman landowners held most official positions in all the districts and a study in 1901 showed that, among the parents of students in colleges and secondary schools, landowners accounted for about 36 per cent and government officials for another 40 per cent, most of whom would have been from landed families. Large zamindars like R. V. K. M. Rao, the Raja of Pitha-puram, with 400 square miles of land, much of it under the Godavari dam, were prominent financiers of the Telugu movement for non-Brahman caste uplift, education, and cultural revival, whose main supporters, like B. Pattabhi Sitaramayya, came 'from rural rather than urban backgrounds. Many possessed vast lands in the villages, even though they were residing in town' where they took up professions in law, education, and medicine.[36] Landed magnates were equally promi-nent in the non-Brahman movements in Maharashtra and Tamil Nadu, as they were in the cultural politics of all the provinces of British India.

Popular movements to promote regional linguistic and cultural identity tended to naturalise the social power of landed families over labourers during a period of history in which labour control became a more difficult and complex project. Political efforts to improve the condition of the poorest, lowliest, landless workers, tribals, and women were subsumed within regional efforts by landed groups to project their own patriarchal values and identity onto regional polities. Agrarian Punjab became synonymous with the cultural identity of landed Jats. Similarly, Rajputs defined Rajasthan and Marathas gave birth to Maharashtra. Vellalas, Vanniyas, Gounders, Kammas, Velamas, Kapus, Lingayats, and Vokkaligas played similar roles in Tamil Nadu, Andhra, and Karnataka. Cultural movements spear-

---

[36] Satyarani, 'Commercialization of Agriculture', pp. 321–48.

headed by landed families from higher non-Brahman castes, lauding traditional culture and fighting against the dominance of the British and the Brahmans, consolidated dominant landed caste control over local communities, where modernity posed a distinctive set of problems and possibilities. Most basically, the terms of labour control were in tumult as farmers needed to bring more labour into production, more regularly, with each passing year. From medieval times, superior status had distinguished the families that combined labour, land, and finance on the farm; for these families, the internal bonds of family ranking and solidarity were supplemented with paternalistic powers over low-status landless labourers, artisans, and service workers. This created various types of bonded and client labour, which were virtually universal in areas of intense cultivation in 1800. The subsequent rapid expansion of farmland and commodity production increased labour demand; government withdrew from the enforcement of bondage; urbanisation dispersed the sites and jobs demanding workers; land privatisation stripped hereditary entitlements from all landless families; and the state bureaucracy invaded the local domain of landowner authority. Clientage and bonded servitude did not disappear. A poor family might actually prefer it to the freedom to starve, and employers might enforce clientage to guarantee labour at peak seasons. At the same time, however, workers might be forced to look for wages by the disappearance of gleaning rights to village land, or they might run away to find better jobs. The impulses that altered labour relations therefore pushed and pulled in different directions, as *dharma* and coercive power continued to structure labour markets. Dominant caste supremacy in modern cultural and political movements certainly did help to solve their local problems of authority in the social relations of labour control, especially when combined with powers of patronage and agrarian finance.

Debt proved to be a powerful, flexible mechanism for lowering the cost of getting workers to the point of production, not only landless wage workers but also men, women, and children from farming families that lacked enough land to support themselves. Landowners were typically the major employers and sources for subsistence and farm loans in a village;[37] and there is evidence that in some commercial

[37] Ashok Rudra, 'Local Power and Farm-Level Decision Making', in M. Desai, S. H. Rudolph, and Ashok Rudra, eds., *Agrarian Power and Agricultural Productivity in South Asia*, Berkeley, 1984, pp. 251–80.

farming areas, land was moving out of the hands of old gentry into the portfolios of investors for whom farming became more of a business, and for whom local credit markets would have been profitable.[38] Current figures on institutional debt (as a proportion of the gross value of farm output) indicate that, even today, rolling over short-term credit remains a good source of power in agrarian localities.[39] Financial powers over workers were also stretched to cover great distances, as we have already noticed in the case of migrant labour from Bihar to Punjab. Indentured workers travelled to British territories in Africa, Malaysia, Sri Lanka, Fiji, and the Caribbean, and many families came to depend for subsistence on circuits of migration that moved among plantations, urban centres, factories, or commercial farms.

Capitalist farming thus developed a strong attachment to family subsistence farming, in which women and children bear the burden of production when the men are gone.[40] Seasonal and circular migration for work in the plains has long provided staple income for many families in the high mountains, most prominently the Gurkhas. In 1876, famine drove workers from the plains to the coffee plantations in the Malnad of Karnataka, and this became a seasonal trek. In Berar, the Jabalpur settlement officer reported in 1894 that Gonds 'flock with their families at the spring harvest to the wheat fields . . . to eke out their subsistence by working as labourers' and farmers often grew a special crop of low-cost grain to feed them, because the wheat they were growing to sell in the market was too valuable for the workers to eat.[41] Market crops – sugarcane, cotton, jute, rice, wheat, tobacco, plantains, tea, and indigo – are much more labour intensive than subsistence crops, especially millet, which they steadily displaced during the expansion of commercial farming. Digging wells and building irrigation, railways, and towns added new demands for mobile labour. Privatisation of village land cut off artisans, servants,

[38] Haruka Yanagisawa, *A Century of Change: Caste and Irrigated Lands in Tamilnadu, 1860s–1970s*, Delhi, 1996, pp. 126–94.

[39] In India, the ratio of short-term credit from all institutional agencies to the total value of agricultural output rose from 9.9 in 1970 to 19.1 in 1995. Compound growth rates in this ratio were 3.93 per cent in 1970–79 and 2.43 per cent in 1980–94. K. P. Agarwal, V. Puhazhendhi, and K. J. S. Satyasai, 'Gearing Rural Credit for the Twenty-First Century', *Economic and Political Weekly*, 32, 42, 18–24 October 1997, table 7, p. 2723.

[40] Gail Omvedt, 'Migration in Colonial India: The Articulation of Feudalism and Capitalism by the Colonial State', *Journal of Peasant Studies*, 7, 2, 1980, 185–212.

[41] Crispin N. Bates, 'Regional Dependence and Rural Development in Central India, 1820–1930', Ph.D. dissertation, Sydney Sussex College, Cambridge, n.d., p. 227.

tribal farmers, and pastoralists from old subsistence resources. By 1900, over half the rural population depended for their living on work for others and/or on farming small plots that did not yield enough for subsistence. A broad social division thus developed between those families who were net buyers and net sellers of labour, respectively. This did not amount to an increasing differentiation of classes because the overall percentage of *landless* families may have been much the same in 1900 as it was in 1800, and the overall distribution of farmland does not seem to have become very much more unequal. The trend is rather toward an increasing number of tiny holdings, too small to support a family for the whole year, and toward a vast increase in the number of people who had to work for others for a wage even though their families might own some land.

In the middle sections of the peasant population, families lost land and bought land, subdivided and rebuilt joint holdings, and rented in and rented out land, losing here and gaining there – which makes any strong empirical trend in land ownership hard to find before 1950. But commodity production and privatisation did change the nature of relationships between families needing workers and families needing work. Small farmers, artisans, and petty traders moved back and forth between these two groups, and kinship groups and castes included families of both types, but a serious division of agrarian society developed which separated families with firm entitlements to food (secured by landed property) from insecure families (who depended on employment to survive). This division helps to explain the social distribution of famine mortality in the Deccan in the 1870s and in Bengal and Bihar in the 1940s and 1970s. Regional cultural and political movements that promoted ethnic, linguistic, and religious identities emerged as locally successful landed employers made their powers of patronage emblematic of solidarity among landowners, employees, and clients. Local leaders of agrarian society thus came to speak for the poor as they became the leaders of movements for social uplift, representing their own identity as that of all the people whose well-being they promoted with their patronage and political activism.

Though, broadly speaking, the social trends that separated land-owners from others and the political trends that produced regional identity movements were similar in zamindari and ryotwari areas, everywhere, landlordism nurtured more radical agrarian politics and more polarised conflict. Tenants fought long and hard for rights to land against entrenched landlord power within a modern institutional setting that sandwiched the zamindars and their legal peers between the tenants and the state. The extreme case of state protection for landlords was Hyderabad, which gave tenants the least legal protection, provided no institutions for conflict resolution or reform, and eventually spawned a revolutionary peasant war against landlords and the state. Suppressing this revolution was a major military challenge for the new Republic of India, and smouldering class war remains the status quo in rural Telangana today. In British India, state power was more flexible and ambiguous in its support of zamindars. Tenants controlled labour, capital, and farming operations during the expansion of cultivation and commodity production; and significant legal powers accumulated in the hands of prominent tenant families in locally high-status social groups, very much along the lines of change in ryotwari tracts. Ranks beneath zamindars became many layered and hotly contested. Though activists and scholars have used the word 'peasant' to designate tenants who led struggles *against* landlordism and *for* property rights, local inequalities were at least as complex here as in ryotwari territories. In Bengal, for instance, the Dufferin Report indicated that, in 1880, 39 per cent of the total population depended significantly for its subsistence on labour alone,[42] and the proportion of landless families appears to have remained fairly stable until 1947. Even depression and famine in the 1930s and 1940s did not dramatically raise the percentage of landless families above roughly one-third of the total.[43] But relations among claimants to land changed dramatically with the expansion of cultivation and commodity production.

In 1800, observers guessed that only about 30 per cent of the cultivable acreage in Bengal was being farmed; by 1900, farms had filled all the lowlands of Bengal, moving into Assam and into the hills on all sides of the deltaic tract, from Chota Nagpur and Orissa to Sylhet and Chittagong. In Bihar, Bengal, and Assam, the local struggles to expand cultivation which defined agrarian polities first pitted settled farming against tribals and *jhum*. From Mughal times, and increasingly after 1750, conflict had occurred between states, farmers, and forest people in the lowlands, foothills, and even the high

[42] Schendel, 'Economy of the Working Classes', p. 552.
[43] Sumit Guha, 'Agrarian Bengal, 1850–1947: Issues and Problems', *Studies in History*, 11, 1 NS, 1995, 133.

mountains. Violence occurred in the central mountains from Gujarat to Bastar, but the major sites of persistent agrarian war involving tribal peoples clustered around Bengal – some continue even today. Conflicts with the largest tribal group, Santals, mark the historical frontier of permanent cultivation. Santals cultivated the forest on the fringe of settled villages in the eastern Ganga basin and in adjacent regions. They numbered among those groups that have a claim to be indigenous though they also have complex histories of migration and resettlement. Santals interacted regularly with farming communities in the lowlands. They cleared land in the jungle with fire and axe, making the extension of perennial farm cultivation much easier for lowland farmers. But before the nineteenth century it appears that Santals did not participate as groups in rituals of rank in agrarian states; so they did not obtain official entitlements to land based upon ranked subordination in official hierarchies. Like other tribal groups, they maintained their own separate social structures and hierarchies, their own rituals of rank. As revenue-paying farmers and zamindars moved into *jhum* lands to expand agricultural territories, Santals were steadily pushed into the forest. By 1850, they had moved out of districts in Orissa, Chota Nagpur, Bihar, and Bengal, following skirmishes in 1811, 1820, and 1830.[44] In 1823, under official protection, large Santal settlements ringed the Rajmahal Hills, in the Daman-i-Koh, 'the skirt of the hills', where, by the 1840s, 83,000 Santals lived in government territory, legally free of zamindar control. Here, Santal leaders sought to establish a permanent homeland free of constant meddling by foreign moneylenders and Company officials. Under the full moon on 30 June 1855, 10,000 Santals are said to have heard a young leader named Siddhu declare his vision from god that Daman must be 'cleared of all outsiders, that moneylenders and policemen be immediately slaughtered, and that Superintendent Pontet be also slain'. In the ensuing war, Company troops and zamindars massacred Santals and their low-caste peasant allies. Mundas around Ranchi and many other smaller groups also waged similar wars to create independent territories in the nineteenth century. None succeeded, but their legacies live in today's regional political movement for regional autonomy in Jharkhand, 'the land of

---

[44] V. Raghavaiah, 'Tribal Revolts in Chronological Order: 1778 to 1991', in A. R. Desai, ed., *Peasant Struggles in India*, Delhi, 1979.

jungles'.[45] As Santals were driven back from the moving borders of zamindari land, the state instituted tribal territories to segregate forest peoples in Bastar, other parts of the central mountains, and regions of the high mountains. This officially segregated the regional histories of the high mountains of the north-east and created the basis for separate national identities in Nagaland, Manipur, Mizoram, and the Chittagong Hill Tracts. As farmers pushed from Bengal into Assam, conflicts among farmers and plains tribals also occurred, and today conflict is raging in Assam that pits Ahoms against Bengalis and Bodo warriors fighting for a homeland.[46]

Inside zamindar territory, expanding cultivation was primarily the work of peasant farmers and superior tenants who combined labour and finance to create new farms and thus produced rights of first possession. A zamindar had many ways to exert power over tenants – legally and otherwise – and these remained until Zamindari Abolition in the 1950s. But expanding cultivation always entailed two distinct moments of power: the *physical* extension of farming and the *political* extension of zamindari property rights. By extending cultivation, tenants made claims to property that zamindars had to subordinate to their own claims, both within the territories of their accepted authority and also outside older zones of cultivation. Collecting rent from tenants was always a political activity that reinscribed ranks into rural society, season after season. Struggles over rights to old farmland might allow tenants to entrench their legal position, as they increased the value of their own land, resisted zamindar claims to rent, or bought tenures. Legal activity formed a basic feature of zamindari polities from the 1760s onward; and Acts of the Bengal government revised the terms of zamindari property law in 1819, 1822, 1859, 1865, 1869, 1876, 1884, 1885, 1886, and 1894. In 1925, the 1819 Patni Regulation Act was still being interpreted by the High Court in legal disputes concerning transfers and encumbrances.[47] After 1859, the state insisted that tenant rights be recorded, which gave tenants new leverage. The comparative strength of tenants in different zamindari territories is indicated by their relative success in getting rights recorded and payments acknowledged in receipts. In Bihar, their

[45] Arun Sinha, *Against the Few: Struggles of India's Rural Poor*, London, p. 32.
[46] Sanjib Baruah, ' "Ethnic" Conflict as State–Society Struggle: The Poetics and Politics of Assamese Micro-Nationalism', *Modern Asian Studies*, 28, 3, 1994, 649–71.
[47] *The All-India Reporter*, Calcutta Section, Nagpur, 1925, p. 962.

position was poor; but in Bengal, the relatively open frontier strained zamindar power, except in old kingdoms like Burdwan. Zamindars always met resistance when they endeavoured to extend their rights over new cultivation, and where open land for peasant colonisation was most abundant, zamindars faced the most difficult challenge. In such areas, a rent-seeking zamindar might most profitably acquire new revenues by allowing effective ownership to devolve into stratified farming communities in which moneylenders and larger tenants established superior rights over farming families. This was typical in Bengal, particularly in the east, north, and south.

The Mughal revenue lexicon entered Company land law and encoded the micro-politics of zamindari property until the 1950s. Broadly speaking, the terms in disputes were as follows. The land outside zamindari territory, *khas* land, belonged to government, which could lease it to farmers or zamindars at will. Extending cultivation onto *khas* might enable a peasant to establish a private right directly with the state; and this was not uncommon – it became increasingly so in the malguzari regions of the Central Provinces. The *sir* land belonged to the zamindar as personal property, for his own cultivation (often with hired labour or under lease to tenants) and here the owner did not need to grant any subordinate entitlements to farmers. The British called this 'the home farm' and it remained zamindar private property even after Zamindari Abolition in the 1950s. Tenant entitlements were of two broad classes: *khudkasht* tenants farmed land inside their own village territory, in which they had rights of first possession or permanent occupancy rights, which derived from the (genealogical) claim that they had brought the land under cultivation themselves; and *pahikasht* tenants cultivated land outside their own villages on temporary leases. In everyday agriculture, the distinction between *khudkasht* and *pahikasht* was like that between *ulkudi* and *parakkudi* (intra-village and extra-village) rights in ryotwari villages in the Tamil country; and some version of this distinction seems to have pertained in most regions. It specifies a domain of ambiguous authority exercised by farmers inside village territories over land not cultivated by villagers themselves. These areas on frontiers of village cultivation – lands held by various groups under various local tenures – were open for the most serious proprietary contestation everywhere. Villages retained legitimate authority over this land and *outsiders* farmed land which *belonged to the village* under the authority of the zamindar. This power *within villages* indicates that zamindari entitlements represented a three-way relationship between the state, zamindars, and villagers, who were composed in turn of powerful tenants, farmers, elders, moneylenders, and other important local patriarchs. In the Company's terminology, a *khudkasht* tenant had 'occupancy rights', whereas a *pahikasht* tenant did not. A zamindar had much more discretionary power over *pahikasht* tenants, whose rights to land were not under village protection. Zamindari recognition of *khudkasht* rights was not always voluntary. Some *khudkasht* farmers had received *farmans* from the Mughals or from Nawabs in Awadh and Dhaka, which were confirmed by the Company.

Struggles over occupancy rights marked zamindar efforts to extend their power over villages on the moving frontiers of cultivation. European indigo planters entered the fray early in the nineteenth century when they purchased zamindar and tenant rights for indigo cultivation in northern Bihar and Bengal. With local powers over land, marketing, and finance, European planters in effect robbed peasant farmers of occupancy rights and combined debt servitude with coercion. Slumping indigo prices from 1839 onward increased pressure on tenants, and finally, in 1860, a tenant strike drove the indigo planters out of Bengal. This event revealed that zamindars had much more power in Bihar, where indigo planting continued until 1930. Sugarcane farmers in Gorakhpur District, in eastern Uttar Pradesh, suffered much the same combination of powers that oppressed indigo farmers. But on open frontiers of cultivation, zamindar and tenant rights were subject to constant local modification and political renegotiation. Whoever controlled the means of production locally had a political advantage in the formulation of property rights. Though custom and coercion played their role, so did law; and legal disputes reveal that all the conflicting interests that pertained in ryotwari regions also embroiled zamindari land, including conflicts between farmers and financiers and between competing village claimants to family property. Only, here, zamindars perched above the tenants. In Bengal, Bihar, and eastern UP, it seems that, symbolically, a zamindar's power to take fruit from bearing trees on tenant land symbolised his superior land rights, even if he could not enforce claims to rent.

Cash crops provided new opportunities for both zamindars and tenants. Jute played a role in Bengal similar to that of cotton and groundnut in the Deccan, as poor families held precariously onto subsistence by growing jute for world markets, living in debt, working family labour on tiny plots, and moving here and there to work for wages. At the same time, jute marketing, financing, and processing provided opportunities for capital accumulation. By 1901, Bengal supplied almost all the jute in world markets, and jute covered 30 per cent of the cultivated land in Rangpur, 27 per cent in Tippera, and nearly 20 per cent in several other districts. Zamindars were often in a good position to accumulate capital in trade and credit markets. This added to zamindar income even as real rental income declined; but the expansion of cultivation and cash cropping also enabled tenants to obtain credit, profit, and occupancy rights. Even in Gorakhpur, on the upland frontier in eastern UP, 'there was an abundance of unoccupied cultivable lands' in the nineteenth century; and, though most of the profits from sugar cultivation may have been captured by zamindars, moneylenders, middle men, merchants, and refiners, tenants increased their occupancy holdings after 1870.[48] Occupancy rights expanded more broadly in Bengal.[49] Legal reforms institutionalised this trend, but its micro-politics were embedded in the dynamics of agricultural expansion. In 1779, the Collector in Sylhet had reported that land was being cleared for cultivation by extended family groups, including several generations of in-laws and distant relatives, and he opined that conflict among families had reduced the rate of land reclamation. Collectors tried to resolve conflicts that impeded the expansion of revenues, and one claimed to have heard over 2,000 boundary disputes in the early 1780s. In 1783, he gave this account of why all his work did not bring in more revenue:

cultivated lands which constituted but a very small proportion were only considered the property of the Zamindars . . . as to the waste of jungle lands they were in the most profuse manner bestowed as Charity . . . nor was any Register kept of such gifts [and] in consequence of this liberality there is not a person . . . not even of the most inferior rank in Sylhet who is not possessed of Lackerage land of some denomination or other and the best richest lands are exempt from Revenue.[50]

Facing the Company's claim to own all the jungle as *khas*, 'the land

[48] Meena Bhargava, 'Landed Property Rights in Transition: A Note on Cultivators and Agricultural Labourers in Gorakhpur in the Late Eighteenth and Nineteenth Centuries', *Studies in History*, 12, 2, NS, 1996, 248–50.
[49] Sumit Guha, 'Agrarian Bengal'.
[50] Sylhet District Records, National Archives of Bangladesh, vol. 292, p. 10.

hungry [zamindar] proprietors [in Bengal] began grabbing jungle land adjacent to their estates by getting them cleared and settled', so that *lakhiraj* or rent-free lands spread across the open frontier. By 1900, virtually the entirety of the lowlands lay under cultivation, except the Sunderbans, and the most prominent forms of entitlement were *patitabad*, that is, tenancies granted 'for the reclamation of cultivable waste'.[51] When land came under secure cultivation, a zamindar would claim that he had made a grant of rent-free land to the tenant as an investment, to facilitate reclamation, and he would seek to resume rent collections after a stipulated period of time. Conflict with cultivators and local financiers would then begin, with everyone claiming their share and their rights. Where a zamindar had strong support and control over village leaders, he could succeed. Toward this end, the Burdwan Raj invented a form of tenure, called *patni*, which replicated zamindari property rights locally, and he thereby produced commercially valuable rights that could generate a local fund of rent for people who financed cultivation. Many kinds of subsidiary rights multiplied beneath the umbrella of zamindari, and local financiers acquired layer upon layer of rights. In Chittagong, as many as sixteen levels of rights existed between the farmer and the zamindar. There, a tenant (called a talukdar) on *noabad* (newly cleared) land would take a *pattah* from government and issue a secondary (*abadkar*) *pattah* to a talukdar who would settle the land with peasant farmers.[52] We have seen that such derivative entitlements had a very long pedigree.

The local powers that combined labour and finance on the farm strengthened local claims to land, and the hold of zamindars weakened whenever open lands came under peasant ploughs. Political struggles over tenant rights in Bengal led to reams of legislation. Court conflict produced major zamindari reform Acts in 1859 and 1885. In 1873, a ruling by a district judge in their favour encouraged a group of Muslim tenants in Yusufshahi to form an Agrarian League to defend tenants in Pabna District against additional rent claims, 'illegal cesses' (*abwabs*), and threats to their occupancy rights. Led 'by men of considerable means such as the petty landlords like Ishan Chandra Roy of Daultapore, the village headmen like Shambhunath Pal of

---

[51] Sirajul Islam, 'Permanent Settlement and Peasant Economy', in Islam, *History of Bangladesh*, vol. 2, pp. 257–62.

[52] Binay Bhushan Chauduri, 'Commercialization of Agriculture', and Sirajul Islam, 'Permanent Settlement', in Islam, *History of Bangladesh*, pp. 257–62, 374.

Meghoolla, and jotedars [major landed tenants] like Khoodi Mollah of Jogtollah', the League's demonstrations to raise support for their cause and to pressure zamindars evoked critical reactions from zamindari interests in Calcutta. But Pabna landlords who fought the League impoverished themselves in the process and the number of perpetual leases jumped up from 627 to 1,633 in the years between 1873 and 1877.[53] This was an omen. In the following decades, movements for secure tenure, lower rents, and restricted zamindar powers welled up under the leadership of high-caste and well-to-do tenants whose families were among those most responsible for increasing cultivation and expanding commodity production. Tenant activists and zamindar allies later moved into regional politics along lines parallel to the Marathas, Jats, Kammas, and Vellalas.

The issues, leadership, and legality of the tenants' struggle remained much the same even as the scale and organisation of their politics expanded. Mobilising was dangerous because tenants could lose everything if the zamindar won, and zamindars had many friends in town. In Bihar, solidarity among upper-caste zamindars and local managers and a scarcity of open land left tenants little room to manoeuvre. Bihar peasants combined fight and flight to make Bihar the largest region for poor peasant out-migration and the most radical ground for peasant movements in the northern basins. Class war developed between the upper and lower castes on zamindari estates, and it continues in village Bihar even today. In Bengal, by contrast, the trajectory of tenant power moved steadily upward as political opportunities increased for the advancement of subordinate property rights. In the east of Bengal, the fact that almost all zamindars were Hindus, whereas tenants were Muslims, produced a symbolic repertoire for popular mobilisation by which leading local families projected their own cultural identity and authority outward into the broad struggle between landlords and tenants. Members of the upper-caste Hindu *bhadralok* projected their own cultural identity out over all of agrarian Bengal, beginning with the writings of Bankim Chandra Chattopadhyay; Muslim tenant leaders did the same, beginning with the organisation of the Agrarian League in Pabna. Zamindar and tenant supporters rejected each other's claims to represent Bengal, and by 1906 their competitive

---

[53] Kalyan Kumar Sen Gupta, 'The Agrarian League of Pabna, 1873', in Hardiman, *Peasant Resistance*, pp. 111–25.

mobilisation had begun to open up a conflict between political groups that was identified publicly as a conflict between Hindus and Muslims. After the death of C. R. Das in 1926, possibilities declined for alliances across the political divide, and the Indian National Congress national strategy of accommodating landlords prevented it from taking up the tenant cause and winning a majority of seats in the Bengal Legislative Council. After 1937, zamindari power was in effect destroyed and Fazlul Haq, leader of the Krishak Praja Party, joined the Muslim League. In 1941, he raised the call for Pakistan and, in 1947, what they called 'partition' in Calcutta was hailed in Dhaka as the arrival of a peasant utopia, a land free of zamindars.

LOCALITY

National independence partitioned South Asia in 1947 and again in 1971. It built new walls against inland mobility. National leaders in their capital cities led the new expansion of urbanism that distinguishes our contemporary agrarian age. The influence of urbanisation today goes well beyond the sprawling impact of huge cities that rank among the world's largest and fastest growing, because, regionally, urban growth is almost inverse to the urban population. Where urban centres were least prominent in 1901, their local expansion became most far-reaching, and the upward trend has accelerated. The percentage of India's population living in urban centres increased by just over 1 per cent (from 11 per cent to 12 per cent) during the first three decades of the twentieth century, by 6 per cent during the next three (1931–1961), and by 8 per cent during the next three (1961–1991). This trend appears in all countries except Sri Lanka, which started with a relatively big urban population (12 per cent in 1901) and now has less than twice that proportion (22 per cent in 1991), whereas India's 1991 figure (26 per cent) is 2.4 times what it was in 1901 (11 per cent). Recent acceleration is quicker in Pakistan, where the urban population increased 70 per cent faster than India's after 1961 to reach 33 per cent of total population in 1991. Nepal's small urban population (9 per cent in 1991) has grown as fast as Pakistan's since 1961.[54] Bangladesh is the most dramatic case. In 1961, its population was only 5 per cent urban, which was only double the 1901 figure. It grew 400

---

[54] Schwartzberg, *Historical Atlas*, pp. 114, 280.

per cent after 1961 to reach 20 per cent in 1991; in the early 1980s, the urban growth rate hit 10 per cent per year. Some of this increase resulted from reclassification. The 1981 Bangladesh census 'extended the definition of urban areas to include small administrative townships and economically significant production and marketing centres . . . which had certain significant "urban" characteristics'. The number of urban centres increased from 78 in 1961 to 522 in 1991, and today more than 500 urban centres have populations of less than 5,000, while the four largest cities contain almost half the urban population, nearly 7 million people.[55] As we have seen in the case of Tirunelveli, such reclassification might actually compensate for previous underestimates of urbanism; and the jump in urban population in the 1980s may well represent a realistic recognition of more rapid urbanisation in smaller centres than was previously recognised in earlier censuses.

Strung along rail lines and roads, pulsing with trains, buses, cars, trucks, cycles, rickshaws, animals, carts, schools, and businesses, thousands of urban centres, large and small, are pushing the intensification of land and labour use in all agrarian regions, as farmland is built over, fields are pressed for more production, and families are leaving agriculture. Between 1901 and 1951, the workforce became more agricultural in South Asia (cultivators and labourers in undivided India increased from 69 per cent to 73 per cent of the male workforce),[56] but the trend has moved in the opposite direction since the 1950s, and today farming accounts for only 57 per cent of the total workforce in Bangladesh, 63 per cent in India, 50 per cent in Pakistan, and 43 per cent in Sri Lanka.[57] During *three* decades after 1950, livestock, net cultivation, and built-up land increased as much as they had during *seven* previous decades, while forest cover declined at about the same rate and population grew about 15 per cent *faster*.[58] Some of today's patterns of change date back to the nineteenth

[55] Shapan Adnan, 'Fertility Decline under Absolute Poverty: Paradoxical Aspects of Demographic Change in Bangladesh', *Economic and Political Weekly*, 33, 22, 30 May 1998, 1338 and 1347, n.4. Schwartzberg has different figures for Bangladesh.

[56] J. Krishnamurty, 'The Occupational Structure', in Dharma Kumar, ed., *The Cambridge Economic History of India, II, c.1757–c.1970*, Cambridge, 1983, p. 535.

[57] It is 93 per cent in Nepal. Bina Agarwal, *A Field of One's Own*, Cambridge, 1994, p. 51, citing World Bank statistics.

[58] For data on thirteen countries in South and Southeast Asia, 1880–1980, see J. F. Richards and E. P. Flint (R. C. Daniels, ed.), *Historic Land Use and Carbon Estimates for South and Southeast Asia, 1880–1980*, Carbon Dioxide Information Analysis Center, Oak Ridge National Laboratory, Experimental Sciences Division, Publication No. 4174. Data from this study are available on the internet.

century. Nearly 1 million people moved into Chota Nagpur from Bihar districts in the twenty years after 1950, as tribal lands were being hacked into industrial sites and mines. Rapid in-migration by farmers and workers has similarly transformed other tribal regions and all of Assam.[59] Every season of distress swells urban centres. Famines and severe scarcities in the 1940s, 1950s, 1960s, and 1970s brought hungry families into Calcutta, Dhaka, and Patna. Dry seasons bring landless workers and poor peasants into Bombay, Delhi, Madras, Ahmedabad, and other cities. After partition, uprooted Punjabis flooded Delhi, many Muslims from India resettled in Karachi and Lahore, and Bengali zamindars retreated to Calcutta, following the path of previous generations. Social mobility also adds to urbanism. After 1950, Dhaka bulged with the rapid self-creation of a new middle class, straight from the village, its energies focused on the university and on careers in government, business, and professions. Nellore District, north of Madras, indicates rural trends. In its villages, real rental rates for land rose by a factor of nine during seventy-seven years between 1850 and 1927, and then doubled again during the fifty-five years from 1927 to 1982. The proportion of rent to output also increased, especially after 1940, and this rental income fuelled social mobility and urban investments. For rent receivers, occupational change 'was mostly a one-way process' leading 'from cultivation and traditional services to business, professions, and [other urban] employment'. The residential trajectory led 'from the native village to a small town, [to] the district headquarters and then to cities'.[60]

The same trajectory also leads to Europe, Australia, the Persian Gulf, Malaysia, Britain, and the United States. Though it is rare for the people who move out of manual labour to move back to the farm, manual workers who go to the Persian Gulf or Malaysia often do return to their village with income to invest in houses, land, and business. Overseas workers from Sylhet, Sri Lanka, and Kerala are significant actors in their local agrarian economies, and young workers fill the airports on their way to and from their distant sites of home life and overseas employment. As we have seen, international agro-business has also established investment centres in profitable farm tracts. Migration, markets, reinvestment, urbanisation, and social

[59] K. S. Singh, 'Agrarian Dimensions of Tribal Movements', in A. R. Desai, ed., *Agrarian Struggles in India after Independence*, Delhi, 1986, pp. 147–8.

[60] Reddy, *Lands and Tenants*, pp. 93–6,159.

mobility by many groups have formed complex links between farms and the world economy. Brahmans, merchants, and other elites play a central role. Urban investors were drawn to irrigated land in the Tamil country from the start of the twentieth century; by then, village Brahmans were already using their rental income to move to town, and selling their land to reinvest in urban careers. By 1925, in Lalgudi Taluk, Tiruchirappalli District, Brahman land was shifting into the hands of non-Brahman business, farming, and labouring castes. This slowly but steadily changed the composition of farming communities and increased the salience of distinctions between local and absentee owners, between poor peasants and rich investors.[61] After 1950, Brahmans almost everywhere were abandoning agriculture and leaving villages where their ancestors had received land grants and rental income. Along with other high-caste groups among the old agrarian gentry – especially Kayasthas, Rajputs, and Baniyas – Brahmans moved out of old zamindari estates into cities across the northern basins and western plains. They left rural Tamil Nadu, Karnataka, and the Konkan coast for Madras, Bangalore, and Bombay. By 1980, many old *agraharams* (Brahman settlements) were abandoned. This Brahman migration became a subject for literature and drama and for films such as *Pather Panchali*.

After 1947, national politics, policy making, and intellectual production became the work of urban elites whose primary task became national development. State development spending soon outgrew the treasury and attracted finance from foreign states and international institutions, as capital accumulation picked up in the 1950s after two hard decades of depression, war, famine, cyclones, and political disruption. Imports, exports, and overseas migration also picked up. Agrarian participation in the world economy was adjusted to the new international system. Primary products declined in value in comparison with the output of industry. Under national control, only tea maintained its world position. Partition disrupted the jute economy of Bengal, separating processing plants in the west from farms in the east, and it proved easier for India to grow jute than for Bangladesh to compete with India for shrinking international sales. India's national policies turned its agricultural markets inward to meet vast urban and

---

[61] H. Yanagisawa, *A Century of Change: Caste and Irrigated Lands in Tamilnadu*, Delhi, 1996, pp. 163–4.

industrial demand. Inside the countries, overall economic trends have favoured non-agricultural sectors, and dividends from growth have disproportionately favoured urban sites, educated groups, commercial classes, and government. Families have set their sights accordingly. At the same time, however, farming communities have remained the foundation of economic growth and political power, because these industrialising economies still remain overwhelmingly agricultural. So, as national leaders in government, industry, and academia have detached their own existence from everyday life on the land, they have also necessarily forged new kinds of relations with the countryside. Politically, the work of building urban–rural alliances animated all the nationalist movements going back to the 1920s, but national development allowed for radical departures as competing urban leaders sought rural support. In every state, government funding for development has been directed toward enhancing the productive powers of the owners of land, who became the backbone of national initiatives to increase production.

Struggles over land and other resources have become more intense over the decades; their legal and political basis had been established by the mid-1960s. In Pakistan, the old landlord class maintained control and the great barons like the Bhuttos of Sindh still retain their vast estates as they lead national political factions. In Bangladesh, the old landlord class disappeared and major tenants became major land-owners. In Sri Lanka and in most of India, individual villagers became the landed electorate, and the best-endowed among them became the core of the green revolution. Where the rising power of tenants met the established power of landlords – each with their advocates in state capitals – the legal reconstitution of agrarian polities in the 1950s and 1960s involved major political struggles. The universal franchise gave the strength of numbers to the tenants and, in this context, Charan Singh (1902–1987) became an architect of India's national system of agrarian alliances. From a Jat family in Meerut District in western Uttar Pradesh, he rose through the Congress ranks, supporting tenant rights, and in 1939 he published his proposals to abolish zamindari. Working against the vein of early Congress policy and fighting formidable landlord influence, he mobilised support for zamindari abolition in UP, implemented reforms, and then prevented tax increases on farmers. His central argument was that 'cultivators in Uttar Pradesh form the largest percentage of any state in India . . . and constitute 77 per cent of the rural electorate', and he worked to make farmers into an aggressive political force.[62] Land reform in other states also followed the logic of state electoral politics.

Everywhere in South Asia, localities assumed an official, institutional form: village communities were organised around socially dominant landed families within the jurisdiction of urban centres that house government offices. All the national regimes re-constituted the village as a natural *social* order to be modernised by the market *economy* and protected by state *politics*. Scholars further naturalised the agrarian social order in theories of culture and modernisation. By 1972, however, when the waves of tumult that established the new regimes had passed – when, in one year, the Dalit Panthers, the first farmers' organisations, the Self-Employed Women's Association, Jharkhand Mukti Morcha, and the All-Assam Students' Union were all formed – it became clear that official institutions faced rampant opposition from many sectors of society. Conflict, inequality, oppression, resistance, and state politics became more visible as constituents of village society. In India, after thirty years of planning and slow, steady growth in agriculture (about 2.5 per cent annually),[63] a Home Ministry study concluded that 'the persistence of serious social and economic inequalities in the rural areas has given rise to tensions between different classes', and some tensions had by then produced serious political violence. A Maoist rebellion in Naxalbari, West Bengal, in 1967, spawned the Communist Party of India (Marxist-Leninist) in 1969, which spread in fragments to Bihar and Telangana, becoming what People's War Group spokesman Var Vara Rao has called 'an alternative to parliamentary politics'.[64] From the late 1960s, many locally organised movements rocked villages as the Congress Party lost control of state governments in Kerala, Tamil Nadu, and West Bengal.[65] In Tanjavur, Bihar, Telangana, and elsewhere, village massacres became news items. The violence predominantly pitted low-caste and Untouchable tenants and agricultural workers and tribals against landowners and financiers supported by the police, military,

[62] Terence J. Byres, 'Charan Singh, 1902–1987: An Assessment', *Journal of Peasant Studies*, 15, 2, 1988, 157–70.

[63] This is figure for the period 1962–1983. See G. S. Bhalla and Gurmail Singh, 'Recent Developments in Indian Agriculture: A State Level Analysis', *Economic and Political Weekly*, 29 March 1997, A-3.

[64] *Indian Express*, 23 May 1997 (worldwide web on-line edition).

[65] Schwartzberg, *Historical Atlas*, p. 277.

and courts, so that subaltern wrath was often turned against the state. In Tanjavur District, Tamil Nadu, one village organiser reported that, having surrounded the police vans, in 1968, 'Several heads would have rolled on the field, blood would have flowed like the Kaveri in flood, if only we had not been restrained by higher-ups.'[66] Quiet, unorganised, conflict may have also increased in agriculture in the past fifty years. In Nellore, the number of landowners grew after 1950, mostly in the category of marginal farmers who had less than 2 hectares, and the number of written rental agreements declined because conflicting parties sought to avoid the courts. At the Home Ministry, policy makers looked for ways to address the tensions that underlay the apparent loss of the modern state's agrarian legitimacy, and, not surprisingly, nine of their recommendations sought to protect tenants, one proposed land reforms to limit family (rather than individual) holdings, one sought to protect tribals from moneylenders, and one called for a minimum wage for agricultural labourers. Echoing Charan Singh, the report concluded that a failure to tackle the problem of inequality 'may lead to a situation where the discontented elements are compelled to organise themselves and the extreme tensions building up with the "complex molecule" that is the Indian village may end in an explosion'.[67]

Village stability remains a state project within modernity; dating back to the early days of Company Raj, it still preoccupies governments and non-governmental organisations that promote political order along with economic growth and public welfare. Grassroots movements have multiplied and exerted their influence inside and outside the electoral system since the 1970s and they have come to represent many contending forces within agrarian societies. At the same time, however, the idea of traditional village society stabilises the modern state as well as the local power of landed patriarchs and protectors of *dharma*. Land reforms to increase the number of landowning families have been a popular policy mechanism for securing stability, expanding equity, and stimulating production in the face of increasing competition for land; and they have continuously pitted the

---

[66] Mythily Shivaraman, 'Tanjavur: Rumblings of Class Struggle in Tamil Nadu', in Kathleen Gough and Hari P. Sharma, eds., *Imperialism and Revolution in South Asia*, New York, 1973, p. 246.

[67] Ministry of Home Affairs, 'The Causes and Nature of Current Agrarian Tensions', in Desai, *Agrarian Struggles*, pp. 36–43.

interests of large landowners against the power of all others who aspire to own land. Also in a vein of modern thinking going back to the nineteenth century, states have regulated landlordism and agricultural finance, with the idea – following Moreland and Nehru – that gross inequalities are 'substantive obstacles to an unleashing of the forces capable of generating economic development, both inside and outside agriculture'.[68]

In India between 1960 and 1990, state policies and land competition shrank the proportion of cultivated land in operational holdings over 10 hectares from 31 per cent to 17 per cent, while holdings of less than 1 hectare increased by roughly the same proportion, from 19 per cent to 32 per cent. A huge population of small landlords and substantial farmers emerged from the ranks of former tenants and ryots. The predominance of medium-sized landowners increased because tiny farms multiplied as large farms dwindled and medium-sized farms (with operational holdings of between 2 and 10 hectares) kept roughly the same proportion of total farmland (about 50 per cent).[69] The picture varies significantly across regions. Very much smaller farms typify wetter regions in eastern and southern India, Sri Lanka, and Bangladesh, and larger farms cover the drier regions of canal and tube-well irrigation in Pakistan and adjacent India. In India, land holdings bigger than 2.6 hectares comprise the highest percentage of land holdings in Rajasthan and Punjab (30 per cent), and also in Gujarat, Madhya Pradesh, and Haryana (20 per cent). They play the least important role in Assam (4 per cent), Bihar (4 per cent), Tamil Nadu (3 per cent), West Bengal (1 per cent), and Kerala (0.5 per cent). Maharashtra, Karnataka, Andhra Pradesh, and Orissa fall in between, averaging 10 per cent. Uttar Pradesh resembles Bihar in that only 3 per cent of the total holdings are bigger than 2.6 hectares,[70] and the resemblance increases in the east, which has 49 per cent of all the farms in Uttar Pradesh that are smaller than 1 hectare. In this as in other respects, western UP more resembles Haryana and contains 40 per cent of all Uttar Pradesh land holdings between 4 and 10 hectares.[71]

[68] Terence J. Byres, 'Political Economy, the Agrarian Question, and the Comparative method', *Journal of Peasant Studies*, 22, 4, 1995, 569.
[69] Centre for Monitoring the Indian Economy, *India's Agricultural Sector: A Compendium of Statistics*, Mumbai, July 1996, table 1.
[70] Shah, 'Food Security and Access to Natural Resources', pp. 50–4.
[71] Zoya Hasan, 'Shifting Ground: Hindutva Politics and the Farmers' Movement in Uttar Pradesh', *Journal of Peasant Studies*, July 1994, p. 176.

Substantial farmers who combine political and economic power at the local and the state level account for much of India's agricultural growth and preoccupy growth-oriented development strategies. Between 1962–5 and 1992–5, the highest annual rates of growth in farm output came in Punjab (5 per cent), Rajasthan (4 per cent), and Haryana (4 per cent). These are also regions in which dominant farmers, mostly Jats and Rajputs, make the strongest political claim to represent their regional cultures. India's north-west quadrant, with the most large farmers and highest per capita state investments in irrigation, had the highest overall growth rate, averaging 3 per ent. Eastern states averaged 2 per cent. Central (2.7 per cent) and southern states (2.6 per cent) fell in between, while Kerala (1.7 per cent), Orissa (1.6 per cent), and Bihar (1.0 per cent) had the least growth.[72] Everywhere, politically well-connected and organised farmers acquire state subsidies for capital-intensive cultivation and their local capital accumulation depends on state-managed electrical supplies, on state prices for petrol, pump sets, tractors, pipes, fertiliser, and hybrid seeds, and on state procurement prices, transport costs, bank charges, and credit conditions. They have thus led the mobilisation of farmers movements. Sugar growers, for instance, led the cooperative movement in Maharashtra from the 1920s onwards and they have also led farmer agitations in Maharashtra and elsewhere since the 1970s. In Uttar Pradesh, under the flag of the Bharatiya Kisan Union, farmer-activists made headlines in 1988 when they 'laid siege to Meerut . . . in pursuit of demands for higher sugarcane prices, lower farm input prices, waiver of loans, higher rural investment and a lowering of electricity and water rates'.[73] Whereas the old-style peasant movements focused on land rights, the new farmer movements that arose in Tamil Nadu, Punjab, Maharashtra, Uttar Pradesh, Karnataka, and Gujarat in the 1970s and 1980s have used roadblocks, marches, and votes to demand better prices and assert 'village interests' against 'urban bias'.[74]

Such grassroots movements express the identity of agrarian regions in the idioms and institutions of nationality and, since the 1920s, the

---

[72] Bhalla and Singh, 'Recent Developments', A-3. Also A.Vaidyanathan, 'Performance of Indian Agriculture since Independence', in K. Basu, ed., *Agrarian Questions: Themes in Economics*, Delhi, 1994, pp. 18–74.

[73] Zoya Hasan, 'Shifting Ground', p. 166.

[74] Tom Brass, 'Introduction: The New Farmers' Movements in India', *Journal of Peasant Studies*, 21, 3, 1994, 3–26. For details, see Dipankar Gupta, *Rivalry and Brotherhood: Politics in the Life of Farmers in Northern India*, Delhi, 1997.

expansive local powers of landed groups have defined *national* agrarian regions in political, cultural, and economic terms. Constitutionally, agriculture is a state subject in India, and agrarian politics is most visible at the state level. New farmers' movements are prominent only in states where capitalist farming has provided a sizeable class of landowners with a coherent set of economic and political demands, where poor farmers from allied castes are willing to march behind their richer neighbours. By contrast, state political culture in Bihar has become a battleground for caste armies representing landlord, peasant, and landless workers; and the limitations of land reform in the state reflect the persistent power of the landed upper castes. The consistently different pattern of electoral outcomes in eastern and western Uttar Pradesh arises primarily from the relative voting power of competing castes in the agrarian electorate. In Maharashtra, Punjab, Andhra Pradesh, and Tamil Nadu, too, the landed upper castes have invested state political cultures with their own identities. In Bangladesh, landed Muslims did the same, beginning in the 1950s, when famine conditions lingered and Pakistani efforts to procure food supplies met resistance from the large landowners (*jotedars*), who blamed Hindu traders and promoted communal animosity. As in Tamil Nadu and elsewhere, a native language movement announced the arrival of the landed rural elite into the Bengali urban middle class; and by 1954 the Muslim League had been permanently displaced from East Pakistan.[75] The Awami League led a movement for regional representation based on rural votes, and, when war began, urban middle-class patriots looked to the peasantry for inspiration. Rustic Bengali warlords who fought for freedom became a lasting political presence in Bangladesh, and, since 1980, Islamicist politicians have struggled to reproduce agrarian patriarchy in the name of the nation. Similarly, agrarian patriarchs in Uttar Pradesh, Haryana, Rajasthan, Gujarat, and Maharashtra have supported the rise of Hindu chauvinism (Hindutva) and promoted traditional values to fight off struggles for equality by women and low-caste workers. Today, both Hindu and Muslim traditionalism seems to have their most decisive political support in the countryside among landed protectors of

---

[75] A. H. Ahmed Kamal, 'The Decline of the Muslim League and the Ascendancy of the Bureaucracy in East Pakistan', Ph.D. dissertation, Australian National University, 1988.

established social ranks who face the challenge of upward mobility and resistance from their status inferiors.

Economically, farmers also propel regional trends, as we have seen; and, to add another, very recent example, agricultural growth has now decelerated in northern Tamil Nadu with economic liberalisation, pushing landed families to accumulate capital in urban match factories, gem cutting, textile plants, leather tanning, metal working, and tool and dye making – all in response to state policies geared to increasing Indian exports for world markets. At the same time, urban agro-industrial investors are pursuing strategies of backward linkage to secure their raw materials from the village. The result is that capital is moving up from villages into towns and down from cities into towns and villages, creating a more and more intricate web of connections between the village economy and the world economy.[76]

For people who lack property and money power and who must therefore work for others – including most women in agrarian society – villages remain the everyday site of power in agriculture. Competing locally for wages from their social superiors and patrons, low-status workers have developed strategies that seek to secure their well-being but also to prevent class alliances across regions. Work is seasonal and working conditions depend on employers in specific settings. Workers seek stable relations with employers, which is more and more difficult as labour is defined in more strictly market terms. With the vast proliferation of tiny holdings, fewer farmers can employ non-family workers with any regularity and more peasants must send their own families out for wage work. Poverty among poor peasants and ambition among substantial farmers combine to make labour contracts increasingly short term and job specific, giving employers more flexibility and workers more insecurity. This same cold logic also erodes loyalty among workers toward employers who need them desperately at critical times, especially to intensify commercial cultivation. As workers are more likely to flee and fight for better conditions, capitalist farmers are more tempted to use non-market means to keep workers at work. In theory, capitalism may mean open labour markets, but it also permits coercion to lower costs and to keep labour in place; at the same time, social and political pressure can undermine

---

[76] Barbara Harriss-White and S. Janakarajan, 'From Green Revolution to Rural Industrial Revolution in South India', *Economic and Political Weekly*, 32, 25, 1997, 1469–77.

these coercive powers, depending upon conditions within specific environments. In Haryana, for instance, according to an investigation published in 1991, the monopoly of Jat farmers over state power allowed village employers to employ bonded labour and physically to prevent workers from taking jobs elsewhere, with political backing from the state government; while in nearby Meerut District, Uttar Pradesh, competitive politics among employers allowed workers' wages to rise in response to outside employment opportunities.[77] In rural West Bengal by contrast, low-caste and tribal farm workers typically live inside the boundaries of village societies where debt, rent, patronage, and social constraints hold them in check and keep their wages down. In Tamil Nadu, low-caste workers routinely get higher wages by moving out into wide circuits of labour migration – to the Persian Gulf and Malaysia – only to suffer the same constraints when they return to live in their home village, where labour discipline involves social intimidation and upper-caste control of village roads and water. In Kerala, despite high minimum wages and relatively free labour conditions, the number of days that employment is available for agricultural labourers is very low, keeping wage income at near starvation levels for many workers.

The institutions of village politics that are bolstered by respect for tradition and by the values of local self-government anchor everyday social power in agriculture. Modern states also rest on the foundation of village administration and stability. This makes widespread class action or broad union movements against village-based landed interests almost impossible. In South Asia, local labour action is the norm, and no workers' party has yet mobilised farm labour across distant agrarian regions. Instead, broad social and political movements seek to improve living conditions for people who live with subaltern entitlements by forming solidarities across dispersed, local settings. These 'new social movements' do not fit into the older categories of class and national politics, but they do reiterate earlier movements as they expand their political possibilities by including a greater diversity of peoples, localities, idioms, and concerns. They all mobilise collective identities in a manner that resembles nationalism. In fact, from the

[77] Partha N. Mukherji, *Report of the Study Group on Social Constraints on Rural Labour*, National Commission on Rural Labour, Ministry of Labour, Government of India, 1991, cited in Jens Lerche, 'Is Bonded Labour a Bound Category? – Reconceptualising Agrarian Conflict in India', *Journal of Peasant Studies*, 22, 3, 1995, 484–515.

perspective of agrarian history, nationality appears merely to be one collective identity among countless others. Though its proponents sought to subordinate other identities during their acquisition of state power, they failed, because nationality has been defined primarily by the upwardly mobile urban middle classes and allied landed groups. As soon as national regimes were stabilised, many forms of conflict became visible which had been developing alongside struggles for national independence. The limits of national movements became more apparent. Even communist parties in South Asia had come to rest on a landed peasant base, and to the extent that they mobilised landless workers, they did so within a national idiom that failed to dislodge the dominance of landed patriarchs and to represent disenfranchised and marginal groups, including tribal peoples and women. In the context of national movements, however, many other *social* identities had also been mobilised, and they forged various *cultural* relations with nationality in the idioms of caste, gender, sect, religious community, and ethnicity. These movements have confronted landed power in the villages by various means. In the early 1980s, for instance, one Dalit official reported that, with local activism, 'atrocities have increased', and he explained that, 'when status changes, consciousness comes, conflict increases', but progress 'starts with elections'.[78] Outside electoral politics, the new social movements have expressed a wide spectrum of *political* alternatives that run the gamut from the violence of the People's War Group in Telangana and of Naxalites in Bihar, to the symbolism of the Neo-Buddhist movement begun by Dr. B. R. Ambedkar, to the poetry of the Dalit Panthers, to the cultural separatism of adivasis and the legal activism of environmentalists and the women's movement.

Since 1980, global networks have visibly altered agrarian territoriality. Since the World Bank and IMF in effect rewrote national economic policies, superseding national governments on critical matters of pricing and state expenditure, the World Trade Organisation has made Trade Related Intellectual Property Rights a major agrarian issue, and multinational firms have worked hard for control of South Asian markets and materials. Struggles over the moving elements of agriculture now proceed simultaneously in local, regional,

---

[78] Marguerite S. Robinson, *Local Politics: The Law of the Fishes. Development through Political Change in Medak District, Andhra Pradesh (South India)*, Delhi, 1988, pp. 258, 264.

national, and international arenas. International labour migrations also affect economies, social relations, and politics in many agrarian regions, as a result, vernacular movements have entered global networks that challenge the authority of national states, the most dramatic example being the Liberation Tigers of Tamil Eelam, in Sri Lanka, whose struggle for a compact homeland along the coast is sustained by activism in South Africa, England, the USA, and Canada.

The struggle over the Narmada Dam indicates some contours of a new formation of agrarian locality in the age of globalisation. Designed before Indian Independence, organised by the Government of India, and financed significantly by the World Bank, the Narmada Dam project was to include 30 large, 136 medium-sized, and 3,000 small dams along the mountainous course of the Narmada river, mostly in Madhya Pradesh. It would irrigate lowland farming tracts, mostly in relatively rich commercial farming tracts in Gujarat. Its artificial lakes would submerge villages housing about 200,000 people, many of whom are Bhils. Popular opposition to the project arose from media accounts of dislocation and hardship imposed upon tribals and the landless poor. Urban activists came to investigate, lead protests, file court cases, and broadcast news to rally opposition that spread overseas as it was translated into the global discourse of environmentalism and human rights. In Europe and the United States, opposition to Narmada – like the much smaller Chipko Movement before it, against commercial logging in the Himalayas – attracted activists with global vision; in their hands the Bhils' plight was submerged by the global decimation of forests and wildlife, by environmental degradation in India's fisheries and around Chernobyl, and by the oppression heaped upon tribal minorities generally, including Iraqi Kurds.[79] Eventually, the movement forced the World Bank to withdraw its support and to reassess funding for all huge dam projects (though the Government of India vowed to continue the work). Today, American college students watch BBC videos about the Narmada struggle along with films about rural women's agitation for liquor prohibition in Andhra Pradesh and about human rights abuse in China. In South Asia, local agrarian histories are now moving into the future on a widening world stage.

[79] See 'India: Cultures in Crisis', special issue of *Cultural Survival Quarterly*, 13, 2, 1989.

BIBLIOGRAPHICAL ESSAY

Because there are too many relevant titles, I limit citations to monographs and anthologies, as much as possible, and cite later work that supersedes earlier scholarship. I omit some citations which have appeared previously in the footnotes. The lists of titles are alphabetical by authors, and each author's titles are listed chronologically. A fuller bibliography, which I will update and expand, appears on my homepage: http://www.sas.upenn.edu/~dludden/.

Intellectual history

Agriculture became an official topic for scholarly analysis under Company Raj. The most useful monographs on agrarian ideas in the Company period are S. Ambirajan, *Classical Political Economy and British Policy in India* (Cambridge, 1968), Ranajit Guha, *A Rule of Property for Bengal* (Paris, 1963), Burton Stein, *Thomas Munro: The Origins of the Colonial State and His Vision of Empire* (Delhi, 1989), and Eric Stokes, *The English Utilitarians and India* (Oxford, 1959). For the later Raj, see B. R. Tomlinson, *The Political Economy of the Raj, 1914–1947: The Economics of Decolonization* (New York, 1979) and Bipan Chandra, *The Rise and Growth of Economic Nationalism in India: Economic Policies of the Indian National Leadership, 1880–1905* (New Delhi, 1966), which is supplemented by Bipan Chandra's editing of M. G. Ranade, *Ranade's Economic Writings* (New Delhi, 1990). For post-1950s official thought, see A. M. Zaidi and S. G. Zaidi, *The Foundations of Indian Economic Planning* (New Delhi, 1979) and A. Moin Zaidi, ed., *A Tryst with Destiny: A Study of Economic Policy Resolutions of the INC Passed During the Last 100 Years* (New Delhi, 1985).

Histories of historical writing, with reprints of scholarly classics, are appearing in the series entitled *Oxford in India Readings: Themes in Indian History*, from Oxford University Press, Delhi – see especially the volumes edited by Sugata Bose, *Credit Markets and the Agrarian Economy of Colonial India* (Delhi, 1994), Sumit Guha, *Growth, Stagnation, or Decline? Agricultural Productivity in British India* (Delhi, 1992), David Hardiman, *Peasant Resistance in India, 1858–1914* (Delhi, 1992), David Ludden, *Agricultural Production and Indian History* (Delhi, 1994), Gyan Prakash, *The World of the Rural Labourer in Colonial India* (Delhi, 1992), Burton Stein, *The Making of Agrarian Policy in British India, 1770–1900* (Delhi, 1992), and Sanjay Subrahmanyam, *Money and the Market in India 1100–1700* (Delhi, 1994). The new Oxford series *Readings in Early Indian History* has opened with a volume edited by Bhairabi Prasad Sahu, *Land System and Rural Society in Early India* (Delhi, 1997), whose introduction is a history of relevant scholarship.

231

Four scholars have had the most profound personal impact on historical writing about agrarian history before 1800: D. D. Kosambi, Romila Thapar, R. S. Sharma, and Irfan Habib. D. D. Kosambi put ancient studies on a material footing that made agrarian issues prominent, and he integrated history with culture, myth, and archaeology; see *An Introduction to the Study of Indian History* (Bombay, 1956), *Myth and Reality: Studies in the Formation of Indian Culture* (Bombay, 1962), *The Culture and Civilization of Ancient India* (London, 1965), and *Ancient India: A History of Its Culture and Civilization* (New York, 1966). Romila Thapar spans ancient and medieval history and her work centres on social history and society–state relations in the first millennium BCE; see especially *Ancient Indian Social History: Some Interpretations* (New Delhi, 1978), *From Lineage to State: Social Formations in the Mid-first Millennium B.C. in the Ganga Valley* (Bombay, 1984), *Interpreting Early India* (Delhi, 1992), *Recent Perspectives of Early Indian History* (Bombay, 1995), and *The Tyranny of Labels* (New Delhi, 1997). R. S. Sharma also covers ancient and medieval history but his most important work is on feudalism and post-Gupta transitions: *Indian Feudalism* (Delhi, 1980), *Material Culture and Social Formations in Ancient India* (Delhi, 1983), *Perspectives in Social and Economic History of Early India* (New Delhi, 1983), and *Origin of the State in India* (Bombay, 1989). Irfan Habib, his students, and his colleagues at Aligarh Muslim University are the central intellectual force in Mughal history. His scholarship covers the second millennium and he is the key figure in debates about agrarian political economy in the early-modern period. See *The Agrarian System of Mughal India (1556–1707)* (Bombay, 1963), *An Atlas of Mughal Empire: Political and Economic Maps with Notes, Bibliography and Index* (Delhi, 1982), *Interpreting Indian History* (Shillong, 1988), and *Essays in Indian History: Towards a Marxist Perspective* (Delhi, 1995).

Southern regions of medieval history have a distinctive literature, which is more centred on the social networks of power and authority in agrarian territory. R. A. L. H. Gunawardana, *Robe and Plough: Monasticism and Economic Interest in Early-Medieval Sri Lanka* (Tucson, 1979) is the foundational study of Sri Lanka. Burton Stein's *Peasant State and Society in Medieval South India* (Delhi, 1980) and *Vijayanagara* (Cambridge, 1989) anchor recent debates on south India; on the cumulative impact of Stein's work, see *South Asia Research* (17, 2, 1997, 113–39).

For the period after 1800, a bibliographical essay that I wrote in the early 1980s considers about 375 titles published before 1981 and remains useful: 'Productive Power in Agriculture: A Survey of Work on the Local History of British India', in Meghnad Desai, Susanne Hoeber Rudolph, and Ashok Rudra, *Agrarian Power and Agricultural Productivity in South Asia* (Berkeley, 1984, pp. 51–99). Today, modern agrarian history seems more coherent than it did then. Six scholars have led the most influential trends. Bipan Chandra represents a national, political history that carries Irfan Habib's mode of class analysis into the twentieth century. See his *Modern India* (New Delhi, 1971, 1976), *Nationalism and Colonialism in Modern India* (New

Delhi, 1979), *India's Struggle for Independence, 1857–1947* (New Delhi, 1988), *Essays on Contemporary India* (New Delhi, 1993), and *Essays on Indian Nationalism* (New Delhi, 1993). Binay Bhushan Chaudhuri is a historian of the Bengal Presidency who exemplifies scholarly work on linguistic regions combining economic, social, and political history, and describing systems and trends of commercial production. See *The Growth of Commercial Agriculture in Bengal* (Calcutta, 1964), 'Agricultural Production in Bengal, 1850–1900: Coexistence of Decline and Growth', *Bengal Past and Present* (88, 1969, 152–206), 'The Story of a Peasant Revolt in a Bengal District', *Bengal Past and Present* (92, 2, 1973, 220–78), 'The Process of Depeasantization in Bengal and Bihar, 1885–1947', *Indian Historical Review* (21, 1, 1975, 105–65), 'The Land Market in Eastern India, 1793–1940, Part I: The Movement of Land Prices, and Part II: The Changing Composition of Landed Society', *Indian Economic and Social History Review* (12, 1 & 2, 1976, 1–42, 133–67), 'Movement of Rent in Eastern India, 1793–1930', *Indian Historical Review* (3, 2, 1977, 308–90), 'Tribal Society in Transition: Eastern India 1757–1920', in Mushirul Hasan and Narayani Gupta, eds., *India's Colonial Encounter: Essays in Memory of Eric Stokes* (New Delhi, 1993, pp. 65–120) and 'The Process of Agricultural Commercialisation in Eastern India during British Rule: A Reconsideration of the Notions of "Forced Commercialisation" and "Dependent Peasantry"', in Peter Robb, ed., *Meanings of Agriculture: Essays in South Asian History and Economics* (New Delhi, 1996, pp. 71–91). A. R. Desai is a sociologist who has pioneered studies of changing social structure and attendant agrarian conflict and peasant struggles, from the nineteenth century to the present; see *The Social Background of Indian Nationalism* (Bombay, 1948) and his edited volumes, *Rural Sociology in India* (Bombay, 1961), *Peasant Struggles in India* (Delhi, 1979, 1981, 1985) and *Agrarian Struggles in India after Independence* (Delhi, 1986). Ranajit Guha has led the group of scholars published in the series *Subaltern Studies: Essays on South Asian History and Society*. See *Elementary Aspects of Peasant Insurgency in Colonial India* (Delhi, 1983), the six volumes of *Subaltern Studies*, which he edited between 1981 and 1989, and David Arnold and David Hardiman, eds., *Subaltern Studies VIII: Essays in Honour of Ranajit Guha* (Delhi, 1994).[1] Dharma Kumar concentrates on the economic history of the Madras Presidency and specialises in the empirical critique of propositions about agrarian class structure: see *Land and Caste in South India* (Cambridge, 1965), and *Colonialism, Property, and the State* (Delhi, 1998). She has also led the historical study of the market economy and development as editor of the *Indian Economic and Social History Review* and *The Cambridge Economic History of India, Volume 2: c.1750–c.1970* (New Delhi, 1983). Eric Stokes focused on the northern basins in the nineteenth century. He positioned himself theoretically at the intersection of political economy and social history, and he set the standard for detailed empirical

[1] There is a web site for everything related to *Subaltern Studies*: http://www.lib.virginia.edu/ areastudies/subaltern/ssmap.htm.

research that integrates the study of agrarian social change with the politics in British India; see *The Peasant and the Raj: Studies in Agrarian Society and Peasant Rebellion in Colonial India* (Cambridge, 1978) and C. A. Bayly, ed., *The Peasant Armed: The Indian Revolt of 1857* (Oxford, 1986).

Studies that influence the direction of historical studies often appear in collections that cover a range of related subjects. The most influential anthologies are those edited by Hamza Alavi and John Harriss, *South Asia (Sociology of 'Developing Societies')* (New York, 1989); Sabyasachi Bhattacharya and Romila Thapar, *Situating Indian History, essays for Sarvapalli Gopal* (Delhi, 1986); Sugata Bose, *South Asia and World Capitalism* (Delhi, 1990); Terence J. Byres and Harbans Mukhia, *Feudalism and Non-European Societies* (London, 1985); K. N. Chaudhuri and Clive Dewey, *Economy and Society: Essays in Indian Economic and Social History* (Delhi, 1979); Alice Clark, *Gender and Political Economy: Explorations of South Asian Systems* (Delhi, 1993); Meghnad Desai, Susanne Hoeber Rudolph, and Ashok Rudra, *Agrarian Power and Agricultural Productivity in South Asia* (Berkeley, 1984); Clive Dewey and A. G. Hopkins, *The Imperial Impact: Studies in the Economic History of Africa and India* (London, 1978); Tim Dyson, *India's Historical Demography: Studies in Famine, Disease, and Society* (Westwood, 1989); Francine R. Frankel and M. S. A. Rao, *Dominance and State Power in Modern India: Decline of a Social Order*, 2 volumes (Delhi, 1989, 1993); R. E. Frykenberg, *Land Control and Social Structure in Indian History* (Madison, 1969) and *Land Tenure and Peasant in South Asia* (New Delhi, 1977); Kathleen Gough and Hari P. Sharma, *Imperialism and Revolution in South Asia* (New York, 1973); Mushirul Hasan and Narayani Gupta, eds., *India's Colonial Encounter: Essays in Memory of Eric Stokes* (New Delhi, 1993); Douglas Haynes and Gyan Prakash, *Contesting Power: Resistance and Everyday Social Relations in South Asia* (Delhi, 1991); Kapil Kumar, *Congress and Classes: Nationalism, Workers and Peasants* (New Delhi, 1988); Morris D. Morris and others, *Indian Economy in the Nineteenth Century, A Symposium* (New Delhi, 1969); Utsa Patnaik and Manjari Dingwaney, *Chains of Servitude: Bondage and Slavery in India* (Delhi, 1985); Tapan Raychaudhuri and Irfan Habib, eds., *The Cambridge Economic History of India, Volume 1: c.1200–c.1750* (Cambridge 1983); Peter Robb, *Rural India: Land, Power and Society under British Rule* (London, 1983) and *Meanings of Agriculture: Essays in South Asian History and Economics* (New Delhi, 1996); Kumkum Sangari and Sudesh Vaid, *Recasting Women: Essays in Colonial History* (Delhi, 1989); and Anand Yang, *Crime and Criminality in British India* (Tucson, 1985).

Histories of ideas that influence agrarian knowledge in the countryside have also begun to emerge in fragments. Shahid Amin, *Event, Metaphor, Memory: Chauri Chaura, 1992–1996* (Berkeley, 1996), reconstructs some elements of one local sub-culture. Mentalities of agrarian subalternity preoccupy Ranajit Guha, *Elementary Aspects of Peasant Insurgency in Colonial India* (Delhi, 1983) and many authors in the volumes of *Subaltern Studies*. Walter Hauser has documented the work of one important intellectual in

Sahajanand on Agricultural Labour and the Rural Poor: An Edited Transla-tion of Khet Mazdoor (Delhi, 1994) and *Swami Sahajanand and the Peasants of Jharkhand: A View from 1941, An Edited Translation of Jharkhand Ke Kisan* (Delhi, 1995). William R. Pinch, *Peasants and Monks in British India* (Berkeley, 1996), analyses local ideas about the historical process of agrarian social mobility. Gyan Prakash, *Bonded Histories: Genealogies of Labour Servitude in Colonial India* (Cambridge, 1990), finds oral epics of worker subordination. Surprisingly, little has been done on the history of popular thinking about scarcity and famine, but David Arnold, 'Famine in Peasant Consciousness and Peasant Action: Madras, 1876–8', in *Subaltern Studies III* (Delhi, 1984, pp. 62–115), and Paul R. Greenough, *Prosperity and Misery in Modern Bengal: The Famine of 1943–1944* (New York, 1982), make a start. Mythology and folklore hold a rich store of knowledge; see for instance *Indigenous Vision: Peoples of India, Attitudes to the Environment*, edited by Geeti Sen (New Delhi, 1992). Scientific ideas about farming have their own kind of history; see M. S. Randhawa, *A History of Agriculture in India*, 4 volumes (Delhi, 1986), and also Robert Evenson and Carl Pray, *Research and Productivity in Asian Agriculture* (Ithaca, 1991).

Approaches to agriculture

Three books present the basic geographical data: Joseph E. Schwartzberg, *Historical Atlas of South Asia* (Chicago, 1978), O. H. K. Spate and A. T. A. Learmonth, *India and Pakistan: A General and Regional Geography* (London, 1967), and Daniel Thorner, *Ecological and Agrarian Regions of South Asia circa 1930* (Karachi, 1996). More specialised volumes cover regions. For Bangladesh, see Nafis Ahmad, *A New Economic Geography of Bangladesh* (New Delhi, 1976), and Haroun Rashid, *Geography of Bangla-desh* (Dhaka, 1977). Rais Akhtar, *Environment, Agriculture and Nutrition in Kumaon Region* (New Delhi, 1980) is a model of thematic geography that merits emulation. For India, see especially J. L. D. Sehgal, K. Mandal, C. Mandal, and S. Vadivelu, *Agro-Ecological Regions of India* (Nagpur, 1990) and Jasbir Singh, *An Agricultural Atlas of India: A Geographical Analysis* (Varanasi, 1974) and *An Agricultural Geography of Haryana* (Kurukshetra, 1976).

Seasonality is a pervasive theme. A good place to begin is Bina Agarwal, 'Social Security and the Family in Rural India: Coping with Seasonality and Calamity', *Journal of Peasant Studies* (17, 3, 1990, 341–412). The best volumes are Robert Chambers et al., eds., *Seasonal Dimensions to Rural Poverty* (Montclair, 1981) and Martha Chen, *Coping with Seasonality and Drought* (Newbury Park, CA, 1991).

Development is the most broadly integrative theme, but only a small portion of work describes farming in its local or even regional environment. Putting Marx's ideas into specific agrarian settings has enabled scholars to theorise a diversity of modern agrarian transformations in South Asia. See particularly Ashok Rudra, *Political Economy of Indian Agriculture* (Calcutta,

1992), 'Pre-Capitalist Modes of Production in Non-European Societies', *Journal of Peasant Studies* (15, 3, 1988, 373–94), 'Local Power and Farm-Level Decision Making', in Desai, Rudolph, and A. Rudra, *Agrarian Power and Agricultural Productivity in South Asia* (Berkeley, 1984, pp. 251–80), *Agrarian Relations in West Bengal: Results of Two Surveys* (Bombay, 1983), and (with Pranab Bardhan), *On the Interlinkage of Land, Labour, Credit Relations in Agriculture: An Analysis of Village Survey Data in East India* (Calcutta, 1978). Rudra's essay, 'Emergence of the Intelligentsia as a Ruling Class in India', *Economic and Political Weekly* (21 January 1989, 151–5), also put historians themselves into agrarian history by arguing that, 'In the last two decades, the intelligentsia has emerged as a member of the ruling class coalition in India, the other two classes being the big industrial capitalists and big land owners.'

My approach in this book is also influenced by Amartya K. Sen's *Poverty and Famine: An Essay in Entitlement and Deprivation* (New York, 1981) and by Joel Migdal, Atul Kohli, and Vivienne Shue, eds., *State Power and Social Forces: Domination and Transformation in the Third World* (Cambridge, 1994). See also Tim Mitchell's article, entitled 'The Limits of the State: Beyond Statist Approaches and Their Critics', *American Political Science Review* (85, 1, 1991, 77–96). Intersections of ecology, environmentalism, ethnography, politics, and history are stimulating the most promising scholarship today, and, in this respect, this book comes at the start of a new period of agrarian studies. For provocative research, see Anil Agarwal and others, *The Fight for Survival: People's Action for Environment* (New Delhi, 1987); Arun Agrawal and K. Sivaramakrishnan, eds., *Agrarian Environments: Resources, Representations, and Rule in Inda* (Durham: forthcoming); David Arnold and Ramachandra Guha, eds., *Nature, Culture, Imperialism: Essays on the Environmental History of South Asia* (Delhi, 1995); and Amita Baviskar, *In the Belly of the River: Tribal Conflicts over Development in the Narmada Valley* (Delhi, 1995).

Regions have their own approaches to the agrarian past. In the same way that southern France and the southern USA have inspired agrarian literature that reflects their own cultural heritage, so has Bengal. Although Tamil Nadu, Punjab, and Maharashtra are well served by agrarian historians, authors from the old Bengal Presidency have shown the most profound rural attachments going back to the early nineteenth century. Only Bengal has its own regional agrarian history in the *New Cambridge History*: Sugata Bose, *Peasant Labour and Colonial Capital: Rural Bengal since 1770* (Cambridge, 1993): whose bibliographical essay is the best guide to the literature. A new cluster of Bengal research is emerging around tribal and forest issues; see Mark Poffenberger, 'The Resurgence of Community Forest Management in the Jungle Mahals of West Bengal', in David Arnold and Ramachandra Guha, eds., *Nature, Culture, Imperialism* (Delhi, 1995, pp. 336–69), and K. Sivaramakrishnan, *Modern Forests: Statemaking and Environmental Change in Colonial Eastern India* (Delhi, 1999). The only substantial compilation of village studies for any region of South Asia is Shapan Adnan, *Annotation of*

Village Studies in Bangladesh and West Bengal: A Review of Socio-Economic Trends over 1942–88 (Kotbari Comilla, 1990).

Long-term history

On pastoralism, the most important reading is in the special issue of *Studies in History* (7, 2, 1991) edited by Shereen Ratnagar, and the most insightful monograph is Gunther-Dietz Sontheimer, *Pastoral Deities in Western India* (Delhi, 1989). On pre-history, see *Ecological Backgrounds of South Asian Prehistory*, edited by Kenneth A. R. Kennedy and Gregory L. Possehl (Ithaca, 1975); and Gregory L. Possehl, *Variation and Change in the Indus Civilization; A Study of Prehistoric Gujarat with Special Reference to the Post Urban Harappan civilization: A Recent Perspective* (New Delhi, 1993). Romila Thapar's *From Lineage to State* is the best general view of ancient transitions and M. S. Randhawa, *A History of Agriculture in India*, 4 volumes (Delhi, 1986), has details on farming from earliest times. For medieval history, first see Brajadulal Chattopadhyaya, *The Making of Early Medieval India* (New Delhi, 1995); B. P. Sahu, *Land System and Rural Society in Early India* (Delhi, 1997), and Herman Kulke, ed., *The State in India, 1000–1700* (Delhi, 1995); then see three important collections: R. Champakalakshmi and S. Gopal, eds., *Tradition, Dissent, and Ideology: Essays in Honour of Romila Thapar* (Delhi, 1996); Tapan Raychaudhuri and Irfan Habib, eds., *The Cambridge Economic History of India, Volume 1: c.1200–1750* (Cambridge, 1983); and Irfan Habib, ed., *Medieval India 1: Researches in the History of India, 1200–1750* (Delhi, 1992).

On the context of Eurasia, see Janet Abu-Lughod, *Before European Hegemony: the World System A.D. 1250–1350* (New York, 1989); K. N. Chaudhuri, *Asia Before Europe: Economy and Civilisation of the Indian Ocean from the Rise of Islam to 1750* (Cambridge, 1990) and *Trade and Civilization in the Indian Ocean: An Economic History from the Rise of Islam until 1750* (Cambridge, 1985); Richard M. Eaton, 'Islamic History as Global History', in Michael Adas, ed., *Islamic and European Expansion: The Forming of a Global Order* (Philadelphia, 1993, pp. 1–36); Andre Gunder Frank, 'The Centrality of Central Asia', *Studies in History* (8, 1, 1992, 43–98); and Andre Wink, *Al-Hind: The Making of the Indo-Islamic World* (Leiden, 1990).

Regional coverage is very uneven for medieval centuries. On Assam, see Amalendu Guha, *Medieval and Early Colonial Assam: Society, Policy, Economy* (Calcutta, 1991). For early Gujarat, see A. K. Majumdar, *Chaulukyas of Gujarat: A Survey of the History and Culture of Gujarat from the Middle of the 10th to the End of the 13th C.* (Bombay, 1956). On Nepal, see D. R. Regmi, *Medieval Nepal* (Calcutta, 1965–1966) and *Ancient Nepal* (Calcutta, 1969). On Orissa, see Hermann Kulke, *Kings and Cults: State Formation and Legitimation in India and Southeast Asia* (New Delhi, 1993), and Shishir Kumar Panda, *The State and Statecraft in Medieval Orissa under the Later Eastern Gangas (A.D. 1038–1434)* (Calcutta, 1995) and *Medieval*

Orissa: A Socio-economic Study (New Delhi, 1991). On Sri Lanka, see R. A. L. H. Gunawardana, *Robe and Plough* (Tucson, 1979) and W. I. Siriweera, *A Study of the Economic History of Pre-modern Sri Lanka* (New Delhi, 1994). For Bengal and the north-east, see especially Richard M. Eaton, *The Rise of Islam and the Bengal Frontier, 1204–1760* (Berkeley, 1994); Abdul Karim, *Social History of the Muslims in Bengal (down to A.D. 1538)* (Dacca, 1959); R. C. Majumdar, *Expansion of Aryan Culture in Eastern India* (Imphal, 1968); Barrie Morrison, *Political Centers and Cultural Regions in Early Bengal* (Tucson, 1970); M. A. Rahim, *Social and Cultural History of Bengal, 1201–1576* (Karachi, 1963); and M. Tarafdar, *Husain Shahi Bengal, 1494–1538 A.D.: A Socio-Political Study* (Dacca, 1965) and *Trade, Technology, and Society in Medieval Bengal* (Dhaka, 1995). For mountain surroundings, the key work is Surajit Sinha, ed., *Tribal Polities and State Systems in Precolonial Eastern and North Eastern India* (Calcutta, 1987), which also treats Rajputisation.

On Rajasthan, Rajputs, and Rajputisation, see B. D. Chattopadhyaya, 'Origin of the Rajputs: The Political, Economic and Social Processes in Early Medieval Rajasthan', *Indian Historical Review* (3, 1, July 1976; 59–82); Richard Fox, *Kin, Clan, Raja and Rule* (Berkeley, 1971); Satya Prakash Gupta, *The agrarian system of eastern Rajasthan, c.1650–c. 1750* (Delhi, 1986); D. Sharma, *Early Chauhan Dynasties: A Study of Chauhan Political History, Chauhan Political Institutions, and Life in the Chauhan Dominions, from 800 to 1316 A.D.* (Delhi, 1975); and Dilbagh Singh, *The State, Landlords, and Peasants: Rajasthan in the Eighteenth Century* (New Delhi, 1990). On Maratha territories, Sumit Guhaa's forthcoming book, entitled *Environment, Ethnicity and Politics in Western India 1350–1991* (Cambridge) will be the fullest monographic study, but Maratha records have sustained many good books. See especially D. K. Dhekane, *Agrarian System under Marathas* (Bombay, 1996); Hiroshi Fukazawa, *The Medieval Deccan: Peasants, Social Systems and States (1500–1700)* (New Delhi, 1991); Stewart Gordon, *The Marathas 1600–1818* (New Delhi, 1993) and *Marathas, Marauders, and State Formation in Eighteenth-century India* (Oxford, 1994); and Andre Wink, *Land and Sovereignty in India: Agrarian Society and Politics under the Eighteenth-century Maratha Svarajya* (Cambridge, 1986). For the Indo-Gangetic basin see Muhammad Taqi Amini, *The Agrarian System of Islam* (Delhi, 1991); Brajadulal Chattopadhyaya, *Aspects of Rural Settlements and Rural Society in Early-Medieval India* (Calcutta, 1990); Iqbal Husain, *The Ruhela Chieftaincies: The Rise and Fall of Ruhela Power in India in the Eighteenth Century* (Delhi, 1994); Sunanda Kar, *Agrarian System in Northern India from the Seventh to the Twelfth Century* (Bombay, 1990); Dirk H. A. Kolff, *Naukar, Rajput, and Sepoy: The Ethnohistory of the Military Labour Market of Hindustan, 1450–1850* (Cambridge, 1990); Harbans Mukhia, *Perspectives on Medieval History* (New Delhi, 1993); and M. C. Pradhan, *The Political System of the Jats of North India* (Bombay, 1966).

For the peninsula, important studies are A. Appadorai, *Economic Conditions in South India 1000–1500 A.D.* (New York, 1981); Nicholas B. Dirks,

The Hollow Crown: Ethnohistory of an Indian Kingdom (Ann Arbor, 1993); Kenneth R. Hall, *Trade and Statecraft in the Age of the Cholas* (New Delhi, 1980); B. S. L. Hanumantha Rao, *Socio-Cultural History of Ancient and Medieval Andhra* (Hyderabad, 1995); Noboru Karashima, *Towards a New Formation: South Indian Society under Vijayanagar Rule* (Delhi, 1992); M. G. S. Narayanan, *Reinterpretations of South Indian History* (Trivandrum, 1976); K. A. Nilakanta Sastri, *The Cholas* (Madras, 1955); K. S. Shivanna, *The Agrarian System of Karnataka (1336–1761)* (Mysore, 1992); K. G. Vasantha Madhava, *Western Karnataka, Its Agrarian Relations, 1500–1800 A.D.* (New Delhi, 1991); Kesavan Veluthat, *Brahman Settlements in Kerala: Historical Studies* (Calicut, 1978) and *The Political Structure of Early Medieval South India* (New Delhi, 1993); and R. Tirumalai, *Land Grants and Agrarian Reactions in Chola and Pandya Times* (Madras, 1987).

Temples have their own literature, mostly for the peninsula, with the notable exception of Hitesranjan Sanyal, 'Social Aspects of Temple Building in Bengal: 1600 to 1900 A.D.', *Man in India* (48, 1968, 202–224). For a general model of temple operations, see Carol A. Breckenridge and Arjun Appadurai, 'The South Indian Temple: Redistribution, Honor and Authority', *Contributions to Indian Sociology* (10, 2, 1977, 187–211). Important studies are in Burton Stein, ed., *South Indian Temples: An Analytical Reconsideration* (Delhi, 1978), whose methodology is carried forward by Cynthia Talbot in 'Temples, Donors, and Gifts: Patterns of Patronage in Thirteenth-Century South India', *Journal of Asian Studies* (50, 2, 1991, 308–40).

Early modern themes

The best compilation of essays on the Mughal era is Muzaffar Alam and Sanjay Subrahmanyam, *The Mughal State, 1526–1750* (Delhi, 1998). For imperial themes, see Stephen Blake, 'The Patrimonal-Bureaucratic Empire of the Mughals', *Journal of Asian Studies* (39, 1, 1979, 77–94; reprinted in Herman Kulke, ed., *The State in India, 1000–1700*, Delhi, 1995, pp. 278–304); Shireen Moosvi, *The Economy of the Mughal Empire, c.1595: A Statistical Study* (Delhi, 1987); Shireen Moosvi, ed. and trans., 'Aurangzeb's Farman to Rasidas on Problems of Revenue Administration, 1665', in Irfan Habib, ed., *Medieval India 1* (Delhi, 1992, pp. 198–208); Tapan Raychaudhuri, 'The Mughal Empire', in *The Cambridge Economic History of India, Volume I* (Cambridge, 1983, pp. 172–92); John F. Richards, *The Mughal Empire* (Cambridge, 1993); and John F. Richards, ed., *The Imperial Monetary System of Mughal India* (Delhi, 1987). On Mughal regions, Irfan Habib's *An Atlas of Mughal Empire* (Delhi, 1987) has the most comprehensive data. Ideas about the agrarian dynamics of Mughal decline are explored in Muzaffar Alam, *The Crisis of Empire in Mughal North India, Awadh and the Punjab, 1707–1748* (Delhi, 1986); Satish Chandra, *Medieval India: Society, the Jagirdari Crisis and the Village* (Delhi, 1982); Chetan Singh, *Region and Empire: Panjab in the Eighteenth Century* (Delhi, 1991); and Andre Wink, *Land and Sovereignty in India* (Cambridge, 1986).

M. Athar Ali gives a good account of the inland geography of early-modern South Asia in his 'Political Structures of the Islamic Orient in the Sixteenth and Seventeenth Centuries', in Ifran Habib, ed., *Medieval India 1*, (Delhi, 1992, pp. 129–40); and, for a wider view, see David Ludden, 'History outside Civilisation and the Mobility of Southern Asia', *South Asia* (17, 1, June 1994, 1–23). For an Asian perspective, see *Emporia, Commodities, and Entrepreneurs in Asian Maritime Trade, c.1400–1750*, edited by Roderich Ptak and Dietmar Rothermund (Stuttgart, 1991); and, for a global view, see Alan Smith, *Creating a World Economy: Merchant Capital, Colonialism and World Trade, 1400–1825* (Boulder, 1991).

The linkages between overseas traders and port city hinterlands imparted a distinctive historical identity to coastal regions. See especially Sinnappah Arasaratnam, *Merchants, Companies and Commerce on the Coromandel Coast, 1650–1740* (Delhi, 1986), and *Maritime Trade, Society and European Influence in South Asia, 1600–1800* (Brookfield, 1995); Ashin Das Gupta and M. N. Pearson, eds., *India and the Indian Ocean: 1500–1800* (Calcutta, 1987); Indu Banga, ed., *Ports and Their Hinterlands in India, 1700–1950* (New Delhi, 1992); and Sanjay Subrahmanyam, *The Political Economy of Commerce: Southern India 1500–1650* (Cambridge, 1990). On overland trade, see Stephen F. Dale, *Indian Merchants and Eurasian Trade, 1600–1750* (Cambridge, 1994).

The substance of networks that connected agrarian regions with the world economy are explored in B. R. Grover, 'An Integrated Pattern of Commercial Life in the Rural Society of North India during the Seventeenth and Eighteenth Centuries', *Proceedings of the 37th Session of Indian Historical Records Commission* (1966, vol. 37), reprinted in Sanjay Subrahmanyam, *Money and the Market in India 1100–1700* (Delhi, 1994, pp. 219–55); Frank Perlin, *Invisible City: Monetary, Administrative, and Popular Infrastructures in Asia and Europe, 1500–1900* (Aldershot, 1993), and *Unbroken Landscape: Commodity, Category, Sign and Identity: Their Production as Myth and Knowledge from 1500* (Aldershot, 1994); Prasannan Parthasarathy, 'Weavers, Merchants and States: The South Indian Textile Industry, 1680–1800', Ph.D. dissertation, Harvard University (1992); John R. Richards, ed., *Precious Metals in the Later Medieval and Early Modern Worlds* (Durham, 1983); Sanjay Subrahmanyam, ed., *Merchants, Markets, and the State in Early Modern India* (Delhi, 1990); and Sanjay Subrahmanyam and C. A. Bayly, 'Portfolio Capitalists and the Political Economy of Early Modern India', *Indian Economic and Social History Review* (25, 4, 1988, 401–24). Bernard S. Cohn provides a good framework for regional history in three essays, reprinted in *An Anthropologist among the Historians and Other Essays* (Delhi, 1990): 'Networks and Centres in the Integration of Indian Civilization' (pp. 78–87), 'Regions Subjective and Objective: Their Relation to the Study of Modern Indian History and Society' (pp. 100–36), and 'Political Systems in Eighteenth-Century India: The Benares Region (pp. 483–500).

Regional studies fill out the picture of early-modern conditions. In addition to studies of Rajasthan, cited above, see Indu Banga, *Agrarian System of the*

Sikhs: Late 18th and Early 19th Century (New Delhi, 1978); Philip Calkins, 'The Formation of a Regionally Oriented Ruling Group in Bengal, 1700–1740', *Journal of Asian Studies* (29, 4, 1970, 799–806); Satish Chandra, *The Eighteenth Century in India: Its Economy and the Role of the Marathas, the Jats, the Sikhs and the Afghans* (Calcutta, 1986); Kumkum Chatterjee, *Merchants, Politics and Society in Early Modern India: Bihar, 1733–1820* (Leiden, 1996); Sushil Chaudhuri, *Trade and Commercial Organization in Bengal, 1650–1720* (Calcutta, 1975); A. I. Chicherov, *Indian Economic Development in the 16th-18th Centuries: An Outline History of Crafts and Trade* (Moscow, 1971); M. H. Gopal, *Tipu Sultan's Mysore: an Economic Study* (Bombay, 1971); S. Gopal, *Commerce and Crafts in Gujarat, 16th and 17th Centuries; A Study in the Impact of European Expansion of Precapitalist Economy* (New Delhi, 1975); Karen Leonard, 'The "Great-Firm" Theory of the Decline of the Mughal Empire', in *Comparative Studies in Society and History* (21, 2, 1979, 151–67), and 'The Hyderabad Political System and Its Participants' *Journal of Asian Studies* (30, 3, 1971, 569–82); and Veena Sachdeva, *Polity and Economy of the Punjab During the Late Eighteenth Century* (New Delhi, 1993).

On pre-modern urbanism, I recommend that readers start with Brajadulal Chattopadhyaya, 'Urban Centers in Early Medieval India: An Overview', in Sabyasachi Bhattacharya and Romila Thapar, *Situating Indian History* (Delhi, 1986, pp. 8–33). For case studies, see Kenneth Ballhatchet and John Harrison, eds., *The City in South Asia: Premodern and Modern* (London, 1980); Indu Banga, ed., *The City in Indian History: Urban Demography, Society, and Politics* (New Delhi, 1991); Balkrishna Govind Gokhale, *Surat in the Seventeenth Century: A Study of Urban History of Pre-modern India* (London, 1979) and *Poona in the Eighteenth Century: An Urban History* (Delhi, 1988); and Hameeda Khatoon Naqvi, *Urban Centres and Industries in Upper India, 1556–1803* (Bombay, c.1968), and *Urbanisation and Urban Centres Under the Great Mughals, 1556–1707, An Essay in Interpretation* (Simla, c.1972).

My discussion of early-modern trends in this volume draws heavily on my own research on the peninsula published in *Peasant History in South India* (Princeton, 1985; Delhi, 1989); 'Archaic Formations of Agricultural Knowledge in South India', in Peter Robb, *Meanings of Agriculture* (New Delhi, 1996, pp. 35–70); 'Caste and Political Economy in Early-Modern South India: The Case of Tinnevelly District', in B. Stein and S. Subrahmanyam, *Institutions and Economic Change* (Delhi, 1997, pp. 105–33); 'Urbanism and Early Modernity in the Tirunelveli Region', *Bengal Past and Present* (114, 218–219, 1995, 9–40); 'Patriarchy and History in South Asia: Three Interpretive Experiments', *Calcutta Historical Journal* (17, 2, 1995, 1–18); 'Orientalist Empiricism and Transformations of Colonial Knowledge', in C. A. Breckenridge and P. van der Veer, *Orientalism and the Post-Colonial Predicament* (Philadelphia, 1993, pp. 250–78); 'India's Development Regime', in Dirks, *Colonialism and Culture*, pp. 247–87; 'World Economy and Village India, 1600–1900: Exploring the Agrarian History of Capitalism', in Sugata Bose, *South Asia and World Capitalism* (Delhi, 1990, pp. 159–77); 'Craft

Production in an Agrarian Economy, India, 1750–1900', in Michael Meister, ed., *Making Things in South Asia* (Philadelphia, 1989, pp. 103–13); 'Asiatic States and Agrarian Economies: Agrarian Commercialism in South India, 1700–1850', *Calcutta Historical Journal* (13, 1–2, 1989, 112–37); and 'Agrarian Commercialism in Eighteenth Century South India: Evidence from the 1823 Tirunelveli Census', *Indian Economic and Social History Review* (25, 4, 1988, 493–519), reprinted in Sanjay Subrahmanyam, *Merchants, Markets and the State in Early Modern India* (Delhi, 1990, pp. 215–41). I have also used 'The Economy of the Ceded Districts, 1800–1828', an unpublished manuscript by Sourindranath Roy compiled from documents in the National Archives, New Delhi.

Modern issues

For a broad view of economic history, see B. R. Tomlinson, *The Economy of Modern India, 1860–1970* (Cambridge, 1993), a compact analysis and excellent guide to the literature. For a wide range of specialised essays, see Dharma Kumar, ed., *The Cambridge Economic History of India, Volume 2* (New Delhi, 1983), and the issue of *Modern Asian Studies* (19, 13, 1985) on the *Cambridge Economic History*. Sumit Guha, *Growth, Stagnation, or Decline?* (Delhi, 1992) presents one important scholarly debate, with classic reprints; for other debates, see Neil Charlesworth, *British Rule and the Indian Economy, 1800–1914* (London, 1982). There is no book that compares long-term regional trends, despite the brilliant, pioneering work by Amiya Kumar Bagchi and Eric Stokes published in *Bengal Past and Present* (95, 1, 1976): 'Reflections on Patterns of Regional Growth in India during the Period of British Rule' (pp. 247–89) and 'Dynamism and Enervation in North Indian Agriculture: The Historical Dimension' (pp. 227–39), which is reprinted in David Ludden, *Agricultural Production and Indian History* (Delhi, 1994, pp. 36–53). Studies of economic development are pushing in this comparative direction, however; see Ambica Ghosh, *Emerging Capitalism in Indian Agriculture: The Historical Roots of Its Uneven Development* (New Delhi, 1988); Manjit Singh, *Uneven Development in Agriculture and Labour Migration: A Case of Bihar and Punjab* (Shimla, 1995); and Surendra Singh, *Agricultural Development in India: A Regional Analysis* (Shillong, 1994).

Comparative studies of agrarian change are still thwarted by the absence of full economic histories for all the regions. There is none for Uttar Pradesh, and most regions, even Punjab, are not fully covered. Two good books on UP focus on a small set of relevant issues: Ian Stone, *Canal Irrigation in British India: Perspectives on Technological Change in a Peasant Society* (Cambridge, 1984); and Elizabeth Whitcombe, *Agrarian Conditions in Northern India: The United Provinces under British Rule, 1860–1900 (v. 1)* (Berkeley, 1972). For Madhya Pradesh, the most useful research is by Crispin Bates, beginning with his 1984 Cambridge dissertation, entitled 'Regional Dependence and Rural Development in Central India, 1820–1930', and his two articles, 'Class and Economic Change in Central India: The Narmada Valley 1820–1930', in

Clive Dewey, ed., *Arrested Development in India: The Historical Dimension*, (Riverdale, 1988, pp. 241–82), and 'Regional Dependence and Rural Development in Central India: The Pivotal Role of Migrant Labour', *Modern Asian Studies* (19, 3, 1985, 573–92). On Bihar, Arvind N. Das makes forceful arguments in *Agrarian Unrest and Socio-economic Change in Bihar, 1900–1980* (New Delhi, 1983), *The Republic of Bihar* (New Delhi, 1992), and *The State of Bihar: An Economic History without Footnotes* (Amsterdam, 1992). There are good specialised studies of Sri Lanka: Jean Grossholtz, *Forging Capitalist Patriarchy: The Economic and Social Transformation of Feudal Sri Lanka and Its Impact on Women* (Durham, 1984); and Asoka Bandarage, *Colonialism in Sri Lanka: The Political Economy of the Kandyan Highlands, 1833–1886* (Berlin, 1983). For Nepal, Mahesh Chandra Regmi's two books are fundamental: *Thatched Huts and Stucco Palaces: Peasants and Landlords in 19th-century Nepal* (New Delhi, 1978) and *An Economic History of Nepal, 1846–1901* (Varanasi, 1988). For Gujarat, Gita Bajpai, *Agrarian Urban Economy and Social Change: The Socio-Economic Profile of Select Districts of Gujarat, 1850–1900* (Delhi, 1989) and Marcia F. Frost, 'Population Growth and Agrarian Change in British Gujarat, Kaira District, 1802–1858', Ph.D. dissertation, University of Pennsylvania (1995), are richly detailed, but the lack of a new general history makes me turn to M. Desai, *The Rural Economy of Gujerat* (Bombay, 1949). On nineteenth-century Orissa, see J. K. Samal, *Agrarian History of Orissa under the British Rule* (Delhi, 1993) and Nabin Kumar Jit, *The Agrarian Life and Economy of Orissa: A Survey, 1833–1897* (Calcutta, 1984). The Bombay Deccan is well covered by Sumit Guha, *The Agrarian Economy of the Bombay Deccan, 1818–1941* (Delhi, 1985). M. Mufakharul Islam's new study of Punjab is meticulous: *Irrigation, Agriculture, and the Raj: Punjab, 1887–1947* (Delhi, 1997); and Imran Ali, *The Punjab under Imperialism, 1885–1947* (Princeton, 1988) covers a somewhat wider range of issues. For Bengal, Sugata Bose's *Agrarian Bengal: Economy, Social Structure, and Politics* (Cambridge, 1986) is the fullest monograph and his *Peasant Labour and Colonial Capital* is the best overview and guide to the literature. The new *History of Bangladesh 1704–1971, Volume Two, Economic History*, edited by Sirajul Islam (Dhaka, 1997) will perhaps stimulate other interdisciplinary collections that focus on specific regions. The model regional monograph remains Christopher John Baker's *An Indian Rural Economy: The Tamilnad Countryside, 1880–1955* (Oxford and Delhi, 1984). For the earlier period in Tamil Nadu, see Arun Bandopadhyay, *The Agrarian Economy of Tamilnadu, 1820–1855* (Calcutta, 1992).

Historians have so far provided the best empirical context for local studies in Bengal, Bihar, the Deccan, Gujarat, Punjab, Tamil Nadu, and Uttar Pradesh. A few monographs have *both* a local *and* a long-term agenda within a broadly comparative, regional perspective: M. Atchi Reddy, *Lands and Tenants in South India: A Study of Nellore District, 1850–1990* (Delhi, 1996); Arvind N. Das, *Changel: The Biography of A Village* (New Delhi, 1996); Tom Kessinger, *Vilyatpur 1848–1968: Social and Economic Change in a*

North Indian Village (Berkeley, 1974); David Ludden, *Peasant History* (Princeton, 1985; Delhi, 1989); and M. S. S. Pandian, *The Political Economy of Agrarian Change: Nanchilnadu, 1880–1939* (New Delhi, 1990). The local characteristics of agrarian regions are emerging primarily from an accumulation of regional studies that concern politics, economy, society, and culture, but tend to obsess on colonialism and nationality; this weighs the literature most heavily toward the study of agrarian administration, development, and politics. Histories of agrarian *social* and *cultural* change have emerged substantially from studies of social movements, for which the best summaries are Sumit Sarkar, *Modern India 1885–1947* (Delhi, 1983) and G. Aloysius, *Nationalism without a Nation in India* (Delhi, 1997). One recent volume has compiled local studies across regions – Peter Robb, Kaoru Sugihara, and Haruka Yanagisawa, eds., *Local Agrarian Societies in Colonial India: Japanese Perspectives* (Richmond, Surrey, 1997) – but focused, thematic studies hold the most potential for comparative history. One compelling effort is Alice W. Clark, 'Analysing the Reproduction of Human Beings and Social Formations, with Regional Examples over the Last Century', in Alice W. Clark, ed., *Gender and Political Economy* (Delhi, 1993, pp. 113–45).

Rebellion and resistance invite cross-regional comparison and provide mountains of evidence on the character of agrarian polities; conversely, geographical, temporal, and institutional contexts condition all agrarian upheaval. Telangana is a glaring example of regional particularity. For its administration, see S. Bhanumathi Ranga Rao, *Land Revenue Administration in the Nizams' Dominions, 1853–1948* (Hyderabad, 1992). The first phase of its revolutionary history began as the first radical phase of peasant politics came to end in British India; see Carolyn M. Elliott, 'Decline of a Patrimonial Regime: The Telangana Rebellion in India, 1946–51', *Journal of Asian Studies* (34, 1, 1974, 27–47); Barry Pavier, *The Telangana Movement 1944–1951* (Delhi, 1981); and I. Thirumalai, 'Peasant Class Assertions in Nalgonda and Warangal Districts of Telangana, 1930–1946', *Indian Economic and Social History Review* (31, 2, 1994, 217–38). The discourse and experience of revolution became uniquely embedded in its agrarian culture; see Devulapalli Venkateswara Rao, *Telangana Armed Struggle and the Path of Indian Revolution: A Critique of 'Telangana People's Struggle and Its Lessons' Written by P. Sundarayya and of 'Postscript' to the Book 'The Great Heroic Telangana Struggle' Written by Chandra Pulla Reddy* (Hyderabad, 1982); Arutla Ramachandra Reddy, *Telangana Struggle: Memoirs* (New Delhi, 1984); and Vasantha Kannabiran et al., *We Were Making History: Life Stories of Women in the Telangana People's Struggle* (London, 1989).

Eric Stokes (*The Peasant and the Raj*, Cambridge, 1978) stressed that rebelliousness needs to be explained in its time and place, and many studies locate agrarian resistance within regional power structures: for instance, Conrad Wood, *The Moplah Rebellion and Its Genesis* (New Delhi, 1987); Jagdish Chandra Jha, *The Bhumji Revolt, 1832–3: Ganga Narain's Langama or Turmoil* (Delhi, 1967); and Kapil Kumar, *Peasants in Revolt, Tenants, Landlords, Congress and the Raj in Oudh, 1886–1922* (New Delhi, 1984).

But the historical meanings of 'revolt', 'revolution', and 'resistance' also merit attention; on this, see T. J. Byres, *Charan Singh, 1902–87, An Assessment* (Patna, 1988) and Charan Singh, *Agrarian Revolution in Uttar Pradesh* (Allahabad, 1957), for revolution from above; and Gail Omvedt, *Reinventing Revolution: New Social Movements and the Socialist Tradition in India* (Armonk, 1993) for popular redefinitions.

Definitions destabilise across regions, periods, and social contexts; and comparisons yield empirical patterns that challenge theory. Gujarat, for instance, could not be more different from Telangana. David Hardiman has explored Gujarati resistance in his *Peasant Nationalists of Gujarat: Kheda District, 1917–1934* (Delhi, 1981), *The Coming of the Devi: Adivasi Assertion in Western India* (Delhi, 1987), and *Feeding the Baniya: Peasants and Usurers in Western India* (Delhi, 1996). In this land without zamindars, the term 'peasant' covers a spectrum from very rich commercial farmers to the poorest family farmers, near-landless workers, and tribal communities, and 'revolt' could be said to have many distinctively Gujarati meanings in practice. On the social and economic background of Gandhian politics, see Crispin Bates, 'The Nature of Social Change in Rural Gujarat: The Kheda District, 1818–1918', *Modern Asian Studies* (15, 4, 1981, 415–54), and Gita Bajpai, *Agrarian Urban Economy and Social Change* (Delhi, 1989). On farmers' politics, see E. J. M. Epstein, *The Earthy Soil: Bombay Peasants and the Indian Nationalist Movement, 1919–1947* (Oxford, 1988); on other leadership, see Ghanshyam Shah, *Politics of Scheduled Cases and Tribes. Adivasi and Harijan Leaders of Gujarat* (Bombay, 1975). On the premier agrarian leader of the region, Sardar Patel, see *The Collected Works of Sardar Vallabhbhai Patel*, edited by P. N. Chopra (Delhi, 1990).

Colonialism is the definitive institutional context of peasant life for many historians – see especially Ranajit Guha, *Dominance without Hegemony: History and Power in Colonial India* (Cambridge, 1997) – but it is obviously only part of the picture. Subalterns work within many institutions that set the terms of their struggles, and differences among local settings are significant. In this book, I focus on regional patterns, on the contrast between intensive agriculture and tribal cultivation, and on institutions that define *modern* subalterns in zamindari and ryotwari terms. Legal institutions distinguish tenant struggles from tribal revolts, and they also help to explain differences between rebellion in Telangana and Gujarat (or Punjab and Bihar). Landlordism has been more particularistic, culturally complex, and changeable than I indicate here. See C. J. Baker, 'Tamil Nadu Estates in the Twentieth Century', *Indian Economic and Social History Review* (8, 1, 1976, 1–44); Nicholas B. Dirks, *The Hollow Crown* (Ann Arbor, 1993); Stephen Henningham, *A Great Estate and Its Landlords in Colonial India: Darbhanga, 1860–1942* (New Delhi, 1990); T. R. Metcalf, *Land, Landlords and the British Raj: Northern India in the Nineteenth Century* (Berkeley, 1979); Nilmani Mukherjee, *A Bengal Zamindar: Jaykrishna Mukherjee of Uttarpara and His Times, 1808–1888* (Calcutta, 1975); Pamela G. Price, *Kingship and Political Practice in Colonial India* (Cambridge, 1996); N. G. Ranga, *Economic*

Conditions of Zamindari Ryots (Dezwada, 1933); D. Subramanyam Reddy, *Agrarian Relations and Peasant in Modern Andhra: A Study of Kalahasti Zamindari* (Delhi, 1990); P. D. Reeves, *Landlords and Governments in Uttar Pradesh: A Study of Their Relations until Zamindari Abolition* (Oxford, 1991); Richard G. Fox, *From Zamindar to Ballot Box* (Ithaca, 1969); and Anand A. Yang, *The Limited Raj: Agrarian Relations in Colonial India, Saran District, 1793–1920* (Berkeley, 1989).

Local power relations differed significantly even among sites of sugar production, which were all marked by strict subordination of farming to capital and of labour to management. In Maharashtra, farmers owned land and expanded their control of investment. In eastern UP, they could not. See Donald W. Attwood, *Raising Cane: The Political Economy of Sugar in Western India* (Boulder, 1992) and Shahid Amin, *Sugarcane and Sugar in Gorakhpur: An Inquiry into Peasant Production for Capitalist Enterprise in Colonial India* (Delhi, 1984).

How does colonial capitalism transform agrarian societies? This remains a critical question for comparative history. On a world scale, it may be that, in the Americas, investors could use the state to remake plantation societies in the interest of world capitalism – see Madhavi Kale, *Fragments of Empire: Capital, Slavery, and Indian Indentured Labour in the British Caribbean* (Philadelphia, 1998) – but, in Asia, capital acquired commodities for world markets without providing Europeans much direct power in agrarian localities. Capitalism and colonialism, like modernity and nationality, varied substantially across agrarian environments; and by sorting out their historical patterns we can better appreciate their local substance and global reach. The distinctiveness of hills, forests, and tribal environments is now receiving more attention. See Tarasankar Banerjee, ed., *Changing Land Systems and Tribals in Eastern India in the Modern Period: Report of a Seminar Held at Santiniketan, 6–7 March 1986* (Calcutta, 1989); Ramachandra Guha, *The Unquiet Woods: Ecological Change and Peasant Resistance in the Himalaya* (Delhi, 1989); J. C. Jha, *The Indian National Congress and the Tribals, 1885–1985* (New Delhi, 1985); Govind Ballabh Pant, *The Forest Problem in Kumaon: Forest Problems and National Uprising in the Himalayan Region (With a Commentary by Ajay S. Rawat)* (Nainital, 1985); Biswamoy Pati, *Resisting Domination: Peasants, Tribals and the National Movement in Orissa, 1920–1950* (Delhi, 1993); Archana Prasad, 'Forests and Subsistence in Colonial India: A Study of the Central Provinces, 1830–1945', Ph.D. dissertation, Centre for Historical Studies, Jawaharlal Nehru University (1994); and Mahesh Rangarajan, *Fencing the Forest: Conservation and Ecological Change in India's Central Provinces, 1860–1914* (Delhi, 1996). On Santals, see Suchibrata Sen, *The Santals of Jungle Mahals: An Agrarian History, 1793–1861* (Calcutta, 1984) and also P. K. Bhowmick, *Dynamics of tribal development* (New Delhi, 1993); A. B. Chaudhuri, *State Formation among Tribals: A Quest for Santal Identity* (New Delhi, 1993); and B. K. Sharma, *Habitat, Economy & Society of Tribal Core: A Case Study of Damin-I-Koh* (New Delhi, 1992). On Bastar, see Nandini Sundar, *Subal-*

terns and Sovereigns: An Anthropological History of Bastar, 1854–1996 (Delhi, 1997).

A number of books which I have not yet cited document the modern history of agrarian polities. On Assam, see Ajeya Sarkar, *Regionalism, State and the Emerging Political Pattern in India* (Calcutta, 1990) and Amalendu Guha, *Planter Raj to Swaraj: Freedom Movement and Electoral Politics in Assam, 1826–1947* (New Delhi, 1977). On Bangladesh, see A. F. Salahuddin Ahmed, *Bengali Nationalism and the Emergence of Bangladesh* (Dhaka, 1994); James Boyce, *Agrarian Impasse in Bengal: Institutional Contraints to Technological Change* (New York, 1987); Haroon-or-Rashid, *The Foreshadowing of Bangladesh* (Dhaka, 1987); Tajul ul-Islam Hashmi, *Peasant Utopia: The Communalization of Class Politics in East Bengal, 1920–1947* (Dhaka, 1994); Sirajul Islam, *Bangladesh District Records* (Dacca, 1978) and *Rural History of Bangladesh: A Source Study* (Dacca, 1977); Atiur Rahman, *Peasants and Classes: A Study in Differentiation in Bangladesh* (London, 1986); and Kirsten Westergaard, *State and Rural Society in Bangladesh: A Study in Relationships* (London, 1985). On greater Bengal, see Partha Chatterjee, *Bengal 1920–1947: The Land Question* (Calcutta, 1984); Joya Chatterji, *Bengal Divided: Hindu Communalism and Partition, 1932–47* (Cambridge, 1995); Ranajit Das Gupta, *Economy, Society and Politics in Bengal: Jalpaiguri 1869–1947* (Delhi, 1992); M. Mufakharul Islam, *Agricultural Development in Bengal, 1920–1947: A Quantitative Study* (Cambridge, 1978); Sirajul Islam, *Rent and Raiyat; Society and Economy of Eastern Bengal; 1859–1928* (Dhaka, 1989); Chitta Panda, *The Decline of the Bengal Zamindars: Mindapore, 1870–1920* (Delhi, 1997); Ratnalekha Ray, *Change in Bengal Agrarian Society, 1760–1850* (New Delhi, 1979); Willem van Schendel, *Three Deltas: Accumulation and Poverty in Rural Burma, Bengal, and South India* (New Delhi, 1991); Willem van Schendel and Aminul Haque Faraizi, *Rural Labourers in Bengal, 1880–1980* (Rotterdam, 1984); and Sunil Kumar Sen, *Agrarian Struggle in Bengal, 1946–7* (New Delhi, 1972).

On Bihar, see Francine R. Frankel, 'Caste, Land and Dominance in Bihar: Breakdown of the Brahmanical Social Order', in Francine R. Frankel and M. S. A. Rao, *Dominance and State Power in Modern India* (Delhi, 1989, vol. 1, pp. 46–133); Bindeshwar Ram, *Land and Society in India: Agrarian Relations in Colonial North Bihar* (Delhi, 1998); Peter Robb, *Evolution of British Policy towards Indian Politics 1880–1920: Essays on Colonial Attitudes, Imperial Strategies, and Bihar* (Delhi, 1992).

On Gujarat, Maharashtra, and the Bombay Deccan, see Neil Charlesworth, *Peasants and Imperial Rule: Agriculture and Agrarian Society in the Bombay Presidency, 1850–1935* (Cambridge, 1985); Shirin Mehta, *The Peasantry and Nationalism. A Study of the Bardoli Satyagraha* (New Delhi, 1984); M. V. Nadkarni, *Farmers' Movements in India* (New Delhi, 1987); Anthony Carter, *Elite Politics in Rural India: Political Stratification and Political Alliance in Western Maharashtra* (Cambridge, 1974); Ravinder Kumar, *Western India in the Nineteenth Century: A Study of the Social History of Maharashtra* (London, 1968); Michelle Burge McAlpin, *Subject to Famine: Food Crisis and*

Economic Change in Western India, 1860–1920 (Princeton, 1983); and Rosalind O'Hanlon, *Caste, Conflict and Ideology: Mahatma Jotirao Phule and Low-Caste Protest in Western India* (Cambridge, 1985).

On Punjab, see Himadri Banerjee, *Agrarian Society of the Punjab, 1849–1901* (New Delhi, 1982); Richard G. Fox, *Lions of the Punjab: Culture in the Making* (Berkeley, 1985); and Richard Saumarez Smith, *Rule by Records: Land Registration and Village Custom in Early British Panjab* (Delhi, 1996).

On Uttar Pradesh and Haryana, see Zoya Hasan, *Dominance and Mobilisation: Rural Politics in Western Uttar Pradesh 1930–1980* (New Delhi, 1989); Walter C. Neale, *Economic Change in North India: Land Tenure and Reform in the United Provinces, 1800–1955* (New Haven, 1962); Gyanendra Pandey, *The Ascendancy of the Congress in Uttar Pradesh, 1926–1934: A Study of Imperfect Mobilization* (Delhi, 1978); Utsa Patnaik, *Peasant Class Differentiation: A Study in Method with Reference to Haryana* (Delhi, 1987); Asiya Siddiqi, *Agrarian Change in a North Indian State: Uttar Pradesh, 1819–1833* (Delhi, 1973); Majid Hayat Siddiqi, *Agrarian Unrest in North India: The United Provinces, 1918–1922* (New Delhi, 1978); and Jagpal Singh, *Captalism and Dependence: Agrarian Politics in Western Uttar Pradesh, 1951–1991* (Delhi, 1992).

On southern India, see David Arnold, *The Congress in Tamil Nad: Nationalist Politics in South India 1919–1937* (Delhi, 1977); B. H. Farmer, ed., *Green Revolution? Technology and Change in Rice-Growing Areas of Tamil Nadu and Sri Lanka* (London, 1977); John Harriss, *Capitalism and Peasant Farming: Agrarian Structure and Ideology in Northern Tamil Nadu* (Delhi, 1982); Barbara Harriss-White, *A Political Economy of Agricultural Markets in South India: Masters of the Countryside* (New Delhi, 1996); Eugene F. Irschick, *Politics and Social Conflict in South India: The Non-Brahman Movement and Tamil Separatism, 1916–1929* (Berkeley, 1969) and *Dialogue and History: Constructing South India, 1795–1895* (Berkeley, 1994); Robin Jeffery, *The Decline of Nayar Dominance: Society and Politics in Travancore 1847–1930* (London, 1976); Susan Lewandowski, *Migration and Ethnicity in Urban India: Migration in to Madras, 1870–1970* (Delhi, 1981); Joan P. Mencher, *Agriculture and Social Structure in Tamil Nadu* (Durham, 1978); J. P. Pandian, *Caste, Nationalism and Ethnicity: An Interpretation of Tamil Cultural History and Social Order* (Bombay, 1987); Chitra Sivakumar and S. S. Sivakumar, *Peasants and Nabobs: Agrarian Radicalism in Late Eighteenth Century Tamil Country* (Delhi, 1993); T. C. Varghese, *Agrarian Change and Economic Consequences: Land Tenures in Kerala, 1850–1960* (Bombay, 1970); and David Washbrook, *The Emergence of Provincial Politics: The Madras Presidency, 1870–1920* (Cambridge, 1976) and 'Caste, Class and Dominance in Modern Tamil Nadu', in Francine R. Frankel and M. S. A. Rao, *Dominance and State Power in Modern India* (Delhi, 1989, vol. 1, pp. 204–64).

INDEX

THE NEW CAMBRIDGE HISTORY OF INDIA

I The Mughals and Their Contemporaries

II Indian States and the Transition to Colonialism

III The Indian Empire and the Beginnings of Modern Society

IV The Evolution of Contemporary South Asia

* Already published   + Available in paperback

STEP BY STEP

THE LIFE IN MY JOURNEYS

SIMON REEVE

LARGE
PRINT

First published in Great Britain 2018
by
Hodder & Stoughton
an Hachette UK company

First Isis Edition
published 2019
by arrangement with
Hodder & Stoughton
an Hachette UK company

The moral right of the author has been asserted

A catalogue record for this book is available
from the British Library.

ISBN 978–1–78541–719–1 (hb)
ISBN 978–1–78541–725–2 (pb)

Published by
F. A. Thorpe (Publishing)
Anstey, Leicestershire

Set by Words & Graphics Ltd.
Anstey, Leicestershire
Printed and bound in Great Britain by
T. J. International Ltd., Padstow, Cornwall

This book is printed on acid-free paper

For Jake

Contents

CHAPTER
ONE

The A-Team

Everything felt wrong. I was damp with sweat, my head was thumping, my limbs were aching as if I'd run a hard race, and I was lying face down on a bed in the early hours of the morning wearing my clothes and muddy boots. I opened my eyes. The room began to spin. I turned on my side and an overpowering sense of nausea welled within me. I staggered to my feet and half-fell against the wall of the hotel bedroom, my limbs now shaking and the room turning over and over in my head. I knew this was serious. Not a hangover, not the flu, not food poisoning, but much worse.

It was 2006, and I was in Gabon, West Africa, filming *Equator*, my first major television series and biggest adventure. For most people, the equator is just an imaginary line running for 25,000 miles around the middle of the world. But the equator is at the heart of the tropics, home to both the richest collection of wildlife on the planet and the greatest concentration of human suffering. Following the line would take me to utter extremes and parts of the world rarely seen on television. The journey was supposed to transform my life. Not end it.

This leg of my series had started on a beach on the coast of Gabon in the middle of nowhere, bang on zero degrees latitude. I had followed the imaginary line across Gabon to the remote east of the country, the wild forest home of impoverished communities and diseased apes suffering from Ebola, a desperate, eyeball-bleeding contagion that sounds like the stuff of science fiction. Now my limbs were aching, shaking and burning. I was feverish and sick. I knew I had to make it to the bathroom before my insides came tumbling out.

With one hand pressed to the wall I fixed my gaze on the outline of the bathroom door and tried to take a step. My feet wouldn't move. I was requesting movement, but nothing was happening. Deep within my brain I was processing my thoughts, but other physical controls were shutting down. The inside of my mouth was burning, and the thudding in my temple was reaching a crescendo. I knew the only way to create momentum to reach the bathroom was to push off from the wall like a rock climber.

I swayed back and forth, fell against the bathroom door, collapsed onto my knees in front of the bath and vomited dramatically. Through the haze of sickness, the dim light and my spinning brain, my mind was still able to flash a stark warning signal. There was blood in my vomit. My first thought was a moment of complete clarity: it must be Ebola. Ye gods. I was screwed. Then I passed out.

It was hours before I came to, slumped on mouldy lino on the bathroom floor. I was shaking, my temperature was rising, and I was scared. But I was still alive. I remember thinking that if I hadn't died, then I had to get up, and I had to carry on. Not make some noise, or call for help, or something sensible like that. Not drag myself back to my bags and my phone and try to ring one of my colleagues or the BBC safety number for a doctor. But get off the floor, rinse out the bloody bath, and get downstairs to see my colleagues, and carry on with my journey. We were supposed to be leaving little-known Gabon and heading east, flying across the neighbouring country, Congo-Brazzaville, and on into the vast Democratic Republic of Congo (DRC). There was an outbreak of Ebola, a viral haemorrhagic fever, on and around the equator in Congo-Brazzaville. There is no cure and a mortality rate of up to 90 per cent. Some victims bleed from every orifice until they die. It is horrific, terrifying, and international medical teams were being attacked by desperate villagers who accused them of spreading the disease. I had been keen to head along the equator into Congo-Brazzaville, but the BBC said it was too dangerous. So instead we were supposed to board a small plane that would leapfrog the insanely dangerous zone, and deliver us into the DRC, scene of perhaps the most violent conflict on the planet since the Second World War. So still not exactly safe, and lacking in advanced medical facilities to treat anyone suffering from Ebola.

Lying there on the bathroom floor, I half-knew all this. I should have called for a doctor. But this was supposed to be the beginning of a whole new chapter for me in television. The few series I had made for the

3

BBC before *Equator* had been fascinating, life-changing and mind-altering, but they had been budget trips shown in the so-called graveyard shift after *Newsnight*, when people were switching on the telly after coming home from the pub. *Equator* had been a bigger idea, a more ambitious proposition, as TV people say, and we had more resources, planning time and dedicated, exceptional cameramen. The end result was supposed to be shown in a primetime slot on BBC Two.

I couldn't let everyone down. The planning for our trip across the DRC alone had taken weeks. And I was excited about the journey. Following the equator around the world — who gets to do that? It was an adventure money could not buy, with the clear purpose of exploring the centre of the tropics, the most beautiful and benighted region on the planet. I might have Ebola, but I was still alive. If I was still alive I wanted to continue. I tried pushing myself away from the tub so I could get to my feet, but my hands wouldn't work, let alone my feet. My mind was swimming in and out of consciousness. I could feel my temperature going through the roof.

With a monumental effort I managed to get up, but my head felt like it was on a spin cycle. Using walls, handles and banisters to remain upright, I dragged my bag out of my room and across the corridor to an ancient lift. When the doors opened I started dry-retching, to the alarm of a couple already inside. My eyes caught theirs and I glimpsed horror, then fear. Everyone in Gabon knew what was happening in

4

Congo-Brazzaville. People were terrified of Ebola. They rushed out of the lift as I stumbled inside. How selfish of me to think only of my journey, or my programmes. If I was a walking Ebola petri dish I should have stayed in my room. Instead I spilled into the hotel lobby, where Sophie and Sam, director and cameraman on this leg of the *Equator* series, were waiting with our Gabonese guide Linel. They saw me sliding along the wall, pulling my bag along the floor, and I could see their mouths drop. I wasn't sweating so much as dripping. Every millimetre of skin was alive with perspiration and yet I was shivering.

"My God, Simon." It was Sam who spoke first. "You look like death."

"Bad night," I muttered. "I was sick in the bath and I slept on the floor. I didn't have the strength to climb into bed." I was swaying back and forth, nothing in my legs but jelly. "I'll be fine. What time is the flight?"

Sophie took a look at me then exchanged a glance with Sam. Taking my arm, she told me the only place I was going was back to bed. By this time I was shivering so badly my teeth were chattering. I was on the point of collapsing again, but the three of them managed to half-carry, half-drag me back upstairs to my room.

"It's Ebola, isn't it?" I mumbled. "You shouldn't be touching me. You need to get me into quarantine."

We had been travelling in Gabon for just over a week. Before starting research for the programme I knew next to nothing about the place, other than it was small, formerly French, and blessed — or cursed — with massive oil reserves. But the BBC team had found me an excellent guide. Linel was a local teacher with a patient but enthusiastic air.

I felt a real thrill filming the opening scenes for the series. We had hired a boat in Libreville, the capital of Gabon, and chugged down the coast. Using a GPS unit and a handful of satellites orbiting the Earth, we found a beautiful and unspoilt beach of pristine sand and palm trees. Yet it was unremarkable. There was no plaque, sign, beach bar or monument marking the point. But it was the stretch of land where the equator made landfall in Africa. It was the middle of the world.

The idea behind the series was simple. I was going to follow or track the equator line through a unique region of the planet, and countries suffering from war, poverty, disease, deforestation and corruption. Following the line would force us to go to remoter areas, to places rarely visited by outsiders, let alone TV crews.

Beyond Gabon months of travel were supposed to take me across Africa to Uganda and Kenya and on to the lawless border with chaotic Somalia. Indonesia, the Galapagos, Colombia's interminable civil war and the vast Amazon all beckoned ahead.

We were expecting endless problems while following the equator. Even chugging to the start point had been eventful. Initially the captain ignored the plan we had agreed and tried to fob us off with a sightseeing trip into a huge lagoon.

"Perhaps we can get to the sea and the line that way," he said, gesturing vaguely towards a peninsula that clearly offered no through-route. "Isn't this good enough for you?"

He only agreed to turn back and out to sea when we at first politely and then sternly insisted we wanted to brave the ocean. Checks on the fuel reserves and life jackets he had assured us were stowed in bench seats revealed he had neither. Two hours were lost fuelling and finding jackets. Linel tied his tight. So did the two crewmen on the boat. None of them could swim, they much later admitted. We headed out to sea towards the zero degrees. The sea was certainly choppy, but the speed at which the boat started to take on quantities of water surprised me. I have a bad reputation among my colleagues for being a bit of a Jonah. Half the boats I travel in while filming seem to nearly sink. By the time we reached the equator we were bailing furiously using buckets and our own water bottles, and I was relieved to be first off the front, leaping into the water, reaching dry land and officially starting my journey. There was no bunting (there is never any bunting), but it was a moment to savour.

Tides and the wind were in our favour on the return journey, and we were soon out exploring Libreville, which boasts casinos, musty hotels, miles of sandy beaches and a handful of handsome seafront buildings with a passing resemblance to those of South Beach. Prior to independence in 1960, Gabon had been ruled from Paris as one of four territories known as French Equatorial Africa. The continuing presence of French soldiers had helped keep Gabon relatively stable, while oil had made a few well-connected locals extremely rich. At one point in the 1980s Gabon had the highest per capita consumption of champagne in the world.

Everywhere I looked the face of President Omar Bongo beamed out from billboards and posters. In power since 1967, he was the longest-serving leader in Africa, and globally second only to Fidel Castro. Critics would point out that perhaps Bongo had not spent Gabon's vast oil revenues entirely wisely or fairly. But he seemed to wield absolute power from a vast and hideous presidential palace. Linel told us nervously that filming it might cause problems, particularly for him, so instead we turned the camera in the opposite direction and I just made sarcastic comments about the leader and the architecture.

Later that day as the team were filming elsewhere in the city, I was wandering the seafront with Linel when a phalanx of motorcycle outriders raced along the main road closing side streets. Five minutes later the President came down the road in a huge convoy of armoured cars, limos, army trucks and an ambulance as medical back-up. I counted forty-five vehicles. Even the US President manages with less. A French attack helicopter swooped low overhead, machine-gunners at the open doors, providing security and a clear sign the autocratic leader still had the backing of Paris. Gallic influence was pervasive in the former French colony. Restaurants were full of oil industry ex-pats drooling over young locals, while pricey supermarkets were stuffed with French wine and *foie gras*.

Linel told me Libreville was one of the most expensive cities to live anywhere in Africa. He took me to a local supermarket where I was amazed by the number of expensive cars parked outside. Mercedes, Lexus and Land Cruisers all had their slots. Inside the store was fruit imported from France and sold at exorbitant prices.

"Isn't this mad?" I said to Linel. "We're in Africa. The sun shines and fruit grows everywhere here."

He shrugged his shoulders. "When you have oil, you can do anything," he said wryly.

But even for those rich enough to afford the supermarket prices, the party was coming to an end. Supplies of Gabon's black gold were dwindling. After Bongo took power the once rich and profitable farming industry had slowly but surely collapsed. There was desperate poverty in Gabon and the supermarket had armed itself with three guards carrying pump-action shotguns to protect against robbery.

We headed to a more traditional street market just a mile from the supermarket, with basic stalls and hungry dogs running loose and hustling for a treat. It was risky for people to talk to us, but one brave middle-aged woman who had been shuffling along the street carrying a basket of vegetables on her head stopped to bemoan the state of the country and the dictator, as she called Bongo with disgust.

"We have nothing. I pray for him to die," she said, before pausing. "But perhaps whoever follows will be worse."

Such was the reality of Gabon. Some of the supermarkets might be stocked with French delicacies.

But most people endured dirt roads and tin-roofed shacks.

Back in our dilapidated hotel I had a moment of terror stuck in the lift while the metal cables groaned and strained. Then I wandered outside and a battered Citroën racing along the coast road suddenly turned sharply and slammed into the thick wall right next to me, demolishing the front of the car, and the wall. The driver slid out of his seat, dusted himself with a dramatic flourish, and calmly walked into the hotel. "I'm fine, thank you, there is nothing to worry about," he said. I gave the car a wide berth as it began to smoulder and hailed a taxi. We drove 40 metres before hitting another car. My driver had been distracted by a completely naked man carrying a bicycle into a shop. Gabon was a weird place.

We packed our kit ready to continue the journey east and made a beeline for the train station. Three times a week trains would leave Libreville and head east, parallel with the equator, on the Transgabonais railway towards Lopé National Park, home to a large population of mandrills and several thousand western lowland gorillas.

With the oil running out, Bongo had decided to tap tourist dollars by exploiting other national assets. With apes, hippos splashing in the sea, pristine rainforest, and nearly 700 species of birds, Gabon is a paradise for naturalists. Absolute power can clearly speed decision-making. The President had recently ordered that 11 per cent of Gabon should be converted into national parks — almost overnight. It was a bold move: Voila! Gabon was being touted and promoted as the "Costa Rica of Africa", an unspoiled high-end destination for wealthy eco-tourists.

I doubt they travelled on the railway. Our carriage was old, wooden, but charming and surprisingly empty. "It's not cheap, and anyone with money drives," said Linel.

The train grumbled and rattled as we rolled slowly along, following, skirting and then crossing the equator in a narrow gulch surrounded by a blanket of bright-green foliage. Ahead was a rickety bridge with a pathetic barrier on one side and nothing but a void on the other. The driver slowed to a crawl. The stanchions sagged under the weight of the train and hairs climbed on my forearms. Linel whispered the obvious.

"The bridge is very unstable," he said.

An elderly man in a suit sitting alone a few rows ahead crossed himself. I stopped breathing. The whole train seemed to sigh and exhale as we reached solid tracks.

At a remote stop called Lopé we left the train and clambered into four-wheel drives for a journey into the rainforest. Roads were terrible, and time and again we had to push and winch the vehicles out of muddy holes.

Eventually we found a place to camp deep in the forest. As darkness fell, it was spell-binding. Light from the moon or stars could not penetrate the canopy, and the forest was pitch-black and filled with a cacophony of nocturnal life. I drifted off, snug in a sleeping bag, hearing the eerie wild cry of primates in the distance. The whole area was riddled with Ebola. Apes had been badly affected and Ebola can spread from primates to humans. Over the previous decade a third of the world's entire gorilla population had succumbed to the awful disease.

When I poked my head out of the tent in the morning the drivers were already up. They looked downcast and embarrassed. Their boss had been on the phone overnight. If we wanted them to take us any further we had to pay an additional chunk of cash, nearly $2,000.

"What?" I said. "Two thousand dollars, are you kidding?"

The driver shook his head. He held up his mobile phone. "The boss," he said. "It's what he told us to tell you."

It was outright blackmail. They took us another hour or so further along the track, but then one of them received a text message ordering them to get the money out of us or turn back. We refused to pay. So they helped us unload our gear and abandoned us, deep in the Lopé forest.

We knew that somewhere ahead was the Mikongo camp, home to a team of researchers, and we set off towards it on foot, each of us carrying a heavy load of kit, clothes and equipment.

Surrounded by tall, dark trees I started to wonder whether we'd be spending a second night on our own in the forest, when researchers from the Mikongo camp appeared, alerted on a radio to our plight, and helped to carry and lead us towards their sanctuary, a scattering of wooden buildings in a sunny clearing.

Researchers at the centre were monitoring the impact of the Ebola virus on the local ape population. They showed us a stack of gorilla and chimpanzee skulls that were victims of the dreaded disease. I picked up a couple for a closer look before the researchers suggested they were best left alone. Washing my hands with disinfectant made me feel safer, but I couldn't shake a nagging feeling something awful from the forest had implanted itself in my brain.

The team based at Mikongo were also studying lowland gorillas in their natural habitat, and they suggested we could trek into the jungle with their researchers. We plunged into the trees led by wiry local tracker Donald Ndongo and began to explore.

Lowland gorillas can wander several miles a day, so in the dense forest the odds of a sighting are not great. Between June and November more than a thousand mandrills can also congregate in the jungle, thought to be the largest non-human gatherings of primates anywhere in the world. I had dreams of an Attenborough-style encounter with huge primates in the jungle. Unfortunately, it was April and we couldn't even find droppings.

But tracking in the jungle was endlessly exciting. The entire ecosystem is alien and surprising. Donald was a mine of information on trees that bled red, and plants used for fighting fever, even as he clucked away noisily to alert gorillas to our presence.

"A surprised gorilla is a frightened gorilla," Donald said sagely. "And a frightened gorilla is not something you want to stumble across. Far better that we let them know we are coming. Then they can decide if they want to say hello."

Pushing through the jungle was a challenge, but after a few hours we finally spotted, followed and filmed putty-nosed monkeys. It was an incredible treat. Sam, our cameraman, had been lugging a heavy camera while we took it in turns to carry the tripod. Long shots of our distant cousins flitting through the trees made the entire experience memorable and a joy — even if we sweated buckets in the equatorial heat and all of us were bitten to pieces by ferocious mosquitoes and insects the size of small sparrows.

Gabon clearly offers both more and less than a standard safari. More, in the sense that, after trekking and sweating through the rainforest, there is the chance of genuine and spontaneous wildlife discoveries. Compare that with a traditional safari in South or East Africa, where you can find yourself watching a bored cheetah on the open savannah while sitting in a jeep with honeymooners from Texas and Bavaria. And Gabon offers less, in that much of the country is thick green jungle, and you might only catch a rear-end glimpse of a mandrill or a gorilla as it heads in the wrong direction. In the rainforest there are no guarantees of a wildlife encounter.

Donald, whose father was a proud hunter ("never a poacher", he added quickly), explained how life was changing since the President decided to target wealthy tourists. Villagers who live in and around national parks had suddenly been banned from hunting in the forests.

14

"It's been a big shock for them," he said. "We try to explain that it's for the benefit of the country, but they need to eat, so they need to see the benefits of tourism quickly."

Donald took us to the village of Makoghé, on the outskirts of the forest, where Jean Jacques, the energetic headman, had been struggling to hold his community together since the hunting ban. Overnight traditional hunting grounds had been taken away and an entire way of life had gone. Jean Jacques told me that as an alternative income for the community he had started organising traditional dances for paying foreigners.

Men from the village started drumming and some of the women started singing and dancing while a small group of visitors watched politely and snapped away with their cameras. It was clearly all very new to the villagers. More than once I saw a lady nudging another and reminding her to lead the next move. But this was their new economy. One young man used a clenched fist as a microphone to announce the dancers while others passed among us collecting payment.

I had a moment with the chief and he asked me to make sure people in the outside world knew they were welcome in Makoghé.

"Tourism is all we have now," he said.

His message was clear: if you want us to stop hunting the wildlife, someone needs to provide us with an alternative means of putting food on the table.

Wildlife across Africa must be protected. But what about the humans? The Lopé forest is a lush wilderness, but it is also a home to thousands of

Gabonese living in villages scattered around and in the middle of the new national park area. With a bit of guidance and training, the villagers of Makoghé and other small communities nearby could be helped to make money from guiding, hosting and feeding tourists. But often conservationists, even the most well-meaning, think that villagers, with their livestock and human diseases, should be forced to move so that national parks can be protected as natural wilderness.

"Now that hunting is forbidden we have animals hunting our cattle and eating our crops," said Jean Jacques. "And if we do anything about it we get into trouble."

I have heard this story in several forms on my travels. Across sub-Saharan Africa, populations are expanding but natural resources are scarce, so humans and animals compete for land, food and water. Villagers find themselves on land that governments or conservation groups want to earmark for animals and exploit for tourist dollars.

Everyone knows that evil corporations push native peoples off their lands for oil or timber. But across the world, some conservation groups have occasionally done much the same, wrecking lives and cultures to create national parks. Bernhard Grzimek, who helped create the Serengeti National Park, and Joy Adamson of *Born Free* fame were both accused of expelling locals from land they wanted for animals.

National parks should be a powerful protection for Gabon's wildlife, but I wondered what would become of Jean Jacques and Makoghé.

16

We left the community and headed back to the station. Our journey further east was blocked by the Ebola outbreak in Congo-Brazzaville, and our incoming train back towards Libreville was late. A herd of drunken elephants had wandered in front of the train deep in the Gabonese jungle. Four of the elephants had been killed, and the engine and two carriages had been derailed. The line was completely blocked.

The stationmaster sweated profusely as he explained the problem to our small group waiting on the Lopé station platform.

"It's the iboga fruit they keep eating," he grumbled, apparently annoyed at the herd's failure to obey railway regulations. "They get intoxicated and stagger around on our lines."

It was another day before the line was cleared and we arrived back in the capital, Libreville. By the time I made it to bed that night my muscles were aching. I dreamt of sickly gorillas. Then woke in the early hours to my very own medical nightmare.

After Sophie, Sam and Linel had half-carried me back to my room they had a hurried chat. We had all been on remote medical courses and were travelling with a trauma kit for injuries and packs of pills for dealing with pain, fevers and infections. We had our common sense but none of us were paramedics and this was clearly something serious. Sophie rang London for advice and help. An expert was lined up on the phone.

My temperature was rising: 39.7, 39.8, 39.9. The room was warm, I was feverish, but I was also shaking and cold. Linel rang a local doctor and asked him to jump in a taxi. Sam remembered that on our delayed returning train we'd briefly met a young German doctor who was working at the nearby Albert Schweitzer Hospital, one of the best research centres on the continent for tropical diseases. It was a chance encounter that ultimately helped to save my life. Sam could remember the doctor was called Jenny but couldn't get through to the hospital on the phone. He jumped in a car and sped off to find her.

I was drifting in and out of consciousness, with a temperature that left me just a shade off brain impairment, and I was hallucinating. I thought Mr T from the A-Team was in the room helping to look after me, with his Afro Mohawk and gold jewellery. It took a while for Sophie and Linel to work out what I was talking about while I mumbled incoherently to my childhood hero. Sophie was able to laugh about it. Linel remained baffled until much later when we had a chance to explain. The A-Team weren't big in Gabon.

Linel's doctor arrived first. I came round in time to find him examining me. I was terrified. I was still convinced I had contracted Ebola.

"Where we were planning to go next," I mumbled. "My brain's not working. I feel so rough."

The doctor spent a few minutes checking me over before he was ready to deliver his verdict.

"What do you think it is?" I asked.

"Malaria."

I've never felt such an immediate relief. Malaria. Thank God. Not Ebola. My eyeballs wouldn't bleed. I wouldn't haemorrhage internally. Anything was better than Ebola.

Then there was a dawning realisation.

Hang on. Malaria isn't good.

Sam arrived back at the hotel with Dr Jenny. She gave the same diagnosis. A medic in London ticked off a checklist of symptoms and also confirmed the judgement.

But Jenny offered some practical help. She had brought a packet of Artemether with her, a newish drug derived from Vietnamese sweet wormwood that was not regulated or allowed in the UK, but was showing great promise as a treatment for malaria in Africa and Asia.

"Look, you will have to check with your people in London whether he can take it, but I think it could really help," she told Sophie and Sam. "The journey is over, at least for now, but this could save his life."

Linel's doctor agreed. The London medic told Sophie the two doctors standing in my room were the best source of advice.

While I had a moment of clarity the team called my partner Anya, at the basement flat where we lived together in North London. They told her what was happening and the drugs Jenny had brought. We talked down the line, or at least I mumbled. I told her Mr T was there looking after me. Anya remained calm. She was cradling the phone and scanning the internet at the same time.

"I think you should take it," she told me. "Simon, can you understand? I think you should take the drugs. It won't be easy. It says here that roughly four hours after you take the pills World War Three will break out in your body."

Artemether works by persuading malarial parasites to launch their attack before they are fully armed and ready. I had no choice. I took the pills. Six chunky tablets, braced with a cocktail of other drugs and paracetamol to get my temperature down. Four hours later I was doubled up with the most intense sickness I had ever experienced. I had a full-blown malarial assault and my temperature leapt around like the bearing in a pinball machine.

The attack went on for twenty-four hours. I was so weak, I could barely lift my head. I spent the next few days just sleeping before I was able to get out of bed. The sickness was a key turning point in my life. Before I had malaria I felt fit, energetic and just a little bit immortal. I've never felt the same since.

Throughout history, malaria has been our greatest enemy. It's thought that up to half of all the humans who have ever lived have died of malaria. Millions of Africans are still infected each year and thousands of children on the continent die every single day from the disease. The mosquito-borne virus is one of the great curses of the tropics, a disease found almost entirely between the Tropics of Capricorn and Cancer. We might have forgotten about it in the temperate West, but in Africa especially it can still dominate life. I have been in some areas of Africa where the incidence of malaria is more than 200 per cent. How is that possible? People are infected more than once a year.

How can you have a fully functioning society when you are permanently dealing with that sort of catastrophe? Malaria is a spectre that haunts the continent. But if malaria still affected Europe, I have no doubt drug companies and governments would be working around the clock to find a way to beat the disease.

I was lucky. As a privileged, foreign TV presenter travelling in Africa I had swift access to qualified help and rare drugs. I was also stupid. I knew I was in a danger zone but had forgotten to take my anti-malaria drugs. It is not a mistake anyone makes twice.

My recovery was slow and in stages. After a few days I was able to lie on some bedding outside in the rough garden of our dodgy hotel. I still felt awful inside, and desperately weak, but I could open my eyes and my brain had started to function.

There was time for reflection, a bit of self-pity and then gratitude. I'd had a good run, I decided. I never thought TV presenting would be much of a career. If it ended then I would have already banked memories to last a lifetime. I had travelled through some of the most remote and beautiful areas of the world. I tried to tot up how many countries I'd visited. It was scores. I lay there in that grotty hotel garden and chuckled away to myself. I was sick and drained of energy. But I was in Gabon. I had been a teenage delinquent who left school without qualifications and went on the dole. I suffered from depression and mental health issues and was a whisker from suicide. But I had overcome my fears and failings, written books, travelled the world and met some of the most inspiring and extraordinary people on the planet.

How on earth had I been so lucky?

CHAPTER
TWO

Mystery Tours

I grew up in Acton, West London, the hinterland between the inner city and the suburbs. We lived in a far corner of the otherwise leafy borough of Ealing, but on the edge of gritty Shepherd's Bush and White City. With my younger brother James, I had a childhood that was small and simple in a modest three-bedroom semi, which our mum and dad bought through years of grafting.

My father Alan was a strong, competitive man who grew up in rural Norfolk as an only child. A champion tennis player in his twenties, he lost a crucial match that would have put him into the Wimbledon championships, and still played tennis hard for the rest of his life. He was young when his father died and his mother had raised him on her own. It can't have been easy, but he struggled and studied, and eventually made it to college, trained and became a maths teacher at a tough comprehensive school in North-West London. Dad was one of the last teachers to qualify without a degree, a huge achievement. But the lack of a university education held him back, which riled him as years ticked by and he was passed over for promotions. Dad never earned vast sums, but he was careful with money and took on private students to supplement his income and pay for our home, the only one I ever knew. My mum Cindy still lives there. She survived a similar start in life to my dad. Her father died when she was young, just nine years old, and she was brought up in a single-parent household by my Grandma Lucy. Mum studied domestic science and then worked in restaurants, kitchens and sold sausages in a supermarket around the time she met my dad. It wasn't the most glamorous of starts, but they look blissfully happy in their wedding photos.

I was born in 1972, and my earliest memory is pain. Extreme pain. At four years old I was sick for a few days and the GP said I had sinusitis. Mum was not convinced. When my condition took a turn for the worse she called the hospital and was put through to a sympathetic specialist.

"That doesn't sound like sinusitis," said the doctor. "That sounds like a serious case of meningitis. Put the phone down, call an ambulance and get him here right now."

It took a doctor, two nurses and my mum to hold down my wriggling, screaming little body while I was given a lumbar puncture to diagnose and confirm meningitis. It is an excruciating procedure where fluid is extracted through a large needle shoved up your spine. Deep within me I still sense the pain and shudder and squirm at the memory. The deadly meningitis was easy compared to the puncture, and after a few weeks I recovered from that only to have tonsillitis. My tonsils were whipped out quickly, just in time for me to contract pneumonia, and I nearly died all over again. It hadn't been spotted by the doctors. I'm only here today because Mum knew something was wrong and wouldn't take no for an answer. I ticked through a few of my nine lives as a tot. I hate to think how many I have left now after years of adventures.

Ours was a small family. Both my parents were only children. James and I had no first cousins, no uncles, no aunts and no grandfathers. When I was five my dad's mother Delsie died. But my Grandma Lucy was a rock of love through my early life with a cosy home nearby in West London that was a loving refuge. Gran was large, cuddly and always ready with a hug and some home-made cakes, especially when life was challenging or things were difficult for James and me at home.

I don't come from a connected family. I didn't grow up in wealthy Westminster or Chelsea. I didn't go to private school or Oxbridge, and I wasn't commissioned in the forces. Nobody in my immediate family has ever gone to university. Go back just a couple of generations on my dad's side and they were fish-hawkers traipsing door to door. One generation further and they were child labourers with no education at all.

Some of my earliest adventures were when my grandma, who for years wore a caliper on her leg due to childhood polio, and always found walking a struggle, would take James and me on magical mystery tours in her adapted car. My gran inspired me when I was a child and her memory remains with me and guides me as an adult. James and I would sit on booster seats and direct her left or right down one street after another. It was completely thrilling, exploring exotic areas like Hounslow, or Park Royal Trading Estate. Gran loved the freedom to drive, and for me, directing a car at the age of six was a real power. I can still remember the sense of excitement as we peered out of the window and discovered the McVitie's biscuit factory from the back of Gran's converted Ford Escort. I don't think I've ever quite lost that thrill of discovery, of seeing what lies over the hill, or round the next corner. I have my gran to thank.

My second favourite treat as a kid was our monthly family meal out. All dressed up in Sunday best, we'd go to our local church, then drive to a huge Makro cash and carry, stack the boot of the car with wholesale quantities of potatoes, baked beans and toilet roll, then troop to the Makro canteen where plates of chewy beef and two veg had been waiting, possibly for a while, behind Perspex pull-up windows. Sunday was bulk-buy day for the small-store and corner-shop owners in West London, and we must have looked ridiculously out of place, but it was what we could afford, and the lemon meringue pie was delicious. A proper Harvester restaurant or Berni Inn was reserved for really special occasions.

My early horizons were local. I had a parochial view of life on the periphery of the most exciting city in the world. I went to the school near the bottom of our road at first and then a couple that were just a bus ride away.

Holidays took me a little further. Year after year we went to Studland Bay in Dorset, where the waters of the English Channel lap a sandy shore that drifts for mile after mile. It was almost a pilgrimage. Dad had seen an ad in a magazine for a house rental near Studland in the small market town of Wareham. The owner was offering it ludicrously cheaply. He only advertised once, and he never raised the price, so we just went back again and again. Every day was the same: we would make a packed lunch, climb into our old Volvo and race down roads packed with holidaymakers. Dad loved overtaking. Once he managed to zip past eight cars in one go on a long straight. That was his record. What was he thinking? No wonder the engine blew up. We'd get to the beach and put up our deckchairs in the same place on the beach, every day, every year, as if it was our patch of sand. James and I spent hours exploring every inch of the dunes, and we were in the sea so long our skin was as wrinkled as wizened old men. At the time it was idyllic. Studland was a gorgeous bit of coast, and we went crabbing, swimming, climbing and digging. It was the 1970s. People didn't travel abroad the way they do now. We went across the Channel once when I was a child — on a camping holiday to France, Switzerland and Italy. I didn't get on a plane until I started working.

My parents had travelled a little further before they had us kids. They went on a cruise on the Med, and Dad took a party of children from his school skiing in the Alps in the late 1960s. Taking state school kids from a poor area of London abroad, let alone to the slopes, was almost unheard of at the time, but Dad was stubborn and determined to make it happen. A first-timer himself, he spent an age lecturing them on the dangers of skiing and how they needed to take it slowly and carefully. He was on the slopes for less than twenty minutes before he fell badly and snapped his leg in two places. The break was so bad he needed a thick metal pin almost a foot long inside his leg to hold it together. We still have it in a drawer in the house in Acton. After it was taken out of his leg Dad used the pin to stir the sweet home-made fruit wine he would make every year from cheap powdered kits you could buy in Boots the chemist. Huge old pots steamed on our cooker, then glass demijohns full of Chateau Reeve sat on top of the kitchen cupboards, popping as they fermented. Bottling and labelling the wine was a ritual, creating cheap and cheerful presents for Christmas. Dad swore his metal rod gave the wine an extra kick.

If there was anything specific that really helped to inspire my adult love of discovery and my interest in the wider world and our billions of stories, it was our local church when I was a small child. We weren't a particularly religious family, and I don't go to church now, but there's no doubt the exposure I had to life at Acton Hill Methodist Church shaped me. But initially it was just a playground. As a tot I was fascinated by a steep cast-iron spiral staircase that led up to the organ loft. Every Sunday I would scale and play on the steps until I finally plucked up the courage to swing down on one of the support poles. Nobody stopped me, nobody

28

worried, it was completely fine for kids to have the run of the place, because it was a community centre and extended family.

By the time I was five Mum says I was a thoughtful lad who would take a knife and chop individual Smarties into four pieces to share among my family, which perhaps suggests my parents had a lax approach to knife safety and I didn't have enough sweets.

From the age of six or seven I was an inquisitive little soul asking tricky questions about the biblical books we were given in Sunday school. My parents passed me on to the minister, an enlightened man who told me he didn't have all the answers and that it was OK to ask questions. There was never any sense of submit and obey. The church gave me the confidence to query. So when religion told me that anything was possible if your faith was pure and absolute, that if you believed something fervently enough it could happen, I decided to put it to the test.

On our next holiday at Studland I stood by the sea screwing up every ounce of belief I could muster, telling myself that if I believed hard enough I would be able to walk on water. I took it seriously. Eyes closed fast, I lifted a foot and let it dangle above the lapping waves before trying to take a step. I told myself I could do this. I could walk on water.

I stood there for an hour. Sadly gravity was against me. It was shattering. No matter what I'd been told, belief was not enough and never would be. It was a mad thing for a seven-year-old boy to do, but that was the day I lost my faith and it has never returned. It was important, a moment when my sense of childhood wonder cracked. I couldn't walk on water, so I never really listened when people at church talked of faith. But I had never really been interested in the service anyway. It was the playtime, friends and stories from the congregation that I loved.

Compassionate and constructive, the church was more like a gathering of UN volunteers than a congregation. Acton was almost ludicrously diverse, and the church doors were open to all. Dozens of countries were represented and national day, when the congregation wore national costumes and clothing, was as colourful as a carnival.

When I was young Mum and Dad would regularly invite lone visitors to the church over for Sunday lunch, so we had a procession of people sharing their stories. George, a research scientist from Ghana, stood out. He was studying the best vegetables for growing in sub-Saharan Africa and was championing the sweet potato as the best option for reducing poverty and hunger. I remember him holding a gnarled old chunk up to the light as if it was sacred and talking about the desperate suffering he'd seen travelling in West Africa. He had me spellbound. Sweet potato became a staple in family meals for years after.

Our house was never full of friends. By the time I was in my teens I was at war with my father and most people stayed away. But when I was still a child other teachers from Dad's school would visit. There was Uncle Ian my godfather, Uncle Eddie the art teacher, a wild-haired Aussie with a glint in his eye who would tell

James and me tales of his travels in the outback, and Uncle Angelo from Sri Lanka, a bull of a man. He told us about tensions, uprisings, and what the Brits had done to his country. He brought tales to our table I had never heard before.

There were also talks in the church that somehow my parents persuaded me to sit through. In one a couple of white aid workers and their young son came to visit and described the wonderful colour blindness of children. Their son was blond-haired and blue-eyed and he had been educated in an African school where every other child was black. His mother described to us how one day when he was roughly five years old he told her they had a new teacher.

"Mum," he'd said. "I was just sitting there when the new teacher came in and none of us had seen him before. He looked straight at me and said, 'You must be Peter.' Well, how did he know my name? Nobody told him. How did he know I was Peter?"

Of course, Peter had been the only white face in the class. I was nine when I heard the story. Even at that age I could see how funny this was but also how profound. I was growing up among every creed and colour and hearing horror stories about racism and discrimination. The wonder and the beauty that skin colour never occurred to younger Peter struck a huge chord. I see it now in my own son Jake, who will mention what people are wearing to identify them rather than their skin colour. We're not born racist. As kids we're all just human.

Other talks and sermons at the church focused on natural disasters, war or suffering. Much of the world was represented in the congregation, and whenever something awful happened elsewhere there was usually someone with a personal connection to the issue or area. Speeches were given. Tears flowed. Money was raised. Then every year we'd have a dedicated week of fund-raising where my family of four would stuff charity envelopes through doors in streets near our home for a specific campaign. James and I would work each side of a street, ducking in and out of gates and crawling through hedges in a race with the other. The envelopes came with mini leaflets that I'd read and studied. They gave me an understanding and appreciation of my own good fortune. I was raised to be mindful and I'm grateful for it. No doubt it sounds worthy, even cheesy, but even at a young age, before I was ten years old, the church, the congregation and fund-raising helped me to realise there was a huge, extraordinary world out there often haunted by an immense amount of suffering.

My mother says I was eight when I told her about global warming. I doubt I could have grasped that concept at such a young age, let alone described it. It's more likely I was telling her about the hole in the ozone layer. TV programmes and teachers were talking about the issue by the very early 1980s. Whatever the issue, Mum says what struck her most wasn't the fact I knew about it, but that I cared about the consequences. I've tried to keep that sense of concern and empathy and not allow the world and its endless horrors and cynicism to strip it away.

I can't claim to have many skills, but when it comes to engaging with people I hope I'm able to empathise without being patronising. When someone tells me their story I really feel what they're going through and can work myself into a complete state internally. I feel it viscerally, deeply. I don't know if that empathy was born of talks in church or wiring from birth, but it was certainly shaped at a young age, and then fed further by hurdles and challenges later in life. I never want to lose it. That early awareness helped to teach me a person's plight or circumstances at any one time should never serve to entirely define them.

By the time I was ten I told my mum I wanted my life to mean something. That I wanted to count. But we were an ordinary, hard-working family and I grew up with no idea of what I would do with my life and no real horizon beyond my corner of Acton. My main ambition was to be a van driver. Then I thought about being a policeman. I was getting serious. Maybe a bit too serious. But then I was given a BMX as a birthday present and I became a little tearaway.

CHAPTER
THREE

Mr G. Raffe

Historians say one of the most significant developments in the lives of ordinary Brits was the invention of the bicycle. Suddenly farm workers and villagers had a cheap way of moving large distances, widening their eyes, their world, and our gene pool. Bicycles transformed Britain.

Nothing broadened my horizons as a child faster than my BMX. By the age of eleven I was on two wheels and exploring Acton and the parks and estates of White City. At the same time James and I were taking the 207 bus every morning from Acton to our school in Ealing Broadway, a 20 minute journey away, with a huge group of other kids, many of them older and infinitely naughtier. The bus journey became like crime academy, with the older kids teaching and encouraging my brother and me how to skive off, muck about and misbehave. Bunking the bus fare was the entry-level game. Those were the days of the old Routemaster double-decker with a conductor and an open deck at the back with a grab pole.

A conductor would approach for a fare and I quickly learned how to glance around completely innocently, with perfect timing, and smile with my eyes. I had just the right air of confidence. He or she would pause for a second and more often than not suddenly seem to remember I'd already paid. Among our group of kids who took the bus together I became one of the best at bunking the fare. I was disarming, and I became a good liar. Even if the wiliest conductors made it past my smile they could still be fooled.

"Ticket?"

"It's right here." I'd fumble confidently in my pocket, then wear an expression of utter bemusement. "Well it *was* here. Hang on a minute, I must've dropped it on the floor." I'd be on hands and knees among discarded sweet papers and cigarette butts.

"All right, if you dropped it you dropped it. Sit down, son. It's not a problem."

If all else failed and a fare was demanded my brother and I could always just leap up, push past the conductor and jump off the bus. Even at speed you could hold the pole and start running in the air, and that would dramatically reduce your chances of going head over heels under a following lorry. Once or twice I had my ears boxed by conductors during a scuffle. And once or twice we leapt off at speed and landed badly. James went into a bus shelter. I went into a bin. But we usually saved our 15p and walked the rest of the way to school, and then just lied about why we were late and got away with it, day after day, which just emboldened us further.

Initially we were just skipping bus fares, playing chicken by lying down on the dual carriageway near our house as cars whizzed close, or making hoax calls from phone boxes to the operator or calling London Zoo and asking to speak to Mr. G. Raffe who was needed urgently at home. The operator on the other end would generally fall for it and we'd hear the request blasting out over the Tannoy. They were just silly pranks for my brother and me, but we soon had a little gang with a few other kids from the same area, and every feral victory was addictively exciting.

Soon we gravitated from bunking bus fares to petty vandalism. We would smash milk bottles, fill car locks with glue and shoplift. For years I held my school record for stealing Kinder Eggs from W.H. Smith in Ealing Broadway: twenty-seven eggs in one go. How I managed it, at eleven, while wearing school uniform, I still don't know. It was ridiculous, of course, and childish. But for me it was completely intoxicating. My poor old mum had no idea what we were up to. James and I told her we were having extra recorder lessons.

At twelve I moved to a high school nearer home with older kids who weren't just thieving sweets. We'd be out late into the evening playing football in the park or causing trouble. One day during the summer holidays a group of us broke into the Barbara Speke Stage School in Acton, which has had soap stars, celebs and Phil Collins as students. For a few years we had butted heads with kids from the private school and in truth we were delighted a fire had broken out and the school had been closed for renovation. Before the work began a group of us decided to see if we could make the builders' job a little bit harder.

We broke in easily enough and then quite literally smashed it to pieces: windows, doors, water pipes and dance mirrors. I ripped a long piece of piping off the wall, watched the water flooding out and then used the pipe to smash the huge floor-to-ceiling mirrors in the hall. Shameful now, but utterly thrilling at the time, gifting a feeling of power and destruction. We broke everything and flooded the rooms. We were out the back playing in a couple of old wheelchairs on a fire-damaged waste dump when the police arrived. We were disarmingly young, and told the police we had seen a bunch of older lads smashing the place and then legging it. It's almost ludicrous with hindsight, but I told the officers "they went thataway", and they believed me. Astonishing. We went back several times to create more mayhem, and other groups of kids did the same. Within a few weeks we were told the damage was so bad the school could no longer be repaired and they had to move to another building further down the road.

Phil Collins kept his link with the school. I met him when we were both guests on the *Chris Evans Breakfast Show* and apologised. To his eternal credit he drummed on an empty box of photocopier paper and let me sing backing vocals to "In the Air Tonight" live on the radio. Perhaps that was punishment.

Time and again as a kid I got clean away with pranks and crimes. Before too long I found myself in stolen cars. I wasn't driving and I didn't steal the cars. I was only twelve or thirteen. But I'd hang out with friends on Acton Vale Estate causing trouble, and then on White City Estate which at the time had a tricky reputation. Cars were regularly set on fire on the estate and the area was considered a major riot risk. This was the mid-1980s, with the Brixton riots a fresh memory, Margaret Thatcher in power and many inner-city areas tense or on a knife-edge. I didn't burn any cars but I knew the young guys who did. More than once they stole a vehicle, set it alight, waited for the fire brigade to show up then lobbed petrol bombs at the firefighters. I don't remember feeling guilty at the time, but I certainly do now.

I was obsessed with fire, burning and explosives as a kid. One time I was by the side of the main road in Ealing setting fire to a rubbish bin at dusk, in the rush hour. There was a line of stationary traffic right alongside. A group of us poured a can of petrol into the bin before lighting it with matches. Nobody yelled at us from the cars. The traffic was nose-to-tail but nobody did anything, and nobody said anything, except for an incredulous young French couple walking by.

"What are you doing?" they said in thick French accents. "Why are you doing this? Don't be so destructive."

We would steal petrol from pumps and cars and start fires. We would nick fireworks from shops or steal money to buy them, then take bangers apart to make larger devices. I remember unscrewing the bottom of a CCTV camera in a stairwell of Ealing Broadway Shopping Centre and packing a small device inside and then watching it blow up before racing off laughing. Why? It was just a stupid, destructive thrill. We ran down the stairs and outside to the back of the shopping centre and I lined up a huge rocket I'd made to fire low across the ground. There was nobody around when I lit it, but at that exact moment a policeman came storming out of an exit looking for us. Everything happened in slow motion. I saw him and looked down at the fuse, which was burning. The policeman was perhaps 25 metres away. I tried to kick the firework away, but it launched. I watched in horror as it spiralled through the air towards him, fizzing and burning. The poor guy tried to leap out of the way, but it hit him in the leg, sickeningly hard, and he went down screaming. We took off, running as fast as we could. He must have put out an "officer down" distress call, because within moments there were dozens of sirens wailing and the police swamped the whole area. I still feel terribly guilty about that moment. I hope to God he was all right.

I was a rebellious kid at school and on our streets, and at the same time at home my relationship with Dad was collapsing. I was cheeky and naughty, and he wasn't sure how to deal with it. I can't remember what had happened or what I'd done but one day during a row Dad was trying to get me to come out from around the table I was hiding behind.

"Come here, Simon," he was saying through gritted teeth. "I want to talk to you."

I hesitated. I knew what a talking to from my father could mean.

"I'm not going to smack you."

Still I hesitated.

"I said, I'm not going to smack you. I just want to talk to you."

I crossed the room to him, and he whacked me.

I stood there staring at him, tears brimming, feeling a colossal sense of betrayal. My dad had given his word and broken it. Who do you trust after that?

Both my parents were only children brought up by single mothers. My dad had lost his father figure as a lad. With no role model to guide him, he only really knew how to relate to me as a teacher.

The school where our dad taught was one of the toughest in London. It had a terrible reputation as a place that was traumatising for the staff as well as the pupils. In those days teachers had more power than they do today. They were able to enforce discipline physically, and sometimes that was echoed at home. Dad was a competitive man, quick to anger, who often didn't think twice before ranting and shouting. His life was the battlefield of the classroom or the competition of the tennis court. Confrontation was often his parenting style.

It wasn't all bad, and I don't feel like I suffered terribly. Dad certainly had a softer side and when James and I were smaller he was fantastic at rough and tumbles. But the relationships in our family became hugely destructive. More than once James and I begged our mum to divorce our father.

At school Dad was used to being obeyed, but at home you can't so easily boss or control a stroppy, confused thirteen-year-old. You have to guide and inspire. Dad wasn't the easiest person to get along with and ours was a tense and sometimes violent relationship. Throughout my early teens we were at loggerheads. We fought verbally and sometimes physically and it was pretty one-sided. Perhaps I would do something stupid or not do something helpful and my dad would fly off the handle. But it wasn't just my father. We all fought. Mum turned the kitchen table over. I had a fiery temper and put my foot through a door and my fist into a wall. The house bore the scars. I bashed my brother and he threw knives at me. There was endless shouting, lots of crashing and banging, and a few times it was so violent we or our neighbours called the police to come and break us up.

As a child the rows were all incredibly upsetting. They dominated my feelings and emotions. Over the years of my middle teens the arguments and upheaval at home fed a sense of despair and depression that slowly grew within me. Now I'm an adult, I blame Dad less, of course. I feel sorry for him. I just think he lacked the skills of compromise and resolution. We fought because we didn't know how to communicate. Too much time, and too many opportunities for happiness, were completely wasted with pointless rows and arguments.

Only later did James and I realise our childhood experiences made us better communicators in relationships as adults. Dad didn't have the wiring to talk issues and arguments through to resolution, but gradually, through the mistakes of others, James and I learned the skills.

My immediate response to our family rows was to skulk upstairs to my room, close the door and simmer and sulk on the bed. Above me was a poster of Whitney Houston, the usual Lamborghini and Ferrari car posters that were obligatory for kids in the 1980s, and on the ceiling directly above my pillow was a poster of an idyllic tropical beach, fringed by palm trees. Whenever I rowed with my dad, which was often, I'd lie on that bed afterwards and immerse myself in the poster, sensing the sun, feeling the sand between my toes. It was a place to escape. That poster was the ultimate contrast with the grey streets of West London. I never imagined, in my wildest dreams, that my feet would ever crunch onto a beach anywhere similar.

Dad's response to our arguments, and me staying out late and sometimes coming home a little blood-stained, was to buy me a couple of books that were supposed to encourage me to stick to the straight and narrow. First the autobiography of my hero, Mr T, which was a jaw-dropping account of his life in a neighbourhood that made mine sound like Windsor. Almost every page was littered with extreme swearing. Dad can't have even opened the book.

The second was *Run Baby Run* by Nicky Cruz, a famous account of gang life by a man who found Christianity and turned his life around. Cruz spent much of his childhood locked in a pigeon loft. His dad would shut him in and leave him with the birds flying around his head. It terrified him to the point that birds dominated his nightmares for years to come. He fled to New York to live with his sister and joined the notorious

42

Mau Maus, rising to become president of the gang. I will never forget the details of his gang initiation. Cruz and another guy were offered the choice of either a savage beating from three or four gang members or they could stand against a target wall, not moving a single muscle, while a knife was thrown. If anyone chose the knife and then so much as flinched they would be jumped and thumped. Nicky decided to take the beating. The other initiate plumped for the knife, but then flinched and cowered in tears against the wall. As a consequence, the Mau Maus grabbed him, spread his arms out in a crucifix, and stabbed him in both armpits. I was just starting my teens when I read that and I couldn't imagine anything worse. I developed a complete phobia of anyone touching or stabbing anything into my armpits. My wife thought I was joking about it when we met, but to this day only my son can tickle me under the arms without fearing an involuntary attack.

I was thirteen when I started carrying a knife. As a kid in Acton hanging out on the streets and even walking home from school I often felt at risk of a random act of violence. Over a few years I was mugged for pocket money, was punched hard in the face by a youth wearing a knuckleduster medallion ring, and was chased by a gang of older boys who threatened to kill me. I was also nearly lured into a car by two men, threatened by another boy with a knife, and had my beloved bike stolen by a gang. My school and streets certainly weren't the most dangerous, it was just an average part of the city. But we were in competition and rivalry with others close by and kids from my school would organise fights with youngsters from nearby Acton High School that would turn into mini brawls. I bought a small flick knife from a friend for pocket money and carried it for protection, or so I thought. It was more for bravado and a sense of power.

Back then you could buy ludicrous weapons by mail order just by ticking a box to say you were over sixteen. I stole money from my dad, used some more cash from a paper round I was doing for less than £2 a week, bought postal orders and sent off for a small combat blade I had seen advertised in a classified-ad paper called *Gun Mart*, even enclosing a letter saying I was a squaddie about to be deployed abroad and so needed it immediately. They wrote back a few days later saying my choice was out of stock, but they thanked me for serving and enclosed an alternative Rambo blade the size of a machete that only just fitted in my school bag.

What the hell was I doing? Right now the news is full of horrific stories of knife crime in London and kids stabbing each other in petty feuds and drug deals. Parents and victims are pleading with youngsters to see sense. Back then, for me, it was mainly about ego.

I revelled in the secret feeling of power and respect carrying a knife gave me. Nobody looks up to a thirteen-year-old. At that age you're on a path to adulthood but you're not respected. People hardly listen to you. Nobody takes you seriously. I thought carrying a knife would give me authority. In the years since I've been held up at chaotic guerrilla checkpoints abroad by kids the age I was back then, carrying Kalashnikovs rather than knives. I've seen the look in their eyes and sensed how they gloried in a feeling of power. It's terrible, and it can result in tragedy. I was a young fool who thought a weapon helped to make me a man. If we want to stop teenagers carrying knives we need to devote resources, school and community attention, to boosting their confidence, self-belief and self-worth.

I also carried a knife partly because of consequences. Or the lack of them. My parents never found my weapons because I was clever at hiding them. I was never stopped and searched by the police, even when I was once caught in a stolen car. Teachers at school never checked our bags. And I never found myself in a situation where I pulled a knife in anger. Thankfully. Because more likely than not it would have been turned around and used against me. There were no dramatic or dire consequences for me. I was never caught carrying a knife. I got away with it. Many, many others were not so fortunate. People I knew ended up committing a crime, were sucked into a serious gang, stabbed someone, or had their own blade pushed into their chest, and bled out in a street and died pathetically early. I was lucky. I used to hang out near a community centre in Acton that was a notorious dive for dealers and trouble. I started smoking at eleven and used to sit around outside on the periphery, puffing away and trying to look hard. Then a bouncer at the centre was shot in the head by a drugged-out guy he turned away at the door. Even I realised it wasn't a good place for a kid to spend their spare time.

I was never a gang member, or a really bad lad, I don't think. I was never a brutal, hard kid. I was never deliberately violent and nobody feared me. I was never hungry, cold, or without a shelter or a bed. But I was very aware of poverty in the lives of friends from broken families, junkie homes, and kids who had fled from towns up north devastated by unemployment. I knew people living seven or eight to a room. My life, even my family life, was cosy by comparison. But ultimately I still managed to sink pretty low.

I'm not proud of everything I did in my early teens, but I mention it now as evidence of what I was and eventually where I was able to get to. In many ways the teenage me is a far cry from the guy on TV. But I'm still much the same person, with most of the same failings and still some of the old fears. I can still see how circumstances could have changed and pushed or led me down alternative paths. Too many people think it's just hard work, study, mindset and focus that determines your journey in life. They're certainly all important, but just a small nudge can throw you off course and change everything. Life, often, is about luck.

The 1980s were a very different era. There were no camera phones, no social media, and our actions were never as visible or informed as they are now. I carried knives, and I'm sorry to say I also sold them to other kids. Then I used the money I made to buy a replica handgun and a covert holster by mail order. It was an identical heavy-metal copy, loaded with blanks, the sort of device that confuses armed police officers, and leads to the idiots and the unstable who are wielding it being shot. I was a child. It was ridiculous. The only time I ever remember pulling it out was when a group of us got into a fight with an older group of travellers in a local park. They were young adults, and fists and anything else were flying around. It was immediately madness. Everyone was screaming abuse, hurling stones and punches, but the other guys got the shock of their lives when I pulled the replica. They scattered, immediately. I might even have fired into the air. It was chaotic and I can't remember. I had an incredible rush of adrenalin. But again I got away with my stupidity. I ducked into a nearby estate, took a longer route home, and hid the gun back in a secret space I had hollowed out under my bedroom floorboards. Eventually I forgot it was there and years later, long after I had left home, my poor mum found it while redecorating.

"Simon," she said calmly when finally confronting me. "Do you have any idea what it was like for me to find a gun underneath the floorboards?"

CHAPTER
FOUR

The Boy on the Bridge

Eventually I was caught doing something stupid. Finally. James and I were hanging around some abandoned tennis courts just a few streets from our home with a group of younger kids, when among the tall weeds and overgrowth we found a stretch of high brick boundary wall punctured by a small hole. Some of us had started kicking a ball around, and some were standing around chatting. One of us must have idly tapped their foot at the loose bricks in the wall and knocked one of them out. That inspired me to kick a few more of the bricks out as well. Then a few kids piled in and rather than talking or knocking the football around we began to completely focus on destruction. We kicked and pushed so more and more bricks came tumbling out. After half an hour or so all that remained was a huge, unsupported arch maybe 8 feet long. It looked precarious, and we stopped to admire our work. Then we crept close and kicked a few more bricks until, in a great cloud of dust, it came thundering down. The noise and dust were terrible. We cheered, knocked out some more bricks, and then wandered away to find our bikes and skateboards. Most of the wall had been knocked down. If any of us had been underneath when the arch fell we would have been crushed or badly injured, but we rarely thought about risk as kids.

For some reason it never crossed my mind that it was a wall belonging to a garden. We left, went home, and I didn't think any more about it until there was a knock on the door. Glancing out of my bedroom window I saw a woman I thought I recognised and instinctively I knew it had been her wall. It was an awful moment. A real chill went through me, like a spider walking on my spine. I knew exactly why she was there and what it meant. After years of shoplifting, setting fires and selling knives, I had never been caught or had to fess up before. And I hated it.

Dad listened calmly to what the woman was saying, apologised, then made me come downstairs to say I was very, very sorry. I cringed. It was crushingly embarrassing. The woman said she would rather avoid calling the police, but we would need to pay to rebuild the wall. There was no bravado from me. Nothing gangster. It was the moment I realised that even if I was trying to be a tougher lad, it was all a front. I had been the oldest kid present when the arch came crashing down, so the burden of paying fell heavily on me. Rebuilding that bloody wall cost me £147, a fortune that I had to pay off with pocket money and cash I had under my floorboards from knife dealing. It wasn't just the money, though; it was the fact that I'd been caught and humiliated. That was what I really hated. I felt like an idiot. And rather than feeling like a big lad who could knock down a wall, I felt like a pathetic little boy. I thought everyone else would think the same, seeing me for what I really was. Ultimately it was the public wounding of my ego that helped bring me to heel, and a painful accident that then knocked my confidence sideways.

Just a few weeks after knocking down the wall I was playing around with my brother and friends in a park near our house. I was behaving a little better already, but some of the other kids were chucking grass at each other and then sods of earth and chunks of stone and rocks. One of the boys grabbed a handful of grass, came up with an old half-brick and lobbed it towards me. I was crouched and facing the other direction when my brother shouted a warning.

"Si!" he screamed. "Look out!"

I stood up, turned around and at the last millisecond saw the half-brick as it hit me full in the face. The edge of the brick raked right across my pupil, scraping my eyeball. I was knocked out. When I came around my crying brother was cradling my bleeding head. In A&E at Hammersmith Hospital I spent a fearful few hours as doctors warned us I could lose my eye. The accident was bad enough, but specialists had to scrape and pick bits of brick, grit and stone out of my eyeball. The pain was excruciating. I had to lie, petrifyingly still, to avoid further damage, even while I could see what the doctors were doing to my own eyeball with tweezers and scalpels. I wince at the memory even while writing this now. For years after the accident anything that was pointed towards my eyes would make me physically recoil. I couldn't even face sitting opposite the corner of a table or a length of wood.

I already had poor vision in one eye, and reasonable vision in the other that just about compensated. The brick, of course, hit my good eye. After the bandages came off I tried to hide the fact that suddenly I couldn't really see, but after a month or two I had to admit reality and went for specs. Nothing designer, there was no money for that. It all happened at the worst possible moment. Testosterone was kicking in. I was suddenly gangly and awkward. My body didn't fit my clothes. Things were terrible at home. I'd revealed, to myself if nobody else, that I was still a silly little boy. And suddenly I had to put two thick bottle tops on my face in a pair of hideously uncool specs.

Then I suffered just about the grandest humiliation an adolescent boy can endure. It was ridiculous, ludicrous, but life-changing. After school one day I was trudging towards home in Acton past a bus stop on the other side of the road that was packed with perhaps 150 kids from the school waiting to head back west towards Ealing. I was wandering along, trying not to look self-conscious, when I spotted a girl I really fancied waiting near the front of the group.

"Adie!" I called out. She turned. I nodded to her and smiled awkwardly. "All right?" I said, pointlessly. She shrugged sweetly.

I had no idea of the disaster, the catastrophe, that was about to befall me. Think of the prom scene in *Carrie*. That comes close. My attention was completely fixed on Adie across the road. I smiled gormlessly back

51

at her, and then walked slap bang straight into a colossal lamp-post. It was a powerful impact. My face connected first, and I went down straight like a tree. My glasses buckled and landed nearby. I found myself sprawled on the pavement, feeling like a frog that had been whacked with a frying pan. I scrambled around to find my specs, and then became aware of the laughter. The entire bus stop of kids was having hysterics at my plight.

Thinking about this now, I feel sorry for the young me. A stronger, more confident, funnier kid could have styled it out. They might have stood up, laughed uproariously at themselves, bowed with style and sauntered off, smoothing themselves down. I did none of that. I struggled hopelessly to get my glasses back on, faffed around on the ground trying to pick up my bag and books, looked in utter horror at the kids opposite, some of whom were bent double at the funniest sight they had ever witnessed, and finally slunk away. It might be amusing now, but it was hideous at the time. Simple little moments in life can have profound consequences.

I was never a star pupil. School had not been going well for me for a while. I was uninspired and deeply uninspiring. I couldn't concentrate and I often struggled in lessons. I don't blame my teachers. They were all caring and thoughtful. Several were charismatic and keen. If there was any failing it was mine. I never really understood, at least until much later, that each of us has to choose life and decide to get involved and active. Rarely can anyone make us. I was too confused, stubborn and perhaps a bit lazy. I just fell through the cracks.

But one book really sparked my interest. Hilary Belden, my brilliant and passionate English teacher, gave our class *Schindler's Ark* to read, by Thomas Keneally.

"There is a chance," she said, as she placed the books carefully on each table in front of us, "that this book might just change your life."

She was right. I didn't entirely realise it at the time, but the book and its story lodged in my mind. Oskar Schindler was a womanising factory owner and Nazi party member who directly saved 1,200 Jews from concentration camps and extermination in the gas chambers of Auschwitz and Gross-Rosen during the Second World War. Calling it an extraordinary story doesn't begin to do it justice. Based on fact and meticulous research, the book gave me a window into the most devastating and intense period of pure human evil. Every page shocked and surprised, yet it was very readable, even as Keneally described the full brutality of the Nazis. It won the Booker Prize and was turned into the movie *Schindler's List* by Steven Spielberg, itself a life-changing film for many viewers.

Up until I read the book my only real knowledge of the war had been gleaned from the pages of *Commando* comics where Tommies fought the Jerries. What I read in *Schindler's Ark* hit me in a way I'd never experienced before. It was an apocalyptic time and the story was uniquely gripping, because the reality of the book was infinitely more powerful and upsetting than any of the young-adult fiction I had read before. It was life, death, survival, and it was brutal, honest, affecting and horrifically emotional. I sobbed. I put the book down. I bit my nails. I picked it up again. Every tragedy I have witnessed around the world as an adult, every desperate act, every wicked demonstration of corruption or abuse is benchmarked against that book. Much later, whenever I worried how futile and pathetic my work was as an adult, I would remember the lives in the book, and feel humbled. Then I recall the moment when Schindler is chastising himself for not saving more of his workers. His accountant, Itzhak Stern, who Schindler protected, consoled him by quoting the Jewish Talmud: "He who saves one life, saves the World entire." It said to me then, and still says to me today, that even when we can't do everything, we can still do something.

The book itself was exceptional, and the story behind it was fascinating, even for me, even as a teenager. Keneally was an Australian writer on a book tour in the US, nearly four decades after the end of the war. He popped into a shop in Beverly Hills to ask about a briefcase in the window. The owner of the store, a Holocaust survivor, heard that Keneally was a novelist and bent his ear trying to persuade him to take the story of Schindler and turn it into a book. The entire astonishing tale had never been told. Only a chance encounter set it free.

Within six years of reading *Schindler's Ark* I would be writing a book of my own. Keneally made me realise that truth and our collective, hidden stories could be not just stranger than fiction, but infinitely more moving and powerful. Yet I cannot say that Keneally's masterpiece inspired me to write as a teenager, or that the dark tragedy of the book encouraged me to accept the privilege of my simple world in my mid-teens and embrace education. I finished the book and my focus shifted quickly back to my own problems.

Life for me felt like it was taking a quick turn for the worse. Dad and I were continually at odds. I had been caught destroying the wall, then nearly lost an eye, and had been humiliated in front of the school. I was also desperate for a girlfriend, but I had completely lost my social confidence. It was maddening. As a young kid I had always been great with girls. When I was in first school I was so naughty I was moved from the table where I sat with my friends and onto a table with three girls who were supposed to keep me in order. It was some sort of punishment, but I thought they were great. It was one of my happiest years at school, and gave me a self-assurance around girls that many other boys envied. In my early teens I was still able to chat happily with girls at school and on holiday. By my mid-teens, though, when I needed it most, my confidence was completely and utterly shot.

I remember going to the annual school disco when I was fifteen or sixteen, and was so low I should have stayed at home. There is surely nothing like a teenage party to broadcast inadequacies and then amplify and ram them back down your own throat. Everyone but me appeared to be dancing. Everyone but me appeared to be snogging in a dark corner. When the music was really blaring my limbs wouldn't move to the tunes. When the slow songs came on I couldn't summon the courage to ask anyone to dance. It's weird and actually a little frightening how that evening is still seared into my mind. I've been around the world, three times, but I can still recall the cheesy 1980s tunes, the crappy striped shirt I was wearing, and how desperately I wanted to chat up a girl called Lisa. I am one of millions scarred by a school disco and that evening I decided dancing was not for me. By the time I resolved my issues and fixed my mind it was a little too late. To this day I do not dance. If there's a party I'm the guy getting the drinks in at the bar, or sitting at a table maybe tapping just one foot. I've faced many fears and been on *Celebrity Bake Off*, but *Strictly*? Forget it.

To add a final layer of topping to my social shame, my parents decided to buy a mustard-coloured Reliant Kitten, the tiny four-wheel fibreglass version of the van driven by Del Boy in *Only Fools and Horses*.

"I mean, come on," I shouted at them, "who would inflict a car like that on their children?"

Of course, much of my downward spiral was self-inflicted and self-indulgent. Pathetic, even. I have since met people around the planet who have suffered, endured and survived astonishing tragedy. I knew that terrible things were happening in the world, and I had only just read *Schindler's Ark*. But everything is relative. I was a fifteen-year-old adolescent with raging hormones and a confused mind, and in just a few short months of bad luck my confidence dripped away.

I went from puffing on light cigarettes to smoking Capstan Full Strength, cancer sticks that carried a picture of a salty sea dog on the front, clearly trying to kill himself as an alternative to the loneliness of the ocean. I began drinking more, sometimes slipping out of school at lunchtime. Being tall, if baby-faced, I could get away with buying booze in off-licences, and I could drink in a few pubs in Acton back then while wearing school uniform, even a stones throw from the police station. I went with friends, but I'd always drink more, and as a complete lightweight I often went back into school worse for wear. There's a photo somewhere of me slumped and slurring in the corner of a classroom. Once I fell asleep drunk in the school library, and some of the kids painted my glasses with Tipp-Ex. When I woke up I thought I had gone blind.

I fell further and further behind at school. Then came exams. I struggled, panicked, and refused to take some of the papers. I scraped a single GCSE, I think, and was somehow accepted to take A-levels. But I rarely appeared for lessons.

Then Mum noticed my fingers were starting to turn blue. I went for tests, had a tube stuck into my heart and iodine pumped through my body so my arteries would show-up on an X-ray, and was eventually told smoking was furring the veins in my neck. If I didn't stop puffing away I would lose my hands. It was all too much for me. I became depressed and withdrawn.

I had already been going for weekly counselling for a year or so at a children's mental health clinic in South Acton. Our GP was concerned about me. On his advice my sessions were upped to two a week. I went for counselling for almost three years from the age of fourteen, with a series of NHS mental health professionals who helped to keep me going and relatively stable just by listening and giving me the space to open up about my feelings and fears. But the counsellors and their centre were woefully underfunded. The building itself was dilapidated concrete, with a dark interior, and grim, grey, empty, dank rooms, like something out of Orwell's *1984*. My heart and spirits sank every time I stepped inside. The staff themselves were stretched. My therapist once broke down in tears as we talked, and I had to comfort them with a pat, a chat, and a box of tissues.

One of my teachers could see I was falling behind. She called me into an office. Far from chastising me, she wanted to know what was wrong. I didn't tell her. I couldn't tell her. I couldn't begin to articulate it myself. She reached out, extending a hand of friendship.

"I can see you're in a bad way. I know things aren't easy for you at home," she said. "I've met your father. I know he can be very . . ." she paused meaningfully, ". . . difficult."

I had started to blub. But now I just looked at her. I was shocked that she could see through me. But at the same time I was also angry with her for talking about my dad behind his back. He wasn't the only one in the family at fault. He was far from perfect, but he was still mine. He was my dad.

If even the teachers knew I was having a tough time, that felt like final proof everyone knew. With the self-regard you only have as a teenager, I thought I must be the butt of every joke. With my specs and the lamp-post disaster, the fact I was getting drunk and stoned on dope — far from making me seem cool — just made me feel even more pathetic. I vaguely remember a school coach trip where I was so spaced out I did nothing as the boy in the seat behind flicked my earlobe every mile of the way.

My final months at school are a bit of a blur. I wasn't studying or preparing for the exams. The thought of sitting down to take tests terrified me, and I had absolutely no idea what I was going to do with my life afterwards.

"What are you doing to do when we leave, just sit in the pub?" one of the lads in my class asked with a sneer.

Going to university never entered my head. Other kids were lining up college and jobs, working in a trade with their father. My only ambition was still to get a job as a delivery driver. But to me even that seemed unlikely. I was becoming seriously depressed and sinking into self-pity and despair. Looking back now I can track how it all happened. A run of apparently insignificant events can turn a life upside down, to the point where you become a shadow of the person you were, and a fraction of the person you should be. My bad luck had left me feeling completely inadequate. One minor perceived humiliation followed another, coming at me from all directions. I started thinking I couldn't go on.

I managed to hold out at school until my final exams but dropped one of the subjects with weeks to go. By the time the actual papers came around I was having panic attacks and I didn't show up to take a couple of exams. I made it into the hall for another one but when I sat down and stared at the questions panic started to well. I was in a complete state. The room began to spin, my mouth flooded with saliva and I knew I was going to be violently sick. I pushed the table away and stood up.

"Simon, are you OK?" shouted one of the teachers in concern. I ignored her, grabbed my bag, rushed through a side door and threw up all over the floor. I walked out of school right then, and I never went back.

My heart breaks for other kids who slip through the net and don't get career or life guidance. Leaving school was an exceptionally difficult time for me. With nothing to do I spent most of my time skulking in my room, watching a tiny, tinny black-and-white TV and ignoring my family when they knocked on the door to check on me. They had no idea how low I was falling. I would get out of bed and wander to the shops to pick up a few cans of Special Brew, then sit in my bedroom alone drinking booze strong enough to stand a spoon in. I felt I had nothing. No education, no girlfriend, and nowhere to go. Within just weeks of fleeing school my thoughts of suicide grew and transformed from passing thoughts to a stronger desire.

Today, the single biggest cause of death among younger men in the UK is suicide. Thousands are killing themselves every year, the equivalent of perhaps sixteen a day. Men aged twenty to forty-nine are more likely to die at their own hand than from road accidents, heart disease or cancer. If any other, more obvious issue caused such tragedy, surely we would be researching it more, studying it harder, and talking about it more openly. We are experiencing a mental health crisis, and we need to spend more time discussing the causes and consequences. Personally I think suicide needs to be thought of like a virus. It can infect through emotions, ego, or as a result of bereavement, failure or loss. Men and lads like me, who are known to the mental health system, are obviously at risk, but so are those with no contact with therapists or a counsellor. Confident, tougher blokes are often less likely to open up when life takes a downwards turn. Women suffer as well, of course, but suicide kills three times as many British men as it does women. Nothing completely explains why. But we know that young men are shockingly vulnerable.

In my case I felt depressed, helpless and hopeless. My family were reaching out to me, but negative feelings and a sense of pessimism about my future were overwhelming. It felt as if a dark weight was hanging around my shoulders, physically holding me down and taunting my mind. Nothing could get through to me and convince me I had a future.

Just a few streets from my house was a footbridge across the Western Avenue, an endlessly busy artery in and out of Central London. For twenty-four hours a day traffic thundered along four lanes. The bridge had been a feature of my life as long as I could remember, a link across what was effectively a dividing motorway. Occasionally we would troop up there as a family at night to watch fireworks over Central London. I would grip the railings as the whole bridge shook when heavy articulated lorries rumbled past below. From when I was a young child my mum had warned my brother and me about playing up by the road and made us swear we would never muck about on the bridge itself.

There was no single moment of disaster that pushed me to the edge. No catastrophe. Just a nudge here and there can shift some of us from what passes for stability to a state of maddening despair.

I thought for weeks about using a kitchen knife on myself, about taking handfuls of pills. I thought about stepping in front of a train, or a tube. Then I thought about falling in front of a lorry. One night I found myself wandering towards the bridge. It was familiar, comforting somehow. I climbed the steps, hopped the railing and shuffled along until I was facing out of London, above traffic heading towards the suburbs. It was windy, noisy. There were no pedestrians to talk me out of it. I looked at the sky. I remember teetering slightly, like a diver on a high board. I was serious, but scared. I looked down just as a heavy lorry passed underneath and a huge horn sounded. Had he seen me from behind? I will never know. It jerked me out of my moment. I started to wonder whether dropping from this low height onto the road would really work. Would I be able to time it so I landed in front of a lorry? Yet the thought of what a heavy vehicle would do to my body was horrific. It was reality, and that might have saved me. In that instant I started to fear the pain of dying more than life. I gripped tightly, nervously. I shuffled back along the side of the bridge and hopped back to safety, shaking with fear. I was choosing life.

It was a turning point for me, of course, but at first nothing changed. There was no euphoria, there wasn't even a sense of relief. I just climbed back over the rail and stood there feeling almost as wretched as I had before. I went home, crept indoors, slipped into bed and had a cry. I had no money, no job and no prospect of getting one either. I'd screwed up my schooling and walked away from my education. I still had no girlfriend; I could see no future. It all looked bleak.

It was a hard time, a painful time, and it is still troubling for me to revisit and admit it all now. But if I hadn't gone through it no doubt I wouldn't be who I am as an adult, or doing what I do today. From the relative comfort of older age, every trauma and darkness that I suffered as a teenager now looks like part of my journey to get to where I am. But I have never stopped to look back, to try to understand my past. Sharing it now is humbling and cathartic.

Every story is unique, every life so frighteningly specific. There is peril in offering further thoughts or advice to others. But perhaps, perhaps, if you are suffering from depression, try to tell yourself there is hope. Try to drown the whispers in your head that are negative with the knowledge, with the stronger and louder certainty that you are wonderful, inspiring and interesting, both now and into your future. Find voices that comfort you and people who hug and help. If you are caring for a young me, just listening is a huge support, but perhaps also remember the human mind is a powerful machine. Many years later I was with a young French special forces captain, in the most dangerous place in the world, on a base under attack from suicide bombers: "People don't change when others tell them they should. People change when they tell themselves they must."

He was talking about countries, but the same thing applies so often to us, as individuals. Sometimes we have to walk our own path, wherever it takes us. In my case I had love around me. I had hugs. But still the darkness was too powerful and overwhelming. It took me to the brink, to a moment from the end.

The days dragged past after I stepped off the bridge and I managed to drag myself along with them. I hadn't changed, I wasn't suddenly brimming with confidence or filled with a zest for life and I had no idea what I was going to do. But I had to do something. Anything. If I wasn't going to kill myself then I needed alternatives. My relationship with Dad improved, to the point that he was able to give me driving lessons without us killing each other. Then he started checking classified adverts and leaving them out for me, but I was nowhere near confident enough to apply for a job. James said I should sign on. I was desperate for a bit of money, so I took a bus into Ealing. From the top deck, I had an elevated view of my world and it felt small and stifling. I wandered over to the DSS office, down a side street opposite the Town Hall, telling myself I was just going to check where it was, but I saw other lads heading inside and followed them in. It had a depressing air and there was a long queue for the counters. But just as I walked inside a man who had been talking to an official near the entrance stood up from her desk. He moved out of the way and she looked straight at me. She had a kindly, wise face and an open smile. She must have dealt with scores of tragedies and desperate souls every single day, but there was no judgement in her eyes.

"Can I help?" she said warmly.

I hadn't really planned to sign on for benefits, but she put me down for Income Support. At £26 a week, I think, it was even less than the dole, but the only option for a seventeen-year-old who had never had a full-time job. I went home and mooched around for a few weeks, still depressed and unsure what to do next. But then I passed my driving test and an idea popped into my head that I can honestly say changed my life. A simple thought that, perhaps more than anything, connects my adult self with that troubled teen. I decided to go on a journey.

CHAPTER
FIVE

The Lost Valley

It just came to me one morning. I felt like I had to face my fears and push myself just a little. But knowing that and doing anything about it were two different things. I would go somewhere, and I would do something. But where? What? I had been so low for so long I wasn't even entirely sure what my specific fears or even my strengths were any more. I was wracked with self-doubt and low self-esteem. Thoughts of doing anything adventurous were frightening.

Initially I had no idea where I would go, or what I would do. Although I had a bit of money from benefits, I wasn't exactly flush. But my mum was desperate for me to get up and out of the house, in the best sense, and she lent me some cash. I bought a cheap train ticket to Scotland, inspired, I think, by nothing more than watching the movie *Highlander*.

Whatever the reason for choosing Scotland, even thinking about going there was a few tentative steps towards recovery. I had been a whisker from suicide, and I knew there was a risk I would be back there again. What if I had a panic attack on the train? What if I couldn't handle it?

I thought back to the lady in the DSS office. I was used to therapy, and even in my brief fifteen minutes with her I had talked openly. I told her I'd left school, with no real qualifications, and that I was pretty low and had no idea what to do next. As I write these words I can feel myself back there, sitting opposite her, as if I have passed through a portal in time, with my hands on her desk as I explained some of my fears. I can remember the sharp raised voices around us, the smell of stale cigarettes and disinfectant in the office, the screw-down chairs in the waiting area, and — most of all — her patient air. I can remember everything about that moment because she gave me simple advice that guided me then, and still does to this day.

"If it's difficult for you," she said, "just take it all slowly. Take things step by step."

I latched onto those words as wisdom. Even in my hopeless state I realised that was the answer. I was no longer a child. I could start behaving like an adult. Everyone seems to think that childhood is without responsibility, but actually you are forever told where to be, what to do and what to study. Now I could claim the freedoms of an adult. If I didn't like something, or didn't want to do something, I could just say no. If I started a journey and changed my mind, I could just turn back. It was OK. I would just take it all . . . step by step.

So, off I went, my first real adventure by way of a train to north of the border. I'd never been anything like that distance on my own. I'd never even been out of London on my own.

As the miles ticked by, I became more and more aware my journey mattered. I got off the train, spent the night in a cheap B&B then hired a car in the morning. A tiny red Peugeot took almost all of the money I had but it got me to Glencoe, which was my jumping-off point. For what, I don't know. I'm not sure what was guiding me, but I like to think it might just have been a bit of fate. By the time I arrived in Glencoe it was far too late in the day to set out anywhere and all I was wearing as outer layers were jeans, a pair of trainers and an old Adidas cagoule. I'd just go for a quick hike, I told myself. I left the car in the car park and ambled up the mountain.

When I started my journey I was an insecure teenager. But the climb changed me, I wasn't conscious of anything as significant as that at the time, but I know it now. Deep within me I must have realised that I had to conquer something. That's what this was about, setting myself a task that seemed unlikely and making sure I achieved it. It would be a tonic, even a cure. Perhaps, deep down, I knew that evening that if I was able to stand on a summit somewhere I would prove something to myself. But initially I just set out, not thinking any further ahead than the next step. I crossed a river, scrambled up a slope and trotted through a wood. I found myself becoming a little bolder. I started selecting specific points in the distance that I promised myself I would get to.

"Step by step," I muttered to myself. If I can reach that tree over there I'll stop and turn back, I thought.

Then when I reached the tree I saw an outcrop of rocks. "I'll just get to them," I said out loud.

Soon it was early dusk. I passed hikers and climbers on their way down. More than one raised an eyebrow when they saw me. I said I was just going to see how far I could go before nightfall.

"Be careful, it's dangerous," one guy in breeches and walking boots told me severely. He was carrying a walking pole and gestured up the way he had come. "It'll be dark before you know it. You're not dressed properly. You've no pack and no sleeping bag, someone will be calling out mountain rescue."

No, they wouldn't, I thought. I hadn't told anyone I was up here.

I promised to turn back, but pressed on, passing others on their way down. I didn't care. I was on a mission. Every step gave me an increased sense of self-worth and purpose. Only I could understand and I wasn't about to explain it to anyone.

I followed a track up rough steps and crested a summit and was initially gutted to realise I had only reached a long flat glen. I now know it was Coire Gabhail, The Lost Valley, where the Clan MacDonald used to hide their cattle, or any they had rustled. It's a rough and rocky walk; all the guides tell you great care is needed and you shouldn't be up there in twilight, never mind darkness. But I didn't think about that.

I looked along the valley and knew I should turn back. There were boulders the size of houses. The glen was surrounded by peaks, but right at the back directly in front of me, I could still see a fold in the mountainside leading up to a high ridge. I wasn't thinking about a summit. I just wandered to the end of the valley to have a look, and then, almost absent-mindedly, I started to climb. Step by step. I didn't think about how I would get down if I made it to the top; I concentrated on taking each step, focusing on targets nearby: a rock, a bush. Onward and ever upward, one foot in front of the other, scrambling on my hands and knees up loose scree, until eventually I was completely committed to the climb and was focused on reaching the ridge above me. I didn't care how dark it got, this was something I was determined to accomplish.

I reached the ridge in darkness, and I stood there feeling euphoric and a tiny bit brave, aware I had really accomplished something. Above me loomed higher peaks, but for the first time in years I felt a sense of physical success. I stared at the stars, lost in the moment and delighting in a sense of achievement. This wasn't how the government wanted me to spend my benefits, but it was a complete tonic. I'd completed a journey, the very first one I had taken alone and the furthest I had ever been. Suddenly Acton seemed small and faraway and the distance offered perspective. With it the panic that had been haunting me seemed to slip away. Then, of course, reality kicked in.

"It's bloody dark," I thought to myself. "How the hell am I going to get down?"

I started back the way I had come but it was really dark and cold. I couldn't see where I was going and it wasn't long before I discovered it was harder to go down the mountain than climb up. I scrambled from side to side on the loose scree until the clouds thinned and I was able to see rocks and holes. I made it back to the valley unscathed and spent a freezing night alone in the car. I didn't care. I was elated.

A day or two later I was back on a train heading south, and, to my amazement, realised I was chatting confidently with a young woman sitting opposite. That climb up the mountain taught me that no matter how bad things might have looked for me, there was hope. When you're a youngster struggling to come to terms with life, it's easy to slip into a trough of despair. But if you can pick yourself up just enough to take a few initial steps, sometimes, just maybe, you can start to climb out of your situation. Life advice often consists of people saying you should "aim for the stars" and plan where you want to be in a year or even five years, but for me that was completely unrealistic. I could hardly see beyond the end of each day. So I set much smaller goals. It worked for me. I had climbed a mountain and my life began to improve.

It wasn't easy and things didn't change overnight. People talk about "getting their mojo back", and mine had been missing for a while. But I could feel a gentle rise in my confidence. I took things slowly. Step by step. My income support helped, as did the sympathy and support of my parents. Dad was calmer, more willing or able to love and compromise, with all of us. He suggested I try for a temporary job, and I managed to get a part-time role collecting trolleys and stacking shelves in a Waitrose supermarket. I loved it. But I still couldn't get a full-time job, so during the week I started volunteering in charity shops. It kept me out of the house, taught me how to negotiate tricky relationships and made me feel like I was actually doing something. It was my job to organise the roster, a role fraught with difficulty. Imagine organising forty occasional volunteers of a certain age. It was a diplomatic challenge to rival negotiating with Pyongyang. Each week I'd figure out what I thought would work in terms of staff then I'd pick up the phone.

"Hi Rose, it's Simon at the Cancer Research Campaign shop. I'm doing the roster for next week. Do you think you might be able to come in?"

"Oh, I can come in for half an hour next Wednesday lunchtime."

"Lunchtime, Wednesday, half an hour. OK, that's a popular slot. I'll see what I can do."

Midday on a Wednesday was when our main bundle of donations arrived from the charity distribution centre. Some volunteers wanted to come in around that time so they could have first dibs on the best clothes. I had to help manage a team, many of them fragile souls, and all for a really good cause. It helped with my self-esteem, as well as giving me advanced training in diplomacy. I stayed for six months or so while schlepping from one job centre to another in a hunt for work and applying for full-time jobs. But I was discovering that when you leave school with no qualifications, no connections and no real idea of what you want to do there's not a lot of help out there.

Everyone told me that any job would be a start, so I went for anything available: porter, janitor, sweeping the floors in the shopping centre. I applied for at least two dozen driving jobs before I finally had a call from the job centre for an interview to drive a small van delivering parcels for a firm on Wembley Stadium Trading Estate. The pay was terrible, but I honestly thought it was a job that was made for me. The sullen owner turned me down straight.

"You're the only one who's applied." He had the keys in his hand. "But I'm still not giving you the van."

I was gutted. I didn't even need to ask him why. The question was written across my face.

He folded his arms across his chest and wagged his head from side to side. "I don't have to give you a reason. I'm just not giving you the job."

I still have no idea why he turned me down and took such malicious delight in telling me to my face. Maybe the job centre had forced him to give me an interview. I had run out of money for my bus fare, and it was a long walk home.

Finally, I managed to get a full-time job with H. Samuel the jeweller's in Oxford Circus. I gave up my part-time job in the supermarket and arrived keen and expectant to start selling watches and earrings. On my first day the manager told me there was one unbreakable, unbendable rule: never, ever, take the keys to the safe home. After a long day I was on the Central Line home to Acton when I found the full bunch in my pocket. It was surely the shortest retail career ever. I went back in the morning and the astonished manager sacked me on the spot. He said it had never happened before, and either I couldn't be trusted or didn't listen but neither was good enough.

Still, I was feeling better than I had in years. I began to think anything was possible. When I wasn't in the charity shop or a job centre, I was in Westminster library looking through magazines and newspapers trying to find a job. I must have read something that sparked an interest in spying, probably Peter Wright's infamous book *Spycatcher*, because I suddenly decided I quite liked the idea of working for MI6. I actually turned up at the then secret headquarters of MI6 in Century House, in Vauxhall, an anonymous office building next to the Tube.

Imagine the scene: a teenager in scruffy jeans and a cheap leather jacket wanders into the global headquarters of the Secret Intelligence Service. The receptionist did a double-take from behind a thick Plexiglas window. Standing in the background beyond her was a police guard cradling a sub-machine gun. His expression spoke for him. *What the hell do you want?*

"Hi," I said to the receptionist. "Erm, I've just come in to see if I can apply for a job."

"I'm sorry?"

"I just wondered if I could apply for a job. Working for, y'know . . ." and then I actually leaned forward and lowered my voice, "M-I-6."

She stared at me with her mouth slightly open, trying to decide if I was for real. Then she started shaking her head. "No," she said, ever so slowly. "No, no; that's really not how things work. You would need to contact the Foreign Office."

"Oh, OK," I said brightly with a glance at the guard. "I'll go and have a chat with them, then."

It makes me cringe now. But I also have a sneaking admiration for myself at that moment. Just a few months before I'd been on a bridge about to kill myself. I was all over the place. One month I was in a state of desperate depression, and the next I was walking into MI6 in some vague hope of becoming a spook.

After that my approach was completely scattergun. I did actually get a job working as a clerical assistant for the Ministry of Defence, albeit by replying to a conventional advert in the job centre rather than ambling into the MoD in Whitehall or stopping an admiral in the street for a chat. I was so nervous when I started the job that I vomited most of the way there on my first day. They made me sign the Official Secrets Act then posted me to a top-secret department at the Empress State Building in Earls Court that handled communications between the nuclear fleet and the land-based command. It sounded important, but then they showed me into the office where I would be working. I was going to be locked into a small room with three middle-aged men with grey hair and grey skin, and my job was to photocopy documents. Thousands of them. Endlessly. Each time the photocopier whirred and clicked a second copy would be put into a locked safe. There was no natural light because of blast curtains, even though we were high in the building, and security was so tight, if we wanted to go to the loo we had to buzz through to a desk and somebody would unlock the door and escort us to the toilets. I was desperate for a proper job, but after an hour in there even I realised I would go mad within a week.

At lunchtime they unlocked the office door and escorted me to the lift so I could pop out for a sandwich. I dodged around a corner, hopped into the Tube and never went back. It caused something of a furore. I'd spent a morning photocopying secret documents and then I vanished into thin air. A day later two plain-clothes police officers showed up at my parents' house and identified themselves as Special Branch. I could hear them talking to my mum at the front door.

"Do you know where your son is, Mrs Reeve? We really need to find him."

Mum stalled for me, muttering something about how I might be out.

"Mrs Reeve? We would really like to speak to him."

"I'm so sorry, officers," she said politely. "But I don't think he wants to see you."

I got off my bed, opened my door and called down. "Mum," I shouted, "tell them I'm not coming out. And I'm not going back."

Short of getting a warrant to search the house there was little they could do.

I sank back into a brief period of depression. I had applied for countless jobs, been ignored, rejected and sacked. After walking out of the only employment I might have been able to hold down I wondered if I would ever manage to find a proper job.

Dad came to the rescue. We'd had our huge, pathetic and violent differences but I knew he wanted the best for me and wanted to see me make something of my life. He didn't pull a few strings, call an old school chum to get me a job, or ring his wealthy friends, because he didn't have any. Instead he helped me find my way in life by spotting an advert in the back of *The Sunday Times*. The newspaper wanted a small team of post-boys and -girls and was holding out the possibility of some journalism training for anyone who worked hard. I thought it was a job that was completely out of my league. I hadn't gone to private school or university, let alone Oxford or Cambridge, still where so many media people are drawn from. There were thousands of over-qualified graduates jostling for any job in the media. But this ad was aimed specifically and exclusively at non-graduates, at people who weren't from traditional media backgrounds or influential families. I had a chance.

I put my all into my application. I had time on my hands and nothing to lose. I turned my CV into my own newspaper and sent it in with an essay I'd written on *Schindler's Ark*. An exec at the paper called me in for an interview on a busy, chaotic Friday and they seemed to like me. I had never lost interest in what was going on in the world and perhaps I was able to impress them with a little knowledge despite my nerves. I was keen, even desperate. They said I fit the bill, that I was exactly the sort of person they had in mind when

77

they placed the ad. It turned out it was the idea of the editor, Andrew Neil. He's had his critics over the years, but I owe him my career. More than 5,000 people applied for the five positions. Two weeks later I was offered one of the jobs. I couldn't quite believe it. Old fears kicked in, of failure and making a fool of myself. This was the most prestigious newspaper in Western Europe — how on earth would a pathetic lad from Acton fit in?

I knew I had to overcome those fears, otherwise they would cripple me. I had to decide that my fear of regret if I didn't take the opportunity was greater than my fear of failure. I decided I had to be just a little bit more positive, hopeful and optimistic. I would take the job, embrace the opportunity and overcome my nerves by taking everything gently and slowly . . . step by step.

CHAPTER
SIX

Foot in the Door

If going for an interview at the *Sunday Times* had been nerve-wracking, travelling there for my first day was horrendous. In the days before I started I suffered from regular panic attacks: dizzy spells, uncontrollable fear, shaking and then incredible nausea. To get there on my first day I had to take my mum along on the Tube for support. I was eighteen, I had been suicidal, depressed, unemployed and out of school for nearly a year. I was a bag of nerves.

The building itself was daunting, a huge old rum warehouse in Wapping split into various departments with the editor Andrew Neil's office at one end, then the picture desk, newsroom, foreign department and investigations, and the post room next to the photocopiers and toilets in the middle. Business, sport, the style section and travel were at the furthest end. The newsroom had a sense of immediacy and urgency you'd be hard pressed to find anywhere else. There was drama and activity, and it constantly felt like a war-room.

When I started most of the staff on the paper seemed to be Oxbridge or Ivy League. I was the least educated person in the room. I often still am today. Everyone on the paper seemed frighteningly clever, brilliant and ludicrously worldly. Some were legends. I'd watched films about two journalists on the *Sunday Times*. One of them was Jon Swain, a foreign correspondent for the paper who had served in the French Foreign Legion, been kidnapped in Northern Ethiopia and held for months in the desert by a group called the Tigrayan People's Liberation Front, and been immortalised in *The Killing Fields*, the Oscar-winning 1984 film set in Cambodia during the slaughter carried out by the Khmer Rouge, which I and millions of others had watched in numbed horror. The other was Peter Hounam, the chief investigative reporter at the paper. I'd seen a TV movie dramatising an investigation he conducted which revealed the existence of Israel's secret nuclear weapons programme. It was a global scoop. Mossad, the Israeli secret service, had kidnapped his source Mordechai Vanunu and smuggled him back to the Middle East. I was going to work near these people. I was supposed to be sorting their mail. Walking in there on day one left me feeling completely awed. My knees quaked.

My nerves and fears lasted for the first few weeks. I shouldn't have worried, but I did. Then I would start feeling nauseous. To avoid being sick I'd skip meals. Yet slowly I realised that I didn't need to be dominated by fear. I was a lowly post-boy, but I felt welcome and useful right from the start. It was a ferociously busy place full of hard-bitten, ambitious hacks, but I posed no threat and from the beginning almost everyone was

80

welcoming and friendly. They made me feel as if I was part of a team, and we were all on a mission. For all my trepidation and churning stomach, the office felt exciting. Even I could sense something tantalising: possibility.

Initially little was expected of me except to be there, often early, and make sure I did what was asked. The four other non-grads who joined at the same time were all at least a few years older. We would either work an early shift starting at 7a.m., or a later one starting at 10. The early shift collected the first post delivery of between ten and twenty sacks of mail from the loading bay, shifted them into the central *Sunday Times* post room in a trolley or over shoulders, and then sorted them by hand. It was a mountain of mail that took hours to clear and I worked at it day after day. I had no pretensions about who I was or what I should be. Never for a second did I think that sorting mail or running errands was beneath me. Quite the opposite. I was bloody grateful for a job and I threw myself into it with gusto.

The end wall of our post room was lined with around a hundred pigeon-holes, which we would sort mail into and then empty every few hours and deliver the contents to people at their desks. It was mundane but perfect for me. I wasn't ready for anything more challenging, and sorting the post gave me an insight into who everyone was and what they did. Most people on the paper were chained to their desks, but I walked miles every day around that old warehouse delivering mail and packages. I knew every inch of the place. I couldn't have asked for a better grounding. It put me in the perfect position to take advantage of the situation.

Right from day one, I realised this was the biggest opportunity of my life. I had a foot in the door. I set about trying to make myself useful, initially just by learning how to use the fax machine and the photocopiers. Long before everything went digital, proof copies of the newspaper pages were made on huge A1/A2 photocopiers and passed to the senior executives for their checks and corrections. The copiers were ancient and forever breaking down. I learned how to fix them and kept them running. In a paper that completely depended on the copier churning out the page proofs it was a critical skill. Being the only one who could keep them alive made me unsackable.

Back then I had nothing going on in my life except that job. I lived at home. I didn't have a girlfriend or see many friends. I would work a full shift sorting the post, then hang around talking to people, volunteering help and slowly, little by little, step by step, picking up confidence and contacts until people were asking me to do small gofer chores for them. Perhaps picking up a package from the couriers, collecting newspaper articles from the cuttings library or getting them tea and a sandwich when they were on a deadline. Then I would offer more help. Cuttings had to be returned at the end of the day, so did they want me to photocopy them? All of them? I'd copy cuttings not just as a bodged job, but carefully and thoughtfully, placing them on the machines so they could actually be read. I remember taking time over those smallest tasks. And never moaning or complaining or getting above myself. I was enjoying everything. I would have worked there for free. And that showed. It made a difference.

After a few months the arts editor David Mills, who was always seen in a three-piece suit, usually tweed, and a homburg hat, asked me to go through the cuttings and find the worst reviews of West End shows to put into a small article. It was a laborious job. I found a few to show him and to check I was getting it right.

"That works, that one doesn't, that one does," he said, mainly to himself, as he glanced through them.

I could have just nodded and checked my watch to see what time I could leave. Instead I said simply: "Why?"

He was rushed off his feet. He didn't need to explain himself to me. But he flicked back through the articles and pointed out what he was looking for. He was happy with what I'd already found, but I stayed there until after midnight in the airless, windowless cuttings library deep in the bowels of "Fortress Wapping" and went through hundreds of articles and reviews looking for more juicy or malicious quotes, wrote them out, and then presented them to him the next morning. I actually found a few that made him laugh. So instead of just working them into an article he put them into a marked-out box on a page in the arts section and added my name underneath. It was my first ever byline, a tiny "compiled by Simon Reeve". Well, I could hardly have been prouder if I had written the splash on the front page. My grandma cut it out and framed it.

Funny how even just a morsel of success can make a person hungry for more. A few key people started to pick up on my enthusiasm. Looking back now, I think I became a bit of a project for some of the older hacks who had entered the profession with ideals and were delighted that some youngsters had been brought into the paper from different and mostly ordinary backgrounds.

One afternoon Peter Hounam, the chief investigative reporter, came to get his mail while I was sorting the post. Peter was big, bearded, kindly, and something of a hangover from the past. A union man through and through, he conducted old-school long-term investigations into corruption, arms dealing and organised crime by doggedly pursuing leads and sources. We started chatting and I mentioned I'd love to help him in my spare time.

It was nothing major at first, just photocopying more cuttings, but it quickly developed. Every success I had led on to something else. Soon I was searching phone directories for him and tracing people he wanted to find who had been involved in dodgy deals, or going out to public record offices and libraries hunting through the electoral roll.

I had only been at the paper for four months when I had my big break. John Witherow, the foreign editor, came marching through to the post room and called me over.

"You've been doing lots of research for Hounam and other people, haven't you, Simon?" he said. I was amazed he even knew my name. "We've got a lead on something. Might be a story. Not sure. Might need you to go to Boston."

Boston! I stared at him. *I'd never even been on a plane.*

He said it as casually as if he was asking me to pop to the canteen and get him a prawn sandwich.

"You're free at the moment, aren't you?"

I nodded nervously.

"I've just got to go into [the editors'] conference now. I'll give you more details in a minute. Just get ready."

He marched off. I wondered whether I should just follow him and tell him I wasn't even sure I had a passport.

I took some post down to the news desk and told the secretaries where I might be going, trying to impress them. I told some friends on the picture desk. They were excited for me. Then I told the researcher on features, the deputy managing editor, the production department and the secretary from the arts section. It's possible I also told one or two of the journalists in home news.

I trotted over to see Peter. I had a pile of cuttings for him. He could see I was flushed with excitement.

"Are you OK?" he asked.

"You won't believe this," I hissed, nodding towards the foreign desk, "but Witherow wants me to go to Boston. Boston!"

Peter cocked a quizzical eyebrow.

"I don't know if I have a passport. I mean, I must have a passport but I have no idea where it is . . ." I rambled on.

Peter cut in.

"Simon, um . . . he means Boston in Lincolnshire. Sorry. They were talking about it after conference."

I felt like a bit of a plum, but also slightly relieved.

Witherow called me to a side office for a quick briefing.

"We've had a tip that two South African neo-Nazi terrorists who are on the run might actually be here in the UK."

"Neo-Nazis?" I queried, stopping him in mid-flow. "Terrorists?" I remember saying the words very slowly, taking it all in.

"Yes." He looked sideways at me, perhaps wondering whether I was ready for this. I tried to look more confident. As if this was normal.

"They blew up queues of people waiting for taxis in the townships. Some say they were given weapons by a rogue South African intelligence unit that's trying to undermine the peace process. The South African police are after them. But we think they left the country overland on false passports and have since flown here. One of them has family in Lincolnshire. We've been given a number," he said, producing a hastily written scrap of paper. "We know it's in Boston, but nobody is answering. I've just tried it again. It's probably a dud lead but why don't you head up there? We'll try to find an address for the number and then you could pop round and knock on their door. Oh, and you could keep trying that number for us," he said, almost as an afterthought.

My mind was spinning.

"If you speak to them tell them you're from the *Sunday Times*. We think they want to talk to us. After that it's up to you. Use your judgement and if you think they'll talk to us and they have something interesting to say, phone me."

He gave me the slip of paper, the foreign desk manager gave me some petty cash and I grabbed my bag and jumped in a taxi to the station. I was breathing heavily, almost hyperventilating. But not just with nerves. With excitement as well. I was a post-room boy on a mission. I felt a real sense of purpose. As I'd been leaving another reporter on the paper told me the men were on the run from the South African secret service, and they were probably being hunted by an armed ANC unit. It was possible MI6 knew they were in the UK or had even let them into the country and was encouraging them to talk to us.

At King's Cross I found a quiet payphone and rang the number Witherow had given me. I expected it to ring off the hook. It was answered almost immediately, but only with silence.

I felt the hairs on the back of my neck stand up. "Hello?" I said nervously. "Hello?"

Silence.

"Hello?" I tried again.

"Who is this?" said an accusing voice with an Afrikaans accent, guttural in my ear.

Inwardly I gasped, then tried to speak. For a second nothing came out. And then everything just clicked into place.

"My name is Simon Reeve. I'm calling from the *Sunday Times* newspaper in London. I gather you might want to share your story with us," I paused for effect. "I'm on my way to Lincolnshire. I hope we can meet up, face-to-face."

My confidence surprised me. I was speaking completely differently, replacing my laddish West London accent with a deeper tone. But I had heard Peter and other investigators talking in this direct, almost commanding way and milking the name of the paper for all of the authority it carried.

There was silence, and the sound of clicks on the line. *My God, was somebody else listening?* "Where shall we meet?" I said, a little less certainly.

"Where do you suggest?" said the voice.

It was working. Bloody hell. I had to think quickly. I looked around for inspiration.

"Let's meet on the station platform?"

"In Boston?"

"Yes. I can be there in three hours."

"How will we know you?" The voice was rasping.

It came to me quickly: "I'll be carrying a copy of *The Times* under my left arm. You do the same." There was a grunt of agreement down the line. By the time I hung up the phone I was shaking.

I took the main line north and then switched onto a branch line to Boston. The train was full of farmers, country gents and schoolchildren. And then there was me, en route to meet two South African terrorists. I must have looked faintly ridiculous, a wide-eyed eighteeen-year-old just a couple of years older than the schoolkids, wearing a leather jacket bought from Shepherd's Bush market and a tie my mum had bought me from the Makro cash and carry. But I felt a surge of pride, and a strange feeling I had rarely experienced before: a sense of purpose and meaning. I was on a mission, and it mattered.

I was late to meet them. I had arrived early but walked into the small market town, not to check if I was being followed or anything professional, but to send a postcard to my mum, telling her I was out of London. When I realised the time I fairly scuttled back to the station with my newspaper tucked firmly under my arm. Boston station is not a large place. There were no trains and no other passengers, save for me on one platform, and two neo-Nazis on the other. It was a surreal moment.

We met halfway across the track and agreed to go to a nearby pub to talk. I had never met anyone like these men. They had committed acts of pure evil. But instead of fearing them, I could see they were pathetic. One was a weaselly-looking thin guy with darting eyes. The other was a much bigger Neanderthal with hairy hands and terrible body odour. They didn't impress me. I wasn't in awe of them and I didn't feel fear. I was a pathetic and nervous lad, but even I could see they were just two thugs full of hate and venom. These two men had been identified as a powerful destabilising force in South Africa, yet to me they seemed amateurish.

Between them they carried two heavy holdalls. One bag contained clothes and weapons. They opened it to reveal handguns, more to show off than as a threat. The other contained documents they said could prove they had been funded, not by a rogue element within the South African secret service, but officially by something called the Civil Cooperation Bureau, an organisation run by the South African Defence Force, which had been involved in the murder and attempted murder of anti-apartheid activists.

They said they had carried out the taxi-rank bombing on the orders of the CCB man who recruited them. They claimed a "third force" was at work in South Africa, trying to pit rival black parties against each other in an attempt to preserve white rule. They told me, and we later confirmed, that before they escaped they had been moved into a hospital from maximum-security prison after they started a hunger strike.

They also said they could prove that South Africa was channelling arms to a guerrilla army in neighbouring Mozambique to destabilise the government there, and the South African Defence Force had given thousands of rifles to the Zulu rivals of Mandela's ANC in the hope of igniting war between the groups. They showed me documents and mentioned specific names of officials and officers.

We sat in a corner in the quiet pub, a few regulars glancing occasionally in our direction, while they talked in hushed tones about their involvement with military intelligence contacts, a "Mr Sting", sanctions-busting arms deals, the white-supremacist Church of the Creator, and the extremist Order of the Boer Nation.

They spoke calmly about what they had done, as if they were merely business transactions. Not once did they question why a teenager had been sent to meet them.

I should probably have walked out. Run out. Called my mum. Panicked. But I didn't. I actually felt that in this dark world I had found my calling. I listened carefully. I made notes. They sounded like the real thing, genuinely awful, and said they would talk to the paper, so I called the *Sunday Times*, spoke to the foreign desk, and told them I would bring the pair to London. Hotels were arranged, tickets immediately purchased.

I suspect all this couldn't happen today. In a time of risk assessments and corporate health and safety, I doubt a newspaper could send an untrained kid to find, debrief and deliver a couple of terrorists. But this was a different time, when risk was more acceptable, and it meant I was able to be involved in investigations that would normally take a degree, training and a decade of experience.

I persuaded them to drop their weapons back at their safe house, and then I took the South Africans, including the nervous wife and daughter of the weasel, who appeared from a car hidden around the corner, back to London. If it had been strange coming on the branch line on the way there, it was ten times more bizarre heading back on the train again with the farmers and the schoolchildren, and two nutjob terrorists.

In London I remember their shock when a police car, driven by a black officer, pulled alongside our taxi.

Weasel nudged Neanderthal and then said to me: "Well, that's not good, is it, Simon?"

I ignored him and looked out of the window. We were nearly back in Wapping. One of the senior journalists met us and took over the babysitting a large article appeared in the paper that weekend. I was just pleased to have been involved. I hadn't fouled things up. Quite the opposite. Everyone was delighted with what I'd done. Critically, I realised that terrorists, who I had always imagined as horned devils, could be worryingly human.

I mentioned it to Peter, and he told me about the philosopher Hannah Arendt, who wrote a seminal work on the war crimes trial of Adolph Eichmann, the Nazi responsible for organising the transportation of millions of Jews to concentration camps during the Final Solution. Arendt described Eichmann as "terrifyingly normal". She coined a phrase: "the banality of evil". It applied perfectly to the South Africans. They were pathetic, but they had still managed to threaten the peace process. Terrorism became something I would study intently. But first, that evening when I got back from Boston, I went straight back in to sort the mail.

My first mission led to many more, often for Peter or the elite Insight team on the *Sunday Times* which also ran long-term investigations. But I was still a post-boy, so I had to juggle two ludicrously different roles. One moment I would be collecting the mail or a bundle of designer clothes for a photoshoot from the courier drop-off point at "Gate Six" at the far end of the

Wapping plant, and the next I'd be asked to work on an investigation into drug smuggling or the IRA. With hindsight, it was absurd.

But the newspaper was a meritocratic sort of place. One of the most brilliant writers on the paper had started there on two weeks of work experience, but he kept his security pass when he was supposed to have left, sat in a corner and waited until he was asked to help on a story. People there were interested in results, not where I had come from, what my background was, how old I was, or whether there were two sacks of mail needing sorting. I found myself involved in investigations into ever more dodgy subjects, including arms dealing and smuggling. The Soviet Union was collapsing and imploding. The world was awash with weapons. One of the investigators took me to a meeting with an intelligence contact.

"Who's this?" said the contact with a smile, shaking me by the hand.

"This is Simon. He might be me in the future," said my colleague with a laugh.

I was stunned. It was an enormous vote of confidence.

"Fair enough," said the intelligence officer. That was good enough for him.

The contact was chatty, garrulous and charismatic. Each meeting I had with him was memorable. It was always on an understanding that we would share gossip and briefings but check and double-check anything we put into print. It might sound like a cosy relationship between the state and the media, but I came to see it as another check and balance on the power of both. He talked to us because we questioned but respected his work. He was ideological and driven by a desire for the world to be a better place. He could have been an aid worker or a campaigner, and we were a safety valve for information he thought should be shared and disseminated. Over the years he opened more doors and guided me into other areas of darkness. But then, he was talking about nuclear weapons.

In the early 1990s the intelligence world was racing to monitor the Soviet nuclear stockpile and prevent it falling into the hands of rogue regimes or terrorist groups. Secret reports suggested Russian scientists had created a strange and exotic substance called "red mercury", that enabled the creation of briefcase-sized nuclear bombs that could be easily smuggled and yet utterly devastating. It was the stuff of a Tom Clancy novel, and years later red mercury became the focus of Hollywood movies. But in the early 1990s, in my late teens and early twenties, I was researching and investigating both its existence and the shadow world in which it was supposedly being smuggled.

Contacts told us their sources in Russia were adamant red mercury could be used to create a pure fusion bomb the size of a football, possibly even a hand grenade, that it was invisible to all available detection measures, and that if used it could wipe out life in a mile or half-mile radius. Documents later claimed to show Boris Yeltsin had issued a licence to a mysterious Russian firm to export red mercury, presumably to rogue regimes. People were talking about multi-billion-pound deals, that red mercury was a substance that could provide clean energy as well as fuel weapons, that it was worth ten times more per gram than gold, then a thousand times more than diamonds. Arms dealers who were thought to be brokering deals were found dead, shot in the head or with plastic bags over their heads. Then a British executive with a South African chemical company was found chopped into small pieces in the trunk of his luxury car in Soweto near Johannesburg in November 1991. His body was covered in a strange black gunk. Intelligence reports suggested he might have tried to sell red mercury to buyers from the Middle East. It was appalling, dark and tangled.

I was sent to Newcastle to speak to his family. I remember the way they looked — ghost-like — as they tried to come to terms with the horror of what had happened. I saw autopsy photos of his remains. They were the most graphic and appalling images I had ever seen. I was nineteen years old. There was no training. My flight to Newcastle was the first time I had ever been on a plane. I didn't know how to put on the lap-belt. I didn't eat the snacks I was offered because I thought you had to pay for them. I was such a kid. I was still sorting the post, for goodness' sake. But I was pitched into ghastly and fascinating investigations.

Peter Hounam became my unofficial mentor, and the newspaper became the education I had missed. It was my college and university. I learned how to investigate difficult and demanding subjects. How to dig, flatter and flirt for information; how to read, understand and mirror people; I learned how to move from chatting with a gang in East London or talking on the phone with a shady business in Dubai, to meeting with an MP in Parliament.

My principal weapon was a telephone, which I would have glued to my ears for hours. The name and authority of the paper helped secure access and kept people on the line. Peter taught me silence is a great way of encouraging others to speak.

Then we had computers linked to public records and, even before the advent of the internet and the World Wide Web, early databases of articles that were a powerful resource, giving an experienced user access to stories and information from around the world. The system we used gave me as much intelligence-gathering capability as that of a small country. Researching the killing in South Africa, for example, I could guarantee that local newspapers in the area would have fresh and different leads from their own contacts that we could also chase up and follow. But the database also had scientific journals, press releases, texts from obscure conferences and government tenders.

Another tool was Companies House in London, where detailed records for all UK limited companies were kept. The elite and the dodgy might be able to hire PR teams and lawyers and hide much of what they were doing, but every firm had to file annual returns and — crucially — list their directors with their home addresses. It was a goldmine. I spent hours going through microfiches looking for people we were investigating, until flicking through the documents on film would give me dizzying motion sickness.

I never hacked phones. But I certainly used tactics that would come into a grey zone of legality. My defence would have been simple. I felt then, and believe still now, as pompous as it might sound, that I was working on investigations that were in the public good. I wasn't involved in any activity my own moral code deemed unacceptable, although I was certainly underhand. I learned to obtain information by pretty much any means possible. I spent days on surveillance jobs sitting in the back of vans watching target addresses, eating cold pizzas and peeing in bottles.

The investigators on the paper were dogged, thoughtful and caring. I thought and still think the work they were doing was a vital check on power, and essential for a healthy democracy. Watching them and learning from them was an education no university could offer.

CHAPTER
SEVEN

Walkie-talkies and Binoculars

It was a tip from a whistle-blower that sent me undercover into the BBC's dirty laundry. One week I had a call from an engineer who worked at the iconic Television Centre in White City. He was worried about fire safety in the passages and corridors down in the bowels underneath the building.

"The whole place is a death trap," he told me. "It could go up at any moment! I've complained over and over again and nobody is listening to me."

We met and talked and agreed I needed to see the issues with my own eyes. The plan was for me to play squash with him at the BBC's internal sports club, then hide until the club closed. When we finished a couple of games he thought the area would be empty, but several people were still working around the club, so I had to hide for an hour in a large wheeled basket underneath dirty towels from the sports club. They stank of stale male sweat, like socks that hadn't been washed for weeks. It was one of the least pleasant experiences of my working life. But when everyone else left for the evening the engineer returned and I was able to hop out.

I had a covert body-worn camera, which I had bought from a spy shop for a previous investigation, to capture images of what the whistle-blower said were extreme breaches of fire safety. But I was carrying just a racquet and still wearing my gym kit, on the grounds we could say I was heading back to the club if discovered, so I had nowhere I could hide the camera. My sports T-shirt was too tight for unsightly camera bulges, so I had to strap the camera around my waist inside my shorts.

We came to an area deep under TV Centre where one fire door seemed to be missing and another was propped open by jerry cans of chemicals. Wood stanchions, posts and rolls of paper were stacked together further along the corridor almost as if they were ready for a bonfire.

"Look, look!" he said, getting very agitated. "Go on, take a photo."

Then I had to pull my shorts down at the front and take a photograph, before quickly hiding everything away before anyone came wandering past.

The whole thing was, of course, ridiculous, and the images I took were too dark for any fire safety expert to verify as a problem.

But I was game, and the newspaper decided to send me on a course in Portsmouth where they taught me shorthand and how to write without libelling people. I shuttled to and from London, still trying to work on projects. I don't know when I ate and I can't recall where I slept, because I was pretty much running on empty. I remember driving back from Portsmouth so tired that a voice in my head said *I'll just close my eyes until I get to the bridge ahead*. The next thing I knew was the wheels rumbling over the cat's eyes. I had tried to take a nap while driving. I'm not sure what Darwin would make of that.

Before long, Peter and other journalists were suggesting I should be writing my own stories. I started by drafting articles for the hacks. They gained by having someone collate thoughts and quotes, but they also had to work through and then rewrite the ramblings of a school-leaver. My first piece was on arms smuggling. Seriously. I sent it over to Peter's computer and sat next to him as he read it. He finished it, sat back in his chair, linked his hands over his stomach and looked at me kindly.

"Always remember there's a thousand ways of writing a piece like this," he said.

It was a brilliant way of telling me it was a pile of manure, without bruising my fragile ego. I watched closely how he wrote the real article, and what he looked for and used from his notes. He picked a few phrases from my words and worked them into his own, which helped my confidence. I learned quickly. I've heard people say that if you start at the bottom in the media the first thing you need to do is kiss it. Very crude. I never had to grovel or suck up to anyone at the *Sunday Times*. There were privileged and brilliant young graduates at the paper. One was a peer, another was the daughter of Michael Heseltine. Several became friends. They all treated me with respect and kindness. But it probably helped that I was open-minded and eager. I watched, I volunteered, I always said yes to a request, even if I was supposed to be heading home, and I was prepared to go an extra mile to do the job well. I tried to give people what they wanted, but equally I tried to show initiative by being proactive and pushing ideas and suggestions.

Pretty quickly I learned that being flexible was also key, and that I couldn't expect everyone to accept me on my terms; I had to be able to adapt to different circumstances and situations. I stopped talking to older people at the paper in the same way I would talk to my mates in Acton. I learned to fit in. Perhaps if I had been less of a blank canvas that would have been more challenging. I think my ordinary background and absence of education actually helped.

Almost every day something would crop up and I would be off investigating or even tailing people, trying to find out where they lived or where they were going. I was part of a small pool of youngsters on the paper with no training, no risk assessment and no thought for health and safety. I didn't care, my confidence was growing every week and I loved the job. It was all very *Boys' Own*.

On one occasion I was part of a small team, armed with walkie-talkies and binoculars, that had to follow an arms dealer from Gatwick Airport into the heart of London. We had received a tip-off he was travelling on a scheduled flight, hiding in plain sight. It was thrilling, even when we realised another surveillance team was on his tail.

Another time I had to drive around London in a hired convertible Mercedes for a weekend while a black investigator drove another identical car to test who would be stopped by the police. I went off script that weekend. At one point I had six friends in the car while we drove to a party with the roof down. I clearly remember thinking that even if I lost my job it was worth it. I was not stopped once. My colleague was stopped within half an hour, and several times afterwards.

I was learning every day and the hours were ludicrous. I was at the paper six or seven days a week. Often I wouldn't make it home at all and would crash on a sofa at a colleague or friend's house and buy a clean shirt in Asda on the way back to work in the morning. Others would leave in the small hours, then come back in early, put their coat on the back of their chair and switch their computers on to make it look as if they were working, and then go back to their car or sit on the toilet for a couple of hours and have a nap. There was a general expectation that you would come in early and leave very late. Every day off I had I slept for twelve hours. Every week of holiday I had I was ill, as if my body knew that finally it was able to give up.

But it was a fascinating place to work. Every day was interesting. Every week had at least a little bit of an adventure alongside the post sorting, whether it was researching, investigating, surveillance, or being sent out to football matches or riots. In the early 1990s the IRA was still very active on the UK mainland. In 1991 three mortars were fired at Downing Street. A couple of weeks after that a bomb exploded at Paddington Station. Later in the year there were explosions on Oxford Street, the National Gallery and at Clapham Junction. Even as a post-boy researcher I would be among a group sent to the scene scouring for information.

I was helping out on the news desk one busy Friday night, just a day after the general election which re-elected John Major as Prime Minister, when the IRA detonated a massive truck bomb at the Baltic Exchange building in the City of London. The *Sunday Times* offices were a few miles away but we heard the blast clearly. For a second everyone froze. Then a few people went outside to see if they could see smoke. Andrew Neil, the editor, emerged from his office and came striding towards us.

"OK, everyone, let's focus," he said, clapping his hands to get attention. "You, you and you," he said, pointing to some of the reporters. "Get on the phones and find out what's happened." He turned to a handful of others that included me. "You four — go there now and see how close you can get."

A couple of us raced to our cars. Someone else jumped on their motorbike, another into a taxi and we headed to the scene in an attempt to glean as much information as we could. Whether we were going to a bombing, a riot or a football match, often it was about seeing with our own eyes what had happened so we could give a visual account for the newspaper, or in this case talking to others who had been close to the blast or were even walking wounded. The Baltic Exchange bombing killed three people, including a fifteen-year-old girl, and injured ninety-one. It was believed to be the biggest bomb detonated on the mainland since the Second World War. Then just a few hours later another large bomb went off at Staples Corner in North-West London, also causing mayhem.

Being at the scene of a riot, or the aftermath of a bombing, can be frightening and upsetting. But I confess it can also be exciting. You feel challenged, on edge, and alive. I managed to slip through the police cordon around the Baltic Exchange and see the damage for myself. There was devastation. I wrote up my notes and sent them on to feature writers who included my copy in their final article.

I can't say I ever actually learned how to write. Eventually I learned how to put words in roughly the right order. I watched how others wrote, sitting quietly next to them for hours and weeks until I could predict what words they would use. I arrived at the paper without preconceptions or skill and I was able to train with some of the best writers in the industry. But I never studied or understood the basic rules. I still cannot define a noun, let alone a definite or indefinite article, or an objective personal pronoun. I rely on spell-check to guide my use of "to" or "too". Does it matter? Colleagues said to me: "If you want to write, just get on and write. Don't wait for a qualification."

Peter asked me to work on an investigation into a dam project under construction in Malaysia. He had finished and published the main investigation and he was about to pen a follow-up article a couple of weeks later when he looked across the desk at me.

"Why don't you write this up instead?" he said. Then he gave me a final piece of superb advice: "Just make every sentence count."

I stayed late into the night with rain rattling hard on the corrugated plastic roof. I worked in every nuance and detail of the investigation, then remembered Peter's advice and stripped it back to the key essentials. I topped it with a drop-intro and tailed it with a pay-off conclusion. It was all I had learned about the style of the newspaper.

The piece went into the system with a few changes, but never made it to print. Yet I was delighted. It was a massive boost to my self-esteem. I wrote a few more short pieces that were tucked on the inside pages and within a short space of time I was writing articles that went into the paper pretty much unchanged. Then the news desk editors began asking me to glance over other copy and "give it a quick tweak". I would take an article in the news desk holding queue and doctor it a little. The way the system worked meant that writers could see where their articles were in the sausage machine that led to the editor's system, subeditors and then "the stone", where type was set into a final layout for inclusion and printing, in the old days using a stone slab. By checking the computer, you could tell exactly where your article was in the line and whether someone had it open on their computer. It didn't take long before experienced journos realised an article they had been slaving over for days was being edited by the twenty-something post-boy. Initially a couple stormed over and asked to know what I was doing. I had to explain that the news editor wanted me to take a look at it, and I was trying to help get it into the paper. Egos were involved, but publication was the ultimate aim for everyone, and most people accepted that if the news editor wanted the post-boy to tweak it then he was the boss.

After a year or so of tweaking articles I became one of the news department's main re-writers. Several of the expert correspondents were specialists from their particular fields rather than trained journalists, and I would sometimes be given their articles to rework into the *Sunday Times* style. I had been promoted out of the post room into the newsroom but people from other sections would still ask me to fetch their cuttings or take a package to the post room. More than once I had to explain I wasn't really working in the post room any more, and I had a frontpage article to copy-edit.

The original *Sunday Times* articles about the Malaysian dam scandal caused something of a stir. Relations between the UK and the Malays soured, legal letters flew back and forth. It became a major diplomatic incident.

The article had helped to reveal that a sale of British weapons to Malaysia had been linked to the provision of hundreds of millions of pounds in UK aid for the Pergau hydro-electric dam scheme in northern Malaysia, a project deemed hopelessly uneconomic by officials in Britain and Malaysia. It remains one of

Britain's biggest aid scandals. In response to the newspaper revelations, the Malaysian Prime Minister, Mahathir Mohamad, imposed a sweeping trade ban with the UK, freezing negotiations for Malaysian government contracts worth billions.

Around the same time a group of British soldiers went missing in Malaysian Borneo and a veteran reporter from the *Sunday Times* was sent out to cover the search. The following Saturday we were working to get the paper out when a phone rang in the newsroom. I picked it up. "Newsroom," I said.

I could hear shouting, the sound of banging, then a voice came down the line, strained, desperate; panic in the tone. "Who is that?" it said.

"It's Simon," I said blankly.

"Reeve?!" I recognised the voice of my colleague.

"Yes. What's going on? Are you all right?"

"No, no, they're taking me. I'm being taken."

I shouted over to alert the news desk and put the call on speakerphone.

"They're taking me away. Get someone from the Embassy."

We heard more shouting, then another voice came closer to the phone screaming abuse in what we presumed was Malay.

The line went dead. It had to be some sort of retribution for our articles about the Pergau dam. The news editor ran into the editor's office. He emerged in seconds and told me to get on the phone to the Foreign Office while someone else called the British ambassador in Kuala Lumpur. The deputy news editor began preparing an article for Reuters, the global news wire. I was on the phone to the Foreign Office as my colleague was tapping away at his keyboard: *A senior Sunday Times correspondent has been arrested in Malaysian Borneo . . .*

An article for Reuters meant the news would spread worldwide in a matter of minutes. I spoke to a senior official at the Foreign Office and asked them to inform the Foreign Secretary and flash an alert to the Ambassador in Malaysia. There was a degree of panic at the other end of the line:

"What are we supposed to do? It's Borneo, for heaven's sake. It's the middle of the night over there. We've only got an honorary consul anywhere near there and he's four hours away."

"Phone him," I said. "Wake him up and get him over there. The editor is demanding you take this seriously."

Twenty minutes or so later they called back to say the consul had jumped in a car and was already driving through the jungle. By now the article was ready to go to Reuters, but before it was sent the news editor suggested that maybe we should try to call a stringer in Borneo, a freelance journalist who had worked on a couple of articles for us in the past. He, in turn, managed to speak to a highly indignant local chief of police. Far from being carted off as retribution over the dam articles, our *ST* man had been embroiled in a heated argument in a restaurant over the price of a lobster. He had strong words with the owner, and then became involved in an unfortunate altercation with a man he thought was a waiter. In reality he was the brother of the owner, and he was also the local chief of police.

We had called the emergency line to the duty officer at the Foreign Office and sent the honorary consul halfway across Borneo. Very embarrassing. When our correspondent was released in the morning and slunk home a few days later, he found a blow-up plastic lobster on his desk. He also found one under his desk and another in his filing cabinet. It should have taught me the importance of checking and double-checking facts before you put them into print.

After I had been on the newspaper for a few years a senior colleague called Maurice Chittenden, a charismatic and witty reporter, wrote a slightly sneering article about a group called "The Lesbian Avengers". The following Saturday afternoon there was a kerfuffle at the door and a bunch of young women burst into the newsroom carrying massive water pistols and shouting slogans. The first person they confronted was Maurice, who stood there in semi-shock as they demanded to know where *Maurice Chittenden* was. He recovered quickly.

"Maurice Chittenden?" he said innocently. "Oh yes, Maurice Chittenden, I think he's in the library, I'll just go and fetch him."

He took off leaving the rest of us to deal with the group, who were chanting slogans as they handcuffed themselves to our computers and filing cabinets, and started soaking everyone with their water pistols. Pretty

109

soon the entire ageing computer system was in danger of exploding.

"If we're still here at 5p.m. can we watch *Brookside*?" one of the protestors said to me, just as an entire regiment of white South African security guards stormed into the building. They had a tendency to direct all of the black members of staff to the car park furthest from the office yet had failed to stop the invasion. Their punishment was to stand in front of the computers while the women sprayed them up and down, before van-loads of police arrived, cut the women loose using bolt-cutters and took them away.

THE EDITOR
60 COPPERS
8 LESBIANS
(AND 4 PAIRS OF HANDCUFFS!)

read the banner headline in the *News of the World*, which ran a full-page article the next day on the "mayhem" and quoted an aggrieved policeman who said: "I was playing football. I can't believe they called so many of us out. There are seven police vans here."

Most of us had a chuckle. But some of the senior executives were outraged by the attack. In a misguided attempt at retaliation one hatched a plan for the newspaper to infiltrate the Avengers. They asked several female journalists on the paper to go undercover in the group, but they pointedly refused. One of the secretaries also turned them down. Then they asked one of the new youngsters in the post room. The most

110

obvious issue was that he was male. When they summoned him to the office to discuss the job they closed the door. That guaranteed they were serious. When he emerged he was pale. The poor lad couldn't believe it. "They want me to wax my legs and put on make-up," he said. "It's crazy. But if I don't do it I'll be out."

It was a ludicrous idea, followed by other idiotic schemes. A star-chart reward and punishment system was introduced as if we were at pre-school. Then I was asked to work on an ill-fated drugs investigation which was proving especially tricky because some of the targets were threatening and powerful. One of our team had his legs broken during a mugging attack that appeared to have been organised by the drug gang.

It was my job to look after a whistle-blower, and it genuinely appeared his life could be in danger. He was a sexually aggressive and odious man who couldn't keep his mouth shut. We were driving from one hotel to another in leafy Surrey and he leapt right across me to lean out of my window and shout at a young woman riding a bicycle in the opposite direction. When I wouldn't turn the car around to pursue her, he turned on me, screaming abuse. We had to keep moving him from hotel to hotel because within an hour of checking in he'd be drinking in the bar and trying to impress the staff with tales of what we were doing. He was a total liability. I began to feel the support and back-up from the London office was inadequate. One senior exec just laughed when I said we had been forced to jump out of a first-floor hotel window and flee in the night when someone tried to get into our rooms. They tried to get a work-experience kid at the paper to take over babysitting him, followed by a young female journalist, even though I said I thought she would be in physical danger if placed alone with him. She had to barricade herself into a room as protection.

One of the final straws for me came when a friend of mine at the paper, a secretary who several colleagues thought looked like supermodel Cindy Crawford, was asked to travel to Kent to interview Alan Clark, the notoriously lecherous Tory Member of Parliament. Clark, who was once described as "the most politically incorrect, outspoken, iconoclastic and reckless politician of our times", had been cited in a divorce case in South Africa, in which it was claimed he had affairs with the wife of a judge, and both her daughters. It was a media sensation, a tale of politics, sex and a dysfunctional family. The interview was scheduled to be at Clark's home. Everyone knew his reputation. I thought she would be a lamb for a wolf. Many of us felt it was outrageous.

CHAPTER
EIGHT

The Towers

On 26 February 1993, a huge bomb exploded underneath the World Trade Center in New York. Six people were killed, hundreds were injured, and America was rudely awoken to the realities of international terrorism. The explosion rocked the towers like an earthquake — tourists one mile away on Liberty and Ellis Islands in New York harbour felt the ground shudder, all power in the towers was severed and the entire building was plunged into darkness. Commuters on the subway below were buried in concrete and twisted metal as the roof above them collapsed. America was stunned.

I was at the *Sunday Times* working on an investigation involving the IRA when news reports first came in from New York. Within an hour I had switched focus and began collating information on the WTC attack.

It took hundreds of firefighters two hours to extinguish the blazes and more than five hours for them to evacuate both towers. Gasping for breath, their faces blackened by soot and muck, thousands of workers and visitors staggered out onto the street and collapsed into the snow, many of them hacking up blood from their lungs. It was a devastating attack. The bombing created more hospital casualties than any other event in domestic American history outside of the Civil War. The New York City Fire Department sent a total of 750 vehicles to the explosion and did not leave the scene for the next month.

For two weeks I researched the attack for the newspaper. Events moved quickly in New York and I kept coming across details and snippets of information about the attack I found extraordinary. Within days investigators had found the vehicle identification number of the truck that had carried the device. A few calls and checks established that it had been rented from a Ryder hire firm in nearby Jersey City by a man whose name appeared on an FBI militant watch list. Staff at the leasing agency told FBI agents the man had actually returned to the office since the bombing to claim a refund on his $400 deposit for the van, which he said had been stolen the night before the explosion. Staff had told him to get an incident number from the police, and he was due back in a few days. The FBI staked out the hire firm and quickly caught three of the men behind the bombing. Within a few more days a man called Ramzi Yousef was identified as the mastermind of the attack. He had fled the US just after the bombing. A global manhunt began. The FBI even extended their famous list of ten most wanted fugitives to eleven to include their new quarry.

We published a comprehensive account of what had happened on the first Sunday and a follow-up piece the next week. But then other terrible things were happening in the world and the newspaper lost interest. I didn't. I became fascinated and then obsessed by the attack. A British intelligence contact told me explosives experts on our side of the Atlantic had been asked to provide assistance, because the device used to bomb the World Trade Center was so rare that the FBI's explosives laboratory believed it had only been used once before in more than 73,000 separate recorded explosions. It was almost unique. In the mainstream media the bombers were portrayed as a small, isolated group of lunatics. But I was being given snippets of information by contacts that suggested there was a much bigger story behind the attack.

Week after week I kept returning to the bombing and the aftermath, discovering more leads and angles. But nobody on the newspaper was interested in taking another story on the attack or approving more research. Peter Hounam had left the paper, along with several other friends and colleagues, and the whole atmosphere there was changing.

The kind of investigations I had previously been involved with were expensive and time-consuming. I was told pockets were no longer as deep as they had been. Gradually there wasn't enough money to fund investigations properly, and I was being moved from deep research on to stories that were more regular news. I found it hard to summon the same levels of enthusiasm.

A prime example was one of my last jobs. I was supposed to drive to a house in Northolt, I think, where a third-rate politician involved in yet another scandal was going to hold a press conference and confess his sins. It was all very last minute. I was late and I wasn't especially bothered about the story. I was sitting patiently in a traffic jam idly wondering whether I would get there on time, when a souped-up BMW came streaking along next to me, driving on the wrong side of the road at high speed. At first I thought it was the police. Then as it whizzed past my line of traffic I caught a glimpse of the driver, who had his window open and was barking into a mobile phone the size of a brick while steering with one hand. I recognised him immediately as a reporter from a rival paper. I knew him vaguely from Friday-night drinks in the pubs around Wapping. And I knew instantly that not only was he going to the same dead-end scandal press conference, but he was infinitely keener to get there, and in that second I realised I never wanted to care so much about filing copy on a grubby politician that I'd weave through traffic risking my neck and the lives of any schoolkids who might step out into the road.

By the time I got to Northolt the press conference was already over. The BMW driver was there, still on his mobile phone talking loudly to the office. I remember smiling to myself. I knew the job was no longer for me. I didn't have the drive or desire. I wasn't actually very good at the job of reporting and finding completely different stories every week. It was research and investigations that I loved, and the writing. I was a fan of what the veteran managing editor at the *Sunday Times* called "a scoop of analysis".

116

I was a staff writer by then, apparently the youngest in the venerable history of Times Newspapers, and I was working on the news desk most weeks writing and rewriting copy and as the deputy night news editor on a Saturday. It was an enormous responsibility for someone as young as me, but I revelled in it. The newspaper was my life, not only professionally, but personally as well. I had grown up there. I socialised with colleagues, moved in with friends I met at work and had a couple of relationships at the paper. I wanted to spend more time investigating subjects I was passionate about, but I hadn't seriously planned to leave. Until, that was, the wrong rugby score was printed on the front page of the paper while I was on the news desk. It was a huge mistake, only spotted in the final edition, which meant hundreds of thousands of copies were printed and scattered around the country. I have a horrible feeling the mistake reversed the result, but I have largely blocked out the memory due to the trauma of the aftermath. It was like the Spanish Inquisition the following week. Several people were culpable, but I was one of those supposed to be in charge, so part of the blame stuck to me. The whole atmosphere there had soured.

I felt it was time to leave, and I came up with a crazy plan to write a book about the World Trade Center bombing and the aftermath. I wrote more than a dozen letters to London literary agents in the hope someone would represent me, then went to see a couple before settling on a lovely chap called Robert Kirby, who I am still with to this day. He had the warm and friendly air of a social worker, and a relaxed confidence that put me at ease. Crucially he was also intrigued by my proposal and by my claim the WTC attack represented a new type of terrorist strike, by a new type of terrorist. I wanted to write a book that would tell the story of the attack and follow the huge investigation and aftermath. Robert thought we had a decent chance of getting it published. That was good enough for me. I negotiated a small redundancy payoff, and I left the *Sunday Times*.

It was 1994/5 and I was barely into my twenties. In a few short years I had gone from being the boy on the bridge to somebody who had the confidence to quit my job with a plan to write a book. I ploughed on with the research and Robert started to look for a publisher prepared to back the project.

At the same time life outside work was taking off as well. I had studied for an A-level at night school, so at least I have one to my name, and with my book still in research mode, I started to wonder about further education. Despite all my chippy comments and views about elite universities I went for an interview at an Oxford college, arranged on the basis that as the youngest staff writer on a newspaper I might qualify as an exceptional candidate. I thought not going to university might be something I always regretted. Sitting in the waiting room with twenty boys, all of them dressed in public-school ties and tweed jackets, and at most two girls, I knew immediately it was too late. I had made a mistake. Arrogantly perhaps, I felt that after all I'd seen and done there was no way I could go back to full-time study. These kids still had spots, for goodness' sake. I was so certain that I stood up, apologised to the gracious staff and left. I was becoming an expert at walking out. They had given me the powerful gift of a second chance, but at least I had confirmed it wasn't for me. I never had another serious regret about my lack of education.

My girlfriend Anna was waiting outside the college. She had been hugely supportive of my idea of going to university, and she was a pillar when I changed my mind. Anna was my first serious girlfriend. Certainly the first woman I tried to move in with. Glamorous, charismatic and fascinating, Anna had fallen in love with Russia and Russian literature, and so of course she went to live in Moscow, sang in jazz clubs and learned to speak the language fluently, with a heavy Georgian accent that to other Russian speakers marked her out as a gangster. She lived in a sunny flat in Hampstead and drove a convertible. We met at work and she started writing a column for *The Times*, partly about my attempts to inveigle myself into her life.

Anna's father was a well-known British journalist and war correspondent. He died, tragically young, after being shot by a sniper while he was covering a civil war in Central America, and she was at university. She had suffered a huge trauma, and she taught me much about grief and life. I'm not sure what I gave back. I think I was a charity case. I remember I kept flooding her bathroom. Then I blew it all by being too jealous and she dumped me.

119

After her my love life was a series of short and often disastrous relationships. There was one girl from Sicily, gorgeous, vivacious; although a bit vague as to why she was in London. It took a while to get at the truth.

"O-K," she finally said in her thick Sicilian accent. "I know you want to know so I'll tell you. My family had a leetle bit of a problem and they decided London was safer for me. The truth is, three of my uncles, they are in prison for twenty-five years for being Mafiosi."

Twenty-five years apiece wasn't minor theft. When I tried to end our relationship — fairly soon after she revealed who my in-laws would be, actually — I'd come home and find messages on my machine left in her distinctive accent.

"Si-mon, Si-mon, where are you?" she'd sing-song. "Why don't you answer my calls? Dar-ling, we have to go on holiday to Sicily. My family really wants to meet you."

I went on a series of holidays, but with my friends, travelling and training across Europe. In a rammed hostel in Paris a mate of mine fell off his bed, landed on top of me and cracked my rib, but I laughed hysterically through the pain. In another hostel dorm we stayed with a Dutch netball team. They made a big impression. Then a group of us were due to go on a lads' weekend to Barcelona. We were all looking forward to some sunshine after dreary weather in London, but at the last moment the tickets were changed to Copenhagen. Still thinking we were going to a beach, half of us showed up at the airport without coats, and three were in shorts and flip-flops.

Copenhagen was freezing. We had no guide book, no idea where we were going and our first port of call became an army surplus store for winter coats. We were all pretty grumpy about the cold and the change of plan, but we dealt with it in the only way possible, by getting hideously drunk. Then we went to Christiania, the self-proclaimed anarchist district of Copenhagen, accidentally ate some spiked cakes, and everything went a little blurry. I vaguely remember walking into a pub in Christiania and feeling like I had walked into an off-world bar from *Star Wars*. I thought there was a polar bear in the corner. Everything was very trippy and psychedelic.

For some reason one of our group then called an ex-girlfriend who lived in the city. She was a construction engineer, and she took it upon herself to take us to the Oresund tunnel and bridge that was being built to link Denmark with Sweden. This was an extremely foolish decision. There were ten of us, and we were drunk and tripping. I can only assume it was her professional enthusiasm. She fitted us out with hard hats and took us down into the huge tunnel. We were stumbling and staggering around, and then several of us were completely spooked by space ships flying down the tunnel towards us, which I now suspect were dumper trucks. A few of us fled through a door in the tunnel wall in a panic and that led to one or two alarms going off, the entire site being put on lockdown and security being called to extract us. Apparently I was hiding under a tarpaulin with a friend and we were

121

hugging each other and babbling when we were rescued.

Fortunately the Danes were very forgiving. Someone explained we were English, and the site manager decided not to press charges. We left and found refuge in yet another bar. We were too well-mannered to be obnoxious, but few countries like wandering drunks. Yet as we staggered around Copenhagen all we encountered was kindness, tolerance and mild amusement. People helped us, advised us, took us to bars, and bought us more drinks.

By the time we went home I couldn't walk, and the others had to push me in a shopping trolley to the train that would take us to the airport. I was half-carried to the plane, and I'm frankly amazed the cabin crew let me on board. For a full week after, I had alcohol poisoning and my poor flatmates graciously cared for me.

At the time I was living with Julie and Elspeth, a couple of friends I knew from working at the *Sunday Times*. We had moved into a cheap flat, with an interior that resembled a shoddy alpine chalet, just around the corner from my ex Anna in Hampstead. Our flat was an awful 1970s block, but we looked out at some of the most beautiful and expensive properties in London. Poor Anna. I bumped into her on the High Street one day and the look on her face didn't need translation — *You've moved around the corner from me? Really?*

Life with Elspeth and Julie was fun and social, like a series of *Friends* set in North London. We had wonderful parties where the flat was full of scores of burning candles and a total mix of characters and pungent smoke. Elspeth was a witty delight who had me in stitches with pithy one-liners and Julie was a bundle of energy and joy who spread love wherever she went. When we entertained, which was often, the floor in the living room would bow with the weight of people dancing. One night after a long party we decided to walk onto Hampstead Heath to watch the sun rise. Twenty of us set off and it was only when we were making our way up Parliament Hill that someone pointed out it was already completely light and people were out jogging and walking to work. We were so far gone none of us had noticed.

Morning recoveries were painful, but then I would start work researching and writing, wearing a dressing gown, of course, like any recently liberated writer. There I was, just into my twenties, trying to live like a Woodstock boho while at the same time researching a book about what was then one of the worst terrorist attacks in US history. I remember one afternoon sitting in my dressing gown on the phone to the Joint Terrorism Task Force in New York, so hungover I was struggling to focus.

I would spend the afternoon researching, the night being social, and then the early hours trying to write to a soundtrack of Ibizan dance and urban jungle broadcast on pirate radio stations run from tower blocks by friends from school in Acton. None of this was a good idea. Inevitably after spending most of the morning sleeping I would have to unpick and rewrite the incoherent stream from the night before. This was not conducive to productivity.

I was following and researching the investigation into the World Trade Center bombing by phone from London. But then my agent Robert managed to secure a UK publishing deal for my book on the attack, followed by a small contract for the US, and I worked myself into a rhythm and a focus, and started to take the whole project much more seriously. The book I ultimately spent five years researching and writing became the single most involving and exhausting project of my life.

My research had two tracks. There was the "Tradebom" investigation into the World Trade Center attack, which was being run by a Joint Terrorist Task Force (JTTF) out of New York, directly comprising perhaps seventy agents drawn from the FBI, NYPD, the US Secret Service, the US Marshals Service, the Bureau of Alcohol, Tobacco, and Firearms, and others. There was also a more secret global intelligence operation studying the wider terror group and emerging connections behind the attack. By phone I was already working my way along a chain of contacts ever closer to the JTTF unit, and soon meetings in London with contacts in MI6 helped my entry into the intelligence world.

On the investigative side my initial approach was to call the media departments of both the NYPD and the FBI and ask to speak to their investigators. It took persuasion, discussion and time, but essentially it was as simple as that. They connected me to agents and detectives who were peripherally connected to the investigation, and I spent hours on the phone milking them for everything they would tell me, going through it all in minute detail. I had a book to fill, after all. Then, after winning their trust and exhausting their patience, I would simply ask if they could pass me on to colleagues working more closely on the investigation for another angle, saying I wanted to accurately capture their professionalism and skill. One phone call led to another and I was passed from person to person until I had a network of contacts.

With the help of the tiny funds from the US edition of my book, which almost covered my international phone bills, my sources ultimately expanded to include the FBI Supervisory Special Agent running the Joint Terrorism Task Force, who was exceptionally generous with his time, and officials from the Directorate for Special Operations and Low-Intensity Conflict at the Pentagon. In London I met contacts from MI6 individually in pubs in Vauxhall and Soho. They passed me on to more contacts in their own world, including in Pakistani intelligence and the CIA. Sometimes it was farcically informal. I still have a pub coaster somewhere with the scribbled telephone number for a former head of Pakistani intelligence.

Why were they meeting me, talking to me and sharing information? It's something I've thought about since. I think there were many reasons. Trust was important. I did not pose a threat. I wasn't going to burn their cover or reveal a source. I was also unassuming, perhaps a bit disarming, and — crucially

— I was interested. Many of those involved in this world felt they were operating in something of a vacuum and that nobody was listening to their concerns and warnings. The prevailing feeling internationally in the 1990s was that the Cold War had been won, the West was unassailable and nothing really posed a threat. Many in the intelligence world disagreed with that idea. They felt the WTC attack was different from anything that had gone on before. So when I popped up on the phone asking questions, people were happy to help. They felt it was their duty. Plus I think everybody wants to feel appreciated. Everyone wants to feel that their work is important, it's human nature. The main reason people answered questions from a wide-eyed, twenty-something Brit, was simply because I asked.

My sources made it clear the scope of the WTC investigation was unprecedented. Every one of the fifty-nine FBI field divisions in the US and every one of the sixty-three global FBI Legal Attachés, known as LEGATs, and each effectively an investigative field office, was involved. The volume of information generated about the attack and the group behind it was enormous. Even just the number of telephone numbers thrown up during the investigation was huge. Three or four agents worked full-time uploading numbers onto computers and identifying suspects. The FBI developed databases based on the names and numbers that were used by investigators for years.

The mastermind of the 1993 World Trade Center attack, Ramzi Yousef, fled the US shortly after the explosion. He could have slipped quietly away and lived out the rest of his life in a friendly dictatorship. But he was determined to launch more attacks. Just months later the detonator of a bomb he was placing to target Benazir Bhutto, the secular candidate for Prime Minister in the October 1993 Pakistani elections, exploded in his face. His right eye was injured but after treatment in two Karachi hospitals, where he told staff a butane gas canister had exploded, his facial injuries healed and he disappeared.

Yousef next appeared on a Philippines Airlines flight bound for Tokyo from Manila in December 1994. He placed a bomb under his seat and left the flight at Cebu, 350 miles from Manila. Two hours later an explosion killed a Japanese man and injured a dozen people sitting nearby. The other passengers on the flight were lucky their plane was not blown out of the sky. The bombing, and an earlier explosion in a Manila cinema, were practice runs for a horrific scheme called the "Bojinka Plot", a plan for simultaneous attacks on twelve airliners. Terrorists would have boarded American-bound flights in the Far East and slipped miniature bombs designed around Casio wristwatches under seats. Undetectable liquid nitroglycerine hidden in contact-lens solution bottles would have been connected to a Casio timer by detonator parts hidden in shoes. Yousef had assembled the parts for his own bomb in the toilet during the flight to Cebu. And then he vanished.

Less than a month later in Manila, police saw smoke rising from an apartment block, raided a flat, and arrested one of Yousef's co-conspirators. It was a crucial breakthrough. A map was discovered tracing the route Pope John Paul II was to take during a visit the next week, as well as a priest's robe, a fragmentation grenade and a timer constructed from the shell of a normal digital watch: all ready for a suicide attack on the Pontiff. Yousef's Toshiba laptop computer was also discovered. But again Yousef himself evaded the authorities, escaped from the country and returned to Pakistan. He became the target of a huge global manhunt.

Yousef, who was probably born in Kuwait to a Palestinian mother and Pakistani father, specialised in inventing bombs that can escape airport searches. He would convert a digital watch into a timing switch and use light-bulb filament to ignite cotton soaked in nitroglycerine explosive. An explosives genius who studied A-levels at the Oxford College of Further Education, he then moved to South Wales to study for a degree in computer-aided electronic engineering at what was then the West Glamorgan Institute of Higher Education, or "Wiggy". When the police raided his flat in Manila they discovered a chemistry textbook from Swansea Library with passages on the manufacture of explosives highlighted.

Everything about the attack and investigation was astonishing. I had some money I'd saved from when I left the *Sunday Times* so I flew to the US. I met senior investigators and FBI "brick agents", a term the FBI uses for the guys doing the legwork; tough, experienced people that are out on the streets literally pounding the "bricks". They took me into bars and mosques in Brooklyn and Jersey City, meeting neighbours of the bombers and people who had prayed with them, and were pious and sometimes militant. I spent hours deep inside the Twin Towers, wandering around with guides so I could understand the layout of the area where the bomb had been placed. I sourced court reports and interview transcripts, and I met officials and agents from the Central Intelligence Agency, the Defense Intelligence Agency and the even more secret National Security Agency. I sat down with nervous, uptight spooks and never discovered their real names, let alone which ultra-secret agencies they really worked for. But on repeat trips to the States I also made contacts working on covert operations who were friendly and worldly, would happily hang out and share their time and a beer, and talk about their childhood growing up around the world with parents who were in the US military.

I was taken to gatherings in a bar near Washington DC that was like a second base of operations for intelligence specialists from different agencies who were studying the wider militant group that emerged at the time of the Tradebom investigation and had connections to the WTC attackers. We know it now, of course, as al Qaeda. They even told me they had a fax machine installed in the bar. I was vouched for by a respected analyst, but not everyone seemed to be aware I was writing a book. On more than one occasion I was mistaken for some sort of junior agent seconded from MI6.

"This is all just between us, isn't it, Simon?" said my guy, looking meaningfully at me and tapping his nose.

I have never really talked about this period before, but I was moving in shadowy circles. Those at the sharp end felt they were encountering an emerging threat to global security. They were talking to me because they believed nobody in power in the US or Europe was taking the threat seriously.

It was Benazir Bhutto, the former Prime Minister of Pakistan, who first mentioned the name Osama bin Laden to me. We were having breakfast together in the restaurant of a small hotel in Kensington, just around the corner from the Royal Albert Hall. There were a pair of Italian honeymooners at the table opposite, some American tourists directly behind us, and Benazir was talking loudly. She said there were links between the 1993 WTC bombing and bin Laden, and she was adamant that bin Laden posed a huge threat to Pakistan, the West and the world. We were sitting at a small table, just the two of us. She kept stressing, and was one of the first to point out internationally, that Muslims were the first victims of terrorism. Then she moved on to tell me how Ramzi Yousef had tried to kill her with a bomb, and then later with a rifle. I was having trouble focusing on what she was saying, because Benazir had a huge blob of strawberry jam stuck to her upper lip. I tried to motion to her, but she was in full flow. I nodded towards and looked at her mouth, but she ignored me. I passed her a napkin.

Finally she paused and flicked it into the cloth with a practised flourish. It was all very bizarre.

Bhutto told me that within two months of the 1993 explosion outside her home, Yousef developed a plan to assassinate her with a sniper's rifle. "I was supposed to be addressing a public meeting in Karachi, and I got a report from one of my party people that according to police sources there was going to be an assassination attempt on me that night," she told me.

Bhutto still went along to the meeting, but by the time she arrived it was "complete chaos". "There were people everywhere and armed men on the stage. In the midst of all this my mother also arrived. So I decided to go up, but the police were not coming to clear the stage. So I had a choice of leaving or taking the risk. So we took the risk and went up there, and it was absolute bedlam. I don't know how I spoke on that stage, or how I got out unscathed, but I did." Only later did Bhutto learn the details of the botched assassination plan. "He was supposed to have shot me. He had gone and done a recce of the place and with his associates he had got on top of the building."

However, a rifle that was supposed to be delivered to Yousef never arrived in time. "So in other words Ramzi Yousef would have shot me if he had got the weapon in time," said Bhutto. "As you can imagine, I was quite shocked by this."

I met Bhutto several times to discuss the emerging threat from al Qaeda. Her second government had been abruptly dismissed by the Pakistani President amid allegations of widespread corruption and economic incompetence. She was travelling with courtiers and a retinue, like a monarch on the move, but we met alone at the same mid-range hotel where she stayed during frequent visits to London. She had a powerful, intimidating gaze. I thought of her as a cross between Margaret Thatcher and Princess Diana.

I had been introduced to Bhutto by the former head of the Pakistani equivalent of the FBI, who was one of her close aides and was also out of office and in exile. I met him successively in a cheap hotel in Swiss Cottage, in a curry restaurant on King Street in Hammersmith, and near his offices on the North Circular Road, where he said he was involved in the petroleum industry. I had been passed on to him by contacts in MI6, and he proved to be a mine of information, sharing extraordinary documents that detailed the scale and spread of the terrorist group we now know as al Qaeda. They included intelligence reports and Pakistani interrogation transcripts. The reports had been transcribed verbatim and could be tough even just to read. There would be a section of speech which would say something like:

[Interrogator] "Tell me the name of your handler."
Silence.
"The name of your handler."
Silence.
Screams.
"Your handler."
More screams.
"Tell me the name of your handler."

I had an endless series of frightening and strange experiences, encounters and adventures working on that book. I was followed by the agents of at least two countries and almost certainly had my phone tapped. During my previous investigations I had been part of a team with the back-up of the *Sunday Times*. Writing the book, I was on my own and there was no one to call should things go pear-shaped.

On one occasion I needed to watch the house of a shady Lebanese businessman allegedly involved in supplying weapons to militants. I was getting a little carried away with the investigation, so I disguised myself as a vagrant and staked out the building. I even peed on my clothes in a misguided attempt to dissuade anyone from taking too much interest in what I was doing. It only encouraged the police to move me on.

Another time I decided I needed to attend a party in a country house outside London that a contact told me various dodgy spies and arms dealers would attend. He wangled me an invite, and for some reason a media friend said that to help me with my cover story they would put me on a list to have access to a convertible Aston Martin DB7 the company was lending out to writers. Then I borrowed an Ozwald Boateng suit from a friend of the fashion designer and set off for the party, feeling bizarrely confident I could pull off my act. I only made it a few streets from the flat. Every time I went around a corner the Aston Martin would lose power and then stall, the power steering would die, and I narrowly avoided crashing into several vehicles. I drove it slowly back home, worried I had damaged an extremely expensive car. An engineer from Aston Martin arrived the next afternoon wearing a suit and carrying a laptop, lifted up a panel in the door sill, plugged in the computer, and ran a diagnostic check. It turned out the person who had the car before me was a motoring correspondent, and he had been driving it at ferocious speeds on tight tracks.

"It has a learning computer that adapts to the driving style," said the engineer. "The guy before you was taking corners at 50 mph, so the computer adjusted the power to account for that. It should have been reset before you got the car. Very sorry."

I drove over to see my mum and dad and took them out for a joyride. They were thrilled. But I never made it to the spies' party.

I had some other near-disasters. I spent all of my savings, earnings and my advance researching the book. I found myself canoeing down a river in South-East Asia, looking for a supposed terror training camp. It seems crazy now. A twenty-something author with no back-up and no one to call, in a wooden canoe with a guide I did not know, trying to locate a terrorist training camp. Talk about overcoming my teenage fears. I was foolhardy, or at the very least naïve, and I had no concerns about where the research might lead or what dangers I might encounter. I never found the camp, but in several dark dreams I've since wondered what would have happened if I had. Can you imagine my canoe bumping up to the shore and some guy with a Kalashnikov springing from the shadows?

"Oh hello, so sorry to bother you. My name's Simon. I was really hoping we could have a long talk."

At the time I really thought I would find them and that they would talk to me. I remember a deep feeling of failure when we finally had to turn the boat around.

Perhaps my most frightening experience at that time came when contacts in Pakistani intelligence put me in touch with a group of bin Laden's supporters in northern Italy. Eventually they agreed to a clandestine meeting.

I travelled on my own. I still didn't understand how dangerous al Qaeda really was, and anyway the money for my book barely covered phone calls, let alone security.

At an Islamic cultural centre I was ushered into a room with six men. I knew from my Pakistani contacts they were "Afghan Arabs" — men who'd travelled from around the world to Afghanistan to fight the Soviets during the 1980s. When the war ended many went home quietly. The men I was with in Italy had gone to the Balkans, fighting the Serbs. They were warriors, and as tough as old boots. We drank coffee and talked through my interpreter, and everything was going fine. I asked them what they believed and what they were trying to achieve. They were radical, for sure, but they weren't hostile.

Then two other men arrived. They had particularly bushy beards and a more hardcore air. The men in the room seemed surprised to see the new arrivals, and they were very surprised to see me, and immediately angry.

I had stepped into a very dangerous world. The mood in the room changed from being slightly threatening to something much darker. I knew that Egyptian and Italian intelligence, and to a lesser extent the CIA, was investigating the Afghan Arabs. They saw me as a threat. I was sitting down, along the back wall away from the door. A few others were sitting, but the two who arrived were among those standing above me, shouting at the others and pointing at me. I felt incredibly threatened. Even my interpreter, who was one of them, looked pale. I knew a few words of Arabic and could tell that not only were they furious about the fact I was there, but they were arguing about whether I should leave alive.

An American source and friend had only just been telling me a few weeks before about a time when he was briefly captured in Somalia and had to fight his way out with fists and bullets. "If you're ever in real trouble, Simon, you'll know it," he told me. "Then whatever you do, don't do nothing."

A thousand things were going through my mind: could I get to the door? Could I leap out of the window? What the hell was I doing there? I was the most scared I had ever been. One of the men was so angry his spittle was flying everywhere. I suddenly felt very stupid and very small. I was playing a dangerous game with very serious men.

I tensed in case I had to rush for the window, while the arguing continued. It lasted for a few minutes but somehow I kept my cool, then things calmed down, my translator found his voice and hospitality prevailed over militancy. The bearded two left with half the group. I tried to sip coffee and appear normal, but my body was shaking. My interpreter was also shaking and we just wanted to get out. I knew I had come face-to-face with the most radical of zealots. It chilled me. I flew home and had nightmares for weeks.

Ramzi Yousef was finally captured in Islamabad in February 1995. Pakistani special forces and the FBI caught him preparing another atrocity: several remote-controlled toy cars packed with explosives. On his flight to New York the next day he told JTTF agents he had wanted to topple one of the Twin Towers into the other, and had deliberately built the bomb to try and shear the support columns holding up the towers. He had also considered a poison-gas attack on the complex, but claimed he had ruled it out because it would have been "too expensive".

In American eyes at the time, Yousef had a legitimate claim to the title of most dangerous man in the world. He was sentenced to 240 years in jail and imprisoned as if he was a virus. He is still the most secure prisoner on the most secure wing of Supermax in Colorado, the most secure prison in the world.

Yousef and bin Laden became the focus of my book, titled *The New Jackals: Ramzi Yousef, Osama bin Laden and the Future of Terrorism*, which came out several years before the attacks of 9/11. It has the dubious distinction of being the first book in the world on bin Laden and al Qaeda. My conclusion was that

Yousef and bin Laden were a new breed of terrorist, men who had no moral restrictions on mass killing.

I quoted a former director of the FBI's Investigations Division, who said: "In the past, we were fighting terrorists with an organisational structure and some attainable goal like land or the release of political prisoners. But the new breed are more difficult and hazardous. They want nothing less than the overthrow of the West, and since that's not going to happen, they just want to punish — the more casualties the better."

It was a debatable comment: by the time the book came out bin Laden had revealed some of his goals, saying publicly he was attacking the West because the US and Europe supported regimes in the Middle East. But my overall point was that we were entering a new age of apocalyptic terrorism. That was my conclusion.

I had worked on the book for years, risked my life and put my all into writing it. You can imagine how disappointed I was when I felt it sank like a stone.

CHAPTER
NINE

Grief

The New Jackals came out in 1998 and hardly anyone read it. My parents went around bookshops moving it from the dusty shelves at the back of stores and placing it at the front. Not only had I said Ramzi Yousef was the first of a new breed of terrorist, but I'd added that many more were being prepared in terrorist training schools dotted around Afghanistan and Pakistan. Nobody was interested.

There was a review of the book in the *Sunday Times*, my old paper, which said I'd clearly had ample access to Western intelligence sources, but that I was scaremongering, and that my "apocalyptic vision" was wrong. It was written by an older expert on the Middle East, who in my view had no idea of how the world had changed, but it was published in my old newspaper, and I felt a sense of betrayal. Even now I remember where I was when my friend Maurice called to warn me and read the review to me.

What could I do? Step by step. I carried on.

While I had been researching *The New Jackals*, I had also been working on other projects to make sure I could pay my rent. I conducted an investigation for

Time magazine into how the Swiss put Jews into labour camps during the Second World War. That caused a stink, and Swiss newspapers paid an infamous private investigator to steal the contents of my bins in an attempt to find some dirt on me. I also worked with my old mentor Peter Hounam at a new investigative publishing company he founded, writing, editing or rewriting a handful of books on such light-hearted topics as biological warfare, organised crime and nuclear smuggling. Peter secured a leaked copy of the Chancellor of the Exchequer's budget speech, some details of which were published in the press, and he won the *What the Papers Say* Scoop of the Year. I was only peripherally involved, but I was questioned by a senior officer from Scotland Yard. To get me to reveal the source of the leak the officer tried to use the fact I had signed the Official Secrets Act years previously when I worked for the government for less than one day. I suggested in somewhat impolite terms that I would love to see him try.

More importantly during those years I was reconciled with James, my younger brother, who had moved into my rented flat after my friends Julie and Elspeth moved out to live with partners. James and I had a sometimes tricky relationship after I left school, and I had seen little of him. Helping him to move boxes into the flat, then cooking meals together and sharing tales and a space, was completely wonderful. He's two years younger than me and I have always adored and admired him more than he realises. There was nobody I wanted to have closer. His first job had been

140

whitewashing the infinity board in the local photographic studio and he was building a career as a photographer after starting at the bottom just like me. He didn't get a degree in photography or media studies; he just threw himself in at the deep end and learned on the job. Enthusiasm and ability meant he began to climb the ladder, and he went on to work as an assistant to some of the world's greatest photographers, and later became an award-winning photographer in his own right. Living together felt like we were placing pieces back into our own emotional jigsaw, rebuilding the people we would have been without the traumas of our childhood. Or at least that's what we decided together after we'd had a couple of drinks.

At the end of the 1990s both of us were also reconciled with our dad, despite all that had gone on between us. He had retired from teaching and become calmer and less combative. He no longer treated us like irritating kids. He talked to us like adults, and we became friends. We all spent time together, went for day trips together and on holidays. I remember James and I taking him to see *Saving Private Ryan* at a cinema on the King's Road in Chelsea. I drove us all there but then couldn't find anywhere to park. I offered to drop them off.

"No, let's stick together," said Dad, smiling. He was savouring a moment with his sons.

We had to park half a mile away, and the film was about to start. We all ran together through the streets, jokingly encouraging each other onwards. We arrived, glowing with sweat. Dad was just beaming with joy and pure delight. At that point, at that moment, more than ever, we felt bonded, and together.

And then after a brief period of illness he was diagnosed with cancer. He became mortal, in all our eyes. It was heart-wrenching, of course, but like so many others we found that illness brought us even closer together as a family and encouraged final forgiveness on all sides. James and I went with Dad and Mum for his diagnosis at Hammersmith Hospital. We held hands together. We cried. James and I were often able to go with him for the interminable rounds of chemo that followed. He seemed to be improving.

I had been working on another book, about the 1972 Munich Olympic massacre of Israeli athletes and officials. Called *One Day in September*, the book was researched and written in parallel with a documentary feature movie of the same title which went on to win an Oscar for best feature documentary. My book, subtitled *The Full Story of the 1972 Munich Olympics Massacre and Israeli Revenge Operation "Wrath of God"*, was published in 2000. Shortly afterwards Dad's sickness worsened. I had been on a book tour of the US, flitting from city to city with my then girlfriend, who was effectively my fiancée. We had planned to go south to Florida for a few days in the sun. I called home from JFK Airport in New York and spoke to Dad.

"It's not good news, I'm afraid, son," he said, trying to sound calm. "The cancer is back, and it seems to be really aggressive."

It was a hammer blow. I put down the phone, changed our tickets right there and caught the first flight home. I moved my office into a tiny room at our family home so I could be around him as much as possible and help Mum to take care of him. We did everything we could, garnered second opinions and tried all manner of treatments and a few quack ideas but nothing had any effect.

He kept telling James and me how proud he was of us. I reminded Dad how he had spotted the advert in the newspaper that kick-started my little journey. I made sure he knew that without his encouragement I would probably never have made anything of my life. I knew and I know he always loved me.

By the spring of 2001 he was largely bedridden. Soon he could no longer make it up the stairs and we had to set up his bed in the lounge. My dad was a strong man, but towards the end he sank fast. It was devastating to watch.

I wrote the following in haste the day he died. It is perhaps the most deeply personal moment of life I can share, but we are too private about both the tragedy and beauty of death.

On the morning of 28th June I arrived at Mum and Dad's just after 11 a.m., made a few phone calls, did a little tidying, and woke up James, who was asleep upstairs in his old bedroom, trying to stay close to Dad. We knew the end was coming. I was on the phone to a funeral director when Mum shouted we should come quickly because Dad was going.

143

I ran into the lounge, and it was obvious Dad was on his last legs. He was sitting up slightly in the bed, resting against my large blue cushion, with Mum sitting by his legs and James sitting on the other side of the bed. The whites of his eyes were turning yellow, and he was breathing slowly and with obvious difficulty.

We sat with him, holding him, telling him loudly that we loved him, and surrounding him with family love. He kept his eyes focused ahead, looking at a photo of Mum, James and me that was stuck on the ceiling directly in front and above him.

We asked him how he was, and he replied with just one word.

"Wonderful."

It was the last word he ever said. We kept up a barrage of love, telling him he had been a great Dad and we would miss him forever, and then I said to him:

"It's OK. You can go now. It's all right. Don't fight it."

Dad winced twice, as if he had a bad taste in his mouth, and then he exhaled deeply. His life flowed out of his body.

We cried, we hugged, and then I went out into the garden, cut some roses, and put them between his hands, which I folded across his chest. James rang 123 to get the right time, and we sobbed some more.

Two hours later, we started to wash Dad, and dressed him in his best pants, vest, shirt, suit and tie. James buffed his shoes with polish and we carefully dressed his body. By the time we had finished our washing and dressing, he looked serene and peaceful.

If a father has to die, it could not be more perfect than Dad's passing. He looked beautiful, restful and content.

I still think about him all the time. I just sobbed for an age when I found the note I wrote about his death buried in my computer. Grief is difficult. It *should* be difficult. Anna, my first serious girlfriend, taught me something vital. Her father died without warning, shot by a sniper. People would say to her things like: "Don't worry, you will get over it. One day you'll wake up and feel better, and you'll face the world again." They were trying to be caring.

"No, I won't bloody get over it!" she would say. "And no, I won't wake up one morning and think, 'Oh, everything is OK and it's fine.' I don't want to! My dad is dead!"

She was adamant, and she was right, that all we can do is try to carry on. To accept. To incorporate death, grief and memory into our lives. People we love never leave us. They *should* never leave us.

Losing my father was desperately traumatic. I miss him still. I have travelled the world and experienced countless cultures but nobody has since managed to change my view that while life can certainly be beautiful and memorable, it is also tragic and desperately, desperately unfair. Why is my father no longer around to see my extraordinary son? Why is there an empty hole in my family? I know he would love Anya my wife and adore my son Jake, his grandson. But knowing it is not enough. I miss him.

We held his funeral at Acton Hill Church. The same church I had grown up in. Then we buried him in the cemetery. Two weeks later my then fiancée left the flat we shared near Ladbroke Grove in West London one morning and went off to work. I never saw her again. I called her that evening when she didn't come home. At first, she didn't pick up my call. When she finally answered, we talked briefly on the phone. She told me she had fallen in love with her boss. She mentioned the money he earned. She was sorry, but she was leaving me.

I was devastated. We communicated by text and arranged for me to be out when she went back to the flat to collect her life. But that was it. We ended.

It had been a difficult relationship, but it was another massive blow. I moped about the flat drinking heavily. Alcohol has never been my addiction, but I turned to it then, and I felt a deep trough opening in front of me.

After losing my dad and my partner, that summer in 2001 was the closest I came to slipping back to where I was as a teenager, teetering on the edge of a bridge. My highs can be very high, but my lows are often still very low. I have never forgotten the feeling of the railings under my hands. The cold metal, the rush of traffic, the lorry horn. It is always within me. Always part of me. I was a slip away from tragedy. I know I am still.

There have been many times since I was a desperate teenager when I have started to feel there was no hope, and no way out. But as I have aged, my experiences and, I think, adventures, have helped me to find comfort and solutions. As a tool for dealing with the lows I stick to my mantra. I put one foot in front of the other and take a step. I do something — anything.

For many years in my early twenties, when I was in a hurry to make my life a success, thinking achievement would keep the dogs of depression from nipping at my heels, I had "MAFA" written on a note pinned to my desk. It stood for "mistaking activity for achievement" and was supposed to focus my mind on being productive rather than faffing. But then I realised, in moments of darkness, when I am staring into an abyss while going through the end of relationships and depression, for me at least, activity *is* achievement. Activity or movement, any movement, rewards me, lifting me up out of the rabbit hole.

As I have aged, acceptance has also helped. Depressive thoughts will probably always be with me. The negative voices can be hushed, ignored, sometimes even laughed at. But doubtless they will always be at least an occasional background whisper. Like grief, my answer is to face them and take them with me. So many of us are taught to think of everything as black or white, happy or sad, depression or normality, high or low. Life has taught me so often that instead everything is just shades of grey. Every life and every journey shares tragedy with happiness and light with shade. Even a simple moment of joy. Because, like life, even a moment ends.

That summer of 2001 I was older and just a tiny bit wiser. I had a breadth of experience to draw on. I stopped drinking after a couple of months, started going to the gym, and reassured myself that one day I *would* find my partner for life. In the meantime, I refused to stand still. I remembered what I'd done after saving myself on the bridge and recalled the still serenity when I stood on that summit in Glencoe. I climbed out of the trough.

Looking back now, my fiancée leaving wasn't the worst thing that could have happened. The relationship was rocky. Marriage would almost certainly have ended in divorce. We wanted different lives. On our first date we met in a bar and she turned up wearing a fake fur coat and next to nothing underneath. Exciting, perhaps. But not exactly a guarantee of a stable relationship.

But that summer was still exceptionally hard. My father had just died in my arms. My fiancée had walked out on me. My beloved grandma was also ill. In a few months she would sicken, and then she would die. I would race to West Middlesex Hospital on the edge of Brentford, driving on the wrong side of the road with my hazard lights flashing and jumping red lights, because I was so desperate to get there before she passed. But I didn't make it. In a blink of a life my brother James, mother and I lost a vital part of our tiny family. We were devastated. I felt completely bereft.

148

And then 9/11 happened. And I had written the only book in the world about the group behind the devastating attack.

CHAPTER
TEN

9/11

My phone rang. It was James. He sounded breathless, and disbelieving.

"Si, have you got the TV on?"

"No, why? What's up?"

"Turn on the TV, quickly."

"Why?"

"Just turn on the TV."

I switched on. The first tower had been hit. The screen was full of smoke billowing above the New York city skyline.

There was a mention of a plane. I knew immediately who was responsible. I felt instantly sickened to the pit of my stomach. I watched for a moment, then dropped the phone, ran to the bathroom and was physically sick.

Everyone remembers what they were doing when those two planes hit the Twin Towers. What Ramzi Yousef had tried to do in 1993 bin Laden had finally accomplished. Everything I had feared had come true. My mind was racing. Sources, contacts, and meetings all flashed through my head.

Like many others I was struck by the obscenity of the scene. By the clear blue sky, and the dart of a plane cruising almost casually into the side of the building. As tragedy but also as horrific drama, it was epic and unparalleled. Although I had no relatives in the buildings or on the planes it was a devastating shock. It was what I had researched and written about. I had warned it was only a matter of time but nobody had taken any notice.

My phone began ringing off the hook before the second tower had been hit. It did not stop ringing for a year and a half.

Initially I did not answer. I realised I had written the only book on al Qaeda and I knew every news desk in the world would be clamouring for someone, *anyone*, who could talk about what had happened. But this wasn't a news event for me, it was personal. I knew people who worked in those towers, I had spoken to them after the first attack. I pictured the inside of the towers. I had spent hours walking around them, and many hours more talking with people who would have been inside when the planes hit. How many were dead? How many were stuck in the fire with no way to get free?

Finally I answered the phone and was pitched into a media feeding frenzy. I couldn't blame them; everyone was desperate to know what had happened, why it had happened, and who was responsible. Within an hour TV news crews found my supposedly secret address and were waiting outside my flat. By the end of the day a Brazilian and a Russian TV crew had each turned up at an apartment where I used to live. Meanwhile I was being shuttled between the studios of US news shows in London. Other people started calling me too, people who should have had their own experts to rely on. I answered one call to find Downing Street on the line requesting a meeting. I didn't see Tony Blair, but I did put words into his mouth.

I spoke to the government and security agencies. I said the same sort of thing to all of them. I didn't have a redacted spiel for the media and a secret one for those in power. I was a writer, and I had laid out what I knew in a book. It was all public.

Then I went to the States, where it was one studio after another, for interviews, comment and discussion. And to talk to the bosses of some of the same spooks and operators I had been following around Washington just a few years earlier. I met senior people from the White House, and had meetings, a lunch and a dinner with people who were portrayed in *The West Wing*. I advised them to go after the culprits hard but pursue terrorists as criminals wherever possible like the British had successfully in Northern Ireland, ultimately helping to bring peace to the Province. I also stressed how important it was to resolve the underlying issues that were driving people into the arms of militants, including the Arab-Israeli conflict and Western support for corrupt regimes in the Middle East. People nodded, and seemed to listen, but those seemed like intractable issues.

One of the great tragedies of the post-9/11 world is actually that the US President didn't use all of the power the crisis gave him. He could have said that not only was the US going to pursue the perpetrators to the ends of the earth, but that the attacks had also shown that the US and the Western world were too dependent on oil from the Middle East, that money from the sale of the oil was partly being used to fund terror, and that there *must* be a peace settlement in the Middle East.

Sadly they didn't listen. I remember having lunch with a close aide to President Bush in the iconic Old Ebbitt Grill restaurant, a fixture on the Washington scene since the 1850s, just steps from the White House. He was focused not on the need to resolve motivating issues, but on a plan to hunt down and kill everyone involved in the attack. I said I could understand that desire, but that if too much force was used, inevitably mistakes would be made, innocents would be killed, and more recruits would rally to al Qaeda. "We have no choice," he said. "They came to us. They attacked us here. It was an act of war. We have to hunt them down. We have to kill them. We have to put their heads on sticks."

I was twenty-nine, and I was sitting down and arguing with officials guiding and advising the leaders of the free world. Why did they want to talk to me? Few others had looked at the issue from multiple angles as I had. Few others, it turned out, had talked to militants, Pakistani experts, Western investigators and intelligence agencies. I was in an unusual position. There were certainly individual analysts who knew chapter and verse about specific issues, but very few had been required to join up the dots the way I needed to do for my investigation and book. Plus in the aftermath of

9/11 the leadership simply did not trust their own experts.

It all became very weird very quickly. Post-9/11 America was a strange and deeply wounded country. Quite frankly — understandably — people went a little crazy. More than once people became completely awed when they saw me.

"You're the guy," said one man, "the guy who knew, and we didn't listen."

Two young women started crying in a restaurant. They literally just wanted to touch my arm. Another woman saw me, paled and backed away, as if I was the incarnation of her loss. The entire country was shocked, wounded and on edge. Some thought I was a prophet of some kind and that I had been able to foretell this tragedy. Others seemed to suspect I might have somehow been involved with the actual event. Profiles appeared in the press asking how this guy from Britain could have known what was going to happen that day in New York. I didn't know it was going to happen, but my research had led me to believe they would attack massive targets. Past experience showed that when the group failed once, they would try again. Nobody should have been hugely surprised that after the 1993 bombing the WTC became a target again. Some of the victims' groups were asking — if I had known — why had the authorities not done anything about it? I had several upsetting encounters with desperately sad people who had lost loved ones in the towers and were trying to make sense of their nightmare. As time passed other books came out claiming I must have been an MI6 agent because of the access I had secured in the States and the intelligence information I had been passed. I can categorically say I was not. I had certainly been asked to work for intelligence agencies, but that was inevitable in the world I was in.

Nobody really read my book before the attacks. Then after the attacks it became a bestseller, one of the biggest-selling non-fiction books in America after 2001. I made money from it, but never a fortune. I have no island. I took only small fees from media interviews to pay my expenses, when I could have asked for six-figure sums. My motivation wasn't financial and it never has been.

I kept feeling that I should have done things differently, and I still wonder today whether if I had shouted louder, banged my drum with more passion or intelligence, perhaps someone would have heard me who could have done something, anything, to prevent the tragedy. I felt deeply, intrinsically involved. I had written a book about al Qaeda and bin Laden and it occurred to me that because I had — other people hadn't. Maybe there was someone out there who would have got the message across better than I did. Were any seasoned writers unable to cut a deal with a publisher because *The New Jackals* had already been written? What if there was someone desperate to write a book who could have made more noise than me?

Heaping further weirdness into my life, suddenly the actor and producer Kevin Spacey was in contact, wanting me to front a TV show. This was many years before he was accused of being a predator. Spacey had seen me chatting on *Good Morning America*, one of the flagship US shows. He had his own company producing movies and shows for television. It was the first time anyone had suggested I present a TV show, and I was intrigued.

Initially I went with my friend Claudia to the premiere of one of his movies in London. At the after-party we were ushered through the velvet rope into the VIP section where champagne was flowing, and then from there into the VVIP section, where a group of Hollywood A-listers were sitting more sedately and drinking cups of tea and coffee. For them this was less of a party and more of a professional requirement. Spacey welcomed me like an old friend. We hit it off. He was political and interested, angry and upset about the world. We chatted, partied, argued and debated for hours. Claudia and I were buzzing by the end of the night.

I was in the back of a cab driving to a party in Notting Hill a few weeks later with friends. Robbie Williams' song "I Will Talk and Hollywood Will Listen" was on the radio. Robbie was singing: "I wouldn't be so alone, If they knew my name in every home, Kevin Spacey would call on the phone", and then thirty seconds later Spacey called me on my mobile. We were all a bit freaked by that. My friend Jason said it was such a coincidence it might make him religious.

I met Spacey a couple more times before he invited me to the Century Club, a private members' club on Shaftesbury Avenue in Soho, London, to meet "his team". Arranged in a line were the head of his production company, his lawyer, his female publicity agent, his manager, all of them deeply tanned, dressed entirely in black, and looking fabulously wealthy and successful. They were the epitome of Hollywood power. Spacey, it turned out, wanted me to front a television talk show, an alternative to the *Charlie Rose* show, which had been a fixture on US TV for decades, and consisted of the eponymous host interviewing all manner of entertainers, writers, politicians, athletes, scientists and sports stars. Anyone remarkable, basically.

"Sounds interesting," I said.

I signed a deal, became friends with Spacey, and when he was in London or I was in New York he would invite me along to a party, a meal or a premiere. Ultimately nothing ever came of the talk show, obviously, otherwise I would probably be on my island by now, but I still met some incredible people through him. He was friends with Hollywood royalty, the Clintons, models, sports stars. I remember after one party sitting with Chelsea Clinton and another friend outside a simple restaurant near Southwark tube station. It was dark and distinctly unglamorous, because our table was lit by the light from the back of a bus shelter.

Chelsea was a real delight; friendly, witty and relaxed, with no visible security. Even when some late-night revellers spotted her and asked for a photo, and then came back ten minutes later and jokingly but physically tried to drag her to a party, she was just bemused and amused. No Secret Service appeared. We talked about life and the world, as you do after a few too many drinks, and for some reason started chatting seriously and I mentioned a powerful article I'd read about a women's health project in the Horn of Africa. I started to explain the issue in simple terms. I had completely forgotten who I was talking to.

"Yep, there are huge health challenges in that area," she said, deadpan. "I've been there a few times." She wasn't cutting me off, just tactfully reminding me of her life.

"With her mum. On Air Force One," said her friend with a slight giggle.

"Sorry," I said.

I met some extraordinary people through Kevin and had a string of short and superficial relationships. I swapped drunken dating tips with George Clooney, went to Naomi Campbell's birthday bash, flew in private planes to parties, misbehaved and drank far too much champagne. Attendance at those celeb events was supposed to be the pinnacle of social success, what many seem to fantasise about while flicking through glossy mags. They were fun, but also forced and hollow. When I eventually started my TV journeys I found them infinitely more memorable and thrilling than a Hollywood party.

Spacey existed in an A-list world and people flocked to him. I was walking along Piccadilly with him and a few other friends one evening and he was talking about how much he loved London because he didn't get hassled like he did in Los Angeles. At that exact

158

moment someone leapt in front of him like a jack-in-the-box.

"It's you!" they shouted. "It's him!" again, to no one in particular. They had a complete celebrity meltdown.

"Keep moving," Spacey said to me. "It's when we stop that it can get chaotic."

But within seconds people had turned and spotted him. It was as if a veil had fallen, revealing him to them, and people began to swarm around him. We all had to jog through a department store to get away.

Obviously this was many years before Spacey was publicly accused of inappropriate behaviour. He never behaved in an unacceptable physical way towards me or in my presence. One time a group of us had been partying and we went back to his private apartment next to the Athenaeum Hotel in Mayfair, which Spacey would book into under an assumed name so the paparazzi couldn't find him. The others left and I was alone with Spacey. We had all been drinking, and I suddenly felt that he might be working up the courage to make a pass at me, so I just laughed and left. Reading the reports now of how he groped young men has been a terrible shock. When I knew him I could tell he was attracted to women and men, but I never saw him behave like a predator. I liked him and thought of him as a friend. I only stopped seeing him much later after I started dating my future wife Anya, and felt the partying and shallower social side of life needed to end so I could focus on my relationship.

That was in the future, though. When I first met Spacey in the early 2000s I was writing, but no longer about terrorism. In the aftermath of 9/11 I was approached by a former Colombian judge who had personally investigated and waged war against Pablo Escobar, at one time the world's biggest drugs trafficker and "narco-terrorist". She had been the target of multiple, extraordinary assassination attempts by an army of hitmen. A surface-to-surface missile had been fired at her home inside an army base. She had helped to defeat the Medellin Cartel, but then had to flee to the United States, where a huge chunk of the federal budget for protecting foreign dignitaries was spent on keeping her alive. She remains one of the bravest, most selfless people I have ever met. I thought she had an extraordinary story that I was sure would make an exceptional and important book. I worked on it for six months. I spent a small fortune researching the story. But nobody was interested. South America was a dead zone, publishers said. They wanted me to write another book on terrorism.

I tried to turn it into a movie. A top female producer came aboard. Then the actress Selma Hayek took out an "option" on the story, basically paying a small sum to secure the rights, and would have been perfect for the main role. But she became pregnant and the whole thing withered away.

I talked with publishers about books, and production companies about TV projects, but nothing really inspired me. One idea that came through was that I should infiltrate al Qaeda for a BBC TV series. I'd had some crazy experiences by that point, but even I thought that was a mad idea.

160

Then one sunny Saturday afternoon I was playing football in Kensington Gardens with a group of friends, including Danny and Tony, who I was living with in a flat near Ladbroke Grove. We sat around on the grass afterwards, sharing beers and chatting. I was saying I needed a project, something of substance, something really involving.

"Mate, you need to try something new," said Tony, laughing. "You need to find yourself a whole new adventure."

I'm not the sort of person who deliberately seeks out an opportunity. I haven't plotted and planned a career. But I have been open to change and chances. From when I was at the *Sunday Times*, I've volunteered, and when people have asked me to try something new I've generally said yes.

As luck would have it a friend of a friend had been playing football and was now sitting with us listening. He was a producer-director at the BBC and we got talking, and he invited me in to the Beeb for a chat. I didn't know it then, but the BBC had already been doing some research on me. By the time I showed up at the White City complex near TV Centre, they had already decided I had potential as some kind of presenter. They had reviewed shows I'd been on, interviews conducted with me, and some of my writing.

I met up with Karen O'Connor, the head of the BBC's international documentary strands, then called *Correspondent* and *This World*. She was a producer and a commissioner. That meant she had the ability to create or pick ideas and had access to the funds to get

161

them made. She was an impressive character, tougher than some of the FBI agents I'd met while investigating bin Laden.

We sat in her small office, surrounded by mountains of tapes, photocopying paper, maps, files, folders and chaos. The whole place looked like a fire hazard. I thought I was there to have early and probably fruitless discussions about presenting some TV shows, but gradually I realised she had already made up her mind to get me involved.

I didn't really have to do anything. There was no interview. I didn't have to take a screen test. We just talked around a few ideas, the most appealing of which was to go on a journey through Central Asia, the countries to the north of Afghanistan, a forgotten corner of the planet that fascinated both of us, and then turn it into a TV series. Karen and I looked at an atlas together. We decided there was no area of comparable size about which so little is known in the West.

We talked about the possible style of the series. We wanted it to be a journey and a real adventure, and we wanted to incorporate both the joy and the darkness of the countries I was visiting, what I called the light and the shade.

"Normally there are travel shows, and then we have current affairs documentaries focusing on specific issues," she said. "What we're talking about is a slightly different kind of TV programme. Something that blends elements from both."

I loved the idea. It sounded completely different and thrilling. I remember Karen turning to me and saying with a terse smile: "What do you think, Simon? Are you interested? It won't be easy."

"All right," I said, perhaps a little too casually. "Sounds exciting. Let's do it."

CHAPTER
ELEVEN

Anthrax and Caviar

I never set out to be on TV. I didn't chase down production companies and bombard them with my show reel. I just worked on books and projects that fascinated me. And eventually, to my surprise, TV came calling.

It might be the pinnacle of popular culture, but television can also be shallow. I was an author, which gave me some credibility, but at least part of the reason I found myself with a BBC series was because I was a thirty-year-old with my own hair and teeth.

Karen had already decided I was going to travel with Will Daws, a former stand-up comedian turned producer-director with a strong reputation. He had the unenviable task of creating and shooting the programmes. We would be joined by a relative youngster called Dimitri Collingridge, an assistant producer who spoke fluent Russian and had an exotic family background that included an auntie who was a Russian baroness and possibly also a Russian spy, and a cousin called Nick Clegg who was an MEP and the future Deputy Prime Minister.

That was it. Three of us. So much for the days when a camel train of people would leave the BBC and head off on shoots carrying hampers. We were supposed to travel light, filming on small cameras in tricky countries and difficult situations.

The three of us would visit Kazakhstan, Kyrgyzstan, Uzbekistan and Tajikistan in a series that Will had wittily titled *Meet the Stans*, which would be broadcast late at night on BBC Two. It was meant to be a one-off, and even while I was helping to research our route and plans I was thinking about what I would do when I returned.

Before we left I was told I would need to complete a couple of health-and-safety courses. I raised my eyes. I had followed arms dealers and terrorists. But the BBC insisted.

"Don't worry. It's not exactly sitting in a classroom," said Karen with a smile.

The first course was chemical weapons training, deemed necessary partly because of the developing conflict in Iraq, the ongoing fighting in Afghanistan, and some of our filming plans for Central Asia. I met Dimitri for the first time when I picked him up from home and we drove down to an army barracks south of London. We got lost three times on the way, which I thought boded badly for the epic adventure we were about to undertake. But then we were locked in a chamber wearing respirators and full nuclear, biological and chemical suits while tear gas was pumped in through openings, and I had other things to worry about.

After release I was told I had to complete something called a "Hostile Environment Course", which was apparently mandatory for anyone from the BBC heading to countries deemed excessively tricky. The course was a six-day residential at Easthampstead Park in Berkshire, a council-run conference centre in a grand, sprawling Victorian mansion.

The joining instructions were all very military. "This is not a hotel. Report by 0800 hours. We have attempted to identify representative tasks for operational deployments to Hostile Environments," said a flurry of emails. "You will need to be able to run 100m in body armour and helmet without stopping, drag a similar size/weight casualty 30m . . ."

On arrival we were drilled by ex-special forces soldiers who taught us how to find hard cover if bullets started flying.

"Don't believe the rubbish you see in films," said one officer. "A car door is like a paper bag to a Kalashnikov bullet. You need to get behind the engine block, a tree trunk, a thick wall, or solid ground." They explained how to identify small-arms fire and large-calibre weapons. They showed us what to do if we found ourselves in a live minefield, were kidnapped, or if we were caught up in a demonstration that turned into a riot.

We were a mixed group. A few of those on the course were working on children's TV shows or an internet project and were going somewhere risky only briefly. Others were veterans of wars and riots, stationed in the Middle East or sub-Saharan Africa, and had only returned to the UK briefly for the course. It turned out that completing the course only provided certification for travel to tricky places for three years. Some people had done the course several times. I've since earned stripes by doing it five times.

Other groups were using the conference centre at the same time. On the second day we were told to walk across the manicured lawn at the back of the mansion and react appropriately to anything we discovered. As we strolled across the grass, certain something awful was going to happen, a gunman in camouflage and a balaclava ran out from among the trees ahead of us carrying a Kalashnikov. He paused, lifted the assault rifle to his waist, opened fire on us with a full clip of blanks, and we all scattered like frightened deer.

As I was running zig-zag towards a fallen tree I glanced up at the mansion. The team from IBM's Southern England Sales Conference were milling around the windows during their tea break. As the gunman changed magazines and opened fire again, I could see their jaws dropping at the scene of horror outside. God knows what the guests at the Berkshire Wedding Fair, which was taking place in another wing of the centre, must have thought. People have got completely carried away on the courses. One senior BBC member who did it leapt over a fallen tree, cracked two ribs and had to be taken to hospital. It was all so surreal I thought it ripe for comedy. I'm amazed nobody has turned it into a sitcom.

After we dusted ourselves down, it was on to the medical side of the course, which was gruesome but fascinating. First we would have the proverbial scared out of us with details and images of bullets travelling through human flesh. Then combat medics showed us how to treat battlefield injuries.

"Get your hands in there and get some compression on the wound," they'd say enthusiastically. "I want to see your fingers covered in fake blood."

We were shown how to turn off the blood supply to the hands by pressing hard into the soft flesh of the upper inner arm, and how and where to press into the groin to halt catastrophic bleeding in a foot, either after someone has stepped on a landmine or been in a car crash. But it also applies if you have injured yourself in the kitchen or cut the top off your finger like I did as a child. It works immediately. We practised on each other, with one person monitoring the pulse in their wrist, and then another turning off their blood supply. Why aren't such basic life skills taught in schools?

The fact we were trained by highly skilled and experienced soldiers made a huge difference. They had shocking stories but also practical suggestions. I learned you can pack bullet wounds with tampons in an emergency, and use a crisp packet and some gaffer tape to save the life of someone with a serious chest wound.

Then we had detailed paramedic lessons from Terry, a serving firefighter, who described in gory but sobering detail the road traffic accidents he had attended around Southampton. "Every time I go to a crash I want to see a friction burn mark across the chest," said Terry, "because that means someone was wearing their seat belt. Even in a war zone your life is most at risk from a car crash. You must always, always wear a seat belt." It was advice I took to heart.

We trotted outside and Terry walked us towards some old tennis courts in the woods. Smoke was rising from two cars that had been arranged as if they had been in a pile-up. A group of instructors were scattered in and around the wreckage, wearing make-up and wounds to simulate a mini-disaster. They had fake wounds hidden under their clothing which spurted blood. We had to assess the situation, triage the victims and treat them as best we could. It felt surprisingly real and the whole course was magnificently organised. If only school had been as dramatically interesting. If you get a chance, sign up for a course or pay to go on one.

The whole week culminated in our entire group being driven to an army training centre an hour away and introduced to the fake country of "Hostalia", where countless disasters befell us. We had to talk our way past fake road blocks, and stop apparently drunk pro-government militia gunmen in camo uniforms from taking away the female members of our group. We drove along a track and there was a huge explosion off to the side. A woman dressed a little too realistically like a Balkan peasant staggered out of the bushes bleeding heavily and clutching her intestines. We dragged her into the back of our Land Rover while she fitted and thrashed around, and then she bit into blood capsules and began bleeding from her mouth. I was quite taken aback by how lifelike it all felt. We later discovered she had been acting on *Casualty* that morning and had then raced down to the training centre, only stopping to buy a bucket of pig guts on the way.

169

Armed government soldiers stopped us further along the track, took the peasant away and shot her. We fled on foot through the trees and arrived in a full-size village where we found a rebel base and a moustachioed commander. He was just starting to tell us about life in Hostalia when a platoon of black-clad government soldiers mounted a full-on assault with mortars and small-arms fire.

Well, I tell you, it was all very dramatic, and not a little exciting. The day finished with an artillery strike on a United Nations compound and the resulting carnage we had to deal with: missing limbs, endless screaming and pints of fake blood.

By the time Dimitri and I drove back to London we felt bonded and ready for anything. Ten miles from the M25 we saw an accident on the other side of the road and immediately went into a response mode, remembering our training and racing to the scene. It was only when we got close that Dimitri pointed out there were two ambulance crews at the scene already and they would probably be able to handle the situation without us.

We landed at Almaty airport in Kazakhstan at three o'clock in the morning to start the journey around Central Asia. It was absolute madness. Even at that time, the arrivals hall was heaving and we had to fight our way through a scrum of people. Somehow our guide Bayan Orumbayeva was waiting to meet us airside to help us through customs and immigration. Bayan was a tiny, fragile bird of a person, with a warm heart but steel for bones. She could persuade anyone to do anything. Bayan had a way about her that people trusted. I have met hundreds of guides and "fixers" in the years since, but Bayan remains my benchmark. She was exceptional.

Outside the airport she ushered us into a van driven by Marat, a former Soviet police captain who happened to have won the Kazakh version of *Who Wants To Be a Millionaire*, and we drove to our hotel. I had only just closed my door to catch a few hours' sleep when two prostitutes with supermodel looks tried to push their way into my room.

I politely declined their offer, wedged the door closed and allowed myself a moment to consider the journey. For weeks I had been reading books on the country, poring over maps and wading through masses of photos. Our rough plan was to travel from Almaty up to the far north-west of Kazakhstan, by the Russian border, then travel by train, helicopter, horse and four-wheel drive across the vast Kazakh steppes towards the Chinese border, then south through Kyrgyzstan and Tajikistan to the Afghan border, and west through Uzbekistan to the ancient Silk Road cities of Bukhara and Samarkand. Finally, we were on the ground. We were starting the journey. I was filled with an incredible sense of possibility and excitement.

On the flight over we had talked about how we were going to work together. This was my first outing as a presenter in front of a camera, but nobody had discussed what I should actually *do* in any detail.

"Without wishing to sound like a total novice," I asked Will, "how do you think I should play this?"

"You need to just be yourself," said Will. "We're going to be filming for weeks. Nobody could pretend to be something they're not for that length of time. So don't play it at all. Don't overthink it."

That sounded like a good idea, but I glanced at Dimitri as if seeking confirmation. He nodded. "Will's right. You have natural empathy. You're interested in people, and you're enthusiastic without being over the top. You've got a way of saying things that's understated and that ought to work well. Just go with the flow and don't try to be something you're not."

I thought about the simplicity of what they were suggesting. It made sense. It's true I felt and still feel a strong sense of empathy with others. I'm interested in people. If I put myself on the couch doubtless I could trace it back to childhood, perhaps to counselling for teenage depression and even the talks I heard at church as a boy. Back then I had been listening remotely to stories from places I never imagined I would ever visit. Now it was the early 2000s and I was sitting on a plane at the beginning of what I hoped would be an incredible adventure, exploring a region that rarely featured on TV. I was delighted, elated.

If the style of my programmes was to be inspired by anyone else, I thought it had to be, of course, the great Michael Palin. Why not try to follow someone declared a national treasure? I watched *Around the World in 80 Days* when it was on the TV and it was a revelation. Michael showed respect to everyone he met along the way, treating them like fellow humans. Gone was the patronising amusement and contempt for local customs, food and traditions that TV travellers displayed before him.

On an old dhow in the Indian Ocean Michael sat with the Indian crew and shared the headphones of his Walkman. He sat down next to them. Not above them, but shoulder to shoulder, with no airs and graces, no Englishman and Johnny Foreigner. A shared seat, shared music; and then the chap next to him nodding his head to Bruce Springsteen. Michael never let anyone's situation define them. He started to break down barriers and helped a generation of viewers dismiss the stereotypes that had plagued our view of other cultures. In a smaller way, a much smaller way, I decided I would attempt to do the same.

I woke in Almaty to a city shrouded in grey. It wasn't depressing, nothing could have depressed me that morning, it was just a blanket of rain. Will put a radio microphone on me linked to his camera, I tucked it under my shirt, then we piled into the van and drove through the streets of Kazakhstan's largest city, and until 1997 the capital. All around us were chilly, grey concrete blocks. Sometimes it was hard to tell the factories apart from the flats. It all felt very Soviet. Bayan saw me staring at a grim factory and smiled.

"It will change, but slowly," she said. "I really hope this programme will be a pathway for future tourists."

I nodded to her, but it was hard to be enthusiastic. The place looked bleak, and our first destination was definitely no local beauty spot.

Bayan took us to a complex of buildings surrounded by a six-foot wall with barbed wire scrolled across the top. It was an old biological weapons factory that had been converted to a research centre for the bubonic plague. Why were we going there? When the Soviet Union collapsed many military installations lost all their funding. Weapons were going missing. It was a huge issue in Central Asia and something we wanted to incorporate into the programmes.

As we drove the camera was already rolling. This was it. We were filming. I made a few general comments and said whatever came into my head, Will filmed, and it all felt very natural. We drove through the gates of the research centre and the first thing that struck me was the lack of security. There were just a couple of guards who waved us through with barely a check on our credentials; no search of the vehicle and no sniffer dogs. Beyond the gate a series of tarmac roadways and paths drifted like tributaries through patches of grass littered with leafless trees. Marat parked outside a faded pinkish building, we got out, and Will readied the camera.

At that moment it could all have gone horribly wrong. Some people who are relaxed off camera go to pieces when a camera is turned directly on them and the recording light goes red. I've seen it myself regularly when filming in the years since. Will had told me to be myself when talking to the camera, but he had no idea if I would start to speak in a staccato tone as if I were on some live link on the ten o'clock news, or whether I would just freeze like a rabbit caught in headlights.

I felt confident I wouldn't stiffen, but I stood watching Will, waiting for him to tell us what should happen next. He was the experienced director, after all. But he didn't say anything, he just turned the lens on me. I waited for him to lead us in, but he said nothing. And then it struck me, one of those moments when a switch just flips in your head. *Ah. So this is how it's going to be. I need to lead, and the camera will follow.*

It was a moment that set the pattern for the style I have tried to employ on my travelogues ever since: no script, no rehearsal, no lead-in, no real recce where a member of the production team goes out in advance and works out where I am going to stand and where the camera will sit on a tripod. From those first frames most of my programmes have been filmed in a relaxed, off-the-cuff style. I walk into situations with the camera rolling and take each moment as I find it. This might not sound fundamental, but many TV programmes are carefully plotted, planned and scripted in advance. Personally, I was never hugely keen on the more traditional TV documentary style where a camera is already set up in a room on a tripod with floodlights burning away, and the presenter walks in and looks around in surprise as if it is the first time they have seen the place. To me at least, those entrances can look just a little fake. So instead I try to make sure the camera and viewer are following me into situations, as realistically as possible.

Sometimes in the years since I have taken the idea of the camera following me to extremes. When I used a home-made zip wire to cross illegally from a remote area of India into a dangerous and virtually unknown corner of Burma while travelling around the Tropic of Cancer, on one of my most dangerous adventures, the team, completely understandably, wanted to send a camera ahead of me so they could capture me arriving on the other bank of the river inside Burma. We had the briefest of barneys about it at the time. I felt I needed to lead from the front and be the first across.

There will always be elements of creation and structuring in making a TV programme, but I was keen to make shows that are as natural as possible, and to knock on someone's door, church or caravan, meet someone on camera for the first time and capture a genuine moment of surprise, as they wipe their hands on a tea towel or something, and then launch naturally into conversation. I craved that sort of authentic moment and interaction, and I have been incredibly lucky to work with cameramen and crews who have been prepared to film in that style. It might not sound much, but actually it's a real challenge for a cameraman to follow me from daylight outside to relative darkness inside a hut or a house. As I walk through a door they usually have to flip through myriad settings so it's not too light outside or pitch-black on the film when inside. Very few cameramen are entirely happy to do that without at least checking the light inside first because of the risk that the resulting footage might look slightly less than perfect. It can be a challenge for the team, certainly, and things can go wrong, of course, but the result, I hope, is the viewer gets a sense of a natural interaction and a genuine meeting.

176

The simple style of most of my programmes was set from that moment outside the plague research centre in Kazakhstan. Ultimately it was Will who made it easy. He just looked out at me from behind the camera, smiled and nodded in the direction of the research centre door. "Go on then," he seemed to say. It was the best instruction I ever had. I looked directly down the lens, said simply, "C'mon then, let's go," and started walking towards the building.

We were welcomed into the plague research centre and shown around by a scientist who led us to a room where the only furnishings were a chipped parquet floor and a selection of old fridges. This was where the researchers kept their store of deadly diseases. Security was woefully inadequate, and the door to the main stock of biological nightmares was secured with a wax seal. So although they would struggle to stop intruders, at least scientists would know if stocks had been stolen after a break-in.

I could see labels on the fridges but the only one I recognised was anthrax. The rest seemed to be differing strains of the plague. The lead scientist unlocked a basic padlock securing the anthrax and took out one of four canisters. As soon as she opened the canister I went to point at it with my finger.

"No, no," she said, batting my hand away from the vials of deadly toxin.

"Did you just try to touch the anthrax, Simon?" said Will from behind the camera.

The scientist replaced the vial again and shook her head at me. "We have to be careful, very, very careful."

But then as she went to put them away she accidentally whacked the fragile glass vials. One of her colleagues gasped in fear. Everybody in the room froze. Nobody dared to breathe. For what felt like an age they rattled like a set of maracas. I thought they were going to fall and shatter on the floor. Fortunately, they settled, she put them away, and nothing was broken and no bacterium was released. But it was a minor moment of horror. If one of those vials had smashed I might have had a very short-lived television career.

Seeing the contents of the cabinets made the lack of security outside even more shocking. This was 2003. Afghanistan, where groups like al Qaeda were training terrorists, was to the south. Other militant groups were springing up in neighbouring Kyrgyzstan and Uzbekistan. It didn't take much imagination to see what kind of mayhem a determined group could create if they made a concerted effort to break inside.

Even if the facility had better security, the director of the institute was not exactly reassuring about the risk of determined terrorists obtaining biological weapons.

"If I need to get a virus, as a scientist I can infect myself, then go outside, infect other people with the virus and then I can cure myself," he said. "I could do this if I was paid enough."

He assured me it wasn't something he would do, of course, but I couldn't help thinking it was an attractive exit for a militant with designs on becoming a martyr.

By the end of the first day of filming I was buzzing with everything we had seen. I knew this was exactly where I wanted to be. The journey was already shaping up to be an unbelievable experience. On day one we had been somewhere bizarre, thrilling and frightening. The journey was already a privilege and responsibility rolled into one. It felt like this was what I had been looking for all my life. It was adventure with purpose, travel with meaning.

From the start we thought that by blending issues into the adventure, mixing the light and the shade, we might encourage people to watch the shows who would normally switch off or change channels when something about Central Asia came on the TV Turning it into a travelogue might just be a way of getting forgotten stories and little-known regions of the planet onto TV. Perhaps it was my chance to make just a bit of a difference, or at least put a gentle ripple across a pond.

We flew north-west to an oil field that seemed to hint at the future. US firms were already working there, as were companies from the UK, Canada, Russia and China. With huge reserves in the ground they had all bought leases as Kazakhstan threw off the shackles of Soviet rule. The Stans are home to some of the largest untapped energy reserves in the world, and the foreign firms were all battling for drilling rights to exploit oil reserves in a replay of the nineteenth-century "Great Game". Optimistic estimates suggested the reserves could rival those of the Gulf States. It was thought oil from Central Asia could reduce Western dependence on oil from the Middle East and help to change the global balance of power.

Before there was oil, there was caviar. A few hundred miles south we were shown a vast, ice-encrusted lake where fish used to swim in huge numbers, and caviar was harvested, before the Soviets over-fished the prehistoric sturgeon that produce it. When I was there the only caviar produced was farmed. Abish Beckeshev, a Kazakh caviar expert (he was once head of the department for the central scientific research institute on sturgeon) showed me the lake and then took me back to his humble flat to meet his wife, who was also one of the world's leading caviar specialists. Abish produced an enormous block from their freezer.

"This is the finest caviar in the world," he said proudly.

He carved a chunk off the side as if it was meat loaf and spread the jet-black pearls on thick bread. The only caviar I had eaten before was cheap and definitely not cheerful. I dutifully put a slice into my mouth, and my eyes widened in shock. Now I knew what all the fuss was about. It was rich, creamy, with a tang of the sea, and completely delicious.

I gorged on slice after slice, then eventually noticed Abish was just eating bread and sipping vodka and tea.

"I have been eating caviar for decades," he said. "I am actually quite sick of caviar."

There was something a little melancholic about Abish that was echoed in Bayan. It felt like a throwback to the time when Kazakhs were under the Soviet yoke, and emotion and enthusiasm could be interpreted as signs of indolence or weakness. She might have been world-weary, but Bayan was an amazing guide. A day or two later we missed our train from the tiny town of Aktobe close to the Russian border after it left an hour earlier than scheduled. The next wasn't due for days, but Bayan went to the home of the local mayor late one evening and hammered on the door. His wife answered wearing a dressing gown and nightdress, and then the mayor appeared on the stairs in his pyjamas. With a combination of guile and charm, Bayan persuaded or forced the mayor to drive to the train station with her, still wearing pyjamas under his coat, where he rang the central despatch for the region and ordered them to stop a train at the station in the morning to pick us up.

It worked. The following morning, waking to snow on the ground, we made it to the station early, and we boarded a train that did not feature on a timetable. I stowed bags then hung out of the window as we left the town behind and rolled through a flat, ice- and snow-bound landscape that stretched to the horizon in every direction like an unending blanket. We were travelling across the vast Central Asian steppe, across which the Mongols and the equally terrifying Scythians had once roared. Now for mile after mile there was nothing to see but telephone poles. It was hard not to romanticise the scale and the distance. It felt like we were on the edge of the known world; in an area so vast and remote almost anything was possible.

I moved through the carriages, where people slept on bunks and slumped in chairs on either side of compartments. The train would roll for days across the enormous interior of the former Soviet Union. We chatted to a few of our fellow travellers and discovered many were ethnic Russians on their way to visit relatives in Moscow.

I talked to one elderly lady who was resting on a bunk with a pillow. I asked how life had changed since independence and the collapse of the Soviet Union. She told me that things were all right, at least at that moment.

"Immediately after independence there was nothing. But now there is food, there are clothes, this means a lot for us," she smiled wanly. "Look, I survived the Second World War, now that was a difficult time."

Two policemen on the train came to check on us and then stopped to chat. Ethnic Kazakhs, they were there to protect the country's borders from drug smugglers and illegal immigrants. Kazakhstan was by far the wealthiest of the four "Stans" and the policemen told us everyone wanted to live there.

One of the policemen was keen to know what I thought of Central Asia. I stumbled a reply, unsure how to tell them I was already finding Central Asia wonderful and eccentric, like a lost world. So instead we swapped stories about growing up on opposite sides of the Iron Curtain.

I explained that for decades we had been told the Soviet Union was about to invade Europe, and that created a sense of fear and suspicion. They nodded in understanding and said they had felt the same on their side. Only when borders are open can reality dawn, said one of them. One of them pulled out his handgun to show it to me, I put my hands up, and we all had a little laugh. It was a brief but sweet little encounter. Clearly things were changing in Central Asia.

Outside the window the landscape never faltered. The view for hours was open, rolling plains. Kazakhstan is the size of Western Europe, with only a quarter of the population of the UK. I saw only the occasional herd of cattle and horses and an odd glimpse of the nomads who tend them. But it was a hypnotically beautiful journey.

Beyond the steppe and the train we rejoined Marat and his van and headed south-west until we found ourselves driving across a sandy desert. Not far from the border with Uzbekistan, we were actually on the bed of what had once been the Aral Sea. The further we went the more surreal the experience became. Camels wandered past the hulks of dozens of rusting ships trapped and then abandoned when the water drained away.

Spreading as far as the eye could see, the land seemed cast in a desperate beauty. I asked Marat to pull over so we could get out and take a closer look at the ghost-like shipwrecks. The Aral was once the fourth largest inland sea in the world. Back in the 1960s Soviet planners pumped chemicals into the sea and then deliberately diverted rivers to irrigate thirsty cotton fields. What resulted was nothing short of environmental disaster. The sea shrank to half its size. When I visited, it was fifty miles away. Parched, contaminated sand blew over villages and sickened unemployed fishermen.

"I remember these ships crossing and the whole thing was full of life," said Bayan, sobbing gently at her

183

own memory of glistening waters. She was dazed by what we found. "The whole thing is dead . . . just like being among ghosts."

But the damage was not limited to the landscape. People were suffering physically. Appalling dust storms were ripping through villages around the old Sea, and the chemical residues in the sand were causing eye infections, stunted growth, reduced fertility, lung and respiratory problems and worse. One investigation discovered that rates of liver cancer doubled between 1981 and 1991. Another study found that by the end of the 1990s infant mortality in the area was much higher than in the rest of Uzbekistan and more than double the rate in Russia. It felt to me like the people had been left, like the boats, just to rot.

We followed one huge camel to a worn-looking village which used to nestle right by the sea. The place looked beaten, the buildings old, flaked and rotten. Villagers who used to catch five or six hundred tons of fish a year were now breeding camels to survive in a desert.

"The people here believe that water will come back," said Bayan. Neither of us was hopeful. We were visiting a graveyard. For me the wasteland of the Aral Sea was a dramatic example of the power of our species to alter an entire landscape.

Early on in my TV travels, in Kazakhstan and elsewhere in Central Asia, I realised I was seeing the world at a time of incredible change, and that we are transforming our planet. Nobody should be in any doubt about that. In the years since, one of my biggest

184

challenges has been trying to show the reality of what's happening to our world. Even today I don't think we quite understand the full extent of what we as a species are doing to the planet. For anyone who doubts the reality of climate change, consider this: how could 7 billion extraordinary humans *not* be having an impact on the climate? Since standing on that empty seabed I have been in dozens of situations around the world where remote and indigenous people have told me, unprompted, their world is changing.

In Kenya people from the Maasai community have warned me that the climate in their region is becoming more extreme, with more intense storms and longer droughts. They wondered how much longer they would be able to roam and herd.

In the mountains of Colombia I have stayed with an indigenous people called the Kogi, who live in huts and wear white robes. Men carry gourds which they stand around coating with their saliva, almost as we would twiddle our thumbs. They are a deeply spiritual people who are the most intact surviving civilisation of the Americas pre-Columbus, and are said to be the inspiration for the peaceful folk in the movie *Avatar*.

The Kogi have survived invasion by the Spanish, by missionaries, and by drug cartels. They are extremely wary of the outside world. But they agreed to let me and a small BBC team visit because they are seeing their patch of the planet changing: mountain caps are melting, rivers have stopped running, there are new diseases, fewer insects, and the climate in their mountains is more unpredictable. The Kogi are very isolated, but they think of themselves as stewards of the Earth. They believe they are "Big Brother", we — the rest of humanity — are "Little Brother", and they are horrified by what we are doing to the world. They told me they have tried to warn us we are destroying our home, but Little Brother isn't listening. Whether it's in Africa, Asia or the Americas, remote people who don't read the *New Scientist* know that something terrible is happening. The climate is changing, and they are frightened.

On the bed of the Aral Sea in Kazakhstan the situation was stark. We left the area feeling very solemn, a feeling accentuated when we came upon an abandoned Soviet missile testing site nearby. It looked like the set of an apocalyptic movie. There were torn-down fences, broken concrete buildings and a few villagers scavenging for scrap iron among the ruins, most of which had already been stripped away. What with that and the Aral Sea, it felt as if Kazakhstan had been invaded, pillaged and abandoned. Despite the oil reserves in the ground, I wondered what the future would bring.

We drove on, and Bayan began to open up. We passed through the remote town where she'd grown up. She told me her parents had been intellectuals banished to the wilds of Kazakhstan by Stalin, along with scientists, writers and musicians from across the Soviet Union. She had grown up surrounded by artists. As a child she'd been taught to play the piano by the aristocratic daughter of the former Russian governor. We popped into a store to buy some meat and cheese for lunch and one of the middle-aged women started flapping around trying to get someone else from the store at the back.

"What's going on?" I asked Dimitri, who could hear what was being said.

A stunning, tall, young woman appeared at the back of the store and strutted down the aisle as if she was on a catwalk. She was wearing a white baker's outfit. The middle-aged woman was fussing around her and talking loudly.

"Ah," said Dimitri. "Bit weird. They think we might be model scouts."

Apparently the young lass was descended from aristocracy, and the middle-aged woman was telling her we might be able to rescue her from the town. She looked gutted when we said we were making a TV show and there were no spare seats in the van.

An hour or two further down the road and for the fourth time that day we suffered a puncture. We were all out of spares. It was almost dark and freezing, but we were told by passing drivers that a police checkpoint was a brisk walk ahead. It was our only hope, and we walked through the darkness until the Kazakh traffic police took pity on us and, thanks to Bayan's persuasive charm, gave us a ride onwards to the town of Kyzylorda, a sleepy provincial capital in the Kyzyl-Kum Desert.

By the time we arrived at a hotel in the town it was 2 a.m., but we had rooms and a special treat waiting up for us. Bayan had arranged for us to meet the Kazakh Beatles, a tribute band who suffered years of state harassment during Communist rule. Striking up on electric guitars and a bass, and with the percussive note of a snare drum, they seemed to know every line, chord and drumbeat of every song, and they played with raw passion.

It was extraordinary to see Western icons in a small hotel in the wilds of Kazakhstan. After they worked their way through the classics we sat in the back of the restaurant, cracked open beer and bottles of vodka, and talked late into the night with Bayan and Dimitri translating. Each of them seemed to adopt the mannerisms of the Beatle they mimicked on stage. They didn't speak much English but every now and again they would inject the conversation with a lyric from their repertoire of songs.

Formed in the darkest days of Soviet oppression, "Paul" told me he had found an old bootleg tape of the Fab Four that had been smuggled into the country and wound its way to the middle of nowhere, having been passed from hand to hand and no doubt copied a thousand times. The music blew him away. It was like nothing he had heard before, because the only music allowed back then needed to be cleared by the authorities.

It was hard for me to imagine. I grew up with Radio One and vinyl, tape decks and then CDs. I used to record *Top of the Pops* onto a tape player held up to the TV, shushing my family when they dared to enter the room. That was all alien to the Kazakhs. When they came across that Beatles tape they were living in a cardboard box of a world where what they could watch and listen to was carefully monitored. I heard it again and again in the former Soviet Union: there had been no colour in life, no taste in the food, and the music was usually soulless and chosen by the government. For those guys discovering that old Beatles tape had totally inspired them. Long before they learned to play, the music transported them to a different reality.

That night in Kyzylorda was exhaustingly inspiring. It was a powerful demonstration to me of the wonder of travel, and the joy to be had from a strange encounter. One by one the Beatles told us how music had changed their world. They had been determined to get hold of instruments and learn the songs and perform for themselves. But they were living in the Soviet Union. For the next few years they managed to keep their love of the real Beatles both secret and alive, even when there was no outlet for their passion. They were not living in Moscow or St Petersburg, where occasional musical dissent was allowed; they were living in a largely closed area of the Soviet Union that was so remote it was used for nuclear tests and missile launches. In Kyzylorda, local scrutiny was much more obvious and clinical than in one of the cities. Yet, somehow, those four Beatles managed to maintain their secret until the walls came tumbling down.

I was tired, but the conversation was fascinating. They told me music was how they were able to stay mentally and emotionally alive, until their world opened up and they could play the songs without fear of being discovered by the state. They poured out their hearts and shared their lives with us that night. We drank and drank and then they played us another couple of songs before we finally went to bed. I didn't find it easy to sleep, and it wasn't just me who was affected. All of us were deeply moved by their story.

A couple of months later, after we'd flown home, Will pulled every string possible and managed to persuade a Kazakh airline to fly the group to the UK so they could play two gigs at the Beatle Week Festival in Liverpool. They actually played at the Cavern, the legendary spot where the Beatles first came to the attention of an adoring public. Their proudest souvenir? They had their photo taken crossing Abbey Road.

CHAPTER
TWELVE

Polo with the Corpse of
a Headless Goat

We rolled out of Kyzylorda with sore heads, and trailed through one broken town after another in a Soviet-era Lada, on a dirt road and across rivers and waterways on makeshift bridges constructed from planks that appeared to have nothing but hope holding them together. On and on we travelled until finally we came to an isolated village where we found people dressed in traditional clothing and a large carpet laid on the ground outside a yurt. Bayan explained she had wanted us to see a traditional baby-naming ceremony, a very special occasion for semi-nomadic Kazakhs. The child himself looked none too pleased. He was bawling his head off.

Beyond the houses, I could see more of the traditional yurts and dozens of small horses saddled and waiting on a patch of open ground. I asked Bayan what was going on.

"It is called *kokpar*."

"And what is *kokpar*?"

"Ha! You will find out, Simon. Just you wait."

I was mystified, but before I could quiz her further the family of the toddler asked Bayan if I would do the honour of naming their child.

"Really?" I said. "Are they absolutely sure?"

"Yes, yes," said Bayan. "I think they have had some alcohol, but they are sincere, and your role is just ceremonial, don't worry."

It was a little absurd. They didn't know me but were affording me a huge honour. I was discovering the power of travelling with a camera crew. Even in a remote corner of Kazakhstan being filmed by the BBC makes people think I must be important. It gifts privilege and access. Alcohol was thrust into my hand, by the villagers rather than by my team, and I tried to play to the gallery by giving a short but still faintly ludicrous and theatrical speech in which I thanked the people of Kazakhstan for their welcome, hospitality, history, culture, and possibly their weather, transport system and caviar as well. There was a surprising amount of applause, perhaps because the Kazakhs were used to ordeals, and I waved a scarf around as instructed and proclaimed the name of the baby, who continued to scream through the entire experience.

Then we had a few more drinks and waited for the mysterious *kokpar* to appear, or begin, or descend — it was initially a bit unclear. Meanwhile neighbouring villages had heard we were filming, and a large crowd began to gather. They treated us like a royal visit.

Finally Bayan explained the *kokpar*. It was a contest between two teams of men on horses (like polo without the champagne) where they would fight over the

192

headless corpse of a goat. When I first heard that last bit I was sure something had got lost in translation.

"Sorry?" I said to Bayan. "The corpse of a headless goat?"

Bayan explained that *kokpar* is as old as Kazakhstan. Some think it was used by the Mongol hordes to train their warriors in the finer techniques of horse warfare. Goats are beheaded, disembowelled and soaked in water for a day or two to toughen them up.

I am not making this up.

Then Bayan explained there was another jolly game called the *Kyz-Kuu*, which mercifully we would not be involved with because it was the wrong time of year. *Kyz-Kuu* is basically a violent form of kiss chase on horseback. A woman sets off on a galloping steed, and then a moment later a group of men on horseback gallop after her. The aim is to catch the girl and give her a kiss while both are still on horseback and at full gallop. A man who tries to catch and kiss her but fails can then be horsewhipped by her all the way back to where they began.

Again, I am not making this up.

Despite being a hopeless horseman, I was invited to play *kokpar*. I have had bad experiences with horses. Because I'm six feet three I am usually given huge and powerful beasts called Storm, Thunder, or Lightning, who rarely do anything I ask, and instead either stand around munching daisies, or race off through trees in an attempt to behead their rider.

Fortunately, my *kokpar* horse was the size of a tough pony. I leapt into the saddle. The other players were delighted. One of the men on the opposite team had the goat partly tucked under his leg just in front of me. The corpse had already been trampled under hooves and dragged around the field. It was in a desperate and bloodied state. But I didn't want to insult my hosts by pointing this out. So I grabbed the body of the goat and tried to take off across the field. My skittish horse seemed about as sure of me as I was of him and kept threatening to buck me off. I managed to stay in the saddle long enough for honour to be satisfied, and for Will to capture a little of the antics on camera. It was an experience that still today ranks among the most bizarre of my life.

As the sun set I was the guest of honour at the village dinner in a huge traditional Kazakh yurt. It was lit by candles inside and looked completely ethereal, like walking into an elvish kingdom in *Lord of the Rings*, or travelling back in time to a feast on the eve of a medieval battle. I wasn't comfortable, but it was nothing to do with the food or hospitality. The problem was my hands. The only way I'd been able to hold the headless goat and keep it close to my saddle was to grip it by its rancid and slippery testicles. There was nowhere to wash my hands before I ate, and the only cutlery was fingers.

I woke in the morning with a dose of food poisoning. I was sick a few times and Bayan arranged for a doctor to see me in my room at our guesthouse. I was drifting in and out of sleep and woke to find a very large woman flanked by two sizeable younger women standing at the end of my bed. None of them were smiling. I had no idea who they were or why they were there. Grabbing at the sheet, I half sat up.

"Who are you?" I squeaked.

"Doctor," the woman poked a meaty thumb at her chest. "Daughters," poking at each of them. They regarded me as if I was a rat in a medical experiment.

"You sick. I make better." Her accent was heavy and priceless.

"Really?" My tone suggested doubt. I looked from her to the two daughters. I wasn't sure why a doctor would show up with her girls in tow. Perhaps she had thought I might have marriage potential.

They started to fuss over me and tugged at the nylon sheet which was all I had to cover myself. It was my shelter and dignity. I held tight.

A wilting plant was struggling to survive in a large yellow plastic flower vase the size and shape of a bucket on the windowsill. One of the daughters took it in her hand, pulled out the potted plant inside and placed it on the ledge, then emptied the remaining water out of the window without checking what was below, and went to the bathroom and gave it what sounded like a rudimentary clean. Then they filled a kettle, let it heat a little and poured the entire contents into the vase.

I stared at them with increasing alarm.

The doctor produced a chunky sachet the size of a Cup-a-Soup and poured a fluorescent purple powder into the tepid water, then gave it a swirl before handing it to me.

"Drink," she instructed. "Drink it all."

Even at the time it worried me that I did what she said without questioning her further. I just thought it better to do as I was told or she might produce a nozzle to force it down me. So I drank. Not just a sip, I had to keep drinking on and on and they made sure I did by urging and chanting at me. I gulped and guzzled till my stomach couldn't take any more. I could feel an inevitable eruption beginning and dashed to the bathroom just in time to vomit an entire bucket of purple puke into the bath. While I slumped on the floor, the doctor looked satisfied. There was a lone piece of meat amid the mess in the bath.

"There," she said triumphantly. "It stuck in stomach. Make sick. Now you better."

And do you know what, she was right. Immediately I started to feel more comfortable. I talked to Bayan about it later. The doctor was a Chechen friend of hers. They were followers of the same Indian mystic called Sai Baba. Bayan looked a little sheepish when I described the scene and questioned whether her friend was an actual medical doctor with an actual medical qualification. But then Bayan reassured me the Chechen had used a remedy from Soviet times, which "always worked". The powder was a potassium mix used in vomit therapy. Certainly effective, but I tell you, it makes a terrible mess.

The following morning, Marat was driving us close to the Chinese border. Nature blesses Central Asia with spectacular scenery usually untouched by tourism or development, and nowhere is this truer than the Sharyn

Canyon, a few hours east of Almaty, which we finally reached after travelling the full width of Kazakhstan.

Marat took us to the floor of the canyon in his four-wheel drive. We slid down a steep, dusty track and crawled slowly around a towering boulder the size of a block of flats and perched so precariously over the track I held my breath as we passed. The canyon is second only to the Grand Canyon in scale, grandeur and natural beauty, but I found Sharyn infinitely more impressive, partly due to the complete absence of other visitors.

We stopped on a gravel precipice and my jaw dropped as I stared into the vast, deep canyon. I was determined to savour the moment, knowing it was somewhere I was unlikely ever to visit again. The canyon seemed to go on forever, stretching miles in each direction and coloured warm rust and golden by the setting sun.

The Sharyn Canyon was a perfect metaphor for the entire region: vast, unspoilt and unknown. The Stans had been a backwater of the Soviet Union, and the Canyon's proximity to the Chinese border rendered it off limits even to Kazakhs. It did not appear on maps, and to this day many Kazakhs remain unaware it even exists. I was falling in love with Kazakhstan. We had been welcomed, embraced and entertained. Everyone had a story to tell, and the rugged scenery carried a drama all its own.

We had wanted to head south from the Canyon, but the road took us back to Almaty, and sharing a few drinks gave us a chance to bid farewell to wonderful

Bayan. Late dinner was followed by a bar called Heaven, which shared the design aesthetics of a counterpart in London or New York but was empty when I arrived at 11.30 with Dimitri. The only other foreigners were a couple of young Australians in town to sell tennis nets. Together we bemoaned the $10 entry fee, a month's wage for most in Central Asia, and then went to leave, but a tank-like Soviet bouncer stopped us by closing the exit just as we approached.

"*Nyet*," he said forcefully, which even I could understand. "You do not want to leave."

I thought we were about to be fleeced or roughed up. But with what passed for a smile in Kazakhstan, he added: "Stay till after twelve." He looked at his watch. "It will get . . . better."

We decided against arguing. Sure enough, the upstairs dance floor opened at midnight, and the club began to fill with a collection of the most glamorous women and men I have ever seen. By 1 a.m. there were confetti cannons firing over a dance troupe from *Moulin Rouge*, and I was doing the can-can while arm-linked with a bunch of lads who appeared to be the Gucci-wearing local mafia.

It was a long road south from Almaty the next day into Kyrgyzstan, the most obscure of the Stans, a land of gorgeous meadows and jagged peaks. Our new guide Kadyr was a twenty-two-year-old local journalist who looked even younger. He had a bright energy that made me feel old. I suddenly felt I had been through a complete transformation since I was his age. Intelligent, thoughtful and enthusiastic, he spoke English with an

198

American accent and told us he'd spent part of his childhood in the United States. We'd found him through our research back in London and he was supremely excited Kyrgyzstan was going to be featured on the BBC.

We hired vehicles and Kadyr took us straight towards the Fergana Valley, a huge area of Central Asia nearly 200 miles long and more than 40 miles wide, which sprawls across eastern Uzbekistan, southern Kyrgyzstan and northern Tajikistan. Home to more than 10 million people, it is by far the most populated area in the region and at the time had a difficult reputation as a hotbed of discontent and developing militancy.

In the early 2000s unemployment was rampant in Central Asia. Poverty, censorship and government repression were the norm. Partly as a result, but also because of funding and encouragement from Saudi Arabia, militant Islam was on the rise. American political support for authoritarian regimes in Central Asia was further fuelling anger and hatred of the West and driving more young men into the arms of new and established groups that supported al Qaeda.

We made for Osh, a small city in the south of Kyrgyzstan where unrest was beginning to spread. We stopped on a bridge when Kadyr spotted illegal posters pasted to lamp-posts calling for the establishment of a Muslim Caliphate across Central Asia. This was long before the emergence of so-called Islamic State. Kadyr was shocked and told us that even to be caught in possession of such material would mean ten years in jail.

Kadyr and other contacts arranged for us to meet an activist in Osh from the shadowy banned militant Islamic group Hizb-ut-Tahrir, which was becoming active across the whole region. One of their stated ambitions was the destruction of Western democracy. Kadyr was nervous. We hired a small bus with curtains and blacked-out windows so we could talk to the activist discreetly without risking taking him back to our hotel. We had no way of knowing who he was, or what he was capable of doing.

Arriving at the agreed contact point, we found a heavy-set, dark-eyed and grim man waiting for us. He was keen to talk despite the fact we were Westerners and, as he kept reminding us, therefore his enemies. We drove out to the edge of the city to avoid any attention from the authorities.

He wagged his finger at me as he was speaking. "America wants to dominate the world but it'll never happen."

"You think that's really true?" I asked him. "You think that's what America wants — to rule the world and crush you?"

The man answered with a sneer. "America will die. Why? Because they're 25 million gays, more than 4 million lesbians, 17 million drug addicts and many people who live in poverty."

He told me that, although he and other militants didn't have an atomic bomb, they had ideas, which were far more powerful. Perhaps one day, he mused, they would get their own bomb. All the talk of bombs was unnerving Kadyr, who was translating. Three times during our talk the militant said he wanted to martyr himself against the West, making Kadyr nervous he was about to blow himself up in our van.

Even as the guy left our van he was ranting. Kadyr told me that as he shook hands, he was repeating that we were his enemies. Kadyr was visibly relieved when he left. He said he had looked closely at the man's clothes to see if he could spot any sign of a suicide vest.

"I was getting ready to jump on him," he said to me earnestly.

Despite goat testicles, militants and sickness, I was loving my time in this forgotten corner of the world. But I had and still have a nagging concern it might still be a future flashpoint for militancy and conflict. I hope I am wrong. But militancy has raised its head in Central Asia before. In the 1990s the battered neighbouring state of Tajikistan, the poorest of all the former Soviet states, endured a violent civil war between government forces and Islamic militants in which tens of thousands of fighters and civilians died.

That night I slept fitfully. So much had happened. How would we fit weeks of intense filming into short late-night programmes? What on earth had we been doing with a militant in the back of our van when this was supposed to be a travelogue? I started to doubt how we would show the madness of *kokpar* one moment, and then a guy who wanted to martyr himself.

But these programmes were always supposed to encompass the extremes of life. The light and the shade. Ironically, one of my favourite moments in

Kyrgyzstan was the night after we met the militant. A pirated version of the movie *Titanic* was showing on the single Kyrgyz TV channel. It was shown almost every single Saturday night for a year, despite the fact it clearly had a banner caption running across the bottom of the screen which stated: "For the consideration of Academy Award voters only".

We were amazed. Imagine a clearly pirated movie showing in peak-time on BBC One. Then Leonardo DiCaprio and Kate Winslet started to speak, and we all had a bout of hysterics. The fact they were showing a bootleg film was bad enough, but it had been dubbed into Russian with just one actor speaking all the lines in a completely emotionless, monotonal male voice.

"Jack! Jack!" cried Rose as she ran through the ship, as her true love answered.

"*Tchack, tchak, rows, rows,*" said the dubbed voice loudly.

Ageing posters and *Titanic* memorabilia were everywhere in Kyrgyzstan. The Kyrgyz version of *Titanic* deserved its own award. It was certainly more entertaining than the original.

Just down the road from Osh was another legacy of Soviet rule. Above the broken former mining town of Mailuu-Suu were more than twenty unstable radioactive waste dumps and pits for uranium waste tailings. Uranium had been mined in Kyrgyzstan for the Soviet nuclear weapons programme, but there was only a cursory clean-up of the sites after the Union collapsed.

There were environmental concerns about the waste dumps, of course, but some experts were also worried people could get access to the sites and be able to steal some of the material and include it in a radiological or so-called "dirty" bomb.

It was definitely a darker side to the story of Kyrgyzstan, and something we all felt we should include in the programme. But of course you can't just *mention* something like that in a TV show; you actually have to go there, and you have to see and film it.

We drove out towards one of the dumps with a local scientist who had been trying to monitor their condition.

"My method of protecting myself from the radiation is twofold: milk and vodka," he told me with a fatalistic smile. "Milk to counter some of the effects of radiation and vodka to forget about it afterwards."

Ours, by contrast, was full nuclear, biological and chemical containment suits. They wouldn't protect us from excess radiation, but they were supposed to protect us from contaminated radioactive dust, which could lodge and linger in our lungs. The site was part of the reason I had been required to do a chemical weapons course before heading out to the Stans.

Getting dressed in those NBC suits felt surreal. We were standing by the side of a dusty track in an unknown corner of an unknown country in an unknown region of the world, and I was putting batteries into a Geiger counter, used for detecting and measuring radiation, and explaining to the camera that we were going to walk into an abandoned Soviet radioactive waste dump to check its condition and assess the security around it. I suddenly thought, *This is completely mad!*

But it was for TV, and I was learning that in front of the camera what otherwise would be absurd can rapidly become normal.

Will and I prised the shiny grey suits from sealed polythene wrappers and pulled them on as we stood by the van, then had our only row of the entire trip when we realised we had forgotten the instructions for the Geiger counter. Kadyr looked on in amazement. We insisted the local scientist wear a suit despite his protestations that he had never bothered before. He produced an ancient map outlining where the various dumps were and which were the most dangerous, and that was it. We adjusted our full-face respirators, or military gas masks, and set off up the hill towards the dumps, sealed in NBC suits and carrying the Geiger counter.

We looked like three alien beings, and within seconds of us starting to walk the sun emerged and we began to bake. Not just swelter, but steam. Within 100 metres we crested a small hill and through the fogged glass lenses of my respirator I could see a couple of locals ahead on a dip in the track trying to push-start a Lada. One glanced round and saw us, then did a double take, tapped his friend on the arm and they backed up against their car in bemused horror.

"*Zdravstvuyte* [hello]," I tried to say as we walked past in slow motion, but through the mask it might have come out as a strangled alien war cry. They gawped at us. I gave a cheery wave and we walked on, past a couple of perfunctory signs warning of radiation. There was no fence and no guards. I looked over my shoulder to see the guys with the Lada still watching. How long had they lived here? Probably decades. Perhaps since they were children, and with no protection.

I pointed back at the men and gestured to our scientist. I thought he should shoo them away, but he just shrugged, as if to say: "What do you want me to do?"

Then I realised there was a village just across the valley, on the edge of the radioactive site, and later the scientist said people had been told the area was safe. But that wasn't what the Geiger counter indicated. It began clicking away, slowly at first, then faster. The whole area was a huge pit where the Soviets had buried radioactive waste, despite the fact the entire region was prone to earthquakes. The dump had been covered in a thin layer of earth and grass, but far from being safe, there were places where the levels of radiation were spiking to more than a thousand times what was normal. We chanced upon a hole somebody had been digging at one radioactive site. Villagers were grazing their cattle on the dump. A few years later Mailuu-Suu was found to be one of the ten most polluted sites in the world in a study published by the Blacksmith Institute.

Radiation wasn't the only hazard, though; to be locked inside one of those charcoal-lined suits for any length of time is like being shut in an oven. The sun was high in the sky, and we were bakingly hot. We all had to stop and have a rest, sitting on the ground on top of the radioactive waste dump. Unbelievable. But the alternative was collapse.

We turned back to the van where Dimitri had been tasked with making sure he got a good shot of our return. As we came over the hill we were clearly arriving much earlier than expected. Despite heat exhaustion I had a giggle as he flapped around trying to find a spare battery for the camera. Will was still filming as we walked, his arm stuck at a permanent right angle. When he finally put the camera down, a strong stream of pure sweat poured from the cuff of his NBC suit.

We finished the last of the water in our packs as we tore off our suits, and then headed to a nearby town, where the delightful Café Rich Man resembled a small Spanish villa. Their water supply had been switched off because it had been raining hard for a few days and the river was muddy. They couldn't draw more water from the river until the sediment had settled.

"So, what should we drink then?" I asked Kadyr.

"There's only one thing for it," he said with a smile. "Soviet champagne!"

Such a bourgeois indulgence didn't seem to fit with the principles of Marx and Lenin. Champagne was produced and Kadyr went to pop the cork. It rocketed out of the top and the champagne erupted everywhere, leaving just a glass or two to drink.

"The champagne shows the power of the Soviet military," said a waiter with a smile.

Relaxing after our sweaty walk, I felt a sense of exhilaration. We weren't just talking about situations from afar, we were engaged in them. Vials of anthrax, the Kazakh Beatles, the Sharyn Canyon, goat testicles. I was surprised what the BBC were prepared to let us do. We were having madcap *Boys' Own* adventures. Whatever I'd thought the job would entail, I had never imagined it would be so brilliant, frightening and sheer, bloody gob-smacking, often all at the same time. Even when it was bonkers, even when we were walking into the madness of a radioactive waste dump, it was exciting and memorable.

We drove on to Lake Issyk-Kul, the second largest and highest mountain lake after Latin America's Lake Titicaca, where a scattering of resort hotels which used to cater for Soviet leaders had plenty of spare rooms. They were, quite frankly, a bit of a dump, yet the Kyrgyz government was hoping to attract adventure tourists seeking white-water rafting and mountain trekking. We stopped at one decent guesthouse which had fresh water and power.

"Who comes here now?" I asked the manager.

"Diplomats, VIPs, and beezneez elite," he replied.

"What exactly does business elite mean?" I asked naïvely.

"Beezneez elite . . . means . . . beezneez elite," he replied with a euphemistic smile. Organised crime is certainly a problem in Central Asia, but rarely for visitors. Local criminals are more interested in the rich pickings garnered from shipping heroin from Afghanistan through Central Asia to Russia and Europe.

We were coming to the end of the first leg of our journey around the Stans, and we arrived at Bishkek, the sleepy Kyrgyz capital, from where we would fly home to rest, recover and plan the next stage of the journey. Our hotel was full of American special forces on leave from Afghanistan. While they lounged in the hotel's dayglo casino, we headed for the national museum, an eccentric celebration of the Soviet past.

The casino now happily accepts the US dollar, but murals in the museum portrayed evil Americans, one of whom bore more than a passing resemblance to George Bush, sitting astride nuclear missiles and laying waste to legions of defenceless women and children. Outside teenagers asked me in English if I liked ganja while they roller-bladed around the base of a statue of Lenin, still standing proudly in the main square.

"We're quite tolerant of Soviet history," said Kadyr, my young guide. "Many people think life was better under Communism."

The main consequence of the end of the Soviet Union seemed to be economic collapse. The Stans were left reeling, and most people I met longed for a return to the financial security of the past. "At least we knew where we were then," said Kadyr.

CHAPTER
THIRTEEN

The Slave and the Tigers

Landing back at Heathrow after finishing filming the first half of *Meet the Stans*, my first ever TV adventure, I was humming with everything I'd seen and experienced. I couldn't wait to see family and friends to regale and bore them with tales from Central Asia.

London felt strange and yet familiar. Going home to the house in Ladbroke Grove I shared with my friends Tony and Danny was particularly difficult. I spent days unpacking, washing kit, cleaning equipment and checking my notes from the journey for the script I would need to write for the programme. After a long and exciting adventure almost everything felt like an anticlimax. I wanted to get a megaphone and tell everyone what I'd seen and done. I wanted to share my tales.

It might have felt to me like I'd been away for months, but in reality it was just a few weeks, and everyone I knew had carried on quite happily with their lives while I was away. Sometimes the comedown from a trip can be instant and intense. I remember coming home after finishing my journey around the Tropic of Cancer, a fairly epic six-part journey around the northern border of the tropics, and discovering the toilets were blocked in the flat I shared with my now-wife. The first thing we had to do, even before unpacking our bags, was get some gloves and wellies on, lift up the manhole cover hidden under the floorboards in the back room, and rod out the overflowing sewers. It was such a colossal fall back down to earth. For a moment I was pretty grumpy about it, but then I smiled to myself: going off on a trip around the world, or an adventure in Central Asia, is not a normal thing to do. It's an abnormal privilege. Rodding out the sewers, washing my kit, or heading to the supermarket, is an equally wonderful normality, and it needs to be embraced and enjoyed.

Once I'd finished my unpacking and washing after my first trip to Central Asia and when everything was under control, I sat around the kitchen table with Danny and Tony and shared a beer and told them a few stories from the road. I didn't drone on for hours, I hope, even if I felt it was what I wanted to do, partly because I could tell the guys were keeping something from me. They looked a little sheepish.

"What's going on?" I said. "What's happened? Why are you looking like that?"

Danny finally came clean.

"All right," he said. "You're going to find out sooner or later anyway. You remember when we moved in, we agreed that with three blokes living together under one roof we could never get a games console?"

"Yeeees," I said slowly.

Tony held his hands up. "I've bought one."

He shrugged. I smiled.

"Rush of blood, out-of-body experience. Before I knew what was going on, I came home with a PlayStation."

We laughed. We knew we were all slightly weak-willed and had banned games because we thought we'd never get any work done. Danny and I were particularly bad. We spent the next week doing nothing but drive a car around London shooting gangsters. In a funny way, though, it was cathartic. We only ever had one game for the console, and once we'd completed it, admittedly by playing all night in one matey beer-fuelled session, we felt as if we'd been through some rite of passage where we had passed from being shallower twenty-somethings to slightly more serious thirty-somethings. Thank God Tony never bought another game or I might never have made it back to the Stans.

Once we had finished the game, I had told everyone I knew about the delights of Central Asia, and had enjoyed a few nights of deep, deep sleep in my own bed, I was itching to get stuck into the preparation for the next trip.

One thing was very clear, my travel kit was completely inadequate. I had just taken my normal clothing and basic equipment bought from a camping shop down the road. As a result, I had been cold, wet, hungry and uncomfortable. So I started sourcing new kit and compiling a now legendary (at least in my family) packing list that has grown over the years to be more than twelve pages long, and is divided under simple headings like: cold, heat, medicine and — most importantly for me — food. I have had to become meticulous, with long lists of stuff I might require that I can then pick from with each new adventure. What's that old saying? Fail to prepare, then prepare to fail.

I have come a long way since I was a kid who climbed into Glencoe wearing little more than an old cagoule. Since I started these TV journeys I have had to become, I now confess, a kit obsessive. In the years since *Meet the Stans* I have sometimes spent eight out of twelve months travelling and working abroad. So I can't afford to forget anything, and my travel kit has to be just right: tough, light, dependable and functional. There is no space in my bags for anything that doesn't work or doesn't last.

Obviously the kit I need varies dramatically from trip to trip. Travelling by road through a former Soviet Republic in the Caucasus during winter is completely different to boating through sweltering southern Colombia. But some old friends are always in the bag. I wouldn't dream of travelling anywhere without a trusty Leatherman and a small, powerful torch, because — time after time — carrying both has saved my skin.

In the capital of Transnistria, an obscure, exotic breakaway state between Moldova and Ukraine, where manhole covers had been stolen and sold for scrap metal, my torch saved me from falling into hellish, pitch-black sewers on unlit city streets. In Botswana's Kalahari Desert, obeying an urgent midnight call of nature deep in lion territory, a sweep of my torch across the bush revealed the silent approach of sets of shiny, carnivorous eyes. Thankfully I was able to scare away their hungry owners by smashing a spade into dry branches.

Travelling for *Meet the Stans*, I took one huge expedition bag that weighed as much as a tractor. In the years since, I've generally taken two bags for the road: one duffel bag, with compression straps to reduce bulk and rucksack straps that mean it can be slung comfortably on my back, and a hardened waterproof case that can withstand a truck driving over it, or the outbreak of thermonuclear war. Sleeping bag, mosquito net, clothes and boots, all go in the duffel. Anything breakable goes in the case. It's a bulky system that wouldn't work for everyone, particularly gappers and backpackers, and it's too much for a normal holiday, but even after Stans 1, I realised that on a filming trip I need to be prepared for almost anything.

Trekking into Burma, illegally and undercover, from a remote region of India, while filming *Tropic of Cancer*, was a particular challenge that required new levels of kit obsession. With my colleagues Jonathan Young and Andrew Carter I travelled to meet the Chin people, who suffer terrible human rights abuses in a remote region of Burma bristling with more than fifty Burmese military bases. We tried to prepare for everything, carrying ropes, machetes, a medical trauma kit, camouflaged hammocks, locator beacons and food. We even had survival kits strapped to our thighs just in case we encountered a Burmese army patrol and had to dump our rucksacks and make a run for it.

But careful planning and preparation encouraged confidence and ensured we were able to deal with all emergencies, major and minor. And the same applies to any trip. If you plan what you want to pack for a holiday well in advance, you won't suffer the stress caused by last-minute packing as you throw your clobber into a bag a few hours before a flight. I now try to leave myself plenty of time to pack, so I can enjoy the reassuring feeling that I have everything I want or need, so I'll be able to cope with any journey challenge, whether it's making sure I have a book for a delay at the airport, or a compass on my watch strap to help me out of the Burmese jungle at four in the morning.

I also don't feel embarrassed that my packing extends to the inclusion of a few edible home comforts. Obviously, I need to be eating the local grub, wherever I am, because that's a vital part of a trip, and a great chance to bank some memorable experiences. But from the second *Meet the Stans* trip onwards, I have taken squeezy tubes of honey, spicy sauce and Marmite to liven up boring breakfasts on the road, and a pack of tea bags for those rare and priceless moments when a hot brew can be slowly savoured. I might be abroad, in some far-flung part of our planet, but careful packing ensures that certain essential standards can be maintained.

While I was faffing around with my packing lists after returning from the first Stans trip, Will Daws had been busy transferring all the raw footage to the editing suite, where the unsung heroes of the television process work their magic.

I saw some of the rushes from the first two programmes and cringed. Not at the landscapes or the way it had been filmed, or the people we met, but at watching myself on camera and the way I came across.

"I'm awful," I said to Will. "People will hate me. My voice is annoying."

"Everyone hates watching themselves on the TV," Will said soothingly. "You're OK, don't worry."

I hated watching myself then, and I still don't like watching myself now. People ask if I sit down in front of the television when my own shows are on. No! Almost never. I'm too self-critical. But from the beginning Will and the BBC reassured me that while I might indeed be annoying, on balance I was probably slightly less annoying than many people would be if they were filmed. I took that to be a good thing.

"And anyway," Will said, "we'll be able to make you look better in the edit."

He had captured a huge amount of material on film, but it had to be funnelled and shaped into a coherent telly programme. What would emerge partly depended on the skill and style of the editor, who has an enormous role in the creation of a show. For several of my early programmes, that was Ryshard Opyrchal. He patiently turned my babble into TV I was proud of, and dozens of other editors have since performed the same alchemy. Nowadays we often have 60, 80, sometimes more than 120 hours of footage from multiple cameras that needs to be wrangled and watched and linked together. Editors sit with the producer-director, often in a windowless room in a basement, and have roughly six weeks to turn it into an hour of TV, struggling and scrolling through the material, looking for moments of clarity from the presenter.

When the editor finishes a composer creates the music, then graders enhance the finished film so it looks glossy and inviting on the TV. Pound for pound nothing improves a programme faster than a skilled colourist sitting in front of a vast *Star Trek*-sized console playing with scores of dials and sliders like Jean-Michel Jarre, tweaking colours and shadows. Meanwhile back in the office there are production co-ordinators and production managers who help to plot the journeys, secure the visas and filming permits, book flights and places to stay, and generally keep an eye on the money. Series producers and executive producers run the journeys and get their hands dirty alongside assistant producers and directors with the research and planning for where we are going and what on earth we will film. Everyone is vital. Everyone does two or three jobs. Some of the newspapers might sneer at the BBC and claim there are too many tiers of management. I see none of that. I see tight, small teams and people working long hours.

On *Meet the Stans* we had a young researcher called Shahida Tulaganova, an Uzbek journalist and fluent Russian speaker living in London who helped to put together the journeys and shows, and was then due to travel out with Will, Dimitri and me on the Uzbek leg of the journey because of the challenges of finding a guide in the country.

Shahida was working with Will to iron out some visa issues, and then we would be back on a plane, heading out to Uzbekistan and Tajikistan. There was just time for me to sit down and consider what I had loved most about my first TV journey.

The landscapes had certainly been epic. Standing and looking out at the Sharyn Canyon had been one of many moments I would treasure forever. The wildlife had been magnificent. As we crossed the steppe I had been captivated by a diving eagle. The food had often been strange and occasionally spectacular. I would remember all of it. Everything.

But what had really stood out were the people. For me the strongest memories from that first trip, and from every trip since, are from my encounters with us, with our inspiring, intriguing, long-suffering, comic, clever and caring fellow humans. When we plan a journey I am always asking and thinking, who are we going to meet? Meaningful encounters with other people in a strange part of the world are the real experiences to treasure. If I'm not meeting people then I'm not on a proper journey.

In Central Asia I was lucky to spend time with locals who were warm, generous and fascinating, and in the years since I have been blessed to meet folk who have been completely inspirational.

Travelling in Kenya more recently, I crossed the great African plains and arrived at a remote Maasai homestead, and the mud-dung hut of a grandmother called Lucy. She was renovating and refreshing the hut, and I was press-ganged into slapping huge cow pats on the sides while Lucy watched and giggled so wildly she had to have a sit-down and a cup of tea.

I loved spending a day with Lucy. Not because of her mud hut, or her traditional Maasai clothing, complete with colourful shawl, bead jewellery and stretched earlobes. Lucy was a proud cattle herder, but her mind roamed so much further than the plains where she lived. As we walked and chatted, Lucy bombarded me with questions, about my travels, the world, our cameras and my life. We were walking together on a vast plain, almost completely empty of humanity, keeping an eye on Lucy's herd of cattle. I was struggling to get a word in edgeways, and then a phone rang. Lucy looked sheepish, then reached into her robes and retrieved a battered mobile. It turned out she would send a youngster fifteen miles to charge the phone each week, proving old Nokias really hold their power. On the other end of the line was her neighbour, standing outside her own hut half a mile away, squinting against the sun and wondering who on earth were those tall foreigners and where was Lucy taking them in the midday heat?

Life for Lucy's family was changing. She had just sold a cow to pay for her granddaughter to go to college 200 miles away to study travel and tourism. Perhaps one day someone reading this will stay in her hotel.

Often the cast of memorable and brilliant people I meet on my journeys are completely inspiring. In Paraguay I met a woman called Margarita Mbywangi who had one of the most extraordinary life tales I have ever heard. She was in her forties, and she emerged from a dark hut in a community of the indigenous Aché people, looking ragged and weary. I found out later she had malaria, and although it had laid her low, she still managed to drag herself out so she could speak to me. She was barefoot, wearing shorts and a singlet and standing about five feet three. Her feverish face still managed to radiate calm and a deep warmth.

Margarita was an Aché *cacique*, or chief, and one of the first female indigenous leaders in the country. Democratically elected by the community, she acted as their point of contact with the outside world. She took me on a walking tour of the village, past some young men who had slaughtered a pig in honour of our visit, while she told me her incredible story. She explained that the first real contact her people had with the outside world was in 1978. Within months trees were being felled, roads laid down and the Aché were being hunted and murdered by farmers and soldiers.

Just a generation before, tribes like the Aché weren't considered to be human by the Paraguayans. Human hunts were organised where "big game" hunters could fly in to track people in the jungle and shoot them. I was astounded. "Indigenous people weren't regarded as citizens until 1991," my guide in Paraguay told me. "Most of the hunting stopped by the end of the 1970s, but in some really remote areas it was still going on until the 1990s."

Mercifully the killings stopped, but the misery went on. With the deforestation growing worse and worse, patches of scrubland were set aside for the Aché to live on, but their traditional hunter-gatherer way of life had already been ripped away. Instead there was casual work on farms with little pay and cheap alcohol.

When Margarita was five years old her village was attacked by Paraguayans and razed to the ground. She was found cowering in the bushes and dragged away. Kidnapped, she was sold into servitude on a farming ranch to serve the family as a slave. She was forced to work cleaning the house and looking after the children of the family. But she did manage to learn Spanish, and when the family left the farm and moved close to a city, she managed to escape. She was caught and returned to the family, but then ran away a second time and made it to the city and got work in a house as a cleaner. She found a local priest and asked him to help her locate her remote village. It took two years to work out where she had been kidnapped, but eventually the priest drove her out to meet the community. By then Margarita had forgotten the Aché language and couldn't tell them who she was. But then a man appeared who recognised Margarita. He threw his arms around her and wailed. It was her brother. He hadn't seen her for fifteen years.

I was almost in tears when I heard all this. It was fantastically moving. But Margarita's story wasn't just one of return. It was one of hope. Of promise. Margarita relearned her language. She struggled with the temptations of alcohol. But she got through it and became a nurse. Then she was made chief of the community of Kuetuvy. Later, she stood for election as a senator in Paraguay. Eventually she became the government Minister for Indigenous Affairs.

I was reeling with each turn of the tale. A slave who became a senator and then a minister. Yet I have travelled across a planet full of stirring human stories, and I have heard astonishing and inspiring stories of profound life-change almost everywhere. Surely that, more than anything, is a reason to travel.

A year after travelling in Paraguay, I went to Bangladesh, and met an extraordinary guide called Tanjil, a bearded and bespectacled slip of a man, who guided me and a crew from the BBC around his country, which, although unbelievably poor, is a place I love with a passion.

Shortly afterwards Tanjil was in London and I invited him over for dinner. He was late and when he finally arrived, he explained that he had stopped to take a call on his mobile phone.

"All because of the tigers," he said with a tired sigh.

"Eh?" I said.

Then Tanjil started to explain that many, many years before he had been on a dangerous trip with a film crew who were looking for huge tigers that had attacked farmers in the Sundarbans region of Bangladesh, an enormous area of river forest. Tanjil and the film crew were travelling on a large wooden river-boat with cabins and kitchens, and on their way into the Sundarbans they stopped in a very poor, very remote village for a few hours. The cook on the boat went out looking for supplies, and eventually he returned to Tanjil and said: "Boss, look, I could really do with a bit of help on this trip, and there's a boy in the village who is enslaved and in shackles."

"Apparently," Tanjil told me, "he had been sold into slavery by his family to pay a debt."

The cook told Tanjil it would only cost a few pounds to pay the debt and the boy could be released and he could help out on the boat.

"No," said Tanjil, "it's dangerous, we're going to look for man-eating tigers, and we don't need anyone else on the boat, certainly not a boy."

The chef pleaded with him: "Oh boss, please, he looks like a bright lad, and I could really do with the help. I'll train him up."

Tanjil sighed and agreed. So they paid off the family debt, and the shackle and chain on his leg was released, and the boy went on the boat with Tanjil and the film crew, and he was given some new clothes and shoes in place of the rags he was wearing, and he helped the cook on the trip.

Tanjil was telling me this in London while sitting at my dining table. The roast chicken was getting cold.

"Well, that's a lovely story, Tanjil," I said, "but what's it got to do with you being late?"

Tanjil looked at me. "That was the boy, on the telephone. He called me as I was walking up your street. He worked for me for years. I trained him. He's now a man, and he was ringing me from Nepal, where he's setting up a tiger conservation sanctuary. He's now a leading expert on tiger conservation. He's co-authored science papers on tigers that have been published in the most prestigious science journals in the world."

222

That boy had been enslaved. He would have rotted in that village. But he had talent and ability, just waiting to be discovered.

CHAPTER
FOURTEEN

The Kalon Minaret

Sitting with Shahida, Will and Dimitri on the plane to Tashkent, Uzbekistan, at the start of both my second TV trip and the second leg of my journey around Central Asia, I was almost sizzling with excitement about the adventure ahead. But there was also apprehension about the country we were due to explore first.

We planned to travel west through Uzbekistan to the ancient Silk Road cities of Bukhara and Samarkand, and then south through mountainous Tajikistan to the border with Afghanistan. The first leg of the journey, through Kazakhstan and Kyrgyzstan, had been an extraordinary tour of a beautiful, bizarre and unpredictable region. Now we were flying to the most violently repressive of the Stan countries.

All the countries of Central Asia had, and still have, political problems, but at the time of my travels in the area Uzbekistan seemed the most troubled. The country was facing the real prospect of armed conflict. Many Uzbeks were angry with their authoritarian leader Islam Karimov and there was talk of revolution. In response tens of thousands of militants and activists who opposed the government were being tortured, jailed or executed. Many men were mysteriously disappearing, often into secret prison cells, but also because they were the victims of extrajudicial killings, simply for growing their beards and being pious Muslims. Sermons at Friday prayers were required to follow government guidelines and the secret police were infiltrating mosques to check rules were obeyed.

Making a TV programme for the BBC draws far greater attention from everyone, including the authorities, than if it was just me on my own writing a book. Will and I had spent ages discussing how we could have an objective guide who would give us a fair assessment of Uzbekistan without the risk of them being picked up by the secret police and potentially tortured the minute we left the country. Shahida was the answer. Guides and fixers are critical on my journeys and Shahida was right up there with the best of them. Strong, clever and erudite, she was also opinionated, young and supremely sassy. She proved to be fantastic company and our merry travel gang of three grew happily to four.

One problem with filming in a repressive regime is that much of the repression often goes on behind closed doors. At first glance Tashkent, the Uzbek capital, appeared to be a relaxed and modern city. We hoped Shahida would be candid and outspoken, and we weren't disappointed. The morning after we arrived she spotted a series of posters depicting Islam Karimov lording it over Uzbekistan as if it were his personal fiefdom. His image was shown next to statements and slogans that echoed the oppression of the Soviet era.

Shahida was contemptuous: "It's a joke," she said. "There's nothing here, an imaginary world. None of what he says is true."

She was right, of course. It was a country with wonderful scenery but a wretched economy. The only growth industry appeared to be personal protection for the new breed of post-Soviet "beezneez elite" as everyone called them. Rich businessmen did not trust the police and so were turning to private security firms.

Shahida took me to visit one training centre where strapping young men were being taught to protect wealthy businessmen by a middle-aged woman wearing a pair of Winnie the Pooh socks. She looked cuddly, like somebody's favourite great aunt, but she was actually a former colonel in the KGB. A Russian national, she had been purged from her state job by the Uzbeks after independence. The BBC producers loved the fact I noticed her socks and mentioned them on camera. It was a minor detail that was perhaps childishly funny and charming, but as far as the Beeb was concerned it humanised both the woman and the story.

The BBC also liked the fact I was happy to front up to one of the most controversial men in the country. Having seen the bodyguards training, I suggested we try and talk to some of the new business elite. A few phone calls later, Shahida informed us we'd been invited to visit the most powerful man in the country.

"The President?" I said. "How did you swing that?"

"Not the President," she chided me with a smile. "Even more powerful."

226

We drove into a leafy suburb of Tashkent, where homes were built behind eight-foot metal fences, and headed to the house of a wealthy businessman involved in what was described as the soft drink and cotton trade. About five feet ten, grey-haired and solidly built, he opened the door of our van as we arrived at his opulent villa and shook my hand with a grip like a Greco-Roman wrestler. With fountains and manicured lawns, the house wouldn't have looked out of place in the Hollywood hills. There were Roman-style piazzas dotted around, as well as guesthouses and garages. We were treated to a feast, but then I started quizzing him about allegations that he was connected with organised crime. Eventually he decided not to talk to us any more, and we politely made our excuses and left. It all made good TV.

Back in Tashkent, Shahida took me for a wander around the centre of the city. A clue to the mindset of the President at the time was the way he was elevating Amir Temur to almost saintlike status. Temur was a fourteenth-century warlord who founded the Timurid Dynasty with a mission to restore the "glory" of Genghis Khan. A few years before, the President had removed the bust of Karl Marx from what had been "Karl Marx Square" and replaced it with a horseback bronze of the new national hero. Many Uzbeks were uncomfortable about being identified with a warlike butcher.

We wandered down what used to be Marx Street but was now Broadway. Young people were wearing T-shirts, baggy jeans, and baseball caps worn backwards. There were market stalls selling clothes, shoes and street food. We could have been anywhere in the world. Then we bumped into Dipsy the Teletubby, who responded positively but unconvincingly when asked if life was better under the Soviets or the President.

On the surface, at least in the capital, it seemed there was nothing wrong. But the economy was in a complete mess, and Shahida explained that almost everyone with an education wanted to leave, including young women whose more obvious assets were mainly physical. We popped into a marriage agency through which Uzbeks hoped to meet wealthy, and usually much older, Western men. There were literally thousands of women on the books. It was rather tragic.

I could understand why people wanted out. The longer we were in Uzbekistan the more obvious it was how limited the opportunities were. The main consequence of the collapse of the Soviet Union, just over a decade before, had been economic disaster. Central Asia was still reeling. Shahida had seen it for herself but managed to pursue a career in London. It wasn't just the lack of opportunity that was stifling; it was repression and ridiculous laws and edicts issued by the President that made many feel they lived at the whim of a medieval loon.

To illustrate the madness, that night Shahida took me to a suburb of Tashkent. We crept behind a burnt-out shop, knocked on a thick iron door at the top of a fire escape, and broke Uzbek law by entering a pool hall and picking up a cue. For no apparent reason, the Uzbek government had decided to ban snooker and pool. Rumours suggested the son of a top presidential aide had lost a huge sum on a game, and his father persuaded the President to ban the popular sport across the entire country in a fit of pique. It seemed arbitrary, but that small-minded and petty action suggested a government that was out of control and might do anything to anyone.

We left the capital in the company of Mr Amir, a human rights lawyer who was a contact of Shahida's. Together we headed out across the country to an Uzbek section of the notorious Fergana Valley, a home to millions of peaceful farmers and villagers but also various old and new radical Islamic groups. Uzbek officials and secret police shadowed us closely, ferociously paranoid anyone we met might express some form of political dissent. They almost had a fit when we went to visit the family of Juma Namangani, the former leader of the Islamic Movement of Uzbekistan, a terrorist group which fought alongside Osama bin Laden and the Taliban.

Before his apparent death during fighting in Afghanistan, Namangani was one of the most wanted men in the world. His brother, however, was running a local village sweet shop, and his sister-in-law insisted we try tubs of their finest vanilla ice-cream and refused to accept payment. We were chomping away when the secret police arrived and tried to force us to leave. Mr Amir, however, lost no time in telling the police they had no right to tail us and no right to force us out. I was squatting on the ground eating ice-cream outside a run-down sweet shop in a far-flung backwater, while

Mr Amir, who was only slightly more than five foot nothing, squared up to a much taller senior policeman and hectored him, literally wagging his finger in his face, lecturing him about arcane sections of the Uzbek constitution, which apparently guaranteed our rights and protection. The policeman was utterly bamboozled.

It was a comic but worrying scene. Small, middle-aged, alone; Mr Amir went up against the might of the dictatorship with a brave but reckless disregard for his own safety. We had no idea whether his outburst would cost Mr Amir dearly after we left. He knew he was taking risks. But he was putting his welfare and possibly his life on the line to campaign for human rights, and to make Uzbekistan a better place to live in. In the years since, I have met countless other human rights workers and campaigners who risk everything to share the reality of their corner of the world. People I have met on the journeys have been harassed, arrested, and even tortured after we have left.

Travelling and filming in Africa a few years later I met a brave young campaigner called Rashid in Western Sahara. Morocco had claimed the territory of Western Sahara after the Spanish left in 1975. In the years that followed there was a bloody war between the Moroccans and a guerrilla army made up of the indigenous Saharawi people, who wanted Western Sahara to be an independent country. We had communicated in coded internet messages, but actually getting to speak to Rashid in person late one night meant sneaking out of our hotel, avoiding secret police and spies, and following him in a vehicle to a safe house. Once inside, he introduced me to a group of other activists and felt able to chat openly, saying what the Saharawi people wanted was their independence, "no more, and no less".

What he said to us was actually very simple. He said there was a lot of oppression, the secret police were everywhere, there was no freedom of speech, and activists couldn't campaign openly for independence. "We can't even raise the Saharawi flag or talk about the history of the Saharawi people," he added. We chatted for a couple of hours and then left.

For talking to us, Rashid said he was later picked up by the secret police, questioned explicitly about what he had said to us, and severely beaten by Moroccan police. He sent photographs of the injuries he said he'd received.

Was it worth it? Rashid thought so. He knew he was likely to be detained. He had told us that he was completely willing to face a beating or worse. Dozens of activists I have met around the world have said the same. They think it is worth taking the risks and enduring the consequences. We always warn them of the possible outcome. But usually they know exactly what is likely to happen. Many of them have endured abuse before. They are brave not once, but often multiple times. And the reason they take those chances and deal with the aftermath is that they are desperate to share their story with our viewers and the outside world. It is humbling, but also profound.

In the Fergana Valley in Uzbekistan the Namangani family were careful not to express anti-government sentiment, but virtually every other family I met in the Valley raged against the government and seemed to have at least one male member in jail. The valley and the country felt tense.

We drove a few hundred miles across Uzbekistan to reach Samarkand, one of the oldest continuously inhabited cities in the world. Central Asia has long been a crossroads between the East and West; it was in Samarkand in the fourteenth century that Chinese traders are thought to have first met Spanish merchants and sparked a new era of globalisation. The centre of the city, graced by the breathtaking Registan, a three-sided square which is perhaps the finest built space in the Islamic world, was a joy. We climbed a secret passage hidden behind a carpet store into one of the famous minarets. I felt a real thrill emerging at the top of the tower to look out at a city that was once one of the centres of the world, a key stop and destination for intellectuals on the Silk Road between Europe and China.

We headed onwards to Bukhara, another ancient city 300 miles west. For years I had heard stories of the place. It sounded evocative and mysterious to me, like Zanzibar or Timbuktu. I was excited as we drew close to the city, but the motion of our four-wheel drive bumping along the road sent me to sleep. The sound of a huge wooden door creaking open finally roused me as we parked, late at night, outside a guesthouse in Bukhara. I picked myself off the floor of the van, where half my body appeared to have slumped rather unedifyingly as I slept, rubbed my bleary eyes, and peered out of the van's rear window, at one of the most powerfully evocative sights I have ever seen.

The guesthouse was next to the glowing domes of the majestic sixteenth-century Mir-i-Arab Madrassa, an Islamic college. Light streamed from tiny windows sparkling along its colossal wall like portholes in a ship and danced over striking blue tiles.

There are very few other places in the world where I have seen such exotic beauty in the architecture. I scrambled out of the van to gasp at the medieval vision. It was a numbingly beautiful sight.

To the side of the madrassa was the chubby base of the legendary Kalon minaret, an elegant mosque tower built in 1187 to call the faithful to prayer, and for centuries lit by fires to guide camel trains travelling through the night. Although Genghis Khan destroyed Bukhara in 1220, he gazed in awe at the Kalon minaret and ordered it spared, enabling later rulers to execute victims and criminals by throwing them off the top.

An ethereal golden glow from oil lamps and elegant lights played over the brickwork as my eyes widened and traced the minaret 160 feet into the dark sky, just as the haunting sound of an Islamic prayer rehearsal drifted from the madrassa towards our guesthouse. It was one of the most intense and emotional sounds I have ever heard. The whole experience was overwhelming. Tears rolled down my cheeks. Even as I remember it now a lump rises in my throat.

The following morning I climbed the steps with a young guide who explained the glorious blue tiles I had admired were thought to derive their unique colour from a mix of human blood.

"Blood?" I said. "Really?"

He nodded. "In the old days people who were sentenced to death were tied up in sacks and carried up the steps." He indicated the stone at our feet. "When they arrived here in the minaret, they were thrown out of this window to their deaths. Their bodies smashed on the tiles and their blood seeped from the sacks to mix with the clay and stone."

It was a good story. Perhaps even true. Then I read in a guidebook about a British adventurer in the nineteenth century who had the temerity to ride into the castle in Bukhara on horseback rather than walking, as was the custom. His story was a solid reminder about the need to understand and obey local customs. Generally, I have found foreigners very forgiving of visitors who commit even the most hideous faux pas. But in the case of the British adventurer no amount of apologising could get him out of trouble. He was thrown into a deep, hideous pit. And then beheaded.

We wandered around the buildings for a little longer, and then Shahida said she was itching to go and see a fortune teller in the city.

Shahida was a very modern Uzbek, but she said she liked the drama of sitting with a teller. "It's like a bit of therapy, Simon," she said. "Come along as well. You will love it."

Fortune telling is generally frowned upon in Islam but even in Bukhara, one of the holiest of cities, there were people practising the ancient art. With a grisly tale and the wonder of the Kalon still in my mind, Shahida took me to see a famous teller in the back room of a building in another part of the city. Wearing a traditional big billowy dress in gaudy yellow and green, and with a single very thick eyebrow, the teller had a mouthful of gold teeth and was quite the character. We warmed to her instantly. She winked at us both when the camera wasn't looking, and then started to put on a good show for the viewers.

With a flourish the teller started by announcing I was clearly a sincere and genuine man with an open heart, and she said that she could see that someone had proposed to Shahida recently, but she'd refused.

"Yeah, that's true," said Shahida.

"Wow," I said, genuinely taken aback. Not by the fortune teller's insight, but because Shahida hadn't mentioned this on our long journey.

The fortune teller rattled on. We leaned forward, desperate for insight. But then Shahida stopped translating.

"What's she saying?" I hissed to her.

"Erm, well, you cannot take their words literally, to be honest," she said mysteriously.

"What are you saying?" I said. "I thought that was the whole idea. What's the point in coming to a fortune teller if you can't take their words literally?"

But Shahida wouldn't budge. She talked about how the teller was just giving her life directions. She mentioned bad angels, good angels, and how only God really knows what would happen. I still don't know what the teller told her.

Instead of receiving a revelation in Bukhara, we all went for a dinner of *shashlik*, skewered and grilled cubes of meat. It was the end of our journey in Uzbekistan, a moment when Will and Dimitri could put their cameras down, and we could all have a moment for reflection.

People often ask me how much and how often we film on a trip. A great challenge on journeys is knowing what to film, but also when not to film, because in a strange and exotic part of the world, almost everything is fascinating. When everything is filmable it can be hard to find a guiding thread for the journey while shooting everything that moves and breathes. And it becomes utterly exhausting for the team if they are lugging a heavy 14-kilogram camera around for twelve or fourteen hours a day, constantly hunting focus and tensing their body to get a stable shot. Instead we have to pick our moments and know when to switch on, even while being ready for moments of spontaneity.

So there are clear moments of down time, usually when we are eating or sleeping. But even then we keep a camera handy, because we never know what will happen. That became a bit of a rule on my programmes after an early journey where I was having dinner with a team on a shoot and a huge car bomb went off near the restaurant. We dived under tables, but had left our cameras behind at our B&B. There's a saying in TV: if it's not on film, it didn't happen. So nothing about the car-bombing or the chaotic aftermath made it into the programme.

236

Sitting with Will, Dimitri and Shahida that night in Bukhara, eating platefuls of delicious *shashlik*, we talked about our time with Kadyr in Kyrgyzstan, and we smiled at the memory of Bayan, the baby-naming and the *kokpar* in Kazakhstan. None of us could stop thinking about Mr Amir, the doughty human rights lawyer. He made a huge impression. He didn't have a camera and he wasn't with an organisation like the BBC. He was alone, risking his own skin to speak truth to power, and to share the reality of Uzbekistan with us. I worried what might happen to Mr Amir. We all worried what might happen to him. But he knew what he was doing, and he wanted us to carry on.

We were now three quarters of the way through the journey, and the distance we had covered was immense. As we headed for the border with Tajikistan Dimitri produced a map and we considered how far we'd actually come. From the far north-west of Kazakhstan to the Aral Sea and the village of Aktobe then all the way across the steppes to Almaty and the Sharyn Canyon. We covered unbelievable distances following the Silk Road, before we had crossed into Kyrgyzstan and then eventually travelled on to Tashkent, Samarkand and Bukhara. Now we were racing towards our final border crossing into Tajikistan. Uzbekistan and Turkmenistan were the most repressive Stan countries, while Tajikistan was wild and lawless.

There was one other country in Central Asia with a leader who could rival the Uzbek ruler for despotic control. Turkmenistan, the fifth country in Central Asia, was at the time ruled by President Saparmurat A.

Niyazov, known as Turkmenbashi, perhaps the most dangerously eccentric leader in the world after the dictators of North Korea. Turkmenbashi stamped his name or face on everything from the local currency to the vodka. Cities, towns and streets were named after him. I had particularly wanted to see the gilded statue of Turkmenbashi with outstretched arms in the capital, Ashgabat, which revolves every twenty-four hours so the leader enjoys maximum sunshine. But the media were banned from Turkmenistan, the borders were closed to all visitors, and BBC requests to visit were rejected.

The country's isolation was a way of keeping out prying eyes. Anti-drugs officials in the region were adamant that senior Turkmen officials were actively involved in smuggling drugs, but the isolation of Turkmenistan meant it was hard for the international community to investigate the allegations.

I still had one more country to visit on the journey, but I could almost see the end ahead and for a moment I was filled with a sense of sadness. Everything about the journey had been magnificent. This corner of the world was absurd, crazy, sometimes dangerous, but always thrilling.

CHAPTER
FIFTEEN

Vodka Terrorism

I crossed into Tajikistan, Afghanistan's small, landlocked and mountainous northern neighbour, on a donkey cart. Usually at a border there is waiting, paperwork, more waiting, more paperwork and then finally you are allowed through to shake hands with the local fixer. At the border with Tajikistan, however, there was also a great chunk of no-man's-land to navigate.

"No filming," a surly guard told Dimitri in Russian. "And no vehicles can cross."

The tract of land stretched more than a mile across hills covered in wild grass and flowers. It looked stunning. But we had a mountain of gear and equipment. Initially we thought we were going to have to make multiple journeys lugging the kit along the only track. It would have taken the rest of the day.

Then we spotted a craggy old man with a donkey cart. His face lit up with glee at the sight of Western travellers and their mountain of equipment. All his remaining birthdays had come at once.

I now consider myself a rather experienced traveller, immune to the flattery and deception of merchants in souks, and attempts by swindlers and conmen to part me from my money or BBC petty cash. However, that elderly trickster with the donkey cart was a genius. He had clearly organised some sort of complicated deal with the ramshackle customs and immigration post because he had a complete monopoly on transport across the border. He counted our bags, looked us up and down, and then he completely fleeced us. A single journey with his cart would cost us the equivalent of nearly £40. We had no choice. We loaded our bags aboard as he tried to contain his smile, then he cackled to himself the entire way across no-man's-land.

But of course it was worth it. Who wants to fly into a bland international airport when you could chug across a border on a donkey cart?

"Welcome to Tajikistan!" said my new guide Noor, a jolly bear of a bloke, as we arrived on the other side.

The poorest country in Central Asia, Tajikistan's economy was still reeling after civil war in the 1990s. At least 80 per cent of the population were living in poverty and wages were as low as £3 a month. Even doctors and government officials earned a pittance. Noor drove us towards Dushanbe, the capital. Burned-out Soviet factories and dilapidated houses littered the landscape. Petrol was sold in old glass jars by the side of the road. "Life was never this bad under the Soviets," was a constant refrain.

Corruption was rife in Tajikistan and the country had terrible roads and infrastructure and very few hotels or even guesthouses. We had arranged to stay in the personal home of an official from the foreign ministry. He had helped to arrange our visas to visit and film in the country, and we thought he was doing us a favour. He said he often gave up his home to visiting dignitaries and we were looking forward to a restful and comfortable night after a long drive and eventful border crossing.

As we pulled up in front of the house the official was ushering his family out through the front door clutching bin bags of belongings. The children were crying.

"I'm not sure you are going to like this," said Noor. "Are you sure you want to stay here?"

"Yes, yes," I said breezily. "It's good for us to see inside a house and get a sense of how people actually live."

The official stuck around just long enough to give us the keys and tell us that he would be back later to take our payment, then he scarpered. There was exceptionally limited internet access in Tajikistan, and no TripAdvisor, so we hadn't seen the house before we arrived. From the outside it looked pleasant enough. It was on a quiet residential street near the centre of the city, which in parts still showed the scars of conflict and poverty. Housing was still intact, but ramshackle. Trees were growing into people's homes. Patches of ground were completely overgrown, as if nature was taking back what the people no longer had the time or money to maintain.

Inside the house, things were a little unpleasant. I had a windowless room with walls encrusted in a stinking, unidentifiable black mould. I looked closely and thought I could actually see it growing. But it was just for a couple of nights, I reminded myself. Then I tried the mattress. It was smelly, and it was sodden. I had already slept on plenty of damp mattresses in dodgy hotels and had been reminded by my packing list before this journey that I should carry a black bin bag, slit at the sides, that I used to cover the worst offenders. But no plastic sheet could have dealt with this mattress. It literally squelched as I pressed it. A small pool of liquid appeared. I had a sniff but couldn't be sure what it was. An indeterminate fluid, I said to myself, possibly bodily in origin? Hard to say. Still, never mind, I could sleep on the floor.

It might sound perverse, but I feel strangely honoured to have bedded down in dozens of guesthouses and hotels untroubled by even medieval hygiene standards. No traveller should return without at least a few tales of squalor and filth. It is part of an adventure.

I went out of the room to the shared sink, turned on the tap and was idly waiting for the water to run from dark brown to clear while I watched two enormous cockroaches either mating or fighting. Then I stepped backwards and trod on the side of an enormous rat-trap the size of a brick, baited with a piece of rancid cheese. *Sod this*, I suddenly thought.

At that moment both Will and Dimitri emerged from their rooms, which were even worse than mine. Will had been trying to clean a creamy mould off his pillow. We looked at each other. Then we all spoke at once.

"This is a bit too crap, isn't it?" said Dimitri.

"Is there definitely nowhere else?" I said.

"Let's get out of here," said Will. "Anything would be better."

Most of our kit was still in Noor's van locked in an old garage. We gathered our personal bags and cameras, checked outside to see if the ministry official was lurking, and then we legged it down the road. We trotted along a few streets to the centre of town, found an old hotel and Dimitri tried to book us some rooms. The lady at reception was apologetic.

"We only have a few rooms, and they're fully booked," she told us through Dimitri. "I'm so sorry."

"Is there nowhere else?"

"I don't think so. We don't have many hotels in Dushanbe. Maybe you could stay in someone's home?"

"Erm, no thanks, we've already tried that."

We were just about to give up and head back to the mould house, when the woman happened to say, almost as a parting apology: "I'm just sorry I can't lower the price for the rooms on the top floor?"

"Sorry?"

It turned out there was a whole suite of rooms that had just been redecorated and refitted, perhaps for visiting warlords and drug barons.

"But you wouldn't want those," she said, smiling but certain, "they are incredibly expensive. We are going to charge . . ." and with that she leaned forward to shock us, "fifty dollars per night for them."

It took us a while to persuade the woman that given the circumstances we could afford them, despite tight BBC budgets. Settling into my luxury suite that night was a delight. The ceiling was painted in stripes a shade of fluorescent yellow, the walls had what looked like carpet for wallpaper, and there was a scattering of pictures in the bathroom that were moving animation waterfall scenes. It was the gaudiest, tackiest place I have ever stayed, and the competition for that title is fierce. But the bed was dry. And the room even came with a free apple and a bottle of vodka.

The next morning the beezneez elite were much in evidence on the streets of Dushanbe. Former warlords, corrupt politicians and mafia bosses were driving around in expensive Western cars. An 800-mile border with Afghanistan, the source of 90 per cent of European heroin, had made Tajikistan a major drug transit route.

The police were woefully underfunded. The main drugs agency in Dushanbe was so strapped for cash they had just one van and the head of the drug squad doubled up as the driver. We had been allowed to ride along with the drug squad as they raided an apartment and captured an unlikely dealer: a forty-five-year-old mother of six trying to sell an undercover officer a kilo and a half of heroin, worth tens of thousands of pounds after it was smuggled down a long chain through Russia to Europe. It was an almost unimaginable sum in Tajikistan. In the West a seizure like that would result in congratulations all round. In Dushanbe the police just shrugged. It was a daily occurrence, they said. Then the head of the drug squad took me back to the police station and showed me his exhibits locker, a single room with half a ton of heroin worth more than £100 million, or more than half the national budget of Tajikistan. I questioned whether they were tempted to sell it. The chief of the drug squad was indignant.

"We may be poor, but we're not criminals," he said proudly.

Tourism was virtually non-existent in Tajikistan. The only foreigners I saw were aid workers or businessmen investing in high-risk ventures. But the country was getting back on its feet, and streets that resounded with gunfire just a few years before were now hosting outdoor cafes and promenading couples. Tajikistan had a long way to go, but personally I loved the place. The Tajiks were friendly, generous, hospitable and devoid of obvious envy, even when a couple of them debating our salaries asked us, wide-eyed, whether we earned more than $10,000 for each camera shot. Anything more than $100 was considered a fortune.

Of course, for visitors seeking an entirely different cultural experience, the isolation of Central Asia should be part of the appeal. Almaty and Tashkent, the capital of Uzbekistan, had a few Western shops, but the rest of the region had been forgotten by Western businesses. Yet we ignore Central Asia at our peril. Economic growth and jobs would be a useful bulwark against political discontent and emerging militant groups.

Geographically the Stans are closer to India and the East, to which they look for cultural leadership at least as much as they look to Mother Russia or the West. At a celebration of the end of the civil war in Dushanbe, I saw teenagers queuing to take photographs with ancient cameras next to cardboard cut-outs of Bollywood stars, not Hollywood icons.

We sat in a café in a square in Dushanbe waiting for food to arrive when I spotted an elderly woman begging from table to table. She was the spitting image of my beloved grandma, who had died just over a year before. I felt the colour drain from my face. The resemblance was uncanny. Noor saw my gaze.

"She isn't a Tajik," he said, thinking he was reading my mind. "She's an ethnic Russian. A lot of them got stuck here after the collapse of the Soviet Union. They still have their homes but they effectively lost their Russian citizenship, and their pensions became worthless due to hyper-inflation."

It was a complete collapse for a society that had previously made a virtue of caring for the weakest. The woman was shuffling around, but she looked at me as she approached our table. I felt uncomfortable, terrible, like a voyeur. But it was as if I was watching the ghost of my grandma.

"There is nothing you can do, Simon," said Noor sadly. "There are so many like her, impoverished to the point where they are reduced to begging in the streets."

I didn't know what to do. When she got to our table I emptied my pockets and tried to give her my money respectfully. It seemed inadequate. One of the hardest aspects of my journeys is that I turn up in a struggling part of the world and find awful suffering among people who have nothing. They are almost always delighted to share their life with us but there is very little we can do for them as individuals. The BBC isn't a charity. We are not allowed to spend licence-fee payers' money on worthy causes abroad. Yes, of course we dip into our own pockets, and our money goes a lot further abroad when given directly to somebody in need. But it is always a sticking plaster.

We left Dushanbe and drove south, guided by Noor and with a Mr Bean fan behind the wheel who told us in broken English his name was Jackie Chan. We met a twenty-two-year-old ex-Etonian called Wills who runs his Canadian father's gold mine, one of the tiny number of Westerners trying to make money in what was effectively a laid-back Wild West. Then, on a dusty, potholed highway which served as a main road across the country, we spotted one of the beezneez elite driving with bodyguards in a brand-new, top-of-the-range white Jaguar. He was a former teacher who had become the president of one of the sports federations in the country, and was a commander in the Ministry of the Interior. I met him later and he said he was hoping Jaguar would put a compartment in the car door which could hold a Kalashnikov. In Tajikistan this is all completely normal.

Noor and Jackie Chan took us up into the Pamir mountains, which dominate the country. More than half of Tajikistan is over 3,000 metres (9,842 feet) above sea level and the Pamirs were completely breathtaking, hundreds of peaks like an army of spears stretched into the distance until the planet seemed to curve. We climbed steep tracks and filmed young herders leading donkeys, goats and sheep to high pasture, travelling deep into an area where people told us they had never seen foreigners before. To the north the Pamirs joined the Tian Shan mountains along the Alay Valley of Kyrgyzstan. To the south they bordered the Hindu Kush mountains along Afghanistan's Wakhan Corridor, which in turn connected to the Himalayas. It felt like we were off the map, and on the roof of the world.

As if drugs and militants were not enough for the Central Asian states to worry about, there are also legitimate concerns about a potential environmental catastrophe. In 1911 an earthquake created a colossal dam 10,000 feet up in the remote Pamir mountains of Tajikistan, behind which now sits Lake Sarez, 50 miles long, a mile wide, and more than 1,000 feet deep. United Nations experts have said they believe an earthquake of around 7.5 on the Richter scale could dislodge the dam, and engineers from the US Marine Corps have predicted the resulting flood could be the greatest in human history. It would pass through several countries and threaten the lives and livelihoods of roughly 5 million people. Perhaps it will take a tragedy of this magnitude before the rest of the world discovers this forgotten region of the globe.

The Pamirs are stunning, but their inaccessibility makes it exceptionally hard to drain the lake to prevent a disaster. Even just patrolling the mountains is nigh impossible. Bandits and smugglers have operated in the Pamirs for centuries. Noor looked at the peaks and stroked his thick moustache thoughtfully.

"You know this terrain is just like the mountains in Afghanistan," he said. Noor had fought in the Soviet

Red Army in Afghanistan against the Western-backed Mujaheddin and men like Osama bin Laden.

"You could go over there with a small team," he said, gesturing across the narrow, rocky valley as we chucked snowballs at each other, "and nobody could see you. You could just watch, wait, and then start shooting."

The Tajiks worry about drugs and militants coming from Afghanistan, so we headed south towards the border, through the spectacular landscape, to see how well it was guarded.

The border region was the real badlands. Militants, drug smugglers and the Taliban were active in the area. So first we had to stop at an army base to meet a Tajik secret police colonel who would guide us, and an armed detachment of border guards. However, there was a problem. The van that was supposed to carry our armed escort was the only one they had along a long stretch of the border, but it was ancient, and lacked a wheel and crucial parts. Young conscripts and a weary mechanic scurried around to fix it, to the embarrassment of all.

The soldiers eventually got their solitary van started and we headed towards the border, finally arriving at a tiny base with barracks that looked more like huts. The few dozen guards were a ragged group of conscript Tajiks. They made a sorry sight, living in appalling conditions, surviving on bits of bread, old potatoes and soup, and wearing ancient, threadbare Soviet uniforms. The soldiers, average age nineteen, were being paid roughly £3 a month to protect one of the most dangerous borders in the world, across which smugglers were passing kilos of heroin destined for the West. The lure of corruption was obvious.

The Colonel from the Tajik secret police strutted closer to the edge of the decrepit army base on the Afghan border and gestured for me to follow. As we shielded our eyes from the sweltering sun, he jabbed a stubby finger across the river dividing Tajikistan from northern Afghanistan, picking out fields of opium poppies and a Taliban training centre clearly visible just a few hundred metres away. It was just two years after 9/11, and across the border the so-called war on terror was raging.

"It is not us who creates these problems," he said angrily. "But we are the ones forced to deal with the drug smugglers and terrorists. Why doesn't the West do more to help us defeat them?"

It was a question I was asked several times during my journey through the Stans, and one I found hard to answer. Although we spend billions hunting for heroin in the West, when I was there Tajikistan had been given just $9 million by the international community to stem the flow of drugs from Afghanistan. Even with those limited resources the Tajiks had seized heroin worth an astonishing $1.4 billion.

Around 90 per cent of heroin in Europe comes from Afghanistan, and much of that is smuggled through the north of the country via Tajikistan and Turkmenistan to Russia and the West. Because we know little about the Stans, we care little about their problems. Yet even just because of the heroin trade, and the misery and crime it causes, Central Asia is critically important to Europe.

For a start, why not provide more support to the Tajiks to detect and capture heroin closer to its source?

Despite empty cupboards, the border guards arranged a minor feast for us with a tin of pilchards. We had been told to leave the border region before dark and quietly because of militants and armed Taliban sympathisers. But as the sun set and we sat around talking a prized bottle emerged. I call this vodka terrorism. It had become a common type of attack in Central Asia, involving an extreme and overwhelming display of alcoholic hospitality to a weary traveller.

Attacks could occur at any time of day, from any direction. Just as Brits would offer a cup of tea, so people in the former Soviet Union would reach into a pocket or a cupboard and produce a bottle of lethal rocket fuel. One time a BBC team and I went to film at a primary school. The school head produced vodka and insisted we drink. It was 8.30 in the morning, and the rest of the day is a complete blur. I don't mind a drink, but I am a complete lightweight, and when a bottle was opened it had to be emptied. And their vodka was strong enough to French-polish my insides.

Lacking the alcohol tolerance of a Siberian miner, I had devised numerous strategies that I now employed with the Tajik Colonel. I used subterfuge. As bowls (bowls!) were being refilled for the umpteenth time, I put mine under the table and tipped it out over a rug. The next round I emptied into a tissue. Another went into my neighbour's glass. He looked like he could handle it. The next two toasts were given standing, so I had to swallow. I was completely hammered, slurring into the camera.

If pre-warned perhaps I could have used the tactic of a former KGB officer I once knew. He claimed he would swallow handfuls of lard before boozy meetings with crucial contacts, because the fat would line his stomach, prevent absorption of alcohol, and keep him sharp and focused. This is still not to be recommended. Without lard, over time I became more professional about my refusal to drink. Generally, I just lie. Claiming my religion or ancestors forbid drinking, or over-eating — another possible method for a hospitality attack — has been remarkably successful. People usually nod sagely and indicate they understand. When attackers in the former Soviet Union now tell me that in their culture an opened bottle cannot be left until fully drunk, I nod and tell them with a straight face that in my culture the bottle must be left half-full so I can take it to greet new friends. I say it with conviction and pride, and it really does work.

However, back then on the Tajik border I was a relative amateur. I had run out of places to tip the bowls of vodka. Then I had a brilliant wheeze. I started tipping it into my boots.

It was after midnight and pitch-black when we finally left the base. The Tajik Colonel had told us that even in daytime we needed to be discreet while travelling in the area and as quiet as possible. But he was the one who produced the vodka. Taliban positions were just to the south. I was competely drunk and we drove back along the border with the lights on in our van, all the

windows open, with Noor and I singing football songs.
Goodness knows what the Talibs thought.

I didn't want to go home. I wanted to carry on to the
east of Tajikistan, to Turkmenistan, to a thousand more
sights and places in Central Asia. I was completely
addicted to the journey, and I loved working and
travelling with the team. They had put up with difficult
locations, often appalling accommodation, truculent
officials and long days with humour and forbearance.
Will, Dimitri, Shahida and all our guides and fixers
were exceptional, and the finest travel companions
imaginable. We had shared an experience, a quest, and
a sense of common purpose. It had been a completely
epic adventure. Was this what making TV was like? I
was a convert.

For me, it was a time of transformation. I had
already travelled the world for fun, love and work. But I
had rarely strayed from the beaten track. My trips had
been holidays. There were laughs, and they gifted me
memories. But they didn't change me. Yet on that first
television adventure, to forgotten corners of Central
Asia, were sights and experiences that made my head
swim and sing.

Until that trip I was relatively happy with the often
lonely life of an author. I had written more than half a
dozen books. But then TV came knocking at my door.
From the start the idea was to blend travel with issues.
To go on an adventure, a real adventure, but also to
learn about the places I was visiting. From the first day
of the first trip, I realised travelling with your eyes open,

and looking for the dark, as well as the light, is a guaranteed way of having an experience that lingers in your soul.

Before I started *Meet the Stans* I told the BBC it would be a one-off. I had a series of books I wanted to write. My author slippers were calling. We flew home after finishing filming on the Tajik border and I was on a high for weeks. My mind was full of the experiences, the images, the smells, the food and the incredible characters I'd met. I was desperate for more. I wrote to the BBC, said I'd loved the experience, and asked if I could change my mind about never doing it again. I suggested a few more ideas. Every trip since then has been extraordinary, every moment a privilege. Travel has gifted me some of the greatest memories of my life.

CHAPTER
SIXTEEN

Hostile Environments

Meet the Stans was an awakening for me. Of all the experiences I'd had in my life, it was among the most profound and intensely memorable. An adventure somewhere remote and uneasy where the joy of discovery had been mixed with real issues — it was an experience and a challenge, and I had to explain those countries both to myself and the viewers.

Back in London after finishing filming I felt more alive than ever before. I was happier, more confident. My friends could see that something had changed. So could my family. Will and Ryshard started putting the shows together and I saw different cuts or versions and sent them endless editing notes and unhelpful comments. Eventually we all agreed on the content of the programmes and I started writing scripts for the commentary that were far too long, far too complicated, and would have involved talking over people on screen. Karen, the boss, gave me a brilliant piece of advice: "Just write to the pictures," she said. Simple. Obvious. But very helpful.

I don't write the best scripts, by a long stretch, but I try to fill them with information. Directors and editors have pulled their hair out with me in the years since as I cram another fact or statistic and another line of commentary into documentaries that are already packed. "Can't we keep a bit of space there?" they plead. "Can't we let the pictures breathe?" We discuss, debate and argue. There are small battles, but no wars. Sometimes I lose, sometimes they lose. Eventually a script and a programme emerges, usually with final changes made on the spot while I am recording the voiceover. It certainly keeps all of us on our toes.

Meet the Stans aired in 2003 on BBC Four and then on BBC Two in a late-night slot and the response was fantastic. Viewers said lovely things about the shows, the BBC were delighted with them, and even the newspapers were generous with praise. The *Guardian* said the shows were "a thrilling postcard from the edge", the *Observer* said it was "a spectacular journey". More importantly, Roly Keating, who was the head of BBC Two, said the programmes were electrifying. "Everyone seems pleased!" said Will in an email. "They might even let us make some more!"

After *Meet the Stans* the BBC and others put me back on the TV presenting a series of programmes. I investigated the Kennedy, Disney and Bacardi clans, the causes of the Iraq War, and the death of Roberto Calvi, dubbed "God's Banker" because of his close links to the Vatican, who was found hanging under Blackfriars Bridge in London. I even went on a long and eye-opening journey around Saudi Arabia for a TV programme, travelling from the cities of Riyadh and

Jeddah down to the troubled border with Yemen and on into the isolation of the Empty Quarter desert.

It was a strange and often bizarre country to visit. I met scores of Saudis, from the most senior princes to desert Bedouin, from Osama bin Laden's former best friend and extremist supporters of al Qaeda to a brave human rights worker and trendy young women. On the streets the fiery bearded Mutawa'een, religious police from the Committee for the Propagation of Virtue and the Prevention of Vice, were enforcing their vision of morality. But an army of youngsters was desperate for change and freedom. Driving along a busy public highway on the outskirts of Riyadh one morning I found hundreds of teenagers and young men crowded by the pavement on the other side of the road watching a high-speed skidding competition.

My Saudi driver had to swerve to prevent one car, driven by a boy aged about fourteen, from crashing into our van. He turned to me, apologetic and slightly embarrassed. "Boys," he said, with a casual shrug of explanation. "They need to let off steam."

There were still few outlets for youthful rebellion in the Kingdom of Saudi Arabia. I was amazed to see youngsters, many weaned on foreign TV shows, scribbling their name and mobile numbers on pieces of paper and then throwing them at someone they fancied when the religious police weren't looking.

We travelled into the remote interior of the Empty Quarter desert and stayed in a Bedouin desert camp. The heat was astonishing. At one point it registered more than 50 degrees Centigrade (more than 120 Fahrenheit), but it was an exceptionally dry heat, and somehow tolerable if you drank litres of water during the day. In the evening a flustered female member of our team came back in a hurry from a chat with local women in their tent and started rooting through her belongings for a pricey gift. Turned out she had idly told one of the Bedouin women her solitary solid-gold ring was beautiful, and the woman had immediately slipped it off and gifted it to her. I suspect the return gift of an iPod didn't quite cut it in her nomadic community.

I was in the Empty Quarter for just a few days with no phone reception. But meanwhile my brother James was in an inaccessible area of Afghanistan, also out of range and out of contact. Our poor mum was obviously worried sick. James was working on a personal project he had devised, photographing activities that were previously banned by the Taliban, including weather forecasting, bird keeping, kite flying and the education and employment of women. When he had first told me he wanted to go to Afghanistan I tried to dissuade him. Initially he wasn't entirely sure what he was going to do there. I thought it would cost him a fortune and he would never get out of a secure compound. Fortunately he didn't listen to a word I said. He took photographs that were breathtakingly beautiful, captured the sense of a changing country, and was recognised by or won multiple awards, including the Observer Hodge Award, the National Portrait Gallery Portrait Prize, and separately, the Professional Travel Photographer of the Year award.

While he was in Afghanistan working on the project and finding a mobile phone signal, I was re-establishing contact with home from Saudi, where I was on a journey that took me to the heart of power. I became one of the few Westerners ever to attend a *Majlis*, an audience with royalty, held under huge crystal chandeliers in a luxurious hall the size of a small football pitch, where Crown Prince Abdullah, the leader of Saudi Arabia in place of his ailing brother King Fahd, would hear the polite complaints and appeals of his male subjects. Unfortunately for me, the Crown Prince was late, I had been drinking several pints of ultra-strong Saudi coffee, and by the time he appeared I was shaking with the effects of caffeine. As I moved through a crowd of tribal leaders to speak to the Crown Prince, I felt like I was drugged. I could see a couple of his guards watching me with alarm, their fingers moving for their triggers.

"Crown Prince, Crown Prince," I said, pushing past a bodyguard with an assault rifle. "Simon Reeve from the BBC, please could we have a word?"

He turned and looked at me patiently. "I'm so sorry," he said. "I have the King of Jordan in the other room, and I cannot keep him waiting."

As excuses go, it was strong.

Still, my journey gave me a vivid insight into the kingdom. I finished my travels down near the border with Yemen. One night in the Empty Quarter desert, in an ancient corner of the world and under stars so bright I could read by their light, my otherwise silent bodyguard suddenly started tapping away on a hand-drum and sang a haunting song to the moon. It was completely spellbinding.

These programmes were all interesting to film, but I was itching for more travelogues like *Meet the Stans* that blended the light and the shade. Safely back in London, I put together proposals and plotted more adventures.

Then one summer night I went with my friends Ben and Antoine to a publishing party held to celebrate the launch of *The Coma*, a book by Alex Garland, author of *The Beach*. I was out most nights at the time when I was in London, socialising, going to parties and generally living the life of a single lad. I drove friends like Mike, Maurice and Dimitri mad with some infuriating rules which meant that if I walked into a bar or a party and there was no one I or they thought was interesting I would often turn around and try to persuade everyone to go somewhere else. Arriving at the packed publishing party, Ben turned to me and said: "At least let's have a drink."

I was just inside the door when I saw her. Towards the back of the party, at least 15 metres away, was a tall, elegant, laughing woman with tumbling blonde hair who stood out in the crowd so instantly it was as if she was lit by a spotlight. She was talking to a couple of men in a way that suggested they were both trying to flirt with her. She looked bright, open, interesting, and she was gorgeous.

Another of my dating rules was no "cold-calling" at a party. I wouldn't just wander over to someone and start chatting them up without at least a tiny indication of interest. It was partly tactical, partly about not hassling lone women, and largely about ego. If there was a second glance then all risks were dramatically reduced. I haven't even mentioned my rules about no Scandinavians, no only children, and no cats.

I moved through the crowd to get a drink, casually keeping my eyes on her, and then as I went to pass in front of her I willed her to look in my direction. It worked. Anya glanced up, our eyes locked, and I smiled. Everything slowed. She held my glance for a wonderful second longer than was merely polite, something fizzed, and I Knew.

Life is always built on tiny moments of chance and circumstance. If her back had been turned, if . . . I got a drink and stood with the lads. "So you're staying then?" said Ben and nudged me in the ribs.

I can't say it was love at first sight. I wasn't a teenager. I thought she was stunning, but looks aren't everything. The Japanese have a word for the feeling that suddenly erupts when you meet someone and know you are destined to fall in love. That was close to what I felt in that moment. I felt excited and confident, but bided my time. Anya was engrossed in conversation with her friend Leanne.

A couple of drinks later and Ben and Antoine were getting impatient.

"Go on," urged Ben. "She won't stay here all night. Go and talk to her." Then he gave me a gentle shove in the right direction.

One of our first dates was lunch in the restaurant inside the British Museum. Anya had been living in Denmark for the past few years. She was half-Danish, spoke fluent Danish, had a degree, worked as a model and had been a camerawoman on wildlife documentaries. She was opinionated, thoughtful and funny, telling tales about a horrific shoot she abandoned when a producer started gluing stick insects to a branch in a garage in Croydon. When we met she was working for her friend, a chess grandmaster from Bolton who used to captain the British chess team, developing links between universities and industry. As we left the restaurant I walked us out past the Rosetta Stone, an ancient slab of rock inscribed with three versions of the same boring decree — one in Egyptian hieroglyphics, another in Egyptian script, and the third in Ancient Greek. It was found by Napoleon's forces, I told her casually, trying to impress her, and used in the nineteenth century to finally decipher Egyptian hieroglyphics and much about the Ancient Egyptian world.

Anya was listening to me thoughtfully.

"Yeeees," she said slowly, straining her eyes to see the top of the rock. "It says . . ."

And then she began reading the Ancient Greek on the stone aloud. I was completely bowled over. Some tourists standing next to her turned and gaped.

"How . . .?" I stuttered.

"Oh, erm, I'm fluent in Greek," Anya said, all very matter-of-factly. "And I can read it. I lived there for a while."

"But . . .?" I stuttered again.

"It's Ancient Greek, but still Greek," she shrugged. "Amazing, isn't it, that the language still has enough similarities after more than two thousand years?"

"Anything else you haven't told me?" I said.

"Well, I speak a bit of Arabic," she said brightly.

And then she realised people around us were staring. She blushed just a little and started to move away. Well, reader, I have to say, I was completely smitten.

One night a couple of weeks later I was in a pub with a few friends having a drink after a game of football under the Westway in West London, just near Grenfell Tower. One of them worked as a shipping agent. He was telling a story about sending some equipment via a place called Somaliland. I cut in.

"Sorry, where? Somaliland?" I said. "Where on earth is Somaliland?"

"It's in the horn of Africa. It's not a recognised country, but I'm trying to send a container there."

An unrecognised country, I'd never heard of such a thing. How could a place like that exist? Something sparked inside me. I grabbed a pen, scribbled the word "Somaliland" on a scrap of paper and stuffed it into my pocket. Then I had a couple more drinks. Of course, I forgot it was there. I wandered home, woke up in the morning, discovered the note and wondered what on earth it was. Then I remembered the conversation, sat down at my computer and discovered it wasn't the only unrecognised state. There were scores of them. All places that technically did not exist.

Although there are almost 200 official countries in the world there are also dozens more unrecognised states like Somaliland which are determined to be separate and independent. These countries are home to millions of people, they have their own rulers, armies, police forces, and issue passports and even postage stamps, but they are not officially recognised as proper countries by the rest of the world. So they can't send a team to the World Cup, have a seat at the United Nations, or even send a singer to Eurovision.

I was fascinated. The more I looked online the more I found. There was a whole stack of unrecognised states with defined borders, governments and infrastructure that weren't officially recognised as nations. When I put them all together I realised there were more than 250 million people who lived in unrecognised countries or considered themselves unrepresented people. Within half an hour I knew this could be a new series. It was an entirely new subject area that nobody knew much about.

Soon I was engrossed in research, and Anya was a massive help.

Together we read up about unrecognised countries and unrepresented people. Both of us thought they were completely fascinating. Each place that we found sounded exotic and unknown: Abkhazia, Assyria, Batwa, Crimean Tatars, East Turkestan, Hmong, Iranian Kurdistan, Khmer-Krom and Ogaden. How can anyone even read the names without booking a flight to learn more? What about Oromo, South Moluccas, Talysh, West Balochistan, West Papua or Western Togoland? Then we discovered a group called the Unrepresented Nations and Peoples Organization (UNPO), which formed some sort of umbrella group for countries that couldn't get into the United Nations. While the UN had a grand headquarters next to the

East River in Manhattan, the UNPO had an office in The Hague. But they had an annual conference coming up in a few weeks. Anya and I looked at each other. We had to go.

I booked tickets, Anya packed her camera gear and we found somewhere to stay. My friend Jo lived in The Hague and said we could use her flat. We arrived to find His & Hers toothbrushes in the bathroom ready for us and rose petals scattered across our bed.

As a quirky destination for a romantic break, the conference in The Hague was simply brilliant. I had never been to a more obscure gathering. Representatives of the most exotic and often persecuted people in the world marched through The Hague and then took their places at a huge circular table that looked like something out of Camelot. Anya and I had a long chat with people from British Cameroon and Nagaland. Then the Crimean Tatars played the Hmong at football.

Talking to the different country reps it was clear to me this was a huge, forgotten story. Almost all of the unrecognised countries were at the centre of past or present conflicts, or were likely to be caught up in an armed struggle in the future if nothing was done to resolve their status. These were people fighting for independence and identity with a voice no one was hearing, even though every tale was strong and emotional, every speaker erudite and committed. There was little interest from the mainstream media. There was no TV coverage of the conference. Anya filmed it for our research and there were a couple of students doing something similar, but that was it. The UNPO was largely unknown. It was a hidden story about our planet.

Back in London we collated all the information we had and put together a list of the unrecognised places around the world that best represented the issues we had heard. Our plan was for me to go on a series of journeys to some of the most obscure places and shine a light on their stories. We turned it into a TV proposal and sent it off to the BBC. Before we knew it, I was back at TV Centre. My second series of travelogues had been commissioned. It was to be called *Places That Don't Exist*, and against stiff competition it remains one of my absolute favourite and most memorable adventures.

There is a certain excitement to arriving somewhere without a clue where to stay or what to do. If you travel spontaneously you often put more thought and consideration into the journey on arrival because you are not following some predetermined tourist trail. You know memories will not be served on a plate, and you have to find them yourself. Spontaneity also means you can wander around a city or a resort area and decide where you want to stay based on reality rather than an enhanced photo on the internet.

Early in our relationship Anya and I booked tickets at the airport and headed to Sharm el-Sheikh, the Egyptian resort town on the Red Sea, for a last-minute break. We walked along the promenade and lazed on the beach for a couple of days, then got bored and took off into the desert. We bought meat from Bedouin, slept out under the stars and then took a daft turn in our little hire car on a complete whim and sank into deep sand in the middle of the desert. It was my fault. I hopped out of the car, looked around for a few moments and realised we were miles from help, then heard a worrying sound coming from the other side of the car. Anya was already down on her knees digging out the wheels and letting the tyres down so we could escape.

"Come on," she said. "Let's get on with it."

Even today our strongest memories of that holiday are the hours we spent digging out the car together. That bonding experience became part of the glue for our relationship. If you want to have a spontaneous adventure, it's always worth remembering that some of the most memorable times can happen when things go a bit wrong. But I still try to follow simple rules: I don't arrive anywhere late in the evening because I want some time to have a look around before finding a bed. I travel light, put cash in my sock, don't get too hung up on review sites, and I try to avoid following the crowd, so I can have my own experiences. Plus I say yes to almost everything.

You can start locally. Upturn a glass on a map and centre it on your home. Then draw a ring around the rim and explore that circle so you know it like the back of your hand. All travel gifts memories, and spontaneity has a place. On my TV programmes we don't write a script in advance and we don't usually have a recce. I don't take a list of questions with me and I am not fed things to say through an earpiece. Spontaneity is encouraged. Much of the time when we are filming we have to make it up as we go along, which can be exciting but also nerve-wracking. If we are set to film a monument in the centre of a city and then spot a demo nearby we will always make the more exciting choice. Hopefully the programmes feel more real as a result.

However, we still need to plan a TV adventure before we go to ensure we reap the full benefits of a trip. We spend at least a few months preparing where we might be able to go and what we might be able to see and do for each shoot or series. Arriving somewhere without a clue about what we are going to do would be profligate. Careful planning and preparation guarantees powerful experiences.

Every journey is different and every production team works differently, but generally an assistant producer or researcher will start drawing up a list of possible stories and adventures two or three months before a shoot actually starts. They use the internet, guide books, newspaper articles and long, long conversations with guides and experts in the countries we are heading towards. Meanwhile we will have meetings, drink tea, look at maps and debate the merits of locations, routes, stories and people we could meet. There are no hard rules for what makes it onto the final list of what we film, but we aim for extremes, whether extremely beautiful, thrilling, shocking or inspiring. I also try to use a technique that has worked well for me in relationships: if someone believes really strongly that we should do something, whether it's the assistant producer or the executive in charge, we generally do it. Enthusiasm trumps apathy. In my relationship at home we sometimes rank things out of ten. Don't laugh. One of us might idly suggest going to see something, and the other isn't entirely keen. The proposer admits they only want to do it "level five", which means they really aren't that bothered, whereas the opposer says they really, really don't want to do it, "level eight". It generally works. You have to be honest and you can't keep dropping level nines or tens, because you just sound mad. Give it a try. Even my long-suffering television colleagues have occasionally played along.

While discussing and debating the ideas for TV shows, the potential shooting team are contacted to check availability, then visas are organised, equipment hired, arms are jabbed with vaccinations, and risk assessments are completed. Eventually we get on a plane.

At the start of *Places That Don't Exist* my first destination was the largely unknown breakaway state of Somaliland, the inspiration for the entire project. A series of trips would also take me to Transnistria (between Moldova and Ukraine), Taiwan, Nagorno-Karabakh, also known as Artsakh, a landlocked region in the South Caucasus, and three regions of Georgia which broke away after the collapse of the Soviet Union. It was a chance to visit some of the most obscure and forgotten parts of the world.

All of the unrecognised nations on my list declared independence after bloody conflicts with a neighbouring state, which I also wanted to visit. In the case of

Somaliland, that's Somalia, one of the poorest countries in the world and at the time perhaps the most dangerous.

I went in with a small team. Just Shahida, my colleague and guide in Uzbekistan, and a producer-director called Iain Overton, a Cambridge graduate who had just been in Iraq filming a frontline fly-on-the-wall documentary about the Argyll and Sutherland Highlanders in Basra. He was ideal for the job, but we didn't actually meet until we were at Heathrow.

Shahida had become a feisty friend, brilliant travelling companion, and assistant producer. She was perfect because she was brave, had a no-nonsense approach to officialdom, and was prepared to take the calculated risks required to go somewhere tricky so we could share the experience with the viewers. There are very few jobs I can think of where you meet one of the people you'll be travelling with into a volcano just as you step off the rim. But that's how it felt on that shoot. I knew Shahida well, but Iain and I hadn't been bloodied together.

That probably sounds dramatic, but flying into somewhere dangerous you need to know what your team can cope with, how they will react in tricky situations, and whether you can trust them to have your back should things go badly wrong. You need to know whether they will carry you, and whether they will literally give you their blood.

We were heading to Somaliland but first we needed to visit neighbouring Somalia and its capital,

Mogadishu. According to reports, it was in a state of near chaos with gun-toting young men on the streets. For years there had been conflict and civil war and the country was in a state of collapse. Kidnap and murder were serious risks. Warlords were feuding over disputed territory. We would need to hire a team of local mercenaries to protect us. As one of the most volatile places in the world the BBC classed it as a "category one hostile environment", and a place of "exceptionally high risk where battlefield conditions prevail". Going there would be the most dangerous journey I had undertaken.

The difference between this adventure and *Meet the Stans* was that this had been my idea from the start, whereas my previous travelogue had been the product of discussion and debate. It wasn't to be a single long journey, it was a series of smaller trips, but still through often tough terrain. We would be off the map, quite literally, and first we had to get through Somalia.

A scheduled flight, with drinks, food and cabin staff, took us as far as Kenya. Then we hopped north before climbing aboard a dodgy propeller cargo aircraft flown by a couple of Ukrainians for the journey across the border into Mogadishu. We were the only passengers on the final flight and just before we started moving I looked forwards to the flight deck. The door was open and I could see the pilot and co-pilot toasting each other with glasses of vodka. In the context of where we were going, this felt completely normal.

Iain and I finally had a chance to chat through our plans on the flight, then we checked the ceramic plates in our flak jackets, adjusted the straps on our ballistic helmets, and Iain cooked up a bean curry on a bench. There was no cabin service.

CHAPTER
SEVENTEEN

Mr Big Beard

The wings of the plane slapped from side to side as we made our final approach, then we smacked into the ground and bounced along a dust-blown airstrip just outside Mogadishu.

From the moment we landed we were thrust into the chaos. Another plane nearby was unloading bundles of *khat*, the local stimulant drug of choice in Somalia. Our local fixer Ajoos, a friendly, smiley man I instantly warmed to, met us at the bottom of the plane steps. Suddenly there was gunfire a few hundred metres away. We ducked, but Ajoos glanced around and told us not to worry.

"They are not shooting at us," he said reassuringly.

We had contacted Ajoos through a guesthouse in Mogadishu that was able to provide us with more than a dozen heavily armed local mercenaries. He introduced us to the men who would be our guards. They were a ragtag group of skinny young men wearing battered clothing, random bits of military gear, flip-flops and faraway gazes. They carried Kalashnikovs and a couple of tripod-mounted machine guns. Several were slung with bandoliers or belts of bullets. They showed us our vehicles. We would be driving around in flatbed pickup trucks with whopping anti-aircraft guns mounted on the back which fired bullets the size of small bottles. The trucks were known as "technicals".

"Like a poor man's tank," said Ajoos with a faint smile.

We were in a situation where everything around us felt potentially dangerous, even life-threatening, like we were barefoot toddlers in a Dickensian glass factory. We had no real idea whether we could trust Ajoos, let alone our guards. We were in a place where we could be shot at any moment or kidnapped for ransom.

Then our plane turned and flew out, and we were on our own.

We loaded our bags into the trucks and I climbed into the back of one with Iain. There was some joking and joshing with the guards as I tried to fit alongside them, and their gun barrels accidentally slapped into my leg. They laughed, I laughed, and after that we got along just fine. We kept that moment in the programme, just to show they were human, and even in a bonkers situation like Mogadishu there was humour, and light in the shade.

We drove into the city. I was quite calm. To my astonishment, I was about to enter a conflict zone with no real back-up and yet I wasn't scared; I was filled with a sense of anticipation and adventure. But the entire time I was there I couldn't get a book out of my mind that I read as a kid. It was a science-fiction story called *The Stainless Steel Rat*, about a space traveller who arrived on an alien world where everything was ferociously dangerous and everything was out to get him. The plants had evolved to eat people, the insects were deadly. That's what being in Mogadishu felt like.

I just had to roll with the situation and behave like an amiable Brit. It helped that I didn't look threatening, and I was with a couple of people who looked equally harmless. All of us were careful to strip out any old military gear from our kit before we flew. A few years earlier some French travellers wearing army surplus clothing in remote North Africa had been shot as spies. Mogadishu was no place to start looking like foreign special forces.

The city was like nowhere I had ever been. It had been destroyed by years of fighting. In some areas almost every building was partially destroyed or at least pock-marked with bullets. Masonry was hanging over streets strewn with debris. It looked like the aftermath of the Battle of Stalingrad, or Grozny. On the streets traffic was light, but there were trucks and other technicals carrying more gangs of young fighters. Ajoos told me corpses were left in the streets for days and locals survived in a state of utter chaos. We passed colonial-era Italian classical buildings, while people scuttled along looking fearful, but also staring at us.

"This is a city of a million people," said Ajoos, "and we think you are the only white people here at the moment."

Even with all that Ajoos was telling us, I cannot say I was particularly worried. I felt alert and alive. It was a shocking and horrific place to be. But it felt like we were somewhere important, where stories needed to be told. We had a chance to broadcast the suffering of a place and a people who had been forgotten.

Our first stop was near the main market. Our guards leapt off the back of our vehicles and fanned out around us to form a secure perimeter. I grabbed our "trauma kit", a shoulder bag full of battlefield wound dressings, and we set off along the street towards the site of a disaster that helped to shape world history.

In October 1993, in an operation immortalised in the movie *Black Hawk Down*, more than 100 elite US special forces and soldiers abseiled out of helicopters into Mogadishu to hunt for two senior warlords fomenting chaos.

The reasons the US got involved had nothing to do with capturing and securing vital oil supplies. They were in Somalia largely from a misguided belief that military power alone could be used to stabilise chaotic regions of the world.

The mission was supposed to take roughly an hour, but everything went wrong when one of the American Black Hawk helicopters was hit by the blast from a simple shoulder-launched rocket-propelled grenade (RPG) fired from the ground. With its tail-rotor severed, it spun in the air and plummeted into a neighbourhood 500 metres north-east of the target zone. Then another Black Hawk was downed. By the next morning, when the group was finally rescued after a ferocious battle, eighteen American soldiers had been killed and more than seventy wounded. At least 500 Somali fighters and civilians were dead and 1,000 injured. It was the longest sustained firefight involving American forces since the Vietnam War.

With Ajoos leading, we passed down streets and narrow alleys where young children peered from behind chipped and broken doors. Then he stopped.

"Here it is," said Ajoos. We had reached what I thought was a pile of rubbish, cactus plants and razor wire next to a group of bullet-ridden buildings. "This is one of the American helicopters."

I felt my whole body chill. The day after the battle in Mogadishu, the corpses of American soldiers were dragged through the streets and paraded in front of television cameras. President Clinton began pulling US forces out of the country and the captured henchmen of warlords were quickly released. The debacle shaped American foreign policy for the rest of the 1990s, making Clinton extremely reluctant to commit US troops to peacekeeping operations and, I was told adamantly while researching my book, to covert operations against bin Laden and al Qaeda. Just one week after the battle in Mogadishu, Clinton ordered US Navy ships to turn back from a peacekeeping mission to Haiti for fear they would be attacked. Within eighteen months the United Nations had packed up and left Somalia. The country was abandoned and left to rot. If those helicopters had not been downed the whole world might have been a different place. Perhaps, even, 9/11 would never have happened. Perhaps Afghanistan, and Iraq, would never have been invaded.

There was still no real government in Somalia, and instead warlords controlled their own territory. Despite the chaos and violence, it was recognised as a functioning country and it had a seat at the United Nations. The suffering of Somalia was horrifying, but the real focus of my journey was Somaliland, to the north, which had split from Somalia. Somaliland was supposed to be relatively stable and secure, but no other nation in the world recognised Somaliland as a proper country.

To illustrate the anarchic situation in Somalia we plunged deeper into the main market. Ajoos led from the front, and Iain and I scurried to keep up. As gunmen from other gangs eyed us with bemusement or suspicion, I tried to play the jolly Brit abroad; no threat, no hidden agenda. Ajoos took us down narrow alleys at the side of the market, past ramshackle stalls and shacks, and our group and guards began to spread out. I started to wonder where on earth we were going, and for a moment my trust in Ajoos wavered. Then we arrived at a small building, our guards took up positions outside and Ajoos ushered me inside and introduced me to a man called Mr Big Beard, who had passports to sell.

"So you've decided to become a Somalian," Mr Big Beard, who had dyed his hair rusty orange, said with a laugh.

There was no government here; no paperwork; no rules other than those of the street and the gun. But the country was still recognised globally and people still travelled abroad. Instead of a government ministry, anyone with money who needed a passport would go to see men like Mr Big Beard. He had liberated a stack of passports and stamps from the official passport office during the chaos of war. He charged me about £50 and in fifteen minutes I had a genuine Somali diplomatic passport, bearing my own name and photograph. No checks, no birth certificate, of course. I still have the passport, and it remains one of my strangest travel souvenirs.

That night we took shelter in a guesthouse compound that was guarded around the clock by our gunmen. It had its own armoury and was built around a central courtyard. Rooms that backed onto the surrounding streets had furniture piled at one end as rudimentary protection against RPG attacks.

But even in the rooms we weren't safe. I pulled a plug out of a ruined socket and accidentally touched the wires. The electrocution blew me backwards across the room. I felt like my arm had been put into a tight vice, and the grip extended round and stopped just before my heart. I felt shaky and nauseous, and my arm was sore for several days. I had a sleepless night, wondering what on earth I was doing in this place, where even a simple plug tries to kill you.

The next morning our gunmen took us to buy their drugs. Everything else in Mogadishu was in chaos, but roadside stalls were still selling fresh bundles of *khat*, or *qat*, an amphetamine-like stimulant that gives chewers a small high. It was also an appetite suppressant, useful when food was scarce, according to Ajoos.

The *khat* is wrapped into a small bundle and chewed. It's legal in the Horn of Africa but there is a serious downside to the drug. At the very least it is psychologically addictive, and regular use can lead to insomnia and anxiety. Often it can make people feel more irritable, and even violent. I spoke to people in Somalia who thought the fact it was chewed by millions of people was holding them and the country back. So Iain, Shahida and I were in a bit of a moral quandary when the men told us we had to pay for their bundle.

"It's something they expect," said Ajoos, who didn't chew. "It's part of the contract with them. And you really don't want a group of gunmen looking after you who are grumpy and missing their fix."

It was a winning argument. No doubt some armchair critics and BBC-haters would have a fit. But on the ground we had no choice. We paid for their drugs. What were we supposed to do? We were in Mogadishu, for goodness' sake. In any situation like that you have to make the rules up as you go along.

After a few days we were friendly with and fond of our guards. They were tough guys, but some of them were also lads just out of their teens. After we finished filming one day I presented a couple of them with BBC pens. They were just cheap rollerballs, but they had "BBC" printed on the side, and the men were completely and totally charmed. It was as if they had never been given a present before.

One of them took his pen and wrote "2Pac", his nickname, on the front of his red beany hat, put the pen proudly into his breast pocket and turned it so the BBC sign faced out (where it remained for the rest of our stay), then laughed to Ajoos.

"He said he's been wanting to write his name on the hat for a year," said Ajoos. "I think you're in trouble now, Simon, they want to give you a special present."

I scrambled to say I didn't want anything in return and that it was just a tiny gift. But it was too late. 2Pac presented me with a loaded Kalashnikov which he put over my shoulder.

"Mind the gap," said Shahida dryly. She had grown up in the former Soviet Union and knew how to handle an AK47. When the safety catch is off there's a clear gap to indicate danger.

"Good point, Shazz," I said.

I flicked the lever to safety. We politely took a couple of photos and then I went to hand the gun back.

"I don't think you understand, Simon," said Ajoos earnestly. "This is an ancient custom. You have given a gift, and now you must receive a gift in return. You would cause terrible offence if you gave it back. You will have to take the Kalashnikov with you to London."

I blanched.

"Ajoos . . . seriously . . . I can't . . ." I said. Then I paused. "Hang on, you're taking the piss, aren't you?"

Ajoos's straight face crumbled. "Yes, don't worry," he laughed. "Give it to me and I'll hide it back in the armoury. They'll never notice."

The next day we were out again, driving north of Mogadishu to where local businessmen were trying to operate a rudimentary port away from warlords. As we drove through the outskirts of the city I had my helmet on my lap and my flak jacket propped up against the side of the vehicle as some protection against small-arms fire. We had decided against wearing the heavy jackets out on the streets for several reasons, but we kept them close at hand in case shooting broke out. Ajoos told us body armour was hard to get hold of in the city and thus extremely valuable to wealthy warlords. "They will attack us and kill you just to get it," he said.

As we drove along I was in the back of the lead technical chatting with Ajoos and piping "Mr Brightside" by the Killers through the car radio, loudly, from a transmitter on my iPod. 2Pac, who was in the back manning the mounted machine gun, banged on the roof and shouted to Ajoos, laughing.

"He says he wants to hear some Tupac or at least Eminem," said Ajoos.

We slowed for a crossroads in a bombed-out area of the city, just as another gang in two technicals came to the junction down another road at the same moment. The other gang started screaming at our guys, and both groups locked and loaded their weapons and turned machine guns and anti-aircraft guns on each other.

For what seemed like an age the world stood still. The anti-aircraft gun on the other technical was pointing right at me. My body armour against the door would not have been the slightest protection. Rounds from an anti-aircraft gun would have shredded the armour, me and the vehicle.

The strangest sensation came over me. A sense of calm descended that I would never have expected. I told myself very quietly and very genuinely there was nothing I could do. Anything I did or said would almost certainly make things worse. It was a moment of acceptance. So I just sat there. Rock still. And I waited, to see if I would live or die.

Wise heads prevailed. The other gang drove off first. We sat there for just a second, as if bound by a spell. Ajoos spoke first.

"Well, let's go on then, shall we?" he said with a casual smile.

A day later we left Somalia on a cargo flight that took us north towards Somaliland. I felt a huge sense of relief when our plane was safely up in the air. It seemed we had been lucky. Other foreigners visiting Mogadishu around the same time were kidnapped. Tragically just a few months after we left, a brave and much-loved BBC producer called Kate Peyton was shot in the back while standing outside a guesthouse in Mogadishu, only hours after arriving in Somalia. She died from internal bleeding after being taken to a local hospital.

Landing in Somaliland everything felt different to Somalia. A smartly dressed immigration official stamped our passports. His presence and uniform were an immediate sign of order. Although rarely found on maps, Somaliland is home to roughly 4 million people. It borders the Gulf of Aden and sits next to Djibouti to the north-west and Ethiopia to the south and the west. Britain is the former colonial power and Somalilanders went to Britain's aid during the Second World War. Somalilanders still feel a strong attachment to the UK, and many struggle to understand why the government in London has not recognised their country.

The international status of many unrecognised states is tied up with geopolitics. One of the problems for Somaliland is that African states have collectively decided that, for better or worse, they will keep to colonial-era borders to avoid sparking wars across the continent as potentially dozens of minorities battle for their own states. The UK, I was told by a British diplomat, will not recognise Somaliland if no African state will recognise it first, to avoid accusations London behaves like a colonial power.

Somaliland faces an added complication because it has a potential port which could become a supply route for cargo to the Horn of Africa if the country was a full member of the UN. But neighbouring Djibouti already makes a fortune from its own deep-water port, so has a vested interest in blocking the recognition of Somaliland and preventing companies from trading with a potential rival.

As we drove into the sweltering capital Hargeisa, I chatted about the issue of recognition with Yusuf Abdi Gabobe, my local guide. He explained that Somaliland voluntarily joined with Somalia after independence from Britain in 1960, but when the relationship soured in the 1980s Somalilanders began campaigning and then battling for independence. Conflict erupted, and at least 50,000 men, women and children are thought to have died in Hargeisa alone as Somali forces and jets tried to quash the independence movement and bomb the city into submission. Up to 90 per cent of the city was destroyed by artillery and aerial bombing by aircraft flown by Zimbabwean mercenaries working for the Somali dictator Siad Barre. But in 1991 it was the Somali dictatorship that collapsed, plunging much of Somalia into decades of chaos. Somaliland then officially declared independence from Mogadishu and set up borders in line with what had previously been called British Somaliland. Yusuf, a towering figure of a man, had been a rebel leader fighting for Somaliland independence during the bitter conflict with Somalia.

Visiting Somaliland was a humbling lesson in survival and self-determination. Hargeisa was being rebuilt with little outside help, and refugees were returning from camps in Ethiopia. The streets bustled with activity, but I was trying to spot something small and understandable that I could point out to the camera, and by extension the viewers, which would illustrate in one moment the differences between chaotic Somalia and ordered, stable Somaliland. And then I spotted the symbol I had been seeking.

I asked Iain if he would follow me with the camera, and we hopped out of our car to film . . . at some traffic lights. Hardly the most surprising thing in cities around the world, but a shock to see in the Horn of Africa. In Mogadishu people had talked almost lovingly about the bright colours of traffic lights, which had all been destroyed long ago in fighting. Somalis told us that farmers and villagers would even trek into the centre of Mogadishu to see the traffic lights because they were so novel, and such a marvel. Their absence in Mogadishu was just a tiny example of the chaos of the city. Their presence in Hargeisa, and the fact drivers all obeyed them and stopped dutifully on red, was a contrasting sign of order. The reality of the whole state boiled down to a set of traffic lights at a particularly busy intersection. I felt they were totemic.

Our driver had been a little too good at obeying the traffic regulations and vanished when the lights turned green, so I followed Yusuf as we walked a short distance across the city to where a Somali MiG jet which had bombed the city sat atop a poignant war memorial.

Yusuf explained that lack of recognition was hitting Somaliland hard. It meant the self-declared state was having trouble securing any investment or foreign aid to help with a terrible drought. Tens of thousands of people were at risk of starvation. He took me to see Edna Adan Ismail, the extraordinary head of the maternity hospital in Hargeisa. She explained that even medical supplies could not be delivered because Somaliland had no international recognition.

"I really struggle to get international help here," she said wearily. "I have had volunteers from abroad, doctors, who want to come and help to train our nurses, but they can't even get insurance to come because the world says that we are part of Somalia." As she gave me a tour, there was a shrill scream from another room, and Edna dashed off to help a mother giving birth.

Edna was a completely inspiring and amazing woman. She was a nurse and midwife, but she was also the dynamic Foreign Minister of the country, and she took me to the President's office and walked me straight into a full cabinet meeting.

I backed out, we waited in our car for a while, and then had a meeting with the President, who was wearing an ill-fitting suit and said he was running the country on just a few million pounds a year, or "whatever we can get". Because nobody would recognise his government it could not get loans, which at least meant Somaliland was not burdened by foreign debt repayments.

The Somaliland Minister for Tourism saw us filming at the cabinet meeting and was elated he finally had a rare foreign visitor he could take to see his country's national treasures.

"Don't worry!" said the enthusiastic minister, as I reluctantly agreed to accompany him to some rock etchings recently discovered at Laas Ga'al outside Hargeisa. "The drawings are beautiful, and it will just be a small detour from the road!"

We headed out on a dirt road bordered by low scrub and spreading acacia trees, then turned off into the bush. After bumping along a parched and pot-holed goat track for long enough for my bones to separate, I started to think my scepticism was justified. But we crested a hill, dodged wiry bushes on a wide plain, and finally scrambled over vast boulders to find exquisite rock paintings dating back thousands of years.

Even under the scorching sun, the paintings had strong, vibrant colours and stark outlines, showing the ancient inhabitants of the area worshipping long-horned cattle and venerating a pregnant cow. In a low cave further up the hill I found human figures dancing along the rock. There are paintings of dogs, camels, a

287

giraffe, and the ancient herders of the region, presumably the people who painted the images. The whole site is an absolute treat. Laas Ga'al is probably the most significant Neolithic rock painting site in the whole of Africa. The rock art has been dated to 9000–3000 BC, but still looks as though it was painted last week.

For a brief moment I felt like an explorer finding hidden treasures, at a time when the entire world seems easy to reach on package holidays. Somaliland is proof there are still areas of the world off the beaten track which can excite and amaze. The territory does not feature on many tourist maps. In fact, it does not feature on many maps at all. According to the international community, Somaliland does not even exist.

Yusuf took us deeper into the mountains and then on to the port of Berbera. "There are tracks along the coast west from here towards Djibouti, and mangroves, gorgeous islands and coral reef," said Yusuf. "If only you had a few more weeks we could head out along the coast. But let's go to the airport instead."

It sounded like a poor alternative. We stopped at an old, dust-blown, abandoned airfield, driving in through a wonky, creaking gate and past a small hand-painted sign: "Wellcome to Berbera International Air Port". A set of passenger steps lay baking in the sun, covered in sand and muck. Yusuf took me up into the dilapidated control tower, and we wiped the windows so we could see outside. It didn't look like much, but then Yusuf explained that at more than 4.5 kilometres, the runway was actually one of the longest in the world. I was stunned.

"It was built during the Cold War by the Soviet Union," he told me. "Moscow based heavy bombers here in Berbera, until the Soviets switched allegiance from Somalia to Ethiopia in the 1970s, and we asked the Soviets to leave."

In their place the Americans arrived, and NASA decided to use the airfield as an emergency landing strip for the space shuttle, apparently paying something like £30 million per year in rent. Yusuf could see that I looked completely disbelieving.

"It's true!" he said with a smile. "It was just in case the shuttle had trouble on re-entry and couldn't make it around the planet and back to the US. You see, we have more surprises to share with you, Simon."

We left and drove further into Berbera in our four-wheel-drive vehicles through the bush, when Yusuf suddenly stopped the car again and leapt out, motioning for me to join him.

"Quick, quick," he said. "Have a look at this beauty."

I followed him for a short distance over to a colossal termite mound standing like a monolith at least six metres tall.

"These wonders were our friends when we were fighting in the bush for more than ten years," he said, his eyes shining. "When I was a guerrilla commander we could hide behind them and even rocket-propelled grenades could not get at us. One time we were attacked by the forces loyal to the Somali dictator Siad

Barre in helicopter gunships and most of us were able to find protection behind the mounds."

He slapped the side. "Feel it, they're like solid concrete."

Termite mounds are astonishing eco-systems with ventilation and natural air-conditioning systems. What you see above ground is just a fraction of what lies below the surface. They are like solid desert icebergs.

Yusuf was a softly spoken, unshockable man who I gradually realised had seen far too much horror. We paused a few hours further up the road, still in the bush, and prepared some food. I dug out a round of food ration packs for all of us and began heating them up. A heating element is put into a bag containing another sealed bag of stew or curry and then a small sachet of water is poured on top. The water causes a chemical reaction in the element that then heats the food.

Yusuf stood watching me as I prepared our meals. He wasn't an easy man to impress, but he couldn't contain himself.

"That is completely incredible," he said. "Incredible . . . incredible . . . How does it work? Oh, if only we had those with us when we were out in the bush, they would have made life so much more bearable. The food was one of the worst things about being a guerrilla fighter."

We sat on the ground and had a picnic, with Yusuf still shaking his head and smiling as he ate each mouthful of the magic stew.

Somaliland made a huge impact on me. The place, unrecognised or not, was a revelation, with stability, democracy, a minister for tourism, women in parliament, a police force, and traffic lights. But it was the Somalilanders themselves who I found most impressive. They are still to this day determined and completely inspiring. Largely ignored by the world, they are building an independent state from scratch.

Sadly, it is still possible that war between Somalia and Somaliland could erupt again. But there is also a much more optimistic future for the country. Perhaps one day Somaliland will have its own seat at the United Nations, and tourists will flock to the rock paintings at Laas Ga'al, and to its stunning beaches to swim at the mouth of the Red Sea.

CHAPTER
EIGHTEEN

Fishing with the President

I was genuinely gloomy about leaving Somaliland. We headed back home and I quickly repacked for the next trip to an unrecognised country on the edge of Europe. Transnistria, a sliver of a place between the former Soviet republics of Ukraine and Moldova, was an unofficial nation thought to be home to 400,000–700,000 people, depending on who was doing the counting.

After the Soviet Union collapsed two thirds of the people in the country that became Moldova were of Romanian descent and wanted to have closer ties with Romania and the West. The remaining third of the population wanted to keep their ties with Russia and Ukraine. There was a short but ferocious war and the land east of the Dniestr River became the unrecognised state of Transnistria.

The little state's campaign for recognition was not going well when I visited. The United Nations and the rest of the world said Transnistria was officially and legally part of Moldova. Only three other states had chosen to recognise Transnistria, and they were also unrecognised, so hardly counted. To get to the breakaway statelet I had to travel through Moldova, the mother country from which it had split, and I headed there with Shahida and Will Daws.

My first impression of Moldova as we drove out into the countryside was that it was clearly staggeringly poor. I had a guidebook with me that talked about "unspoilt landscapes", "rural pastures", "charming backwater", which I think translated as something like: "grinding poverty", "high unemployment", "no development", "most people have left".

The statistics showed that many people in Moldova were earning less than £2 a day. I confess I had no idea such abject poverty could exist right on the doorstep of the European Union. We drove through the Moldovan countryside on roads of mud, passing villages so poor that buildings were barely standing. Most of the countryside was empty of people except for young children and the grandparents who looked after them.

Moldova was officially the poorest country in Europe. I was stunned by the conditions people were enduring. I have travelled through rural regions of Romania and Hungary, but they don't even get close to Moldova for poverty. I saw an elderly woman trying to pull a small wooden plough across a field like a two-legged donkey. We drove to one village that was in such poor repair, with roads pitted with rocks and potholes, that we had to get out of our rugged four-wheel drive and walk. People who remained in some communities were so utterly impoverished they had resorted to the most desperate methods possible to earn money.

In the heart of one village we walked up a steep muddy track, past broken fences until we came to a green metal fence with a small house, beyond which scrawny chickens were penned and dogs barked incessantly. My guide, local journalist Liliana Vitu, introduced me to three of the remaining men in the village who had sold one of their kidneys to foreign buyers desperate for a transplant.

They sold a kidney.

For an example of the reality of poverty, in its most basic form, it was utterly shocking. And on the edge of Europe? I was stunned.

The men showed me scars that ran from the base of their ribs almost to their armpits. Most had been paid less than £2,000. One man had used the money to buy a washing machine and some clothes for his children, another bought a cow and redecorated his house. As I spoke to them, I couldn't quite believe this was happening in the twenty-first century.

These poor, desperate people had done something extreme in a vain attempt to survive, in a country with no economy to speak of, and had then squandered the money they had been paid. All the men said they were experiencing sickness and weakness.

Walking through their village I started to wonder how Moldova could ever build a functioning economy. Huge areas of the country were the preserve of kids, grandparents, the sick and the weak. They were empty of young adults.

Around a million Moldovans were thought to have travelled abroad. There were only 3 million people remaining. Across much of the country there was almost no one left of working age. Most had fled in a desperate search for work in Europe or Russia.

For me it was a stark illustration of an aspect of the migration debate in Europe I had never previously considered. People inside the borders of the EU often discuss the pros and cons of migration into Europe based on a relatively selfish idea of what is good or bad for Europe. "*What do immigrants do for us?*" is often the tone of the debate.

Very rarely does anybody talk about the consequences for less-developed countries of seeing their ablest and fittest leaving in search of work. In ghost communities in Moldova I saw the effects. Moldova had lost an entire generation, and society was reeling and listless as a result.

I have since been in many other countries which have lost millions of people to migration, from the Philippines to Mexico, from Bangladesh to sub-Saharan Africa. Many of those left behind complain their brightest and best are being poached by the West through complicated immigration quotas, often so they can work as taxi drivers and pizza chefs, rather than staying at home to develop their own businesses and the national economy.

Take healthcare workers. The International Organisation on Migration (IOM) has concluded there are more Ethiopian doctors working in Chicago than in the whole of Ethiopia. One study found that an astonishing 77 per cent of physicians trained in Liberia were actually working in the US. More than half the doctors born in Sierra Leone, Tanzania, Mozambique, Angola and Liberia are now working in wealthy Organisation for Economic Cooperation and Development (OECD) countries.

In the UK more than a quarter of doctors received their primary training outside of Europe, and the main countries providing doctors to the UK from outside the EU include India, Pakistan, Nigeria, Egypt, Sri Lanka, Iraq and Sudan.

The money the UK saves by recruiting Ghanaian health workers may well exceed the money Britain gives Ghana in aid for health. African and East Asian states in particular spend a fortune on the education and training of nurses and doctors only to see European countries actively recruit them, often straight out of college. It is just one of a hundred ways poorer countries continue to subsidise wealthier nations. The NHS is especially dependent on migrant healthcare workers. The government Office for Budget Responsibility admits that without them the NHS would be in "dire straits". We should be paying more to the countries that train our doctors and nurses, compensating them for fixing our own skills shortage.

Consider what happens when your nation is drained of the young, able, middle-class professionals and the educated. In several countries in the Caribbean 70 per cent of people educated above high-school level have fled or left their countries for opportunities elsewhere. By one estimate Jamaica has lost 85 per cent of university educated workers. It is infinitely more difficult to run a state without a middle class and the tax revenue they generate. They help to pay for schooling, welfare and medical care. If they are absent the country is crippled.

I can understand why individuals leave, of course. But collectively the consequences can be a state that never stands on its own two feet.

Some economists say that increasing "immigration flows", as they call them, could have enormous economic benefits. If the developed world took in enough immigrants to enlarge their workforce by just 1 per cent, they claim, the additional value created could be worth more to those migrants than all of the foreign aid payments in the world combined. I have no doubt that could well be true.

But a benefit to the relatively small number of people from developing countries who have migrated abroad does not necessarily mean benefit to the hundreds of millions left behind.

Other supporters of migration — large corporations, for example — say that countries like Moldova or Bangladesh receive huge sums in "remittances", the sums sent home by migrants. But those remittances do not help to create communities; they often become what Australian Aboriginals call "sit-down money", a welfare cheque received without any requirement to find work. Often they can help to entrench poverty by encouraging people in remote communities empty of employment to do little but drink, fester and wait for the next handout from their relative abroad.

I am not completely opposed to migration. I am not saying immigration is always a bad thing. I just think the debate in Western countries concentrates on the effect it has on us. We are selfish. There should be more discussion about the effects on the poorer, developing countries and communities that people are leaving. Because on the ground in rural Moldova, and in dozens of other places I have visited in the years since, the consequences are often tragic.

We went to visit the President of Moldova. You can do that when you're a BBC TV crew making a documentary about Transnistria. Along with the poverty, unemployment and migration, the breakaway state was perhaps the biggest issue affecting the nation. Liliana explained that President Vladimir Voronin's mother lived in Transnistria and for the past two years he had been unable to visit her because of the border dispute with the breakaway territory.

I feared my time with the President would involve a formal chat. But as we drove through a set of iron gates, arrived at the palatial presidential property and discovered that President Voronin wanted to take me fishing on his very own well-stocked lake. My only other memory of fishing was when I was twelve, and I slipped off a bank, fell into the River Piddle up to my neck, and then had to walk through the local village while people lined pavements to laugh at me. President Voronin helped exorcise my demons. A couple of ornate, gilded state chairs were set up on the bank by the lake for us to relax in, slices of watermelon were brought out, and the President tried to show me how to cast a line.

A lifelong Communist, Voronin was white-haired, in his sixties, and had been the head of a bread factory in a small Moldovan town before he entered politics. He still had the air of someone involved in provincial middle-management. I asked him what he thought about Transnistria and whether anything was going on there that the rest of Europe should be concerned about.

"It's a hole," he said. "I cannot go there. I cannot see my mother; the place is nothing more than a black hole of corruption and trafficking." He was angry, but it was an oft-repeated speech.

"Moldova has a 480-kilometre border with the Ukraine and the section in Transnistria is not controlled, and via this there's uncontrolled migration, contraband, arms trafficking, the trafficking of human beings and drugs. These operations are being legitimised by the separatist regime. There are thirteen enterprises in Transnistria that are producing arms non-stop."

At that moment the President broke off from the chat because his aide announced he had caught a fish. Then he asked me to join him on a tour of his wine cellar. It must have been a quiet day for the President, because he decided we needed to celebrate Moldovan national independence day, and went straight for vodka and his favourite cognac. He insisted we weren't about to get drunk.

"I'm just very proud of Moldovan cognac and I want to promote it," he said.

We were all finishing a second bottle when his wife came in from the shops, complete with plastic carrier bags, told him to stop teasing and playing with the foreign film crew, and we staggered out.

You don't have to travel far to discover the exotic appeal of an unrecognised state. It is only around an hour by bus or car from the leafy Moldovan capital Chisinau to the border with Transnistria. Officially it was still part of Moldova and the border did not exist. But the reality on the ground was tanks, armed guards, bunkers, fortified positions, and reams of razor wire. I was surprised at how tense the situation was. We were visiting years after actual fighting had stopped, but each side feared it might erupt again at any moment. Just before we arrived Transnistria had upped the stakes by banning the teaching of Moldovan in schools, allowing only Russian. Moldova had responded with an economic blockade. If you looked at the situation on paper it would seem that tiny Transnistria could not survive the siege, but still they held out.

We showed our passports to surly guards and soldiers, then drove and walked through what was essentially a demilitarised zone before crossing into Transnistria. I had arrived in my second breakaway state and felt a gentle sense of elation.

Transnistria was quite the experience. I thought I had gone through a time warp. It was like visiting a Soviet-themed adventure park. In the capital Tiraspol the hammer-and-sickle emblem of the Soviet Union had pride of place outside many buildings, and a statue of Lenin dominated the street outside the House of Soviets.

My new guide Larissa, a teacher with a kindly soul, met us at the crossing. I asked whether the Soviet symbols meant people looked back fondly on the past.

"No, we just do not carry out war with monuments," she said with a grin.

Moldovans had warned me hungry armed men roam the streets of Transnistria, but although the border was tense, the leafy streets of Tiraspol were full of cafes and restaurants. People sat outside on cheap plastic chairs as old cars chugged past. Fighting talk was limited to thoughts on political strife in neighbouring Ukraine and the impact on the price of *salo*, pig fat, a major Ukrainian export. Transnistrians were eating it covered with chocolate, partly as a joke, and partly I think to show how hard they were. I had to try it, just for research purposes. Sweet on the outside and extra salty on the inside, after a moment of chewing it just tasted like raw bacon rind. It was unappetising, but not quite as bad as it sounds.

Larissa spoke English well and was thoughtful, with well-considered views. She said she had no doubt that breaking away from Moldova and keeping ties with Russia was the right decision. She talked optimistically about the future. "We are young," she said, "but there is work here for the people, and you can't say that about Moldova."

Then she showed me her Transnistrian passport. It looked more convincing than my Somali diplomatic offering. I asked her who recognised it as a legitimate travel document.

"We do," she said, and she laughed.

"Does anyone else?"

"No," she said. "Not yet."

Transnistrians celebrated their National Independence Day while we visited, an event which bore a striking resemblance to old Soviet May Day parades. Small children in uniforms sang "our army is the best army" with evident pride, and the army goose-stepped along the main road past a platform of officers awarded medals by the kilo. Having always wanted to visit Red Russia, I watched goggle-eyed.

But I also felt sorry for them. Years since they split, the ongoing tension between Moldova and Transnistria ensured both states were economically depressed and continued to suffer.

The President of Transnistria, Igor Smirnov, was happy to explain why independence was so important. "It means the protection of all the generations that live here regardless of their nationality," he told me. But then, realising that he had set himself up for a tricky follow-up question, he added that there were forty-six different nationalities in Transnistria and begged: "Please don't ask me to list them all."

There was a party atmosphere in Transnistria the day they celebrated independence. Cafés served great flagons of beer and we ate heartily. The rest of the time Transnistrian cafés were some of the trickiest places to eat on the planet.

Each one had a menu the length of a telephone directory, as if they were listing all the food available on the Eurasian land mass. We would request something, and the waiter would go to the kitchen and ask if it was available. Then they would return, shake their head almost imperceptibly, and say simply in Russian: "*Nyet.*" I like the people of the former Soviet Union and I missed them during the past few years while I was travelling in the tropics. I missed their hard shells and inner warmth. I missed their culture, their language, their resigned shrugs, and their ability to talk without moving their lips or using facial muscles. But ordering a meal in Transnistria became a right saga. After a couple of requests for meals were rejected we thought it best for the waiter to simply tell us what was available. He went off again, returning five minutes later.

"Chicken. And potatoes."

The first time we ate a meal in Transnistria we saw our food being chased around the yard outside. We knew it was fresh but then we waited two hours for it to be served. Cafés in Transnistria, I can say with absolute certainty, are the slowest on Planet Earth. So the next day we tried to ring ahead. Despite assurances to the contrary, nothing was cooked until we arrived, and we waited another hour. The next day Dimitri went ahead to order, pay and browbeat them into cooking, but the chef walked out in a huff. Apparently, it was the custom for everyone to be sitting, waiting, before anyone would even start boiling water. The long, long waits gave time for repeated karaoke rehearsals of the uplifting

Transnistrian anthem. In dark moments I can still hear it rattling around in my head.

Bulgaria and Romania were both waiting to join the European Union when I visited Transnistria. After they entered the bloc in 2007 that put the breakaway state right on the eastern edge of Europe. The EU is supposed to be a gathering of nations committed to improving life for all, but critics say it has failed to adequately press for reform and change in Transnistria and other post-Soviet "frozen conflict" zones.

When I visited, Transnistria was thought to be a haven for smuggling. It certainly had a Wild West feel. Time and again we discovered that a business, stadium, restaurant or factory was run by a single mysterious firm controlled by former Red Army officers who seemed to have bottomless pockets and a penchant for flashy, top-of-the range vehicles.

International investigators claimed they were unsure what was going on, hardly surprising when there were no foreign embassies and few foreigners visiting the extraordinary little state. Rumours and undercover reports suggest it was a major producer of illegal arms, and the border with Ukraine was said to leak like a sieve. We drove to the south-east of Transnistria and I crossed the unguarded border on foot. I could see for myself how easy it would be for smugglers to traffic arms to the Black Sea port of Odessa and from there to anywhere on the planet.

One of the main reasons for making the series was to highlight the risks of leaving unrecognised countries isolated, and Transnistria was a classic example. Guns from Transnistria have turned up in conflicts around the world.

Russia was said to be calling the shots in Transnistria, so we drove north for a few hours and then crept through bushes to try and get shots of a secret Russian military base that was roughly half a mile away.

"They'll never see us over here," I was blithely saying to Will Daws, who was filming behind the camera, when there was a squeal of tyres, a couple of old Ladas screeched up and four KGB heavies in trench coats jumped out. It was like a scene from a 1950s spy movie.

The KGB had never been disbanded in Transnistria, and we were detained, marched away, and trucked off to cells in the secret police headquarters. Perhaps I had seen too many Cold War thrillers, but I had visions of being held for years and having to write escape plans in blood using my toenails for nibs. We were taken from the cells individually and questioned. Over and over they asked in halting English what we were doing in Transnistria and why we were trying to film the base.

"Are we being arrested?" I asked the officer.

"No," he said. "You are being . . ." he searched for the word, "*detained*."

The way he said it left me feeling nervous. "Arrest" was a procedure. "Detained" was more open-ended.

Fortunately for the team and me, I'd been gassing away to my guide Larissa about how my family's solitary claim to fame was a distant link to the man who rebuilt much of London after the Great Fire.

"Not Sir Christopher Wren?" Her eyes had lit up.

"Yes," I said, surprised. "How did you know?"

"We studied London as a module in Soviet times: Buckingham Palace, Regent's Park, Saint Paul's Cathedral." Larissa was supremely impressed. My local stock had risen dramatically.

Larissa heard we'd been detained and turned up at the KGB headquarters in the middle of the night, literally banging on the door and demanding to see the officer in charge.

"You cannot arrest these people," she wailed at him. "One of them is related to the Queen of England. You will bring terrible shame on Transnistria."

There was a great banging of doors and clanking of keys. We all thought something awful was going to happen. Then a senior KGB officer appeared and apologised for the misunderstanding. "Perhaps we can go for a drink to smooth this over," he suggested. We were all released into the night and agents gave each of us KGB cap badges as souvenirs.

We left Transnistria in a hurry fearing the KGB would change their minds and seize our tapes. We separated them out between us, hid them in our bags and in our clothing, and left the territory in taxis, buses and cars, just to reduce the risk if one of us was stopped and detained. Again I was disappointed to leave. It was a crazy place, but edgy and fascinating. We escaped with a precious travel experience to share with viewers and I had a tale to bore my son with for years to come.

We headed east, across the Black Sea and Turkey towards the Caucasus, never the most stable part of the world, and Georgia, which had no less than three regions which broke away when the Soviet Union collapsed: Ajaria, South Ossetia and Abkhazia. In the ensuing conflicts thousands were killed and the whole region has suffered ever since.

Yet initially Georgia felt safe and impressive. For a couple of days we set the scene by exploring and filming ancient monasteries, old sulphur baths, trendy new bars in the capital Tbilisi, and ate meals with a population that delighted in drinking endless toasts to family, country, friends and football teams. Georgia gave the world a Golden Fleece and Stalin, who they commemorate with a museum. When our local guide vanished I was able to sit on Stalin's personal toilet and strike my own small blow against the veneration of a murdering madman. Then we drove back to the capital, and a meeting with the young Georgian President "Misha" Saakashvili, who was trying to re-unify the whole country and drag it into the twenty-first century.

We were waiting for the President in his offices when someone said he was dashing outside to talk to a crowd of demonstrators, so we jumped into the same small lift. He was completely unfazed.

"Mr President, Simon from the BBC," I said.

"Hi, how are you?" he responded, in American-accented English.

I asked him what was going on with South Ossetia, the main breakaway state in Georgia. "It looks like Russia wants to stir up trouble on the border," he said, "but we are trying to keep things calm. We don't need any other bloody clash there."

I asked him how difficult the situation was at that moment.

"It's a very small piece of territory," he said, striding out of the lift and across the ground floor of the presidential offices, "but it looks like for Russians it's kind of a Maginot line of defence, but God knows for what interest. There is a chance there will be a clash, but we hope it won't happen."

With two bodyguards, wearing obligatory sunglasses, he dived into the crowd and told them he was praying for peace every single night.

Emotions were running high on the border between Georgia and the breakaway region of South Ossetia, which had its own government and army. Just a day before we arrived there fifty Georgian soldiers had been taken captive by South Ossetian forces, who were being trained, backed and encouraged by the might of Russia. We tried to cross into South Ossetia but became trapped in a no-man's-land by Georgian soldiers who said we were not allowed to go forwards or backwards because of the risk of kidnap or detention by South Ossetian and Russian forces.

Moscow had placed "peace-keepers" along the border. Georgians viewed them as "piece-keepers" — desperately trying to keep the old Soviet Union alive. It was one of President Putin's early and successful attempts at meddling in a former Soviet state that wanted closer ties to the West.

We were only released from the no-man's-land when a Russian general, who said his forces were preventing fighting, agreed to chaperone us into the breakaway region. We crossed into South Ossetia, the land of the Ossetes, who told me they speak a different language to Georgians and are determined to remain independent.

President Putin was a hero in Ossetia. His poster was everywhere, looking down on the leafy streets of a tiny territory that seemed stuck in another 1970s Soviet past. Old Lada cars spluttered along on potholed roads, and gaunt, elderly civilians with hollow cheeks sold vegetables from baskets on overgrown pavements. Russia was not gifting them a marvellous alternative to rule by Georgia. The place was desperately poor.

The Ossetes were hugely suspicious of foreigners, partly because our minder kept telling people I was from London in America. After I explained London was on the edge of Europe, young soldiers shared a drunken birthday toast and vowed to fight and die rather than rejoin Georgia.

"We will never allow the Georgians to rule us, because throughout Ossetian history they have always tried to push us around," said one young soldier, idly twirling a dagger around in his hands. "We've never submitted to that, and we never will."

The soldiers were drinking, but they were friendly and engaging, and they invited us to sit with them in an outdoor area behind a restaurant and let us film. I swapped tales from my travels for their stories of life on the front line, and then the youngster offered his dagger as a gift. I refused, but he insisted. I was genuinely touched and gave him my watch in return. I still use his knife as a letter opener.

Even after years of conflict with Georgia, the Ossetes were noticeably edgy. People were scared about the prospect of renewed fighting with Georgia. With some rudimentary Russian I nearly caused a riot in a local fruit market by accidentally insulting a female fruit seller while I was trying to buy some apples. Years of travel should have made me a paragon of diplomatic virtue, the very embodiment of the culturally sensitive adventurer. But my inadequate grasp of languages has repeatedly tripped me up. Sometimes a broad smile has got me out of trouble, and sometimes a rapid exit is the only available option. Employing a translator is no guarantee of social safety. "I'm here to grasp your private parts," was how an interpreter translated President Jimmy Carter's opening comment when visiting Poland.

The Ossetian market seller was livid. She was throwing apples at me and shouting to other stall-holders. Someone claimed I had asked if she had a penis. I had to be rescued by our furious Ossetian government minder, and I swore to stick to the most basic local phrases. It was an uncomfortable visit, and we were shadowed everywhere by the secret police.

Back in Georgia we found American and British troops training Georgian soldiers, and entire trains loaded with troops and tanks, waiting for the call to head to the front line. It was clear war could erupt between Georgia and South Ossetia at any time.

310

Heading west across Georgia an overnight train took us to the western Black Sea coast and Ajaria, a holiday destination and summer paradise with beaches that attracted tourists from across the former Soviet Union. It was rejoining Georgia, largely because of local anger at the former strongman dictator. His son would close the best road every night and race his Lamborghini up and down the seafront. Strangely, this did not go down well among locals earning £20 a month. They kicked out the strongman and were welcomed back into Georgia. But they still had a thing or two to learn about leadership: the new governor took us to a restaurant which was immediately cleared of other customers by henchmen who looked like extras from *The Sopranos*.

Abkhazia may well be a lovely place to visit, but we barely made it across the border before the Abkhaz government kicked us out. No Western government operates in Abkhazia, although organised crime gangs are thought to be based there.

All of the breakaway regions of the country were a shock, but perhaps the single most bizarre and chilling place I visited in the region was actually a former secret Soviet military base inside Georgia. The sprawling base had been abandoned when the Soviet Union collapsed, and even when I visited, more than ten years later, it still contained thousands of tons of almost completely unguarded high explosives in artillery shells and anti-aircraft munitions. A local scientist, who had taken it upon himself to rally some help from other retired experts and deactivate some of the weaponry, showed me into a corrugated-iron shed, locked by a single piece of string, inside which were 30,000 rusting shells still containing the military high-explosive TNT. He claimed that if any explosives at the base detonated, the chain reaction would destroy most of the hill the base was sitting on and register on seismic charts around much of the world.

Then to really put the fear of God up me, the scientist took me further up a grassy, overgrown hill and showed me dozens of rocket pods holding even more powerful surface-to-air missile systems. Each one contained, he told me, more than 200 kilograms of TNT.

"One can destroy almost anything, they are extremely powerful," said the scientist. "For example, a skyscraper, no problem."

He was clearly frustrated, exhausted and worried. I asked him how easy it would be for someone to take out the explosive and use it in a terrorist weapon. He smiled wanly.

"Everything is inside," he responded, "that's why a small spark or static discharge will detonate them. You could detonate one with a small battery."

I looked around at the edge of the base. There were fence posts, but no fences. The scientist told us that some houses in local villages had been destroyed when locals tried to extract explosives from some of the smaller artillery shells. He also said he had no money for petrol for a lawnmower, which meant long dry grass had grown around the missile systems, creating a real risk that a fire could detonate the weapons. Nobody was willing to cut the grass with a hand scythe because the area was infested with snakes. The situation was set to get worse.

"Soon, the base will be reclassified," said the scientist. "At the moment it has five guards, but soon it will no longer be a military base, so even those five guards will be removed, and the base will be completely and totally unguarded. Isn't this crazy?"

I had to agree.

Militants were active throughout the volatile region, but there wasn't even fencing around the base to protect the missiles from theft. I found it astonishing governments were warning us of the threat from terrorism, and troops were hunting for weapons of mass destruction in Iraq at the same time, yet so little was being done to safeguard powerful weapons abandoned in the former Soviet Union. The scientist had rung the US embassy to warn them the stockpile could be stolen, but nobody even bothered to return his calls.

I wanted to move on across the Caucasus mountains to breakaway Nagorno-Karabakh, a small, mountainous, landlocked region in the South Caucasus. But on the phone from London we had only been able to find one person there who spoke English and could act as an interpreter. His name was David, and he was on holiday visiting relatives. We had to delay our journey for a week until he returned, so instead we headed to Azerbaijan, which had gone to war over Nagorno-Karabakh.

Historically Nagorno-Karabkh had been mainly Armenian Christian, but Stalin, who was skilled at using division to control people, gave it to Azerbaijan, which is mainly Muslim.

After the Soviet collapse Azerbaijan and Armenia got their independence. When Nagorno-Karabakh then wanted to become independent, neighbouring Armenia sent troops into battle and helped the Karabakh army push out local Muslim Azeris who had been living there for decades.

Both sides committed terrible atrocities during the conflict. When I visited, Azerbaijan was still officially at war with Armenia. With a young, passionate guide called Tural we started our journey on the Azeri front lines looking into Karabakh. Active conflict had halted, but it was still one of the world's forgotten hot spots. Azeri soldiers spoke of their fury at losing family homes just across the front lines. They seemed genuinely determined to get them back. Some still had keys to homes now occupied by Armenians. Ethnic Muslims were forced to flee, leaving towns and villages destroyed so there was no way they could return.

It might have been the twenty-first century in the rest of the world, but on both sides of the border between Karabakh and Azerbaijan young soldiers were still manning trenches. We had to sprint across the open ground of no-man's-land to avoid sniper fire. I heard shots, but nothing came close.

The conflict over Karabakh actually began in the dying years of the Soviet Union. Back in 1988 there were demonstrations in Karabakh and Armenia calling for unification. Then an Azeri march degenerated into a riot and clashes in which there were deaths and injuries on both sides. Azeris and Armenians had lived among each other for generations on both sides of the border, but more outbreaks of violence erupted and people began fleeing to safety, often running through the night with their families. Armenians fled back to Armenia, Azeris to Azerbaijan.

I remembered reading about the conflict and the war that followed while still a teenager. Back then it had seemed like an unfathomable conflict in a very faraway corner of the world, in countries I could not understand involving people I could not comprehend. Now I was there. Talking with them. And their motivations were completely understandable. I could see clearly how a chain of individual events, dislikes, hatreds, connections and disconnections, had led to tragedy.

Reading about the situation from afar I had been tempted to criticise and condemn when I arrived. But it's all too easy for outsiders to misunderstand and underestimate the complexity of relationships and situations that lead to such conflict. Nagorno-Karabakh was one of my first real tastes of what I had always thought of as medieval hatred and tension. So often we don't understand situations and try to suggest or impose simplistic solutions. Yet the problems between the Armenians and Azeris had developed over generations. People from both sides might have got stuck in the past, but for them that past mattered. Understanding that was a starting point in my own attempt to try and fathom what had happened, and I reminded myself that Europeans were in no position to criticise, given the wars we had started and the conflict that raged across our land mass just a few decades before. Anyway, criticising wasn't my job, then or now. I wasn't there to cast simple aspersions. I was there to try and offer a balanced view of the situation, show an unrecognised state to the viewers, and encourage them to learn more about the chaos and tragedy that exists in our world.

We drove back into Azerbaijan and discovered there were still thousands of refugees from the war living in appalling conditions. Although the country has vast oil wealth, and once used to supply half the world's oil, children and the elderly were surviving in rusty train carriages on a railway siding.

We walked among washing lines strung between the boxcars like a community from the Great Depression. It was bitterly cold and dozens of families were trying to survive with no electricity, no water and no heating.

Walking past one boxcar I heard children's voices and our guide told me it housed a small school. Inside teenagers were being taught with almost no resources. I spoke to one teenage girl and asked her how long she had lived there.

"We came in 1993," she said. "I was very young, I don't remember before. This is the only home I remember."

I struggled to comprehend. She had spent more than a decade living in a railway car designed to carry freight. If I hadn't seen it with my own eyes it would have been inconceivable. No one was giving up hope of going home, but, as is often the case, refugees like this had become pawns in a bigger game. Azerbaijan didn't want to assimilate the refugees into the country and give them proper homes, because if they did they could no longer be used as evidence of loss. Integration would be a tacit acceptance that they were never going to get Nagorno-Karabakh back, and the government and the country could never allow that. The desire to maintain a hold over a breakaway state would keep those refugees exactly where they were on a railway siding at the border.

We drove on, feeling sombre. Everyone mentioned the war. We stopped to grab something to eat in a wooden hut of a cafe that, at one time, had been a brothel. A wandering minstrel came in to sing us a melancholy song. He explained it was about the homeland he had lost and longed for. The emotion was heartfelt.

The border between Azerbaijan and Karabakh was closed, so to get there we took a monumental detour across the border into Georgia, passing through stunning snowy mountains and then on into Armenia.

The journey took a few days and the camera rolled most of the time because we knew just about anything could happen. Our car skidded off the road and had two punctures. We had a row with some truck drivers, spent hours listening to strange Azeri and Georgian music on cassettes, and ate plates of unidentifiable food at mountain truck stops. It was a challenging but brilliant adventure, so I was gutted when the programme was later put together and so little of the journey made it into the cut. But we only had thirty minutes and the other footage we had filmed was much stronger.

Finally we headed south over icy mountain passes and into Karabakh. A sign set above a snow-capped landscape bade us welcome. It was early evening and the moon was out. I felt snow crunch under my boots as I looked out at the disputed landscape. A twisting, empty road through the mountains led to Stepanakert, the capital, past eerie, burnt-out villages destroyed after the Azeris left.

In Soviet times Stepanakert, which sits on a high plateau, had been a provincial town under Azeri control. Now the only inhabitants were Armenian-Christian Karabakhians. It was a town stuck in a mindset of continual conflict. In the morning I was taken to visit a school, where young men were being trained to strip down a Kalashnikov blindfolded.

The scenery and churches of Karabakh were impressive, but it was difficult to visit without asking awkward questions. Before Karabakh declared independence from Azerbaijan its population was split between Azeris and Armenians. After the bloody war only a handful of Azeris remain.

Everyone in Karabakh had their own, very different take on the conflict and division. It was the other side of the story. But it was also another side of the truth. Two peoples can go to war and endure decades of conflict and division, but both can still be right. Both can still deserve our sympathy. We can go through the events that created the situation and identify who on each side made mistakes and who committed crimes, but when the end result is long-term suffering, everyone deserves understanding.

David took us back towards the border region, much of which had been mined. We were walking through a gully at the side of a road when we saw the skeleton of a cow. Its back legs had been blown off. Then someone screamed: "Don't move, we're in a minefield!" I froze rigid. We were there for a few moments, calling to each other and trying to reassure everyone that we would be all right. We knew how to get out of a minefield but it is, of course, exceptionally dangerous and takes hours. Then we heard a vehicle pull up on the road above the gully, and an army officer in a camouflage uniform appeared.

"Don't worry," he said, "there are only tank mines here, so your weight will not detonate them."

We retraced our steps. Very carefully.

David took us to see the work of the magnificent British charity, the HALO Trust, which runs demining operations around the world, has cleared vast areas of mines and saved countless lives. They were working hard to clear mines in Nagorno-Karabakh and a former British Army officer showed us a plot they were surveying. I wanted a closer look so he lent me a flak jacket and a thick curved perspex mask supposed to deflect at least some of a blast.

Walking towards the minefield was nerve-wracking. One of the teams was working close to a village. They told me pigs occasionally wandered onto mines, sometimes when deminers were working in the same area. The HALO deminers explained to me that whenever they saw pigs or other animals straying into a minefield they would have to suspend their work and retreat, rapidly.

There are hundreds of different types of landmines. Some only detonate after they have been trodden on three times, or ten. Some explode immediately with a blast directed upwards. Some are designed to leap half a metre into the air before blasting hundreds of ball bearings around a huge radius, severing limbs and turning attacking soldiers into casualties that become a drain on their colleagues. Others will spray ball bearings at head height over an area the size of a football pitch. One mine detonation can cause others to explode, like dominoes. They are astonishing works of evil, and they can sit in the ground for a decade or much longer, just waiting for the unwary to stray across their path.

We got down on our hands and knees and crawled to the edge of the minefield, ready for them to begin demining, poking very slowly through the ground with plastic spikes designed to identify but not trigger a mine. Whenever they found something they would need to place a marker on the ground and then, very slowly, excavate the area to remove the deadly threat. I was learning all about this while we were on the ground right on the edge of the minefield, when suddenly we realised there were people, villagers, actually walking through the minefield in front of us. One of them was carrying their shopping bags. I couldn't believe anyone could be so stupid. They had crossed into a clearly marked minefield.

I did just about the exact opposite of what I was supposed to do. Rather than burying my body in the ground, or leaping up and running away to find hard cover, I stood up and started shouting at the villagers.

"What are you doing?!" I said, in English, rather unhelpfully "Go back, go back!"

In fairness, other people were roaring at them as well.

Rather than standing stock-still and begging for help, the villagers just looked irritated. They actually wandered over to our position, causing me to raise my hands to the heavens in despair.

"What are they doing?!" I said in vain to the lead HALO deminer.

"It's very tricky, because they can live somewhere like this for years and perhaps nobody gets injured and so they stop being afraid of the minefield and become blasé about it," he said. "We often find people letting their cattle wander through areas that we know and they know are littered with ERW [explosive remnants of war], or using the minefield as a short-cut to get to shops or even school."

He was despairing, and I really felt for him. His team were already risking their lives on demining operations, and they also had to deal with foolhardy local villagers. What a task.

Despite the willingness of people in Nagorno-Karabkh to wander through minefields, they seemed to be a surprisingly long-lived people. My guide David took me to a cemetery high in the mountains where we found headstones of both men and women who had lived to become centenarians. David was convinced people from the region lived longer than anyone else on the planet. It sounded unbelievable when first suggested, but then I found a headstone in the cemetery for someone who died aged 115.

One other gravestone indicated the plot contained a husband, and had space ready for the wife, whose date of birth was already inscribed on the headstone. But there was no date of death, and David said she was still alive. I stared at the date, did a quick calculation, never my strong point, and realised that if she were still alive she would be 120. It is most likely she had been displaced in the conflict and never made it to her resting place, but David was convinced she was still alive. "If we had international recognition," he said proudly, "then everyone would know people in Nagorno-Karabakh live longer than anywhere else in the world."

In the years since I have heard similar claims in other mountainous regions of the world. Perhaps it's the fresh air, perhaps it is the organic mulberry vodka people kept pouring down our throats, or perhaps it is the fact mountain people are forever walking up and down the hills, and exercise keeps them fit and healthy. Whatever it is, I think someone should investigate.

We left the cemetery and drove back to the plateau. I suggested we should finish our time in Nagorno-Karabakh on the front line. We took another long drive up into the mountains and hiked to a remote outpost manned by young men, boys really, and looked out to the Azeri trenches in the distance where we'd been just under two weeks before. It all felt very sad and remote.

Although international recognition seems highly unlikely, wealthy Armenian exiles in the United States still provide massive funding to encourage the Karabakh government's claims for independence. This annoys many Armenians, who are sick of the conflict dominating their lives and draining their government budget.

There seems no easy end to the situation. In 2016 dozens were killed and a helicopter gunship and a tank were destroyed in ongoing clashes between Azeri and Armenian forces battling over Nagorno-Karabakh. One day full-scale conflict may erupt again, causing huge problems for the supply of oil from Azerbaijan and the Caspian region to the outside world. Perhaps it's only when oil pipelines are switched off and petrol prices in the West rise as a result that the rest of the world will wake up to the ongoing crisis of breakaway states.

CHAPTER
NINETEEN

The "Golden Age" of Travel

Failing all else, surely the threat of World War Three should alert people to the risks surrounding unrecognised nations.

We left the Caucasus and headed to the Far East. Lack of international recognition is not limited to poor countries. The island of Taiwan has one of the most powerful economies in the world and it has been the tenth largest trade partner of the US, but it has no seat at the United Nations and no major state recognises it as a proper country It is the wealthiest and most powerful unrecognised nation on the planet, the ultimate place that doesn't exist.

When Chinese Nationalists were defeated by Mao's Communists they fled to Taiwan and took over. Taiwan has since become a stable democracy, but Beijing views Taiwan as a renegade province, wants it back, and has repeatedly said it will use extreme force if necessary. Successive US presidents have said they will support, protect and even defend Taiwan.

Everything hinges on recognition. For the past forty years both Beijing and the authorities in Taipei, the Taiwanese capital, have had a tacit understanding that

Taiwan is actually part of China. Taiwan exists in a strange diplomatic limbo where it takes part in events like the World Cup and the Olympic Games, but generally uses a name like "Chinese Taipei", which China will accept, rather than "Taiwan", which would suggest it is a state, and might provoke fury or worse from China.

Despite sometimes flirting with the idea of declaring independence, Taiwan has never gone the whole hog. In return China has held back its vast army from invading and taking the island. But China has said, repeatedly, that it will go to war, against anyone and anything, even the US, if Taiwan tries to split itself permanently away from China.

It all sounds quite extreme. I wanted to visit Taiwan and see what all the fuss was about. First, of course, I had to visit China.

We flew into Beijing in the mid-2000s when it was a building site. The country was going through the most spectacular and profound transition imaginable, as it transformed from a nation of poverty and peasantry to an economic powerhouse. I had never visited China before, and I felt a sense of awe. For all the human rights abuses, the decades of suffering and starvation, the Chinese government was now lifting more people out of extreme poverty than any other leadership in world history. It was a stunning time to visit.

With a young guide called Rock, who seemed pretty relaxed for a guy who was taking the BBC around a state with all-powerful authoritarian rule, we started our journey by heading to one of the symbolic centres of Chinese power: Tiananmen Square, where demonstrators had been massacred in 1989. Guards did try to stop us filming, but in fairness they let us continue after checking our permits.

Tiananmen Square is colossal. It's where Mao Zedong proclaimed the founding of the People's Republic of China in 1949. Visiting from abroad, and seeing it for the first time, I felt like a witness from a very small, distant land. China seemed so huge, its population so vast. Even at twenty to nine in the morning, hundreds of Chinese visitors were queueing to see Mao in his tomb, and revolutionary and Communist propaganda statues and slogans still dominated public spaces.

But much was changing. We found a Rolls-Royce showroom, something completely unimaginable just a few years before. Then we went to the main antiques market and found piles of Mao memorabilia. In the past he had to be venerated. By the time I was there, he had become for many a curiosity, even a figure for amusement, with his image on clocks and hip-flasks. In a dusty shop I found and bought a poster dating back to the time of the Cultural Revolution which had a slogan that said, effectively, "We must recover Taiwan! We must get it back!" It was classic state propaganda imagery, with five sturdy male military figures carrying a red flag and a picture of Mao. But there was something slightly worrying about it as well. A country that had retained such a focus on one issue for so long would surely find it hard to simply let it go.

There are no direct flights from Beijing to Taipei, so we flew there via Hong Kong, met up with a guide and translator called Sen-lun Yu, and travelled on to the tiny Taiwanese island of Kinmen, just off the Chinese coast. Taiwanese soldiers on the island fought a twenty-year artillery duel with the Chinese. During one forty-four-day period the Chinese lobbed 474,000 artillery shells at Kinmen. Eventually both sides came to a gentleman's agreement to bombard each other on alternate days. For more than a decade the two sides agreed the Chinese would bombard on Monday, Wednesday and Friday, and the Taiwanese would return fire on Tuesday, Thursday and Saturday. On Sunday everyone took the day off.

Then the Taiwanese built the world's largest neon sign and the world's loudest loudspeakers on Kinmen and bombarded the mainland with propaganda. They released balloons designed to carry anti-Communist propaganda pamphlets into China, and a few more bizarre offerings: one balloon that apparently drifted to Israel was found to contain see-through underwear. Times have changed and local shops now melt old artillery shell casings into kitchen knives for visiting tourists. I still have a set in my kitchen drawers.

We drove to the coastline which remains the front line against possible invasion. A multitude of signs warned of mines in the sand, but our driver said it was safe so we made our way down to the beach. Just a few miles away the south-east Chinese city of Xiamen was clearly visible through the haze. Sen-lun Yu was a little overwhelmed. She had never seen China before.

I asked her what she had been told about the Chinese when she was growing up and her reply said much about the nature of propaganda.

"Here we grow bananas and we get to eat bananas, and over there they only get to eat the skins of bananas," she said. It was comical to hear, but telling all the same.

I asked Sen-lun what sort of messages the loudspeakers had been broadcasting to China.

"They used to say, 'Taiwan is a treasure island, we are free China, we will come to save you from hell,' " she told me with a smile.

Thanks to Sen-lun's skills of persuasion, we were allowed to board a Taiwanese coastguard cutter. Chinese fishing boats were encroaching into what the coastguard said were Taiwanese waters, and they were being turned back.

But what completely fascinated me were boatloads of Chinese tourists on packed pleasure cruises who had come out to have a look at an island, and an enormous propaganda sign on a hillside, which they had previously only seen from afar or in news bulletins. The sign had the snappy line "Three Principles of the People Unites China", and was a slogan the Taiwanese used to represent their belief in nationalism, democracy and the livelihood of the people. The principles were said to be the basis of Taiwanese prosperity and featured in the first line of the Taiwanese anthem.

The coastguard crew were grumpily telling the boats to turn around and head back to China, never appearing to realise how ironic it was that until recently they had been desperately trying to convince the Chinese that life was so much better on the capitalist side of the strait. The pleasure cruises were right next to us and turning so fast it was as if their crews were pulling handbrake turns, and the Chinese tourists on board were waving enthusiastically at us and the stony Taiwanese crew on our boat. I actually became a little emotional seeing their eager, excited faces, and the coastguard captain looked at me, baffled, and asked if something was wrong.

I knew they were a symptom of profound change, and the vanguard of a Chinese tourist revolution. Tens, perhaps hundreds, of millions of people across on the mainland were deciding they wanted to do what much of the rest of the world had been doing for ages, and get out and explore. On my journeys since then I have seen an ever-growing number of Chinese tourists just about everywhere.

I watched them for ages, really feeling the joy of people who had rarely had the opportunity to travel, before it was time for us to leave and we headed to the Taiwanese capital.

The city is completely dominated by Taipei 101, then the tallest building in the world. It hadn't fully opened when I visited, and there was still a smell of fresh paint inside. But we were allowed to take a superfast lift to the top, saw a giant ball on a pendulum that was supposed to balance the tower during an earthquake, and then emerged blinking into the light on top of the building, so high up we could see planes flying beneath us.

I loved Taipei. For me it was a great mix of bling and grime, of culture and excess. The city has some of the finest restaurants in the world, but instead of filling ourselves somewhere classy, we went for noodles in a night market which was also selling medical remedies made from honey mixed with cobra blood. A sign in English said: "The snakes sold and cooked at this store are definitely not protected animals. Welcome and taste!" Clearly some other concerned travellers had been there before us.

Taiwanese cities felt like cleaner versions of locations in *Blade Runner*. Neon signs lit skyscrapers and the night market, while girls from the Chinese mainland sat outside obvious brothels.

To give you an idea of the options we would consider as a team when heading somewhere for filming, and the research I would put together as the presenter, I have dug out a document buried on my computer with the title "Taiwan things2do". Four pages long and 2,457 words of scribbled notes in total, it stands up reasonably well to scrutiny many years later, and includes simple notes for me to remember for "PTCs" (pieces to camera, where I look directly down the lens and talk to the viewer):

Mainland China is a one-party state. Taiwan is a functioning democracy. China locks up anybody who threatens Communist party rule. Taiwan is alive with combative politics and a lively free media.

Thoughts about what we could do:

Be good if we could try to show how an advanced breakaway state/unrecognised nation develops and matures: e.g. musicians sing about Taiwan and political repression in the Taiwanese language (which used to be banned!).

We ticked that box when Sen-lun took me to see a Taiwanese boy band, who sang of their pride at being Taiwanese, not ethnic Chinese like their parents.

There were also quick notes on what was changing in Taiwan:

And the first passports with the word Taiwan on the cover have been issued.

Some background stats:

According to an annual poll taken by Taipei's Chengchi University, the proportion of Taiwan's residents who consider themselves exclusively Chinese has plummeted to 10 per cent from 26 per cent in 1992, while the number who think of themselves as exclusively "Taiwanese" has jumped to 42 per cent from 17 per cent.

And the sort of imaginative wish-list things you can only request at short notice if you are filming a documentary for the BBC:

Very keen to go on 1 of Taiwan's 2 combat-ready subs. They're seen as being crucial to defending the island and the US is planning to sell Taiwan more of them — much to China's fury.

My favourite line, however, is the first:

Is it possible for us to meet the President?? Perhaps he could take us for a Taiwanese meal?? Worth a try.

We never managed to wring a meal out of the Taiwanese President, but he did fly us to see a firework concert in Taiwanese Air Force One, then refused to speak to us and dumped us in a muddy field. I still have a couple of souvenir Air Force One sick bags in my van.

We had a series of strange encounters and experiences in Taiwan, but one of the most memorable was visiting what used to be the biggest school in the world, with more than 5,000 pupils. The children would arrive before 8 a.m., clean the school, raise the Taiwanese flag — yes, they do have one — then be drilled like little soldiers and march back to their classes after an outdoor assembly.

Taiwan is a huge success story. After the Second World War it was one of the poorer countries in Asia. In the decades that followed it built a super-high-tech economy and became one of the top twenty economies. Taiwanese firms make 90 per cent of the world's laptops. Its success has been partly built on the back of one of the finest education systems in the world. When I last visited it was ranked fourth in the world for maths teaching and second in the world for science teaching. It is an astonishing achievement, partly down to huge investment in education, and partly down to the quality of the teachers — who all have PhDs, and deserve the bow they are given by children at the start of each lesson, even at primary school.

Children at the school were motivated, and encouraged to be competitive, but they were not robots. They were cheeky and fun, leaping around in front of our camera and gurning into the lens. They knew when they could have fun, and when they had to be serious. So how on earth did the teachers keep them in line?

I asked the head teacher, a surprisingly relaxed and friendly woman in a pink suit who carried two walkie-talkies, and was in charge of maintaining order.

"It's like controlling a line of Taiwanese donkeys," she said, with an honesty that instantly made me smile. "They're all connected to each other by ropes, so you just have to know which one to pull and the rest will follow."

All too soon it was time to leave Taiwan, and come to the end of the *Places That Don't Exist* series. I thought back to my time across the water in mainland China. We had travelled west out of Beijing to visit a section of the Great Wall of China. We puffed our way to the top of a hill on a broad section of steps. It was breathtaking, of course, quite literally. I was amazed by the height of each step, which meant even I had to lift my foot almost to my waist to climb up. Were the ancient Chinese giants? The view out was spectacular, but I was more taken by the view when I turned around, and the words of a guide. "Everyone thinks that the Great Wall was just built to keep bandits out," he said to me. "But the wall was also built to control movement of people, and to try to unify the country within."

That last bit was crucial. For a large part of its history China was split into fiefdoms. For hundreds of years Chinese leaders believed one of their greatest challenges was to keep the country together, and the people, who are mainly Han Chinese but also come from dozens of other ethnic groups, as one. The fear for generations has been that if Taiwan was allowed to declare independence and break from the motherland, then other provinces might try to follow. Only by unifying the people, leaders have said, can China remain strong.

It was a realisation that helped to shape my thoughts about China, a country that I think many of us still get very wrong, labouring under the misconception the Chinese are automatons broken by decades of Communism who do the bidding of their masters almost without question. Our image of them is often still as little more than units of production on a factory line, churning out plastic consumer goods for eager buyers in the West. If we think any more of them it is usually as money-grabbing *nouveau riche*. It is a perception that is completely unfair.

From the first time I visited China I met men and women who were strikingly individual and eccentric. Since China began to open up millions have turned back to interests which reveal their depths. They have become intellectuals, Buddhists, vegans, enthusiastic pet owners and artists. Often it is not easy under the heavy hand of one-party rule, but still culture endures. How could it be any other way when their history stretches back thousands of years? The Communist period is barely a moment in the overall history of an ancient civilisation.

I've had far too many experiences getting slightly drunk with Chinese tourists singing karaoke on ferry boats on the Yangtze, or meeting experts on the architecture of Iceland or the work of Banksy, to find the country anything other than captivating.

I remember one moment when we were in a far-flung part of the country in a city which was rapidly becoming a megalopolis. We were walking back from a distant restaurant, heading for the godforsaken hotel the BBC had booked us into, and I could hear jazz saxophone playing on a radio. We were a bit lost and went around a corner or two and the music became louder and louder. Then I realised it was coming from the basement of an office complex. Idly looking in as we passed, I suddenly saw a security guard sitting inside in front of banks of CCTV screens he was supposed to be monitoring. He was crammed into the cubicle, but he was rocking back in his chair, wearing a pair of *Blues Brothers* sunglasses and playing a polished saxophone like a 1920s Harlem master. It was a perfect travel discovery.

Life has changed spectacularly fast in China, of course — more dramatically and quickly than anyone thought possible. And perhaps the authorities in China are not always the terrifying human rights abusers many of us might imagine. Filming in another remote city we stopped our cars outside a major Buddhist temple. We didn't realise at first but our drivers had parked illegally and were partially blocking the entrance to a fire station. As we stood a short distance away filming the temple a stern policeman appeared, but didn't bash the drivers around with a truncheon. Instead as he was walking towards the vehicles he produced a handy-cam and started filming the parking violation, presumably as evidence for a fine or prosecution. I was surprised. In turn, the drivers, far from being in fear of this agent of the authoritarian state, attempted to stand in front of him and his camera to stop the filming. The interaction was similar to what you might find someone doing to a traffic warden in the UK.

I am not saying the Chinese police are representatives of a benevolent state, or could give lessons in community policing to a Swedish village cop. But I think we still swiftly criticise China without adequately acknowledging the country has lifted more people out of poverty in the last generation than has ever been achieved anywhere in the world. By contrast I think India, for example, often gets an easy ride despite being a place of appalling poverty and suffering. I have seen situations in India that would result in howls of outrage if they were happening in China and result in aid appeals if they were happening in sub-Saharan Africa.

As we were getting a parking ticket in China next to the temple, despite the loud protestations of our drivers, I noticed a large permanent sign on the wall nearby which our translator (when he had also stopped shouting at the police officers) interpreted for us: "I'm your district police chief, and if you have a problem please get in touch." The police chief was a woman, as were both her deputies, who were also pictured underneath. Three female law enforcement officers in charge of the borough of a massive city, complete with their names, direct phone numbers as well as their email addresses. That police plaque was not evidence of a faceless bureaucracy. It might not be Denmark, which remains one of my benchmarks for an inclusive and well-run society, but it was hardly *1984*.

Yet there are of course many lines that cannot be crossed in China. You certainly wouldn't want to be an opposition activist, or a bookseller offering anti-Party material. Amnesty International is clear: "Freedom of expression is severely restricted in China and anyone who speaks out against the authorities faces harassment, arrest and detention. Torture is widespread across the country and justice is elusive for many." Investigating corruption is forbidden, as is questioning the rule of the Party or China's ownership of Taiwan.

Back in the mid-2000s in Beijing before heading to Taiwan I took some time out to wander around the magnificent Forbidden City, which was home to the emperors and their households for almost 500 years. Then I did something I try never to do in my programmes: I went to see a government man in a suit.

"Taiwan has never been a country," said the senior official, who had the task of leading Chinese policy on Taiwan. "It is still not a country. The Chinese people will not allow Taiwan to be separated from the Motherland. The Chinese people will safeguard their sovereignty and territorial integrity and we have the ability to break any intention to make Taiwan independent."

It was couched in a bit of official-speak, but not much. The sentiment was strong. But how far would China go? I wondered. I asked him whether the Chinese government was concerned that a conflict between China and Taiwan might involve the United States.

"I don't believe the American people will be prepared to spill their blood for Taiwanese independence," he said.

For many years Chinese plans for the invasion of Taiwan were jokingly referred to as "the million-man swim", because the Chinese navy was so weak compared to the Taiwanese forces. In the last decade, however, China has upgraded and rebuilt a powerful military machine, complete with aircraft carrier and submarines.

Chinese policy back in the mid-2000s was to get Taiwan back, and it remains the policy now. Nobody should be under any illusions. China is still ready and willing to go to war over Taiwan.

Visiting places that don't exist left me wide-eyed. They are quite literally off the map, with eccentric customs, the energy of upstarts, and with patriotic locals desperate for the rest of the world to recognise their existence. It had been a series of incredible journeys and adventures.

Going to Taiwan, in particular, made me realise I could make a travelogue exploring the light and shade of life almost anywhere. It wasn't a style that only worked in a country that was dark, poverty-stricken or at war.

We just needed to find moments that were quirky and countered a prejudice or revealed something telling about a place. Often that could come from a jokey interaction with someone. But it could also come from something I spotted and identified to the camera. In Taipei, for example, I realised that telephone junction boxes were works of art: local artists had been commissioned to paint murals on the street-side green boxes. A place that can think about beautifying street furniture is clearly at an advanced stage of development.

Taiwan might be better run than Switzerland, but there was still darkness to explore, as there is everywhere. Wherever I go now part of my aim is to look for the alternative to whatever stereotype dominates the perception of a place. This could be something positive or even fun in a troubled country, perhaps playing *kabaddi* in poor Bangladesh; or the opposite in an affluent country, such as discovering a dark rubbish island in the otherwise paradise world of the Maldives. The point is to overturn preconceptions, starting with my own.

Taiwan worked for me as a destination for a documentary because I explored the place with my eyes open. If I had gone there just looking at history, or landscapes, there

339

would have been fewer dimensions to the journey. Getting off the beaten track and learning more about the places we visit — both the light and the shade — always makes for a more interesting experience, a more rounded adventure. I don't think travellers need to ignore darkness. I haven't been anywhere where people won't talk about issues or problems. For most people it's cathartic to share with outsiders.

Other travellers might not be mad keen to copy some of my hairier journeys, but I still think many could benefit from injecting a few elements into their next holiday. Apart from exploring the light and the shade, my trips have been memorable, for me at least, because they combine adventure with a clear plan and destination.

More of us should try turning a break into a proper adventure with a healthy dose of purpose and meaning. It almost guarantees a lifetime of memories. You could follow a river from source to sea or start a trip in one location and then head to another, exploring along the way. Taking chances is often where the best memories are, and the richest rewards in life come from a bit of risk-taking. We can all benefit from pushing ourselves, our partners, friends or family, out of our respective comfort zones. On a holiday that can be as simple as not wasting your life lying horizontal by a swimming pool. Personally, on any trip I try to push myself a little and follow a simple set of rules: go to strange places, take chances, ask questions, do things that are exciting, eat strange foreign food, and dive into the culture of the world and embrace risk.

A proper adventure is now more possible than ever before. You can go almost anywhere and do almost anything. We are often sold a vision of the world as a dangerous and frightening place. In reality the world is friendly and astonishingly hospitable. And the further you go from the tourist traps the warmer the welcome and the more authentic and unforgettable the experience. Some people think the "Golden Age" of travel was when steam wafted from trains, crystal clinked in dining cars, and air stewardesses wore long white gloves. I think the real Golden Age of travel is actually now, when it is cheaper and safer than ever. It's also a guaranteed way of tingling your senses, enhancing your life and gifting you a huge stock of memories, encounters and experiences.

CHAPTER
TWENTY

Exorcism at the Monastery

I came back from filming *Places That Don't Exist* and began plotting a new adventure, this time around the equator. It was a much longer, more ambitious journey than I had attempted before, and the first programme we shot did not end well. I spent a couple of weeks sleeping and recovering from malaria, and a couple more considering whether to continue the journey. Anya and I talked about it not just in terms of career options, but from the perspective of my health. I'd had a brush with death and I felt I would never be the same again. She wanted me to take at least a moment to consider the future.

As I mooched around, friends and family came to see me, offering commiserations about my illness, and then ribbed me about my trips as if they were holidays.

I started talking about the hardship, the dangers, and the endless pieces of heavy camera kit which daily need to be lugged in and out of four-wheel drives and dodgy hotels. "These journeys really aren't holidays," I said earnestly.

Then I regaled them with tales of sleepless nights in godforsaken villages, scuzzy hotels and even unmade beds in part-time brothels. I offered up a couple of recent experiences, like the joy of sleeping head to toe with colleagues in a tiny African hut, where the smell from our pile of unwashed sweaty clothes was enough to ward off all local insect life.

I moved on to the Groundhog Day experience of eating identical meagre meals together with three colleagues day after day and week after week. I droned on about one of the most difficult aspects of filming while travelling: the fact we're constantly on the move. On every journey I make there are always half a dozen places where I would love to pause to savour the surroundings. Filming in Bukhara, for example, I would have given anything for a chance to relax for a few days and explore. If I was travelling for pleasure I could simply have decided to halt the trip and unwind. But on filming trips we have the briefest of stops to shoot, then we're back on the road.

I say "road". On many trips, roads were often just connected potholes. Travelling for months meant I was spending large chunks of my life being bounced around in small cars. The result was backache and spinal pain that earned me a loyalty card from my local osteopath. Finally, I would tell friends and family about the bureaucracy and paperwork. It's an aspect of the journey we never show on TV, simply because it is hideously boring. But the meetings we have to attend and forms we have to complete just to be allowed into a country to film are enough to try the patience of a particularly calm nun.

But who was I kidding? Filming trips certainly aren't a holiday, but they are still a glorious treat. Filming for the BBC opens doors. I have seen and done things and gone to places most folk can only imagine. I have met some of the most incredible and inspiring people on the planet. Filming a TV series while on a journey is one of the most spectacular ways to travel. It is enlightening, entertaining, and it provides a purpose and reason for adventure.

How could I turn my back on the madness? How could I turn my back on the light and shade? Even the first part of *Equator* had been magnificent. I spoke to the BBC about my illness and what should happen next. A lot of time and money had been spent planning *Equator* and they were keen for the journey to continue. But they were still concerned for my health. It was up to me. I thought about it briefly, but I knew there was no way I could turn my back on a chance of adventure and experiences, or the near-guarantee of meeting people I would remember forever.

Within two months of returning home in the aftermath of malaria, I was flying back south from London to continue my journey following the equator eastwards across Africa. It would become one of the most humbling journeys of my life.

I felt fragile and mortal. I had no idea if I would sicken again, and I was flying to the Democratic Republic of Congo, one of the most dangerous countries in the world, a nation the size of Western Europe, where medical cover was extremely limited.

But the team were brilliant. Sophie Todd, the producer-director who helped save my life in Gabon, had agreed to take me back on the road. A tough and adventurous sort ready for a challenge, Sophie was joined by an assistant producer called Jamie Berry, a great shooter who was young but enthusiastic and rarely fazed.

We arrived into Kinshasa, capital of the DRC, and together met up with Brian Green, a South African war cameraman who had flown in from his home in Johannesburg. Straight from the off it was clear Brian was a bit of a card, in the best possible way. Witty, brave and resourceful, Brian had dodged bullets and artillery shells during the Bosnian War, was marvellous at using humour to dilute tricky situations and would amuse us all by slipping into the kitchens of slow cafés to help cook the food when we were in a rush. He owned a shopping centre in South Africa but loved the excitement of an adventure and the chance to record a moment of history.

We had a briefing chat in Kinshasa with officials from the United Nations, who seemed determined to put the fear of God into us. They explained there was still fighting in the east of the DRC. Following the equator would take us through an active conflict zone, but first we went north towards the small city of Mbandaka in a tiny Cessna Caravan plane flown by a missionary called Dan from Colorado.

Flying through blue skies we tracked along the vast Congo River, a mirror for low, fluffy cotton-wool clouds. It was just a tiny corner of the DRC, the largest country in sub-Saharan Africa, but it was breathtaking. Endless green forest stretched in every direction, broken only occasionally by remote villages and dirt tracks. My eyes were glued to the view, my mind following every slope to a peak and every curve along the river. Everything was fascinating; everything was wondrous. To be a stranger in a strange world such as this, as travellers have for thousands of years, keeps wonder alive. It exercises astonishment, even awe.

I looked out of the window to the west, towards Congo-Brazzaville, a separate country, and also crossed by the equator line. The Ebola outbreak in Congo-Brazzaville had actually worsened since I was in Gabon, and we had no option but to avoid the country altogether and land on the outskirts of Mbandaka in DRC. The moment I stepped off the plane I knew I was back on the equator. I had forgotten how hot it could be. The sun was merciless.

By this point in the mid-2000s I had explored several dozen countries, recognised or otherwise. But everywhere new still felt different and surprising. Each country still does today. I have never lost the sense I am doing something exceptional. Perhaps the reality of my past is part of the reason. Hardly travelling when I was younger, let alone exploring exotically, helps ensure these experiences feel remarkable as an adult. I have never felt jaded. On each new journey I sense possibility, discovery, and most especially in a country like DRC, enormous challenge.

Emery Makumeno, a wonderful, warm and softly spoken fixer, was to be our guide and translator in the

DRC. Somehow he had managed to find us four-wheel-drive vehicles in one of the poorest areas of Africa, and we set off to find a place to stay.

Mbandaka, like the rest of the country, was desperately, appallingly poor. There were hundreds of people walking and some cycling on the dirt roads, but very few cars, and those were mostly UN vehicles travelling in convoys. There were no hotels to speak of, and no running water or public electricity.

The DRC was, and remains, in a desperate state. Two wars had ravaged the country. They were often described as civil wars, but they involved forces from nine countries and perhaps two dozen armed groups. They were Africa's world wars. The death toll was simply astonishing. By the time I visited in the mid-2000s at least 4 million people had died since 1998.

We stopped in the street in central Mbandaka and I looked around. I had been focused too closely on my own selfish recovery and personal journey. Suddenly the reality of where I was hit home. There was a dirt road, busy with people walking and cycling past, balancing metal pots on their heads and long pieces of thin timber on shoulders. To the sides were old one-storey concrete buildings and shanty huts, in front of which weary women ran basic stalls selling vegetables, clothes and single-use sachets of washing powder and shampoo.

It might sound perfectly pleasant, but there is rarely anything romantic about poverty. Most people had next to nothing. Children looked ragged and malnourished.

The country was staggering from crisis to crisis. Some there told us it was cursed.

Yet there were few obvious scars of conflict. No bullet holes like I had seen everywhere in Somalia. Often the weapons of choice during the conflict in the DRC, as neighbouring ethnic groups attacked and hacked at each other, were machetes.

We found rooms in a spooky, semi-abandoned monastery. At dusk we lit candles next to our wooden beds and incense coils to drive away mosquitoes. I dug out my travel kit, covered myself in natural repellent, screwed my mozzie net into the ceding and unrolled a black plastic sheet and sleeping mat. Then I grabbed my head torch and went off to find a toilet.

If you really want to feel like you've travelled and experienced a completely different culture, you need to bid farewell to bleach and flushing loos. A bit of personal discomfort actually helps to create priceless travel experiences guaranteed to linger in the memory. Travelling abroad and realising it is all a bit mucky helps put our own lives into context and reminds us how lucky we are to have running water at home.

But the toilet in the monastery was astonishing. Round the side of the main building I followed the remains of a path to a derelict outhouse with a small platform and a huge pit. The fumes were so overwhelming and so combustible I nearly collapsed into the black swamp.

For sheer danger that experience competes strongly with a coastal village in Indonesia I reached later on my equator journey. I was shown to a drop toilet in a small outhouse made of rotting branches perched precariously over the sea. It was low tide, and as I attempted to let nature take its course an entire pack of enormous, ravenous pigs fought their way up through the hole in the floor, their sharp teeth snapping at my undercarriage. Children watching outside giggled, but I very nearly lost more than my dignity.

I can hardly complain. Experiencing and briefly enduring the reality of life has been an education. That night at the monastery scores of local villagers began to gather in the overgrown grounds. At first we thought it was for a church service. Then the darkness was pierced by a series of bloodcurdling screams, flaming torches were lit, and a terrifying exorcism began. It all came as something of a shock. We wanted to start filming.

"No, that would not be a good idea," said Emery calmly. "I think we should try to find a way of locking our doors."

When the sun rose every one of the villagers had vanished. Sophie and Jamie did some yoga in the grounds, which made all of us feel much better, before we set off for a community on the equator that had suffered during Congo's endless fighting. I wanted to see what life was like in the aftermath of the deadliest conflict on the planet since World War Two.

Beyond Mbandaka we passed an old colonial mansion that had long since succumbed to the jungle. Surrounded by grassland, trees had taken root in verandas before twisting around pillars and porticoes to break through tiles on the roof. It was close to the

Botanical Garden of Eala, once a lush and tended reserve home to thousands of trees, flowers, shrubs and bushes. But that was long ago. Many of the trees had been felled for firewood and what was left was neglected and astonishingly overgrown. Standing by the entrance track the reserve had an end-of-the-world feel, as if civilisation had vanished and left just a few survivors.

I spotted a lone figure walking slowly towards us. He was carrying a bundle of thin pieces of firewood across his stooping shoulders. Brian grabbed the camera to get a shot of him approaching. He was barefoot, tiny, ancient, and wearing just a ragged pair of old knee-length shorts. I sidled up to him as he drew level.

"How far have you come?" I said to him as Emery translated.

"About four kilometres."

"That's a long way."

"Yes," he replied through Emery. "And I still have a way to go yet."

Emery and I helped him with his load so he could rest for a couple of minutes.

He said his name was Ngozi. He was so skinny his ribs were visible. His arms looked wizened and wasted.

"Thank you," he said, as he shook my hand. "*Merci beaucoup.*"

"It's heavy," I told him. "It was heavy for me and all I did was lift it down from your shoulders."

"It is heavy," he said, stretching his old limbs, "but that's the price I pay in order to survive."

We sat on a rock and he laid the machete he used to cut the wood across his knees. Bright-eyed and smiling, he seemed completely unperturbed by our presence or the camera. It was as if he had been expecting us. Like it was fate our paths had crossed.

"Do you mind if I ask you a cheeky question?" I said to him.

"Not at all."

"How old are you, Ngozi?"

He smiled. "Sixty-eight. I look older because I work so hard. I'm not strong any more. Carrying so much wood makes me weak."

"What do you do with the wood?"

"I pick it from the forest and then I take it to the market and I sell it. Sometimes it can take a whole day, working from dawn to dusk. Everything I get for my survival comes from the forest."

I asked him how much money he would get for the wood he had been carrying. He thought for just a moment. Then told me he would earn perhaps 400 francs per day. Emery did the calculations, checked with Ngozi, then turned to me. It was roughly 42 pence. Per day. I was horrified, but I tried to make sure it didn't show.

"It's not enough to buy the food I need," said Ngozi thoughtfully. "But it's all I can get for the wood. This is what I have to do in order to support myself."

I shook his hand again and thanked him for talking to us. It was just a brief moment. But it lives with me. How could it not? There is hardly a day that goes past when I do not think of Ngozi or the other humbling

351

souls I met on that trip. This was the journey, more than any before or since, that helped convince me of both the personal value of an adventure, which at its best should challenge, enlighten and fulfil, and the merit of taking a camera to a remote part of the world.

Capturing a sense of how our fellow humans, our brothers and sisters, struggle to survive in parts of the world enduring conflict and poverty can be a potent reminder of reality for those watching in less blighted corners. I still believe it has value. Even years after this series aired I would be stopped by a viewer who would sidle close or put their hand on my arm to convey the sharing of an experience and tell me they also remembered Ngozi. A young woman once sought me out to say she watched this journey on the television, changed her university course to study remote medicine and was about to become the only doctor in a faraway refugee camp. She was telling me the ripple of the programmes had an effect. Making a television series is surely not enough, but at least it is something.

Emery wanted us to see a village called Ngamba-Kinshasa, where a school teacher was waiting to talk to us. To get there we had to journey up the Congo River. We stopped at a busy jetty, watched in amazement as a man walked past with a small crocodile on his head, then hired a long dugout canoe fixed with an outboard motor.

We set off with a breeze coming off the muddy water and locals bathing close to the banks. They were waving and chanting as we passed them, so I waved back.

"They're taunting you, Simon," said Emery, laughing.

"What are they saying, then?"

"It's a song. *White man — your breath stinks.*"

We pulled alongside a huge barge. In a country with only 300 miles of paved roads, the river was the lifeline and main thoroughfare, and barges carried basic trade and people wanting to move from place to place. This barge was completely rammed with travellers. It looked like an entire village was living aboard, under tarpaulins strung up on poles.

"Have you done that, Emery?" I asked him, smiling away rather naively as if nothing could be more pleasant than a barge trip on the Congo.

"Travelled on the barges? Of course, many times."

I gazed across the water to where the people on one massive barge were all but spilling over the sides and asked him how long he would have to wait until a barge was ready to leave.

"Minimum is a month," Emery said.

"A month?" I was incredulous. My smile vanished.

"Maximum is three months."

I couldn't believe it.

"Conditions are terrible," he told me. "You can have four or five hundred people and only two toilets for all of them."

I was silent for a while after that. The DRC often left me numb. You can read about a place as much as you like, but only by going and seeing can you truly appreciate both the beauty and the tragedy. The DRC had both in epic quantities.

It was explorer Henry Morton Stanley, he of "Dr Livingstone, I presume" fame, who really helped begin the subjugation of the people of the Congo basin. Under the colonial rule of King Leopold II of Belgium 5–10 million people died in what is now the DRC. Some historians argue it is the hidden holocaust.

Independence from Belgium was no salvation. The country set sail on its own with just a couple of dozen graduates in the entire country and not a single person with a university degree in law, medicine or engineering. The Belgians had prevented almost anyone from getting an education.

Just as you can't run a country if all the educated people leave, so the DRC then floundered. A dictator called Mobutu Sese Seko took over, ran a kleptocracy for thirty-two years and deliberately didn't build any roads so nobody could attack him in the capital. He milked the country for personal wealth and created a culture that enrichment through the state was standard. Corruption remains endemic.

Today there is enough fertile land in the DRC to feed the entire continent and enough hydroelectric potential to power most of it as well. But the DRC is astonishingly poor.

Finally, we arrived by canoe into the village of Ngamba-Kinshasa, a simple settlement of wood-and-thatch houses built on stilts, and pulled our boat up onto the bank, next to fishermen who were mending small nets using random pieces of string.

Jose, a young teacher from the community, took us to see the basic school. He said he hadn't been paid by the

354

state in months but was still trying to give some kind of education to the next generation.

"There's no money, but I do the best I can," he said. He led me through a church which doubled as a school. The floor was open planking with no desks, just rough pews for kids to sit on.

"There are no books," he admitted sadly, "no tables where they can write, they just rest the paper on their thighs."

"How many children are there?" I asked him.

"Sixty. They're split into different forms, first and second because of the different ages. I place one form on this side, another on this side and so on. We have nothing, and we need everything, blackboard, books, chalk."

We visited Jose's home where he and his wife were not only trying to raise three children of their own, but three more children of family members who had died of disease, including malaria. Jose's youngest son Johnson, who was just a year old, had also contracted the disease. I felt my heart wrench. There were no German doctors who could rush round to see them.

This was the harsh reality of poverty, corruption, and life in the DRC. An astonishing 60 per cent of children were dying before their fifth birthday. Even those who survived into their teens faced enormous challenges from afflictions such as malaria. Life expectancy for a man was just forty-two years.

We flew further along the Congo river with the help of Dan from the Mission Aviation Fellowship (MAF).

355

With his crisp white shirt, moustache and pre-flight clipboard checks, Dan seemed slightly out of place in the jungle. I asked him whether he felt he had a calling to be in the DRC. He laughed and said if he didn't there would be no reason to be there. "I'm not getting paid enough to do this," he added.

I have always been taken by a line used by Archbishop Desmond Tutu about the arrival of Christianity on the continent: "When the missionaries came to Africa they had the Bible and we had the land. They said 'Let us pray.' We closed our eyes. When we opened them, we had the Bible and they had the land."

Even in recent decades other missionaries in other parts of the continent have done wicked and appalling things in Africa, reportedly only agreeing to help people in one area if they would be tattooed with a cross on their forehead, ensuring their annihilation when persecutors returned to town. But MAF pilots seemed completely selfless, shuttling missionaries but also lepers, cancer patients, the injured and anyone needing urgent help around the DRC and other areas of the world lacking infrastructure and roads. You can book a flight via their website. Dan didn't lecture or hector us about faith. But he did slip a couple of leaflets into my bag.

Dan was one of the few people prepared to fly into the east of the DRC despite the ongoing conflict.

"What's the situation like there at the moment?" I asked as I sat in the co-pilot's seat with grasslands and waterways unfolding beneath me.

"Flare-ups," he said. "One after the other, there's continual fighting. The Ugandans keep coming across the border. There's the Hutu and the Tutsis who are always fighting it out. The cattle people fight with the farmers. It's anarchy."

DRC was a collapsed state. The United Nations was the life support.

Dan flew us to a UN base just north of the equator and we landed on tarmac surrounded by a multitude of helicopters used to ferry thousands of troops around the east. The UN was running the largest peacekeeping operation in the world in DRC to prevent the country slipping back into a devastating regional war. They were trying to disarm well-armed militia groups and also train the nascent Congolese army, which still had a terrible reputation.

As we drove to our lodgings we passed a troop of Congolese soldiers exercising in the middle of town. Dressed all in black they looked more than a little menacing. People moved swiftly out of their way. Emery summed up the local feeling.

"It's all right in the middle of town here," he said. "Lots of people around and the UN soldiers are everywhere." His voice was low as if he was worried someone might overhear. "In the middle of the bush, though — if we met them there — I wouldn't be anything like as happy."

"Why?"

At first, he seemed a little reluctant to answer. "It's common knowledge. The army, or some of them at least, rob the population."

Much of the fighting had been about gold and diamonds. The DRC was and is fantastically rich in mineral deposits. I wanted to visit a gold mine, but all the roads were blocked or too dangerous even with an armed escort. But the United Nations agreed to take us on a UN helicopter flight to a mine. A detachment of Pakistani soldiers came along for our protection.

As we came in to land I could see more soldiers in pale-blue UN helmets guarding the strip to make sure we didn't come under attack from militia groups with rocket-propelled grenades. We lurched through the bush in the back of Land Rovers to reach a lucrative mine which had changed hands on five separate occasions during the war.

It was an astonishing sight. In a vast pit of mud and water, perhaps a mile long by half a mile wide, hundreds and hundreds of men, women and children toiled, up to their waists and often deeper. The work was often impossibly hard. Passing heavy pans of sludge and mud from hand to hand they would then tip it out and purify it over a water bed padded with carpet that would hold small flecks of gold.

There was very little machinery. Almost everything was done by hand. The mine was under the control of a powerful local militia which charged miners a daily fee to work there. If anyone found any gold the militia would then take a hefty commission. It all looked, sounded and smelt absolutely horrific.

I asked one of the miners whether he thought gold had been a blessing or a curse for the DRC.

His answer chastened me. He said that people were poor, but at least with the mine they could earn a little money. Without the gold, he said, life would be unbearable.

I took a photograph in that mine of a youngster standing on the rim, in front of a vast hole in which tiny bodies look like insects. I have the photo on the wall in my office. I see it every day, and it reminds me not just of the humbling endurance of the Congolese, or their apparently eternal suffering, but also how sheer bloody lucky I am to not be working for twelve hours a day, seven days a week, up to my waist or my neck in sucking mud and filth.

The Pakistani UN force invited us to their base for dinner that night. It was a matter of honour for them that we ate well.

There was no alcohol on offer, of course, but we talked late into the night and they spoke with horror and wonder about the state of the DRC. Men from the deserts of Balochistan, they said they were astonished to discover when they arrived that people in the region were starving.

"This is a place where you drop a seed in the ground and by the next year there is a tree," said one captain. Gradually the Pakistanis realised they were dealing with an entire society that had been traumatised by endless and apocalyptic conflict. People had lost touch with fundamental skills and leadership was completely absent. Refugees began gathering around their base begging for help and advice, so men from the deserts of

Pakistan began offering crash courses in smallholding. By the time I visited there were vegetable stalls lining the roads near their base, and malnutrition rates, in their area at least, had fallen dramatically.

Each time I have visited a UN military contingent they have gone out of their way to both protect and feed us. Elsewhere in the DRC a contingent of Moroccan UN soldiers were especially proud of their food, and had spices, dried apricots, fruit and meat flown in weekly. "Our own special aid flight," one of their senior officers said with a smile. The best UN food I have eaten was, perhaps a little predictably, a meal with an Italian force. They had flown in not just fresh garlic and vegetables, but pasta, cheese, wine and their own chef.

But a posting with the UN in the DRC was no cushy job. When I visited in the mid-2000s there were 17,000 UN troops working not just as peacekeepers, but peace enforcers, authorised to fight warring factions. Dozens of UN soldiers had been killed and they were taking no chances when out on patrol.

The next day we headed out with the Pakistanis on a patrol that is often described as "force projection", a show of power designed to intimidate enemies and reassure friends. Driving around flanked by UN armoured cars with mounted machine guns was nerve-wracking. Attacks with RPGs were still worryingly common.

We were taken to a district where an astonishing 50,000 had died in fighting between different ethnic groups battling over land that one side wanted to use for crops and the other to graze their cattle. Whole communities had been wiped out. The UN dropped us off in the village of Nizi, where locals from the Hema tribe told me they had been attacked by the neighbouring Lendus. The village chief took Emery and me to see a mass grave where victims had been buried.

"How many are there?" I asked as I looked out over a forest of wooden crosses.

"One hundred and fourteen. All killed in one attack." His eyes narrowed at the memory. "They were mostly women and children."

"How did it happen?" I asked him.

He took a moment before he responded. "Early morning, just as the sun was coming up they attacked the village with machetes." He pointed into the distance, towards the Lendu village from where the attackers had appeared. "They massacred women and children, hacked them down wherever they came upon them."

An older man appeared, clearly traumatised. He struggled to contain his emotions as he described the attack. He escaped with his life, but his arms and hands bore the scars of machetes and his right ear and head had been split with a heavy blow.

"They tried to hack me to death," he told me. "I don't know how I survived."

"How many members of your family did you lose?"

"All of them. They killed my wife and all my children. There is no one left, the Lendus took everyone from me."

Emery and I were both deeply moved by the suffering we heard in the village. We had a quiet hug after meeting that poor man, before we headed back into the town of Bunia in search of a reflective beer. On the dirt road outside our guesthouse was a bar with a sign at the door showing a crossed-out sub-machine gun and the legend "Pas d'armes / No weapons". It was perfect. We sat outside and Emery, as decent a human being as you will find on this planet, told me he was optimistic about the future. He showed me his voter registration card for upcoming elections and said he would guard it with his life.

Emery had faith in the democratic process. In the years that followed the President of the DRC, Joseph Kabila, secured repeat terms in office in 2006 and 2011, then refused to leave when his term expired in December 2016. Further fighting has erupted in the north-east, with more suffering and tens of thousands forced to flee. Meanwhile in Mbandaka there have been Ebola outbreaks even within the town. It seems the people of the DRC must continue to endure the endless consequences of climate, colonial rule, conflict and sapping corruption.

CHAPTER
TWENTY-ONE

The Open Prison

We flew east to Uganda, and then travelled on overland to Kenya, the most stable African country on the equator, where my guide Michael Kaloki has since become a firm favourite on repeated trips. Keep your ears open for his name, because he often pops up on the radio. Tall, thoughtful, and the sort of bloke who keeps a pen in his pocket, partly to chew and partly to make notes on anything that interests him, Michael is also one of Kenya's (unsurprisingly few) ice-carving champions.

"How on earth did you discover ice-carving?" I asked him when another colleague mentioned his slightly eccentric skill. Michael remains much too modest to brag.

"I was a journalism student in Canada," he said, "and I happened to see the winter carnival in Toronto." Michael was captivated by enormous, glistening, almost transparent sculptures. Back in Kenya he persuaded a friend who sculpted more traditionally in stone and wood to turn to ice and they found tools to use on small blocks they produced from home freezers. Eventually they were allowed to use a walk-in freezer at a hotel in Nairobi to practise, and Michael has since represented Kenya at ice festivals in Canada, Finland and in a competition on the sidelines of the Turin Winter Olympics.

With Michael leading us, we set off across Kenya, keeping our eyes peeled for anything odd or interesting that might be happening. We didn't have to go far. Michael heard about a village close to the equator that was holding a weekend festival. Some traditional circumcisers would be attending. The rite was performed in Kenya on some boys aged around twelve as part of their transition to manhood. I wasn't sure if I was looking forward to it or not, but we tracked along the equator until we were driving through the outskirts of the community, and we found huge bulls being marshalled through the streets by groups of men wielding sticks, clubs and long spears. Obviously Brian, as an intrepid war cameraman, was out of our vehicle in a shot, racing towards the action. He was carrying a 14-kilogram camera on his shoulder, but I still struggled to keep up. We managed to get in front of the bulls and I asked Michael what on earth was going on.

"It's a bull fight," he said.

We made our way beyond a series of broken-down buildings to a spacious patch of grass that seemed to form the bull-fighting arena. The animals looked confused and not even slightly itching for a fight. One guy appeared to be baiting his bull with a pair of hand-held bells that resembled maracas.

"He's psyching him up," Michael said as my eyes took in the scene. Another bull was half hidden in a crowd of chanting men.

At that point a man wearing a long pink dress and a gorilla mask pulled me into the throng, past another bloke who had what appeared to be a dead rat on his head.

"Can someone explain what the hell is going on?" I said somewhat plaintively.

Michael came puffing towards me and said that it was the local tradition for people at bull fights to wear animal skins: their costumes were supposed to protect them. I raised a cynical eyebrow, but then the gorilla-man drew me towards two bulls that were being pushed closer together to lock horns.

"How do you know who wins?" I shouted over the chaos to gorilla-man.

"Eh?" He could barely hear me.

"How do you know who wins?"

"When one of the bulls runs off."

As he was speaking the contest came to an abrupt end. A giant black-and-white bull saw off a brown bull, which turned tail and ran with everyone whooping and chasing after it. It was, I should point out, nothing like a Spanish bull fight where razor-sharp spears are thrust into an agitated beast. The Kenyan version is nothing to celebrate, in my view, but was still a much less violent affair. Two bulls would push and shove at each other for a moment or two, and then one would run away. That was it. The crowd, many of whom were drunk or at least jolly, seemed much more at risk.

I watched as the owner of the winning bull was hoisted onto shoulders and carried around the arena and onto the road. A few minutes later we had a quick chat. He was clearly delighted at the prospect of a victory payout.

"The loser gets a little too," he said. "In the old days the winner would get a sheep and the loser would still get a cockerel."

"It's just a bit of country fun really," said Michael with a smile. So long as nobody gets seriously hurt.

Amid all the chaos Michael spotted one of the circumcisers we were supposed to be meeting — a young guy wearing a brown shirt, an animal skin and a massive wig, with his face and arms painted with leopard spots.

"Seriously, Michael?"

"That's him."

"Would you trust him with your todger?" I said to Brian. "I wouldn't."

Just a moment later another of the bulls turned during a fight and raced off through the crowd, catching a young man on his leg. Chaos turned to bedlam.

People were attempting to drive off the bull with shouts and chants as another man with a megaphone tried to marshal the crowd.

"Can someone please put the boy into a vehicle and take him to hospital?" he begged. The boy was bleeding from a loosely tied bandage.

"What's happened?" I asked one of the men carrying him.

"He's broken his leg."

We had the only suitable car, a large four-wheel-drive vehicle used for game-spotting on safaris, so Michael intervened and volunteered our transport.

366

And that is how, ten minutes later, I found myself in the surreal situation of sitting in the back of a makeshift ambulance with a lad called Magnus who had been injured by a rampaging bull, a Kenyan ice-carving champion, a South African war cameraman and two knife-wielding traditional circumcisers dressed in animal skins.

Michael had dragged the circumcisers along with us on the way to the hospital, and they helped us lift the lad out onto a hospital gurney. Rather ironically, he was the son of the chairman of the bullfighting association. Nurses in starched uniforms took him away, and we went for a chat in a bar with the circumcisers. The older of the two was called Thomas and he brandished a rusty-looking blade as he explained the procedure. I listened intently, sitting with my hands fisted in my lap and a grimace on my face.

"Thomas, that sounds really painful."

"That's how he becomes a man," the circumciser assured me. "Then he can sit with the other men."

"Are you very busy?" I said. "Do you do the procedure a lot?"

He nodded. "We can circumcise a hundred boys an hour."

"A hundred?" I said. "Don't they mind you working so quickly?"

"That's the way it's done. You can become crazy."

Now I was really mind-blown. "What do you mean?" I said, shaking my head with a strained smile. "What do you mean, you can become crazy?"

"There is singing, it's frantic." Thomas was wild-eyed. "It gets into your head. You're in a frenzy and just continue to cut, cut, cut."

Legs crossed, I'd heard enough. We gave the circumcisers a lift home, then drove on along the equator towards Kenya's Lake Nakuru National Park. It was said to be home to the most fabulous bird spectacle in the world. How could we resist?

The lake itself is relatively small and shallow, but that helps to keep the water warm all year round, which feeds the growth of algae, which in turn is the major draw for a vast population of flamingos.

As we hopped out of our vehicles we were met with an almost perfect filming moment. Brian was thrilled. I was in raptures. In the foreground were buffalo and rhino, even a hyena trotting along with a bird in its mouth for breakfast. Behind them, around them, above them and almost everywhere, in fact, were perhaps a million flamingos which had gathered in huge numbers at the lake edge but then seemed to reach right across the water like a scattering of pink petals.

This was the Kenya travellers wanted to see; this was wildlife and landscape in all its splendour.

We drove up to a vantage point over the lake called Baboon Cliff, which gifted a panoramic view of the lake, but also gave me a series of understandings and insights that inform me to this day.

Thousands of photographs have been taken from Baboon Cliff, almost all of them showing the wildlife of the park. Documentaries have been shot in Nakuru showing animals roaming majestically free. Indeed, down below I watched a giraffe out for a stroll around the edge of the lake, its stilt-length legs looking as though they were moving in slow motion.

But turn eyes and cameras just slightly to the north, and there in clear sight is the busy town of Nakuru, a home to more than 300,000 people.

I was stunned at the proximity of park and people. And at that moment I saw through the fantasies and illusions of advertisers and documentary makers, who for years with their careful shots and photographs have peddled an idea that Lake Nakuru and much of the planet is still properly wild. A bubble suddenly popped in my head.

At first glance Lake Nakuru might appear to be a wilderness, but in reality it was a managed park, controlled by humans and at risk from humans, who were right at its borders.

It was another moment where the journey became an education. I was learning every hour of every day on the road. Even here, while watching a giraffe out for a morning amble.

Countless times in the years since I have been confronted by the reality that we have been lied to for decades. By advertisers? Well, that's hardly surprising. But documentary makers have also gone to extraordinary lengths to create wildlife porn that bears no relation to reality.

While filming in Madagascar a few years after travelling around the equator I visited Berenty, a tiny wildlife reserve that has featured in numerous nature documentaries and become synonymous with iconic lemurs. Unique to Madagascar, lemurs are the descendants of primates that travelled across the Indian Ocean from the mainland millions of years ago on rafts or logs. They are stunning and delightful creatures loved by all. Documentaries about them are hugely successful and sold around the world. Chances are, if you have seen a documentary about lemurs filmed in Madagascar, then it was at least part-shot in Berenty, even right around the offices, bungalows and restaurant of the reserve, with cameramen straining to keep the buildings out of shot.

The founders of Berenty cleared huge areas of forest and left just a token sanctuary that now provides habitat for a small number of lemurs. The reserve is only the size of a London park, and is surrounded by a huge expanse of agricultural land. When I visited, tens of thousands of acres around Berenty were being used to grow sisal, some of it apparently destined to become environmentally friendly packaging for Europe.

Yet often TV programmes about places like Berenty or Nakuru completely fail to show that reality, or the truth about what we humans have done and are doing to our world. The producer of one wildlife film on Madagascar told my colleague their team had been given explicit instructions to just make their programmes look good and avoid mention of deforestation and destruction. Partly as a result, I fear, many viewers do not fully understand just how humans are transforming and ravaging Planet Earth.

Because my brief from the outset has been to mix elements of both beauty and darkness, light and shade, we haven't needed to follow the same rulebook. Sitting up there on Baboon Cliff after wallowing in the beauty of the lake we were able to pan our cameras across to point at Nakuru town. We mentioned the proximity of the buildings, and then later went into the urban centre to film and hammer home the point that humans are right on the borders of wild areas, nibbling away at their edges, and posing a fundamental threat to the wildlife within.

Steve, a senior ranger from the Kenya Wildlife Service, then gifted me more understanding. He explained that Nakuru was being surrounded by a 50-mile-long electric fence, not to keep the wildlife in, but to keep the humans out. Farmers had tried to encroach on the park looking for more land, and poachers were a constant threat.

"This is our Ark," said the ranger, holding his arms out as if he wanted to hug it. It was a light-hearted comment, but he was so right. The national parks of Africa and marine reserves around the world, which are basically national parks in the sea, have indeed become wildlife Arks. They are our last chance of protecting iconic life.

I was mulling all this over on Baboon Cliff, as good a place as any for moments of revelation, when Steve pointed towards the park entrance.

"Look," he said. "Here come the guests."

It was early in the morning. Three car-loads of tourists were arriving at the park on a game drive. They headed straight for the edge of the lake, then hopped out to start snapping away at the glorious scene.

Steve was smiling.

"You think of them as guests?" I said. "That's very positive."

"Of course. They pay our wages," he said with a laugh.

It was another light-bulb moment. Of course, tourism *can* be a powerful force for good. *This is what I love about these journeys,* I thought. *This is the reason to go back on the road after a brush with malaria, and to keep on travelling as long as I possibly can.* From the comfort of home, I used to imagine that tourism could only be a disaster for the environment. But up there on Baboon Cliff I realised national parks and marine protected areas are incredibly dependent on money from travellers. Entrance fees from tourists pay for guides, guards, patrol boats, salaries, uniforms and electric fences. If we don't visit national parks and marine protected areas around the world, and pay our entrance fees, those wildlife Arks will be poached to annihilation, turned into palm-oil plantations, or fished to death, or logged.

When I talk to guides and rangers in places like Nakuru I invariably discover either they or their parents were poachers or hunters before they started working in the park. By creating a park, and then providing jobs and salaries to local communities, we give economic incentives to people to protect what all of us surely want to preserve. It is something absolutely critical that travellers can do to help protect iconic life.

If you doubt the role you can play, take a look at the small-print "About" section on the Kenya Wildlife

Service website. Their mission statement, as daft as those things sometimes are, is profound: "To save the last great species and places on earth for humanity". And how do they do that? They collect fees and charges in parks, money from filming and hotels, then they plough that back into parks and for "benefit sharing with communities living in wildlife areas".

I am, of course, completely aware of the environmental consequences of travel. All our holidays and adventures, whether for hedonism or political enlightenment, have a deep impact on the planet. Forests are logged and marshes are drained to provide land or materials for more hotels and resorts. Planting trees to offset carbon emissions from our long-haul flights just legitimises our unsustainable lifestyles. But almost everything about our Western lifestyles is environmentally catastrophic. I remember paling when I read one study that estimated each and every Google search uses the energy it would take to boil two cups of water.

Just to be absolutely clear, I believe we are in a struggle for the future that I would liken to the Second World War for importance. The human and environmental challenges that I see around the globe are urgent and critical. We absolutely have to give a damn, and campaign, fight, demonstrate and agitate for profound change and immediate and dramatic environmental protections.

Yet tourism doesn't just have to be about exploiting and ruining. When it is managed sustainably and meaningfully it can really help to protect and preserve a place. So get up, get out there, and experience the best this world has to offer. Seek out authentic and immersive holiday experiences, something you will be able to look back on and remember forever. And pay your entrance fee for a park or a day pass for a marine park and know that you are helping to preserve some of the greatest wildlife on the planet.

My time in Kenya was supposed to be coming to an end. I was due to travel on along the equator to the coast of southern Somalia, where the African leg of the adventure would finish. In the distance ahead were journeys following the equator across southern Asia, and then from the Galapagos across South America to the mouth of the Amazon.

But at dawn on the morning of our flight to Somalia we were told heavy fighting had broken out in the very area we were due to visit. The BBC High Risk team said they were sorry but there was no way they could authorise our trip.

So instead I decided to fly along the equator as far as I could, to get as close as possible to the border with Somalia. It was to be a decision that, in a positive way, has deeply affected my life, shaping my travels in the years since.

Right on the equator in eastern Kenya are the Dadaab refugee camps. We pottered through the skies in a tiny plane, flying above endless rusty-coloured desert scrub and low brush, then dropped down towards a landing strip in the middle of nowhere.

All around the land was flat, arid, and devoid of obvious features save for a dusty road, and a vast encampment of myriad huts, tents and makeshift shelters. This, at the time, was the largest refugee camp in the world, a home to hundreds of thousands of refugees from the relentless fighting across the border in Somalia.

We landed, met up with UNHCR, the United Nations refugee agency, who ran the camp and were very used to flighty television crews passing through their world, and then went to find new arrivals who had just made a long trek to the camp and were waiting to be processed by the UN.

It was tragic and pitiful. There were families with absolutely nothing to their names, squatting in the dirt waiting for someone to help them. I spoke to a woman who had fled fresh fighting in Mogadishu.

"Why did you come here?" I asked her.

She spread her palms in a hopeless gesture. "The fighting was very bad. The worst I've ever seen."

"Are you here with your family?"

"Some of them." Her face masked immense pain. "I had to leave two of my children behind."

I was stunned, trying to imagine how appalling that must have been.

"I could not bring them," she told me. "I don't know what's become of them."

She was absolutely desperate. My heart broke for her.

"We were attacked," she went on. "I lost them in the fighting. I don't know what happened to them. I had to flee. I brought my other children but I don't know where those two are. I had no choice but to leave."

She told me her group had walked for almost three full weeks to get to the camp. Along the way their meagre supply of food ran out and there was nothing to survive on but rainwater. I had been to Somalia. I had some small sense of the violence they had fled. I knew the world had largely forgotten them. They were victims of a conflict that the region, let alone the West, no longer had any time for. I wondered how long they would remain there, on the edge of nowhere, with no way out, no hope and nothing to look forward to.

And then I met Fatima, a young Somali woman, aged twenty-three, who had been in the camp for an astonishing seventeen years. I was instantly reminded of the families and children living in railway boxcars near the border of unrecognised Nagorno-Karabakh. Both prisons, in their own way. Fatima was calm, assured and gentle. She appeared to be so worldly it was hard to believe she had never lived anywhere but this desert camp. She led me to her home, a simple hut made from saplings of acacia with a roughly fenced yard, and we sat down together to talk.

"Fatima," I said, "have you really been here for most of your life?"

"That's right."

I asked her if she thought she would ever go home to Somalia. She replied clearly: no.

Would you want to? I wondered.

No, she said, never. "Because I know the problems, I know that my people have been killed there."

Fatima and thousands of other refugees in the camp did not want to return to Somalia, they wanted to integrate into Kenya. But the Kenyan government was concerned their presence would destabilise communities near the Somali border and as a consequence would not let them move deeper into the country to settle or work.

What that meant, Fatima explained, was that no one from the camp was allowed to travel more than twelve miles from the perimeter. They were stuck there. Fatima was literate, well educated, fluent in English and bursting with capability and promise. It was a positive camp run by caring aid workers, but it was also a forgotten prison. She was trapped in the desert, unable to go home because of conflict and chronic instability in her home country and forbidden from travelling more than a few miles from the camp by the Kenyan government.

While she was stuck, I was moving on, the fundamental difference between us just the place and circumstances of our birth. Backpack over my shoulder, I walked with her to the edge of the camp.

"This feels so wrong," I told her. "I'm leaving. I have a British passport which gifts me freedom and a chance to travel. I'm on a journey that will take me around the world and yet you're stuck here."

Fatima gazed out across the empty landscape.

"We call this an open prison, that's what we normally tell people," she said, "where we're free to go just so far and no further. The nearest town is 90 kilometres away and to get there you have to have a vehicle. We don't have cars and, even if we did, the police would stop us and ask to see our ID cards. We don't have ID cards so they would know we came from the camp and we'd be sent straight back."

Fatima had only left the camp twice. Once for a meeting of youth leaders in the town, and once for a volleyball game, of all things. Apart from that, for nearly two decades, she had been stuck out in the desert.

Meeting Fatima hit me like a bolt. I had spent the last couple of months being treated and recovering from malaria and then pondering whether to continue the journey of a lifetime. Yet here was someone denied the most basic freedom of movement. Unable to go home because of conflict in Somalia, Fatima had spent almost her entire life trapped in a tiny patch of desert. Her story haunts me. I remember her every single time I reach for my passport.

Before we met I had felt the compelling joy of travel, but Fatima was tangible proof that travel was still an extraordinary luxury, and an intense privilege. Those of us who can fly must never forget how lucky we are, and that travel is still the preserve of a fortunate minority. Standing with Fatima I thought back to my own dear grandmother, who first sparked my love of discovery with her magical mystery tours in her adapted car. Both women had been trapped by circumstance, while my renewed health and passport now gifted me a licence to explore.

In that moment, I knew I never wanted to stop travelling, and discovering. I knew that for as long as I could I needed to use each journey to enrich my mind, heart and life. I would take chances, go to strange places, and dive into the culture of the world. And I would never take it for granted.

"Thank you for showing us around," I said to Fatima.

"You're very welcome," she said. "Thank you to you and your team. I really appreciate you coming and seeing my home."

We both smiled. I had a lump in my throat.

My travels along the equator in Africa were coming to an end. But my journeys around the world were just beginning.

Acknowledgements

I would like to thank Robert Kirby and Rosemary Scoular, my lovely agents at United Agents, who encouraged me to put fingers to keyboard to make this book a reality. Rupert Lancaster, the charitable publisher at Hodder and Stoughton, has been badgering me for years to tell a few more tales about my life and travels, so must also share some of the credit and the responsibility. Huge thanks also to Cameron Myers at Hodder, and Natalia Lucas and Kate Walsh at UA.

Jeff Gulvin helped tease out and structure my stories and did much of the initial heavy-lifting for the book. Friends and family carried me along the way, as they have done through so much of life, especially my mum Cindy and my brother James, who both racked their brains to recall and discuss events and moments from what initially felt like a distant past.

This book covers more than three decades of my life, and sadly I cannot express gratitude to everyone who has guided me along the way. You would be reading a phone directory. But to all who have nudged, inspired and encouraged me I thank you from the depths of my heart. Most of all my thanks go to Anya, my wife and partner in life, who has tolerated, supported and inspired me since the day we met, and to our wonderful son Jake, who fills us both with joy and purpose, and to whom I dedicate this book. Love you son.

.

Matt Wilven was born in Blackpool in 1982. After receiving an MA with Distinction in Creative Writing, he spent the next ten years moving around, working various jobs and honing his craft. *The Blackbird Singularity* is his debut novel. He lives and writes in London.

You can discover more about the author at www.mattwilven.com

THE BLACKBIRD SINGULARITY

Two years after the death of their son,
Charlie, Vince and his wife Lydia are still
struggling to come to terms with the loss.
Vince was prescribed lithium for his stress-
induced bipolar disorder, diagnosed after a
nervous breakdown — but the medication
also makes him feel confused and fuzzy. So
when Lydia announces she is pregnant again,
he secretly decides to quit cold turkey. But as
withdrawal kicks in, Vince can barely hold his
life together. Somewhere between making
friends with a blackbird in the back garden
and hearing his dead son's footsteps in the
attic, he finds himself lost and alone,
journeying through a world of chaos and
darkness — completely unaware of the
miracle that lies ahead . . .

MATT WILVEN

THE BLACKBIRD SINGULARITY

Complete and Unabridged

CHARNWOOD
Leicester

First published in Great Britain in 2016 by
Legend Press Ltd
London

First Charnwood Edition
published 2017
by arrangement with
Legend Press Ltd
London

C463490465

A catalogue record for this book is available
from the British Library.

ISBN 978–1–4448–3217–4

Published by
F. A. Thorpe (Publishing)
Anstey, Leicestershire

Set by Words & Graphics Ltd.
Anstey, Leicestershire
Printed and bound in Great Britain by
T. J. International Ltd., Padstow, Cornwall

This book is printed on acid-free paper

For Saskia

Foreword

From Dr Eleanor Longden

'Madness,' says Shakespeare, 'must not unwatch'd go.' And certainly, for those of us who experience a serious breakdown, there is a level of spectating and scrutiny. Society stares at us, science dissects us, our lives fall apart, and we are forced to watch it happen. When I was eighteen, I went mad. It occurred in a sputtering cauldron of trauma, loss, injustice and despair, and for many years I simply gave up hope and surrendered to the loss of myself and the life I'd been supposed to have. *Gone mad* people sometimes say, as if madness is a discrete destination or place, and this is also true. Such extremes of suffering are a journey which we often need to make, and are forced to travel alone. Maddened, then, yes — driven mad. But not ill. To me, the term 'illness' privileges biology. It's suggestive of random aberrance, an arbitrary, catastrophic misfiring of neurons. I believe very strongly that what happened to me was not a piece of biological bad luck. Rather, it was a sane and understandable response to deeply insane and abnormal circumstances. A narrative not based in disease and disability but in meaningful distress and a struggle for survival. In the years since, this has been the emphasis of my professional career: that what gets labelled mental illness is in fact an intelligible, ordinary reaction

1

to incomprehensible and extraordinary pain, and that the therapeutic response demands we bear witness to the person's story. Not *'what's wrong with you?'* but rather *'what's happened to you?'*

The Blackbird Singularity charts the journey of someone driven slowly, exquisitely, excruciatingly mad by the weight of his own anguish and unresolved grief. In discontinuing his medication, Vince is forced to confront the unspoken and unspeakable. It is a voyage that is both catastrophic and liberating: beautiful and tortured in turns. As readers, we witness the visceral complexities of a man being undone and remade as he attempts to engage with a past he believed to be buried; yet which is ultimately proved to be buried alive and desperately demanding acknowledgement. There are considerable risks in abruptly withdrawing from psychiatric drugs, and *The Blackbird Singularity* deals honestly and unflinchingly with these. Vince's struggles are not romanticised or sanitised: we are never in any doubt of his desolation; never unaware that this is a man clawing together every possible resource — mind, body, soul — to fight for his life. The novel explores some profound issues: what does it mean to be mad? To be sane? Who makes that judgement, and how permeable are the boundaries of reason and rationality anyway? How can creativity, imagination and invention complement positivism and logic? As such the book can be enjoyed on several levels — a puzzle box of questions with no easy answers — and all handled by Matt Wilven with considerable deftness, wit, wisdom and compassion.

Any novel, and particularly a first novel, that can engage with mental health issues in such an engaging and intelligent way is to be warmly recommended. But one does not need personal experience of emotional distress to appreciate the nuances and pleasures of a good story, well-told. If you have known what it is to love, to lose, to persevere, to laugh with friends and sigh with family, then you will find something that resounds with you within *The Blackbird Singularity*. My own personal resonance I would like to share here. It was several years ago, and I was sat on a bench overlooking London's Parliament Hill with my then-partner as I told him more details than I ever had before about my life. It was a story in several acts: trauma, degradation, madness, redemption. Of suffering, sadness and senseless loss; but also of hope, healing and transformation. I disclosed the years of abuse that had driven me mad in the first place, the pessimism and pathology that came after, the schizophrenia diagnosis, and — finally — the freedom that came from reinterpreting my distress as something meaningful to be understood, explored and acknowledged. It took a long time, and when I looked over I could see tears in his eyes.

'Someone died in that place,' I said quietly, although I didn't really know what 'place' I was referring to. Somewhere ineffable, I suppose; that dark, wretched wasteland called The Past.

'I suppose someone did,' he replied, and there was pause. 'But you know, someone else was saved.'

3

On the way to the Tube station, we stopped for a drink. The pub was playing a Beatles medley, and I remember 'Blackbird' beginning as we took our seats. One of the lyrics had a curious relevance: the reminder that even if one's wings have been broken, it's always possible to learn to fly again.

★ ★ ★

Eleanor Longden, PhD's TED talk, *Learning From the Voices in My Head,* was featured on the front page of the *Huffington Post* and has been named by the *Guardian* newspaper as one of 'the 20 online talks that could change your life'. It has been viewed over 3 million times and translated into 36 languages.

FIRST
TRIMESTER

1

An event horizon is a mathematically defined boundary around a black hole. It is the point from which light can no longer escape the pull of the centre and all possible paths lead further into the hole. Beyond it, gravity is thought to be so powerful that it stretches and tears matter into subatomic strings. Outside, observers see it as a black surface upon which things darken and disappear. They can use the boundary to calculate a few simple facts — such as mass, spin and charge — but they can only theorise about what happens in the space beyond it.

Lyd leaves the house for work around 7:30am. I'd been listening for the sound of her shower to stop but drifted off. I sit up and rub my face, annoyed about missing her. Lithium doesn't discriminate between the important and unimportant moments in life. My mornings are always fuzzy.

After using the toilet I look at myself in the bathroom mirror. The tired man behind the glass has aged a lot in the last two years. His black hair is mottled grey at the temples. The skin around his eyes is dark, bruised almost, but not on the surface; the beating has come from the inside. There is a discrepancy between the perceived morbidity of his character (someone in his late fifties) and the age of his physical body (somewhere in its mid-thirties) but his end is definitely closer than his beginning.

Downstairs, I make myself a coffee and a couple of slices of toast and listen to a John Lee Hooker compilation. The phone starts ringing after my first bite. I leave the music on and continue eating, letting it ring out. Lyd's left half an old packet of sultanas on the kitchen counter with a yellow Post-It note stuck to the front. It reads: *For the birds.* It's impossible to fault her pragmatism, thinking about feeding the neighbourhood birds minutes after seeing me sleeping through one of the definitive moments in our relationship.

I open the pack and smell them. They look sticky and are beginning to ferment so I open the sliding door and dump them on the frosty lawn. The majority fall out in one big clump and break into three pieces when they hit the hard earth. It's too cold to bother scattering them properly.

I slide the patio door shut, pull a chair away from the kitchen table, wrap my hands around my cup of coffee and watch the white lawn. Within seconds a blackbird arrives, and then another. Soon there are nearly a dozen of them fluttering about, raising tiny clouds of hoar frost and trying to win a few moments on top of one of the sultana clumps. I'm not sure how long I sit watching them but, for the first time in a long time, I experience the creative glimmer of a new idea.

After a couple of minutes the idea is outshining my interest in the birds so I venture upstairs to my writing desk. Words flow out of me all morning. There's no double-checking my email, no scrolling through news sites or vacantly gazing at lists of jobs. I don't even turn my computer on. I just sit down and write in my notebook for four hours.

Around lunchtime the broken images of the story stop appearing in my head and the words clog up. I realise that I've forgotten to take my lithium. I consider taking it now but what I just wrote felt like a breakthrough. I want to keep hold of this clarity of mind. I bite the inside of my right cheek and decide not to take it. I go out for a twenty-minute jog instead.

After a shower and some lunch I head back to my writing room. I stop at Charlie's bedroom door. It's been over six months since I've faced it, and Lyd doesn't like it when I go in, but I feel like I have to. My hand trembles as I reach for the knob. I wonder if I'm already withdrawing from my medication or if I'm genuinely afraid.

The room is exactly the same — off-white wallpaper with pleasant childhood objects dispersed like polka dots, planetary-themed carpet, *Toy Story* bedcovers, wardrobe cluttered with cartoon stickers and scribbled crayon drawings, plastic whiteboard with a picture of our family drawn in stick man form, a cheap wooden trunk too small for all the toys — typical stuff for a four-year-old raised in a London suburb. The only unique thing is the low-hanging moon I made for him in one of our make-believe sessions. I push it with the tip of my toe and watch it sway back and forth.

His favourite soft toy lies by the pillow on the

bed. He was probably the last person to touch it so I don't want to disturb its position. It always looked like a limp, dead ferret, even when it was new, and we could never get it away from him. Where did it even come from? I look around and find myself sighing. The sound that comes out contains an unintended groan.

I pick up a retro 1960s robot from the windowsill; a toy we bought as an ornament. It's red, quite heavy and shaped like a squat cone. Its mouth is a chrome grill and the eyes are blue sirens. There is nostalgia in its naïvety, cuteness based on the fact that the original creator had been unable to form a clearer vision of the technological future. My jittery hands fumble and drop it.

The robot is motionless on the floor, part of the wrong future. I scowl at it, hate it, and find myself stamping on it three times. It doesn't break. It's surprisingly sturdy. The pounding hurts my foot through my shoe. Grimly amused by my failure to destroy it, I pick it up and put it back in the same position on the windowsill. My hands are steady again.

I begin to feel like I'm loitering so I leave the room and go back to my writing. I find myself working on another new story. It's set in a completely different time and place but it belongs in the same universe as the one I was writing this morning. I don't know how or why I know this. I just know that I feel alive in a way that seems forgotten. I'm focused and productive. Time is moving so fast that I almost can't believe it when I hear Lyd's key in the front door.

When people ask Lyd what she does for a living she usually answers with something self-deprecating like, 'Sums.' Sometimes, when pushed, she says, 'I'm a physicist.' Until four years ago she was an unsung hero in the world of particle physics and a sometime lecturer at Imperial College London. Then her book *Mini-Novas: The End of Science or the End of the World?* became a crossover hit (her publishers forced the subtitle — it upset Lyd for weeks but also ensured that she sold a lot of books). It's about the role of particle accelerators in the future of science and, specifically, the potentiality of mini black holes. Now she occasionally does interviews on the news when they need someone to balance out a regressive or scaremongering perspective. She used to work much longer hours but a mixture of success and grief has put her in a position to choose her own working pattern.

I rush downstairs to meet her at the door. She looks tired but her mood lifts slightly when she sees that I'm smiling. I pick her up off the ground with a hug. Outside's chill covers her.

'Wait,' she protests. 'Let me get my coat off.'

I put her down.

'Hello, lovely.'

'Hello?' she says, curious. 'What's up? You seem pretty buzzed.'

'It's just good to see you.'

'*Okay.*'

'I'm sorry I fell back to sleep this morning.'

'It's fine,' she says, hanging up her coat and grabbing her leather satchel back up off the

11

floor. 'What've you been up to?'

She walks through to the kitchen, dumping her things on the counter.

'Writing. A new thing. A couple of new things actually. They might be part of the same thing. I don't know yet.'

'Oh? That's good.'

'The first taste is always the sweetest.'

'Great. Angela's going to be happy.'

(Angela's my agent.)

She kisses me, a peck.

'How was your day?' I ask.

'Dull. Busy. Mostly dull. I think the problem I'm working on might be impossible. And pointless. Impossibly pointless.'

'In the simplest terms?'

'Diffeomorphism covariance.'

'Should I pretend to — '

'No. It's fine.'

'Prawn stir-fry sound good?'

'Later.' She pulls an opened bottle of white wine from the fridge. 'I've got a headache.'

I accidentally lower the right side of my mouth as she pours out a glass.

'What?' she asks. 'One won't hurt.'

'No. One's fine.'

I can tell from her slightly aggressive manner that she doesn't want to talk so I go back up to my writing room for an hour. After a quiet dinner we watch a couple of episodes of a political drama that we've been hooked on for the last few weeks. I can't follow the story because our silence feels like the most prominent thing in the room. I rest my hand on her thigh. I kiss the side of her face. She doesn't turn to me once.

Around 10pm we go up to read in bed but I can't focus on my book either. I pretend to leaf through the pages for a few minutes and then put my bookmark back where it was when I started. Once she's finished her chapter she turns her bedside light off and lies with her back to me. I turn my light off and nestle up behind her. When I put my arm over her she rests her hand in mine but doesn't say a word.

★ ★ ★

It's 10:56am. I've slept in. I can feel the lithium depleting in me. It took me hours to get to sleep last night. I feel sluggish and depressed. I must have turned my alarm off and gone back to sleep but I have no recollection of doing it. Lyd's long gone.

I put some coffee on, pour myself a bowl of cereal and stand looking out into the back garden. One of the blackbirds is back. He keeps searching the grass and then jumping up onto our birdbath, turning his head sideways and, seemingly, staring at me in the house. He is more slight and agile than the typical adult male and moves quicker, with more poise and grace. I like the look of him.

After a couple of renditions of this lawn-and-birdbath routine I realise that he isn't searching the grass for bugs or food, he's pretending to. It's a show. He's begging, but not in a desperate fashion. He's like a busker or an entertainer. He doesn't want to work for a living, he wants to sing for his supper.

Intrigued as to whether I'm truly being manipulated by a blackbird (and amused enough to participate), I open a new pack of sultanas and throw out a handful for him. After cautiously flying up onto the garden fence when I slide the patio door open he quickly flies back down onto the lawn and hops from one sultana to the next, pecking and swallowing them. When he's done, before he flies away, he makes an oddly distinctive chirping sound:

— *chink-chink, chook-chook, chink-chink, chook-chook* —

The experience of watching him and being tweeted at cleanses my mind in some unfathomable way. The phased-out feeling I woke with dissipates. I close the sliding door, put my bowl in the sink, pour myself a black coffee and take it upstairs, ready to start writing.

It's already later than when I usually take my lithium and what I wrote yesterday felt so clear and concise. Right now, I need that clarity. The light fuzz of lithium can be a gift, it keeps me level, but when I'm trying to use my mind as a quick, sharpened tool it slows me down.

I spend all afternoon typing up and editing my work from the previous day. I cut all the abstract language and useless similes then eke out the right grammar and piece it into something more structured and interesting. Once it's in a readable state I go out for a jog.

I'm still in the shower when Lyd gets home from work. I can hear her on the telephone

14

whilst I'm getting dressed. From her tone of voice and the cadence of her laughter (scathingly ironic but innocent of malice) I immediately narrow the person on the other end of the line down to her sister, Jayne, or her friend Gloria. I head downstairs.

'Yeah, he's here now . . . No. How could he? He never leaves the house. Ha, ha . . . Let me look at him . . . Yeah, he seems to be on pretty good form . . . Okay, I will . . . Okay. Bye, love.'

She hangs up.

'I'll have you know I've been out running,' I say, 'today and yesterday. Was that Jayne?'

'Gloria,' she replies, quickly descending from a world of open and carefree friendship into a more stressed and evasive mood.

'Did you tell her?'

'Tell her what?'

'About the pregnancy.'

'No. Jesus, Vince.'

'Sorry. How is she?'

'She says hi. She's good. Sergio's being a dick though.'

'Oh?'

'He's hounding her. Asking who every text's from and if everyone in the office wears clothes like she does. I thought he was better than that.'

'Come on, Serge is a good guy.'

(Me and Sergio were friends before her and Gloria but now they meet up more than we do.)

'He's acting like an ape.'

'She has changed though. She used to wear all those dark jumpers, loose trousers, everything covered up. They've been married eight years and she's suddenly started dressing provocatively. What's he going to think?'

'She can dress however she wants,' says Lyd. 'It's good that's she's coming out of herself.'

'I didn't say she couldn't, or shouldn't, just that — '

'If Sergio can't deal with the fact that his wife wants to feel good about the way she looks — '

'It's not that. I think he just — '

She sees that I'm flustered by her aggression and restrains herself.

'We said we wouldn't do this,' she says, smiling, changing tack. 'And she does seem a little bit *too* relaxed lately, doesn't she? I wonder if she'd tell me if she was sleeping with somebody else. Sometimes you just can't tell. Who really knows anybody?'

'What if there were no rhetorical questions?' I quip.

Lyd rolls her eyes.

'So, good day?' she asks, insinuating that I'm chirpy again.

'I'm getting a lot out of these new ideas I'm working on. But I'm not really ready to talk about them yet.'

'Still in the delicate stages?'

'Yes, like you,' I say, moving in to hold her.

She tries to turn her head away from me.

'Hey,' I protest, gently moving her face back towards me. 'We've got to talk about it at some point.'

'Not yet.'

'After dinner?'

'Maybe.'

'Definitely?'

'Maybe,' she repeats, slipping out of my arms and grabbing some of her things to take upstairs.

'Do I not even get a kiss?'

She comes back and petulantly kisses me on the cheek. It's supposed to be funny but I watch her disappear with concern. Her wit is an act that has no joy in it.

I take my time making dinner to give Lyd some space. I cook an onion paste and a curry paste. I roast lots of sweet root vegetables in olive oil and seasoning. I mix them all together and add lots of tomatoes and cream. Then it's just a matter of waiting for it all to simmer down whilst I put the rice on.

Lyd loves curry and comes into the kitchen inhaling the aroma with her eyes closed.

'Smells delicious,' she says, approaching the fridge and taking out a quarter-full bottle of white wine.

'Five–ten minutes,' I say, adding some cloves and coconut milk to the rice and quickly checking to see if she's pouring out the whole quarter-bottle.

She is.

'What?' she asks, spotting my glance.

'Nothing.'

I open the crockery cupboard and begin setting the kitchen table. Lyd helps and then takes her large glass of wine over and sits down.

'You know,' she says, 'my mum smoked twenty a day back when I was a bunch of mushy cells.'

'And you blame her for having a small lung capacity whenever you get the chance.'

I give the curry a stir.

'I'd have found another axe to grind.' She takes a sip with a smile. 'She knows I love her.'

'I can never imagine your mum smoking . . . So, it's sinking in a bit?'

She looks at me blankly.

'The mushy cells?'

'A bit,' she sighs, looking away from me, towards the steamed-up glass of the sliding doors.

I test the rice, there's still a tiny bit of crunch.

'We're going to have to talk about Charlie's room,' I say.

Lyd skips a couple of beats before replying.

'No. We're not.'

I turn to her.

'No?'

'There's plenty of other things to talk about first.'

'True,' I concede.

'It's early days.'

'I know.'

'You're always off in the future.'

'I'm just trying to make sure we're ready for what's coming.'

'Like I said, it's still early days. Try not to get carried away.'

'Okay. But don't start using caution as an excuse not to talk about it.'

'I'm not.'

'I hope not.'

I drain the rice in a colander and begin dishing out our food. I've made enough for four or five. It will serve us twice so I get some plastic boxes out and put the surplus in them.

'Are you okay, honey?' asks Lyd. 'You seem very . . . lucid.'

'Me? I'm fine.'

I nod, perhaps a little bit too enthusiastically. Lyd tilts her head slightly.

'Okay.'

We don't talk much over dinner. The curry has taken a while to cook so we're both hungry. We barely look up from our plates. Once we're done, Lyd says that she's tired. She can't seem to shift her headache from yesterday. I can leave the pots and pans. She'll do them in the morning.

I stay downstairs and do the washing up anyway. Cooking, cleaning, tidying up; I don't mind doing chores. I find them calming. And since Lyd is the only one earning any real money at the moment, doing most of the housework seems fair enough.

Drying my hands on a tea towel, I notice that they're trembling again. I grip and release the tea towel three times, slowly and firmly. I'll have to be careful Lyd doesn't notice these tremors. My promise to keep taking lithium is an important part of our relationship but my gut is telling me to stop. I have to stay sharp, get back in touch with myself.

I lie on the couch in the living room, staring at the ceiling. My mind wanders back to Charlie in the hospital, the day of his death. Astrocytomas are devouring his brain and spinal cord. We're entrenched in the stress cycle of his procedures: CT scan, MRI scan, biopsy, surgery, radio-therapy. We're hardly sleeping and rarely going

19

home. Charlie has been having fits, losing his hair, vomiting in his sleep. It's beginning to seem like the hospital is trying to kill him, not save him. It's an institution of torture.

We've been living on the precipice of his death but when we're warned that today might be the day it seems like we haven't had a chance to prepare. There has to be something we should be doing, something we haven't thought of yet.

We sit on either side of him, both hold a hand and wait for the cancer to eat that final cell which will turn out his light. It takes sixteen hours. He's unconscious but makes soft, intermittent whimpers. When the sound of his flatline finally comes it tips all of my darkness out into the world. At first, Lyd thinks I'm crying but it's laughter, manic laughter so deep that it's silent.

Months earlier I asked one of the doctors why it's called *astrocytoma*. He told me it's because the cancer eats star-shaped brain cells. After this I started thinking of Charlie's brain as a universe plagued by a tiny black hole, swallowing all his stars. He started with a billion, you could see them in his eyes, and the cancer ate them up one by one until there were almost no stars left.

In the instant that I hear the flatline I imagine that Charlie's universe is the actual universe and that our sun, the last of the stars, has just been devoured. Everything is submerged in total blackness, the world is falling off its orbit, the moon is crashing into the Pacific Ocean, violent black winds are throwing clouds of people and cars and trees across countries and continents.

20

Within moments there will be only chaos and death.

All this in a second.

Then I realise that the black universe where everything is about to die is not Charlie's, it's mine. This is the joke, where the laughter starts. It's the irony of not being connected to my emotional self. My feelings are in a dream universe. My actual body is relieved, happy, escalating towards euphoria. I'm divided in two. Reality's a trick. It's all one big joke.

After the laughter everything turns white. Credit card receipts tell a story of three manic days where I manage to spend much more than our life savings on hundreds of powerful torches and expensive lighting devices. At some point I crash our car. I vaguely remember telling everyone I meet that the night sky is a memory, that the stars are already dead, the light's about to end, we all need torches.

My delusions spike in a dark police holding cell where I keep demanding, in a shrill, loud voice, that the universe turn the sun back on. But every time I shout *sun* I start having these visual flashes of Charlie, dead in his hospital bed. Eventually, I figure out what's going on and have a fit of despair. They send me to a psychiatric ward.

After a couple of weeks of deep, silent grief, I start seeing the hoops they are holding up so I begin jumping through them. After another couple of weeks they diagnose me with stress-induced bipolar disorder. Apparently, it's a relatively common way of not dealing with problems properly.

21

They prescribe a lifetime of lithium. It makes me feel confused and fuzzy so I intend to shrug it off once I get out but Lyd says that she won't take me back unless I promise to stay medicated. She is weak and barely able to talk but her relative resilience and strength fill me with inadequacy and shame. She has dealt with our son's funeral on her own whilst I was out there ruining what was left of our lives. I can't believe that anyone could have the depth of character to forgive me, but she does.

This was almost two years ago.

When I asked her why she had taken me back she answered:

'You loved him so much that you lost your mind.'

★   ★   ★

I'm still on the couch when I wake up. It's morning, already light outside. There's a yellow Post-It note on my forehead: *If you're an idiot, read this*. I produce an almost non-existent snigger and sit up. My bodyweight is heavier than usual. I feel woozy and morbid.

Lyd's laptop is on the coffee table. I look up *lithium withdrawal* on the Internet and find that the only real side effect is a fifty-fifty chance of relapsing into mania. This dark gravity inside of me is all my own. My hands should *stop* trembling, not start, yet they tremble as I type. I clear the search history and go into the kitchen for some apple juice.

Outside, in the back garden, the blackbird

from the day before is back and when he sees me through the window he starts doing his lawn-and-birdbath routine. I grab the bag of sultanas from the cupboard and open the sliding door. He flies up onto the fence. It's a chilly morning but, since I've woken up fully clothed and full of heavy shadows, I decide to take my apple juice outside and sit on one of the patio chairs. The blackbird watches me warily. When I throw a handful of sultanas onto the lawn he chirps up into the air:

— *choo-chin-chink-chica-chin-chink* —

After a few moments of anticipation he flies down and starts eating. It seems his call went out to his friends because, one by one, five more blackbirds fly down onto the lawn and begin eating the sultanas with him. As each bird arrives, the joy in me increases. I feel the sort of vacant serenity that I used to feel when I watched Charlie playing with his toys, unnoticed from his doorway. I'm looking in on a secret world. I've had a big hand in creating it but I'll never be able to truly join in or fully understand it.

Tensing all of my muscles against the bite in the air, I keep feeding them. Every time I throw more sultanas they all panic and fly up onto the fence and then, one by one, make their way back down onto the grass; always my little friend first.

After ten or twenty minutes, my feet go numb and my fingers turn blue but I feel inspired and capable and I'm wondering if the blackbirds have anything to do with my newfound creativity. I go up to my office and lose myself in

23

yet another new story. Words fall through my pen with ease. I'm picking all the right details. The momentum is electric. Writing hasn't given me this much pleasure in years. I get into it so deeply that when Lyd comes home I'm still unshowered and in yesterday's clothes.

I go downstairs sheepishly to say hello. She's standing in the dark behind the front door in her long beige raincoat, holding her briefcase and handbag, eerily still.

'Lyd? *Lyd?*'

She drops her things, falls to her knees and hunches over.

'What's going on?' I ask, rushing over to her.

'I can't do it,' she whimpers.

I stroke the back of her head and sit down next to her in the dark hallway.

'Talk to me,' I say.

She's silent.

I rub her head so she knows that she's the centre of my thoughts. I prompt her to speak a few times but she either ignores me or repeats, 'I can't do it.' When she eventually sits up, she wraps her arms around her legs and tucks her face behind her knees. I swivel round next to her, in a similar position, with my back to the front door. We've been staring down the dark corridor for a long time when she finally speaks:

'Remember when we took him to the duck pond and he shouted, '*A golden fish!*' and that whole family smiled at us? Even the kids.'

'And then he kept saying it because he knew it was cute.'

'Yes. Was that the day when he first saw a

24

caterpillar? What was that sound he used to make?'

'*Woooaaah,*' I say, impersonating Charlie.

Lyd starts to laugh but chokes up with sadness.

We reflect a while.

It's the first time she's started a conversation with a memory of Charlie in over a year. For months after I got back from the psychiatric ward almost every silence was followed by, 'Remember when . . . ' He could come up in the middle of anything: talking about the electricity bill, making a cup of tea, watching the shadow of the television pass along the carpet. Our grief was so all encompassing that remembering him was the only thing we were ever really doing.

After about six months Lyd didn't want to talk about Charlie anymore. She turned her back on the idea of him, wouldn't visit his grave, closed his bedroom door, and punished me with terrible moods if I brought him up. Even these days she doesn't really like to talk about him so this mentioning of him seems like a step forward.

'I know it sounds stupid,' she says, eventually breaking the silence, 'but I didn't believe I could get pregnant again. I thought that part of me was dead. I never even imagined . . . In my head, we were these shadow people, and all we could ever have was a shadow life. That's one of the reasons why we had to stay together. It wouldn't be fair to whoever we met next. It wouldn't be real. You know?'

'Sure.'

I put my arm over her shoulders.

'But now, with this . . . I don't want to be some kind of shadow family. It's not right. It's not how it's supposed to be.'

'It doesn't have to be like that.'

'How could it be any other way?' she asks.

'It's impossible to know how a baby will change things.'

'Maybe.'

'This could be the best thing for us.'

'I doubt that,' she says.

'But maybe it's time for us to start trying a little harder?'

She nods and looks at me with a frown.

'Why are your hands shaking?'

I look at my right hand on her shoulder. The tremble has expanded into a shake.

'I haven't really eaten properly today,' I say, pulling the hand away from her. I try for humour, 'And it's emotional, down here, behind the front door.'

She smiles, with love, sadness, but also an unanswered question behind it all.

'Come on,' I say, shifting the weight off my pelvis. 'Let's get up.'

She begins to stand. I rise with her.

'What's for dinner?' she asks. 'Do you want me to make something?'

'I've not really thought about it. There's that leftover curry.'

'Sounds good.'

We walk in the dark towards the kitchen. My hand hovers along the wall and starts feeling for the plastic of the light switch. I stop, stroke up and down, move my hand around in circles. It

26

seems to have moved. Lyd steps up and reaches for where she thinks it is but she doesn't find it either. We grope around in the shadows for a few seconds.

'Is this even the right wall?' she asks.

'I can't remember,' I say. 'Is it over there?'

2

Not many animals adapted to the cities but certain kinds of scavengers thrive on human waste: pigeons, rats, mice and squirrels. Foxes too, with their guile and their burrows, made headway. But something happened to these animals in the transition. They became dirty and dishevelled, sooty and infested. However, one of the earliest colonisers managed to maintain its natural dignity: the common blackbird. After hundreds of years living in cities the civilisation still slips right off them. Sometimes a person hears one singing the song of the car alarm or the mobile phone but these whistles are not the tainted echoes of the technological era, they are full of imitative joy. The blackbirds are singing about a subject larger than the city, the thing above and below it, inside and out: boundless, endless Nature.

Two weeks later. Saturday morning. There's no ice on the ground but it's still cold. Lyd is out shopping for a meal for her family. We're going to break the news to them tonight. Most people wait a couple of months but Lyd is too close to them to keep anything big like this quiet.

I stand in the back garden drinking my morning coffee with a pack of sultanas in the pocket of my dressing gown. A week ago I bought a separate supply especially for the blackbirds so that Lyd wouldn't notice our normal pack depleting. I keep them hidden at the back of the tea towel drawer. I don't know why.

'Blackie,' I say, following with a quick, fluctuating whistle.

He flies out of our evergreen and down onto the lawn. I throw out a single sultana at a time and smile continuously as he chases after them. He's become very used to my presence. The sliding of the screen door doesn't scare him away and he happily lets me stand and watch him. The others only play or eat on the grass if I sit down and remain very still.

Lyd has told me in advance that she'll be stressing out and that it will probably be better if we stay out of each other's way until people start arriving at 7pm so, when I hear her car in the driveway, I quickly come in from the garden, stash my sultanas at the back of the tea towel drawer, run upstairs and go to my office.

The novelty and excitement of my new ideas have passed but my need to keep writing the story is still great. I imagine it similar to how an archaeologist must feel when his tool first strikes an ancient set of bones. Exhilaration comes first, having found something rare, but that is short lived. The real work still needs to be done.

The trick is to let the hidden object do the talking: sense its lines, move unflinchingly along its curves, allow something deeper to take over, work selflessly and relentlessly until you gradually reveal something alien and unimagined. That's the stage I'm entering: climbing down into my writer's pit and scraping and brushing the bones of my story every day.

I write and edit in my office all day whilst she prepares for her family's arrival. I make sure I'm done by 5:30pm to give myself plenty of time to lift my head out of the writing pit and get cleaned up. I wear my smartest jeans, a checked cotton shirt and brown suede ankle boots.

Lyd's parents, Fee and Dom, arrive first with their overnight bags and a display of civility and goodwill that cleverly disguises their concerns about the fact that their whole family has been invited over on the same night. They are both dressed in simple and inscrutable smart-casual clothing chosen logically and with candour for exactly this sort of occasion.

We sit them down in the living room and serve Prosecco in champagne flutes, which they receive delightedly. After spending a couple of minutes welcoming them and asking about their journey, Lyd excuses herself and goes back to the kitchen. I ask them what they're currently reading and we arrive at the next ringing of the doorbell without any awkward pauses.

It's Jayne at the door, Lyd's big sister, Fee and Dom's middle child. She's brought a bottle of red wine and a worried curiosity that she's masking in amusement.

I take her coat.

She's wearing an electric-blue pencil skirt, an eighties' blouse with an eye-straining black-and-white pattern, yellow tights and shiny red brogues. 'Clashing' is her style, and it oddly opposes her facilitating nature.

In a social context, Jayne almost always focuses on putting the most nervous and uncomfortable person in a group at ease. When we first met, I thought she really liked me. Now I'm a little bit ashamed of how long it took her to move on from looking after me.

After getting Jayne a glass of Prosecco, I help Lyd in the kitchen whilst those three catch up in the front room. Her stress levels are peaking and her creased brow-line means she's feeling emotionally vulnerable so I stay quiet, only asking for new jobs when she's pausing for breath.

She asks me to watch the hobs whilst she pops upstairs to change and reappears less than five minutes later in a sleeveless red dress with a high neck, dark tights and a pair of black ballerina flats. She looks great and I tell her this but she's already worrying about the food again.

The doorbell rings.

It's Lyd's brother, Peter, the eldest. He's brought a date who hasn't been invited. This is typical of Peter. Lyd envisioned an intimate meal where she could carefully tell her immediate family that she's expecting a baby. Now it's going to be an evening about meeting Peter's new girlfriend.

'Come in. They're all through here.'

Peter's inflated sense of self-worth makes me despair and I find it impossible to understand how nobody else can see that he clearly has a drug problem; cocaine and benzodiazepines, I think. I also hate the way he parades women around in front of his family as though his vulgar

31

prowess says nothing about his emotional problems or his inability to commit to a relationship.

The worst thing is that they all devour his charm hook, line and sinker. Even Lyd, a perfect critic of all things patriarchal, has a blind spot where he's concerned. I once made a blasé crack about the fact that he always wears Prada suits because he's a narcissistic egomaniac and Lyd got depressed for a week because she didn't know how to forgive me.

'Vincey Vince Vincent and the Vince Watergate Band,' he says, with his arms open — this is his jovial way of greeting me and simultaneously saying that I'm a pathetic creative egotist.

(Watergate is my surname which, unlike most terrible surnames, escaped ridicule and attention until it captured the imaginations of the freaks and geeks at university.)

'Hello, Peter,' I reply, not taking the bait and certainly not moving into his giant arm span to be crushed by an overzealous and impersonal hug.

'This is Pascale.'

'Nice to meet you.'

I extend a hand.

'And you,' she says, taking the hand for a second, very sweetly.

She's a nervous creature but the pinch of the thumb says sensual and self-possessed too. She is petite, has a slight French accent, a dark bob haircut and is wearing a simple black dress. As usual, Peter has ensnared a beautiful and intelligent young woman.

I close the front door (Peter uses these two seconds to grope Pascale, as though my eyes lack peripheral vision) and then they follow me through the hall to the living room.

'Guess who?' I say into the living room doorway.

They cheer for Peter's visage when it appears before them.

'Rumours of my death have been greatly exaggerated,' says Peter, motioning with his hands for his admiring fans to now sit down.

They all laugh, relishing his irony.

Pascale creeps out from behind him with a coy smile, clutching a bottle of gin.

'And here is my exquisite aperitif,' he says. 'The young French lady holding it is called Pascale.'

Even though he has introduced her like a misogynistic gameshow host, there is another bout of laughter.

'Pay no attention to him,' says Jayne, rising to introduce herself to Pascale whilst Fee and Dom look her up and down with vacant smiles.

'I'll go set another space,' I say. 'Drinks, anyone?'

'A G&T would go down a treat,' says Peter, snagging the gin from Pascale and passing it to me.

'Oh, yes,' agrees Fee.

'Mmm,' confirms Dom.

Jayne and Pascale, great friends in seconds, spare a moment to nod.

'Five Gee and Tees,' I say, walking to the kitchen to prepare them.

'Peter?' asks Lyd.

'And *Pascale*.'

'You're kidding?'

'Afraid not.'

'What am I going to do?'

'I'm just making them all a gin and tonic then I'll set another place at the table. You want one?'

'Yes. But I can't, can I?'

'Sorry, honey. I forgot.'

'Shit. Shit. Shit.'

'It's going to be fine.'

Lyd's face freezes in a distorted grimace. It can go one of two ways from here: angry meltdown or resilience. She rubs her forehead with the back of a hand that holds a large kitchen knife.

'There's not going to be enough food,' she says.

Resilience.

'We'll make it stretch,' I reply.

'Squiddy-pants,' says Peter, entering the kitchen.

'Isn't it bad luck to see the chef before the dinner?' I ask, cutting lemons for the drinks, buying Lyd a couple of valuable seconds.

'Nonsense.'

He approaches her.

She relaxes, becomes his loving little sister and embraces him, still holding the knife.

'Hey, bro.'

'I hope you don't mind, I brought a guest.'

'I don't, but a little bit of warning wouldn't have gone amiss. I'm cooking for six here.'

'I *literally* couldn't. She just got back from

34

France two hours ago. I didn't think she'd make it. Besides, she eats like a mouse. I promise.'

'She better. Now, shoo. I'm busy.'

Peter does as he's told with a cheeky grin and a wink.

I serve the gin and tonics and take out a small tray of smoked salmon with cream cheese on tiny pieces of rye bread. They are all happy and chatting so I put a collection of Bach's cello suites on quietly in the background for them.

Back in the kitchen I set a seventh place at our four-seater kitchen table.

'Do you still want to tell them?' I ask.

'I think so,' says Lyd. 'Let's see how it goes. Maybe a stranger will make it more normal.'

'That's true.' I walk over and kiss her. 'I hadn't thought of that.'

'We're almost ready here.'

'I'll just pop up and get my office chair for Pascale, then I'll call them through.'

'Go on then, quick.'

I run up and grab the chair and, as I rush out onto the landing, I almost knock into Charlie playing in the hall. I turn my hips to the side, raise the chair a little and say:

'Oopsy-daisy.'

When I get to the top of the stairs I stop dead and all the hairs on my arms and neck rise. I don't dare look back. I take a deep breath, walk downstairs and stand in the living room doorway.

My head is still upstairs on the landing. I didn't actually see Charlie, I reason. His face was not part of the experience. It was just the notion of his presence, an awareness of his body filling space. Not a hallucination, something else.

When I become aware of myself again everybody is looking at me vacantly holding an office chair in the doorway.

'Dinnertime,' I say.

Dom gives Fee a look of concern, seemingly referring to something they've spoken about earlier. Jayne glances at me and then focuses on taking Pascale's attention away from me. Peter stares at me like a car crash, brimming with morbid pleasure. Realising I'm now redundant, I turn from them, distracted, and head to the kitchen to put the chair in place.

The silence I created behind me soon fills up with chatter again. I sit down. Lyd says something but I don't hear it.

Did I actually see anything? The top of his head?

'*Vince.*'

'Hmm?'

'Can you grab these soups?'

I nod and stand up as the group comes through.

'You guys take the chairs. Me and Vince will sit on the stools,' calls Lyd.

They arrange themselves around the table and I begin playing waiter.

'What's this?' asks Fee.

'Oh, erm. Soup,' I say.

Peter laughs out loud.

'French onion,' calls Lyd, looking at me with confused derision.

It was just a silly moment, I tell myself. People

imagine things all the time. They just don't speak about them.

The table is cramped with seven of us. Pascale apologises for her presence. Fee says she is being silly and Dom says it's cosy, rubbing her shoulder in a way that makes Pascale uncomfortable and Jayne explode with laughter.

The conversation starts with the usual pleasantries about the food but soon takes a detour into the current state of left-wing politics. I slowly become engaged again (I catch Lyd looking at me approvingly). Everyone is pleased that Pascale has a humanitarian agenda and briefly feels sorry for her when Peter takes pains to expose the naïvety of her position on global poverty.

After this, Lyd serves goat's cheese and roasted pine nuts on rocket and we all isolate Peter from the conversation for a while. Jayne and Pascale continue to hit it off, laughing whilst me and Lyd speak to her parents about whether or not they are making the most of their retirement.

Once everybody has finished the starter Lyd puts her hand on my leg. She's getting nervous (I presume she intends to make a toast before the main meal). I rub the top of her hand and give her a sympathetic smile. She refills her glass of wine; something tells me it's not the first time but I make no attempt to confront her about it even though I know I should.

I help clear the plates and set up the table for the main dish. I manage to get Lyd to myself in a spot by the cooker.

'How are you feeling?' I ask, putting my hand on her hip.

'It is what it is,' she says.

'Are you going to say something before we eat?'

She nods.

I kiss her quickly and take two trays of chunky cod fillets that have been cooking in white wine, garlic, cream and capers over to the table. Everybody makes appreciative sounds as they see the size and amount of cod and smell the aroma drifting around them.

I put the potatoes and green vegetables in the centre of the table whilst Lyd serves out the fish. Then I top up everybody's wine, put another bottle of white and red on the table and sit down. Lyd remains standing and puts her hand on my shoulder. Peter shoves a large mouthful of cod into his mouth.

'Before we begin,' says Lyd, raising her glass. 'We have an announcement to make . . . ' She chokes up, almost crying, and looks down at me. 'Vince? Could you?'

I stand up and put my arm around her.

'It's been a tough couple of years, as you all know, and it wasn't planned, but now it's happened we're going ahead. It feels like the right thing to do . . . Lyd's pregnant.'

'How beautiful,' says Pascale, clasping her hands together adorably before noticing the quiet anxiety in the room all around her.

The toast disintegrates. Nobody raises their glass.

'Good for you, honey,' says Dom, suddenly

kicking into gear and having a semi-symbolic sip of his drink. 'It's time to move on.'

As Lyd raises an unimpressed bottom lip to her father's response, Jayne, cringing humorously at him, stands up and walks round to give her a hug.

'I love you so much, Squid,' she says to Lyd. 'Let me know a good day for lunch next week.'

Lyd nods and they kiss each other on both cheeks. Jayne continues her response by moving towards me.

'Check you out, Mr Fertile!' She prods my side, smiles widely, and expands her arms for a quick hug that connects at the collar bone (at which point she whispers), 'I hope it all seems manageable, darling.'

'Thanks,' I say, touched but mildly offended.

Fee is still in quiet contemplation. Pascale is looking at Peter with a question mark on her forehead and Peter is shaking his head subtly to say, *Not now*. Dom is wringing his hands with a nervous smile waiting for his wife to say something.

'Of course, it's great news,' says Fee, finally realising that things are now resting on her response. 'Congratulations.'

She doesn't get up. She descends straight back into deep thought. Lyd's face droops into disappointment and then fights back, deciding to find it all amusing. She looks at me and raises her eyebrows. I mirror her expression, kiss her and we both sit down.

'Congrats, sis,' says Peter, in an untouched tone.

'Thanks, bro,' says Lyd, impersonating him in a robotic monotone (to which he raises his glass and swallows half of his wine in one gulp).

Maybe I'm being paranoid but the message I'm receiving is, *Poor Lydia. She's well and truly stuck with him now.*

There's much more introspection throughout the rest of the meal. Pascale's eyes are flitting around from face to face nervously. Peter is scowling with amusement, as though life is a series of sadistic jokes and the punchline, today, is that his little sister has been impregnated by me . . . again. Dom and Fee are busy mentally reforming the essence of their united front. Jayne continually fails to engage anyone with whatever comes to her mind. I start thinking about Charlie playing upstairs on the landing. Lyd is becoming so visibly upset that, one by one, all any of us are thinking is, *Please don't cry.*

Eventually, the cello suites in the other room finish and, even though we've barely been able to hear them, the silence they leave behind is cavernous. Somebody has to speak and this is exactly the kind of time when I'm no good at talking. We wait, most of us taking a moment to glance at Lyd. I can hear myself chewing and so begin moving my jaw more delicately. The sound of cutlery on plates is excruciating.

'Remember, whenever it got tense, Charlie would just burst out laughing like a maniac?' says Lyd, laughing sadly.

Jayne almost chokes on her food with relief and joy. Everybody else looks more anxious.

40

'I remember that,' says Jayne. 'He was a right little psycho.'

Fee and Dom both look at me cautiously, obviously equating Charlie's maniacal streak with me. I ignore them and smile at Lyd.

'He got that from his aunty,' I say.

'Hey!' protests Jayne.

'No,' I grant her. 'Not really. He always laughed like a villain, didn't he? No matter what he was laughing at.'

'Charlie was their son,' Peter whispers to Pascale.

Pascale frowns with sadness and pity.

'He was so weird,' says Lyd. 'Half the time we had no idea what he was laughing about.'

Again, Fee and Dom glance my way. It annoys me the second time because they both loved Charlie deeply. Underneath their silent insinuation that he was a bizarre boy because of me there rests the faintest allegation about the unpredictability of his cancer and death.

'What do you miss about him?' I ask in their direction.

'Oh, the whole lot,' says Fee. 'That cheeky look in his eyes. He could get round anybody with that look.'

Me and Lyd smile. We know the look she means.

'Oh yes,' agrees Peter. 'Butter wouldn't melt anywhere near him. He could turn shit to gold, that one.'

We all laugh.

'He was an extremely crafty young boy,' says Dom. 'A trickster. Not many children can make

41

me laugh but he always managed it.'

This is the first time we've reminisced about Charlie as a family. Since the conversation has been broached there's no going back. We carry on drinking and start telling stories about him, forgetting about dessert until it gets late. We apologise to Pascale half a dozen times but then carry on. We speak for so long and with such good cheer that everything seems alright again.

When Peter decides to call it a night, and Jayne follows suit, it's agreed by everyone that a lovely night has been had. We set up a double mattress in the living room for Dom and Fee and say goodnight with smiles on our faces.

It's only afterward, lying in bed, that the evening begins to seem gloomy. The new baby barely made an impact. Nobody even mentioned the pregnancy at the end of the night.

Lyd is out like a light, exhausted from all the cooking and worrying, but I find it impossible to sleep. Since I've cut out my lithium I'm struggling to get six hours a night. This evening it's worse still. I have indigestion, cold sweats and I'm inadvertently drunk. Black waves of dizziness crash against my skull, the world spins out of control, icy oceans rise into the sky.

I roll around for hours until my legs are aching.

When the tides of drunken chaos finally settle the blackbirds are singing outside. I hear Blackie up on our drainpipe, and maybe six or seven other blackbirds that are further away. The dark tales of winter are gone from his song. It's more matter of fact now.

It's all going to be starting soon, his tone says.

My ears release their focus and I listen to the entire dawn chorus for a while. Is it a giant conversation, parts of it whistled across from Asia? A grouping of territorial sound barriers? A musical collaboration? Calls of romantic longing? Utter randomness? Ancient black secrets?

Lyd wakes me up with a nudge.

'Come on, Vince. Time to get up. They're both up and showered.'

My eyes feel like they have knitting needles in them. I can't have slept for more than a couple of hours.

'How much did you drink last night?' she asks, seeing the struggle on my face.

'Couldn't sleep.'

She sighs.

'Okay. They've already had cereal and want to get out. I'll take them for a walk on the Heath. They want to buy us lunch before they go. You've got two hours.'

'They'll be glad to get you on your own.'

'Two hours.'

'Thank you.'

I sense her eyes rolling but sleep still has its hooks in me. I slip out of the bedroom and back into the blackness.

'*Vince?* Are you not even up? You've had nearly three hours.'

'Huh?'

'It's almost twelve. Come on. You're not exactly doing much to save your image here.'

'I'm up,' I say, swinging my legs over the edge

43

of the bed and sitting up with my eyes still closed. 'Sorry.'

I stumble to the bathroom and have a quick shower, mulling over Lyd's 'save your image' comment.

When I get downstairs, Fee and Dom smile but their eyes are wondering how I look as bad as I do given that we all went to bed at the same time. Seeing how alert and vitalised they are makes me want to crawl into a cave and disappear for a month.

'Morning,' I say.

'Only just,' says Lyd.

'You didn't sleep well?' asks Dom.

'I'll live.'

'Glad to hear it,' says Fee.

We walk up Archway Road for lunch at a local café that does expensive Italian breads, niche fillings, strong coffees and fresh juices. Fee and Dom both ask for the daily special: baked eggs on spinach with Parmesan and tomato toast. Fee wants an apple, pear and cherry juice and Dom a blueberry, strawberry and apple juice. Lyd orders tomato, mozzarella and pesto in piadina with an orange, mango and banana smoothie. I get a Parma ham ciabatta and a double espresso.

The conversation is stilted. Fee and Dom drink their juice in sharp, bitter sips. It's obvious they've been talking about me all morning.

I'm sighing a lot. Lyd keeps looking at me. I can't think of anything to say. One thing is clear; nobody wants to talk about the baby.

As my sandwich arrives I anxiously reach up

44

to take the plate from the waiter and see that my hand is trembling quite badly. I recall my arm as casually as possible (not very) and he puts the plate down with a quizzical smile.

Thankfully, everybody else's food is served within moments, distracting them from my weird arm flinch, but Dom manages to flick a surly glance my way before smiling and nodding gratefully for his baked eggs.

'So my writing's going really well at the moment,' I say.

Dom coughs and splutters. He's choking on his first bite of Parmesan and tomato toast. To be fair, it does look very dry but it feels like he's choking on my ambitions.

The cough turns into a fit, which slowly settles and then has a second wave. Fee pats his back and glares at me with scathing disinterest. She does this for so long that I look over my shoulder and see that there is absolutely nothing offensively boring behind me. Finally, Dom catches his breath.

'But you're not really ready to talk about it yet, are you, honey?' says Lyd.

'No, I guess not.'

The coffee is not working. Tiredness is draining all the accuracy from my perceptions. Everything is grey and dull. My eyes are lilting.

'Lydia tells us that you had an interview last month. Writing campaign copy for Freedom From Torture, was it?'

Fee inhales violently up through her nose. This throws me off. Did she ask or did he? I answer into my sandwich.

'Hmm, yes. It was quite a tortuous interview, actually.'

Nobody laughs.

'I didn't get it.'

'He does apply for things when he sees something he likes,' says Lyd.

I flash a quick frown at her.

'There's just so little in the world I seem to like.'

I say this looking directly at Fee. Her throat does a small, repulsed lift. Dom watches her in anticipation. Lyd squeezes my thigh. I'm about to take a bite of my sandwich but a deep tremor in my right hand and arm means I barely get the thing anywhere near my mouth. I pretend I'm looking at the bread, admiring it close up, and then put it down on my plate with a bit too much of a clatter.

'A household needs two fixed incomes these days though, doesn't it?' says Fee. 'Not everybody has the luxury of choosing a job they like.'

'But some jobs barely cover the cost of childcare, do they?' I reply.

'Some of your three-month royalty cheques barely seem to cover one week's shopping,' says Fee.

'It's tough for your generation. We're not denying that,' says Dom, pulling my angry glare off his wife.

'And we appreciate everything you've done for us,' I say, through gritted teeth.

We eat in silence.

My ciabatta is tough and floury. The taste of

46

Parma ham is hardly noticeable. I've finished my coffee and my mouth is getting dry. They all have big glasses full of fresh juice, colours so bright they're searing my eyes. I cough a floury cough.

'Maybe something else will come up,' I say.

This is my first mild appeasement and Lyd rewards me for it with a quick touch of the shoulder.

'Let's hope so,' says Fee.

Her tiny snipe makes me want to slam my arm down on the table, swipe all the stuff off it and rage-tip every object in the restaurant over. I'm clenching my teeth and trying to smile. I recall that this isn't the first time I've felt like this in the last few weeks and tell myself to calm down because I'm suddenly warning myself, *Irrational violence is a symptom of mania.*

I try to bring it down a notch. I breathe slowly, chew through my tough floury bread, and ease into a calmer self. I say and do nothing and gradually revert to the prior tired mess.

After this wave of anger the meal doesn't get any better, worse or any more interesting. Lyd manages to grab the conversation and take its focus off me.

'Wasn't Pascale lovely?'

'Her English was perfect.'

'Oh, yes, great girl.'

Luckily, my weird hands seem to be flying beneath the radar but there's a definite sense of my oddness getting through. I'm still getting glances from Fee. It's taking a great effort for me to remain within the parameters of normal social decorum. I can barely chew and swallow properly, let alone sit up straight.

'And so pretty too.'

'I just hope we get to meet this one again.'

Why is nobody talking about the baby? I want to scream all of a sudden, my rage popping back out for an encore. I clench my teeth and breathe slowly through my nose, closing my eyes. They carry on singing Pascale's praises.

It's obvious why the baby is not up for discussion. There's something very concise getting in the way of making it an appropriate subject: me. I am the priority problem. The baby is the next problem.

They think it's selfish and irresponsible for me to want anything besides an income and some stability but my mind is fast and clear for the first time in years. I have to keep writing my new novel. I have to prove that I don't need lithium. I can't be a father who gave up on himself.

3

When the air loses its chill and the courtship rituals of the mating season begin, life of almost every kind begins to thrive. Tiny curled-up leaves bud on tree branches. Tulips, daffodils and bluebells rise bravely. Early birds scurry in the undergrowth looking for the next special twig that looks like home. On any given day a million flying insects might suddenly burst into the skies as though a secret voice, connected to the dreams of every one of their kind, has called, 'Wake up! Your wings are ready! It's time to fly! It's time to fly!'

I'm listening to Bessie Smith whilst I eat my breakfast in the kitchen. The sliding door is open, letting in cool, fresh air. An ineffective sun is shining in a mostly blue sky. Blackie's on the lawn courting a slender brown female with a slightly speckled breast. He's dancing around her, running with his head bowed and beak open, singing a strange low song. This morning ritual has been going on for days.

After putting my empty bowl in the sink and grabbing my sultanas, I stand on the lawn in my dressing gown and slippers. The two birds fly into the evergreen when I step onto the patio but when I give my usual whistle, Blackie pops out, lands on the lawn and chirps at me.

— *chink-chink, chook-chook, chink-chink, chook-chook* —

(I've taken to loosely interpreting him and imagine this frequent and distinctive chirp he sends my way means both *Hello* and *Goodbye*.)

I warm him up by throwing single sultanas for him to chase after (he occasionally lets out a little chirp of protest if he feels the distance was too far between the two).

After a few minutes the real training begins. I leave a sultana on the edge of the patio and stand back. He jumps up and gobbles it down. I move forward and put another one down but closer to the house. He flutters back to the middle of the lawn.

— *pook-pook-pook, che-che-chook* —

(*You're too close.*)

I move back a little.

He jumps onto the patio, eyes up the situation, slowly edges forward and then runs and grabs the next sultana. Once he has it he rushes back to the edge of the patio.

I leave one even closer to my feet this time. He flies onto the lawn again.

— *pook-pook-pook, che-che-chook, pook-pook-pook* —

(*Way too close.*)

I move back a tiny bit. The sultana is about half a metre away from me. He climbs onto the patio, goes left, looks at it, goes right, looks at it. He takes a hop. He's really close. He lunges in for the sultana, runs away quickly, but stays on the patio looking at me, wondering what kind of game I'm playing.

I take a step back, into the house, and leave a sultana outside on the patio, another on the small white ledge beside the sliding door and one inside on the kitchen lino. He slowly hops diagonally left, diagonally right, diagonally left again. He twists his head to analyse the situation and decides he can risk the first one. He jumps over to it.

I can't see him because he's too close to the house. I wait, stretching onto my tiptoes, watching the ledge. I wonder if he's hopped away. I'm about to go and check when he jumps up onto it. I smile. He looks sideways at me, down at the sultana, back at me and then eats it. He sees the sultana on the lino but hops back onto the patio.

— *pook-pook, chickachicka-choo-choo, choo-chook* —

(*I don't trust you enough yet.*)

I repeat this previous step but the first sultana I leave out is the one on the ledge. I put three more on the lino inside the kitchen. He eats the first sultana but stops on the threshold, stares inside for a while and goes back onto the patio. I put another sultana on the ledge and stand back. The same thing happens.

The third time, after eating the first sultana and staring at the others for twenty or thirty seconds, he finally hops into the house and takes a sultana off the lino. He then immediately flutters back out onto the lawn (because I accidentally release a loud breath of delight).

Over the course of an hour I repeat this exercise again and again but, up on the edge of the breakfast counter, I place a big pile of sultanas in his direct line of sight. When he gets comfortable coming inside I only leave one sultana between the sliding doors and the breakfast counter and sit down on the stool furthest from the big pile of sultanas. He comes in for the single sultana four times, staying inside and eyeing up the big pile for longer and longer until, on the fifth time, he finally flies up onto the counter and buries his beak in the heap.

I am frozen on my stool but ecstatic. My spine is tense. I daren't even move my head. His attempt to eat from the counter causes about ten or fifteen sultanas to fall to the floor. Even though he has made this commotion, the sound of their dropping onto the lino unsettles him.

— *pook-pook, twit-ta-twer-choo-choo, twit-ta-tewah-tewah* —

(*I don't like this anymore. That's enough for today.*)

He jumps off the counter and flies out the door, across the garden and back into the evergreen. I can't stop smiling for about fifteen minutes. The spike in my happiness makes me decide that today is the day that I'm going to pack up Charlie's room. Our baby is only the size of a grain of rice but I've been off the lithium for a month and suddenly feel capable of facing it. I want to do it before the feeling goes. I'm more and more aware that it has to become the baby's room as soon as possible. It's time for things to change.

★ ★ ★

The local shop doesn't have any cardboard boxes. I have no luck at the supermarket either. I don't believe the woman who tells me (she's very distracted, asking every colleague who passes if they've seen Shaniqua, and she's unwilling to leave her post) but there's nothing I can do about it. She has a special way of standing guard against my need to progress into the store and ask somebody else, a silent threat. I have to concede to the fact that free things no longer exist and spend an unbearable amount of money in a shop that is tagged on to the front of a storage facility. The boxes are good quality and they all match so this offsets some of the resentment of paying.

Back home, I mentally prepare for the task at hand, warning myself that sentiment and nostalgia are the enemies of efficient packing. I try to enter Charlie's room with my emotions on mute. The first thing that has to go, before I start filling boxes, is the low-hanging moon. This dead pendulum has the ability to ruin the momentum of the entire day. It is too unique and holds too many special memories.

When Charlie's garbled toddler noises began turning into understandable words and phrases it quickly became apparent that he had been waiting to tell me that he wanted to play Fire Engines on the Moon. I never got to the bottom of why he was so inexplicably obsessed with the idea of this game but I was always quietly proud of how much imagination it displayed. He requested the game so often that I ended up making him a moon. I took two square cushions from the couch, lots of scrunched up newspaper, and wrapped it all in lots of string and sticky tape. Then I gave it a surface covering of white printer paper and hung it from a hook in the ceiling. It swung about a foot from the floor so it was easy for Charlie to play with but just slightly too high for him to climb on. Being so low, it also gave him the opportunity to imagine that it was part of the sky that emanated from his planetary carpet.

Slowly but surely I decorated it, at Charlie's request, with craters, roads for the fire engines and some of his other random inspirations (a lollipop lady, a shipwreck, Big Ben). He loved his moon.

When he didn't want to play Fire Engines on the Moon it also served as an excellent wrecking ball. Decimating piles of his books and toys gave him lots of pleasure and I would frequently hear him laughing on his own at the naughtiness of it all.

Whenever I carefully chastised him about this destructive game he would protest his innocence by saying, Moon Around the World. This was his way of suggesting that an interesting and fun science experiment (that I initiated by showing him how orbits work) had gone a little bit wrong. He always managed to distance himself from trouble in this way, not because he believed in the validity of deceit but because he knew that I would find his lies amusing.

I unhook the moon and hold it in my hands, staring at it for a while. I think about keeping it, packing it in a box, but remember my initial ruling — no sentiment and no nostalgia. I bring a pair of scissors up from downstairs and begin to cut into it.

It's been so long since I made it that the colour of the two cushions inside it is more vibrant than the ones downstairs. I pat them down, fluff them up and put them back in the living room. I put the rest of the scraps in a bin bag.

It was a good decision. After this I feel capable of dealing with anything the room can possibly throw at me. The entrance to the attic is in Charlie's room so I clear as I go, climbing up and down the ladder all afternoon; a box of clothes, a box of bedding, two boxes of toys, one box of books with all his pictures and paintings on top, a box of cuddly toys (horrible ferret teddy included), two trips for the dismantled toy chest, one for the toy whiteboard.

It's going really well. I've got every loose object packed up. The boxes are labelled with marker pens, stacked neatly. Everything is in its place. I just have the bulky furniture to deal with. Then I notice the windowsill. The retro 1960s robot should be in a toy box but the toy boxes are taped up and at the bottom of a pile of boxes in the attic. This single, defiant object brings the gravity of the situation falling upon me.

In violent despair, I grab the wardrobe and heave it over. It crashes into the middle of the room. I grab the retro 1960s robot and jump onto the back of it, smashing the robot down again and again. Somewhere along the way the

MDF backing cracks and I fall into the main body. Trying to destroy the rest is difficult. I keep stubbing my fingertips and knuckles. When my thumb cracks on a side panel I cry out in pain and stop. The robot doesn't have a scratch on it. I drop it in with the rubble.

My arms are full of adrenalin. I fall over trying to stand up. Looking at the mess I've made, I begin concocting the most plausible lie for Lyd: I had to smash it because it wouldn't fit in the attic. All the dints on the main body, I'm not so sure about. I'll probably have to work things so that it never sees the light of day again.

By the time I hear the front door open downstairs I've taken up the sides and doors of the wardrobe, filled a bin bag with broken pieces of MDF and tossed the retro 1960s robot behind the piles of boxes in the attic. I'm in the process of taking screws out of the slats on the child-sized bed.

I try to stay calm about Lyd being home but immediately fail. Blood rushes to my head as I hear her on the stairs. My arms feel light and jittery. My hands begin trembling. I try to maintain my conviction about my decision to do all this but I suddenly want to cry.

She is craning her neck to see if I'm in my writing room as she passes but then stops dead, noticing that Charlie's bedroom door is open.

'No,' she says, looking through the doorway.

She's wearing her black trouser suit with a white blouse which either means she woke in a highly emotional state and needed the suit to feel solid and professional or she had an important and stressful meeting today. Whichever it was, there is gloom in her eyes and it's rapidly expanding into damnation.

'I can't believe you did this.'

She walks away.

'It had to be done,' I call after her, getting up and moving into the corridor.

She stops before our bedroom door and turns back to face me: vacant, inhuman. I stay by Charlie's doorway, defending my decision to box up the room.

'I know you're not ready for this,' I say, 'but we have to face what's coming.'

She walks up to me.

'I don't have to face anything,' she says.

She punctuates the sentence by pushing me in the chest. I stumble back and jar my spine on the doorframe. After looking at the floor for a couple of seconds, trying to calm herself, Lyd launches at me, flapping her arms wildly.

'Heartless. Bastard.'

'Stop. Stop!'

I grab her wrists and restrain her.

'There was still time,' she whimpers, limp and instantly defeated now that I've grabbed her.

'Time for what?'

'It's not too late.'

I move my head, trying to gain eye contact. She evades my attempts.

'I don't have to go through with it,' she says.

'Go through with what?'

'I don't have to keep the baby.'

'An abortion?'

'It's my body,' she says, looking off to the side.

'But . . . we told your family.'

She turns away from me but doesn't walk off.

'Is that what you really want?' I ask, putting my hand on her upper arm.

Her shoulder flinches. I take my hand away.

'It's too late,' she says. 'We can't keep him now.'

She walks into our bedroom. I follow.

'What are you talking about?'

'Forget it.'

'It needed to be done. Baby or no baby. Do you really want an abortion?'

She sits on the bed and puts her face in her hands.

'I just want everything to stop, just for a minute. I'm tired, and nauseous. My whole body is sore. I have constant headaches. And you're on me as soon as I get through the door. The house is never empty. I've got this *thing* inside me. I'm never alone.'

I'm trying to make my face express sympathy rather than confusion.

'I'm sorry,' I say. 'I'll give you more time to yourself.'

'You should have told me . . . '

'I'm sorry.'

'I didn't get a chance to say goodbye.'

I sit by her on the bed.

'I'm sorry,' I repeat. 'I didn't think. Do you want to look through some of the boxes?'

'I don't want anything to do with it.'

It's clear that she needs to be alone. I put my hand on her back for a moment. She looks repulsed by the physical contact so I stand up

58

and leave the room. I think about going downstairs and making her a nice dinner but I have to stand by my decision so I go into Charlie's room and carry on dismantling his bed.

When I've put the pieces of the bed up in the attic and am in the process of sliding the ladder up into its mechanism, Lyd comes to the doorway. Seeing the room empty makes her turn her head away, raising one hand to her mouth and resting the other on her stomach.

'You should come in,' I say.

'I can't even look at it.'

I know what she means. My guts feel hollow. I step into the corridor and close the door behind me.

'I don't want an abortion,' she says.

'No?'

'I don't know why I said that.'

'No?'

'I know it's not . . . I need a drink. Do you want one?'

'Sure,' I say, struggling not to reproach her for all the alcohol she's still drinking.

We go downstairs to the kitchen and she pours from an open bottle of Rioja. I wonder to myself when she opened it.

We sit at the kitchen table. After a large first sip, Lyd sighs with relief.

'I didn't mean to go crazy up there,' she says. 'I guess I thought we'd be using your study as the baby's room.'

'I'm sorry. I thought it was the right thing to do. What about this abortion? This idea must have come from somewhere?'

'I'm tired. I was being spiteful. I hate feeling this irrational.'

'Do you want to talk about it?'

She thinks for moment.

'The past keeps changing,' she says.

'What do you mean?'

'Everything's slipping away. None of it's real. Last time, we were so young, so wrapped up in ourselves. We had no idea what it meant to be a family. We changed so fast, learnt things so quickly.'

'We had to.'

'There were all these new, spaces, inside me . . . When he was taken away they didn't disappear. I'm so lost inside myself. I'm a mother. You know? I never stopped being his mother.'

'He wasn't taken,' I say, correcting her.

'No,' she confirms.

'Sorry, but I can't think of it like that.'

'No. I know.'

We pause.

'You'll always be his mother.'

'But I'm not. I'm not a mother. Not anymore. Knowing that a part of our life with him was still here, that it was real, that was important to me.'

'His room . . . '

'It's never going to feel like a baby's room. It's Charlie's room.'

'We have to start looking forward. We have to try to make it feel right.'

'Something in me was kept alive, knowing that all his things were behind that door; it was like Schrödinger's cat.'

At this last remark she almost laughs but sighs grief through her nostrils instead.

'We can't cling to our old life. We have to get ready for our new one.'

'I don't want it . . . '

I sip my wine quietly.

'The thing in Charlie's room,' she says. 'It's gone for ever. That part of me. I can't be that mother again. The mother I'm going to be. That's somebody else.'

'Whatever's coming, we have to accept it.'

'Why?'

'Because it's coming whether we like it or not,' I say, raising my voice a little.

This hint of aggression does nothing but subdue Lyd further.

'I can feel it changing,' she mumbles, before slugging down the last of her wine. 'He's not here anymore.'

'He was already gone.'

'No, he wasn't,' she says. 'Not completely.'

She stands up and leaves the kitchen. I look at the sliding door absently, wondering how much of him I took away from her. I can faintly hear Blackie whistling up on the drainpipe. It soothes me to think of him out there, alone in the world, singing in the face of it all. Listening to him, I'm slowly guided back to the idea that packing up the room was the right thing to do.

4

Lithium was one of the three stable elements synthesised in the moments of primordial fusion after the Big Bang. It rarely occurs freely in nature but there are traces of it in almost everything. Nucleosynthesis calculations present a 'cosmological lithium discrepancy' because, in the atmosphere of dwarf stars, lithium abundance is often three times lower than expected. The amounts of hydrogen and helium (the other two stable elements synthesised) tally perfectly with predictions but the irregular lithium levels throw all of stellar physics and Big Bang nucleosynthesis into question.

Lyd is making a rocket, walnut and avocado salad. I'm pacing around the kitchen, being a bit useless. We're listening to Robert Johnson on the stereo. Whenever Lyd moves I seem to be standing in her way. Things have been strained since I packed up Charlie's room. Lyd seems to think that I've crossed a sacred line, undermined all the fundamental things we hold dear, and she's now applying the theory that I lack empathy to almost everything I do.

'I just think you should have told her in person,' she says.

'What's the difference? I probably would have waited another two months if I didn't feel bad about the fact that your family already knew.'

'You're constantly punishing her for remarrying, without even thinking about it.'

'It didn't even occur to me that there was a proper way of doing it.'

'Maybe it did,' she says, scooping out an avocado. 'Maybe it didn't.'

'I've admitted that I'm not particularly bothered about seeing my stepdad and stepsister.'

'John and Chelsea,' she corrects me.

'She only ever calls me when they're both out the house. She cuts me short if I call when they're in.'

'She's just trying to keep everybody happy. You want her all to yourself, and they want her all to themselves.'

'In her eyes, I'm part of a previous life.'

'We all have our separate lives.'

I turn the music off.

'Are you ready?' I ask.

'Not really.'

'Come on, I've been waiting ages.'

'Fine,' she says, putting down the knife, 'but you can make the dressing.'

We're griping at each other but I'm not going to let this ruin all my hard work. I've been building up to this moment for weeks. Lyd has promised she'll stay in the kitchen doorway, quiet and still. She moves into position.

I leave a small pile of sultanas on our breakfast counter, open the sliding door, sit on the usual stool and whistle. Seconds later Blackie flies out from the evergreen, across the lawn, through the open doorway and lands on the edge of our breakfast counter.

We've been eating our breakfast together like this most mornings. One day this week, when I slept in, I found him waiting at the sliding door and when I finally appeared he pecked at the glass to attract my attention.

He sees me sitting on my stool with a bowl in front of me, the usual pile of sultanas at his end, and presumes everything is normal. As promised, Lyd watches him peck at the sultanas silently from the kitchen doorway but only for about fifteen seconds before she says:

'This is really creepy.'

Blackie looks at Lyd, back at me and releases a very angry and disapproving sound:

— *SEEEEE, POOK-POOK-POOK!* —

Then he flies back out of the sliding doors, across the lawn and into the evergreen.

'You annoyed him,' I moan.

'And he annoyed me,' she says. 'I don't want his gross little bird feet on my breakfast counter. I don't know where he's been. What if he craps in here?'

'He doesn't. He won't. He's smarter than that.'

'He's not smart. He's just figured out a new way of getting food.'

'No,' I say, 'he likes coming in because he's brave. He's a risk-taker. He likes showing off.'

'Why can't you make real friends instead of pretending some flea-ridden bird loves you?'

'I have real friends.'

'I don't want you encouraging wild animals to come into my kitchen,' she says. 'It's weird.'

'*Your* breakfast counter? *Your* kitchen?'

'You know what I mean.'

'I think your parents are finally getting through to you.'

'Don't be stupid. Of course they're not.'

I realise that I want to talk about this even less than she does and so redirect our attention to the bird.

'I like having breakfast with him. It feels special, like it's a part of our new life.'

She shakes her head and rolls her eyes.

'That sounds like it could be your mum outside.'

'Lyd, don't be like this. I thought you'd think it was, I don't know, cool.'

'Go and let your mum in.'

I stand looking at her. The doorbell rings.

'Vince. Go.'

'He's a good omen. I'm telling you.'

I hear her mutter as I leave the room:

'Of course he is.'

When I answer the door my mum's face erupts into a happiness that's going to be very difficult to follow through on. She rushes forward, puts her arms around my neck and makes a faux-excited vowel sound:

'*Eeeeeeeeeeeee.*'

'Hi, Mum.'

She lets go and shuffles back with an excited wiggle to get a better look at me. She's wearing this season's Smart Look range from Next. Green and metallic tones, monochrome patches, premium fabric; she looks good but very much of the High Street. When I was little we were poor so now she treats herself.

John is looking up and down the street, unimpressed (as he is by everything). He wears grey old-man trousers (he's had them so long that I already know the rear seam is poorly restitched with white thread) and an untucked peach pastel shirt that the nineties forgot to take with them. If I had to signify the word boredom with one object it would be his large, drooping, grey moustache.

'John,' I say, acknowledging him and holding out my hand.

'Vinny,' he says, in his flat monotone, giving my hand one firm shake with a nod to match.

(Nobody calls me Vinny.)

'Little sis,' I say to Chelsea.

She glances up from the screen of her mobile phone for half a second, screws up her face a little bit and then looks back down. She's wearing blue Nike tracksuit bottoms, Reebok classics and a cheap stripy sweater that says *C'est la vie* across the front in a handwritten font.

'Can I take madam's bag?' I ask her.

Chelsea takes a step away from me without looking up.

'Are you two okay?' my mum asks, looking into the house. 'Where's Lydia?'

'Good, thanks,' I say, taking her bag and grabbing John's from him. 'She's in the kitchen.'

'I hope she's not going to any trouble. We had Kentucky on the motorway. Didn't we, love?'

'Aye,' says John. 'We did.'

'I'm sure it's fine,' I say, ushering them in. 'I'll just take your bags up.'

Charlie's room is empty besides our visitor's

double mattress and a chest of drawers. I stripped the wallpaper and whitewashed the walls at the start of the week. Every time I walk into the room I feel like my heart has been scraped out. Lyd hasn't even looked at it yet.

I drop the bags by the mattress and rush down to save Lyd from any social calamity that might be ensuing but, on the contrary, she's still in the kitchen and they have made themselves at home in the living room. The TV is already on and blaring out heinous advertisements. Lyd is putting cling film over the top of her bowl of salad. The kettle is on.

'Just making them a brew,' she says, smiling at me with as little aggression as she can manage.

'Did they even say hello?'

'Your mum did.'

'I can't believe they ate fried chicken on the way here,' I say. 'I told them you were making lunch.'

'It's just a salad. It will keep for tomorrow . . . Or whenever.'

'But you bought all that nice fresh bread.'

'Forget about it. They're here now. Let's just try and keep them happy.'

'Good luck.'

Lyd smiles. She likes how anxious and critical I become around my family. It's a shame she's struggling to forgive me for Charlie's room.

'Remember, it's your mum you want to see. As long as she's alright.'

I nod and kiss her on the cheek.

'Take these through.'

I take the two teas to the living room and put

them on the coffee table.

John already has his laptop out. Chelsea is still glued to her mobile phone. Mum is watching the TV. Their lifestyle is like a chain restaurant; everything around them is completely inter-changeable. They have the charmless ability to pick up their world and somehow dump it in your front room within five seconds.

'Ta, love,' says Mum, smiling gently and then raising both eyebrows and smiling with an extra ecstatic theatricality.

'Aye, ta,' mumbles John, his face made even duller by the light emanating from his laptop.

'She drinks all this fancy coffee now,' says Mum, rolling her eyes happily (which means Chelsea won't be happy unless she has a fancy coffee).

'Oh, right,' I say. 'What kind do you like?'

'You haven't got it,' states Chelsea. 'I like Starbucks.'

'Lattes?'

'Aye, yeah, that's it. Latty.'

'I'll see what I can do.'

I go back to the kitchen.

'Chelsea wants a *latte*,' I say with a smirk.

'Well, isn't she a very sophisticated fourteen-year-old girl?' says Lyd.

We eye each other wickedly. This visit could be good for us.

I make a filter coffee and warm some milk in the microwave.

'This is the best I can do, I'm afraid,' I say, passing Chelsea my concoction.

Chelsea sneers over the rim of the cup, smells

it and takes a sip. Pathetically, I'm eagerly awaiting her response.

'It's not like Starbucks,' she says.

My mum lowers her head and smiles at Chelsea with a distinctly non-threatening face that nonetheless implies that she could perhaps, please, try to do a little bit better than that.

Chelsea sighs and takes another sip.

'It's good though,' she says. 'It's better than what she makes.'

I put my hands together like a camp waiter, almost say, *Thank you*, restrain myself, and then walk back to Lyd in the kitchen.

'How long before they leave?' I ask.

She laughs.

An hour later we all get the Tube to Oxford Street. For Lyd's family eating together and being social is the main event but for my mum it's shopping — in this case, buying us lots of things for the new baby. We leave John in PC World (so he can stare dully at laptop specifications) and Chelsea in Starbucks (so she can drink lattes and get Wi-Fi on her mobile phone). We arrange to meet them in three hours outside Next (where my mum will have her final blow-out — buying something for everyone).

Meanwhile, we go inside every baby shop we come across and visit the baby sections in all the big department stores. Me and Lyd both hate shopping (and it's the last thing she wants to do whilst she's pregnant) but we put a brave face on because it's a good chance to communicate with my mum whilst she's in her element.

'So, what have Lydia's parents bought you?'

Mum asks, as she looks at overpriced wooden toys in a shop called E is for Elephant.

'Nothing yet,' I say.

'*Nothing?*'

'No, I don't think so.'

'Nothing? Lydia? Is that right?'

'No, they never take us shopping. Do they, Vince?'

I shake my head with a smile. Lyd is great with my mum.

'Well, we'll have to fix that, won't we? You'll be needing all sorts.'

Mum is full of provider's pride now, and on a shopping mission that only a veteran shopper of her standing can complete within three hours. She rushes us to a more standardised baby shop and zooms around it.

'Going to need one of them, definitely one of them, one of those . . . that's nice . . . and one of these . . .'

We fail to keep pace with her and end up standing by a play area where toddlers are grabbing at an oversized abacus and some giant square cushions that double as building blocks. We stare at the children playing, mildly depressed.

'Charlie would have been six now,' says Lyd. 'You forget they keep growing, don't you?'

I take her hand.

When Mum finds us again she's managed to attain a trolley. I haven't seen anybody else with a trolley. God knows where she found it. She's filled it with all manner of products. At a glance it seems to be a mixture of bare essentials and completely superfluous tat.

'Mum. That's way too much. We don't need all that.'

'Nonsense. This is just essentials.'

'How is this essential?'

I pick up a tacky-looking blue teddy bear.

'Weeeell, they all need a teddy. Show me one baby without a teddy.'

'It's too much, Mum. You can't afford all this.'

'I can afford what I want to afford and don't think I'm done affording things yet.'

Me and Lyd look at each other and smile with affection.

'We appreciate it, Linnie,' says Lyd. 'But he's right. It's too much. Besides, we've still got a lot of this kind of stuff up in the attic . . . from before.'

My mum's face sinks.

'Oh, yes. I'm not thinking, am I? I'm not thinking at all. I'm thinking it's your first. But it's not, is it? Oh dear. I'm sorry, loves. I just didn't think.'

'Mum, it's okay.'

She's tearing up.

'You're just going to have to take out what you've already got. God, I'm sorry. I just didn't think.'

Lyd goes to the trolley feigning a deeper interest than she actually has.

'It is lovely stuff you get here though, isn't it?' she says. 'And it's nice to have *some* new.'

My mum's face immediately reverts from sad to excited.

'That's what I say. It's nice to have some new,

isn't it? And it is lovely stuff.' She grabs Lyd's elbow and pulls her away. 'Come and have a look at this comforter. It's a bit much but . . . '

I'm left waiting with the trolley.

In the evening Lyd gets out some takeaway menus and suggests we order a couple of large pizzas and eat them with the salad she made earlier. This idea sinks into the abyss without even being acknowledged. She puts the menus down on the coffee table and looks around to see what's wrong.

'What you getting?' Chelsea casually asks John, picking up the menu she deems appropriate, making sure Lyd knows that her salad idea has been derailed without debate.

When the menu has been passed around I order for us all. John: stuffed-crust mighty meaty. Mum: medium Hawaiian. Chelsea: stuffed-crust double pepperoni. Lyd: medium vegetarian. Me: medium Mexican chicken. Then there are the obligatory extras: garlic bread, dough balls, chicken dippers and stuffed jalapenos.

While we're waiting for it to arrive we let Chelsea run loose with the remote control, signing us up for a 'TV and film on-demand' service. It's the only time she speaks with any enthusiasm to any of us about anything all day. My mum looks at me and Lyd sweetly, thanking us for making her so happy, which makes us both despair about the girl, but we both smile back awkwardly.

When the pizza comes my mum rushes to the door to pay.

Chelsea chooses the first film; a terrible

coming-of-age comedy about a bunch of Californian girls with way too much of everything in their lives — like *Clueless* but without the irony. John chooses the second; an inane thriller set in Boston about a financially motivated kidnapping gone wrong.

Both films are put together well enough to hold their own but the plots and characters are pitifully transparent. That seems to be part of the fun though. Chelsea, in particular, likes pointing out (in a semi-aggressive fashion) who is going to do what and how they are going to end up.

'She's going to be the popular one at the end.'

'They'll break up and he'll get off with her.'

'She'll escape with him.'

'It'll be him fighting him at the end.'

When all our pizzas are finished my mum pulls out a bag of chocolate that she's brought from home and passes different bits around until at least a kilogram of sugar disappears into the spaces between the seemingly indigestible lumps of dough in our bellies. Throughout the night Chelsea gulps down a litre and a half of Coke, John empties six cans of bitter, my mum drinks four cups of tea and me and Lyd have a glass of Coke and a couple of teas.

By the end of the evening me and Lyd have terrible stomach aches and they seem to interpret this as a metropolitan softness and laugh at us. They're not suffering in the same way and instead give heavy sighs and stifled burps that seem to signify deep pleasure.

I've got through the day without any weirdness but, today more than ever, I've noticed that all three of my family members constantly deflect emotional contact. They hardly ever look people in the eye and rarely talk about anything except the things they want. It doesn't seem a particularly healthy way to behave but it does create space for your own anxieties to float around freely, ungazed upon. When we say goodnight I realise that it hasn't been a stressful day.

★ ★ ★

An hour later, staring at an all-too-familiar watermark on the ceiling, I'm hoping that tonight's wakefulness might be caffeine-related or due to the fact that I'm uncomfortably full. Maybe I'll start getting drowsy after an hour or so. But the tiredness doesn't come. Feelings of hopelessness sweep through me instead.

The sight of Lyd sleeping by my side, growing a human being in her womb, fills me with guilt. Pregnancy is a real risk to her body and it will change the shape of her bones for ever. Meanwhile, I'm betraying her, taking a needless risk — skipping my lithium every day — and all in the name of rediscovering a version of myself that might not have even existed in the first place. Crushing that pink pill and rinsing it down the sink is just part of my daily routine now. It makes me a liar, a coward, a fool. Why do I even imagine that I deserve a life with her?

★ ★ ★

I don't know what day it is, what time, what year. I'm not thinking like that. My sleep has been broken at least four times. Yesterday and tomorrow are islands I'm swimming between. My brain is pulsing. I can hear the beat of blood between my ear and the pillow. The darkness is an alien blue. There's a cold sweat on my back. A distant noise sounds on the edge of my senses, pulling me further into a waking state.

A mouse in the walls?

I sit up and sigh, reaching for the glass of water on my bedside table. I drink half of it and decide to relieve my bladder. Sometimes, even if I don't need to, squeezing out a few drops of urine is enough to convince myself that I've only woken up because I needed the toilet. Afterwards, getting back to sleep is the obvious next step. I have to avoid thoughts like, *Waking in the middle of the night is a symptom of the manic cycle.* I have to think stealthily.

I hear it again whilst I'm in the hallway, something shuffling somewhere. It's an animal of some kind. It lacks the inane lifelessness of a house noise. I stop on the spot and listen quietly, poised, my perceptions soaring.

There it is again.

It has a distinct direction. It's coming from Charlie's room. I move towards the doorway. As my hand hovers over the doorknob it begins to shake. I'm looking at my vibrating hand but it doesn't seem like my hand. I can't feel the shaking. I can only see it.

Another sound.

Above me this time.

Something scurrying in the attic. I rub my arm up and down and listen carefully but the noises seem to have stopped. The tremors in my right hand are settling down. The feeling is returning to my extremities.

I begin to picture Lyd catching me standing in the hallway in the middle of the night, lurking by Charlie's door, and I suddenly remember that it's not Charlie's door, my mum and John are in there. Chelsea is downstairs on the couch. Charlie doesn't exist. I feel disorientated, aggrieved. It's been a long time since I've had to realise that he's dead. It used to happen every morning. This time it was smaller, less intense, but it was there.

I go to the bathroom and then head back to bed.

★ ★ ★

We planned to take my family for a walk on the Heath, let them stare down at London from Parliament Hill and bring them back for a healthy lunch before sending them on their way, but they all stay in bed until 11 am. Chelsea goes upstairs to shower and then Mum and John come down with their bags packed. I offer them breakfast, drinks, anything, but they're set to go.

'Chelsea wants McDonald's,' is all Mum says, clearly a little bit upset.

On the doorstep Mum comes up close and sneaks fifty pounds into my hand.

'No,' I say, trying to give it back. 'You already bought too much yesterday.'

She tenses her teeth and widens her eyes, begging me not to draw Chelsea or John's attention to it, then clasps my hand around it.

'It's for that *demanding TV* thing. You didn't have to do that. It made her night, that did.'

'I'm far too old for this,' I whisper in protest.

'You're never too old for a treat from your mum.'

She kisses my cheek and then pinches it and wobbles the flesh around with a wink.

Getting into their car, Chelsea looks over at us, sizes us up, almost says something that looks like it could have been a compliment, sort of nods and then climbs in. John starts the engine and raises a dull salute. My mum gives Lyd an intense hug.

'Look after him, won't you, love?'

'I will, Linnie,' she says.

Mum comes back to me and squeezes her arms around me.

'And you look after her.'

'I will,' I say.

'And at least think about getting a proper job, so you can take her out and buy her something nice.'

'Okay, Mum. I'll think about it.'

After they drive away, I stumble into the kitchen, lean on the counter and begin despondently eating grapes from the fruit bowl.

'That wasn't too bad, was it?' says Lyd, following me in and quickly clearing up the last traces of having had guests.

'No, I guess not.'

'What's up?'

'Nothing. I'm just being dramatic.'

'Go on.'

'I don't know. It's just that I really want to be able to connect with her, but we never quite manage it.'

'She seemed to have a nice time?'

'I know. Like I said, I'm being dramatic. I didn't sleep well. After I see her I can never quite shake this feeling that neither of us was really there. We try to reach each other but we can't.'

'That's sad, honey. But everything seemed fine to me.'

'Maybe I just want too much.'

'I don't understand,' says Lyd. 'What isn't there?'

'Feelings, I guess. They're there, but they're behind glass. We can see them in each other but we just can't feel them.'

'Your childhood was quite complicated.'

'I just wish we got more out of it. And I wish those two would respect her a little bit more, see how lucky they are to have her.'

'I'm sure they do . . . People can't go around feeling things and expressing things all the time.'

'No. I know. But they're so *cold* with each other. It scares me that families can be that way. They're all so separate. They don't even know they're depressed.'

Lyd finally understands.

'It's okay,' she says, coming to me and wrapping her arms around my shoulders. 'Our family will be nothing like that.'

This is the first time Lyd has referred to the future in a positive way since we found out she was pregnant. It's the first time she's held me since I packed up Charlie's room. I grab onto her. I don't want the moment to end.

5

The Green Man, one of folklore's oldest gatekeepers, is said to present his face in leaves and foliage. Those who see him before they enter a wood must beware the tricks he might play. His summer trees are catchers of light and beneath his green skin is a daytime twilight and a starless night of the truest dark. Though the gateway his face creates is impassable, and investigation reveals only dissolution, time spent in his shadows can unearth portions of his world beyond. He is sometimes said to send out woodland creatures to give obscure messages or play pranks and it has also been told that, on very rare occasions, he can blow the entire spirit of the natural world right through a person and shake them to the very core of their being.

On my computer screen this morning there was a yellow Post-It note: *Call Sergio.* I first met Sergio living in a shared house in Hackney after university. He was having trouble finding a decent job and I was unemployed and struggling with my writing so we became daytime dependents, meeting up in the kitchen for chats and cups of tea. Despite being vastly different we formed a bond that mattered to both of us so, even when he became a wealthy business lawyer and I remained a destitute writer, we stayed in regular contact.

When Lyd got close with Sergio's wife, Gloria, we mostly started seeing each other as a group of four. Lots of couples become friends because their children are similar ages, or they have a similar income and like to do similar things. We got on well despite our differences. They are second generation British-Spanish, much richer than us, unable to have children and completely uninterested in literature or science. Yet, somehow, it worked from the outset. We always had good times together.

When Charlie arrived we didn't pull towards other couples with children and they didn't pull away as a couple who couldn't have children. Me and Lyd were insistent that parenthood wasn't going to define us as completely as it did for others and Sergio and Gloria enjoyed the proximity to Charlie. The five of us were like an extended family. They babysat for us all the time. In some ways, they got to take on the portion of the parenting identity that we didn't want and they couldn't have. When Charlie died they were devastated and that kept us tight, even through the dark times.

When I see Sergio, he's walking towards the entrance of the café/bar where we always meet. He, or I, would usually just wait at the table. He's wearing a designer polo shirt, beige chinos and brown, tasselled moccasins; the usual preppy stuff that I constantly mock him about.

'Long time, buddy.'

He offers me his hand with an intense smile.

'Good to see you,' I say.

But this handshake is slightly too formal. We usually hug.

He glances over his shoulder nervously. He seems a little bit hyper. I'm now working on the assumption that this meeting is a set-up. I'm about to be analysed in some horrible, probing way.

'There's someone I want you to meet,' he says.

This could be worse than I expected.

A shrink?

An intervention?

I follow him, scanning all the tables. There's no one I can imagine we're going to end up sitting with. The person we're heading towards makes the least sense of all: a teenage Japanese girl with large breasts and a surly glare.

Sergio sits down beside her and proudly puts his arm around her shoulders in a possessive and sexually satisfied way. His smile is beaming. She seems underwhelmed. I sit down apprehensively. This isn't about me at all.

'This is Mitsu,' he says. 'Mitsu, Vince.'

I was wrong about her age. Now that I'm up close, she looks to be in her mid-twenties. Her face is stubborn and gloomy. It was her schoolgirl look that threw me off: crisp white blouse, black cardigan, pleated grey skirt, white ankle socks with frilled edges and flat-bottomed patent leather shoes with a strap. Three of her blouse buttons are undone, revealing the wispy edges of what must be an enormous tattoo that creeps up onto her cleavage from all directions.

'Hi,' I say, offering my hand.

She reaches for it limply, barely makes contact and is seemingly appalled by the formality of the gesture. She has the vacant disinterest of an extreme masochist and radiates emotional trauma. I smile awkwardly and look back at Sergio.

'I'm in love,' he says.

Mitsu looks at him disapprovingly.

'So I see,' I say. 'When did, *this* happen?'

Unable to bear hearing what Sergio is about to say, Mitsu slides off her chair and walks towards the toilets. I can't help but watch her walk away. Her nonchalance, alongside the thinly veiled sexual statement her clothing makes, is hard for the libido to ignore. Every man in the place watches her lustily, even the family orientated proprietor at the cash desk. I notice that she has the word *December* tattooed in red ink on the back of her right calf.

'*December?*' I ask.

'Isn't she amazing?' he says, shrugging.

'What's going on, Serge?'

He tries to compose his face, project some seriousness, or empathy, but he is full of lust for his overgrown schoolgirl.

'I know,' he says, unable to control the glee creeping onto his face. He takes a breath and tries again. 'I know.'

'Does she know?'

'That I'm married?'

'No. Does Gloria know?'

'I've left her,' he says, pausing for a second before asserting himself with a single nod.

'When?'

'This morning . . . I've never felt like this, Vince. She blows my mind.' He looks over his shoulder. 'She does anything I say. *An-y-thing.*'

83

'Please,' I say, holding a hand out for him to stop.

'You should hear some of things that come out of her mouth. She's from a different world.'

He smiles, shrugging again.

'And Gloria?'

'I've never felt like this . . . It's passion. Real passion.'

'Is Gloria okay?'

'Gloria?'

'Yes. *Gloria*.'

'She doesn't know. Not yet.'

'Doesn't know what?'

'Well, anything . . . But I can't go back there, Vince. That life is over. It's done.'

'Okay. Okay. Stop. Do you realise what you sound like?'

A flash of resentment passes across his face but is quickly displaced by joy.

'I don't expect you to understand.'

'What *do* you expect?'

He glances over to the toilets.

'I need you to tell Gloria for me.'

'*What?*' I say, standing up, intuitively beginning to leave.

He jumps up, runs around the table and stands in front of me. He has somehow grabbed a white envelope during these quick movements and now holds it in front of him.

'Please. Just give her this.'

'No way. I'm not implicating myself in this,' I say. 'She'll think I knew.'

'The letter explains everything.'

'So? Drop it through the letter box.'

84

'She deserves more than that.'

'No shit,' I say, laughing with disbelief. 'You've been married eight years.'

'But no kids,' he adds, with a half-smile, as if this is a saving grace.

'Lyd said you'd been accusing *her* of cheating.'

'She's been at it for months. Trust me. I know she has.'

'No. I'm not getting involved in this. You can talk to her yourself.'

'I *can't*,' he says, his smile beaming for a split second as he sees Mitsu exiting the toilet. His expression is suddenly urgent. 'Mitsu says it has to be gung-ho, just the two of us, no turning back, Bonnie and Clyde, Micky and Mallory, you know?'

'You're married. She's . . . I don't know what she is.'

'I know. I know. But you're the only person I can ask. *Please.*'

He looks her way again and desperately forces the envelope onto my chest. I shake my head, fold the envelope and put it in my pocket. He mouths *Thank you*, and tries to insist that I sit back down as she slouches onto her seat. I refuse but I'm still too intrigued to leave.

'How did you two meet?' I ask, standing by the table.

'Casino,' says Mitsu, lethargic, a slight accent.

'You're not gambling again?' I ask Sergio.

'Not anymore.'

'When was that?'

'Three weeks ago,' says Mitsu, bored.

'Three weeks. And now you're . . . Jesus . . . I

should go . . . Sorry, Mitsu. Something came up whilst you were . . . in there.'

She does not acknowledge this. Sergio jumps up and follows me for a couple of steps.

'Thanks for this, Vince,' he whispers, patting my shoulder.

'Yeah,' I say, walking away.

★ ★ ★

I step up to Sergio and Gloria's house and ring the doorbell. Gloria answers in a frilly black negligée, stockings and a silk robe that is open and hanging by her sides. Her face is heavily made up. The sight of her breasts bulging and her curvy thighs pinched by the stockings is a complete surprise to me. Up until recently, this would have been completely out of character. When me and Sergio get drunk together, he sometimes whinges about their sex life; how she never goes down on him, how their sex can never just be about fun or fucking, how there's too much inhibition and emotional preciousness, how, unprovoked, during bedroom conversations, she needlessly lectures him about her refusal to be 'a man's prize', or about sex not being a fantasy of power and worship. These are not the irks of a man whose wife has an outfit like this.

Seeing me, the initial sexual confidence drains from her face, her spine slouches and she quickly closes her robe and ties it up.

'What are you doing here?' she asks, poking her head out the doorway, looking both ways and then grabbing my arm and dragging me inside. 'You're going to have to be quick.'

'Jesus, Gloria.'

'What?' she asks, impatiently. 'What?'

'Nothing. It doesn't matter.'

She slants her head at me as a warning.

'What is it? Dinner? The four of us some time? Message for Serge? Something from Lydia? What?'

I take the envelope out of my pocket.

'Message *from* Serge,' I correct her.

'Fine, fine,' she says, snapping it out of my hand, barely recognising the irregularity of this. 'Go. Go.'

'Okay,' I say. 'I just want you to know, I didn't know anything about it until this morning.'

It now dawns on her that this situation is strange. She closes the door with a confused expression, glances at me critically and then opens the letter. Reading it, her frenetic energy depletes in seconds. By the time she's turned the first page she is sitting at the bottom of the stairs barely able to keep her head above her shoulders.

The letter is long. As she is reading the final page the doorbell rings. Gloria looks up with a dumbfounded expression, as though she's not sure what the noise signifies. Her eye make-up has run down her cheeks. Her crying has been silent.

'I'll get rid of them,' I say.

'No!' she shouts, suddenly coming into herself.

She panics, flings the letter aside and runs towards me.

Bemused, I look through the clouded pane of

87

glass by the side of the front door and see the blur of a familiar figure that I can't quite place.

'No!' repeats Gloria, trying to forbid me to even look.

She stands in front of the door and pushes me away. Intrigued, and fairly certain that I know the person outside, I try to reach around Gloria's waist for the door handle but she thrusts her breasts out at me, forcing me to take a step back and desist.

'Don't,' she says, serious, broadening her stance.

To my horror she seems to be implying that there could be an accusation of assault in store for me. She's desperate.

The doorbell rings again, twice in quick succession, and is followed by immediate, heavy knocking.

'Gloria? I can hear you. What's going on?'

The voice is muffled. The identity of this person is dangling just out of reach, it won't come to me, but Gloria sighs, her protective stance slumps, and, presuming that the game is now up, she opens the door.

Peter, Lyd's big brother, is standing in the doorway in a Prada suit, holding a chilled bottle of Cristal. His face does not falter from its relaxed, overconfident smile when he sees me.

'Alright, Vince? What are you doing here?'

★　★　★

Back home, sitting in a chair on the patio after a late lunch, my feet up on the round outdoor table, I can barely stay awake. The stress of the morning was exhausting. Gloria and Peter have forced me into a corner, making me swear that I won't tell Lyd about them. I hate lying to her. I'm deceiving her enough as it is. The hope of getting things back to our usual open and honest state is the only thing keeping me on course. Another secret feels like too much, a step too far.

I'm also worried about what Sergio and Gloria are doing to each other and, even though it is a relatively small aspect of the situation, I feel personally betrayed by their lack of regard for the friendship the four of us share. There was a time when we could sit around this outdoor table without a negative thought crossing between us. With these affairs, those days are gone. They've thrown what we had away.

I try to think about writing to distract myself from the pressure of all these lies and betrayals. There's a quote on a Post-It that I've stuck on my desk that's been working its way into the story. Something Kant wrote. It's slowly becoming a theme in the work, connecting the different narratives.

On the great map of the spirit only a few points are illuminated.

I say it to myself a few times, trying to mull on how it relates to the fictional events, how I can make it resonate, but I can't concentrate on concepts or imaginary people. The sun is shining and, today, after Mitsu, after Peter, brightness is enough.

Next door's cherry blossoms are blooming; glorious pinks and whites. The sunlight makes

89

them look unreal, blurring all the edges with the intense purity of their colour, creating clouds of candy floss and marshmallows.

My eyes keep giving in to sleep. My head lolls, dips, and then jerks up, awake. I do this again and again and, between the snoozes, through the cracks, the colours of the trees gleam. Each time I slip away it's for a little while longer. It starts with a second, two seconds, four, gradually moves up to a minute. Somewhere along the way I'm unconscious long enough to call it sleep. Five minutes. Ten minutes. I start waking with my chin on my collarbone and a crick in my neck. Finally, I sleep for so long that I lose track of time altogether.

A dull strain in my ankle wakes me. I open my eyes and see that Blackie is standing on the tip of my right foot, sideways, in profile, his black left eye with its golden ring piercing me intensely. His shiny yellow beak is glistening in the sun, clouds of pink-and-white blossom pulsate behind him. This is the first time he has come to me since I annoyed him over a week ago. It's the first time he's ever come to me without my coaxing him with sultanas.

He stands in silence. He's not here for food. He is here to show me his true self. But he is extremely disappointed in me. After seeking and gaining his trust, and making him a part of my journey to a new self, I showed him off like a trained pet. He must gaze into me and see if I have the conviction and integrity to see my journey through. I'm not sure how he tells me all this. It is implicit.

He jumps, turns one hundred and eighty degrees and faces the opposite direction, still on my foot, looking at me with his other eye. Uneasiness rises in me. Showing me his profile like this is a demonstration of his power. He is turning himself into a symbol, a pure being, and by doing so he is opening a chasm into another realm. Behind him, in the amorphous pinks and whites, there is an ancient world, older than I can imagine, and he is one of its messengers.

He jumps again, this time he lands facing me. His eyes contain the unflinching supremacy of nature. There is no compassion in their black depths. He sees me for exactly what I am. I feel deep and sincere shame and this shame forms a bridge between us, connects us. His beak opens and, as I look down his throat, something, an idea, a message, pours out from inside him, from beyond him:

I will save you if you try with all your heart. I will protect you. But if you are weak, I will leave you to be devoured. I will stand aside as your world falls apart.

'I'll try,' I whisper. 'With all my heart.'

★   ★   ★

My eyes are closed. I'm not sure how long I've been asleep. The entire blackbird experience could have been a dream but when I open my eyes I find myself face down on the lawn. My head is throbbing. I have no idea how I got here.

Blackie is standing in profile about a metre away from me on the grass. He jumps one

91

hundred and eighty degrees and my headache calms slightly. He jumps one hundred and eighty degrees again and I feel almost normal, as though nothing has happened. He is just a bird on my lawn.

— *chink-chink, chook-chook, chink-chink, chook-chook* — *(Goodbye.)*

He flies away.

6

Human beings have three types of photoreceptor in their retinas: red, green and blue. This is the reason they see the range of colours that they do. Their spherical eyes are only able to focus on one thing at a time, changing the way they perceive, understand and interact with reality. Birds, on the other hand, have four photoreceptors and their cones' maximal absorption peaks are higher, enabling them to see ultraviolet light and countless additional variants of colour. Their eyes are also flatter so they can focus on lots of things at once. However, the unfathomable difference is the fourth cone. Birds see a whole field of visual information that is beyond human comprehension. People can try to guess what it is by studying the behaviours and attributes of birds (some experts say polarised light, others magnetic fields) but in the end they have to accept the limitations of the imagination and admit that birds can see an entire dimension that people are unable to envision.

I wake up at around 5:30am and decide to get up and make Lyd breakfast: orange juice, porridge with seeds and sliced dates, coffee, toast with butter and honey — a basic but broad weekday breakfast. I listen to Lucille Bogan as I prepare it.

After showering, Lyd arrives in the kitchen

93

wearing her white robe. The idea of me eating into the few private minutes she has in her day annoys her at first. She relaxes when she sees the breakfast laid out for her and even more when I turn my music off.

'I won't have time to eat all this,' she says, almost apologetically, running her fingers through her hair to distribute whatever product she puts in whilst it's still wet. 'I've got a big day.'

I approach her.

'I know,' I say, reaching for her waist. 'I just wanted to treat you.'

She lifts an eyebrow and registers how tired I look.

'What are you doing up at this time anyway?'

'Just woke up,' I say, reaching for the knot at the front of her robe.

She flattens my hands to her stomach.

'I usually just grab an apple,' she says.

'You should be eating properly. All the critical growth happens around this time. Organs, all that stuff.'

She's amused that I know more about her pregnancy than she does.

'*Really?*'

'Really.' I submit to her amusement with a smile. 'I've been reading up.'

I slide my hands from under hers, around her hips and down her robe until I'm touching the skin of her lower thighs. At the first indication of upwards movement, she takes a step back and looks at me with a playful warning.

'We don't want to interrupt the critical growth, do we?'

I move away with a half-amused, half-rejected smile, wondering when we last had sex. My libido is pointlessly blazing. It has been for days. Lyd walks over to the breakfast counter and pulls herself onto a stool with a sigh.

'You not eating?' she asks, skipping the porridge and spreading honey on a piece of toast, no butter.

'Too early,' I say, patting my stomach.

'For you or your little friend?'

She drinks half of her orange juice, whipping an amused glance at me.

'He doesn't come anymore.'

She glances again, this time with a frown, but quickly dispels the need to worry. She begins eating her slice of toast.

'Oh well,' she says. 'I'm surprised he kept it up for as long as he did. Maybe he got bored of sultanas?'

'Maybe,' I say.

It doesn't occur to her that I would lie about the importance of Blackie's role in my life, or that my heart might be racing at the mere mention of him.

'He'll probably come back,' she offers, but with a tone that suggests that it's unimportant either way. 'Creatures and habits and all that.'

'It doesn't matter,' I say, fighting the blood gushing through my veins, attempting to project an image of normality. 'It's mating season. I think he's paired off.'

She looks out through the patio doors as though she's only just registered that it's spring. The brightness makes her wince.

'You okay?'

'Just another headache,' she says.

'Can I get you anything for it?'

She shakes her head, puts her elbow on the breakfast counter and clamps her middle finger and thumb around her temples, moving them in tiny circles. With the other hand, she pushes her plate away. I start clearing up.

★ ★ ★

When Lyd leaves the house it feels empty and I'm uninspired, almost afraid of writing. Words seem to have abandoned me. I stare at a blank page in my notebook and then check my email.

The inbox is full of the usual stuff from websites I'm signed up to — books I should read, music I should hear, tickets I should buy, films I should watch, jobs I should apply for, clothes I should wear, old web accounts I should tend to, competitions I should enter, food I should order, discounts I should take advantage of — an algorithmic world scarily close to correct but, thankfully, just slightly wrong. There's nothing from the magazines I sent the last batch of short stories to, nothing from old friends, nothing from an actual person.

I check my junk mail.

It's even worse in there: offensively transparent scams and corporate click-bait that even my corporate email provider thinks is too invasive. I'm careful with my email address so it took them fifteen years but the Viagra spam I've heard so much about has finally started arriving. In amongst the devious titles designed to get me to click there's:

From: *CHARLIE*

Subject: (1) Re: contact me please . . .

I delete it along with all the rest of the junk.

When I click back on my inbox my junk folder has (1) next to it. I click it and look.

Email from: *CHARLIE*

Subject: (2) Re: contact me please . . .

I click delete again and it pops back into my junk inbox, instantly this time.

Email from: *CHARLIE*

Subject: (3) Re: contact me please . . .

I start deleting it again and again until my head falls into a spiral. When I stop clicking it says:

Email from: *CHARLIE*

Subject: (56) Re: contact me please . . .

It must be a clever new kind of junk mail, a tracker in it or something. I'm not technologically gifted but I know better than to open it.

The word CHARLIE flashing back onto my screen again and again has made me feel like he's in the house somewhere. Behind me. Around me. I need to get out, see a fresh face; somebody separate from the entanglements of my intimate life but close enough to understand them. The only person who fits into this category is Jamal. I stand up impulsively and leave, heading towards him.

I don't see a single blackbird on the twenty-minute walk over to his house but I can hear them everywhere; hiding in bushes, behind houses, in trees. My knock on the door is slightly desperate, like I need to escape the noise.

Jamal answers the door with an unlit joint hanging out of his mouth, squints at outside's brightest and motions for me to follow him inside. His long, greying dark hair is held back in a ponytail. He's wearing his usual black T-shirt and ripped, oil-stained jeans. As always, the entire floor of his house is lined with newspaper and covered with small chunks of steel and aluminium that have neat lines of washers, pieces of plastic and nuts and bolts next to them. It smells of spray oil, tar and cannabis resin. There are carefully exposed foot-shaped holes in the newspaper to indicate how people must navigate the room. The couch, the chairs, the coffee table and the kitchen table (from a sideways glance) are all covered with newspapers and motor parts. Each stair has a carburettor sitting on a newspaper, pushed over to the right-hand side.

Upstairs there are two bedrooms. He uses one as a workshop, for more serious work, but his actual bedroom is where he spends most of his time, polishing pieces of metal cross-legged on his bed and putting things together so he can sell them on the Internet and make his meagre living (he inherited his house from a childless, divorced aunty who always favoured him over her other nieces and nephews).

A quick look into his bathroom reveals a bathtub full of engine parts soaking in a murky grey liquid which is giving off noxious fumes. I fleetingly wonder how he cleans himself but realise I haven't seen him without oil-stained skin for almost ten years. I'm not sure he does wash.

In his bedroom, he carefully takes the four corners of a newspaper, gathers up the pieces of a camshaft and puts the bundle in the foot of his wardrobe, revealing an old wooden chair for me to sit on in the process. He steps up onto his bed as though navigating the ledge of a fifty-storey building (there are lots of loose pieces of metal on sheets of newspaper) and gestures towards the chair. By the time I get to it and sit down he has relit his slightly oil-stained joint and is scraping rust from the main section of a crankshaft.

Until now Jamal has been silent. He can only talk properly whilst he works. He's better at engaging when his mind is diverted.

'So,' he says, 'what can I do for you?'

'Just needed to get out of the house.'

'Spliff?'

He offers it to me and glances at my legs, jigging up and down.

'No, thanks,' I say, putting my hands on my thighs to stop them moving. 'Feeling a bit edgy as it is.'

'Yeah? What's going on?'

'Nothing. The usual. Life stuff.' I stand up and walk over to the window, evading little piles of scrap on the floor. 'Do you know Serge and Gloria are cheating on each other?'

I met Jamal in the same shared house as the one I lived in with Sergio after university. Whilst Sergio was seeing Gloria in the evenings, we often smoked weed and had long philosophical discussions. Jamal and Sergio share a passion for vintage cars so they always stayed in touch a little bit. Occasionally, they go to a motor show or trade fair together. I sometimes think they keep it up because I'm an umbilical cord between them — this could be sheer narcissism though.

'It was always going to happen,' he says.

'You think?'

'Yeah, man. She constantly forces her presence everywhere in his life, undermines him in front of his friends, emasculates him. He'll be having a fling with someone who lets him cut loose a bit, most likely younger. And Gloria's probably realised that she bullies Serge so much because she wants someone more macho, someone who won't put up with all her oppressive shit.'

'Do me a favour. Never tell me what you think about me and Lyd.'

He laughs at this, but he's also frowning at the way I've started treading back and forth across his room. I can't help it though. I can't stay still.

'You two are a good match. Yin and yang. And probably not the way around you imagine.'

'Maybe. And you're bang on. Serge *is* running off with someone younger. East Asian girl. I guess he's cutting loose but, in some ways, she seemed to have him by the balls too. Gloria's been sleeping with Peter.'

'Peter, Peter? Peter Bateman, Peter?'

'Yep. The psycho himself.'

Jamal shakes his head and scrubs with more ferocity.

'Is there anyone that guy doesn't end up

fucking? He truly doesn't know where to draw the line.'

(Peter once seduced and had sex with Jamal's little sister in Serge and Gloria's downstairs bathroom when she was drunk at their summer barbeque.)

'I try not to think about it,' I say. 'The world's depressing enough without wondering why all intelligent and beautiful women seem to want to sleep with him.'

'Does Lydia know?'

'No. Not yet. I told them I wouldn't say anything but I can't keep lying to her. With Lyd, it's like the truth is always there, talking to her, even if I'm not saying anything. It starts twittering in my ears. The only upside is that she's pregnant, and I don't want to upset her. So at least there's actually a reason to keep quiet.'

He raises his eyebrows and stops scraping at his metal.

'Lydia's pregnant?'

'Yeah.'

'You can't just slip the P-bomb in like that. Pregnant?'

'Yes. Pregnant.'

'This is major, life-altering news, man. No wonder you're treading the boards like a caged tiger . . . Unless you're trying to talk it down? Is that what you're doing? Do you not want to talk about it?'

He starts scraping again. I continue pacing between the far wall and window, careful not to step on any motor parts.

'I don't mind,' I say. 'But I think I might be

unravelling a bit. Not because of the pregnancy. Well, maybe. I don't know.'

'So you've come to your guru for some sage advice.'

'You wish you were my guru.'

He smiles.

'Congratulations, by the way.'

'Thanks,' I say. 'I think it could be good for us.'

'So what's *unravelling*?'

I peer out the window. There's a blackbird pecking for worms down on a bare patch of the mostly overgrown lawn.

'Oh, nothing really,' I say, with an overwhelming and slightly frightening intuition that I'm not allowed to tell him about Blackie now that I've seen this blackbird. 'Nothing specific.'

The blackbird flies up into a tree. I feel a pang of relief and turn to face Jamal. He sucks on his joint a couple of times and puts it back in his ashtray, confused. I have to tell him something.

'I stopped taking my lithium when I found out about the pregnancy.'

This statement earns me a rare second of eye contact.

'Good for you, man,' he says, nodding and then looking back down at his crankshaft. 'That's great. What does Lyd think about it?'

'She doesn't know.'

'So that's the real secret. Not this stuff with Peter.'

'I just didn't want to be . . . I don't know.'

'I never thought you should have been put on that stuff in the first place. You know how I feel about people medicating trauma and depression. All that chemical balance bullshit.'

'Ironic given your lifestyle choice.'

He lifts up his joint and smiles at it.

'Hey, I'm not depressed, man. This stuff just helps me think straight. Most men need a woman. I need this. I thought you'd lost a couple of pounds.'

'Really?'

'You look less bloated. More like you. Do you want some chai?'

'Sure.'

He gets up and leaves the room, grabbing a darkly stained mug on the way.

I look around with a sigh. The room, and the impossibility of a woman spending the night in it, make me feel momentarily sorry for him but I also empathise with the level of solitude he has sought out. On the surface it might seem like the house of a disturbed kleptomaniac but it's also the systematic domain of a cleverly integrated and highly functioning recluse. There is strength and self-assurance in the environment, motivation and attainment. In his presence, I never feel pity or concern. In fact, I envy his resolve. It is only when he leaves the room that the loneliness of it creeps over me. And that is my loneliness, not his.

He comes back with two cups of chai, strong and black. I take mine with a nod and he carefully gets back into his cross-legged position on the bed. He takes a sip, leans over and puts the cup on his bedside table (which is covered with miscellaneous washers and nuts and bolts).

He picks up a small, curved toothbrush with metal bristles and gets back to scraping and scrubbing his crankshaft.

'I'm so glad you're off that shit,' he says. 'It was no good for you.'

I nod in agreement, quickly, anxiously.

'If she finds out though . . . ' I say, pausing with dread. 'And, I mean, I can barely sit still. I'm awake all night. I feel like I've got electricity running through my veins.'

'But that can't last, can it? That's not how you used to feel, before?'

'I don't think so. It can't be. But if she finds out . . . '

He pauses and takes a look at me, wondering if anybody could see anything but a nervous wreck. He doesn't seem to decide either way but he's excellent at concealing his thoughts when he wants to be.

'How's the queen of the subatomic dealing with being pregnant?' he asks, deciding to balance his view of the situation with an interpretation of Lyd's current state.

'She's busy. Working all the time, as ever. I think she might be drinking too much. Well, for someone who's, you know. But I can't really get a handle on her. At the start it seemed okay. She seemed to be working it out. She's gone more distant now. I thought I'd got through to her a few weeks back but I've started getting the feeling she's not really there again.'

'Sounds about right. She's always been evasive. She likes to work things out on her own. But she always seems to get there in the end. She

104

always comes back to you.'

I nod, fearing the hope he's trying to give me.

Jamal always has a pragmatic and assured tone of voice. His words come out spoken as singular truths. More often than not, he's extremely objective and insightful but he occasionally misses the mark completely. This tone of his is part of the strength that comes from his solitude, because he never has to mediate his opinion or compromise for somebody else, but I've come to realise that I can't always trust it.

I watch him scraping at his metal, grateful for his friendship. All the things that soothe and satiate his being happen with mechanical precision; rolling joints, cleaning scrap, fitting things together, taking things apart. Everything is always straightforward with him. The world holds no secrets. All the parts fit together.

'And you're alright?' he asks. 'The withdrawals aren't too bad? You're not seeing pink elephants or anything?'

'No, no,' I say, looking out the window. 'Just, you know, a bit anxious. A bit mental. Because I can't really show it.'

He nods absently.

'Good. That's good, man. She can't say your heart's in the wrong place, can she? That's what I'm taking from this. I know how she feels about you towing the line, and why she wants it that way, but you don't want to be some kind of zombie-dad, do you?'

This is all I wanted, to hear somebody say that I'm doing the right thing, but part of me is appalled that he can say I'm on the right track.

'Thanks,' I say. 'But please don't tell anyone I'm off it.'

'You know me better than that. You must think it's the right thing to do though, for the baby.'

'I just need to get back to me.'

'Cutting out the lithium has got to be the best way to go about it.'

I nod and start pacing back and forth again, taking compulsive sips of my chai. I finish mine before he even reaches for his second sip. He's deeply engrossed in bringing the shine back to the surface of the curved hunk of steel he's holding. He eventually puts it down, lights his joint and reaches over for his cup.

'It's such a relief to tell somebody,' I say.

'No wonder you're on edge, man, trying to keep something like this locked up.'

'I hope you don't mind. I feel like I've just got to . . .'

I put my cup down on the windowsill and loosen my arms. I pivot on the balls of my feet, shake my hands and release a bizarre, nasal roar: 'Uuuunnncchhhhrrrrrr.' Jamal puts the end of his joint out in the ashtray, exhales with a grin and takes a big gulp of his chai.

'That's it,' he says. 'Wig out, man. Let it all hang loose.'

I allow my arms to flop down and shake my body and head from side to side. Jamal laughs and starts making another joint.

'That feels good,' I say. 'I'm so coiled up.'

'You've got to let out your weird, man.'

'I really do.'

I shake my face, bounce up and down and

make more, strange guttural noises. Jamal is increasingly amused and impressed. He is the only person I know who I could behave this way in front of. A lot of the major decisions he has made in life have been due to his difference, and his fear of the normal. Moments like this only confirm the meaning of our friendship for us.

Feeling accepted for who and what I am, I dance further into my weirdness. My meat and bones begin to feel slack and loose. I jolt and jerk, twist and spasm. My body is a living concept, nebulous and unique. I'm a demented ballerina, an electric chicken. I'm thrashing and twirling, shaking and writhing, completely lost in the pleasure of it all.

When I finally stop, out of breath and pleased with myself, I notice that Jamal isn't smiling anymore. He's looking fixedly down at the fresh joint he's making, reluctant to raise his eyes. I can see the wilfulness in his refusal to glimpse my way.

My smile drops. I look at the floor. Somewhere along the way I've kicked one of his piles of scrap and scattered it across the floor, mixing it in with two other piles.

'Shit, sorry,' I say, bending down, beginning to gather it up.

He pulls up his right cheek in a tense, forced smile and continues to look down at his joint.

I quickly pluck out the pieces of metal that look out of place, because they don't fit in any neat lines. But once I've gathered up all the obvious ones the piles become confusing. Lines of bolts appear in two directions at once, crossing each other. Everything looks increasingly random. There's no order. After moving a big piece of aluminium over to the kicked pile I begin to get anxious that I'm making things even worse, that I've completely shuffled the order of everything and it will be better if I just stop.

'I think I got it back how it was,' I say, sitting back down on the wooden chair, knowing that there is no way that I've managed to put things back in their original place.

He gives the same nod and forced smile, looking at his joint.

I sigh and look towards the window. My legs are still and the anxiety has gone but it took too much. I went too far. There must be something wrong with me. Jamal is looking downwards too intensely. I think I'm going to leave.

SECOND
TRIMESTER

1

In June's warmer, longer days growth and replenishment replace the struggle to reproduce and survive. Food becomes abundant and rearing is in full swing. Poppies, orchids and foxgloves add blush to fields. Ducklings, goslings and cygnets waddle behind their parents. Grasshoppers and crickets begin to chirp in meadows. Butterfly wings unfurl and take flight. Dragonflies hover over water. Female bats suckle inch-long pups. House martins, swifts and swallows swoop and glide, diving for insects. Fawns fall and antlers rise. Baby badgers squint at their first night sky. Though much is lost or stolen, destroyed or killed, more is found and given, created and born. The rustling of life is everywhere.

We have the dating scan this afternoon so Lyd's taken the day off. I'm sitting at my desk pretending to write, realising (because of Lyd's presence in the house) that I haven't been working properly since Blackie messed with my mind in the back garden. I have six chapters, a whole bunch of scraps and no focus or momentum to put any of the rest of it together. Nothing correlates. All the chapters are about different people, in different times, in different places. I no longer have any idea what I'm working on.

Two weeks ago I used editing as an excuse to

scroll down the same six chapters again and again. On the Friday I sent my first three chapters to my agent, Angela 'not the dead novelist' Carter, and convinced myself that this was enough of an achievement for a week.

Last week, along with the pointless scrolling and unfocused rereading, I was checking my email for a response from her thirty, forty, fifty times a day. Constantly clicking, scrolling, clicking. She still hasn't got back to me.

Usually, when I send Angela pages, she at least acknowledges them. Later, she gets back to me with ideas about where we might send extracts for some advance publicity or else she suggests areas that could do with a little bit of tightening up. I'm beginning to think that she's so embarrassed by what I sent her that she's ignoring me.

I try to forget about it and instead focus on why I've ground to a halt. I revisit my archaeology metaphor where the unmapped charters of fiction are the entire landmass and the seed of inspiration, the excitement of the new thing, is like the first moment, after months of methodical digging, when the archaeologist reveals a small portion of an ancient bone. What follows — the real work, dusting away at the bones, following alien curves, revealing unforeseen crevices, allowing the hidden object to reveal itself — that's where I got lost.

I have to start again where I left off; that's what Lyd's presence in the house tells me. I need to reconnect with the bones, let them surprise me, trust that slowly following them will lead me further into their deeper structure. Their subterranean world is full of incomplete fragments but I have to believe in my initial feeling; that this is a special project, the different strands are part of a singular structure, I have to keep going and see it through.

The doorbell rings. A distraction. I rush down the stairs but Lyd's already there. She opens the door to her brother, Peter, whom she is extremely surprised to see.

'Oh. *Hi*. Did I tell you about the scan?'

'The what?'

'What are you doing here? Come in, come in.'

'Vince . . . ' he says, seeing me on the stairs and nodding, 'erm, told me you'd be around. Did he not tell you I called?'

I make my way down the rest of the stairs. He looks at me with a pitiful need for me to corroborate his story. He did not call. He must be here to see me. He would have thought Lyd was at work. She turns her head to face me.

'Sorry. I forgot,' I say.

Tension drifts out of both of their faces.

'Maybe he did mention the scan,' Peter concedes, unusually generous. 'I just remembered that you were going to be at home. I thought we could . . . eat.'

He holds up a brown takeaway bag.

There's something different about him. He's sniffing a lot, which probably means he was snorting coke last night (hopefully not this morning), but it's not that. It's beneath that. His face has softened. He looks mildly worried, less reptilian.

113

'Yeah. I'm pretty sure I mentioned it,' I say.

We walk through to the kitchen.

'Can you eat before this thing?' he asks.

'Yes. And I have to drink at least a litre of water. We don't have long though. What did you bring?'

'Sushi.'

'It looks fancy,' she says, impressed and coming round to the idea of his unplanned appearance.

'It is. I'm told the chefs are very good.'

'It doesn't seem like much for three,' I say.

'It looks like plenty,' says Lyd, looking at me insipidly.

My ego is a little bit drunk on the fact that Peter seems unable to belittle me for a change. I have to be placated and fed posh sushi. This must be about Gloria.

(Lyd now knows about Sergio running off with Mitsu and that Gloria has been sleeping with someone else but she doesn't know that Peter is that someone.)

'So, why aren't you at work?' I ask him.

Lyd walks over to the cupboards and starts gathering plates and chopsticks. Me and Peter sit down facing each other, leaving the middle seat for Lyd.

'Oh, you know, business lunch.'

'You finance boys don't do a thing in your big offices all day,' I say. 'I bet you could disappear for a year and they wouldn't notice.'

'*Vince*,' says Lyd. 'If you're trying to say thank you for the lovely food I think you're getting it a bit wrong.'

114

'He's probably right,' says Peter, attempting a laugh but failing. 'Sometimes I look at what's in front of me and I'm not even sure what I do.'

'I'm sure that's just because it's complicated,' she says, putting plates down on the table.

'Maybe,' he says, sighing.

Lyd opens the boxes of sushi and starts putting the pieces on a big central plate.

'Are you . . . ' Lyd pauses, looking at me sharply before settling back on Peter tenderly, 'okay?'

'Of course. You know me,' he says, with a complete lack of the piercing charm he is so well known for.

He takes two hosomaki rolls off the middle plate and covers them in soy. Lyd finds a little tub of wasabi at the bottom of the brown paper bag and passes it his way. She serves out the rest of the sushi, puts the empty boxes back in the bag and leaves the bag on the floor by her chair, out of the way, for recycling as soon as she's done eating.

'How's the writing going?' asks Peter, smearing wasabi on the vinegared rice of one of his rolls.

'You should probably avoid the tuna,' I say to Lyd. She looks baffled. 'Mercury.' She rolls her eyes and takes a tuna and avocado futomaki from the centre. I look at Peter. 'I've been in a bit of a difficult patch. I think I might be coming out of it now.'

'Are you allowed to tell us what it's about yet?' he asks.

'I'm not very good at talking about my work,' I

say. 'I'm better at describing the process.'

'Oh well,' he says. 'Keep trucking and all that.'

Lyd's head is moving back and forth between us, mildly suspicious about how polite her brother is being.

'How are things with you?' I ask.

Peter pauses at the question, his chopsticks hovering. He sniffs, looks down at his plate and a desperately lonely smile creeps onto his face.

'I think I might be in love,' he says.

'That's great,' says Lyd, sympathetic now that she feels that she has the missing link. 'Pascale is so perfect.'

Peter looks up at her, confused, the momentary wet sheen on his eyes dull again.

'Who?' he asks.

'Pascale,' I say, for her.

'Yes . . . Pascale . . . No . . . I'm not in love with Pascale.'

I take a large spicy salmon temaki from the centre.

'It must have been a whirlwind romance,' I say.

Lyd shows me the whites of her eyes.

'Not really,' he replies. 'It's been on the cards for a while. It just seemed . . . impossible. Like it couldn't really be happening. Pascale was just a distraction. I'm done with Pascale.'

'So, who's the lucky lady?' I ask.

'Yes. Who is she?'

'I can't . . . I mean, I'm not ready to talk about her.'

'Just the process,' I say.

'Yes,' he replies, with an amused lilt.

We eat the rest of the sushi. Peter, besides sniffing occasionally, is quiet. I tilt the conversation towards the dating scan. Lyd looks puzzled. I can see that she's already building a deep defence against this woman whose love has dimmed the sparkling elegance of her brother.

I clear the plates once we're done and leave them to chat for a minute while I wash up and put the recycling out. When I come back in from the bins I hear Lyd say:

'Right, I'm going to pop to the loo before I have to drink all this water.'

The second she leaves the kitchen Peter stands up and rushes over to me.

'You *have* to talk to her for me, Vince. I *need* to see her.'

'Gloria?'

'She won't answer my calls. She's not answering the door. I'm afraid there might be something wrong with her. Something might have *happened*.'

His gruff intensity is suddenly back, but fuelled by anxiety rather than the usual egomania. My raised palms are doing nothing to ease him away from me.

'Slow down,' I say. 'Calm down.'

'I'm serious.'

'You can't pull me further into this thing. I feel bad enough about lying to Lyd as it is. Have either of you thought about when you're going to tell her?'

'I'm going out of my mind here. I know you don't like me. I know Sergio's your friend. But *please*. I just need you to do this one thing.'

117

'Did you hear me? You need to tell Lyd. You're ruining one of her favourite friendships. You're forcing me into a position where I have to lie to her. Does any of this mean anything to you?'

'I wouldn't ask unless I was desperate.'

I'm momentarily astounded by this admission. His honesty coerces me the way his charisma coerces others. I find myself nodding.

'Okay. I'll pop round,' I say. 'But this is the only time I'm getting involved. I don't want to know about this stuff. You need to keep me out of it.'

He puts both of his huge hands on the sides of my head.

'When? *When?*'

'Today, if I get a chance. Tomorrow, maybe. But remember, I'm only doing this so you two can talk about how to tell Lyd. Whether it's over or not, one of you needs to tell her.'

'Let me know as soon as you've seen her. *Please.* And let me know if it's going to be tomorrow. I can't sit around all night not knowing.'

'I'll text you later.'

He releases my head and hugs me with forceful gratitude.

'Thank you, Vince. I mean it.'

He lets go of me and waits around for Lyd, unable to meet my eyes. Purpose fulfilled, ashamed of his display of weakness, he's ready to leave. When Lyd walks back in he quickly perks up and grabs her for a hug.

'Got to dash, sis. Got to go and sit in my office and pretend to do some work.'

118

'Okay,' she laughs. 'You seem very chipper all of a sudden.'

'He's a good man, this one,' he says, unclasping one of his arms from her and pointing at me. 'You keep hold of him.'

He kisses her cheek and sees himself out.

'Bye,' she calls.

'Bye,' I echo.

Lyd looks at me with disbelief and, as soon as the front door closes, asks:

'What was that about?'

'I have no idea.'

'What did you say to him whilst I was gone?'

'I just fed him some line about love. I can't remember.'

'I knew you'd grow on him eventually,' she says, a deep confirmation forming within her. 'You're good with people when they're down.'

'Sure,' I say. 'It was bound to happen sooner or later.'

'Still, he was acting weird. I'm a bit worried about him.'

'Yes,' I agree. 'Not himself, was he?'

After drinking a litre of water, Lyd drives us to the clinic. In the waiting room her leg is jigging up and down. She already needs to urinate and, because she doesn't understand why she isn't allowed to, she's feeling aggressive and annoyed about it. Her arms are crossed and her elbows are hunched up. I stare at the other couples in the waiting room and decide that we're the best one, the one I want to be a part of.

We're called through.

The sonographer has the self-satisfied posture

of a person who feels like he is doing something good with his life. His smile gives the impression that, because he thinks that he lives in the presence of miracles, he has different priorities and understandings to the rest of us. He is only slightly grounded by the occasions on which he has had to deliver serious or bad news and goes about his work with an air of mild bliss.

I am envying his charmed mind. Lyd is half sitting/half lying on an electronic examination bed staring at him, trying to scratch out his harmless conceit with invisible claws.

'Can you just hitch your top up to your ribs for me?' he says.

She does.

'That's great. You might have to undo your trousers and pull them down but they've got quite a low waist so let's see if we can get a peek without. I'm going to rub some of this gel on your stomach. It'll be quite cold and I'll have gloves on so it might feel a little bit strange, okay? I know you're probably bursting for the toilet, and there's going to be some pressure on your bladder, but try to relax.'

Lyd smiles with discomfort, glad that her situation has been acknowledged, and nods.

Once the skin over her womb is covered in lubricant he wheels over a machine that is much more hi-tech than the one that was used at Charlie's ultrasounds. It has a thousand knobs and dials, a touch pad, devices with curly wires hooked onto the side, a big monitor on top and a large vaginal probe sticking up on the right-hand edge.

The sonographer grabs the transducer from the nodule beneath the probe and moves it over Lyd's lubricated stomach. Four grainy images immediately flicker onto the monitor, and dials and bars light up all over the machine's surfaces. He presses a few buttons on the touch screen and twists a few knobs. Lyd's initial unease from the pressure on her bladder quickly dissipates into curiosity, knowing that all the lights and measurements are derived from her body and its systems.

'Nicely placed . . . It's over seven centimetres and just starting to curl so you must be around fourteen weeks . . . The heartbeat looks good . . . No major structural abnormalities visible, but we'll know more about that next time. Have you had any bleeding? Light spotting?'

'No. Nothing like that. Would that be bad?'

'Not necessarily.'

My eyes are fixed on the screen but I can't see anything. I don't even have an inkling of what they could be looking at. I have a creeping suspicion that we're not seeing the same thing. My screen is blank. It's empty. There's no life, just a bit of green fuzz.

'Everything looks great,' he says.

'It's got a face,' says Lyd. 'Oh my God. It's got a face.'

She squeezes my hand.

'Yes,' he confirms.

'Yeah,' I agree, but it still seems like a blank womb full of pointless squiggles and dots to me.

I don't want a new baby, I hear myself think, but not in my own inner voice. It's something

121

more direct, more instantaneous, coming from nowhere.

'Can we tell if it's a girl or a boy?' asks Lyd. 'Wait. I'm not sure I want to know.'

'You're a bit further on than we thought, so we could have a good guess, but think it over. You'll be able to know for sure at your anomaly scan.'

The word *anomaly* makes my stomach turn.

'No, actually. I don't think we want to know,' she says. 'Not yet.'

'No,' I mumble, in agreement.

I feel light-headed.

The sonographer says something I can't hear, takes the transducer off Lyd's stomach and gives her some tissues to wipe off the gel. I'm still looking at the blank screen wondering why I didn't see it.

* * *

After the scan Lyd goes to try out a yoga class for pregnant women that she's found online. Whilst she's out the house I take the opportunity to visit Gloria. It's less than a fifteen-minute walk from ours.

Sergio's vintage mahogany MGB GT V8 is parked in the driveway. Sitting in the passenger seat, Mitsu waits with her arms folded, disgusted with everything. She is dressed like a schoolgirl again but with an additional neo-western shoestring necktie clasped with a silver skull.

I wave, keeping my enthusiasm in check. Her eyes slowly track over towards me, acknowledge nothing and move back to their prior position. I

122

sarcastically give her a false suburban smile and salute. She stares gloomily ahead.

The front door is open so I put a foot inside and crane my head over the threshold. I can hear Spanish words violently slashing through the air from upstairs.

'Hello?'

The two voices continue to bicker.

'*Hello?*'

There is a momentary lapse in sound before the squabble starts up again, getting louder and louder until I can pretty much gauge the full volume of it coming down from the top of the stairs. Sergio is shouting with amused disdain. Gloria is screaming with the emotional volatility of somebody surprised about how hurt she is.

Sergio comes down the stairs with two suitcases. Gloria is throwing shirts and trousers down the stairs after him, along with torrents of verbal abuse. Seeing me, Sergio frowns for a moment before shouting back up the stairs:

'Whore!'

'Pervert!' she shouts back.

A shoe flies down at him. He flinches, trying to move out of the way, but it hits his shoulder.

'Psycho!' he shouts.

He picks up the shoe and throws it back up the stairs at her before turning and walking quickly past me, barging my shoulder and ignoring me. He looks terrible. The last few weeks with Mitsu have aged him. Perhaps he is just sleep deprived from an overactive sex life but I get a deep sense of loss and loneliness from his eyes.

Sergio rushes to his car, throwing his suitcases into the boot. Gloria screams in Spanish again and comes rushing down the stairs with rage so blind that my stomach lifts. She doesn't even notice me as she rushes out the front door holding the shoe that was thrown back and forth between them.

Sergio climbs into the driver's seat and pushes down the lock just in time. Gloria is pulling on the door handle and when one of her fingernails snaps she screams up into the air, cursing his 'stupid, precious car', and then starts hammering the heel of the shoe down on the windscreen, where his face is.

She manages three ineffective smashes before something occurs to her. She looks around the garden with fierce alacrity and rushes over to the garden wall as Sergio reverses out of the driveway.

'Jesus,' I hear myself mutter as she runs out of the garden with half a brick poised above her head.

Sergio, seeing her coming for him, slams the accelerator down but he's not quite fast enough. The brick crunches against his rear right tail light, which pops and shatters, leaving a trail of red plastic and clear glass as he speeds away.

Gloria immediately starts stamping her way back up the driveway. There is a tiny flicker of recognition as she sees me standing in front of her house.

'Gloria,' I begin, in an apologetic tone, 'it's about Peter.'

She strides past me and into the house.

'Fuck off, Vince,' she says, before slamming the door in my face.

I think about knocking on the door but turn to leave instead. Sergio's shoe is still in the middle of the driveway.

2

The dawn chorus becomes particularly loud and full during the mornings around the summer solstice. Skylarks, song thrushes, robins and blackbirds chime in first, before the sun has risen. Then sparrows, finches and buntings add their twitters and trills. Warblers and wrens wait for the sunlight but soon catch up. Adults call. Chicks cry. Each kind uses a different frequency and only sings to its own but together the birds fill the sky with a song that is as predestined but chaotic as the pathway a growing tree takes to the sun; all the gaps are filled, not a drop of silence is wasted.

Since the dating scan I can't get it out of my head that our baby doesn't exist but I also vaguely remember having some trouble with screens after Charlie's death; a bus that was heading to *Black Hole*, a shadowy cashpoint where every option was *Death*. I don't feel like I've lost my grip on reality to that extent but I have to be careful this doesn't go too far. A few days ago I woke in the middle of the night and said:

'The photo. There must be a photo.'

Lyd stirred.

'Where's the photo?' I asked her. 'The photo of the baby. The sonogram.'

'Go . . . sleep,' she mumbled.

126

'Did we get a photo, a picture, at the dating scan?'

'No . . . forgot.'

She rolled away from me.

For a brief moment, I thought I'd saved myself.

It's the weekend now and I don't want it to be. The weekend means I have to face Lyd and I'm so anxious at the moment that I'm afraid I won't be able to hide it for the full two days. I managed to get through the weekday evenings by being quiet and staying out of her way.

She's already left the bedroom when I wake up. I get up and look out the window. The sky is low and dull. There have been showers and bursts of sunshine all week; mild drizzle, warm sunny patches, rainbows, cold hard rain, fast clouds breaking apart. Today the sky has no shifting characteristics, just a low, paper-white ceiling that will last all day.

I've still not heard anything from Angela about the chapters I sent to her so I'm currently trying to blame her for a lot of my feelings of anxiety (unsuccessfully). I quickly check my email before I go downstairs: still nothing.

In the kitchen, Lyd is holding a cup and staring out into the back garden with a mildly confounded look on her face.

'What's up?' I ask.

'Huh?'

'You look confused?'

'No,' she says. 'Not really. The birds woke me up at four thirty this morning, they were ridiculously loud, and it's bright so early at the

127

moment, I couldn't get back to sleep, we really need better curtains by the way, but, have you noticed, they're not singing at all now? The birds.'

I listen. It's true. There's no birdsong in the air. I shrug, open the sliding door, wait a few seconds and whistle. Blackie doesn't appear.

'I wonder why they've abandoned us,' she says.

'Maybe a sultana factory exploded and they all went to visit.'

Lyd smiles.

'You've got *me* fixated on the bloody birds now,' she says, dismissing her curiosity.

I step out onto the patio. There's a little bit of birdsong but it's sparrows and robins and other small birds. The loud and distinctive blackbird solos are the main thing missing. I walk out into the middle of the lawn and look up and around. Turning back towards the house a dark shape catches my eye. I approach it for a closer look.

A female blackbird lies on her back, her wings inaccurately flailed out, head turned to the side, motionless, dead. Her stomach has been ripped open and an inch and a half of her pink-and-red guts are hanging out.

My throat is closing. I'm getting dizzy. Breathing is difficult. I close my eyes and take a moment to inhale and exhale slowly. It's just a dead bird but I feel overwhelmed by its death. I have to get away from it. I go back into the kitchen.

'What's wrong?' asks Lyd, as I walk towards her.

I fall on my knees in front of her and wrap my

arms around her pelvis, pulling her melon-sized womb towards my head.

'Nothing,' I say.

'Vince? What's going on? What are you doing?'

As my disorientation passes I realise that this is not normal behaviour. Lyd is trying to wriggle away from me. I let go, stand up and try to make light of it.

'Nothing. Really. I'm fine. I just wanted to listen to the baby for a minute . . . Sorry. I didn't mean to freak you out.'

'You wanted to listen to the baby?'

'I had an uncontrollable urge.'

'Right.'

'I think I solved the mystery, anyway.'

'Mystery?'

'Next door's cat's killed a blackbird in our garden. Must have scared all the others off. Her guts are hanging out.'

'Gross,' says Lyd, putting a hand on her stomach.

'I don't feel like I can just throw her in the bin. It's not like finding a dead mouse.'

'No?'

'I think I might bury her in the garden. If that's okay?'

'Put some Marigolds on. They're full of parasites.'

'Okay.'

My hands are trembling as I dig near the fence with a trowel. I can feel Lyd's glare burning my back. I'm trying not to make a big show of it but I am trying to appease the blackbirds. This is a test, or a sign, part of their system of guidance, but it also feels threatening, dark, like they want me to live in fear. By burying her I'm showing that I respect their lives and hold their species in high regard, that I will contemplate the meaning of this sacrifice.

The grave is around seven inches deep when I'm done. I put the bird in and scatter mud over her. When she's covered I feel the need to enact some form of ritual but I don't know what to do. I think of priests reciting prayers and making the sign of the cross but these things don't apply to me so I simply bow my head to offer a moment of quiet reverence.

When I get back inside Lyd kisses me on the cheek. There is a dismissive sympathy in the way her lips make contact with my skin that makes me feel awkward and judged.

'Chuck them out,' she says, pointing with her eyes down at the yellow rubber gloves.

I smile and put them in the bin. She goes through to the living room. I follow her in. She's picking up a thesis that's been sitting half-read on the coffee table for weeks.

'Do we have anything planned for today?' I ask.

She looks up from her pages and around the room. Something occurs to her.

'What?' I ask.

'Are there more cushions than there used to be?'

'What do you mean?'

'More cushions.'

'No,' I say.

'There never used to be this many cushions.'

'There's been this many for ages.'

'Where did they all come from?'

I sigh.

'There were two in Charlie's room.'

'In Charlie's room?' she asks.

'In the moon.'

'You destroyed the moon?'

Lyd grabs one of the cushions and holds it to her stomach. I sigh again.

'What was I supposed to do with it?'

'I thought you boxed everything up? What else did you throw away?'

'Nothing. I just had to throw that thing away. I couldn't keep it.'

'How have I not noticed all these cushions?'

'I don't know.'

'If we could have only kept one thing I'd have said keep the moon.'

'Of course you would.'

'I *would*. He loved that thing.'

'Some things are too painful to keep.'

'And some things are too painful to throw away.'

'Can we not do this, please? It's done. There's nothing I can do about it.'

'Fine.'

She shuffles her legs beneath her, still gripping the cushion firmly. She puts the thesis down.

'Let's go and buy a crib,' she says.

'What? Really?'

'My headaches and soreness are beginning to level off. And I'll be the size of a planet before long. I'm in the sweet spot for getting things done. Besides, we're not going to have a good

131

time today. We may as well tick a box.'

'Sounds fun.'

Lyd drives us to a place that's a bit like IKEA. It stands alone off a busy dual carriageway, has the same drawn-out shopping procedure and the same homogenised but stylish produce, but it's more expensive. I think IKEA does 'style on a budget' well, so you may as well get the cheap stuff, but Lyd likes to spend a little bit more and feel like she has quality products. She says that materials matter and I agree, but I don't think they use better materials. Still, that's where we go. Since crashing the car during my breakdown, she's the one who drives.

In the car I'm trying to look at Lyd and think about her beauty and the happiness of our future life together, the simple but stylish furniture we'll be surrounded by, but she's grimacing.

'What's wrong?' I ask.

'I can hear the blood in my veins,' she says, flicking a wrist around as though shooing the sensation away.

'*Hear* it?'

She nods, clutching the steering wheel with disgust.

'I wonder if you're hearing through the baby's ears?'

'I doubt it.'

'Amazing.'

'Not really. It's making me feel sick. I don't want to talk about it.'

'Okay.'

The gigantic car park is full. We have to drive around aimlessly waiting for someone to pull out. For a couple of minutes we slowly follow a man carrying a huge box of flat-packed wood until he gets so edgy that he stops to let us past. We stop too, thinking he's at his car, and the three of us end up looking at each other in a confused triangle. Eventually, somebody pulls out twenty metres ahead of him so Lyd floors the accelerator, which makes him flinch and lose his grip on his giant box.

Walking towards the ugly, grey warehouse with its glassy, corporate entranceway a low flying blackbird swoops above my head releasing a flurry of loud tweets:

— *chuck-chicka-chink choo-chucka-chucka pook-pook-pook* —

(*Watch out. The chaos is coming.*)

My stomach turns and the speed and proximity of its flight makes me duck slightly.

'What's wrong?' asks Lyd.

'Did you see that?'

'See what?'

'You must have heard it.'

'What?'

I'm unsure if she's daring me to draw attention to *yet another* blackbird or if she didn't see or hear it at all. I look up at the empty white sky.

'Never mind,' I say.

I catch a glint of disgust in Lyd's expression and note that I've seen her look at me like that a few times in the last couple of weeks.

We walk towards the entranceway with a metre between our shoulders.

'You know, we still have a crib,' I say, as the automatic doors slide open. 'In the attic.'

This comes out at the worst possible moment. It's my version of a nervous tick. I have a knack for finding the exact wrong thing to say at the exact wrong moment. Lyd is aware of this facet so she just glances at me sullenly. Thankfully, she's forgotten that I stopped doing this when I started taking lithium.

'I want everything new,' she says. 'I don't care what we've already got.'

'That's going to be expensive.'

'It's my money.'

'I'm aware of that.'

As we turn the first corner we find ourselves standing at the foot of a corridor of fake living rooms full with a near-impenetrable amount of people. In this shop you can't just find the thing you need and buy it. You have to walk through a whole labyrinth of jumbled produce, note down everything that you want and wait to see if they have it in stock when you get to the end.

Lyd glances at me, subtly amused, knowing that this is many of my least favourite things crammed into one experience: a packed crowd, a cynically inefficient system, overpriced products, pretentious parents, identikit individualism, squealing children ... My teeth are firmly clenched.

Lyd is much more well adjusted than me and sees this place as a gift to consumers with good taste. To her it's a chance for people of average wealth to afford the luxury of excellent design without the hackneyed feeling that it is too cheap and commonplace.

'Let's just get this over with,' I say.

'Lead the way.'

I push through the centre of the crowd in silence, evading cellulite hips and bony shoulders, moving forward at four times the normal customer rate. We get to the children's bedrooms before the baby rooms. I've stopped because I've seen Charlie's wardrobe. Lyd notices what I'm looking at.

'I don't mind so much about that sort of thing,' she says. 'Maybe we could re-use the wardrobe? He didn't spend any time in it. Touching it. You know?'

'No.'

'No?'

'We should get all new, like you said.'

'But . . . '

'The wardrobe's got his stickers all over it.'

(And I smashed it to smithereens.)

'I suppose you're right. Do you think we'll need a wardrobe straight away? When did we get one for Charlie?'

I shrug and Lyd carries on talking about other things we might need but I'm not listening properly. I'm looking around for the red 1960s robot as if, by some trick of fate, it will be decorating one of these fake children's bedrooms and I'll be able to grab it and use it to smash the whole store to pieces.

'So?'

'What?' I ask.

'What planet are you on today?'

'We probably won't need a new chest of drawers,' I say, clutching at an echoed memory of her speaking.

'I thought you just said you didn't want us to reuse anything.'

'There's no stickers on the drawers. I left them in the room. We don't need more drawers. They won't fit up the hatch into the attic. There's no point throwing drawers away and getting the same replacement drawers.'

'What's wrong with you?'

'What are you talking about?'

'You're clenching your fists. Your knuckles are white.'

'I just hate it in here.'

'Come on. I can see a crib down there.'

We take down the product number, buy the overpriced crib and get out of there. It's a simple white thing. Yet, for all its simplicity, back home, it takes me about four and a half hours to construct. The whole time I'm thinking that I must be a terrible writer because Angela still hasn't been in touch. I know my expectations are usually too high when I give people things to read but she was so positive about my first two novels. The way she responds to my work has changed my life. Now she doesn't even have a response.

The crib is done but the baby room still looks undefined. It's devoid of character, completely white, just the bare essentials. It isn't Charlie's room anymore though. Charlie has been whitewashed out of the space. For some reason, this notion reminds me of the blank screens at the dating scan. There's nothing in Lyd's womb. There's no baby. Why do I keep thinking this?

I go to my office and check my email. Still nothing. Nothing from anyone. I click on my junk folder, select all and delete them. Immediately, that weird piece of junk email returns:

From: *CHARLIE*

Subject: (276) Re: contact me please . . .

★ ★ ★

I decide that it's finally time to open it and click on the title.

Dear Sir/Madam

I am Charlie a Banker working in bank in London Until now I am account officer to most government accounts and I have since discovered that most of the account are dormant account with a lot of money in on further investigation I found out that one particular account belong to the former minister MR Dennis McShane, who ruled Rotherham from 1994–2012 and this particular account has deposit of £146,000 with no next of kin.

My proposal is that since I am the account officer and the money on the account is dormant and there is no next of kin obviously the account owner the former president of Rotherham has died, that you should provide an account for the money to be transferred.

The money is floating in the bank right now and I want to transfer to your account for our mutual benefit. Please if this is okay by you I will advice that you contact me through my direct email address.

Your reply will be appreciated,
Thank you.
CHARLIE

I'm glad that I've finally read it. Having deleted it so many times, it was beginning to seem like an unstoppable force in my life. Its persistence had made me think that it really might be from Charlie, because it was behaving like my memory of him behaves. I'm amused by how relieved I am about the fact that it's just the usual sort of scam but then I feel sad about Charlie, sad that I've been whitewashing his memory out of our lives. Then it occurs to me why I saw a blank screen at the ultrasound. I click reply and start writing.

Dear Charlie,

I hope you know that you are still a very real part of my life. The pain of losing you was so intense that I had a breakdown. When I started putting myself back together again there was a little part of you in every single piece. You became part of me, so I could never lose you.

As you know, me and your mum are going

to have another baby. I don't want you to be jealous about this. Nobody will ever replace you. I know you probably want me to forget about the new baby but I have to be its father and try to love it. I want us all to stay together. Please try to understand. Try to let me be happy.

Love from,
Daddy

I click send. A couple of seconds later a new message appears in my junk folder.

From: *CHARLIE*
Subject: (1) Re: direct contact . . .

I click the cross in the top right corner and close the Internet window. That's enough communicating with my dead son for one day.

After a near silent dinner, I spend the rest of the evening reading through my first six chapters again; deleting an adverb here, changing a comma there, wondering what it is that links these stories together. I don't dare write for fear of casting my net too wide, creating blind alleys and unanswerable questions. I need the idea to talk to me before I move forward but the project has become silent and inert.

Lyd is asleep when I get into bed. She looks peaceful. Sometimes I forget how much grief there is inside her whilst she's awake. This is how her face used to be, especially in the mornings, before all the mathematics and physics started creeping back into her head.

I'm trying to stay still so I don't wake her but I can tell that it's going to be another sleep deprived night. I've always been unable to wind down at the end of the day. It seemed like I spent half of my childhood lying awake in bed. This is something that lithium helped me to forget. Its chemical fuzz allowed me to slip into sleep in minutes.

Thirty or forty minutes later I'm trying to control my breathing, easing my brain into unconsciousness, when I hear the pitter-patter of tiny feet run across the ceiling. My body tenses up and my heart starts beating fast. Lyd, sleeping next to me, rolls over, momentarily disturbed, and makes a quiet moaning sound.

I get out of bed and walk down the dark hallway. As I get to the baby's room I stop and put my ear to the door. It's silent in there. I turn the doorknob and walk in. The curtains are open so it's marginally lighter than the hallway. Everything is still. The room is white, soulless. The empty crib sits in the corner.

Little feet run along the ceiling again, directly over my head.

'Charlie?' I whisper.

I pull the string that unlocks the attic door and lower the pull-down ladder, slowly to make doubly sure I don't wake Lyd. The thin metal crossbeams hurt my feet as I ease my weight onto each step. My heart is racing. My throat is dry.

My head emerges above the floor of the attic.

'Charlie?' I whisper again.

There's a faint giggle, over in the corner.
'Charlie?'

I climb up into the attic and after two steps nearly trip over a box of Christmas decorations. I stop still, listening for Lyd. I don't think I've disturbed her.

Moving the box aside, I remember tinsel in Lyd's hair and Charlie banging his spoon about in his high chair, cranberry sauce all over his face. A new toy fire engine that he wouldn't eat without is knocked to the floor. He doesn't cry, he giggles. I hear this same giggle to the side of me.

I keep a torch by the edge of the hatch so I grab it and turn it on. I shine it to the right side of the attic, where the giggle came from. The yellow spot of illumination passes over Charlie's empty high chair.

There's a lot of his stuff up here now; his crib, boxes full of bottles and bibs. Then there's all the things from his room. Everything he ever had.

A round shadow swings across the back wall and disappears behind the boxes full of Charlie's toys.

I close my eyes for a couple of seconds. I try to tell myself that these sounds and shadowy movements are not real, they are symptoms, but either way I know I have to face them. A tear slips down my right cheek, my hands are shaking. What if I see his face?

I approach the pile of boxes where the round shadow vanished. A new noise is coming from behind the boxes now, one my brain can't decipher. My ears are struggling to hear Charlie

141

but the dots don't connect. The sound is distorted, lost between two places, like a dream language scrambling into nonsense as I wake.

I move towards this fuzzy sound and peer behind the boxes. The noise becomes louder, more high-pitched. I shine the torch into the corner and see something tiny moving down on the floor. My eyes won't inform me as to what it is. To get a closer look, because of the slope of the roof, I have to get down on all fours.

As I lower myself, my knee crunches on a horrible cone-shaped object full of painful little nubs. I almost cry out but breathe through the sides of my teeth instead. I shine the torch towards the object and see the red 1960s robot. I stand it up by the sidewall and look back into the corner.

After this small bout of pain everything is clear and focused. There are three little fledglings chirping in a small round nest. A quick look around reveals that there's a crack in one of the nearby roof tiles through which the mother must have been coming and going.

'Vince?'

I crawl backwards, sliding the nest along with me, then stand up and see the silhouette of Lyd's head popping up from the hatch.

'It's okay, honey,' I say. 'Go back to bed.'

'What are you doing?'

'It's just a nest of chicks. I heard them chirping. That dead bird today must have been their mother.'

'Chicks?'

'Yes.'

'Are they okay?'

'They're distressed. I'm going to take them outside, put them in the evergreen next to the other nest.'

'Now?'

'Yes. They'll die up here on their own.'

'You scared me.'

'I'm sorry, honey,' I say, carefully lifting the nest.

'I thought it was Charlie.'

'What?' I ask, quickly turning my head towards the hatch.

'I hope they're not starving.'

'They'll be fine,' I say. 'Go on.'

'Do you want me to leave the light on down here?'

'No, my eyes have adjusted.'

'Okay. Night.'

'Night, love.'

I carry the nest over to the hatch and carefully sit down with my heels on the ladder. I turn off the torch, leaving it in its usual place, and descend the rungs slowly, putting my weight onto my pelvis, sitting on each crossbeam to stop my heels from slipping out from under me.

By the time I make it to the ground the three chicks are frantic, squealing for food, scared. I hold them towards the window to see them better. They have no feathers and there are still shards of egg around them. Their skin is purply-pink and their eyes big and blind.

As I walk them through the hall, Lyd calls:

'I can hear them.'

'Do you want to see?' I ask.

'No. I think it might upset me.'

'Okay. I'll be up in a bit.'

I carry the nest downstairs and through to the kitchen. I have to put them down on the counter whilst I open the sliding door. Brisk air rushes in. I'm still barefoot and in my boxer shorts but I can't be bothered going to get dressed. It will only take a minute. I'm worried about exposing the featherless chicks to it but I decide that most chicks are outside and that it might be warmer in the middle of a bush. This is their only chance.

Out in the back garden, their chirping is dampened. They seem quieter and smaller heard alongside the sounds of the wind and the moving leaves and branches. Or perhaps, beneath the sky, they have sensed danger and actively become more discreet; a warning from their genetic memory.

I walk over to the spot where Blackie and his partner live. At the foot of the evergreen I hold the nest forward and try to move one of the bigger branches aside with the outside of my wrist. As I do this I hear an aggressive:

— *SEEEEEEEE!* —

An extremely irate female blackbird rushes out of the bush and flies at my face. I fall backwards and drop the nest. I have no time to regroup and check the chicks because the bird, Blackie's partner, is following through with her attack.

I feel a sharp peck on the top of my head.

— *SEEEEEEEE!* —

A tiny talon scratches my cheek.

The fluttering of wings seems to be every-where. I turn my back to her and scramble away from the bush. There's another peck on the back of my neck, one on my shoulder and then one at the back of my ankle. After that she's gone, back to her nest and chicks.

I sit on the edge of the patio to collect myself for a moment. The surface is cold and quickly brings me back to my senses. I cautiously step sideways, moving back towards the bush with my head lowered and my elbow up. The nest is upside down on the lawn.

As I get closer I see one of the chicks about thirty centimetres from the nest. It's still and quiet and has died at some point in the commotion; perhaps from the fall, maybe I scrambled over it.

I lurk down even lower, sending my knees out sideways, and tip up the edge of the nest. Beneath, the two remaining fledglings immediately raise their beaks into the air and begin chirping. I delicately place them back into the slightly dishevelled nest. One of them tries to feed from my finger as I lift it. It occurs to me that I might be issuing these chicks a death sentence (without their mother to keep them warm) but I don't know what else to do. I go to the other end of the garden and embed them as deep into the evergreen as I can.

I pick the dead chick up off the lawn, careful not to split its thin skin open, and carry it to its mother's grave. It's still warm. I scoop out a couple of handfuls of dirt and then bury it. I tell myself that this does not have to be a sign. My life and the blackbirds' lives are not cosmically engaged. It could mean anything. If it was a test it could have been to see if I would feel a sense of duty, a need to nurture, a desire to protect. I'm making a vested effort not to think the worst.

Wincing at the chirps of the chicks I have left alone in the bush, I head back inside, wash my hands, check to see if Blackie's partner broke my skin (she didn't) and climb back into bed. Lyd is asleep and keeps her back to me. I stare up at the ceiling, wondering if I'll ever hear those pitter-pattering feet again.

3

In an old myth, a prankster promises two lovers that one day they will find a pot of gold at the foot of a rainbow, just so long as they hold on to each other. Wandering through the greenest lands, they rush towards each rainbow they find with their arms and shoulders entwined, the promise finally coming true, but as they near the point where the colours touch the ground the pair always find their arms untangling and their hands pulling apart. They are never quite heading in the same direction and, at the vital moment, they always separate, each blaming the other for running the wrong way. All their lives they never once imagine that they are seeing two separate rainbows. It's right there in front of them, right in the centre of their world.

After signing in at reception and getting a visitor's card, I swipe through the barriers and walk into the lobby. It's a vast space. The back wall is a fifty-foot black marble monolith. The six lifts and two stairway entrances are framed with brass. The sidewalls are white-polished oak. The floor is covered with giant black rectangular tiles with embedded flakes of silver and crystal. I can't remember which side I'm supposed to get the lift on.

Two black marble doors open in the centre of the shiny back wall; an executive elevator I didn't know was there. Curious, I look over to see who's coming out and immediately fill with disgust. It's Ajwan White; a writer whose work I hate.

He's one of these accidental zeitgeist novelists who continually trades off the success of his first book. His work is gimmicky and full of cheap tricks but a passing fashion for 'spiritual postmodernism' meant that he was given a big marketing budget. All his main characters are narcissistic idiots who have big epiphanies and then change for the better.

I'm trying to look away, to choose between right or left, but something seems to be wrong with him. He moves his spine diagonally backwards. He ducks down and runs forward. He scratches manically at his ear with both hands. He turns one hundred and eighty degrees, ducks lower, then turns one hundred and eighty degrees again. Just as he looks like he's going to calm down, his spine jolts and he flings his right arm out in a big arc.

Watching him, I feel a little bit light-headed. The black marble swells and distorts. I close my eyes for a couple of seconds. When I open them he is looking around, panicking again, and he starts running back towards the lift. The black marble doors are sliding closed, he's not fast enough, and he ends up pushed against them. He quickly turns and looks in the air around him. His nerves begin to settle. He walks away from the shiny black wall grinning and shaking his head.

I'm standing in the centre of the lobby and

still haven't chosen left or right. Despite the fact that I'm clearly just watching him I'm also eager to imply that I'm not interested in the fact that he's walking towards me.

'Did you see that?' he asks, smug, amazed by something pitiful, probably about to 'change' for the better.

I look over my shoulder to check for other people. He's talking to me. The bastard is talking to me.

'What?' I ask, annoyed with myself for engaging.

He laughs, leans down, puts his hands on his knees and breaths deeply for a second. He's bathing in my attention. Pathetic.

'Phew! There was a wasp waiting for me when the lift doors opened. It came right at me.'

'A wasp?'

'I *know*.'

'I thought you'd lost it.'

'I nearly did . . . I'd love to know if they get a kick out of doing that to people.'

'I doubt it.'

He looks around and decides he can finally be fully calm.

'Sorry, but you're Vincent Watergate, right?'

'Vince,' I say, he doesn't seem to be offering his hand so I'm not either. 'And you're Ajwan White?'

'Adge . . . I heard we were at the same place. Come for your monthly bollocking?'

'Something like that.'

'I don't want to keep you. But after the wasp I felt like the ice was already broken . . . I just

149

wanted to say that I thought *All the Leaves Have Fallen* was . . . well . . . you wrote a beautiful book. Really underrated . . . I can't believe it didn't take off.'

'Thanks.'

'The relationships, the emotional spectrum, so understated, but so complex. We don't know who to love or who to forgive. Everybody's so . . . human.'

'Thanks.'

'Really. I never do this.'

'I appreciate it.'

'You should be the one doing all the interviews and signings.'

'I wouldn't want to,' I say. 'I read *I Is No More Than the Man Who Says I.*'

'A mouthful, isn't it?' He laughs. 'God knows how it sold so well.'

'Yes. I imagine you sold more than Barthes ever did.'

'Thank you,' he says, accidentally accepting a compliment that he hasn't been given. 'And it's nice that you got the reference. Not many people did. Like I said, a miracle it took off the way it did.'

'Advertising,' I say. 'I suppose corporate investment creates a sense of value.'

He finally senses that I'm not a fan. He's not an acute observer.

'Well,' he says, amused by my disdain, 'I just wanted you to know, you know, how much I enjoy your writing.'

He waves awkwardly and walks away shaking his head. At the barriers he pulls out his wallet

150

and holds it over the scanner. It detects the magnetic strip of his entry card inside. The guard nods and smiles at him as he walks out the front door. He doesn't hand in a visitor's card. They must have given him his own card. He can come and go as he pleases.

I take a lift on the left and get lost in a labyrinth of identical corridors, small offices and kooky bureaucrats. After a few horrible minutes I knock on a door and get directions from a woman who looks like I asked if she had a spare kidney.

My agent, Angela 'not the dead novelist' Carter, has frizzy brownish-blonde hair cut like an old lady (even though she's not even sixty) and huge glasses that have been in and out of fashion twice since she bought them. Unlike every literary critic in the country, she loved my first two novels.

'Vince. Good to see you.'

She says this like a grandmother who once had high hopes for her now disappointing grandson.

'You don't represent Ajwan White, do you?'

'I wish. Ha! No. He's a top-floor author.'

'He's a hack.'

'Of course he is. Sit down. Sit down . . . Do you want a drink?'

'I brought you some more pages.'

I try to hand her my fourth, fifth and sixth chapters but she puts out her hand in a halting motion, forms a mock-repulsed pout and shakes her head.

'That's not why you're here.'

'I'm writing some really good stuff.'

'I don't doubt it.'

She pulls out two crystal glasses and a decent bottle of Glenfiddich from her bottom drawer, pours over an inch into both and offers me the fuller one. I take it.

'It's a little bit disjointed but that's the point. At least, it is at this stage.'

'It's great that you're writing again.'

'I know it might take readers a little bit of getting into, but I'm pretty sure the pay-off will be worth it in the end.'

'Vince, stop. They're turning the screw. Tightening belts. We've got to get rid of our three lowest earners and replace them with one new writer who we're willing to take a risk on. A risk. Ha! That's one way of putting it.'

'Shit. Am I one of them? One of the lowest three?'

'You're *the* lowest, darling. I'm sorry. But we've never made a penny out of you. It's like they constantly tell me when I go upstairs: we're not a charity.'

'But this is the one. I can feel it. I just need to, wait, do you think Ajwan White is one of his agent's bottom three?'

'I very much doubt it. Why? What's all this Ajwan White talk? Is this book more like what he does?'

'No. *No.* Jesus.'

'Too bad.'

'It's going to sell. I promise you.'

'It's out of my hands.'

'So what happens? Do I take my deal somewhere else?'

She sighs.

'That's the other thing I need to tell you. There is no deal.'

'What do you mean?'

'I was waiting for the right time. I thought I might be able to sell the rights on to somebody else.'

'I don't understand.'

'You missed three deadlines, lovey. I know it's been a tough couple of years, and writing's no science, but they can't sit on their hands these days. You signed a contract. Maybe if we were further along . . . What's it going to be called?'

She picks up a notepad and pen.

'I'm not sure yet. But, wait. I still don't understand. There's no book deal?'

'No.'

'So I can't send it to them directly?'

'There is no them. The ship has sailed, come back and sailed again. You'll have to send it to agents, like you did with the first one.'

'I got fifty-four rejections before you took it on.'

'So you're well-practiced.'

'Are you joking? Is this a joke?'

'You can send it to me. When you're done. I'll put it to the top of the slush pile.'

'The slush pile?'

'Don't make this harder than it has to be,' she says. 'Drink your drink.'

I take a sip.

'Please. You can't drop me. Lyd's parents already think I'm a failure. This is the only thing I have going for me.'

153

'Right now, the top of the slush pile is the best you can hope for.'

'So . . . I'm fired?'

'Ha! Sorry. Did you ever read your contract? Writers are never really hired, darling. They get picked up.'

'And dropped.'

'Unfortunately. But it's a business, Vince. And business isn't booming. It used to look good, having a certain spread of talent on the books, but they can't afford to carry people anymore. The culture is changing.'

'That's it then?'

'There'll be some paperwork in the post.'

'Paperwork?'

'Options. From the publisher. For repaying your advance.'

'*Repaying?* I've got a baby on the way. I don't have any income.'

'A baby? Congratulations,' she says. She means it. 'That's wonderful news. But really, doll, how are you surviving? Most of my writers have a second job. Even the successful ones. There's all these creative writing courses popping up. Have you thought about teaching?'

'This can't be happening.'

'I'm sorry. I really am. You know I always loved your prose. Do you want another drink?'

'What? No. Thanks.'

I get up from my seat.

'Let's not end on a bad note,' she says.

'No, of course.'

But I'm not with her anymore. I'm retreating, spurned and wounded. I need air. I'm halfway out the door and I don't hear the last thing she says. I'm in the lift swaying and sinking. I'm swiping and swiping but the stupid barrier gate isn't opening.

Rushing out, I get called back by the receptionist. I can't face looking into the eyes of another human being so I pretend I haven't heard her. This only makes the security guard by the door move into the middle of the entrance way. Caught out, I turn back towards the desk. The woman is friendly but I can't communicate. I can barely focus on the portion of the page she wants me to sign after I've given her my visitor's card. She mentions that I should write in the time but this is a step too far. I push the clipboard and her generic pen back at her and walk out past the security guard with my eyes fixed on the ground.

The London streets are full of bright sunlight and car fumes. July is just beginning to get hot. Everybody is dressed for different weather. The busyness of the general street environment is too much for me. I can hear blackbirds singing but I can't see them. Their whistles are mixing with the traffic and people, creating a wall of random, jittery sound. When I put my hands over my ears the birdsong seems louder.

Welcome to the chaos, it says. *Feel free to break down and scream at the sky.*

I rush to the nearest Underground. When I'm on my own I usually prefer the bus but I just want to disappear and reappear where I need to be, get away from this barrage of noise. On the Tube I keep my hands over my ears and rock back and forth in time with the vibrations and whirring and clucking sounds, trying to ignore the jolts and bangs.

When I get back to the house I slam the door on the twittering skies. I hear wittering in the kitchen, faint chirruping behind me. I walk through the hallway to the kitchen. Fee and Dom are sitting at the table with Lyd. They look concerned to the point of tense and Lyd is on the verge of anger.

'What's going on?' I ask. 'Why aren't you at work?'

I have not been warned about this visit. I was expecting an empty house. I wanted to lie face down on the bed and shout into a pillow, scrawl neurotic rants about literary agencies and birdsong in my notebook. This is the opposite of what I wanted.

'Lydia needs to talk to you,' says Fee.

Lyd whips a warning glance at her mother. I'm struggling to repress thoughts of madness and failure. I take a deep breath and wipe the sweat from my forehead with the back of my hand.

'Lyd?'

She's unsure how to proceed. There is a long pause whilst she tries to phrase things correctly.

'We think you might need some help,' says Fee, butting in.

'*Help?* Help with what?' I ask.

'Mum, can you not?' says Lyd.

'We're worried that you're becoming unstable again,' says Fee.

'We? Who's we?'

'Myself and Dom,' she replies. 'And Lydia.'

'We're not attacking you,' says Dom.

I raise my hand to him.

'Just say what you came to say.'

I force myself to take a seat with them at the table. They have had tea and biscuits and a calm, resolved talk in the build-up to this. By comparison, I got denounced by the one thing that set me apart from being a complete failure. I can't even try to project the visage of a calm, centred human being. My legs are jigging and my eyes are wild. I'm holding onto the edge of the table like it's the edge of the Earth.

'Look at yourself,' says Fee. 'You can barely even sit at a table.'

I look at Lyd. She turns away. Dom coughs.

'We just think you maybe need to start seeing someone,' he says. 'Nothing too serious.'

'Lyd, could you please tell me what the hell is going on here?'

'Vince, *stop*,' she says, finally looking me in the eyes. 'I know . . . we know that you're not taking your medication.'

'What?'

'I've known for months.'

I glance at Fee and Dom. I hate to admit this breach of trust in front of them.

'Was it Jamal?' I ask. 'Did Jamal tell you?'

'Jamal knew?'

'No. I mean . . . I just thought he might . . . '

'You can tell Jamal but you can't tell me?'

'No. It's not like that.'

'And he knows exactly what happened to you. I'm going to kill that little stoner the next time I see him.'

I glance at her parents. They are both fidgeting twitchily after hearing the word 'stoner'.

'I'm sorry,' I say. 'Really. But I don't need it. I never did. I lost my grip when Charlie died. That's all. It makes me too fuzzy. I walk into a room and I don't know what I've gone in for. How am I supposed to write when I feel like that?'

'God forbid you should be unable to write,' says Lyd.

'We're worried that the news of this baby has set you off again,' says Fee.

'Brought up old feelings,' says Dom.

'I really can't do this in front of your parents.'

'No,' she agrees, 'I know.'

Lyd stands up, glares at her mother and leaves the table. Fee lifts her head diagonally with forced pride to show that she stands by her behaviour. Lyd walks out of the kitchen. I follow her. She turns to me in the hallway.

'This isn't coming from you,' I say, quietly. 'Do *you* think I should be seeing someone?'

'You should at least see your doctor. You can't just stop taking lithium like that. The rest is up to you.'

'I swear, I don't need it.'

'I'm still paying a credit card bill that says otherwise.'

'Every pill I swallowed was for you.'

'And you stop when I get pregnant?' she snaps, folding her arms.

'I just wanted to be me again. For us. For the baby.'

'I lost you when I needed you most. I'm not

158

going through that again. I can't risk it. Not with a baby in the house.'

'Okay. So we need to talk about it. I know we're not very good at that but we get there in the end. Why did you have to get your parents involved?'

She looks back towards the kitchen and sighs.

'I didn't mean to. I planned to talk to you before they arrived. I meant to do it last night but I lost my nerve. I'm so used to you being free, I forgot about your meeting this morning . . . I'm going to stay with them for a while.'

'You're *leaving*? You can't leave. What about work?'

'There's plenty I can do with an Internet connection. And I'm in Geneva for a fortnight after next week anyway.'

'Can you fly?' I ask. 'Is it safe?'

'I think so.'

'But . . . What about us?'

'I have no idea what's going on with us. I just know I have to leave.'

'When did you decide all this?'

Lyd leans back against the wall and looks up at the ceiling.

'It's too tense for me here. We're in completely different worlds. Things haven't been right since we found out I was pregnant.'

'No. But I thought we were working on that. I didn't expect you to run back to your parents.'

'I'm not running back to my parents,' she says, aggressively. 'I've made a decision that I need some distance. The stress here isn't good for me. This is the best way around it.'

'You're leaving me, aren't you? They're going to talk you into leaving me.'

'Forget about my parents, Vince. It doesn't matter what they want. I'm sorry you had to walk in to that but this has nothing to do with them.'

'I stopped taking it for you. I swear.'

Lyd shakes her head with disbelief.

'This is broken,' she says. 'What we have. Here. Surely you can see that? You can't talk to me. I can't talk to you. If we can't be honest about what we're going through then we need to go through it alone.'

'Please. Don't do this. Don't leave me.'

'Not that you've noticed, but this isn't about you. I've got my own stuff to deal with.'

She breaks eye contact, no longer receptive to anything I might say. I know this obstinate look from experience. There's nothing I can do. I try anyway.

'Whatever it is,' I say, 'you can tell me. I know I've been too self-involved lately but you can always talk to me. I'd never judge you.' Her look hardens. My desperation increases. 'Can you at least tell me when you're coming back? Are you ever coming back?'

She doesn't respond.

4

Polaris (the North Star) always points true north. This casts the illusion that all the other stars in the sky pivot around it but its actual role in the celestial body is not central and only seems this way due to its relative position to Earth. With its heightened gleam and consistent position, Polaris almost certainly instigated the earliest discoveries of astronomy but it no doubt also helped to elongate the belief that humanity was at the centre of an orchestrated cosmological plan. After all, it is much more probable that the night sky's point of true north would be black, not the brightest star in the sky.

I have a new routine. I wake up at 5am, make myself coffee and toast, feed Blackie and his children and then write and edit in my dressing gown for as long as I can manage. For the first three hours or so my nerves are settled and assured. I invent things, solve problems, make progress, whittle away at words. I don't seem to worry about the value of what I'm doing, or whether all the different stories are ever going to join together. At 5am I can work without doubts.

It's the remaining fifteen hours of my day that I find more difficult. Around 8am my legs begin agitating. The hours ahead seem lonely and vacant. My stomach starts turning. My jaw clenches until my temples ache. I can't imagine the world inside the words I'm working on. The emptiness becomes bigger and wider and harder to ignore until I lose focus completely and I have to face it.

Today, delaying this inevitable confrontation with the big nothing, I visit pregnancy websites and read about the different aspects of the second trimester. Our baby should be beginning to wriggle. It is around six inches long (having doubled in size during the last two weeks). Currently, it's covered in a fine, downy hair called lanugo and a waxy coating called vernix. It has eyebrows, eyelashes, fingernails and toenails. It can hear and swallow. It can make its father feel completely alone.

When the postman comes I close my Internet window and go downstairs to retrieve the letters. Only one of them is for me. I separate the junk for recycling and put Lyd's in a pile that I intend to forward to her parent's address at the end of the week.

I open mine.

The cover letter is from a lawyer detailing how much I owe my publishing company (£14,654) and what my options are for repayment (very few). The next page is a receipt of monies owed and a breakdown of the coming interest and charges. The last page is a note from an account executive at the publishing house offering me the opportunity to buy the remaining stock of my books at a reduced rate (from as little as £2.16 per unit for all 1,278 units, ranging up to £3.91 per unit, for a minimum of 10 units). I'm still reading the final page of the letter when someone knocks on the door.

I look through the frosted glass and see that it's Jayne, Lyd's sister, so I run into the kitchen and hide behind the breakfast counter. When the knocking returns I wonder what I'm doing, why I've panicked, and since I've acknowledged the fact that I'm squirming by the counter I tell myself that I have to walk through the hall and face her. I can't plead temporary insanity. I'm a coward if I don't go.

I open the front door to a blast of brightness, Jayne's silhouette and a loud burst of birdsong. The discordant melodies are so loud that they almost seem to be connected to the sunlight. They throb in my eyes and brain in the same way. I try to focus on Jayne.

'This is unexpected,' I say, squinting, my right eye twitching all of a sudden. 'Come in.'

'Have you just got up? I could come back after work?'

She glances down at my hand. I look at it too. I'm scrunching up the letter in my fist. I manage to angle it so she can't see the letterhead but my fist has given off a general air of tension.

'I've been up for hours,' I say. 'I just like working in my dressing gown.'

'Okay. Sure.'

She steps into the hall. She's wearing a sixties-style paisley dress, cherry-red Dr Martens and purple tights with white polka dots. She doesn't have much in common with Lyd (on any level) but in their physical forms I always register a resemblance around the neck and shoulders, and they both have the same curves on their legs.

These simple lines, these echoes of Lyd, make me want to reach out and hold her, embrace her, but I have enough clarity of mind to know that only a desperately lonely man would do that.

'Do you want a drink? Tea? Coffee? Juice?' I ask, closing the front door and walking towards the kitchen.

She follows me.

'Maybe a glass of water,' she says.

I quickly stash my disturbing letter behind the fruit bowl on the way past and then pour her a glass of filtered water from the fridge.

'How's it going?' she asks, glancing at the fruit bowl.

'I miss her.'

Jayne nods and meets my eyes sympathetically, mirroring my sorrow as she accepts her glass of water. My right eye twitches and I wonder if she sees it.

'It must be hard,' she says.

'We should be together. Preparing for the baby.'

My eye twitches again. Jayne breaks eye contact and moves away from me. I'm pretty sure she's seen my eyeball juddering around in its socket and is going to phone Lyd the second she leaves to tell her that I've gone completely mad.

'How's the writing?' she asks.

'My book? Good. I'm over half way through the first draft now. It's getting there, slowly but surely.'

'I do wonder about creative people; where it all comes from.'

'Anyone could do it. Honestly. It's nothing special.'

'I imagine it's a very spiritual experience, writing a book.'

'People think writers are creative authorities who work up in the castle but really we're just fools prattling around in the village. We spend our days chasing imaginary people, misinterpreting messages, doing dull chores. Have you read *The Castle*?'

She shakes her head.

'It's good that you're keeping on top of it,' she says. 'With everything that's going on.'

'I feel like, maybe, if I write a good book it might prove to Lyd that I'm on the right track. She'll know I haven't lost it.'

'I don't think she'd care if you wrote a masterpiece.'

'Probably not.'

A tapping sound comes from the sliding door. My face jolts towards the noise. It's Blackie, drumming his beak against the glass. My right eyeball flutters and my stomach turns. Jayne looks over, with normal curiosity. An unsettling sense of being watched comes over me. I feel exposed. I can faintly hear the birdsong on the other side of the glass.

'Oh, yes, that's right,' she says. 'Lydia told me about this little guy. Doesn't he come for his breakfast or something?'

She walks towards the sliding door and Blackie flies away, back onto the lawn.

'Sometimes.'

'Look at his little kiddies badgering him.

They're almost as big as he is.'

I go to the cupboard, grab a handful of sultanas, pull the sliding door across and throw them out onto the lawn. Birdsong floods into the kitchen. Most of the birds fly up onto the fence or on top of the evergreen. Blackie stays on the lawn, quickly takes the opportunity to eat a couple of sultanas and then adds to the whistling rumpus:

— *chink-chink, chook-chook, chink-chink, chook-chook* — (*She can see your eye twitching.*)

I quickly slide the door shut and turn my back to the garden. Jayne watches as the birds all fly back down onto the grass. My right eye is now twitching more than it's still.

'Look at him feeding them all. Why can't they just pick up the raisins themselves?'

'Sultanas,' I say.

'Do they always have so many chicks?'

'No. They usually just have two or three but a cat got the female from another nest so the male moved on. This one looks after their chicks as well as his own.'

'Aw, that's sweet.'

'He looks after his people.'

Jayne turns towards me.

'You know, she's miserable without you.'

'*Really?*'

'You don't have to sound so happy about it.'

'Sorry,' I say, rubbing my eye. 'It's just . . . she left.'

'Yes. She left. But she could have kicked you out.'

166

'Do you think that means something?'

'Yes. Of course. Even if *she's* too stubborn to admit it.'

'You think I have a chance?'

'Definitely.'

'What should I do? I don't dare call her. I don't dare do anything.'

'You could start by taking your medication.'

'That's not going to happen,' I say, sighing.

'I know you think you stopped taking it for the right reasons but this pregnancy has brought a lot up for Lydia. It's the worst possible time to try something like this.'

I grab a small glass from the draining board, walk to the fridge and pour myself some orange juice.

'I think it's the best time,' I say.

I close my eyes for a second whilst I put the juice back in the fridge and my back is turned to her, trying to relax, but my eyeball jitters around behind my eyelid.

'This is why you've ended up living on your own. You think you're doing this for Lyd and the baby but you're doing it for yourself. You're living on your own, you're writing your book instead of looking for work, you're not taking your medication, and you're doing all this because it's what *you* want. You're going to end up on your own completely but you don't see it.'

'I see it. I do. But it's worth the risk. I don't want us to live in the shadows.'

'Whatever that means.'

'It's one of Lyd's phrases.'

'Personally, I don't think she's ever really

forgiven you for running off like that. Leaving her to deal with all that mess. This is just throwing it in her face.'

'I know you're her sister, and I'm sorry to say it, but you don't know her like I do. And you don't know our situation, how it feels. She forgave me for all that. She had to, so we could grieve together. This is something else.'

'Forgiving and forgetting are two different things.'

I gulp down my juice, take the glass to the sink and look out the kitchen window. Blackie is still feeding his five pestering children. Jayne's right. He shouldn't have to feed them all. They're big enough to feed themselves. Why does he put up with it? Why does he let them twitter at him and bounce around him and make him do whatever they want? It's too stressful a sight. I have to turn my back to it.

'Vince . . . Do you have any plans?'

'When you look back at how she was when she was younger you all see the scientist in her, the high achiever, and that's good because you're proud of her, and you love the role she plays in your life, but she's not really like that. Not at heart. None of you see how deeply sensitive she is, how soft her humour is, how forgiving she is, how she always puts those she loves before herself. The decisions she makes reflect who she is, how she thinks and feels. We would have never got back together if she hadn't forgiven me.'

I turn to face Jayne. She's looking at me, unsettled, because I'm resting the palm of my hand over my right eye. I'm not sure how long it's been there. I lower it and my eye starts twitching again. I screw up my cheek to try to stop it in its tracks but it doesn't work, it just makes me look like I'm pulling a strange face.

'You obviously don't want to talk about your plans. But we can talk about Lydia if you want. Why do you think she left?'

'I don't know.'

'I want to help you, Vince. That's why I'm here. I think you're good for her. I think you're right for each other. You probably do know her better than I do. And with a baby on the way it makes sense for you to be together. But you have to face up to the reasons why she might have left you. You have to be willing to change.'

'Into what?'

'I don't know. You know Lydia. She doesn't talk about this stuff. But decisions have to be made. You're living in a house she's paying for, for a start.'

'Do you think you can get her to talk to me?'

'Do you really think you're ready?' she says. 'No offence, but you need to do something with yourself.'

'You mean get a job? That's all it ever comes down to for you lot.'

'No. That's not what I meant. But since you brought it up: what if Lydia did stop supporting you? How would you afford your own place? How would you be a father if you had to separate? These should be eventualities you're preparing for. You have to be able to look after yourself. Otherwise, how will anyone think you can look after a child?'

'Charlie was happy and my life, the way I lived, was no different to how it is now.'

'When Charlie was born your first novel had just been published and your writing career looked promising. Mum and Dad had helped you both get on the property ladder so you were cushioned from all of that. When it turned out your books weren't selling, Lydia's book suddenly made lots of money. So it made sense for you to stay at home and look after Charlie, because you could. Everything's changed since then. Lydia's quite well-off but you're back at the start again. Surely you see that?'

'I do. I know.'

'You have to start looking after yourself or you're going to lose her.'

I suddenly decide that I can't stand another second of this. I feel like my eye is going to explode. I approach Jayne, put one hand on her lower spine and the other on her shoulder and begin to usher her out of the house. Her eyes bulge with surprise but she accepts her fate without a challenge.

'Thanks for coming,' I say. 'I'm really going to think this through. I'll try harder. I promise.'

I open the door for her. All the brightness and birdsong rushes in. I screw up my face and urge Jayne out onto the doorstep. She steps out. I'm just about to close the door on her when she turns around and says:

'Vince.'

She's holding something out. Her glass of water. I take it from her.

'Look after yourself,' she says. 'Think about what I've said.'

I close the door.

I should have stayed crouched by the breakfast counter.

★ ★ ★

After Jayne's visit I can't concentrate on writing or editing so I turn off my computer and draw blackbirds in my notebook to pass the time, trying not to think about the version of me that Jayne would be happy with. The first image is a terrible attempt at a realistic depiction, unmeasured and mutant. The second actually looks like a blackbird but it's more of a generic sketch. The third one is cartoonish and looks more like a crow.

It's a relieving change to watch the black ink from the nib of my fountain pen creating lines rather than words. The twenty-six letters of the alphabet seem so oppressive compared to the casual strokes a picture uses to gradually acquire its meaning. The hand moves more freely. The system is less restrictive.

I gradually start producing smaller and more emblematic images until I've developed a simple glyph. It's made up of two hooked and curved lines that give just the right impression. As I'm drawing these glyphs I start to hear Blackie up on the drainpipe. His whistle is entwining with the hooks and the curves of the lines. My mind is sinking and the symbols on the page are swelling and losing focus. I can't see the nib of my pen.

My writing hand is shaking.

When Blackie releases a distinctive flurry of tweets a thought strikes me, true and bold. I rush to the baby's room, pull down the ladder and climb into the attic. The plastic white board is directly behind me, by the wall, covered by an old sheet. I grab the torch, fling off the sheet and illuminate Charlie's family portrait.

He depicted the house from the back, not the front. You can see this from the amount of wall that the doorway takes up. The sliding door is the entrance to inside. He was by no means a housebound child, we took him out all the time, but to him the outside world is the back garden.

The first figure is Mum. Her arms are a horizontal yellow line: love, acceptance. He has been very careful to give her a red smile.

The central figure is Charlie. He also has a red smile. His head is oversized, bigger than either of ours, and his body is a tiny lump. His arms are black: one pointing up at his mother, one pointing up at me.

I have a smile too but mine is black. I'm very tall. Relatively, Lyd could be my child. She's closer to his size. My arms are a purple diagonal line: one end points down towards him and the other up.

I follow the line of my arm up the image and there it is, the thing I'm looking for. I've stared at this portrait a hundred times and never made anything of it. Up on the top right corner of the house are two very small, very purposefully placed, hooked black lines. They are strikingly similar to my glyph. They represent a blackbird.

I stare at these two small, interlocking black hooks for three or four minutes. Did Charlie know about the blackbirds? Did Blackie speak to Charlie? Is Charlie speaking through Blackie? Is there a link? The picture provides no answers. It only adds weight to the creeping feeling that blackbirds are in control of my fate.

My contemplation is broken by the absence of solitude. There's something behind me. Eyes are on me. I know it's Charlie but I don't want to look. My heart is racing. My hands tingle and begin to sweat. I can feel his smile in the air around me. Almost hear his giggle.

I slowly turn around but, as I do, the feeling goes, the smile wanes. It's not Charlie. It's Blackie, standing in the middle of the floor. He doesn't move when I shine the torch on him. He must have got in through the cracked tile, the route the dead mother took to build her nest in here. His presence is filling me with dread. There is a plan and Blackie is a part of it. He opens his beak:

— *chink-chink, chook-chook, chink-chink, chook-chook* —

5

Photons, the principal particles in electromagnetic fields, transmit electromagnetic radiation. A small frequency of this radiation is called the visible spectrum, or light (waves of which interact with retinas and amass into the sensation of sight). For this reason, photons are often referred to as 'messenger particles'. In laboratory settings, human exposure to certain frequencies of electromagnetic fields produces altered emotional states including fear, panic and disorientation, or relaxation, relief and contentment. Tests have also stimulated hallucinations and feelings of being watched, talked to or followed, in both malevolent and comforting contexts. This is to say, electromagnetic fields and their photons don't just affect what people see and believe, they are what people see and believe. Yet, their messages, when perceived, are not necessarily aligned with the objective truth. Subtle fluctuations in a brain's electromagnetic field changes the way the photons' 'reality message' is received and interpreted.

Lyd's standing in our doorway with a lonely and angry look on her face. It's the day of the anomaly scan and she's come to pick me up. She's wearing a yellow-green chiffon maternity dress and, despite her despondent mood, she's glowing and looks beautiful. Her life-forming, five-month bulge makes me feel like I'm emerging from a world where nothing real grows.

'You look rough,' she says. 'Have you lost weight?'

'It was the medication, bloating me up. I'm slowly getting back to my old shape. Do you want to come in for a minute?'

'No.'

'Okay.'

I follow her out to the car, ignoring the birdsong in the air and Blackie on the telephone wire across the road.

It's all under control, I tell myself, as I get in the passenger seat. *Act normal, don't freak out and everything's going to be fine.*

The fact that Jayne created this opportunity doesn't necessarily render it meaningless. There's a slim chance Lyd could be ready, piece by piece, to let me back into her life. Of course, she might want nothing to do with me but think that I deserve to be part of the major moments in our child's development. Whatever the answer, I don't want to get off on the wrong foot. As Lyd drives I move over safe ground and don't mention the fact that I've got a feeling we're being followed by the red car behind us.

She's been out to the Large Hadron Collider in Geneva doing freelance work for CERN (she's been going once or twice a year since the second year of her PhD). She loves it there (it's her only chance to get away from numbers and do some 'real engineering') so I stay conscientiously quiet and coax her into talking about her trip. I

175

manage almost five minutes before making a huge blunder.

'It felt strange,' I say, 'not quite knowing if you were away or not. We've never been apart like that.'

She glances at me harshly and then looks back at the road with amused disbelief.

'That's funny,' she says, 'because I have a distinct memory of planning a child's funeral without quite knowing where you were.'

Again, it's that skill I have for drawing attention to exactly the wrong thing. We drive in silence for a few minutes.

'So was there anything interesting at this conference you mentioned?' I ask. 'After Geneva?'

'I went to see an astronaut speak,' she says.

I wipe my palms on my thighs and look over my shoulder through the rear windscreen. The red car is still behind us. The driver is a shadowy blur.

'An astronaut?'

'Really charismatic for an American guy.'

'Uh-huh.'

'It was supposed to be a respite in the schedule, something non-taxing in the middle of all the serious science, but he ended up getting the majority of the press.'

'How come?' I ask, watching the red car turn right in the side mirror.

'He was speaking about his perspective after being up in space so many times. Mostly the reformed environmentalist stuff you'd expect — beautiful blue ball, terrible wars, pointless borders, reckless use of resources, all that. Obviously, being American, he didn't politicise any of his views, he just kept talking about now being the time to act, but he did have a couple of interesting ideas.'

'For example?'

'Like, in the twenty-first century, Western children grow up with interactive, digital images of Earth at their fingertips and, whilst they're barely beyond the mirror stage before most of them have met people outside the family, a lot of them are self-identifying as citizens of a planet floating in space. For the first time, a toddler's conception of the world is finite. Earth is their home. He thinks this is an unprecedented conceptual upheaval that will change the way future generations will come to think of their identity and where they live.'

'There's only one place a toddler really knows about,' I say, 'the centre of the universe.'

My witticism doesn't even earn me a grin and, under the circumstances, I felt like I'd done spectacularly well. Lyd continues talking as though I'm not really involved in the conversation.

'He was quite eloquent about how the sky isn't a limitless expanse and how, when seen from above, our atmosphere is a relatively thin collection of gases hugging the earth, protecting our entire ecosystem from the decimation of outer space, and how it's completely conceivable that we're changing the nature of this minuscule force-field by filling it with the wrong kinds of gases.'

177

'Sounds like a soft-pot,' I say, trying to amuse her again. 'Don't they weed out the jelly brains in these astronaut programmes?'

She smiles this time, so quickly it could be a twitch. She doesn't want us to enjoy each other's company. She just wants to avoid talking properly by talking about this astronaut. Whilst this is relieving (because I don't want to have to lie about how I'm feeling and what I'm currently going through) it's also agonising because important things are purposefully going unsaid and our relationship feels all the more hopeless for it.

'I agree with most of what he said,' she says, 'any humanitarian does, but I want to know how such a sentimental subject can take centre stage at a supposedly world-renowned physics conference. The bottom line is that he's just another middle-aged man trying to validate his Messiah complex.'

I quickly look over my shoulder. The road behind us is clear. There must be someone just slightly out of sight because I still feel like we're being followed.

'People eat that stuff up though, don't they? It appeases their guilt.'

'The worst thing is that he's filled with awe by a nature that doesn't even exist. It's like watching a mushroom cloud rising over London and saying how beautiful it is. His perspective makes no attempt to deconstruct what's actually happing, or solve any real problems. Meanwhile people making breakthroughs in grand unification, super-string, inflationary cosmology — breakthroughs

178

that will change the way we understand the universe forever — they're being ignored.'

'You know, I'd still be looking at the world with seventeenth-century eyes if it wasn't for you.'

She ignores this compliment and glances down at my lap. My hands are tightly gripping my thighs. I release them and try to find a relaxed stance but everything seems decentred and forced.

'His new-found respect for the planet is bullshit,' says Lyd, more conviction behind her anger now. 'He has absolutely no idea what's going on in the world, or how complicated its problems are. At a push he's, what, a glorified mechanic, a pilot? Who cares what he thinks or if he's had a vague, transcendental experience whilst sitting in a spaceship? He probably has a carbon footprint the size of Asia with all that rocket fuel and all those planes he takes to go and do his talks. And Eastern philosophy has been saying what he's saying for thousands of years. Maybe he should have just read a few books and become an environmental activist. It's such a naïve and pointless perspective.'

My usual response to Lyd's anger would be to gently probe to see if there was something else upsetting her. This time, I simply nod in agreement because if there is something it's probably me.

'You're right,' I say, massaging the back of my neck with my dank right hand. 'Completely right.'

We remain quiet for the rest of the journey. I

179

try to sit as still as possible in order to attract no attention. I ban myself from looking in the mirrors. Nothing is following us, even if I feel it.

★ ★ ★

In the waiting room, twenty minutes after our appointment time, Lyd is still trying to get through a large bottle of mineral water. She's extremely tense. I'm looking around, reading the health posters on notice boards and jigging my right leg.

We're finally led into the ultrasound room by the same assistant as last time. The sonographer is different. She's a mole-faced woman with a big nose, tiny screwed-up eyes, wrinkled lips and greasy brown hair. Her voice has a nasal quality.

'Sit down, lie down, get your feet up,' she says. 'And pull that dress up. Let's have a look at you.'

Lyd gets on the examination bed and hitches up her dress, resenting the speedy, matter-of-fact instructions because she thinks most medical professionals are sadists and that stripping people of their dignity and confidence is all part of a game they pretend they're not playing.

The sonographer starts moving fast and explaining little. Within moments Lyd's bulging stomach is covered in gel and the mole-woman is racing through a series of checks and measurements without explaining a single thing to us.

'If you're thinking of finding out the sex today you can forget it,' she says. 'Little blighter has its legs crossed.'

'Oh,' says Lyd, trying to sound disappointed

180

instead of antagonistic.

'Maybe we could wait a couple of minutes?' I suggest.

'Could be two minutes, could be two weeks but I haven't got time to find out,' says the sonographer. 'Behind schedule as it is.'

'We know,' says Lyd.

Again, the sonographer sets off on a series of nozzle twists and writes little encoded notes on a form that I'm sneaking glances at but can't decipher.

'There's not much point getting a sonogram either,' she says. 'It's in a funny position. You won't be able to see the face.'

'But you can tell if everything's okay?' says Lyd. 'It looks fuzzy. Why is it so fuzzy?'

'Everything's fine . . . Fine, fine, fine. You can book again if you really want a clearer picture.'

'*What's that?*' I ask.

My anxious tone peaks Lyd's interest. She looks at the screen and tries to see what I'm seeing.

'What's what?' asks the sonographer, eager to get through this as quickly as possible.

'That,' I say, pointing at the top half of the screen.

'That's your baby,' she replies.

Lyd's staring at me. My lower spine is trembling. I must be hallucinating. What I'm seeing can't be what I'm seeing because what I'm seeing isn't a baby. It's something else: some kind of deformed mutant, a disfigured runt, a grotesque homunculus. A wave of nausea rushes through me. A cold sweat quickly follows.

Not now, I'm thinking. *Not now*.

Lyd has a disgusted look on her face, like my existence is contaminating the air and making it unpleasant to breathe. I look around the room, increasingly dizzy, and see a small metal bin over in the corner. I run towards it and drop down onto my hands and knees.

For a second it seems like it's passed and I've just humiliated myself for nothing but when I look at the contents of the bin, at the disposed rubber gloves, paper towels and thin plastic condoms covered in lubricant, I'm suddenly dry heaving and retching. Deep undulations are curling through my spine and whipping out of my gullet. It's not real vomit, it's just air and drool, but it sounds harsh and insane.

6

In Plato's allegory of the cave, Socrates describes underground prisoners who are chained up facing a blank wall. Above, a procession of people and objects pass before a fire and their shadows project down onto this wall. Over time the prisoners give names to these shadows and come to accept them as real things. They become more and more skilled at perceiving them and predicting the order of their procession. When one of the prisoners is freed and sees the source of the shadows and the world above, he realises that his fellow prisoners will never believe that they are only looking at a puppet show and that the real world is above them. They will think that his eyes have been ruined, that he no longer sees the truth. Socrates argues that, by default, the free man now understands that the body is the real prison and that truth lies beyond the material world. He does not discuss what would have happened to the man if he went deeper into the cave.

I wake up late, thirsty, with a headache. There's a heat wave outside, trying to get in. My lithium tablets are on the bed. I fell asleep thinking about taking them again, feeling like I'd ruined everything.

Downstairs, Blackie is waiting for me at the sliding door. He pecks and pecks at it, trying to get my attention, but I ignore him. Birdsong is quietly bouncing off the walls and windows. I can't deal with any of it today so I pull the blinds shut and go around the house closing all the curtains.

Staring at the living room ceiling, lying on the couch, I doze on and off all day, the house slowly warming through. I have no motivation to get up and I'm not tired enough to sleep. My consciousness weaves in and out of itself, hearing house noises and dream noises at the same time, neither here nor there, lost between spaces.

When it finally gets dark and the birds are asleep I feel a bit more awake. It occurs to me that Lyd might have contacted me via email. I go and check. She hasn't. After deleting my junk mail, the message from *CHARLIE* (Subject: (24) Re: direct contact . . .) pops back into the folder. I decide to write him another message and stare at the flashing cursor in the blank message box. I type, *Why are you doing this to me?* and the moment I press the key for the question mark the sound of tiny feet pitter-patters across the ceiling above me.

In the baby's room, I pull down the ladder. Looking up into the square of darkness, I no longer feel alone. As my head breaches the attic I smell the faint whiff of Charlie that permeates from all of his things. I turn on the torch, look around at his stuff and climb the rest of the way in. There's definitely somebody up here.

I step over the small box of Christmas decorations and hear shuffling behind the pile of boxes where I discovered the abandoned chicks.

I approach the corner the boxes create and shine the torch down the slope of the roof. My stomach flutters as the beam of light passes over a physical object which twists and morphs, forming strange colours and bumps, until my eyes finally understand that it's a scrunched-up child: Charlie, sitting with his hands over his face. He's wearing red dungarees, a blue T-shirt with thin neon stripes running through it and a pair of blue shoes with red laces. It's the outfit he's wearing in my favourite photograph of him, the one I keep in my wallet.

'Who are you hiding from?' I whisper.

When I speak he disappears and I hear running across the middle of the floor behind me. I follow the direction of the sound, slowly navigate the floor space with the torch pointing ahead of me and eventually find him again, this time beneath the wardrobe doors that are leaning against the sidewall.

When the light of the torch passes over his face he wriggles with excitement.

'Charlie? Why are you hiding?' I ask.

He disappears again and, behind me, I hear the sound of his feet running across the middle of the floor. I realise that he might be playing hide-and-seek so this time I put on a mock-spooky voice, count down from ten and narrate my journey to find him.

Listening for audible clues, I hear him squirming and writhing over by his old cot so I dramatically lengthen the game, pivoting around his position and raising the tone of my voice until he makes a thrilled squeal, at which point I

sweep the beam of the torch onto him and cry:
'Got you!'

Again, he disappears and I hear him running through the darkness.

We play like this for close to twenty minutes. There aren't all that many hiding spots but I know that his pleasure is mostly derived from the anticipation of waiting to be found so I try to make the build-up as tense and enjoyable as possible.

When I hear him behind the first pile of boxes again, I can't resist. It feels like he's really here, we're really playing this game. Hope has taken root in me so, instead of raising the volume of my voice and springing towards him, I kneel down in front of him. I still haven't seen his face. I have to see it but I daren't. I rest the beam of the torch on his chest and take a few breaths.

I desperately want to reach out and hold him. I inch the beam up to his neck, the dip of his chin, but there's no face, just blackness, death; a small black shadow scurries towards a crack in a roof tile and disappears. The attic is empty. I'm alone. There's no running sound in the darkness. I sit in the attic for hours, just in case, but he doesn't come back.

★ ★ ★

On the couch, it's getting light and I can't sleep. I'm haunted by his absence. Every time I get close to nodding off I hear him in the distance — a giggle, a squeal, running feet. I need him. More than ever. I can't let go.

186

Hours? Days? All I know is that the heat wave continues, ignoring the closed curtains, moving through every object in the house, into every tiny space and crevice. I idle around — lying on the couch, leaning against walls, getting warmer, sweating, drinking water, questioning why I saw Charlie, thinking about why I want to see him again so much, wondering how the birdsong is getting through the walls and into my ears. Every peek through the curtains reveals a blackbird conspicuously close to the house. Now and again I hear the clicking sound of a beak pecking on the sliding door in the kitchen.

Outside is pure bombardment: light, heat, birdsong, blackbirds, huge buildings, millions of people, sweat, garbage, technology, decay, carbon dioxide, pot holes, chewing gum, coffee shops, pushchairs, mobile phones, double-decker buses, advertisements, cars, traffic lights, lamp posts, paving stones, tarmac, double yellow lines, clothing, faces, hair, train tracks, tunnels, barriers. Everything is unnaturally connected; welded, wired, waged. It's all too much.

Inside, I might have a chance. Me and the house have a long-standing mutual dependency. Here, I'm not just a lost and hopeless man living in his partner's house, I'm in a safe place, fighting to get through a dark time, taking an isolated opportunity to try to come to terms with some of the blind spots in my mind. If I stay here everything might work out. I just have to avoid going outside, where everything's connected, where they'll see that I'm not part of it all.

I sweat. I drink water. The couch becomes

slightly moist. Darkness falls and rises. Birdsong quietens and swells. Distant traffic and plug sockets hum. Heat clings to everything. Time is completely unpunctuated until I finally hear the faint sound of scurrying in the attic. I stand up but have to stay still for thirty seconds while the blood rushes into my head and out again.

When I get up there Charlie is sitting in plain sight. He isn't trying to hide from the beam of my torch. I can see his face. He's smiling, glad to see me, wearing those red dungarees again. I drop to my knees and release a mournful groan. Emptiness and sadness twist in my guts. He begins to fade out of sight so I fight my feelings, rock my spine, clench my gut, rein everything back and force it down. When I'm done he's still sitting there.

'Do you want Daddy to read you a story?' I ask, almost whimpering.

'No,' he says, definite, shaking his head.

The presence of this word, the reality of it, shocks me. I didn't expect him to speak. Last time his movement made noises and he made a few reactionary sounds but it all lacked the immediacy of an independent mind choosing a word and projecting it at me. It could have all been in my head. But hearing him. Hearing his voice. It makes me see that he's really here. He has wants and needs and I don't know what they are.

'Do you want to play with your cars?'

'Make pictures,' he says.

My hands shake as I scramble through a couple of boxes, trying to remember which one his crayons and felt-tip pens are in. I eventually find them on top of some books underneath lots of his drawings and paintings.

There's no paper so I rush down the ladder to the printer in my office. As I grab a few sheets I have a morbid moment of self-reflection where I imagine the pain of rushing up into an empty attic but he's still there waiting patiently when I get back.

I put the blank pieces of paper in front of him and he begins scribbling. Lines and colours form on the page and I follow their appearance keenly, pointing the torch at the emerging picture so he can see.

I forgot how intensely honest and creative he is. There is no pause for thought in his drawing and colouring, no doubt or reflection. He is lost in the process. Not a single moment is wasted worrying about how his image will be perceived. This is art as id, image as dream, self as symbol, and it's untainted by creative block, lack of focus or the pursuit of value.

When he is done he grabs the corner of the page and, without checking the image over, knowing that it is exactly as he intended, holds it out for me.

'Look,' he says.

I take the page from him and inspect it. It is a version of Lyd in stick man form. Her arms are open. Her big face is smiling. A large messy block of yellow starts in her belly and almost takes over the whole page. Above her there is a black scribble in the sky. Below there are green lines and a pair of hooked black lines.

'Is this Mummy?' I ask.

He nods but he isn't looking at me. He's busy drawing the next picture. It takes him a long time to finish. It's another picture of Lyd. This time he only uses black. Lyd's mouth is sad. Blackness is protruding from her stomach.

'This one's not very happy, is it? Is there something wrong with Mummy?'

'Yes,' he says, nodding his head.

'Is she sad?'

He shakes his head.

'Is she poorly?'

He shakes his head again.

'What is it then?'

'Mummy doesn't love Charlie,' he says.

'Of course she does.'

'Mummy loves baby, not Charlie.'

'That's a horrible thing to say.'

'Baby's going to die,' he says.

'Please, Charlie. Don't say that.'

'Baby's going to die.'

'Charlie, no,' I say, reaching for his shoulders.

The second I reach for him he doesn't exist. His shoulders aren't there. His felt-tip pens and crayons are scattered around on top of blank pieces of paper. There are no drawings anywhere. The pictures have gone. He's taken them with him. I think I hear a little scratching sound behind a pile of boxes but when I look there's nothing there.

⋆ ⋆ ⋆

The house is too hot. Outside is still impossible. The only thing that matters to me is seeing

190

Charlie again. I decide to move up into the attic. This way, whenever he's around, I'll be there to see him straight away. I won't miss a moment.

I take up an extension cable, plug in a small lamp and fashion a makeshift bed. I empty all the bottles I can find and fill them with water. I even fetch the mop bucket and bleach so I won't need to visit the toilet more than once a day.

After putting all the tinned food that doesn't need cooking in a bag I notice a yellow Post-It note at the back of the cupboard: *If you can read this we need more food xxx*. It jars me for a second. I forgot about Lyd's notes. I close the cupboard door with a flinch.

When I'm all set up I feel safe. There are no windows for blackbirds to tap on and, although I can still hear it, the birdsong is quieter up here. Time — or its overabundance — is the only problem. The hours are long and uninterrupted. There's no night or day. It's endless.

Ten hours? Fifteen? There's still no sign of him and my eyes are worn out so I quickly go downstairs and retrieve the stopwatch I sometimes use to time myself when I go jogging. It makes sense to rest in short bursts because, if I spread my sleeping out throughout the day, there's a greater probability that I won't miss him entirely. I use the stopwatch as an alarm and trial sleeping for half an hour and then staying awake for three hours.

After three, maybe four rounds of this I struggle to stay awake for the full three hours so I have to keep reducing the sleeping and waking times. It gets blurrier and blurrier but I eventually find a good balance sleeping for three minutes and waking for ten.

Meals are reduced to sporadic grazing. I'm never hungry but now and then I notice a strange twinge in my stomach and eat a couple of sultanas. After a single bowel movement my digestive system slows down to a near stop. I only have to go down to empty the mop bucket into the toilet once. The light level surprises me. The edges of the blinds gleam and lint collides with golden photons slipping through into the room. The whole house is thick with warmth.

It's hard to know if he's ever going to show up again but occasionally I wake and sense that he's been and I've missed him, or else that he's getting close but choosing to stay absent. This makes me feel so empty that my stomach cramps and folds me in half.

More and more I find myself crying. Occasionally, my nervous system is attacked by electric convulsions. My back arches, my limbs tense up and the back of my head slides around on the floor, banging into cardboard boxes. My spine is constantly shaking near the pelvis. My hands shiver. My right eye twitches. Sweat drips off my back. The air gets thicker and thicker. I'm awake, I'm asleep, I'm awake, I'm asleep.

Soon enough my attention is not so much focused on seeing Charlie but on feeling his presence in the space. I have to make myself ready to receive him. It's a process. The first two were flukes. All the conditions were accidentally right. Now I have to work for it.

Everything changes when he's near. When he's

close by I lie back and try to feel him washing through me, try to summon him through my body. I have no appetite for anything else. This feeling is the only thing I'm hungry for.

When he finally appears weeks might have passed, months, but it's as if he's come from nowhere, as if I've put in absolutely no effort and he was always going to simply show up at this moment. This is the fated time. I should have known all along.

'Charlie?'

He ignores me.

'Charlie?'

He starts grinning. He's playing the ignoring game. My tension subsides.

'Do you want to play a game?' I ask him.

He's still trying to win at the ignoring game.

'Charlie. You're terrible at ignoring. I can see you grinning.'

He laughs and looks at me.

'Is that what you want to play? The ignoring game.'

He shakes his head and looks around.

'Fire Engines on the Moon,' he says.

'We can't play that one. There is no moon.'

'*Daddy*. Please. Fire Engines on the Moon.'

'Okay,' I say. 'Don't go anywhere. I have to get some things.'

I rush downstairs and get two cushions from the living room, then string, paper, Sellotape and lots of old newspapers. Charlie is still there when I get back and sits dutifully by my side, marvelling at my handcraft. It takes me almost an hour to make but I recall the process of creating the first moon very clearly.

When the final piece of paper is attached, I remember one last thing and so descend the ladders into the baby's room, remove the small hook from the ceiling, take it up to the attic and screw it into the highest roof beam. Charlie claps his hands together with glee when he sees the new moon hanging a foot from the attic floor.

'See? It's just like the old one.'

'Please, Daddy. Fire engine,' he says.

I open one of his boxes of toys, find his favourite fire engine and put it by his side.

'Do you want to see how the moon travels around the world?' I ask. 'Or do you just want to play fire engines?'

'Yes,' says Charlie, with a nod. 'Moon Around the World.'

'Sit there then.'

I point to a spot on the floor and grab hold of the moon. Charlie shuffles into position with coy excitement, holding onto his fire engine.

'Close your eyes for a minute and imagine you're floating in space,' I say. He closes them, his expression becoming slightly concerned. 'You're the whole world, the big blue planet Earth, where we all live. Way over in the distance is the bright yellow sun. And that's what the world spins around all year long. Okay, you can open your eyes now. This, in my hand, is the moon — '

Charlie covers his face with his hands in excited anticipation.

'Not yet, Charlie. Wait for it.'

He parts his fingers and looks through them with a smile.

'This is the moon. And when do we see the moon?'

Charlie mumbles.

'I can't hear you. When do we see the moon?'

'Night-time.'

'That's right. We mostly see the moon at night time, when the sky is black. The sun shines onto it from the other side of the world and lights it up shiny and white. And what does the moon spin around?'

'Me,' says Charlie, covering his eyes again.

'No, Charlie. What does the moon spin around?'

'Moon Around the World.'

'That's right. And what are you?'

He giggles and hides his face in his lap.

'Charlie. What are you?'

He peeks up.

'World,' he says.

'That's right,' I say. 'You're the world. And the moon goes around world . . . like this.'

I push the moon in a small circle around Charlie and he laughs infectiously and intensely, like he almost can't bear how amused he is.

'See,' I say, pushing it round. 'The moon travels around the world.'

After a few revolutions Charlie loses his timid fear, sits up and follows the moon's path with delighted eyes. Unconscious of his own wonderment, he raises his fire engine into the air as though it is caught up in the motion of it all. Occasionally, he releases a spasmodic burst of laughter.

His intense happiness is having a shimmering

effect on my vision. Lamplight is passing through him. I can see the space behind him. My hands are sweating and beginning to shake so intensely that I can feel the reverberations in my elbows. I'm pushing a big white ball around an empty space. A toy fire engine is sitting still by my side.

The next time the moon comes around I clutch it in my jittery hands, hold it to my chest, tuck my chin down into it and stare at the empty space where he was, trying — but failing — to will him back into existence. I don't ever want to let it go.

'I won't,' I promise the warm air all around me. 'I won't.'

7

A black hole's entropy is proportional to the size of its event horizon, not its inner volume. Since a black hole is space in a state of maximum entropy, this can be taken to mean that there is an elemental spatial entity — a region of space that allows for one unit of entropy — and that this space is a surface area, not a volume. To put it another way, it might reveal that the universe works in a similar way to a hologram. If true, a physical, linear existence in space and time is a false construct. Every moment, from the beginning of the universe to the end, already exists on a flat surface, surrounded by inconceivable dimensions. Time is a circle, space is an illusion and reality is relative to the number of dimensions that something exists in.

I'm standing on Suicide Bridge, my eyes tracing the skyline. The rumble of speeding traffic rises from below. London is cloaked in fumes and heat. The city is a single thing, a single word, a single idea. It has survived plague, fire, bombs, war. It's over two thousand years old. I'm not even a speck of dust falling off its skin. I grip the bridge's black metal bars. My legs are agitating. Someone pulls up beside me on a vintage pushbike. An unnecessarily enhanced startle reflex passes through my body.

'Don't do it,' says the cyclist, mock-seriously.

197

In a petrified stupor, staring at the sunlight in his ginger beard and the sweat glistening on his freckled skin, the attributes of the stranger slowly form a memory of words: Dieter, bookshop, barge, mushrooms. With them, his flat, meaningless face takes on form and character.

'No. Never. Good. Hi, Dieter. Hi.'

'I didn't take you for a jogger. I almost didn't recognise you. I can't stand it. Bores the hell out of me.'

He's talking about my clothes. I put on my jogging outfit because I wanted to be invisible. I wanted people to see a jogger, not me. Dieter saw me anyway.

'All that time in the cave,' I say. 'No movement.'

'I don't know how you do it. I'd go out of my mind, cooped up on my own all day . . . I'm not disturbing a profound moment here, am I?'

'No. Far from it.'

'Good.'

'It's all surface. It looks real but it's just memories piled on top of each other.'

'Okay.'

'Lyd was right. It's best to keep the door shut. Keep the cat in the box.'

I let go of the bars and look at Dieter. He's looking down the street beyond me. His cheeks are bunched up and his squinting eyes are awkwardly imagining his own back, cycling away.

'How's the mushroom farm coming along?' I ask.

'Erm, yeah . . . I'm still at the bookshop at the moment. Can't get the funds together. My mate in Wales wants me to partner up with him. It's the only place where there's a real mushroom scene at the moment.'

'Sure.'

'But I'm in a really serious relationship with my yoga teacher. And I don't want to sell my barge. How's the writing going?'

'I'm trying not to force it. Wait. Listen. See what comes. Don't judge it.'

'Are you writing another novel then?' he asks, looking out at the view.

'Stories about delusions . . . Different times. Different places.'

'Sounds interesting. Can you believe this weather? Best summer we've had in years.'

'You don't want to sell your boat?'

'Barge. No. But I can't get it to Wales. And this yoga teacher . . . '

'You have to learn how to hear the surface. Stop hearing too much. You know? Just hear her.'

'I'd love to wax lyrical about her, really, but I have to get to work.'

'Sure.'

'See you later.'

He cycles off. I start jogging. Blackie swoops down and lands on the end of Suicide Bridge. I stop before him, waiting for a message or instruction but he just wants to demonstrate his power for a moment. He flies up onto the roof of the first house and whistles diagonally across the road. Over there, the way he calls, another Blackie acknowledges him and tweets further down the road to another Blackie who's standing on a lamppost at the crossroad ahead. I set off

199

jogging again and as I pass each bird it chirps to the next one:

— *tck-tck-tck-tck-tck-tck* —

(*Keep watching him. It's nearly time.*)

Blackbirds talk about me all the way to Hampstead Heath. Every time I think I might be imagining it another one is looking at me, whistling to the next one. The park is full of people. The sight of them is overwhelming, almost too much. Their flat, desperate souls are jumping out of their eyes. I stick to the paths through the woods and stay away from Parliament Hill and the main fields so that I don't come across any crowds. I have a bench in mind that I want to sit on — over by the boating pond — but first I want to run the lap I used to walk with Charlie.

As I speed along by the playground I find myself slowing down and standing still, watching the children and their parents. I'm aware of how I might look — that I live in an era where I can't glance at a child without its paranoid parents thinking that I want to sexually abuse and kill it — but Charlie loved coming here with me. I used to be one of those parents, beyond the gates.

There are twenty-three children on the playground, eleven parents and four pushchairs lined up against the perimeter. One girl in a yellow-and-white polka dot dress is screaming on the swings so loudly that it's beginning to embarrass her mother. I quickly make all the connections between the parents and the children. Two boys are here with a man text-messaging on a bench (he keeps glancing at them). Four of the bigger girls, about nine or ten years old, are the children of three women standing together over by the monkey bars. One rogue girl and boy are here alone. Of them all, only one boy is unaccounted for. He's sitting in the box compartment the children go into before crossing the blue rope bridge. He's sad, morbid, hiding on his own. He's not playing with anyone, not talking. Nobody's checking on him or looking for him. He doesn't look like a boy who would be left to roam free. Even from this distance I can see that his haircut is more expensive than mine.

I'm getting increasingly worried about this little boy. My legs are jiggling. The birdsong is getting loud and intrusive, swelling out from the surrounding trees. I pointlessly wipe my damp hands across my sweaty face. He's only three or four. He shouldn't be left unattended. Maybe his mum or dad popped out to get him an ice cream, or get themselves a coffee.

Maybe I'm his mum or dad, I think, and then sneer.

I decide I better stay here and look out for him in the meanwhile, just in case.

The group of three mums over by the monkey bars start glancing over at me. I jump three times, bringing my knees right up to my chest. I can't stand still. One of the mothers is particularly unsubtle. At the precise moment she covertly points at me, a child's hand clasps tightly around the index finger of my right hand, the way Charlie used to hold it. She thinks I'm a demented paedophile who has just stolen a child.

I look down but Charlie's not there. When I look back at the playground I can't see the four-year-old boy. I scan all the places he could be. One of the fathers has joined the three worried mothers by the monkey bars and is looking my way. My rising panic tells me that they will think I'm crazy if I try to warn them about the child who just went missing. I should just start jogging, look like a jogger.

Before I set off I look around for a sign and, sure enough, Blackie's standing on the backrest of the nearest bench, watching me, waiting. If I sit there, it's near enough to show that I'm not fleeing and it faces away from the playground and so displays that I'm not predisposed to constantly look at children. I head towards it.

— tck-tck-tck-tck-tck-tck —

(*We're watching. Everybody's watching.*)

Blackie flies away as I approach.

Sitting on the bench, I take a sip of my water and then spread my arms out. I wait seventeen seconds before I twist my neck to glance at my accusers. They're all looking in another direction now. I follow the line of their stares and see a man who is wearing the same shorts and t-shirt as me. He is walking away from them. A four-year-old boy is holding his index finger. It's the boy from the playground.

The man standing with the three mothers breaks away from them to use his mobile phone. From his urgency, and the way he keeps eyeing the man and the boy, it seems like he's calling the police.

I stand on the bench, trying to glean more of the scene, and start waving my arms around. I'm trying to get their attention and show them that the man with the boy and me are different people, but they won't look. They're too intently focused on them.

'It's not me!' I find myself shouting. 'My boy's dead!'

A happy family who are out to walk two golden retrievers and grandma in her wheelchair are talking about me, glancing, staring. The birdsong is getting louder again. Twittering chaos flitters through the air. I hop off the bench and start running away from the playground.

I must be running too fast because people are looking at me like a criminal. I slow down and jog over to the boating lake trying to avoid people's eyes, trying to jog like a jogger.

An old man is sitting on the bench I planned to sit on. He has a Jack Russell on his lap. The bench before him is free, as is the one further along, but I sit next to him anyway. It could be a sign. I might have to talk to him.

As I sit down his dog immediately erupts into a whirl of barking and spinning. The man looks at me sidelong, well aware that the other benches nearby are free, and pins his dog down onto his lap, reassuring it with whispers.

'My little boy's dead,' I say. 'He used to smile when I whispered in his ear. Astrocytoma. If you could tell your dog one thing what would it be?'

I reach towards his lap to stroke the Jack Russell. It growls and its flews tremble. I snap my hand back. The old man shoos it off his lap.

At first the dog looks back at him with its tail raised, waiting to see if he is about to stand, but with no movement or instructions from its master it decides to run after a goose about fifty metres away on the grass behind us.

'Merdre,' says the old man.

I'm only half sure that this is the word he says. It could have been a dismissive and inaudible grumble. It's not likely that he used a made-up word from the *Ubu* trilogy that has the double connotation of 'shit' and 'murder'. Nonetheless, I decide to move forward as though this is the word he's uttered.

'Sure, sure. *Ubu Roi*. The realm beyond metaphysics. A dog would get that.'

'My little dog's dead,' says the old man.

I look over my shoulder. I can't see it anywhere.

'Sure, sure,' I say, my legs bouncing up and down four and a half times a second. 'Dead. I don't think so. What else would you tell him?'

'Life is plentiful,' he says, 'but cheap.'

'A literary theme. Nineteenth-century Russian realism. Twentieth-century Southern Renaissance. I never got to read a decent book with Charlie.'

'Dead.'

'Sure. Sure. Your dog's dead. Do you hear all that birdsong?'

The old man looks up at the empty sky, screwing his face up. I close my eyes and wiggle my fingers about, trying to capture the cadence of the sound.

'Ubu!' the old man shouts. 'Ubu!'

His Jack Russell is running back towards him. He's standing up to leave. When he looks back at me he has a different face. I try to ignore this and look at the bright squiggles of light drifting along the surface of the water on the boating pond. After a couple of minutes everything I look at drifts sideways in both directions. The world is just a surface. Everything that connects up and down, left and right, forwards and backwards, is just random nonsense that easily comes undone.

I'm lost in golden light and birdsong, everything twittering and unreal, when a muscly gym freak with tribal tattoos and a head like a rock tears through my world with an angry voice. He's shouting into his mobile phone. I can't hear the words but I find his anger fascinating. I stand up and start following him.

His vest has the slogan *I could bench you* on the back. His neck and both wrists have chunky silver chains hanging around them. He's holding a rope that could be a dog's lead but there's no dog. He walks with a swagger (it's unclear if he does this because of the nature of his bulk or because he wants to possess as much space as possible).

Once he enters a path through the woods and puts his phone back into his pocket I walk fast and catch him up. Now that we are beneath the trees the birdsong is even louder.

'Why are you so angry?'

'Get fucked, bro,' he says, mildly startled by my sudden appearance. 'I'm seriously not in the mood for a whack job today.'

205

I look up into the nearest tree. Blackie's up there, looking down. The giant demented song is all around me, becoming noisier and more confounding.

'Sure. Sure. Sure,' I say, speaking louder so that I can hear myself over all the noise. 'But was there even anyone on the other end? Does it matter? Where's your dog?'

'Get the fuck away from me, yeah?'

He shoves me away. I almost fall but keep my balance. He's marching away. His vest now says *Blackbirds protect you* so I spring back towards him.

'Sure. Sure. Sure,' I say. 'Pure, unmotivated, irrational violence: the unifying element in all mankind. Inescapable aggression until the end of time.'

He stops, raises his head to the sky and turns back towards me wrapping the rope for his non-existent dog around his fist.

'Listen, psycho. I'm gonna snap you in two if you don't stop following me. Get me?'

He walks on.

'You're the boss,' I say, continuing to shadow him.

He tries to speed up but I'm quick on his heels. He stops and turns, stamping down his left foot and raising his right fist.

'Have you got a death wish or summink, bro?'

'Now, Blackie,' I cry into to the trees. 'Attack!'

He ducks his head with a slight flinch and slowly looks up to where Blackie is standing on a tree branch. He sees nothing of note. The anger in his face disperses into exasperated disbelief.

'Last chance, nutjob. I mean it. Wrong guy. Wrong day.'

He lowers his fist and carries on walking. I'm quick to his shoulder.

'Sure, sure, sure. Maybe you're grieving. Anger is part of that. Maybe your dog died and this is our big cosmic coincidence that's going to create a perfect collision of meaning.'

He pivots towards me. A powerful right hook smashes into the side of my head. Everything goes black. I fall to the ground. A huge thudding pain begins to throb on the side of my head and in half of my brain. A foot slams into my gut.

'You don't know when to quit, do you?'

Crimson drool connects me to the floor. London's subterranean world vibrates through the liquid strand, ancient and overloaded.

Another kick, this time the toe of his running shoe flies piercing into the left side of my ribcage. A squealing wheeze involuntarily surges through my throat.

'Sick fuck,' he says. 'You wanted this.'

I roll onto my back.

Four or five more kicks. I loose count. Kidney, ribs, shoulder, neck, ribs. I'm in foetal position after the second, trying to protect my head. I feel swells of pain that could be kicks but might just be aftershocks bouncing through my body.

His rage is quelled once I'm limp. He spits on the ground next to me and walks away. I catch a glimpse of the rope he's carrying, hanging like a noose.

'I thought you were protecting me,' I mumble, incoherently.

— tck-tck-tck-tck-tck-tck —
(*He's ready.*)

My mouth is filling up with saliva that tastes of copper. Everything looks different when I close my eyes. My pain has patterns, symmetries. I can see it. A woman asks if I'm alright, if I need any help.

'Pain is terrible,' I mutter.

She repeats herself.

I shake my head and hold my hand out, implying that I don't want her to do anything. She walks away, looking back at me, taking out her mobile phone. This brings me back into a more present state. I remember that there are eyes everywhere. If they see me like this they'll take me away, lock me up, force-feed me chemicals.

I manage to lurch onto the grass verge and crawl far enough into the trees that people on the path can't see me. It's cooler here, but darker. The musky scent of insect life is in my nostrils. My skin itches. My face bleeds slowly. Birdsong stabs at my ears. I can't see any birds.

I struggle to sit up, my back against a tree trunk. My spine jars against the hard nubs and wrinkles. Tiny, silent midges float around like hyperactive lint. A grey squirrel scurries up a distant tree. My right eye slowly swells shut. The birdsong reverberates with the pain in my head, a migraine made of tinnitus.

It's been such a hot summer that the leaves are all limp and lifeless. These floppy edges have created lots of little gaps where thin shards of sunlight shoot down to the undergrowth. I pass a hand through the warmth of a couple of them and, as I do this, Blackie swoops down and lands on the toe of my right running shoe.

He jumps and turns one hundred and eighty degrees and all the foliage behind him blurs and turns into a gold-and-green blur. He jumps and turns one hundred and eighty degrees again and I see faces everywhere, evil green faces made out of leaves, flat, monstrous, screaming in agony.

Blackie jumps to face me, still perched on my right foot, both yellow-ringed eyes looking at me. His bill opens. I can see down his throat. A message is coming from inside him, from the deep beyond. It pierces my skull and splits through my brain:

Nothing is connected.

An intense electric pain rips through my nervous system. I hold my head and close my eyes. The pain crashes and explodes, smashing around in chaotic clusters. I writhe and twist. My body judders and flinches, jerks spasmodically. I weep. Twitch. Flinch. Gravity is crushing me. I'm falling. Everything is broken. Everything I care about is gone. There's nothing left. The despair is bottomless.

THIRD TRIMESTER

1

Many of the unification theories in scientific discourse accept the universe as a series of inevitable occurrences caused by the underlying laws of nature and the initial conditions of life. In this sense, science's crowning achievement, its theory of everything, might merely add credence to one of humanity's most ancient ideas: that the universe is governed by the principle of fate. If true, people will come to see their lives as part of a grand cosmological equation, predetermined by the initial conditions on the tip of time's arrow. Questions about the nature of freewill would be resigned to history but the feeling of freedom would continue to confound.

I spend the day slowly tidying up the attic and bringing all my things back down the ladder. My body is weak and sore. I have to take long rests between journeys. I feel lost and lonely, starved of contact with people and the world, afraid that things will never feel as connected or as meaningful as they once did.

Putting the cushions from the centre of the moon back on the couch, I receive a text message from Jamal asking me to pop over. Jamal never sends texts. Sometimes he doesn't even answer his front door when I'm knocking on it. His rare invitations always inspire a sensation of amused validation in me; being chosen by somebody who chooses so few. In this state, with my face swollen and bruised, my reality shaky and delicate, the pride aroused by this invitation rises through me with unexpected power. Jamal is suddenly the exact person I want to see. His message seems like a fated gift.

As always, Jamal answers his front door with an unlit joint hanging out of his mouth. His cautious, socially awkward eyes don't meet mine. He just stands aside and gestures for me to enter with a subtle smile on his face.

Inside, all the newspapers and engine parts are gone. The curtains are open. It almost looks like a normal person's house. The odours of oil and cannabis smoke still cling to the air, but not as intensely.

'Where's all your stuff?' I ask.

He shuts the front door.

'You've seen it like this before.'

'No. I definitely haven't.'

I walk into the centre of his living room and look around.

'I didn't even know you had a carpet.'

'Shit, man,' he says, catching sight of me. 'What happened to your face?'

I touch my swollen eye gently.

'I tripped.'

'Isn't that what victims of domestic abuse say?'

'This whole house used to be a victim of domestic abuse. What's going on?'

'I do this sometimes,' he says, eyeing me quizzically. 'I time it so all my projects end together, so I can cash in and focus on one big thing for a while. I take it you don't want to talk about it? It's okay. We don't have to.'

'We'll get to the bruises. Give me a chance.'

'Sorry. Your face is a real mess though.'

'I've definitely never seen your house like this,' I say, forcing the shift.

'You have.'

'I haven't. It's so tidy.'

'Come on,' he says, frowning at my bruises and forcing himself not to mention them again. 'I want to show you something.'

He jogs upstairs, almost excited. I follow, intrigued. There are no carburettors resting on top of newspapers. I can walk straight up the middle of the staircase. It feels oddly freeing to lack constraint in Jamal's house. I'm used to tiptoeing around.

At the top of the stairs he turns right instead of the usual left. I notice that even the bathroom is clean. There are no giant pieces of scrap soaking in noxious liquids in the bathtub. The tiles are white. The sink lacks its faded black oil stains down the sides.

'Have you started seeing someone?' I ask.

Jamal's standing in front of the spare room which he uses as his workshop.

'God no,' he says. 'I wouldn't know where to start. Come and see.'

I approach the doorway and look in. This is where all the mess is hiding. Shelves full of rusty pieces of metal line the two sidewalls like a library. The back wall's window has been covered with hardboard and has tools hanging on it. In the centre of the floor space, on a purpose-built workbench, there is a large, freshly polished engine.

I walk into the room.

There are bigger, stranger parts than usual: giant springs, huge bars of steel, long bending tubes, tyres, sheets of glass, a pile of black metal slats stacked against each other.

'What am I looking at?' I ask.

'An original 1965, one hundred and seventy-two horsepower, six point two litre, eight-valve Silver Shadow. Engine, chassis, body. The whole thing. I'm getting the upholstery redone with a specialist.'

I look at him, none the wiser.

'It's a vintage Rolls Royce.'

'Is this the thing that was in your bathtub last time?'

'Some of it. Look at that engine. Isn't she a beaut?'

'It's definitely an engine . . . ' I say, walking around the workbench. 'Is it worth much?'

'Money? After all the overheads, not really, no. More of a passion project. When you learn about all the relationships these pieces of metal have with each other . . . it's hard to explain. Let's just say, the Silver Shadow is a beautiful machine.'

'Silver Shadow,' I say, inspecting it and trying to see something special. 'Sounds like a superhero. Is this why you invited me over? I mean, I'm sorry I'm not more impressed. I'm sure it's a big deal.'

'No, man,' he says, still smiling, looking at the engine. 'I just wanted you to see why I'm buzzing about like a bee in a flower shop. I actually wanted to see how you were doing, after

216

last time. You know? It's been a while.'

He glances at me, concern simmering beneath the robotic flicker of his eye muscles.

'Who installed your empathy programme?'

He walks out of the room grinning and shaking his head. I follow him to his bedroom. He climbs into his usual cross-legged position and relights the unlit joint in his mouth.

'So? How are things?' he asks. 'Besides the bruises we're not talking about.'

I think about playing it cool and trying to enjoy our friendship without thinking or talking about everything that's going on (and Jamal would let me without probing) but sorrow rushes to my eyes and throat and I have an overwhelming need to be honest with him.

'She left me,' I admit, trying to breathe slowly.

Jamal forces himself to look into my eyes.

'For good?'

'I don't know. Maybe not, at first. But I think I've messed up my chances. I was stupid. I kept too much back.'

'She found out about the lithium?'

'She figured it out.'

'But she left you in the house?'

'For now. It was a good job she did, to be honest.'

'Is she staying at her sister's?'

'No. Her mum and dad's.'

'Shit.'

'I know.'

Jamal's knees are beginning to bounce up and down. His eyes are wide. The emotional aspect of the conversation has made his muscles rigid,

217

but he is still answering with sound empathy.

'Just give her time,' he says. 'She'll let you know what she needs. You don't want to see her whilst you look like this anyway.'

'Can we talk about this later?' I say. 'I was doing okay for a minute there.'

'Of course. What do you want to talk about?'

I stand up and look out his window, down at the patchy, overgrown lawn. Jamal, though struggling with it, is being unusually receptive and I'm uncomfortably aware that this reflects that I'm on a low ebb, and that it's clear, even to him, that I need care and attention.

'Do you believe in signs, or messages, in nature?' I ask.

He shifts his weight on his spine and furrows his brow, but he nods slightly, motioning that he will move forward with this strange subject because talking about it might be the thing that helps me.

'I believe in a guidance system,' he says, 'a genetic memory, I suppose. Signs and messages can be a part of it. Like black and yellow for poison, or red for danger. It can be more complicated than that, obviously.'

'I mean, more like spirit guides, that kind of thing.'

'Why, what have the sprites been whispering?' he asks, trying to grin.

'Nothing I can explain without sounding crazy.'

'Try me.'

'No. It doesn't matter.'

'Seriously. I know loads about that sort of stuff.'

218

'No, you don't.'

'I do. I'm constantly reading anthropology.'

'You are?'

'You know I am.'

'I thought you just read car manuals and newspapers these days.'

'I was reading about the difference between Neanderthals and Homo sapiens this morning. Look.'

He reaches down by the bed and hands me a book with a badly designed cover and a terrible title, *Monkey See. Monkey Do. Man Imagine*. It looks like it had a print run of about fifty. There's a picture of a professor on the back dressed like a hiker who wants to die a virgin. I hand the book back to him, dismissive of its content.

'It's too hard to explain,' I say. 'I made friends with this blackbird. It was following me around, telling me things, warning me, guiding me . . . Sorry. This sounds insane. Talking about it ruins what it was.'

'Not at all. I was reading a book on Palaeolithic religion before this one, about totems and rituals. It's all fresh in my head.'

'If you're about to spend half an hour calling me a Neanderthal . . . '

'No, man,' he says, leaving his joint resting in the ashtray and picking up a squat tube of metal and some wire wool, starting to scrub. 'Neanderthals were atheists by nature. They weren't capable of symbolic thought. At least, not to the extent that we were.'

'Isn't the whole point of atheism the choice?'

'When Homo sapiens started believing in

things they couldn't see, that's when they became human. It had nothing to do with their intelligence. Well, it did, but this book argues that the modern world has misconceived what human intelligence is.'

'Enlighten me.'

'So, most people think intelligence is like focus, or alertness, being objective, being able to measure things quickly and accurately, all the qualities that are valued by science, but this book says that Neanderthals were more intelligent than us in this primary way.'

'So why aren't they sitting here having this conversation?'

He puts down his chunk of metal and lights his joint again.

'Think about it. Discoveries come from inspiration, visions. If Homo sapiens had objective minds there would be no culture or invention, no science or technology. We'd still be living in alpha-dominated packs.'

'Why no science?' I ask.

'Because first you have to invent a theory, conceive a method, put two and two together. That's not how an objective mind behaves.'

'So Homo sapiens started daydreaming and inventing things.'

'Exactly.'

'I don't see what this has got to do with anything.'

'Okay,' he says, inhaling smoke deeply. 'First of all there were a select few Homo sapiens who started having visions. They taught the others how to see them by pointing them out with pigments — effectively, drawing things on rocks. Back then, a picture was inconceivable to the majority of people and the seers would have to teach them all how to see it, even after they'd drawn it.'

'The seer was like a shaman or a priest or something?'

'This book just calls them seers. They were the ones who could see the pictures in the first place, before they'd marked them out for the others. And once these artworks started appearing, the seers began telling stories about where these pictures were coming from. They created entire belief systems around them. Painting a picture was like catching a spirit, bringing it into the physical world.'

'I still don't see where this is going.'

'I'm laying groundwork, man. Chill.'

'Fine.'

'Okay, so the interesting thing, the relevant thing, is that one of the most recurring things we hear about these seers, from deepest Africa to Western Europe, is that — without any contact or communication between tribes — they consistently documented the fact that they had spirit animals, usually birds, protecting them and guiding them to the truth.'

'Birds?'

'A spirit animal was considered a badge of honour, given directly to the seer by the great spirit of nature. In those days it was the equivalent of having a well-funded research laboratory. If you had recurring visions of a spirit animal, or if a certain kind of wild animal was consistently tame in your presence, then your theories and inspirations were believed to be nature's sacred truths.'

'Basically, you're saying that forty thousand years ago society would have deemed me an important person but now I'm just a whack job who should have studied science.'

Jamal laughs smoke out through his nose and stubs out the end of his joint.

'People who experienced periods where they couldn't see reality were revered as sacred and wise.'

'You are. You're saying my brain has been stuck in some kind of retrogressive caveman state.'

'No. You're not getting it. The Homo sapiens' ability to imagine and interpret complex imagery, to make contact with meaning and project it onto the world, that was what marked their heightened intelligence. That was how they evolved beyond the animals.'

'So imagination is a kind of intelligence?'

'The human kind. Basically, when a seer conceived of his totem, that was the sign he was becoming more intelligent, figuring something out. It meant that the two sides of his consciousness had started communicating with each other. His tribe would put up with all sorts of shit from him because when he came back to reality he always brought something with him: knowledge, stories, ideas.'

He starts to build another joint.

'But you're also saying that all those seers were crazy.'

'No. I'm saying that, in the first instance, insight is subjective.'

'Still, you're saying that all the spiritualism was imaginary. None of these seers ever truly had a spirit animal.'

'The seers didn't know how to differentiate between good and bad visions, true and false ones. Psychosis, creativity, it was all just supernatural and mystical and therefore true. But the codes and laws they formed over time, the things we kept hold of — science, law, narrative, art, ritual — these are the things that make us human, what makes society worthwhile.'

'But you said these seers, thousands of miles apart, all claimed to have spirit animals. Maybe that's what happens when people connect to a deeper facet of nature. We just forgot how to do it.'

'It's more likely that spirit animals were the first severance from nature, the beginning of culture.'

'When it was happening, I knew it wasn't real, I knew it could never be measured, but, equally, it was just as convincing as reality. There was something incomprehensible all around me, nothing to do with time or space. The blackbirds, Charlie, they were just the signs it chose to guide me.'

Jamal, about to lick the gum on his new joint, stops and looks up.

'Charlie?'

'I saw Charlie. A few times.'

'Shit, man.'

'I know it wasn't him. Not really. But I don't think it was me either.'

He seals his joint, prods it with a match and lights it.

'I can't help seeing it the way I do,' he says. 'Take the engine across the hall, when I get it running it'll sound like it's got a life of its own, the power it creates will seem like it's coming from nowhere but it comes from the fact that it's part of a system, gathered over the years, slowly getting more and more complex, until lots of knowledge is crammed into a tiny space. It might not look like it's got anything in common with a rowing boat's oars but it does. The collective power of all the previous engines is carried forward within it. It's the same with the unconscious mind. There's some inherent knowledge passed down from our ancestors, more than just instincts, something that can help us understand what's true, how to move forward, how to deal with life. We project it onto the world around us because that's the way our brains work. That's how we find meaning.'

'But why are you so sure? Why can't you accept reality as an incomplete idea, something we can never fully grasp? There's no telling what's in here with us, what sends us meaning, what lies beyond us, what can't be measured or understood. We have to accept the uncertainty of it all.'

'I guess that's why you're the writer and I'm the mechanic.'

'Maybe,' I say, standing up and walking towards the door.

'Where are you going?' he asks. 'I've not annoyed you, have I?'

'No. Everything you've said makes complete sense.'

'What's wrong then?'

'It just . . . it makes *too much* sense.'

'What does?'

'Sorry, I've got to go.'

'Why?'

'I've just realised what's going to happen in my book.'

I leave the room.

'Your book?'

'*On the great map of the spirit only a few points are illuminated*,' I call back.

'But you haven't even told me where you got your bruises.'

'Another time,' I shout, from the stairs. 'I've got to go.'

2

There are four fundamental forces in nature. Quantum mechanics' probabilistic theories led to the comprehension of three: the strong nuclear force, the electromagnetic force and the weak nuclear force. Gravity was understood slightly earlier, using the classical rules of general relativity. However, since the micro quantum-universe is mathematically incompatible with the macro classical-universe, a singular framework that incorporates all four fundamental forces has not yet been discovered. Physicists know what the forces are and what they do. They know how to measure and predict their behaviours. They just can't prove that they exist in the same universe.

I've spent the last month in a very different kind of isolation, writing and editing as much as ten hours a day; lonely but focused and productive. My novel has been finished and redrafted many times over but I keep reading and reading it, just to make sure. The first read-through took over twelve hours but now I'm so familiar with the material I can get through it in four. I'm at the point where there's nothing else I can do without somebody else's opinion.

The end has come at a good time. Today's going to be the first chance I've had to see Lyd since she walked out of the anomaly scan whilst I was heaving over a bin. I go out for a run in the hope of vitalising myself, so I don't seem like somebody bound to a desk, starved of human contact. I avoid Hampstead Heath because I'm not quite ready to re-enter that strange land where I lost myself. My psyche is still slightly raw and my body has only just healed. Instead, I do a couple of slow laps around the much smaller Waterlow Park and then walk over into Highgate Cemetery.

This is the cemetery where Charlie is buried. We were lucky to get him in here, apparently. They only accept thirty new bodies a year. His grave is small and discreet. I have no idea how much it cost but it must have been expensive. I don't even know who paid for it.

I stop, like always, at George Eliot's small cenotaph. I take a moment to think about her writing, her insight and empathy, her commitment to realism. She was always one of my greatest inspirations and, at a formative age, gave me the first sensations of psychological transcendence that made me want to become a writer. Her work is like a friend that I'm always glad is inside me and her grave always calms me before I move on to see Charlie's.

Walking on, I recall my obsession with Charlie's decomposition. For months, rolling around in bed, I would find myself imagining the state of his dead body in its coffin. Again and again I wished he'd been cremated but I was too scared to share this with Lyd. Not only because I had been too manic and too far gone to attend the funeral (or even conceive of it) but because I didn't want to bring a new and unimagined kind of torment down on her. There was a chance that she hadn't even thought of his body rotting and decaying in its coffin.

When I see his grave I'm glad that he's buried. Cremation tiles, all bundled together, are less personal. The dead become a brick in a wall. There's no space for memories to breathe. Here I can pull away weeds, tend to old flowers and keep his little garden under control. The bones beneath are proof that he truly existed — an anchor: invisible, but adding weight and stillness to my memories.

The grave also adds a sense of settlement to my life in London. Highgate once seemed like an alienating suburb that I shouldn't be able to afford to live in, part of a city too big to call home. Now, this tiny plot of land makes me feel like I really belong here, because someone I truly loved is buried in its earth.

I realise that this is the first time I've stood at Charlie's graveside and felt like he's really dead. I don't sense his essence lurking or shining in the world around me. The feeling of his being, my collected memory of him, comes from the inside instead of outside. I still long for him but the longing is distant, less brutal.

At home I shower and shave and then pick up fresh fruit and vegetables for a healthy lunch. I feel prepared, ready to face life head on. Rather than pick me up, I've arranged to meet Lyd at the NHS antenatal services centre because I don't want her to feel like she has to drive me around, or that I rely on her to do practical things.

I arrive early and wait outside. The NHS building was once an affluent Georgian home, probably converted in the early fifties. There's space to park eight cars in what was once a front garden. Being on a residential street, it looks slightly out of place but there's also a dentist's office, a solicitor's office and two nursing homes.

Lyd arrives in a taxi looking tired. I can't believe how bulbous she is. She's walking on her heels like an obese person. She hardly says a word to me when I greet her. We walk into the building with our heads bowed; lone agents of parenthood. I have an image of a room bathed in soft white light, with modern furnishings and laminate floors, where a circle of loving couples sit toboggan-style, four hands on every bump, forging lifelong friendships whilst me and Lyd sit side by side struggling with our proximity.

The clinic is all beige and pale greens. There are pin boards, health posters, tables of flyers, acrylic signs, plastic chairs, dozens of health-and-safety notices and laminated notifications from the staff who are trying to make their own jobs easier. The round wooden reception island exhibits a level of carpentry and quality of wood that suggests it predates the cheap eighties' refit. Old kinds of death and suffering seep through its cracks and scratches.

Lyd speaks to the receptionist and we're directed to a classroom. The whole building is austere and downtrodden. Parts of the corridor are barely even lit. It's a long way from the bright twenty-first-century pillar of technology where we went for our ultrasounds but it's the only

229

place we could find that would take us on such short notice (our communications and arrangements regarding the pregnancy had fallen by the wayside over the last few months).

The set-up of the room and the people populating it are nothing like my projected image. Twenty tired couples sit in uniform rows on cheap plastic chairs barely speaking to each other. The room is what I imagine night school looks like, but with lots more posters of babies and no desks. Me and Lyd approach the second row to take the last two chairs, causing a calamitous recession of pregnant bellies and awkward men as we make our way past.

The room, with over forty people in it, is eerily quiet. Blue light bouncing off the projector screen seems to have drawn everybody into a hypnotic state of submission. We all wait for a stout, depressed-looking midwife to connect wires and fiddle with a laptop.

Eventually, an image is projected. It has a white, baby blue and soft yellow colour scheme and is brimming with bad clip art. The stout midwife closes the blinds, turns off the electric lights and proceeds to spout over an hour of obvious, common sense information whilst clicking a little button and making exactly what she's saying appear on the screen behind her. It is the epitome of a bad presentation.

At the hour mark I look at Lyd and see that she is loathing the dull woman at the front as much as I am.

'Want to go?' I ask her in a whisper.

She looks at me like I just spat on our unborn

baby and did I not know that the important bit was coming up in just a minute?

When the presentation finally comes to an end, after each of the seven subheadings has had its bland ten minutes (1: Health, 2: Exercise, 3: Labour and Birth, 4: Pain and Relaxation, 5: Care, 6: Emotions and 7: Health — again!), the midwife turns the lights back on and, in a monotone, announces:

'Okay, everybody stand up and move your chairs to the sides of the room. We're going to swap partners and try a little role play.'

Lyd's shoulders slump and hang low. She looks at me with adolescent reluctance.

'Fine,' she says. 'Let's get out of here.'

I jump to my feet and hold my hand out behind me before she changes her mind. She grabs it and I lead her through a corridor of knees, distended wombs, shoes and thin metal chair legs. As we reach the door the midwife's dreary voice calls after us:

'Shyer couples can sit this one out if they prefer.'

We both look back at her and shake our heads with feigned amusement and ambiguity, trying to imply that something else is pulling us away from this interesting and essential class.

Once we are out in the corridor we both sigh with relief and smile at each other. Realising we're holding hands our smiles become awkward so we let go and begin walking towards the exit.

'Why do the extroverts who script these things always assume that introverts are broken versions of themselves who just need a little bit of repression workshopped out of them?' asks Lyd.

'Probably the same reason we think they're self-indulgent idiots who need a little bit of self-reflection and doubt forced into them.'

'I know it's just a team-building exercise, making everybody feel like they're in it together so they can break down barriers and make friends, but I really can't abide it when things are that psychologically transparent. It's embarrassing. Anyone with any intelligence feels forced to respond ironically or knowingly and then they find themselves trapped in a rebellion that's even more pathetic than engaging with the process.'

'And then all the rebels have to try to mockingly justify their appeasement to the process when they inevitably join in.'

'Whilst the more self-pitying of them wonder why they can never find a comfortable role in a group.'

'And the more confident of them ponder why everybody appropriates a psychological type whenever a group forms and thinks they're so clever to keep their strong individual self so hidden but so present.'

'And the rest of the group are thinking, we all know that this exercise is stupid. You lot are just the maladjusted idiots who want lots of attention because you didn't get any love in your childhoods.'

'But really we deserve all the attention because we were well-behaved children and that's why Mummy and Daddy stayed together and loved us.'

'I hate it,' she says, smiling.

'Me too.'

We've just left the building but our conversation feels so natural and amusing that we carry on walking together. At the end of the street we turn left and go into the first coffee shop we see without even acknowledging that we've made a decision to stay together. This excites me and there's a tiny sparkle in Lyd's eyes that reflects the same.

'Maybe we are a bit too antisocial,' I say, as we stand in the queue.

'Undoubtedly. But that doesn't affect the world in any negative way. There's no reason to surround ourselves with people if we don't enjoy it.'

'We're just not built for groups.'

'Some people are more useful on the peripheries.'

'Exactly,' I say. 'And we do okay. We're good in smaller, more tight-knit groups.'

'Sometimes,' says Lyd. 'Personally, I think we both thrive when we're alone. I've got so much more work done since I've been at Mum and Dad's.'

'Me too actually,' I admit, reluctantly.

At the counter, even though I'm desperately poor and thinking that today might be a good opportunity to bring up the fact that I can't afford the electricity bill (the only bill in my name), I make a point of buying the drinks: black coffee for me and peppermint tea for Lyd.

We sit at a small table by the window. Now that we're facing each other the easy mood has become more difficult. There is a long silence.

Lyd's expression is serious and solemn. I fiddle with a sugar packet until I notice her scrutinising my twiddling fingers.

'I'm sorry,' I start. 'I should have handled things better.'

'Please, don't launch into a big thing.'

'But we need to talk.'

'Shall I sum up what you're about to say and save us both a couple of hours?' she says. I shrug, half prompting her. 'Okay. It goes like this — I was wrong. But I was also right. I'm sorry I was right. But I was right. I'm really sorry being right upset you. You were right too. And no less right than me. In some ways, everybody's always right. Isn't life confusing? Have you forgiven me yet?'

'Be fair.'

'That's your standard apology.'

'I hate it when you do that.'

'What?'

'Mock me for trying to be honest.'

'You always want to talk but it doesn't change anything.'

'I think it helps, even if you just sit there parodying me. It's getting something out there.'

'It doesn't help me.'

'We've barely spoken for months.'

'We didn't need to. We needed time . . . You know, I thought we might be able to have one drink where we weren't weighed down by things we need to get through. You know? Something light.'

'I'm sorry. I want that too.'

She looks away from me, out the window.

'Too late,' she says.

'I guess . . .'

'I don't think we can be good parents. We're too messed up, too self-involved.'

'So? I hate good parents. Good parents make me want to kick children in the face.'

She smirks.

'I think we might function better apart.'

'No.'

'I'm afraid that I might not love you anymore.'

She looks at me for a moment, and then down at the table. Her hand passes over her stomach and she frowns.

'When it kicks it always feels so far away.'

'Come home with me, Lyd.'

'I'm not coming home.'

'We can make it right together.'

'No. We can't.'

'I don't understand.'

'Don't pull that face. I'm just being honest.'

'At least come back to the house. I can sleep on the couch, stay at Jamal's; whatever you need. Surely your parents give you less space than I could?'

'I still need time away from the house.'

She puts both hands on her stomach now. There is a note of melancholy in her eyes, as though her hands are ears that hear nothing.

'If you need time, you need time,' I say.

'I do.'

'What are we facing here? Do you think we'll ever be together again?'

'I'm sorry, Vince. I can't answer that.'

'Why not?'

'Because the answer is no . . .'

She looks at me apologetically.

'I'm hoping the answer is going to change,' she says.

'But I'm out of the woods. I'm better. I've been working, focused. My book's finished . . .'

At the mention of my writing Lyd looks at her watch.

'I better get back. Peter's coming to pick me up.'

'No. Wait. Can we talk more? I want to spend time with you. We can make it light.'

'No, we can't, Vince. That's the problem . . . I've got to go.'

'Why is Peter picking you up?'

'He's going to take me back to Mum and Dad's, have a meal with us. I got the train this morning.'

'Let me walk you to the car.'

'No. You don't have to. You're closer to home here.'

'I want to.'

'Fine. You can walk me to my brother's car.'

We leave the coffee shop.

Lyd wraps her elbow around mine, cautiously, as though testing for feelings. At one point she rests her temple on my shoulder and grabs my arm with her other hand — still placid, still wondering. My left side fizzes with nervous pleasure. My manner becomes more stiff and cautious because I'm trying to avoid the inevitable moment when I say the wrong thing or act the wrong way and lose her fragile affections. This anxiety is immediately intuited by Lyd and she lets go, walking with her eyes fixedly ahead. The last thirty metres was a tactile indulgence that we are now supposed to pretend didn't happen.

Peter is already waiting in the antenatal centre's small car park, sitting in his two-seater Audi. He gets out of his car when he sees us.

'They all came out five minutes ago.'

'Sorry,' says Lyd.

'Hi, Peter.'

He nods at me, half able to reveal his contempt for my existence now that he thinks his sister might be leaving me.

'Where've you been?' he asks.

'We went for a hot drink,' says Lyd. 'It was horrible in there.'

'We should get going or we'll hit the traffic on the way out.'

'I forgot to book my appointment with the midwife. Sorry. I won't be a minute.'

Lyd walks back towards the entrance. I'm left standing with Peter. He sniffs every couple of seconds. The comedowns from the cocaine and benzodiazepines are beginning to make his eyes sink and withdraw. He's not too far away from the point where I'll have to object to Lyd getting in a car with him. For now he's a highly functioning addict but he's definitely treading the border between overconfidence and self-annihilation.

'What happened with you and Gloria in the end?' I ask him.

(I know that it didn't work out but I can't help myself.)

'*Gloria?*' he says, mockingly. 'I haven't thought

about her in months.'

'No?'

'On to pastures new.'

'You seemed pretty set on her last time I saw you.'

A flicker of hatred crosses his eyes. He wants to destroy me for having seen him in a state of weakness. He needs everybody to believe that he is strong.

'I should have known better than to get involved with any of your people,' he says.

'My people?'

'She'd rather scream at a gambling addict than have something good in her life.'

'I hear coke-heads make much better partners.'

'You don't know anything about me.'

'I know adultery isn't the best foundation for a relationship,' I say, 'especially with your sister's friend . . . I'm sorry you got hurt though.'

'She did me a favour.'

'Why's that?'

'She reminded me how duplicitous women truly are.'

I turn away from him with a smile of disbelief.

'You should be grateful you felt something,' I say. 'I didn't even know you had feelings.'

'You talk like a teenage girl. It annoys me that you can even annoy me. If it wasn't for . . . '

'What?'

He squares up to me and glances at the entrance to the building.

'You know, don't you? That you don't deserve Lydia?'

He takes a breath, leaning back, and claps his hands in front of my face. I try but don't wholly manage to restrain a flinch.

'She always went for the fuck-ups,' he continues, pivoting away from me. 'You just happened to be the fuck-up who got her pregnant.'

'You have no idea what me and Lyd have been through,' I say, my spine trembling slightly, my bladder tightening.

He steps back towards me.

'We're not talking about Charlie here, Vince. Don't hide behind that. We're talking about you being a waste of space. Why don't you just piss off out of that house and leave her to get on with her life?'

His expression is desolate. My heart is beating fast. There are no words in my head. I feel inferior, undeserving of his sister's love.

Lyd reappears in the doorway.

Peter finds instant resolve and smiles for her. I take a deep breath. For the first time, I see a kind of moral strength and integrity in Peter. He might be a sociopath, but he also loves his sister.

'You two look very serious,' she says.

'We've just been having a chat,' says Peter.

'I hope it wasn't about me?'

'It wasn't about you,' I say.

'We were talking about his future.'

Lyd shrugs her shoulders.

'I think you two are really starting to get to grips with each other, aren't you?'

I smile at her.

'Come on,' says Peter. 'Let's beat that traffic.'

3

People used to believe that the gateway to the Otherworld opened for a short while at the end of the harvest season, allowing all the dead souls to pass through. Places were set at tables and food was offered to dead ancestors out of respect and remembrance. Fare was also left outside to keep darker spirits' mischief and trickery at bay. These ritual offerings gradually became the sweets and chocolates that home owners gave to wandering children dressed as the dead, who, on their reception, announced the option, 'Trick or treat?' By this point in time the gateway to the Otherworld had been long presumed closed. Darkness was just empty space. The dead were just dead.

I had to do a lot of preparation to end up looking like Frankenstein's monster. I have bolts stuck on my neck, grey-green skin, a tattered black jumper and overcoat, black trousers and big black boots. The real work went into adding the latex cap that adds two inches to my forehead and gives me that deformed, receding monster look.

I already had this outfit. Lyd has the Bride of Frankenstein wig with the two white zigzag stripes up the sides. She wears it with a long white nightgown, white face make-up, dark eyes and bandages all up her arms. We've been to three Halloween parties together dressed this way and it always seems clear, even when we're standing apart, that we're together. Lyd won't be wearing her Bride of Frankenstein outfit tonight. It's still in the box at home.

Gloria and Sergio's house is decorated with fake spiderwebs, expertly cut pumpkins and plastic insects and ghouls. The lights are low. In the front room there's a projection of a ghost that loiters on the living room wall. Every five minutes or so, it turns into a giant skull with a wide open jaw and a loud scream rips through the room. All the songs are themed. So far we've had 'Monster Mash', 'I Was a Teenage Werewolf' and 'Ghostbusters'. The house is full of people in fancy dress. I don't know any of them.

Sergio's friends are all corporate lawyers and efficiency experts, and other jobs that require a psychopathic streak (or, like Sergio, a series of mini — and early — midlife crises). They have mostly come as famous murderers. There's a lazy guy who's just hung a plastic chainsaw around his neck and put it over the top of his work suit — a Patrick Bateman cop out (yet uncomfortably convincing). Freddy Krueger, Myra Hindley, Leatherface and a man in a miscellaneous orange jumpsuit are all seemingly talking about their favourite kill and laughing.

Despite Gloria's profession being similar her friends are a broader mix of people: some university friends, people from an old workplace, others from leisure activities and a few select people from her current job. There's a tendency toward the sexy in the women — cats, witches and rabbits in tiny skirts and fishnets — and lots

241

of zombies and a couple of vampires amongst the men.

The only two I can't work out are a couple who have come as Magenta and Riff Raff from *The Rocky Horror Picture Show*. Sexy and psycho, they must be mutual friends of them both.

I can't see Lyd anywhere.

I'm on my second pumpkin punch (which is surprisingly good — I get the feeling professionals might have done the decorating and put on the spread). It's served in a white plastic cup in the shape of a skull. Sergio, dressed as Gomez Addams, sees me standing alone and heads towards me. Gloria is dressed as Morticia. They are extremely well-suited to their roles, which are extremely well-suited to hosting a Halloween party at home, so they are both fairly proud of how they look.

'I hate your friends,' I say.

'Me too. Me too,' says Sergio, looking around.

'Who *are* they?'

'They're not all completely evil,' he says. 'I met Freddy Krueger over there at my gambling group. He's a sweet, sweet man. He's been through hell.'

'How come all your buddies came as serial killers?'

'It's Halloween.'

'I've been *psycho*analysing the costumes.'

'I'm sure you have. Me too actually. Don't you think zombies are very working man? You know, powerless sheep stumbling through life until the next payday.'

'The zombies are the only ones I want to talk to.'

'That's because you're attracted to depression.'

'You talk such rubbish. Did you invite Jamal?'

'Every year.'

'Has he ever come?'

'Nope.'

'Any sign of Lyd?'

'About that,' he says. 'I wanted to tell you in person . . . I'm sorry I wasn't there for you when — '

'We've been through this.'

'I know but I feel like — '

'I told you not to worry about it. You had your own thing going on.'

'I know but . . . anyway . . . I don't think she's here yet.'

'How are things on the home front?'

'Are you asking or are you being polite?'

'I'm asking.'

'Fucking tough. I messed up big this time.'

'She messed up too though.'

'You only know half of it.'

'Do I want to know?'

'Let's just say the roulette wheel took a couple of Porsches out the bank on either side of Mitsu. And staying in hotels for three months wasn't cheap either.'

'Shit.'

'She screwed around. I screwed around. Lust is a tricky bastard. Everyone knows that. When things get rough it's easy to mess things up that way. The gambling though. That's separate. I promised her I'd never do that to us again. The trust is gone.'

'Totally gone?'

'Not like when I lost the house, but bad.'

'What happened to Mitsu?'

'The less you know about Mitsu the better.'

'Fair enough. Does Lyd know that it was Peter yet?'

Sergio grimaces.

'Yeah. She's had it out with Gloria already. You wouldn't know to look at them. Hey, hey, hey, look who it is.'

I turn my head. Gloria is walking Lyd through to the kitchen. Lyd is wearing a nineteenth-century gothic black dress with test tubes in a utility belt. It has long sleeves and a high neck. Her bump looks huge in it. Leatherface and Patrick Bateman leer over Gloria's cleavage as they pass.

'I shouldn't have come as Frankenstein's monster,' I say. 'I should have come as Venkman or something. I don't want her to see me like this.'

'Frankenstein's your thing,' says Sergio. 'It's literary.'

'No. It's *our* thing. She's supposed to be the Bride, remember? It's cinematic. Halloweeny. I'm going to have to change. Have you got a white sheet or something?'

'Vince, take a breath. She wouldn't have come if she didn't want to talk to you. I thought things were getting better? You were making progress?'

'What does she expect me to say? Last time I saw her she said all this weird stuff about us being better off alone. Since then we've just been talking rubbish on the phone, trying to prove I can make things feel light again.'

'As far as I'm concerned, her coming all this way can only be a good sign. This could be the first night you get to take her home again.'

'You think?'

'Definitely. Why else would she travel fifty odd miles or whatever it is to come to some lame Halloween party? You think she wants to stay in Peckham with her sister when yours is just down the road?'

'I'm so embarrassed. I should have got a new costume.'

He takes me by the shoulders.

'Vince. Forget about the costume. She doesn't care about the costume. She's pregnant with your child.'

'You're right. You're right.'

'Take a deep breath and down the rest of that punch.'

I do what he says.

'Now, go get her.'

'If this goes wrong I'm going to be Cousin Itt next year, living in your basement.'

'That's it. Summon up some of that famous Watergate positivity.'

He slaps me on the back as I walk towards the kitchen. Seeing me approach, Gloria stops talking and fixes her eyes on me until Lyd turns her head. They stare at me with bad smells in their noses.

When I get to where they're standing, before I speak, Gloria rests her hand on Lyd's shoulder sympathetically. Lyd turns to her, forces a smile and nods. Gloria gives her shoulder a little squeeze and walks by me with a blank face.

'Who are you?' I ask. 'I mean, what's your costume?'

'Marie Curie,' she says.

I shrug.

'The first woman to win a Nobel Prize?'

'Sorry,' I say, apologising for my ignorance.

I look at her large bump sticking out, our child.

'I see you're the monster again . . . '

I smile awkwardly. Lyd replies with a twitch of her right cheek. It's supposed to be a polite flash of a smile but it doesn't make an impression on her lips.

'So,' she says, almost a question.

'Lame party.'

'Yep.'

Riff Raff and Magenta have come into the kitchen and are showing off their creepy sibling lovers' handshake to a pirate and a vampire. I watch them and wonder what to say. Lyd runs her right hand across her stomach. Magenta is beginning to perform the opening dialogue to the 'Time Warp'. Riff Raff joins in. I have to look away.

'How's work?' I ask.

'There's never a dull moment below the Planck length.'

'The plank what?'

'Never mind.'

My mobile phone vibrates in my pocket. Quickly glancing at the screen I see that it's my mum calling. I think about all the possible inanities that I could ignore but none of them cover this time on Halloween night. I walk a couple of steps away and answer.

'Hi, Mum. Everything okay?'

'Hi, love. I don't know how to say this. Are you at home?'

'I'm at a Halloween party. Say what?'

'It's your dad.'

'My *dad*?'

'Yes,' she says.

'What about him?'

'The hospice rang. He only has a few days left . . . He wants to see you.'

'He wants to see me?'

'He's dying. Cancer.'

'He's dying and he wants to see me?'

'That's what they said.'

'Why?'

'You're his son, Vince.'

'I know that.'

'That's all they said. He wants to see you.'

'I don't know about this.'

'You might regret it if you don't go.'

'I might regret it if I do.'

'You can stay with us, if you come. John will drive you up there if Lyd's not . . . well, you won't tell me anything about what's going on. If she doesn't, if she's not — '

'I need to think about this.'

'You don't have time to think about it. You either come or you don't. He's on his last legs.'

'Okay,' I say. 'I'll ring you in the morning and let you know.'

'Remember he's your dad, Vince. Whether he was a good one or not, he's still your dad.'

'I know, Mum. I've got to go.'

Being dressed like Frankenstein's monster suddenly seems ridiculous, as does dressing up in general. The whole party is surreal and absurd. I need to leave but my first instinct is to tell Lyd about the phone call. She is my barometer of truth. By talking to her I'll know how I feel. It also occurs to me that this is a serious thing, an important moment, and, as such, if I'm still important to her, I'll be able to see in her response where we stand.

I turn back to her.

'My mum,' I say, waggling my phone before I put it back in my pocket. 'Apparently, well, my dad's dying.'

'Your *dad*?'

'Cancer. He wants to see me.'

'He wants to *see* you?'

'So she says.'

'Are you going to go?'

'I don't know.'

'Do you want to?'

'I guess. More for curiosity than anything.'

Lyd is fully immersed in my situation, sympathetic, but she catches herself at it. She forces her emotional tides to recede, moving heaven and earth so that she can seem resolved in her decision not to share the burden of my problems. I see this struggle in her face and find it hard to blame her, especially after seeing that her instinct was to come forward, towards me. Her reticence is born of trauma and pain. Her hand wanders over her pregnant stomach again.

'Sorry you have to go through this,' she says, deadpan now, rational. 'It's bad timing.'

'I'm not sure I'm going through anything,' I say. 'I can't go anyway.'

'What do you mean *can't* go?'

'I don't want to talk about it.'

'Tell me.'

'I can't.'

'Tell me.'

I stare at a plastic bat hanging from a light fitting. Beneath my green make-up my cheeks are burning. I'm glad that some portion of my embarrassment is covered but I know that Lyd will be able to see it in my eyes.

'Well?' she says.

'I can't afford the train ticket.'

'Are you kidding me?'

'I can barely afford food.'

'You're a child, Vince, a *child*.'

'I know.'

She shakes her head with an exasperated grin. 'Fine.'

'What?' I ask.

'I'll take you.'

'You'll take me?'

'Yes, I'll take you. If you want to go?'

'I think so,' I say, grabbing the opportunity to be with her for an extended period. 'I mean, I do.'

'You're hopeless. You know that, don't you?'

I nod but, beneath my shame, beneath my dying father, beneath my overdraft limit, there is a tiny glimmer. She could have just offered me the money for the train ticket but instead she's coming with me.

4

The objective truth is a concept formed within subjective realities about a wider reality. Words and numbers are constantly added to this extremely complicated concept, expanding its sign system. When its underlying rules are wholly understood and the objective truth has been fully expressed, further signs and significations will only ever enhance and readdress what is already known. Having come of age, the objective truth will be celebrated and made available to everybody. People will analyse more or less of it, tell stories about it, make discoveries with it, progress or regress because of it, believe in it or dismiss it, but, most importantly, they will remain separate from it.

London recedes like a sea we've been swimming in. We drive past inert industrial zones, warehouses, piles of stones and sand, silos and long chutes. Monolithic chunks of concrete fly backwards, glass flashes, wires bounce, brick walls smear into clay smudges. Dirt and soot taints the first fields but the colours gradually become more vibrant and natural. Birds begin to outnumber aeroplanes. There are more orange and red tree roofs than grey and terracotta house roofs.

My MP3 player is plugged into the car stereo, set on random. 'Venus in Furs' by the Velvet

Underground begins to play. Fixing my eyes on the middle distance, the fast-moving tarmac and traffic seems almost stationary. John Cale's discordant viola and Lou Reed's wooing voice send me into a reverie about when I first met Lyd.

A large group of us were out in Victoria Park for Bonfire Night. She was a friend of a friend of a friend, just starting out as a particle physicist, obsessed with M-theory and mini-black holes and unable to talk about anything else. I found her passion fresh and exciting. Unlike me, talking with self-interest about the novel I was working on, her work sounded important, it was new ground, it was adding to how people would understand the universe in the years to come. She made me appreciate how selfless and meaningful the pursuit of science was.

I remember watching her face as light from the fireworks glowed on her skin. Her expression did not contain the same vacant joy of the others. It was philosophical, but not pretentious. She was bathing in the chemistry of gunpowder, the physics of light and sound, space and time. She was as infatuated with the mysteries of science as I was with her.

At the end of the night we exchanged numbers, promised each other coffee and soon found ourselves in constant contact, sharing stories and spending all our free time together. I couldn't believe she wanted to know me. I felt so lucky.

'What are you thinking about?' asks Lyd.

Another song is playing now, something by

251

Creedence Clearwater Revival. I can't remember the title. The vocal is full of passion and honesty and the rhythm guitar is chugging and rolling. The tarmac passes quickly beneath the car. I'm full of sad love for Lyd.

'I don't know,' I say. 'Nothing really.'

'Your dad?'

'No. Not him.'

We sit in silence for a while. I watch her driving from the corner of my eye and take a moment to imagine the position of the baby inside her bump.

'Do you ever think about death?' she asks.

'Sure. All the time.'

'No, I mean, what it actually is.'

'I wonder whether it's an actual force of nature, something inside time that makes things deteriorate and die, or if it's more like an abstract drive in our minds and all the physical stuff is just part of the nature of systems.'

'No. I'm talking about the afterlife, nothing-ness, that kind of thing.'

'Do you, think about it?'

'Sometimes. Since. You know.'

'When I was a kid, from when I was about five until I was eight, I became obsessed with this idea that when you died you met God and he showed you every single thing that was ever said or thought about you. So it didn't matter what people said or thought about you now because you'd find out everything when you were dead.'

'That's cute,' she says, with a smile. 'And an ingenious way of beating your socially obsessive streak at its own game.'

'I don't really believe in identity after death though,' I say. 'Not really. A mind and a memory are part of a brain and a body. Even if I could stretch myself to believe in some kind of energy transference, or a bigger life force, it wouldn't make much difference to what a person became when they were dead. Why do you ask?'

'I had this weird dream that made me start questioning a few things.'

'What things?'

'It was one of those big dreams. You know, the kind that seem as important as real experiences, when they change something inside you. It was based on the idea that what you do in life is what you're stuck with after you're gone.'

'Go on.'

Lyd tenses her arms, grips the steering wheel tight, takes a breath and loosens up again.

'So in this dream, I'm dead, and I know I'm dead, and I'm in this empty blackness, like outer space. There are no stars or planets or anything like that. It's just this endless nothing, but I also know that it's where all the dead souls go. Nothing happens for ages, aeons. It's really boring. But I'm slowly understanding that I haven't retained my human form. Instead, everything I ever said, everything I ever did or thought has been transformed into this bizarre spirit sign. I'm like a ghost but also a signpost — it's me, every single aspect of me, transformed into the language of the dead. I never get to see my own spirit sign, I just know that that's what I am now. Eventually, I start bumping into other dead souls. And they're completely exposed

253

before me, as I am to them. One glance is everything, all at once. All their strengths and weaknesses, all the moments they're ashamed of, all the right and wrong, how they felt and behaved, what they regretted, who they were, who they wanted to be. And all this is signified with strange emblems and foreign markings, wood, eyeballs, gemstones, feathers; all kinds of crazy stuff. I couldn't communicate with the other dead souls because everything I could ever say was said during this one second of exposure. I didn't have a mouth anymore anyway. The frequency of bumping into the dead souls was varied. The dream seemed to go on for months. Sometimes it was like rush hour in Holborn but other times I spent days in the black before I bumped into anyone. Pointless, eternal, in death you became everything you ever were in life, forever.'

I laugh.

'That's pretty messed up. And, for you, very moralistic.'

'But it was relative moralism. The morals of the person were part of the context of the spirit sign: they gave insight into their behaviours. It really made me think about how I'm choosing to live my life.'

'And did you feel the need for any major changes?'

'I'm not sure. The thing was, I bumped into your dead soul.'

'My dead soul?'

'Uh-huh.'

'And?'

'And it was beautiful. I really liked it. We just kept looking at each other and even though there were all these new dark bits and these weird bits we didn't know about, it just felt right.'

'I wish I could have a look at your dead soul.'

'Well, I've seen yours.'

'And then what?'

'Then I woke up.'

The implications behind telling me about this dream might suggest she feels like she has treated me too harshly, that we only have so much time on this planet and we should be spending it together, but hopelessness stops me from responding as though this is the context of the story. Lyd has not been directing any love my way.

'Let's just hope death is the end of it,' I say.

'I think it probably is.'

'Me too.'

We both look ahead.

The hypnosis of the motorway pulls us back in. The cities we edge around become smaller the further north we go. After the Northern Belt, cities give way to towns, towns to villages, villages to farms. When farms give way to reserves there is suddenly more nature than civilisation. Particularly after Lancaster, the views of the Lake District and the North Pennines on either side of the car keep us quiet and satisfied. I feel like London has made me forget what the planet is made of. And here it is: the greater truth.

As we pass through Eden Valley there is an enormous cloud of starlings in a murmuration, whipping and bulging in perfect synchrony above a wood of red and orange trees. The sky is a crystalline dark blue with diamond stars beginning to glow. There must be a hundred thousand starlings, many of them recent migrants, here for England's mild Gulf Stream winter. Their flight patterns resemble the movements of magnetised metal but there is no giant magnet being waved around, no conductor. They fly freely, each with their own individual will, and collectively, definitively part of their cloud.

'You know, I read somewhere — '

'Here we go. Vince read somewhere. Probably the Internet but let's pretend it was the National Archive.'

'Okay, okay,' I say, smiling.

'Sorry. Go on.'

'In the 1890s this guy, Eugene somebody, he was obsessed with taking all the birds mentioned in Shakespeare's plays over to America. Anyway, he released one hundred starlings in Central Park. Most of the species he took over there didn't survive but by the 1990s there were two hundred million starlings in North America.'

'I think the same thing happened with blackbirds in New Zealand.'

I try to ignore this.

'The strange thing is, in the same period, clouds of starlings disappeared from London altogether. There used to be thousands living underneath London Bridge. There were once so many of them perching on Big Ben's minute hand that the clock came to a standstill. Now

256

there's hardly any. There hasn't been a cloud of starlings above London in decades.'

'If I was a bird I don't think I'd live in London.'

'Probably not. But I wonder what the breaking point was. How did they all decide to move away?'

'Things only live where they can survive.'

I nod.

We've been on the road for over four hours. The sky is darkening. The roads are narrowing. Hedgerows and ditches replace grass verges. There are no lamp posts and, a little further along, no cat's eyes. Trees obscure the sky. Twigs scratch at the doors. The speed of the car's movement is beginning to feel dangerous. The way ahead is full of blind corners and potential collisions. When the road dips our headlights illuminate less than a metre in front of us. The blackness is immediate, and infinitely dense.

★ ★ ★

We pull up to my childhood home (in a village outside Carlisle) and drop our bags off. On the doorstep my mum enacts an overly sympathetic sadness even though there is a smaller and more honest sadness behind her eyes. My stepdad, John, shows solidarity by standing up, away from his laptop, next to Mum. Chelsea lurks by them too, kindly keeping her mobile phone in her pocket (though the tips of her left-hand fingers are passing over the bulge to make sure that it's still there).

It occurs to me that they are making this man's death about me even though I barely knew him. I'm not sure if I'm supposed to say something meaningful or make a throwaway statement to ease them out of their sympathy. Maybe I'm supposed to have a feeling and express it. Even Lyd's looking at me now. It was my mum who loved him and had a child with him but her emotions are shielded by her new family. I'm the one whose life this changes. He is my family, nothing to do with hers. Yet, if he is my family, I don't have a family. I only have Lyd, the baby growing inside her and my dead son.

'Don't worry about me,' I finally manage to say. 'I barely know the guy.'

This brings tears to my mum's eyes. John nods with a gruff manly respect as though he thinks I'm only being strong for my mum. Chelsea stares at me like an alien. Lyd puts her hand on my shoulder. I have no idea why they're all so sorry for me.

When me and Lyd get to the hospice I ask the woman at reception whether we can visit Alan Watergate and she looks through a computer printout attached to a clipboard, tells us to hold on for a second and makes a phone call with a well-practised inaudible voice.

After she hangs up she flicks her eyes across at us, smiles a tight-lipped smile and gets back to work on her computer. For the first ten seconds I think she might be doing something regarding us and then I realise that she's ignoring us. Just as I'm about to ask her for some information two nurses and a doctor, all female, approach. The doctor looks over at the receptionist, back at us and then back at her. The receptionist nods. The three of them approach us.

'Mr Watergate's son?' asks the doctor.

'Yes,' I say, though I don't particularly agree with the terminology.

'I'm afraid your father passed away about an hour ago.'

'Oh.'

'I'm sorry.'

'Thanks.'

'Would you like to see him?'

I look at Lyd and at the two nurses, they all expect me to want to.

'Okay,' I say.

'Follow me,' says one of the nurses.

The doctor and the other nurse immediately branch off and head in another direction. I look back; Lyd's not coming with me. The look on her face reassures me that she thinks she's doing the right thing, that she has no right to see this dead man's body because she's never met him. The problem is that I don't particularly feel like I have the right either. I must have seen his living body less than ten times in my life.

After walking down a couple of squeaky-floored corridors I'm led into a room that has a plastic plaque inscribed, *Viewing Room*. It's just the same as the other rooms we passed on this corridor, with space for four patients, but in this room all four curtains are closed around the beds and there are no machines or extra pieces of furniture.

The nurse stands by the curtain. It crosses my

259

mind that she might whip it open like a magician but she doesn't. She just stands there.

'Take as long as you need,' she says, before walking away.

I find the gap in the curtain and step over to the bedside. The corpse looks like it had been very ill. Its cheeks are sunken and the skin yellowed with decay. Its eyes are closed and palms crossed neatly. He's not an old man. His hair is grey but he's not started balding. He looks a bit like me, or I look a bit like him. I don't feel much beyond a slight awkwardness. It's a shame he didn't get to see me, not that he deserved to.

I stare at him and try to think of feelings I might need to address. Loss isn't one. Abandonment almost touches a nerve but I pretty much got beyond that in my teenage years. Anger doesn't come, he's too dead. Denial is a possibility but I'm pretty sure I'm fully functioning and not repressing anything. Acceptance is the one and only feeling. It's simply happened. My father, who I never really knew, has died.

Rather than leaving the room at my first inclination I spend a couple of minutes standing over him, focusing on him, his body, his death. I force my mind back to him when it skips to Lyd, to the baby. I think about a time he turned up out of the blue when I was about six. I was shy and full of fear and wouldn't go near him. Mum grabbed me and put me on his knee out of charity. His breath smelt of sour coffee and ashtrays. The stink made me squeal and wriggle away from him, back to my toys. I remember his disappointed smile as he left. I glanced but didn't go to him. I had no idea who he was. I felt nothing. I feel nothing now. Perhaps the sadness of a missed opportunity. Perhaps not.

When I get back to Lyd she stands up and looks at me, desperately worried, pregnant, beautiful, alive.

'I'm fine. It was a bit weird but I'm fine.'

'I'm sorry you didn't get to say goodbye,' she says, hugging me.

'You don't miss what you never loved.'

She laughs sadly and clings to me, and I hope that she's glad that I'm still here, still present.

★ ★ ★

Back at the house my mum is behaving manically because her first husband is dead and she can't figure out whether me and Lyd are back together and she doesn't dare ask. We're tired from the drive and, for a change, we would really welcome my family's usual sitting around and doing nothing philosophy but they're dressed for cold weather and there are no plans for dinner.

'It's Bonfire Night,' says Chelsea, stopping herself from rolling her eyes in an act of sympathy.

I'd forgotten and my stomach sinks at the mention of it. I look at Lyd who is feeling similarly awkward. We always took Bonfire Night as our anniversary because we couldn't remember when we first made anything official.

261

Apparently, we have to go to Bitts Park for the *Fireshow*, eat pie and peas, hotdogs, toffee apples, burgers, candy floss, treacle toffee — 'Whatever you want' — and watch the bonfire and fireworks display. I think about saying I'm not up for it but I've already implied that I'm fine. I look at Lyd and try to indicate with an expression that we could stay in if she's willing to blame her pregnancy for wanting to stay off her feet but she shrugs, unable to get my meaning, and we accept our fate.

'Sounds good,' I say. 'A bit of distraction.'

We all pile into the car and head to Carlisle city centre. There are no parking spaces anywhere and some of the main through roads are closed. John knows how to manoeuvre around it all but we end up having to leave the car a ten-minute walk from Bitts Park (which makes Chelsea huff and grumble).

As we get closer, Chelsea keeps informing us that she can smell smoke so we must have missed the start of the bonfire and that we better not miss the start of the fireworks. Mum keeps calling her back, reminding her that Lyd is heavily pregnant. Random fireworks go off from people's back garden displays and each time my mum cringes slightly. I can't figure out if she's getting more nervous as she gets older or if she's so afraid of Chelsea's mood swings that she's flinching against the idea that the fireworks might have just started without us. Lyd suggests that they walk ahead but Mum says we'll never find each other if they do. John looks at his watch and assures us all that we'll make it in plenty of time.

The park is absolutely packed. I didn't know there were this many people in the whole of Cumbria. John informs me that thirty-five thousand people were expected. The crowd has turned all of the grass underfoot into muddy sludge. Most people (including my mum, Chelsea and John) are wearing wellies. Me and Lyd, unprepared, are wearing normal, not particularly waterproof shoes.

Embers and flakes of carbon are wafting by more and more frequently. Noise from a couple of fairground rides and a number of pounding speakers mixes with the general hubbub of the crowd. As we finally see the enormous bonfire, Chelsea speedily breaks away from us.

'Where are you going?' calls Mum.

'To meet Becca.'

'Have you got money?'

'Yeah.'

'Where will we see you?'

'I've got my mobile.'

Chelsea disappears into the crowd.

'That's why her knickers were in a twist,' says Mum. 'She didn't want to miss her mates.'

The bonfire has been made out of pallets, nailed together in a pyramid structure about twenty feet high. The wood is quick burning and there are lots of gaps for air so the flame is tall, sweeping and yellow, rising ten feet above the structure. The sides are already beginning to collapse inwards even though it must have been lit less than twenty minutes ago. All the way around the fire, about ten feet from its edge, is a seven-foot anti-climb metal barrier fence. It's see-through, for the most part, but the best view of the bonfire seems to be in a region where its heat is ineffectual. We find a sweet spot on a raised bit of ground where we can see the fire over the fence and just about feel the heat.

I have a memory of being here as a child, standing extremely close to the naked flame of a bonfire made of logs, wooden cabinets, shelves and old couches, poisonous green flames rising from seat covers, sticky toffee all over my burning cheeks, forgetting I was with anyone, looking at the fire until my eyes were so dry that I couldn't blink. Was I with my dad?

The bonfire crackles and pops loudly, bringing me out of my daydream. Thousands of tiny cinders fizz up into the sky. About a fifth of the crowd releases a vowel noise. Mum tells us to wait where we are whilst she and John get us all pie and peas. When Lyd says she doesn't want meat, Mum represses a mini-meltdown and says she'll do the best she can.

When they're gone I put my arm around Lyd's waist. She takes a step away, puts her hand on her stomach and looks at me.

'It's still not right,' she says.

'You and me?'

'The bump.'

'They always say pregnancy's different every time.'

'Not this different. I can't feel the shape of it. And when it kicks, it doesn't feel right. I can't explain it.'

'So it's not a big kicker.'

'Knock on my stomach.'

'I'm not going to knock on our baby.'

'Well, just feel it then.'

I put my hand on her stomach. It's incredibly firm and solid.

'Sometimes you see women who look like they've got a beach ball inside them,' I say. 'I think it's a good sign that you're so big and firm.'

'I've had weird cravings. Mud. Twigs. I wanted to eat worms last week. I'm constantly exhausted. It feels like something really weird is happening in there.'

'The sonographer said everything was fine.'

'I know.'

'We could probably arrange another ultra-sound, even now?'

'Maybe I'm just a bit delirious. I can't believe how tired I am. I was still working when my water broke last time.'

'And five minutes after it broke.'

She smiles.

'Don't take this the wrong way,' I say, 'but you were six years younger then. That's a long time on the biological clock.'

'I know. Maybe I'm just getting old, and paranoid.'

'It's completely understandable.'

'Is it?'

'Of course. It's precarious, giving birth. Dangerous. It must be scary seeing a bump that big and knowing that it's got to come out of you.'

'I guess so. I just wanted everything to be right by now. If it wasn't for this . . . '

'What?'

'Nothing. We shouldn't be talking about me. You've just lost your dad.'

'I want to talk about you.'

'You're dealing with it so well. I think you really might be back to your old self, better than your old self.'

'I know you think I'm being brave but I'm not. I feel like I came to Carlisle to see a stranger's dead body. And I know it's my dad and that should make me feel something, but it doesn't. If anything, it's made me realise that John's the closest thing I've got to a dad. I didn't have a father. You know? It felt like a bit of a shame, like there were things I'd never know, but mostly it was just a dead guy.'

Lyd looks at me. I look at the bonfire.

'Vince, I don't want you to think it's more than it is, but I'm going to move back in. I'm not saying we're getting back together. I just think it's time I came back.'

I'm about to respond when Mum and John arrive with four portions of pie and peas. Mum's frantically excited because they had cheese-and-onion pies so Lyd doesn't have to miss out. The rest of us have steak, which is actually mincemeat. The pastry is rubbery and the filling is sparse but I'm unexpectedly famished now that I'm holding something warm. I eat quickly and keep glancing at Lyd.

A local radio DJ is announcing the countdown to 'the best fireworks show in the North' on a stage that we can't see on the opposite side of the bonfire. The heat from the thirty-foot mound of flame has dried my face. My cheeks are taut. After the countdown there is a desolate four seconds where thirty-five thousand people quietly look up at an empty black sky.

When the fireworks begin squealing their way up into the air I look at Lyd as she watches the explosions. Her face is incomparable with the one I first saw on Bonfire Night nearly eight years ago. Now, after her love for Charlie, the worry that came with it, and her loss, the grief of it all, and with this new child inside her, exhausting her, her face has been robbed of its scientific appreciation for coloured gunpowder exploding in the sky. In its place is the face of a strong woman, a mother, someone who has seen beyond herself, loved and lost something so powerfully that it has destroyed her but also shown her how to rebuild a life from rubble. She is full of the wisdom of experience and, whether she knows it or not, she is going to be an excellent mother. Those first-child temptations are gone: the need to spoil, to over-love, to imagine everything is perfect and will go on being perfect forever. In their place an emotional realism has taken hold, an affinity with the struggle of life. There will be no pretence, no over-happy fixation. This child will see the lines in its mother's face and gradually intuit the pain that love can cause, the complexity of emotions that life can instil, and it will walk into the wider world a little bit more prepared because of it.

Lyd glances at me.

'You're supposed to be looking up there,' she says.

267

'Are you really coming home?'

She nods but there is a warning in her eyes, *Don't let one thing mean another*. I nod back and put my arm around her waist. She lets me keep it there. I catch my mum glancing and smiling, nudging John (who can't figure out that she wants him to look at us). I look up. A group of red fireworks fill the sky.

'That's lithium,' says Lyd. 'The red ones have lithium in them.'

'Is it?' I say, trying to cling to my hopes.

5

In physics, a singularity is a theoretical space at the centre of a black hole with zero volume and infinite density. In mechanics, a singularity occurs when a system or machine reaches a position or configuration where the subsequent behaviour cannot be predicted. In mathematics, a singularity is the point at which a mathematical set fails to be 'well-behaved'. In all these cases, there is a singular point of incomprehension, where logic undoes itself and change is absolute. It goes against everything that has come before, yet somehow epitomises it.

Lyd waddles down the stairs behind me, reading my book. I have a letter in the morning post. It's official-looking and I'm anxious about receiving demands for the thousands of pounds I owe my ex-publisher. One of the terms set out in the big relationship talk me and Lyd had is that the publisher's debt is my problem. There will be no financial bailout.

I've spent the last few weeks morosely contemplating my options. English teacher? Can't afford the course fees. A profession? Can't afford the training. Set up my own little printing press? Can't afford the start-up costs. Any job, anywhere? Don't have the experience. I've been thinking about setting up a creative writing course in a night school somewhere but it's been

269

looking more and more like I'm going to have to swallow my pride and find something menial and unskilled so that I can pay off my debts.

I open the letter and read it as I make my way to the kitchen.

'What is it?' asks Lyd, looking up from the A4 pages, noticing the consternation on my face.

'I don't believe it.'

'What?'

'My dad left me some money. Whatever's left after the house is sold and the debts are paid off.'

'Will there be much?'

'They're predicting about eighteen thousand.'

'That's — '

'Enough to pay off the publisher.'

'And buy the final stock.'

'Do you think I should bother?'

'You can sell them at readings when this one comes out.'

'*If* it comes out.'

'I can't put it down.'

'You have to say that.'

'I do and I don't. I don't have to say it like that. There's something about these last few chapters especially.'

'Where are you?'

'The last chapter, I think. It's all coming together really well.'

'I had this creative surge. I wrote the last five chapters in about two weeks.'

'It's the best writing you've ever done.'

'I'm worried what you'll think about the ending.'

'There's not all that much that could go wrong at this stage.'

'Just wait,' I say.

'Eighteen thousand?'

'I know. It never occurred to me that he might leave me money. I suppose I presumed he didn't have any.'

'It's about time you had a bit of good fortune.'

'Maybe I should spend it on teacher training?'

'You've spent the last fifteen years learning your profession. You're a writer, not a teacher.'

'I know. But writing's not really a profession anymore.'

'It is for some people.'

'Not many.'

'Everything seemed more problematic before I read this. Let's just see how it lands.'

I kiss her neck just behind the ear.

'Stop building my hopes up,' I say.

'What? It's good. But leave me alone,' she says. 'I want to finish it.'

'You can't. We've got to go and meet Serge and Gloria.'

'But it will only take about quarter of an hour.'

'We promised. I think they're trying to make an effort to get back on track with things.'

'Okay. But I'm taking it with me. I'll finish it on the way.'

'I'm feeling very bolstered by all this praise.'

She smirks.

'Well, don't be. Everybody else might hate it.'

★   ★   ★

271

Walking down Archway Road towards the café that does the fancy bread, Italian fillings and decent coffee, I'm looking over Lyd's shoulder, reading the last chapter with her. She's just coming up to the last four pages and my stomach is turning.

'I want you to stop now. I don't want you to read the end. It's too weird.'

'Shh. Leave me alone. You're ruining it.'

'Sorry.'

'Get away. Let me read it.'

'Okay. Okay.'

I pull away from her and smile to myself. Her interest in my work makes me feel whole. Whatever I write, she's my chosen audience. Her heart has the only ear I want to whisper into. As long as she responds to my words, thinks they're good work and were worth writing, then it doesn't matter so much what the rest of the world thinks.

My ears pop and start ringing.

As my hearing comes back it dawns on me that there's birdsong everywhere, blackbird song. I look up and see hundreds of black males on the rooftops, orchestras of yellow beaks. At this time of year most of the blackbirds in London have migrated to Cornwall for the milder air. And blackbirds don't gather like this. They occasionally play together in spring but they're too territorial to perch besides each other or fly together. This type of clustering, particularly at this time of year, is unheard of. The sight of all the black feathers and the sound of all the whistling is making me feel light-headed.

Nobody else on the street seems to have noticed them.

'Have you seen all the — '

I turn to Lyd but she's no longer by my side. I look around, panicking. The birdsong is so loud that I can't hear anything else. I finally catch sight of her. She's so engrossed in the last few pages of my novel that she hasn't registered a kink in the road. She's veering away from me. She doesn't stop or look up where I expect her to. She takes an extra step and her foot twists on the edge of the kerb, forcing her to take three quick steps so that she doesn't fall down onto her stomach. She's suddenly standing in the middle of the road, confused, holding three hundred pieces of A4 paper. There is a screeching sound. A black van with a yellow trim is sliding along the road. Lyd doesn't have time.

'Baby!' I cry, reaching a hand forward, watching helplessly.

The van slams into Lyd's pregnant stomach, knocking her a metre through the air and onto the floor, coming to a squealing stop with its bumper above her knees. Hundreds of blackbirds fly up into the air. Small wings flap in a million different directions, chaotically wafting me around as I move towards her, as she clutches her stomach, cries with pain.

I can see blood on her face, on her hands. Pages of my novel scatter in the wind. Familiar words blow past my eyes. My brain feels high up. My body is toppling. As I get close to her I stumble, somehow spinning one hundred and eighty degrees, but I just manage to save myself from falling. I spin one hundred and eighty degrees back towards her but my legs are giving in, I'm sinking, scratching at the blackness, trying to get back to my mind so I can help, but the inward pull is too great. I'm gone before I hit the ground.

★   ★   ★

I wake up in an ambulance.

'Where is she?' I ask, trying to sit up with a paramedic's hand restraining me.

'She's here,' he says. 'Look. Right there.'

I look across to the other side of the ambulance. Lyd is on the main medical bed. I'm on a foldout thing that has been pulled down from the wall.

'Lyd? *Lyd?* What's going on? Why can't she hear me?'

'She's unconscious,' says the paramedic.

'The baby?'

'We're not sure,' he says.

'What do you mean you're not sure?'

'There seems to be some kind of anomaly,' he says.

My stomach turns.

'Is there a heartbeat? Is it alive?'

I try to sit up and he attempts to restrain me again but I catch a glimpse of blood between Lyd's legs and rip him away from me. A confused medic is moving his stethoscope around on her pregnant stomach which now looks like a rocky mountainscape. Mucus-thick red blood covers her crotch area and is drooling down from the bed onto the floor of the ambulance.

'What the hell is going on?' I wail. 'What are you doing? Why aren't you saving her?'

'We don't know what we're dealing with,' says the paramedic.

'You're dealing with a pregnant woman who got hit by a van!'

'No,' he says, very certain and very sternly, 'we're not.'

When we get to the hospital everything becomes a blur. No matter how much I struggle, they won't let me go with Lyd. They take me to a waiting room where I rock back and forth on an uncomfortable chair. They make me sign things that seem completely irrelevant.

Finally, they tell me she's prepped for an emergency operation that might or might not be a caesarean section and that if I really want to, and they advise against it, there's an observation window I can watch from.

I go with them.

A surgeon makes a long, deep incision in Lyd's bumpy abdomen. His hands are quick. I close my eyes for a moment. The surgeon makes lots of precise adjustments to the incision and cuts away some fatty tissue whilst a male nurse dabs at the blood. When the surgeon makes a vertical cut into Lyd's womb, a litre of thick red albumen pours out of her. The surgeon recoils and looks at his colleagues, confused, asking for advice. The viscous red gloop pours over her hips and between her legs, off the sides of the operating table and onto the floor. One of the nurses runs out of the theatre and comes back with a bucket and mop.

After a little debate the surgeon goes in with some forceps and pulls out a shard of something bluish white. He does this again and again, pulling more and more strange white shards out of her, dropping them into a metal tray. His brow is knitting tighter and tighter. Though the pressure has eased, the red albumen keeps oozing. The nurse mopping the floor just seems to be spreading the thick red slime around.

After five or ten minutes pulling out increasingly smaller white shards from Lyd's womb, the surgeon seems satisfied and goes in deeper with the forceps. All the people around the operating table lean in to see.

The thing he pulls out has big, fuzzy purple bulbs on top of its head and a yellowish fleshy flap instead of a face. Its arms are hooked over, webbed, speckled with what look like wet black feathers. One male nurse runs to a bin to vomit, another nurse holds her hand to the patch over her mouth. Two doctors take the creature to a separate table whilst the surgeon begins to take more white shards out of Lyd.

I don't know where to look. There is too much thick red albumen. It's everywhere. It covers every apron, it's on every bare arm, it almost covers the floor. Over by the creature two doctors are scratching their heads, looking really closely at the centre of it. They seem to have come to some sort of agreement. They bend over it with medical tools I can't decipher the functions of. I can't see what they're doing.

276

On the main table a nurse is vacuuming Lyd's insides and the surgeon is shining a light into her womb. The two nurses holding the wound open are looking away, squeezing their eyes closed. The gurgling sound the suction device makes inside her is making me queasy, even though the sound is muffled by the glass.

Back on the small table the two doctors put something that looks like a large orange turkey wing with tufts of black feathers into a metal tray. They look at each other and nod, leaning back in. Thirty seconds later another raw, limp turkey wing is put in the metal tray. Now, they both move in very close and work very carefully.

The gurgling stops.

Over on the operating table they expertly sew Lyd's womb, tissue and skin back together.

One of the two doctors over with the creature puts a long yellow flap and a cap of skin with two furry purple bulbs into the metal tray. Both doctors look at each other with amazement, carefully pull some loose strips of skin away and put them in the metal tray, and then pass something small and purple to one of the nurses. She goes to wash it in a sink.

Lyd's wound has been dressed. I can see the machines she's attached to and nothing is flashing or making irregular noises.

A nurse comes towards the door to the viewing room with something wrapped in a small green sheet. As she approaches everybody in the room gathers around her. In the doorway she doesn't say a word. None of them do. When she passes it to me I don't expect to see what I do.

It's a baby. I look up at them all. They are all peering down.

'What is it?' I ask.

All of them are silent. I have to open the blanket and find out for myself.

It's a girl.

I wrap her back up and bob her up and down. Relief gushes through me, tears and joy and confusion. She's so light and precious.

'I don't understand,' I say.

Nobody responds.

'I don't understand.'

One of the two doctors who put the hooked wings and yellow flap into the metal tray steps towards me.

'Neither do we,' he says. 'They should both be dead. But it looks like they're both going to make it.'

I look down at our little girl's face. She is still immersed in non-being but signals are beginning to prod at her: light on her translucent eyelids, new temperatures, the emptiness of air compared to liquid, the coarseness of cotton over flesh, weight and gravity, disconnection. It's too early for her to grasp any of this but her brow wrinkles. An ancient black secret escapes her. She pulls back towards nothingness but life has her. She is slowly coming into being, stuck here. She cries. She wants to go back, where all the secrets and miracles hide.

6

I am the forgotten connections, the untold stories, the lost sensations, the useless facts. If somebody needs to hear a song, I sing it. If somebody needs to see a sign, I show it. I had never saved a soul. I had never touched the truth. I was no more than a thing that said I . . .

'Vince.'

I'm sitting on the couch holding my fountain pen with a plain black notebook resting on my thigh. It's open on the first page, blank. Lyd is nursing Merula beside me.

'Huh?'

'You were miles away.'

'I was thinking about when we were first getting together.'

I chuckle.

'What's so funny?'

'You were always talking about string theory. Constantly.'

'So what?' she says, smiling.

'At first, everything that came out your mouth was completely baffling but then, after about the third time we met, you started dumbing it down for me.'

'Ohhh, that must have been when I realised you were an idiot.'

'Around then, yes. I remember you said that everything in the universe might be made of

279

these tiny strings, and if it was, all space, all matter, light, gravity, everything, when you looked really close, would look similar to sound waves. And what made one thing a rock and another thing a sunbeam was just the way it vibrated. Everything was made of the same thing. It was all just vibrations travelling through vibrations, like a giant symphony.'

'It seems so long since I've had the time to think like that. I've been so entrenched in the details.'

'That's when I knew how successful you were going to be. I knew if you could get me to understand it you could get anyone to.'

'I think those chats were the preamble to writing my book,' she says.

'I'm glad I could help.'

'I've actually been thinking about writing another.'

'That's great. What about?'

'Probably supersymmetry. It seems like the right time.'

'Definitely.'

Merula stops nursing and milk drools down her chin. Lyd wipes it away gently with her thumb and tucks her breast away. I lean over and give Merula a kiss on the cheek.

'I think it might be a while before I can write anything again,' I say.

'You deserve a break. You wrote a novel in nine months. That's quicker than usual isn't it?'

'I guess.'

'You can't just bounce from one thing to the next.'

I look at her, supporting Merula's little head, close the notebook and move closer to them.

'I just don't like being at a loose end,' I say. 'I need a project to be getting on with.'

'I've got an eighteen-year project for you right here.'

I take Merula whilst she buttons up her shirt.

'I know,' I say. 'But it's not the same.'

'It'll come. Don't worry. Did Angela get back to you yet?'

'Not yet. She said she'd put it to the top of the slush pile. If I don't hear anything within a couple of weeks I'll start putting in the administrative grind, try and get it into the right hands.'

'And in the meanwhile?'

'Just keep following my nose.'

'You'll think of something.'

'The words always find me in the end.'

'Exactly.'

★ ★ ★

Jamal opens his door and stands aside for me to enter his front room. The floor is covered with pieces of scrap metal and motor parts on newspapers. It's just as crowded and inhospitable as it used to be.

'I see you've taken up your old habits again.'

'Not all of them,' he says, shutting the front door.

'Just the worst ones?'

'A man who starts again usually chooses the same path.'

281

'Are you going all Zen master on me already? How many joints did you smoke this morning?'

'Shut up. Let me show you something.'

'Here,' I say, handing him a print-out of my book. 'Take this first.'

'Great, thanks, man. I'll get started on it later.'

He puts it down on top of a car battery on the coffee table and heads up the stairs (each of which has a carburettor pushed to the right-hand side on top of a newspaper).

At the doorway of his workshop, after looking into the room for a couple of seconds, he turns and looks my way.

'Isn't it beautiful?'

I approach him and look through the doorway. He's built an entire Rolls Royce in his workshop. But it is no longer a workshop. All the shelves have been taken down and all the tools are gone from the back wall. The walls have been painted white and the room is lit like a car showroom. His black Silver Shadow is gleaming. It looks like it just rolled off the assembly line.

I start laughing.

'You're crazy,' I say.

He walks around the side, opens one of the bedroom windows (which were previously covered by the hardboard wall of tools), feeds out a hose pipe connected to the car's exhaust pipe and closes his new thick black curtains. He then reaches up and clicks the side of a big box that is hanging from the ceiling, a projector.

'Turn the lights off,' he says, grinning.

As I do this he sits in the driver's seat. A bright blue rectangle is projected across two of the walls and then replaced by the image of his desktop (I didn't know he even owned a computer). He rolls down the passenger window.

'Come on,' he says. 'You're riding shotgun.'

I shake my head with a smile and get into the car.

'Only you would build a beautiful car in your spare bedroom. What's the point if you can't drive it?'

'Who says I can't drive it?' he says, starting the engine.

The machine hums and vibrates at a smooth, even level.

'We're not going to die of carbon-monoxide poisoning, are we?'

'You just saw me put the pipe out the window.'

'Still . . . '

'I'm alive, aren't I?'

'Sort of,' I say, with a smirk.

'Quiet a second,' he says, indicating with a hand to his ear that I should be listening to the engine. 'Isn't it beautiful? I could listen to that sound forever.'

'It definitely sounds like a car.'

'Come off it,' he says, squeezing the accelerator. 'Tell me that's not beautiful.'

'It sounds great,' I admit. 'I don't think you'll get very far though.'

I gesture towards the walls in every direction.

'There's all these videos you can download. They're amazing. I've cruised down Route 66, put in sixty laps at Silverstone, I even did the Rally de Portugal. I felt a bit sick after that one.'

I'm laughing.

'There are these great railway ones too,' he continues. 'I know it's a bit weird, sitting in a car, but I did a four-and-a-half-hour trip from Glasgow to Mallaig last week. It goes over Fort William. Such a lovely journey.'

'You have taken recluse to a whole new level.'

'Who needs to leave the house when you have this? I never thought I'd get into the Internet, any of this technological stuff, but, you'll see. I'm going to do the Trans-Siberian Railway at some point. I've got the full six days of footage. And there's Big Sur, Nurburgring Nordschleife, Ruta 40, Conor Pass, Karakoram Highway, so many great drives. And people are just giving these videos away. I couldn't afford to do all these trips in real life even if I wanted to.'

'I have to hand it to you,' I say, 'you have assimilated into your suburban isolation with a great sense of adventure.'

'I got one especially for you.'

'Ominous.'

'Not at all,' he says, beginning to click though folders. 'Here it is.'

'How have you got the screen so big?' I ask. 'It's in the side windows.'

'Just a bit of keystoning. It's a decent projector. It's got two heads.'

'Look at you, part of the twenty-first century.'

'Shush, just feel the engine vibrating through your feet and watch.'

'Aye, aye, Captain.'

The room goes black. It's immediately apparent that he has the car wired up for sound, very good quality sound.

The room lights up.

We're in the desert, with rocky mountains on the horizon and scaffolding in the foreground. A hissing noise slowly builds and builds until it explodes into a roar. The Rolls Royce shakes with the bass of it, the engine gently purring beneath. The scaffolding falls away. The camera spins slowly and we begin to rocket upwards. The huge mountain range quickly begins to look flat. Everything rumbles and vibrates. We pass a layer of small intermittent clouds. The desert below looks fuzzy from the heat. The roar goes on.

Long thin strips of white cloud slowly sink around us. The desert and the mountains shrink and shrivel. Over half of the view is blue sky. The sun makes me squint as it passes across the windscreen. For a couple of seconds everything beneath us is a mixture of vapours that the eye can't see through but then a misty cloud falls away, revealing the surface below.

The roar thunders on. The flat horizon begins to curve. The desert is now just a small portion of the Earth which is mostly ocean. The sky's upper horizon starts bending, shifting through all the deepest blues until there is an encroaching curve of blackness. This blackness pulls down, further and further, until the portion of blue that accounts for the sky is a thin, ethereal blue ribbon wrapped around a blue and white marble floating in nothingness.

A bright white light, a spotlight that used to be the yellow sun, with a centre that the camera cannot interpret as anything other than its brightest and whitest pixels, crosses the blackness as our rocket rotates, travelling diagonally, looking for nothing. The roaring of the scorched fuel settles into brassy reverberations. A booster pack is released and slowly floats backwards.

My stomach lifts.

The sound is dead.

We're suspended in the vast blackness of space, spinning slowly, almost unnoticeably. The stars begin to multiply. The darkness between them deepens. It crosses my mind that, before the universe, there was an endless black hole, an infinite singularity, and that our universe is expanding into it. Our black holes are bubbles of that spaceless and timeless truth beyond us: death. And this death should not be feared as an evil, decimating force. It is formless and eternal, complete and inconceivable; part of a truth we cannot measure or judge.

Floating in an imaginary vacuum, suspended in disbelief, I get the sensation that the universe is expanding. This death beyond the stars is in retreat. I've almost forgotten that I'm sitting in a stationary Rolls Royce in a bedroom in Highgate. I don't hear the rumble of the engine, the hum of the projector, the pause in my breath. The camera spins slowly. The world is edging back into view.

We do hope that you have enjoyed reading this large print book.

Did you know that all of our titles are available for purchase?

We publish a wide range of high quality large print books including:
Romances, Mysteries, Classics
General Fiction
Non Fiction and Westerns

Special interest titles available in large print are:
The Little Oxford Dictionary
Music Book
Song Book
Hymn Book
Service Book

Also available from us courtesy of Oxford University Press:
Young Readers' Dictionary
(large print edition)
Young Readers' Thesaurus
(large print edition)

For further information or a free brochure, please contact us at:
Ulverscroft Large Print Books Ltd.,
The Green, Bradgate Road, Anstey,
Leicester, LE7 7FU, England.
Tel: (00 44) 0116 236 4325
Fax: (00 44) 0116 234 0205

MY NAME IS LEON

Kit De Waal

1980: Leon is nine, and has a perfect baby brother called Jake. They have gone to live with Maureen, who has fuzzy red hair like a halo, and a belly like Father Christmas. But the adults are speaking in low voices and wearing Pretend faces. They are threatening to give Jake to strangers. As Leon struggles to cope with his anger, certain things can still make him smile — like chocolate bars, riding his bike fast downhill, burying his hands deep in the soil, hanging out with Tufty (who reminds him of his dad), and stealing enough coins so that one day he can rescue Jake and his mum . . .

THE ITALIAN'S CHRISTMAS SECRET

BY

SHARON KENDRICK

MILLS & BOON

First published in Great Britain 2017
by Mills & Boon, an imprint of HarperCollins*Publishers*
1 London Bridge Street, London, SE1 9GF

Large Print edition 2018

© 2017 Sharon Kendrick

ISBN: 978-0-263-07342-3

C463776248

This book is produced from independently certified FSC™ paper to ensure responsible forest management. For more information visit www.harpercollins.co.uk/green.

Printed and bound in Great Britain
by CPI Group (UK) Ltd, Croydon, CR0 4YY

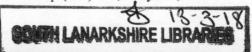

For the vivacious and beautiful
Amelia Tuttiett—who is a great raconteur
and always fun to be with. She is also
a brilliant ceramic artist.

Thanks for all the inspiration, Mimi!

CHAPTER ONE

'MR VALENTI?'

The woman's soft voice filtered into Matteo's thoughts and he made no effort to hide his exasperation as he leaned back against the leather seat of the luxury car. He'd been thinking about his father. Wondering if he intended carrying out the blustering threat he'd made just before Matteo had left Rome—and if so, whether or not he could prevent it. He gave a heavy sigh, forcing himself to accept that the ties of blood went deeper than any others. They must do. He certainly wouldn't have tolerated so much from one person if they hadn't been related. But family were difficult to walk away from. Difficult to leave. He felt his heart clench. Unless, of course, they left you.

'Mr Valenti?' the soft voice repeated.

Matteo gave a small click of irritation and not just because he loathed people talking to him when it was clear he didn't want to be disturbed. It was more to do with the fact that this damned trip hadn't gone according to plan, and not just because he hadn't seen a single hotel he'd wanted to buy. It was as much to do with the small-boned female behind the steering wheel who was irritating the hell out of him.

'Cos' hai detto?' he demanded until the ensuing silence reminded him that the woman didn't speak Italian, that he was a long way from home—in fact, he was in the middle of the infernal English countryside with a woman driver.

He frowned. Having a woman chauffeur was a first for him and when he'd first seen her slender build and startled blue eyes, Matteo had been tempted to demand a replacement of the more burly male variety. Until he reminded himself that the last thing he needed was to be accused of sexual prejudice. His aristocratic nostrils flared as he glanced into the driver's mirror and met her eyes. 'What did you say?' he amended, in English.

The woman cleared her throat, her slim shoulders shifting slightly—though the ridiculous peaked cap she insisted on wearing over her shorn hair stayed firmly in place. 'I said that the weather seems to have taken a turn for the worse.'

Matteo turned his head to glance out of the window where the deepening dusk was almost obscured by the violent swirl of snowflakes. He'd been so caught up in his thoughts that he'd paid scant attention to the passing countryside but now he could see that the landscape was nothing but a bleached blur. He scowled. 'But we'll be able to get through?'

'I certainly hope so.'

'You hope so?' he echoed, his voice growing harder. 'What kind of an answer is that? You do realise that I have a flight all geared up and ready to go?'

'Yes, Mr Valenti. But it's a private jet and it will wait for you.'

'I am perfectly aware that it's a *private jet* since I happen to own it,' he bit out impatiently. 'But I'm due at a party in Rome tonight, and I don't intend being late.'

With a monumental effort Keira stifled a sigh and kept her eyes fixed on the snowy road ahead. She needed to act calm and stay calm because Matteo Valenti was the most important customer she'd ever driven, a fact her boss had drummed into her over and over again. Whatever happened, she mustn't show the nerves she'd been experiencing for the past few days—because driving a client of this calibre was a whole new experience for her. Being the only woman and the more junior driver on the payroll, she usually got different sorts of jobs. She collected urgent packages and delivered them, or picked up spoilt children from their prep school and returned them to their nanny in one of the many exclusive mansions which were dotted around

London. But even mega-rich London customers paled into insignificance when you compared them with the wealth of Matteo Valenti.

Her boss had emphasised the fact that this was the first time the Italian billionaire had ever used their company and it was her duty to make sure he gave them plenty of repeat business. She thought it was great that such an influential tycoon had decided to give Luxury Limos his business, but she wasn't stupid. It was obvious he was only using them because he'd decided on the trip at the last minute—just as it was obvious she'd only been given the job because none of the other drivers were available, this close to Christmas. According to her boss, he was an important hotelier looking to buy a development site in England, to expand his growing empire of hotels. So far they had visited Kent, Sussex and Dorset—though they'd left the most far-flung destination of Devon until last, which wouldn't have been how *she* would have arranged it, especially not with the pre-holiday traffic being what it was. Still, she wasn't being employed to sort out his schedule for him—she was here to get him safely from A to B.

She stared straight ahead at the wild flurry of snowflakes. It was strange. She worked *with* men and *for* men and knew most of their foibles. She'd learnt that in order to be accepted it was better to act like one of the boys and not stand out. It was the reason she wore her hair short—though not the reason she'd cut it in the first place. It was why she didn't usually bother with make-up, or wearing the kind of clothes which invited a second look. The tomboy look suited her just fine, because if a man forgot you were there, he tended to relax—though unfortunately the same rule didn't seem to apply to Matteo Valenti. She'd never met a less relaxed individual.

But that wasn't the whole story, was it? She clutched the steering wheel tightly, unwilling to admit the real reason why she felt so self-conscious in his company. Because wasn't the truth that he had blown her away the moment they'd met, with the most potent brand of charisma she'd ever encountered? It was disturbing and exciting and scary all at the same time and it had never happened to her before—that thing of looking into someone's eyes and hearing a million violins start playing inside your head. She'd gazed into the darkest eyes she'd ever seen and felt as if she could drown in them. She'd found herself studying his thick black hair and wondering how it would feel to run her fingers through it. Failing that, having a half-friendly working relationship would have satisfied her, but that was never going to happen. Not with a man who was so abrupt, narrow-minded and *judgmental*.

She'd seen his expression when she'd been assigned to him, his black gaze raking over her with a look of incredulity he hadn't bothered to disguise. He'd actually had the nerve to ask whether she felt *confident* behind the wheel of such a powerful car and she had been tempted to coolly inform him that yes, she was, thank you very much. Just as she was confident about getting underneath the bonnet and taking the engine to pieces, should the need arise. And now he was snapping at her and making no attempt to hide his irritation—as if she had some kind of magical power over the weather conditions which had suddenly hit them from out of the blue!

She shot a nervous glance towards the heavy sky and felt another tug of anxiety as she met his hooded dark eyes in the driver's mirror.

'Where are we?' he demanded.

Keira glanced at the sat-nav. 'I think we're on Dartmoor.'

'You think?' he said sarcastically.

Keira licked her lips, glad he was now preoccupied with staring out of the window instead of glaring so intently at her. Glad he was ignorant of the sudden panicked pounding of her heart. 'The sat-nav lost its signal a couple of times.'

'But you didn't think to tell me that?'

She bit back her instinctive response that he

was unlikely to be an expert on the more rural parts of the south-west since he'd told her he hardly ever visited England. Unless, of course, he was implying that his oozing masculinity was enough to compensate for a total lack of knowledge of the area.

'You were busy with a phone call at the time and I didn't like to interrupt,' she said. 'And you said…'

'I said what?'

She gave a little shrug. 'You mentioned that you'd like to travel back by the scenic route.'

Matteo frowned. Had he said that? It was true he'd been distracted by working out how he was going to deal with his father, but he didn't remember agreeing to some guided tour of an area he'd already decided wasn't for him, or his hotels. Hadn't it simply been a case of agreeing to her hesitant suggestion of an alternative route, when she'd told him that the motorways were likely to be busy with everyone travelling home for the Christmas holiday? In which case, surely she should have had the sense and the knowledge to anticipate something like this might happen.

'And this snowstorm seems to have come from out of nowhere,' she said.

With an effort Matteo controlled his temper, telling himself nothing would be achieved by snapping at her. He knew how erratic and *emotional* women could be—both in and out of the workplace—and had always loathed overblown displays of emotion. She would probably burst into tears if he reprimanded her, followed by an undignified scene while she blubbed into some crumpled piece of tissue and then looked at him with tragic, red-rimmed eyes. And scenes were something he was at pains to avoid. He liked a life free of drama and trauma. A life lived on his terms.

Briefly, he thought about Donatella waiting for him at a party he wasn't going to be able to make. At the disappointment in her green eyes when she realised that several weeks of dating weren't going to end up in a swish Roman hotel bedroom, as they'd planned. His mouth hardened. He'd made her wait to have sex with him and he could tell it had frustrated the hell out of her. Well, she would just have to wait a little longer.

'Why don't you just get us there as safely as possible?' he suggested, zipping shut his briefcase. 'If I miss the party, it won't be the end of the world—just so long as I get home for Christmas in one piece. You can manage that, can't you?'

Keira nodded, but inside her heart was still racing faster than it should have been considering her sedentary position behind the wheel. Because she was rapidly realising that they were in trouble. Real trouble. Her windscreen wipers were going like crazy but no sooner had they removed a thick mass of white flakes, there were loads more their place. She'd never known such awful visibility and found herself wondering why she hadn't just risked the crowds and the traffic jams and gone by the most direct route.

Because she hadn't wanted to risk a displeasure she suspected was never very far from the surface with her billionaire client. Matteo Valenti wasn't the kind of person you could imagine sitting bumper to bumper on a road of stationary traffic while children in Santa hats pulled faces through the back windows. To be honest, she was surprised he didn't travel round by helicopter until he'd informed her that you got to see a lot more of the natural lie of the land from a car.

He seemed to have informed her about quite a lot of things. How he didn't like coffee from service stations and would rather go without food than eat something 'substandard'. How he preferred silence to the endless stream of Christmas songs on the car radio, though he didn't object when once she changed the station to some classical music, which she found strangely unsettling—particularly when a glance in the mirror showed her that he had closed his eyes and briefly parted his lips. Her heartbeat had felt *very* erratic after that particular episode.

Keira slowed down as they drove past a small house on which an illuminated Santa Claus was driving his sleigh above a garish sign proclaiming *Best Bed & Breakfast on Dartmoor!* The trouble was that she wasn't used to men like Matteo Valenti—she didn't imagine a lot of people were. She'd watched people's reactions whenever he emerged from the limousine to cast his eye over yet another dingy hotel which was up for sale. She'd witnessed women's gazes being drawn instinctively to his powerful physique. She'd watched their eyes widen—as if finding it hard to believe that one man could present such a perfect package, with those aristocratic features, hard jaw and sensual lips. But Keira had been up close to him for several days and she realised that, although he looked pretty perfect on the surface, there was a brooding quality underneath the surface which hinted at danger. And weren't a lot of women turned on by danger? As she clamped her fingers around the steering wheel, she wondered if that was the secret of his undeniable charisma.

But now wasn't the time to get preoccupied about Matteo Valenti, or even to contemplate the holidays which were fast approaching and which she was dreading. It was time to acknowledge that the snowstorm was getting heavier by the second and she was losing control of the big car. She could feel the tyres pushing against the weight of the accumulating drifts as the road took on a slight incline. She could feel sweat suddenly beading her brow as the heavy vehicle began to lose power and she realised that if she wasn't careful…

The car slid to a halt and Keira's knuckles whitened as she suddenly realised there were no distant tail lights in front of them. Or lights behind them. She glanced in the mirror as she turned off the ignition and forced herself to meet the furious black stare which was being directed at her from the back seat.

'What's going on?' he questioned, his tone sending a shiver rippling down Keira's spine.

'We've stopped,' she said, turning the key again and praying for them to start moving but the car stayed exactly where it was.

'I can see that for myself,' he snapped. 'The question is, *why* have we stopped?'

Keira gulped. He must have realised why. Did he want her to spell it out for him so he could shovel yet more blame on her? 'It's a heavy car and the snow is much thicker than I thought. We're on a slight hill, and...'

'And?'

Face facts, she told herself fiercely. You know how to do that. It's a difficult situation, but it's not the end of the world. She flicked the ignition and tried moving forward again but despite her silent prayers, the car stubbornly refused to budge. Her hands sliding reluctantly from the wheel, she turned round. 'We're stuck,' she admitted.

Matteo nodded, biting back the angry excla-

mation which was on the tip of his tongue, because he prided himself on being good in an
emergency. God knew, there had been enough
of those over the years to make him an expert
in crisis management. Now was not the time to
wonder why he hadn't followed his instincts and
demanded a male driver who would have known
what he was doing, instead of some slip of a
girl who didn't look strong enough to control a
pushbike, let alone a car this size. Recrimina-
tions could come later, he thought grimly—and
they would. First and foremost they needed to
get out of here—and to do that, they needed to
keep their wits about them.

'Where exactly are we?' he said, speaking
slowly as if to a very small child.

She swivelled her head to look at the sat-nav
for several silent seconds before turning to meet
his gaze again.

'The signal has cut out again. We're on the
edge of Dartmoor.'

'How close to civilisation?'

'That's the trouble. We're not. We're miles from anywhere.' He saw her teeth dig into her lower lip as if she were trying to draw blood from it. 'And there's no Wi-Fi connection,' she finished.

Matteo wanted to slam the flat of his hand against the snow-covered window but he sucked in an unsteady breath instead. He needed to take control.

'Move over,' he said roughly as he unclipped his seat belt.

She blinked those great big eyes at him. 'Move over where?'

'Onto the passenger seat,' he gritted out as he pushed open the car door to brace himself against a flurry of snowflakes. 'I'm taking over.'

He was pretty much covered in ice by the time he got into the car and slammed the door shut, and the bizarre thought which stuck in his mind was how deliciously warm the seat felt from where her bottom had been sitting.

Furious for allowing himself to be distracted

by something so basic and inappropriate at a time like this, Matteo reached for the ignition key.

'You do know not to press down too hard on the accelerator, don't you?' she said nervously. 'Or you'll make the wheels spin.'

'I don't think I need any driving lessons from someone as incompetent as you,' he retorted. He started the engine and tried moving forward. Nothing. He tried until he was forced to surrender to the inevitable, which deep down he'd known all along. They were well and truly stuck and the car wasn't going anywhere. He turned to the woman sitting beside him who was staring at him nervously from beneath her peaked cap.

'So. Bravo,' he said, his words steeped in an anger he could no longer contain. 'You've managed to get us stranded in one of the most inhospitable parts of the country on one of the most inhospitable nights of the year—just before Christmas. That's some feat!'

'I'm so sorry.'

'Saying sorry isn't going to help.'

'I'll probably get the sack,' she whispered.

'You will if I have anything to do with it—that's if you don't freeze to death first!' he snapped. 'If it were down to me, I would never have employed you in the first place. But the consequences to your career are the last thing on my mind right now. We need to start working out what we're going to do next.'

She reached into the glove compartment for her mobile phone but he wasn't surprised to see her grimace as she glanced down at the small screen. 'No signal,' she said, looking up.

'You don't say?' he said sarcastically, peering out of the window where the howling flakes showed no signs of abating. 'I'm guessing there's no nearby village?'

She shook her head. 'No. Well, we did pass a little B&B just a while back. You know, one of those places which offer bed and breakfast for the night.'

'I'm in the hotel trade,' he said silkily. 'And

I'm perfectly aware of what a B&B is. How far was it?'

She shrugged. 'Less than a mile, I'd guess—though it wouldn't be easy to reach in this kind of conditions.'

'No kidding?' Matteo eyed the virtual white-out which was taking place outside the window and his heart thundered as he acknowledged the real danger of their situation. Because suddenly this was about more than just missing his flight or disappointing a woman who had been eager to make him her lover; this was about survival. Venturing outside in this kind of conditions would be challenging—and dangerous—and the alternative was to hunker down in the car for the night and wait for help to arrive tomorrow. Presumably she would have blankets in the boot and they could continue to run the heater. His lips curved into a grim smile. And wasn't the traditional method of generating heat to huddle two bodies together? But he gave the idea no more than a few seconds' thought before dismissing it—and not just because she didn't look as if she had enough flesh on her bones to provide any degree of comfort. No. To take the risk of staying put while the snow came down this fast would be nothing short of madness, for there was no guarantee anyone would find them in the morning.

He ran his gaze over her uniform of navy blue trousers and the sturdy jacket which matched her cap. The material curved over the faint swell of her breasts and brushed against her thighs and was hardly what you would call *practical*—certainly not appropriate to face the elements at their worst. He sighed. Which meant he would have to give her his overcoat and freeze to death himself. 'I don't suppose you have any warmer clothes with you?'

For a few seconds, she seemed to brighten. 'I've got an anorak in the boot.'

'An anorak?'

'It's a waterproof jacket. With a hood.' She removed her peaked chauffeur's cap and raked her fingers through her short dark hair and Matteo felt inexplicably irritated by the brief smile which had lightened her pale face.

Was she expecting praise for having had the foresight to pack a coat? he wondered acidly.

'Just get it and put it on,' he bit out. 'And then let's get the hell out of here.'

CHAPTER TWO

KEIRA HAD TO work hard to keep up with Matteo as he battled his way through the deep snow because his powerful body moved much faster than hers, despite the fact that he'd insisted on bringing his suitcase with him. Thick, icy flakes were flying into her eyes and mouth and at times she wondered if she was imagining the small lighted building in the distance—like some bizarre, winter version of an oasis.

Despite putting on the big pair of leather gloves he'd insisted she borrow, her fingers felt like sticks of ice and she gave a little cry of relief when at last they reached the little house. Thank heavens she *hadn't* imagined it because she didn't like to think about Matteo Valenti's reaction if she'd brought him here on a wild goose chase. He might have insisted on her borrowing his gloves, but even that had been done with a terse impatience. She saw his unsmiling look as he kicked a pile of snow away from the wooden gate and pushed it open, and she stumbled after him up the path to stand beneath the flashing red and gold lights of the illuminated sign overhead. She was shivering with cold by the time he'd jammed his finger on the doorbell and they heard some tinkly little tune playing in the distance.

'Wh-what if…wh-what if nobody's in?' she questioned from between teeth which wouldn't seem to stop chattering.

'The light's on,' he said impatiently. 'Of course somebody's in.'

'They m-might have gone away for Christmas and left the lights on a timer to deter burglars.'

'You really think burglars are going to be enticed by a place like *this*?' he demanded.

But their bad-tempered interchange was brought to a swift halt by the sound of a lumbering movement from within the house and the door was pulled open by a plump, middle-aged woman wearing a flowery apron which was smeared with flour.

'Well, bless my soul!' she said, opening the door wider as she peered out into the gloom. 'You're not carol singers, are you?'

'We are not,' answered Matteo grimly. 'I'm afraid our car has got snowed in a little way down the road.'

'Oh, you poor things! What a night to be outside! Come in, come in!'

Keira felt like bursting into tears of gratitude as Matteo's palm positioned itself in the small of her back and propelled her inside the bright little hallway. During the seemingly endless journey here, she'd been convinced they weren't going to make it, and that their two frozen figures would be discovered the next day, or the day after that. And hadn't she been unable to stop herself from wondering whether anyone would have actually *cared* if she died?

But now they were standing dripping in a

small hallway which had boughs of holly and strands of glittery tinsel draped absolutely everywhere. A green plastic tree was decked with flashing rainbow lights and from a central light hung a huge bunch of mistletoe. Keira's eyes were drawn in fascination to the row of small, fluffy snowmen waddling in a perfectly symmetrical line along a shelf—her attention only distracted by the realisation that puddles of water were growing on the stone tiles beneath their feet. Years of being told to respect property—especially when it *wasn't your own*—made Keira concentrate on the mess they were making, rather than the glaringly obvious fact that she and her bad-tempered Italian client were gate-crashing someone else's Christmas.

'Oh, my goodness—look at the floor!' she said, aware of the faint look of incredulity which Matteo Valenti was slanting in her direction. 'We're ruining your floor.'

'Don't you worry about that, my dear,' said the woman in her warm West Country accent. 'We get walkers coming in here all the time—that'll soon clean up.'

'We'd like to use your phone if that's okay,' said Matteo, and Keira watched as the woman looked at him, her mouth opening and closing comically as if she'd only just realised that she had six feet three inches of brooding masculine gorgeousness in her house, with melting snow sliding down over his black cashmere coat.

'And why would you want to do that, dear?' questioned the woman mildly.

Matteo did his best not to flinch at the over-familiar response, even though he despised endearments from complete strangers. Actually, he despised endearments generally. Didn't they say that you always mistrusted what you weren't used to? Suppressing a frustrated flicker of anger at having found himself in this intolerable situation, he decided he needed to own it. Better to calmly spell out their needs, since his driver seemed incapable of doing anything with any degree of competence. 'Our car has become

imbedded in the snow just down the road a little,' he said, directing an accusing glare at the
woman who was currently pulling off her bulky
waterproof jacket and shaking her short dark
hair. 'We should never have taken this route,
given the weather. However, what's done is done
and we can't do anything about that now. We
just need to get out of here, as quickly as possible, and I'd like to arrange that immediately.'

The woman nodded, her bright smile remaining unfaltering. 'I don't think that's going to be
possible, dear. You won't get a rescue truck to
dig you out—not tonight. Why, nothing's going
to get through—not in these conditions!'

It was the confirmation of his worst fears and
although Matteo was tempted to vent his rage, he
was aware it would serve no useful purpose—
as well as insulting the woman who'd been kind
enough to open her house to them. And she was
right. Who could possibly get to them tonight—
in weather like this? He needed to face facts and
accept that he was stuck here, in the middle of

nowhere—with his incompetent driver in tow. A driver who was staring at him with eyes which suddenly looked very dark in her pale face. He frowned.

Of all the females in the world to be stranded with—it had to be someone like her! Once again his thoughts drifted to the luxurious party he would be missing, but he dismissed them as he drew in a deep breath and forced himself to say the unimaginable. 'Then it looks as if we're going to have to stay here. I assume you have rooms for hire?'

The woman's wide smile slipped. 'In December? Not likely! All my rooms are fully booked,' she added proudly. 'I get repeat trade all through the year, but especially at this time of year. People love a romantic Christmas on Dartmoor!'

'But we need somewhere to stay,' butted in Keira suddenly. 'Just until morning. Hopefully the snow will have stopped by then and we can get on our way in the morning.'

The woman nodded, her gaze running over

Keira's pale cheeks as she took the anorak from her and hung it on a hook. 'Well, I'm hardly going to turn you out on a night like this, am I? Especially not at this time of the year—I'm sure we can find you room at the inn! I can put you in my daughter's old bedroom at the back of the house. That's the only space I have available. But the dining room is completely booked out and so I'm afraid I can't offer you dinner.'

'The meal doesn't matter,' put in Matteo quickly. 'Maybe if you could send something to the room when you have a moment?'

Keira felt numb as they were shown up some rickety stairs at the back of the house, and she remained numb as the landlady—who informed them that her name was Mary—opened the door with a flourish.

'You should be comfortable enough in here,' she said. 'The bathroom is just along the corridor though there's not much water left, and if you want a bath, you'll have to share. I'll just

go downstairs and put the kettle on. Make your-
selves at home.'

Mary shut the door behind her and Keira's
heart started racing as she realised that she was
alone in a claustrophobic space with Matteo Valenti. Make themselves at home? How on earth
were they going to do that in a room this size
with *only one bed*?

She shivered. 'Why didn't you tell her that we
didn't want to share?'

He shot her an impatient look. 'We are two
people and she has one room. You do the math.
What alternative did I have?'

Keira could see his point. Mary couldn't magic
up another bedroom from out of nowhere, could
she? She looked around. It was one of those
rooms which wasn't really big enough for the
furniture it contained. It was too small for a double bed, but a double bed had been crammed into
it nonetheless, and it dominated the room with
its homemade patchwork quilt and faded pillow
cases on which you could just about make out

some Disney characters, one of which just happened to be Cinderella.

There were no signs of Christmas in here but on every available surface seemed to be a photo. Photos of someone who was recognisably Mary, looking much younger and holding a series of babies, then toddlers, right through gangly teenagers until the inevitable stiff wedding photos—and then yet more babies. Keira licked her lips. It was a life played out in stills. A simple life, probably—and a happy life, judging by the smile which was never far from Mary's face. Keira was used to cramped and cluttered spaces but she wasn't used to somewhere feeling homely—and she could do absolutely nothing about the fierce pang of something which felt like envy, which clutched at her heart like a vice.

She lifted her eyes to meet Matteo's flat gaze. 'I'm sorry,' she said.

'Spare me the platitudes,' he snapped, pulling out the mobile phone from the pocket of his trousers and staring at it with a barely concealed lack of hope. 'No signal. Of course there isn't. And no Wi-Fi either.'

'She said you could use the landline any time.'

'I know she did. I'll call my assistant once I've removed some of these wet clothes.' He loosened his tie before tugging it off and throwing it over the back of a nearby chair, where it dangled like some precious spiral of gunmetal. His mouth hardened with an expression of disbelief as he looked around. *'Per amor del cielo!* Who even uses places like this? We don't even have our own bathroom.'

'Mary told us we could use the one along the corridor.'

'She also told us that we'd need to share a bath because there wasn't enough hot water!' he flared. *'Sharing a bath? Not enough hot water?* Which century are we supposed to be living in?'

Keira shrugged her shoulders awkwardly, suspecting that Matteo Valenti wasn't used to the vagaries of small-town English landladies, or the kind of places where ordinary people stayed.

Of course he wasn't. According to her boss, he owned luxury hotels all over his own country—he even had some scattered over America, as well as some in Barbados and Hawaii. What would he know about having to traipse along a chilly corridor to a bathroom which, like the rest of the house, obviously hadn't been modernised in decades?

'It's an English eccentricity. Part of the place's charm,' she added lamely.

'Charm I can do without,' he responded acidly. 'Good plumbing trumps charm every time.'

She wondered if he was deliberately ignoring something even more disturbing than the bathroom facilities…or maybe she was just being super-sensitive about it, given her uneasy history. Awkwardly she raked her fingers through her spiky hair, wondering what it was which marked her out from other women. Why was it that on the only two occasions she'd shared a bed with a man, one had been passed out drunk—while the other was looking at her with nothing but irritation in his hard black eyes?

He was nodding his head, as if she had spoken out loud. 'I know,' he said grimly. 'It's my idea of a nightmare, too. Sharing a too-small bed with an employee wasn't top of my Christmas wish list.'

Don't react, Keira told herself fiercely. And don't take it personally. Act with indifference and don't make out like it's a big deal.

'I expect we'll survive,' she said coolly, then began to rub at her arms through the thin jacket as she started to shiver.

He ran a speculative gaze over her and an unexpected note of consideration crept into his voice. 'You're cold,' he said, his eyes lingering on her thighs just a fraction too long. 'And your trousers are soaking.'

'You don't say?' she said, her voice rising a little defensively, because she'd never been very good at dealing with unsolicited kindness.

'Don't you have anything else you can wear?' he persisted.

Embarrassment made her even more defensive and Keira glared at him, aware of the heat now staining her cheeks. 'Yes, of course I do. I always make sure I carry an entire change of clothes with me whenever I embark on a drive from London to Devon,' she said. 'It's what every driver does.'

'Why don't you skip the sarcasm?' he suggested. 'And go and take a hot bath? You can borrow something of mine.'

Keira looked at him suspiciously, taken aback by the offer and not quite sure if he meant it. Without his cashmere coat he stood resplendent in a dark charcoal suit which, even to her untutored eye, she could tell was made-to-measure. It must have been—because surely your average suit didn't cater for men with shoulders as broad as his, or legs that long. What on earth could Matteo Valenti have in his suitcase which would fit *her*? 'You carry women's clothes around with you, do you?'

An unexpected smile lifted the corners of his mouth and the corresponding race of Keira's heart made her hope he wasn't going to do a lot of smiling.

'Funnily enough, no,' he said drily, unzipping the leather case. 'But I have a sweater you can use. And a soap bag. Here. Go on. Take it.'

He was removing the items from his case and handing them to her and Keira was overcome by a sudden gratitude. 'Th-thanks. You're very kind—'

'*Basta!* Spare me the stumbling appreciation. I'm not doing it out of any sense of *kindness*.' His mouth hardened. 'This day has already been a disaster—I don't want to add to the misery by having you catch pneumonia and finding myself with a wrongful death suit on my hands.'

'Well, I'll do my best not to get sick then,' she bit back. 'I'd hate to inconvenience you any more than I already have done!'

Her fingers digging into his sweater, Keira marched from the room to the bathroom along the corridor, trying to dampen down her rising feelings of anger. He really was the most hateful person she'd ever met and she was going to have to endure a whole night with him.

Hanging his sweater on the back of the door, she quickly assessed the facilities on offer and for the first time that day, she smiled. Good thing *she* was used to basics. To her the avocado-coloured sink and bath were nothing out of the ordinary, though she shuddered to think how Mr Cynical was going to cope. When she'd been growing up, she and her mother had lived in places with far worse plumbing than this. In fact, this rather tatty bathroom felt almost *nostalgic*. A throwback to tougher times, yes, but at least it had been one of those rare times when she'd known emotional security, before Mum had died.

Clambering into the tiny bath, she directed the leaking shower attachment over her head and sluiced herself with tepid water before lathering on some of Matteo's amazing soap. And then the strangest thing started happening. Beneath her massaging fingers she could feel her nipples begin to harden into tight little nubs and for a moment she closed her eyes as she imagined her powerful client touching her there, before pulling her hands away in horror. What on earth was *wrong* with her?

Leaving the plug in situ and climbing out of the tub, she furiously rubbed herself dry. Wasn't the situation bad enough without her fantasising about a man who was probably going to make sure she got fired as soon as they reached civilisation?

She put on her bra, turned her knickers inside out and slithered Matteo's grey sweater over her head. It was warm and very soft—it was just unfortunate that it only came to mid-thigh, no matter how hard she tugged at the hem. She stared into the mirror. And the problem with that was, what? Was she really naïve enough to think that the Italian tycoon would even *notice* what she was wearing? Why, judging from his attitude towards her up until now, she could probably waltz back in there completely naked and he wouldn't even bat those devastatingly dark eyelashes.

But about that Keira was wrong—just as she'd been wrong in making the detour via Dartmoor—because when she walked back into the bedroom Matteo Valenti turned around from where he had been standing gazing out of the window and, just like the weather outside, his face froze. It was extraordinary to witness, that unmistakable double take when he saw her, something which never normally happened when Keira walked into a room. His eyes narrowed and grew smoky and something in the atmosphere seemed to subtly shift, and change. She wasn't used to it, but she wasn't going to deny that it made her skin grow warm with pleasure. Unless, of course, she was totally misreading the situation. It wouldn't be the first time, would it?

'Is everything okay?' she asked uncertainly.

Matteo nodded in response, aware that a pulse had begun to hammer at his temple. He'd just finished a telephone conversation with his assistant and as a consequence he'd been miles away, staring out of the window at the desolate countryside and having the peculiar sensation of realising that nobody could get hold of him—a sensation which had brought with it a surprising wave of peace. He had watched his driver scuttle off towards the bathroom in her unflattering navy trouser suit, only now she had returned and...

He stared and swallowed down the sudden lump which had risen in his throat. It was inexplicable. What the hell had she done to herself?

Her short, dark hair was still drying and the heat of the shower must have been responsible for the rosy flush of her cheeks, against which her sapphire eyes looked huge and glittery. But it was his sweater which was responsible for inflicting a sudden sexual awakening he would have preferred to avoid. A plain cashmere sweater which looked like a completely different garment when worn by her. She was so small and petite that it pretty much swamped her, but it hinted at the narrow-hipped body beneath and the most perfect pair of legs he had ever seen. She looked…

He shook his head slightly. She looked *sexy*, he thought resentfully as lust arrowed straight to his groin, where it hardened and stayed. She looked as if she wanted him to lay her down on the bed and start kissing her. As if she were tantalising him with the question of whether or not she was wearing any panties. He felt he was in a schoolboy's fantasy, tempted to ask her to bend down to pick up some imaginary object from the carpet so he could see for himself if her bottom was bare. And then he glared because the situation was bad enough without having to endure countless hours of frustration, daydreaming about a woman he couldn't have—even if he was the kind of man to indulge in a one-night stand, which he most emphatically wasn't.

'*Sì*, everything is wonderful. *Fantastico,*' he added sarcastically. 'I've just made a phone call to my assistant and asked her to make my apologies for tonight's party. She asked if I was doing something nice instead and I told her that no, I was not. In fact, I was stuck on a snowy moor in the middle of nowhere.'

'I've left you some hot water,' she said stiffly, deciding to ignore his rant.

'How will I be able to contain my excitement?' he returned as he picked up the clothes he had selected from his case and slammed his way out of the room.

But he'd calmed down a little by the time he returned, dressed down in jeans and a sweater, to find her stirring a pot of tea which jostled for space on a tray containing sandwiches and mince pies. She turned her face towards him with a questioning look.

'Are you hungry?' she said.

It was difficult to return her gaze when all he wanted to do was focus on her legs and that still tantalising question of what she was or wasn't wearing underneath his sweater. Matteo shrugged. 'I guess.'

'Would you like a sandwich?'

'How can I refuse?'

'It's very kind of Mary to have gone to the trouble of making us some, especially when she's trying to cook a big turkey dinner for eight people,' she admonished quietly. 'The least we can do is be grateful.'

'I suppose so.'

Keira tried to maintain her polite smile as she handed him a cup of tea and a cheese sandwich, telling herself that nothing would be gained by being rude herself. In fact, it would only make matters worse if they started sparring. She was the one in the wrong and the one whose job was on the line. If she kept answering him back, who was to say he wouldn't ring up her boss and subject him to a blistering tirade about her incompetence? If she kept him sweet, mightn't he be persuaded not to make a big deal out of the situation, maybe even to forget it had ever happened and put it down to experience? She needed this job because she loved it and things to love in Keira's life happened too rarely for her to want to give them up without a fight.

She noticed that he said nothing as he ate, his expression suggesting he was merely fuelling his impressive body rather than enjoying what was on offer—but Keira's hunger had completely deserted her and that was a first. She normally had a healthy appetite, which often surprised people who commented on her tiny frame. But not today. Today food was the last thing on her mind. She broke off the rim of one of the mince pies and forced herself to chew on it and the sugar gave her a sudden rush, but all she could think about was how on earth they were going to get through the hours ahead, when there wasn't even a radio in the room—let alone a TV. She watched the way the lamplight fell on her client's face—the hardness of his features contrasting with the sensual curve of his lips—and found herself wondering what it might be like to be kissed by a man like him.

Stop it, she urged herself furiously. Just *stop* it. You couldn't even maintain the interest of that trainee mechanic you dated in the workshop—do you really fancy your chances with the Italian billionaire?

A note of desperation tinged her voice as she struggled to think of something they could do which might distract her from all that brooding masculinity. 'Shall I go downstairs and see if Mary has any board games we could play?'

He put his empty cup down and his eyes narrowed. 'Excuse me?'

'You know.' She shrugged her shoulders helplessly. 'Cards, or Scrabble or Monopoly. Something,' she added. 'Because we can't just spend the whole evening staring at each other and dreading the night ahead, can we?'

He raised his dark eyebrows. 'You're dreading the night ahead, are you, Keira?'

A shimmer of amusement had deepened his

voice and Keira realised that, not only was it the first time he'd actually used her name, but that he'd said it as no one had ever said it before. She could feel colour flushing over her cheekbones and knew she had to stop coming over as some kind of unworldly idiot. 'Well, aren't you?' she challenged. 'Don't tell me your heart didn't sink when you realised we'd have to spend the night here.'

Matteo considered her question. Up until a few moments ago he might have agreed with her, but there was something about the girl with the spiky black hair which was making him reconsider his original assessment. It was, he thought, a novel situation and he was a man whose appetites had been jaded enough over the years to be entertained by the novel. And Keira whatever-her-name-was certainly wasn't your average woman. She wasn't behaving as most women would have done in the circumstances. She had suggested playing a game as if she actually meant it, without any purring emphasis on the word *playing*, leaving him in no doubt how she intended the 'game' to progress—with him thrusting into her eager body. People called him arrogant, but he preferred to think of himself as a realist. He'd never been guilty of under-assessing his own attributes—and one of those was his ability to make the opposite sex melt, without even trying.

He focussed his gaze on her, mildly amused by the competitive look in her eyes which suggested that her question had been genuine. 'Sure,' he said. 'Let's play games.'

Picking up the tray, she went downstairs, reappearing after a little while with a stack of board games, along with a bottle of red wine and two glasses.

'There's no need to be snobby about the vintage,' she said, noticing his expression as he frowningly assessed the label on the bottle. 'It was very sweet of Mary to offer us a festive drink and I'm having a glass even if you aren't.

I'm not driving anywhere tonight and I don't want to offend her, not when she's been so kind.'

Feeling surprisingly chastened, Matteo took the bottle and opened it, pouring them each a glass and forcing himself to drink most of his in a single draught as he lowered himself into the most uncomfortable chair he'd ever sat in.

'Ready?' she questioned as she sat cross-legged on the bed, with a blanket placed discreetly over her thighs as she faced him.

'I guess,' he growled.

They played Monopoly, which naturally he won—but then, he'd spent all his adult life trading property and had learnt early that there was no commodity more precious than land. But he was surprised when she suggested a quick game of poker and even more surprised by her skill with the cards.

Matteo wondered afterwards if he'd been distracted by knowing her legs were bare beneath the blanket. Or if he'd just spent too long gazing at her curling black lashes, which remarkably didn't carry a trace of mascara. Because wasn't the truth that he was finding his pocket-sized driver more fascinating with every moment which passed? She was certainly managing to keep her face poker-straight as she gazed at her cards and inexplicably he found himself longing to kiss those unsmiling lips.

He swallowed. Was she aware that her coolness towards him was fanning a sexual awareness which was growing fiercer by the second? He didn't know—all he *did* know was that by the time they'd drunk most of the bottle of wine, she had beaten him hands-down and it was an unfamiliar experience.

He narrowed his eyes. 'Who taught you to play like that?'

She shrugged. 'Before I became a driver, I worked as a car mechanic—mostly with men,' she added airily. 'And they liked to play cards when the workshop was quiet.'

'You worked as a *car mechanic*?'

'You sound surprised.'

'I am surprised. You don't look strong enough to take a car to pieces.'

'Appearances can be deceptive.'

'They certainly can.' He picked up the bottle and emptied out the last of the wine, noticing her fingers tremble as he handed her the glass. She must be feeling it too, he thought grimly—that almost tangible buzz of *electricity* when his hand brushed against hers. He crossed one leg over the other to hide the hard throb of his erection as he tried—and failed—to think of something which didn't involve his lips and her body.

'Mr Valenti,' she said suddenly.

'Matteo,' he instructed silkily. 'I thought we agreed we should be on first-name terms, given the somewhat *unusual* circumstances.'

'Yes, we did, but I…

Keira's words tailed away as he fixed her with a questioning look, not quite sure how to express her thoughts. The alcohol had made her feel more daring than usual—something which she'd fully exploited during that game of cards.

She'd known it probably wasn't the most sensible thing to defeat Matteo Valenti and yet something had made her want to show him she wasn't as useless as he seemed to think she was. But she was now aware of her bravado slipping away. Just as she was aware of the tension which had been building in the cramped bedroom ever since she'd emerged from the bathroom.

Her breasts were aching and her inside-out panties were wet. Did he realise that? Perhaps he was used to women reacting that way around him but she wasn't one of those women. She'd been called frigid by men before, when really she'd been scared—scared of doing what her mother had always warned her against. But it had never been a problem before, because close contact with the opposite sex had always left her cold and the one time she'd ended up in bed with a man he had been snoring in a drunken stupor almost before his head had hit the pillow. So how was Matteo managing to make her feel like this—as if every pore were screaming for him to touch her?

She swallowed. 'We haven't discussed what we're going to do about sleeping arrangements.'

'What did you have in mind?'

'Well, it looks as if we've got to share a bed— so obviously we've got to come to some sort of compromise.' She drew a deep breath. 'And I was thinking we might sleep top and tail.'

'Top and tail?' he repeated.

'You know.'

'Obviously I don't,' he said impatiently. 'Or I wouldn't have asked.'

Awkwardly, she wriggled her shoulders. 'It's easy. I sleep with my head at one end of the bed and you sleep with yours at the other. We used to do it when I was in the Girl Guides. Sometimes people even put pillows between them, so they can keep to their side and there's no encroaching on the other person's space.' She forged on but it wasn't easy when he was staring at her with a growing look of incredulity. 'Unless you're prepared to spend the night in that armchair?'

Matteo became aware of the hardness of the overstuffed seat which made him feel as if he were sitting on spirals of iron. 'You honestly think I'm going to spend the night sitting in this damned chair?'

She looked at him uncertainly. 'You want *me* to take the chair?'

'And keep me awake all night while you shift around trying to get comfortable? No. I do not. I'll tell you exactly what's going to happen, *cara mia*. We're going to share that bed as the nice lady suggested. But don't worry, I will break the habit of a lifetime by not sleeping naked and you can keep the sweater on. *Capisci?* And you can rest assured that you'll be safe from my intentions because I don't find you in the least bit attractive.'

Which wasn't exactly true—but why make a grim situation even worse than it already was?

He stood up and as he began to undo the belt

of his trousers, he saw her lips fall open. 'Better close those big blue eyes,' he suggested silkily, a flicker of amusement curving his lips as he watched all the colour drain from her cheeks. 'At least until I'm safely underneath the covers.'

CHAPTER THREE

KEIRA LAY IN the darkness nudging her tongue over lips which felt as dry as if she'd been running a marathon. She'd tried everything. Breathing deeply. Counting backwards from a thousand. Relaxing her muscles from the toes up. But up until now nothing had worked and all she could think about was the man in bed beside her. *Matteo Valenti. In bed beside her.* She had to keep silently repeating it to herself to remind herself of the sheer impossibility of the situation—as well as the undeniable temptation which was fizzing over her.

Sheer animal warmth radiated from his powerful frame, making her want to squirm with an odd kind of frustration. She kept wanting to fidget but she forced herself to lie as still as possible, terrified of waking him up. She kept telling herself that she'd been up since six that morning and should be exhausted, but the more she reached out for sleep, the more it eluded her.

Was it because that unwilling glimpse of his body as he was about to climb into bed had re-inforced all the fantasies she'd been trying not to have? And yes, he'd covered up with a T-shirt and a pair of silky boxers—but they did nothing to detract from his hard-packed abdomen and hair-roughened legs. Each time she closed her eyes she could picture all that hard, honed muscle and a wave of hunger shivered over her body, leaving her almost breathless with desire.

The sounds coming from downstairs didn't help. The dinner which Mary had mentioned was in full flow and bothering her in ways she'd prefer not to think about. She could hear squeals of excitement above the chatter and, later, the heartbreaking strains of children's voices as they started singing carols. She could picture them all by a roaring log fire with red candles burning on the mantle above, just like on the front of a Christmas card, and Keira felt a wave of wistfulness overwhelm her because she'd never had that.

'Can't sleep?' The Italian's silky voice penetrated her spinning thoughts and she could tell from the shifting weight on the mattress that Matteo Valenti had turned his head to talk to her.

Keira swallowed. Should she pretend to be asleep? But what would be the point of that? She suspected he would see through her ruse immediately—and wasn't it a bit of a relief not to have to keep still any more? 'No,' she admitted. 'Can't you?'

He gave a short laugh. 'I wasn't expecting to.'

'Why not?'

His voice dipped. 'I suspect you know exactly why not. It's a somewhat *unusual* situation to be sharing a bed with an attractive woman and having to behave in such a chaste manner.'

Keira was glad of the darkness which hid her sudden flush of pleasure. Had the gorgeous and arrogant Matteo Valenti actually called her *at-*

tractive? And was he really implying that he was having difficulty keeping his hands off her? Of course, he might only be saying it to be polite— but he hadn't exactly been the model of politeness up until now, had he?

'I thought you said you didn't find me attractive.'

'That's what I was trying to convince myself.'

In the darkness, she gave a smile of pleasure. 'I could go downstairs and see if I could get us some more tea.'

'Please.' He groaned. 'No more tea.'

'Then I guess we'll have to resign ourselves to a sleepless night.' She plumped up her pillow and sighed as she collapsed back against it. 'Unless you've got a better suggestion?'

Matteo gave a frustrated smile because her question sounded genuine. She wasn't asking it in such a way which demanded he lean over and give her the answer with his lips. Just as she wasn't accidentally brushing one of those pretty little legs against his and tantalising him with her touch. He swallowed. Not that her virtuous attitude made any difference because he'd been hard from the moment he'd first slipped beneath the covers, and he was rock-hard now. Hard for a woman with terrible hair whose incompetence was responsible for him being marooned in this hellhole in the first place! A different kind of frustration washed over him as the lumpy mattress dug into his back until he reminded himself that apportioning blame would serve little purpose.

'I guess we could talk,' he said.

'What about?'

'What do women like best to talk about?' he questioned sardonically. 'You could tell me something about yourself.'

'And what good will that do?'

'Probably send me off to sleep,' he admitted.

He could hear her give a little snort of laughter. 'You do say some outrageous things, Mr Valenti.'

'Guilty. And I thought we agreed on Matteo—

at least while we're in bed together.' He smiled as he heard her muffled gasp of outrage. 'Tell me how you plan to spend Christmas—isn't that what everyone asks at this time of year?'

Beneath the duvet, Keira flexed and unflexed her fingers, thinking that of all the questions he *could* have asked, that was the one she least felt like answering. Why hadn't he asked her about cars so she could have dazzled him with her mechanical knowledge? Or told him about her pipe-dream of one day being able to restore beautiful vintage cars, even though realistically that was never going to happen. 'With my aunt and my cousin, Shelley,' she said grudgingly.

'But you're not looking forward to it?'

'Is it that obvious?'

'I'm afraid it is. Your voice lacked a certain… enthusiasm.'

She thought that was a very diplomatic way of putting it. 'No, I'm not.'

'So why not spend Christmas somewhere else?'

Keira sighed. In the darkness it was all too

easy to forget the veneer of nonchalance she always adopted when people asked questions about her personal life. She kept facts to a minimum because it was easier that way. If you made it clear you didn't want to talk about something, then eventually people stopped asking.

But Matteo was different. She wasn't ever going to see him again after tomorrow. And wasn't it good to be able to say what she felt for once, instead of what she knew people expected to hear? She knew she was lucky her aunt had taken her in when that drunken joy-rider had mown down her mother on her way home from work, carrying the toy dog she'd bought for her daughter's birthday. Lucky she hadn't had to go into a foster home or some scary institution. But knowing something didn't always change the way you felt inside. And it didn't change the reality of being made to feel like an imposition. Of constantly having to be grateful for having been given a home, when it was clear you weren't really wanted. Trying to ignore all the

snide little barbs because Keira had been better looking than her cousin Shelley. It had been
the reason she'd cut off all her hair one day and
kept it short. Anything for a quiet life. 'Because
Christmas is a time for families and they're the
only one I have,' she said.

'You don't have parents?'

'No.' And then, because he seemed to have
left a gap for her to fill, she found herself doing
exactly that. 'I didn't know my father and my
aunt brought me up after my mother died, so I
owe her a lot.'

'But you don't like her?'

'I didn't say that.'

'You didn't have to. It isn't a crime to admit
it. You don't have to like someone, just because
they were kind to you, Keira, even if they're a
relative.'

'She did her best and it can't have been easy.
There wasn't a lot of money sloshing around,'
she said. 'And now my uncle has died, there's
only the two of them and I think she's lonely, in

a funny kind of way. So I shall be sitting round a table with her and my cousin, pulling Christmas crackers and pretending to enjoy dry turkey. Just like most people, I guess.'

There was a pause so long that for a moment Keira wondered if he *had* fallen asleep, so that when he spoke again it startled her.

'So what *would* you do over Christmas?' he questioned softly. 'If money were no object and you didn't have to spend time with your aunt?'

Keira pulled the duvet up to her chin. 'How much money are we talking about? Enough to charter a private jet and fly to the Caribbean?'

'If that's what turns you on.'

'Not particularly.' Keira looked at the faint gleam of a photo frame glowing in the darkness on the other side of the room. It was a long time since she'd played make-believe. A long time since she'd dared. 'I'd book myself into the most luxurious hotel I could find,' she said slowly, 'and I'd watch TV. You know, one of those TVs which are big enough to fill a wall—

big as a cinema screen. I've never had a TV in the bedroom before and it would be showing every cheesy Christmas film ever made. So I'd lie there and order up ice cream and popcorn and eat myself stupid and try not to blub too much.'

Beneath the thin duvet, Matteo's body tensed and not just because of the wistfulness in her voice. It had been a long time since he'd received such an uncomplicated answer from anyone. And wasn't her simple candour refreshing? As refreshing as her lean young body and eyes which were *profundo blu* if you looked at them closely—the colour of the deep, dark sea. The beat of his heart had accelerated and he felt the renewed throb of an erection, heavy against his belly. And suddenly the darkness represented danger because it was cloaking him with anonymity. Making him forget who he was and who she was. Tempting him with things he shouldn't even be thinking about. Because without light they were simply two bodies lying side by side, at the mercy of their senses—and right then his senses were going into overdrive.

Reaching out his arm, he snapped on the light, so that the small bedroom was flooded with a soft glow, and Keira lay there with the duvet right up to her chin, blinking her eyes at him.

'What did you do that for?'

'Because I'm finding the darkness…distracting.'

'I don't understand.'

He raised his eyebrows. 'Don't you?'

There was a pause. Matteo could see wariness in her eyes as she shook her head, but he could see the flicker of something else, something which made his heart pound even harder. Fraternising with the workforce was a bad idea—everyone knew that. But knowing something didn't always change the way you felt. It didn't stop your body from becoming so tight with lust that it felt like a taut bow, just before the arrow was fired.

No,' she said at last. 'I don't.'

'I think I'd better go and sleep in that damned armchair after all,' he said. 'Because if I stay here any longer I'm going to start kissing you.'

Keira met his mocking black gaze in astonishment. Had Matteo Valenti just said he wanted to *kiss* her? For a moment she just lay there, revelling in the sensation of being the object of attraction to such a gorgeous man, while common sense pitched a fierce battle with her senses.

She realised that despite talking about the armchair he hadn't moved and that an unspoken question seemed to be hovering in the air. Somewhere in a distant part of the house she heard a clock chiming and, though it wasn't midnight, it felt like the witching hour. As if magic could happen if she only let it. If she listened to what she wanted rather than the voice of caution which had been a constant presence in her life ever since she could remember. She'd learnt the hard way what happened to women who fell for the wrong kind of man—and Matteo Valenti had *wrong* written on every pore of his body. He was dangerous and sexy and he was a billion-aire who was way out of her league. Shouldn't she be turning away from him and telling him yes, to please take the armchair?

Yet she wasn't doing any of those things. Instead of her eyes closing, the tip of her tongue was sliding over her bottom lip and she was finding it impossible to drag her gaze away from him. She could feel a molten heat low in her belly, which was making her ache in a way which was shockingly exciting. She thought about the holidays ahead. The stilted Christmas lunch with her aunt beaming at Shelley and talking proudly of her daughter's job as a beautician, while wondering how her only niece had ended up as a car mechanic.

Briefly Keira closed her eyes. She'd spent her whole life trying to be good and where had it got her? You didn't get medals for being good. She'd made the best of her dyslexia and capital-ised on the fact that she was talented with her hands and could take engines apart, then put them back together. She'd found a job in a man's world which was just about making ends meet, but she'd never had a long-term relationship. She'd never even had sex—and if she wasn't careful she might end up old and wistful, remembering a snowy night on Dartmoor when Matteo Valenti had wanted to kiss her.

She stared at him. 'Go on, then,' she whispered. 'Kiss me.'

If she thought he might hesitate, she was wrong. There was no follow-up question about whether she was sure. He framed her face in his hands and the moment he lowered his lips to hers, that was it. The deal was done and there was no going back. He kissed her until she was dizzy with pleasure and molten with need. Until she began to move in his arms—restlessly seeking the next stage, terrified that any second now he would guess how laughingly inexperienced she was and push her away. She heard him laugh softly as he slid his fingers beneath the sweater to encounter the bra which curved over her breasts.

'Too much clothing,' he murmured, slipping his hand round her back to snap open the offending article and shake it free.

She remembered thinking he must have done this lots of times before and maybe she should confess how innocent she was. But by then he'd started circling her nipples with the light caress of his thumb and the moment passed. Desire pooled like honey in her groin and Keira gave a little cry as sensation threatened to overwhelm her.

'Sta' zitto,' he urged softly as he pulled the sweater over her head and tossed it aside, the movement quickly followed by the efficient disposal of his own T-shirt and boxers. 'Stay quiet. We don't want to disturb the rest of the house, do we?'

Keira shook her head, unable to answer because now he was sliding her panties down and a wild flame of hunger was spreading through her body. 'Matteo,' she gasped as his fingers moved down over her belly and began to explore her molten flesh. He stoked her with a delicacy which was tantalising—each intimate caress making her slide deeper into a brand-new world of intimacy. Yet strangely, it felt familiar. As if she knew exactly what to do, despite being such a novice. Did he tell her to part her legs or were they opening of their own accord? She didn't know. All she knew was that once he started stroking his fingertip against those hot, wet folds, she thought she might pass out with pleasure. 'Oh,' she whispered, on a note of wonder.

'Oh, what?' he murmured.

'It's…incredible.'

'I know it is. Now, touch me,' he urged against her mouth.

Keira swallowed. Did she dare? He was so big and proud and she didn't really know what to do. Swallowing down her nerves, she took him between her thumb and forefinger and began to stroke him up and down with a featherlight motion which nearly made him shoot off the bed.

'*Madonna mia!* Where did you learn to do *that*?' he gasped.

She guessed it might destroy the mood if she explained that car mechanics were often blessed with a naturally sensitive touch. Instead, she enquired in a husky voice which didn't really sound like her voice at all, 'Do you like it?'

'Do I like it?' He swallowed. 'Are you crazy? I love it.'

So why was he halting her progress with the firm clamp of his hand around her wrist, if he loved it so much? Why was he was blindly reaching for the wallet which he'd placed on the nightstand? He was pulling out a small foil packet and Keira shivered as she realised what he was about to do. This might be the craziest and most impulsive thing which had ever happened to her—but at least she would be protected.

He slid on the condom and she was surprised by her lack of fear as she wound her arms eagerly around his neck. Because it felt right. Not because he was rich and powerful, or even because he was insanely good-looking and sexy, but because something about him had touched her heart. Maybe it was the way his voice had softened when he'd asked her those questions about Christmas. Almost as if he *cared*—and it had been a long time since anybody had cared. Was she such a sucker for a few crumbs of affection that she would give herself completely to a man she didn't really know? She wasn't sure. All she knew was that she wanted him more than she'd ever wanted anything.

'Matteo,' she said as he pulled her into his body.

His eyes gleamed as he looked down at her. 'You want to change your mind?'

His consideration only made her want him more. 'No,' she whispered, her fingertips whispering over his neck. 'No way.'

He kissed her again—until she'd reached that same delicious melting point as before and then he moved to straddle her. His face was shadowed as he positioned himself and she tensed as he made that first thrust and began to move, but although the pain was sharp it was thankfully brief. She saw his brow darken and felt him grow very still before he changed his rhythm. His movements slowed as he bent her legs and wrapped them tightly around his waist so that with each long thrust he seemed to fill her completely.

As her body relaxed to accommodate his thickness, Keira felt the excitement build. Inch by glorious inch he entered her, before pulling back to repeat the same sweet stroke, over and over again. She could feel her skin growing heated as all her nerve-endings bunched in exquisitely tight anticipation. She could feel the inexorable build-up of excitement to such a pitch that she honestly didn't think she could take it any more. And then it happened. Like a swollen dam bursting open, waves of intense pleasure began to take her under. She felt herself shatter, as if he

needed to break her apart before she could become whole again, and she pressed her mouth
against his sweat-sheened shoulder. Dimly, she
became aware of his own bucked release as he
shuddered above her and was surprised by the
unexpected prick of tears to her eyes.

He pulled out of her and rolled back against
the pillows to suck in a ragged breath. With a
sudden shyness, Keira glanced across at him but
his eyes were closed and his olive features shuttered, so that suddenly she felt excluded from
the private world in which he seemed to be lost.
The room was quiet and she didn't dare speak—
wondering what women usually said at moments
like this.

Eventually he turned to her, his eyebrows
raised in question and an expression on his face
she couldn't quite work out.

'So?'

She wanted to hang on to the pleasure for as
long as possible—she didn't want it all to evapo-

rate beneath the harsh spotlight of explanation—but he seemed to be waiting for one all the same.

She peered up at him. 'You're angry?'

He shrugged. 'Why should I be angry?'

'Because I didn't tell you.'

'That you were a virgin?' He gave an odd kind of laugh. 'I'm glad you didn't. It might have shattered the mood.'

She tucked a strand of hair behind her ear. 'Aren't you going to ask me why?'

'You chose me to be your first?' His smile now held a faint trace of arrogance. 'I could commend you for your excellent judgment in selecting someone like me to be your first lover, but it's not really any of my business, is it, Keira?'

For some reason, that hurt, though she wasn't going to show it. Had she been naïve enough to suppose he might exhibit a chest-thumping pride that she had chosen him, rather than anyone else? 'I suppose not,' she said, her toes moving beneath the rumpled bedclothes in a desperate attempt to locate her only pair of panties.

'I just hope you weren't disappointed.'

'You must know I wasn't,' she said, in a small voice.

He seemed to soften a little at that, and brushed back a few little tufts of hair which had fallen untidily over her forehead. '*Sì*, I know. And for what it's worth, it was pretty damned amazing for me, too. I've never had sex with a virgin before but I understand it's uncommon for it to be as good as that the first time. So you should feel very pleased with yourself.' He began to stroke her hair. 'And you're tired.'

'No.'

'Yes,' he said firmly. 'And you need to sleep. So why don't you do that? Lie back and let yourself drift off.'

His words were soothing but Keira didn't want to sleep, she wanted to talk. She wanted to ask him about himself and his life. She wanted to know what would happen now—but there was something in his voice which indicated he didn't feel the same. And mightn't stilted conversation destroy some of this delicious afterglow which felt so impossibly fragile—like a bubble which could be popped at any moment? So she nodded obediently and shut her eyes and within seconds she could feel herself drifting off into the most dreamy sleep she'd ever known.

Matteo watched as her eyelashes fluttered down and waited until her breathing was steady before removing his arm from where it had been resting around her shoulders, but, although she stirred a little, she didn't waken. And that was when the reality of what he'd done hit him.

He'd just seduced a member of staff. More than that, he'd taken her innocence.

Silently, he cursed. He'd broken two fundamental rules in the most spectacular way. His chest was tight as he switched off the lamp and his mind buzzed as he attempted to ignore the naked woman who lay sleeping beside him. Yet that was easier said than done. He wanted nothing more than to push his growing erection inside her tight body again, but he needed to work out the most effective form of damage limitation. For both of them.

He stared up at the shadowy ceiling and sighed. He didn't want to hurt her and he could so easily hurt her. Hurting was something he seemed to do to women without even trying, mainly because he couldn't do love and he couldn't do emotion—at least that was what he'd been accused of, time after time. And Keira didn't deserve that. She'd given herself to him with an openness which had left him breathless and afterwards there had been no demands.

But none of that detracted from the reality of their situation. They came from worlds which were poles apart, which had collided in this small bedroom on the snowy outreaches of Devon. For a brief time they had come together in mindless pleasure but in truth they were nothing more than mismatched strangers driven by the stir of lust. Back in Italy he had been given an ultimatum which needed addressing and he needed to consider the truth behind his father's words.

'Give me an heir, Matteo,' he had breathed. *'Continue the Valenti name and I will give you your heart's desire. Refuse and I will sign the estate over to your stepbrother and his child.'*

Matteo's heart kicked with pain. He had to decide how much he was willing to sacrifice to maintain his links to the past. He needed to return to his world. And Keira to hers.

His jaw tightened. Would he have stopped if he'd known he was her first? He might have *wanted* to stop but something told him he would have been powerless to pull back from the indescribable lure of her petite body. His throat dried as he remembered that first sweet thrust. She had seemed much too small to accommodate him, but she had taken him inside her as if he had been intended to fit into her and only her. He remembered the way she'd touched him with that tentative yet sure touch. She'd made him want to explode. Had the newness of it been responsible for her joyful response—and for the tears which had trickled against his shoulder afterwards, but which she'd hastily blotted away?

Suddenly he could understand the potent power wielded by virgins but he could also recognise that they were a responsibility. They still had dreams—because experience hadn't yet destroyed them. Would she be expecting him to take her number? For him to fly her out to Rome for a weekend of sex and then see what happened? Hand in hand for a sunset stroll along Trastevere, Rome's supposedly most romantic neighbourhood? Because that was never going to happen. His jaw tightened. It would only raise up her hopes before smashing them.

He heard her murmur something in her sleep and felt the heavy weight of his conscience as he batted possibilities back and forth. What would be the best thing he could do for Keira—this sexy little driver with the softest lips he'd ever known? Glancing at his watch, he saw from the luminous dial that it was just before midnight and the rest of the house had grown silent. Could he risk using the landline downstairs without waking everyone? Of course he could. Slipping from the sex-scented bed, he threw on some clothes and made his way downstairs.

He placed the call without any trouble, but his mood was strangely low after he'd terminated his whispered conversation and made his way back to the bedroom. With the light from the corridor flooding in, he stared at Keira's face, which was pillowed on a bent elbow. Her lips were curved in a soft smile and he wanted to kiss them. To take her in his arms and run his hands over her and do it all over again. But he couldn't. Or rather, he shouldn't.

He was careful not to touch her as he climbed into bed, but the thought of her out-of-bounds nakedness meant that he lay there sleeplessly for a long, long time.

CHAPTER FOUR

A PALE LIGHT woke her and for a moment Keira lay completely still, her head resting against a lumpy pillow as her eyes flickered open and she tried to work out exactly where she was. And then she remembered. She was in a strange bedroom on the edge of a snowy Dartmoor—and she'd just lost her virginity to the powerful billionaire she'd been driving around the country!

She registered the sweet aching between her legs and the delicious sting of her nipples as slowly she turned her head to see that the other half of the bed was empty. Her pulse speeded up. He must be in the bathroom. Quickly, she sat up, raking her fingers through her mussed hair and giving herself a chance to compose herself before Matteo returned.

The blindingly pale crack of light shining

through the gap in the curtains showed that the snow was still very much in evidence and a smile of anticipation curved her lips. Maybe they'd be stuck here today too—and they could have sex all over again. She certainly hoped so. Crossing her arms over her naked breasts, she hugged herself tightly as endorphins flooded through her warm body. Obviously, she'd need to reassure him that although she was relatively inexperienced, she certainly wasn't naïve. She knew the score—she'd heard the men in the workshop talking about women often enough to know what they did and didn't like. She would be very grown up about what had happened. She'd make it clear that she wasn't coming at this with any *expectations*—although, of course, if he wanted to see her again when the snow had been cleared she would be more than happy with that.

And that was when she noticed the nightstand—or rather, what was lying on top of it. Keira blinked her eyes in disbelief but as her vision cleared she realised this was no illusion as she stared in growing horror at the enormous wad of banknotes. She felt as if she were taking part in some secretly filmed reality show. As if the money might suddenly disintegrate if she touched it, or as if Matteo would suddenly appear from out of hiding. She looked around, realising there *was* nowhere to hide in this tiny room.

'Matteo?' she questioned uncertainly.

Nobody came. Of course they didn't. She stared at the money and then noticed the piece of paper which was lying underneath it. It took several seconds before she could bring herself to pick it up and as she began to read it she was scarcely able to believe what she was seeing.

Keira, he had written—and in the absence of any affectation like *Dear* or *Darling*, she supposed she ought to be grateful that he'd got her name right, because Irish names were notoriously difficult to spell.

I just wanted to tell you how much I enjoyed last night and I hope you did, too. You looked so peaceful sleeping this morning that I didn't want to wake you—but I need to be back in Italy as soon as possible.

You told me your dream was to spend Christmas in a luxury hotel and I'd like to make this possible, which is why I hope you'll accept this small gift in the spirit with which it was intended.

And if we'd been playing poker for money, you would certainly have walked away with a lot more than this!

I wish you every good thing for your future.

Buon Natale.

Matteo.

Keira's fingers closed tightly around the note and her feeling of confusion intensified as she stared at the money—more money than she'd ever seen. She allowed herself a moment of fury before getting up out of bed, acutely aware that for once she wasn't wearing her usual nightshirt, and the sight of her naked body in the small mirror taunted her with memories of just what she and the Italian had done last night. And once the fury had passed she was left with hurt, and disappointment. Had she really been lying there, naïvely thinking that Matteo was going to emerge from the bathroom and take her in his arms when the reality was that he couldn't even bear to face her? What a stupid fool she'd been.

She washed and dressed and went downstairs, politely refusing breakfast but accepting a mug of strong tea from Mary, who seemed delighted to relay everything which had been happening while Keira had been asleep.

'First thing I know, there's a knock on the door and it's a man in one of those big four-wheel drives,' she announced.

'Which managed to get through the snow?' questioned Keira automatically.

'Oh, yes. Because Mr Valenti ordered a car with a snow plough. Apparently he got on the phone late last night while everyone was asleep and organised it. Must have been very quiet because nobody heard him.'

Very quiet, thought Keira grimly. He must have been terrified that she would wake up and demand he take her with him.

'And he's ordered some men to dig your car out of the snow. Said there was no way you must be stranded here,' said Mary, with a dreamy look on her careworn face. 'They arrived about an hour ago—they should be finished soon.'

Keira nodded. 'Can I pay you?'

Mary beamed. 'No need. Your Mr Valenti was more than generous.'

Keira's heart pounded; she wanted to scream that he wasn't 'her' anything. So the cash wasn't there to pay for the B& B or help her make her own journey home, because he'd already sorted all that out. Which left only one reason for leaving it. Of course. How could she have been so dense when the bland words of the accompanying letter had made it perfectly clear? The comment about the poker and the disingenuous suggestion she take herself off to a luxury hotel were just a polite way of disguising the very obvious. A wave of sickness washed over her.

Matteo Valenti had *paid her for sex.*

Operating on a dazed kind of autopilot, Keira made her way back to her newly liberated car, from where she slowly drove back to London. After dropping the car off at Luxury Limos, she made her way to Brixton, acutely aware of the huge wad of cash she was carrying. She'd thought of leaving it behind at Mary's, but wouldn't the kindly landlady have tried to return it and just made matters a whole lot worse? And how on earth would she have managed to explain what it was doing there? Yet it felt as if it were burning a massive hole in her pocket—haunting her with the bitter reminder of just what the Italian really thought of her.

The area of Brixton where she rented a tiny apartment had once been considered unfashionable but now, like much of London, the place was on the up. Two days before Christmas and the streets had a festive air which was bordering on the hysterical, despite the fact that the heavy snows hadn't reached the capital. Bright lights glittered and she could see Christmas trees and scarlet-suited Santas everywhere she looked. On the corner, a Salvation Army band was playing 'Silent Night' and the poignancy of the familiar tune made her heart want to break. And stupidly, she found herself missing her mother like never before as she thought about all the Christmases they'd never got to share. Tears pricked at the backs of her eyes as she hugged her anorak around her shivering body, and never had she felt so completely alone.

But self-pity would get her nowhere. She was a survivor, wasn't she? She would get through this as she had got through so much else. Dodging the crowds, she started to walk home, her journey taking her past one of the area's many charity shops and as an idea came to her she impulsively pushed open the door of one. Inside, the place was full of people trying on clothes for Christmas parties and New Year—raiding feather boas and old-fashioned shimmery dresses from the crowded rails. The atmosphere was chaotic and happy but Keira was grim-faced as she made her way to the cash desk. Fumbling around in her pocket, she withdrew the wad of cash and slapped it down on the counter in front of the startled cashier.

'Take this,' Keira croaked. 'And Happy Christmas.'

The woman held up a hand. 'Whoa! Wait a minute! Where did you—?'

But Keira was already pushing her way out of the shop, the cold air hitting the tears which had begun streaming down her cheeks. Her vision blurred and she stumbled a little and might have fallen if a steady arm hadn't caught her elbow.

'Are you okay?' a female voice was saying.

Was she okay? No, she most definitely was not. Keira nodded, looking up at a woman with platinum hair who was wearing a leopard-skin-print coat. 'I'm fine. I just need to get home,' she husked.

'Not like that, you're not. You're not fit to go anywhere,' said the woman firmly. 'Let me buy you a drink. You look like you could use one.'

Still shaken, Keira allowed herself to be led into the bright interior of the Dog and Duck where music was playing and the smell of mulled wine filled her nostrils. The woman went up to the bar and returned minutes later with a glass of a brown mixture resembling medicine, which was pushed across the scratched surface of the table towards her.

'What's this?' Keira mumbled, lifting the glass and recoiling from the fumes.

'Brandy.'

'I don't like brandy.'

'Drink it. You look like you're in shock.'

That much was true. Keira took a large and fiery swallow and the weird thing was that she *did* feel better afterwards. Disorientated, yes—but better.

'So where did you get the money from?' the

blonde was asking. 'Did you rob a bank or something? I was in the charity shop when you came in and handed it over. Pretty dramatic gesture, but a lovely thing to do, I must say—especially at this time of the year.'

Afterwards Keira thought that if she hadn't had the brandy then she might not have told the sympathetic blonde the whole story, but the words just started tumbling out of her mouth and they wouldn't seem to stop. Just like the tears which had preceded them. It was only when the woman's eyes widened when she came out with the punchline about how Matteo had left her a stack of money and done a runner that she became aware that something in the atmosphere had changed.

'So he just disappeared? Without a word?'

'Well, he left a note.'

'May I see it?'

Keira put the brandy glass down with a thud. 'No.'

There was a pause. 'He must be very rich,'

observed the blonde. 'To be able to be carrying around that kind of money.'

Keira shrugged. 'Very.'

'And good-looking, I suppose?'

Keira swallowed. 'What does that have to do with anything?'

The blonde's heavily made-up eyes narrowed. 'Hunky Italian billionaires don't usually have to pay women for sex.'

It was hearing someone else say it out loud which made it feel a million times worse—something Keira hadn't actually thought possible. She rose unsteadily to her feet, terrified she was going to start gagging. 'I… I'm going home now,' she whispered. 'Please forget I said anything. And…thanks for the drink.'

Somehow she managed to get home unscathed, where her cold, bare bedsit showed no signs of the impending holiday. She'd been so busy that she hadn't even bought herself a little tree, but that now seemed like the least of her worries. She realised she hadn't checked her phone messages since she'd got back and found a terse communication from her aunt, asking her what time she was planning on turning up on Christmas Day and hoping she hadn't forgotten to buy the pudding.

The pudding! Now she would have to brave the wretched shops again. Keira closed her eyes as she pictured the grim holiday which lay ahead of her. How was she going to get through a whole Christmas, nursing the shameful secret of what she'd done?

Her phone began to ring, the small screen flashing an unknown number; in an effort to distract herself with the inevitable sales call, Keira accepted the call with a tentative hello. There was an infinitesimal pause before a male voice spoke.

'Keira?'

It was a voice she hadn't known until very recently but she thought that rich, Italian accent would be branded on her memory until the end of time. Dark and velvety, it whispered over her skin just as his fingers had done. Matteo! And despite everything—the wad of money and the blandly worded note and the fact that he'd left without even saying goodbye—wasn't there a great lurch of hope inside her foolish heart? She pictured his ruffled hair and the dark eyes which had gleamed with passion when they'd looked at her. The way he'd crushed his lips hungrily down on hers, and that helpless moment of bliss when he'd first entered her.

'Matteo?'

Another pause—and if a silence could ever be considered ominous, this one was. 'So how much did she pay you?' he questioned.

'Pay me?' Keira blinked in confusion, thinking that bringing up money wasn't the best way to start a conversation, especially in view of what had happened. 'What are you talking about?'

'I've just had a phone call from a…a *journalist.*' He spat out the word as if it were poison. 'Asking me whether I make a habit of paying women for sex.'

Keira's feeling of confusion intensified. 'I don't...' And then she realised and hot colour flooded into her cheeks. 'Was her name Hester?'

'So you *did* speak to her?' He sucked in an unsteady breath. 'What was it, Keira—a quickly arranged interview to see what else you could squeeze out of me?'

'I didn't plan on talking to her—it just happened.'

'Oh, really?'

'Yes, really. I was angry about the money you left me!' she retorted.

'Why? Didn't you think it was enough?' he shot back. 'Did you imagine you might be able to get even more?'

Keira sank onto the nearest chair, terrified that her wobbly legs were going to give way beneath her. 'You bastard,' she whispered.

'Your anger means nothing to me,' he said coldly. 'For *you* are nothing to me. I wasn't thinking straight. I couldn't have been thinking straight. I should never have had sex with you because I don't make a habit of having one-night stands with strangers. But what's done can't be undone and I have only myself to blame.'

There was a pause before he resumed and now his voice had taken on a flat and implacable note, which somehow managed to sound even more ominous than his anger.

'I've told your journalist friend that if she prints one word about me, I'll go after her and bring her damned publication down,' he continued. 'Because I'm not someone you can blackmail—I'm just a man who allowed himself to be swayed by lust and it's taught me a lesson I'm never going to forget.' He gave a bitter laugh. 'So, goodbye, Keira. Have a good life.'

put him down for his nap before we sit down to eat,' she said hopefully.

Aunt Ida's mouth turned down at the corners, emphasising the deep grooves of discontentment which hardened her thin face. 'That'll be a first. Poor Shelley says she hasn't had an unbroken night since you moved in. He's obviously an unsettled baby if he cries so much. Maybe it's time you came to your senses and thought about adoption.'

Keira's teeth dug into her bottom lip as the word lodged like a barb in her skin.

Adoption.

A wave of nausea engulfed her but she tried very hard not to react as she stared down into the face of her sleeping son. Holding onto Santino even tighter, she felt her heart give a savage lurch of love as she told herself to ignore the snide comments and concentrate on what was important. Because only one thing mattered and that was her baby son.

Everything you do is for him, she reminded

CHAPTER FIVE

Ten months later

'I HOPE THAT baby isn't going to cry all the way through lunch, Keira. It would be nice if we were able to eat a meal in peace for once.'

Tucking little Santino into the crook of her arm, Keira nodded as she met her aunt's accusing stare. She would have taken the baby out for a walk if the late October day hadn't been so foul and blustery. Or she might have treated him to a long bus ride to lull him to sleep if he hadn't been so tiny. As it was, she was stuck in the house with a woman who seemed determined to find fault in everything she did, and she was tired. So tired. With the kind of tiredness which seemed to have seeped deep into her bones and taken up residence there. 'I'll try to herself fiercely. *Everything.* No point in wishing she hadn't given away Matteo's money, or tormenting herself by thinking how useful it might have been. She hadn't known at the time that she was pregnant—how could she have done? She'd handed over that thick wad of banknotes as if there were loads more coming her way— and now she just had to deal with the situation as it was and not what it could have been. She had to accept that she'd lost her job and her home in quick succession and had been forced to take the charity of a woman who had always disapproved of her. Because how else would she and Santino have managed to cope in an uncaring and hostile world?

You know exactly how, prompted the ever-present voice of her conscience but Keira pushed it from her mind. She could *not* have asked Matteo for help, not when he had treated her like some kind of *whore*. Who had made it clear he never wanted to see her again.

'Have you registered the child's birth yet?' Aunt Ida was asking.

'Not yet, no,' said Keira. 'I have to do it within the first six weeks.'

'Better get a move on, then.'

Keira waited, knowing that there was more.

Her aunt smiled slyly. 'Only I was wondering whether you were going to put the mystery father's name on the birth certificate—or whether you were like your poor dear mother and didn't actually know who he was?'

Keira's determination not to react drained away. Terrified of saying something she might later regret, she turned and walked out of the sitting room without another word, glad she was holding Santino because that stopped her from picking up one of her aunt's horrible china ornaments and hurling it against the wall. Criticism directed against her she could just about tolerate—but she wouldn't stand to hear her mother's name maligned like that.

Her anger had evaporated by the time she

reached the box-room she shared with Santino, and Keira placed the baby carefully in his crib, tucking the edges of the blanket around his tiny frame and staring at him. His lashes looked very long and dark against his olive skin but for once she found herself unable to take pleasure in his innocent face. Because suddenly, the fear and the guilt which had been nagging away inside her now erupted into one fierce and painful certainty.

She couldn't go on like this. Santino deserved more than a mother who was permanently exhausted, having to tiptoe around a too-small house with people who didn't really like her. She closed her eyes, knowing there was somebody else who didn't like her—but someone she suspected wouldn't display a tight-lipped intolerance whenever the baby started to cry. Because it was *his* baby, too. And didn't all parents love their children, no matter what?

A powerful image swam into her mind of a man whose face she could picture without too much trying. She knew what she had to do. Something she'd thought about doing every day since Santino's birth, and in the nine months preceding it, until she'd forced herself to remember how unequivocally he'd told her he never wanted to see her again. Well, maybe he was going to have to.

Her fingers were shaking as she scrolled down her phone's contact list and retrieved the number she had saved, even though the caller had hung up on her the last time she'd spoken to him.

With a thundering heart, she punched out the number. And waited.

Rain lashed against the car windscreen and flurries of falling leaves swirled like the thoughts in Matteo's mind as his chauffeur-driven limousine drove down the narrow suburban road. As they passed houses which all looked exactly the same, he tried to get his head round what he'd learned during a phone call from a woman he'd never thought he'd see again.

He was a father.

He had a child.

A son. His heart pumped. In a single stroke he had been given exactly what he needed—though not necessarily what he wanted—and could now produce the grandson his father yearned for.

Matteo ordered the driver to stop, trying to dampen down the unfamiliar emotions which were sweeping through his body. And trying to curb his rising temper about the way Keira had kept this news secret. How *dared* she keep his baby hidden and play God with his future? Grim-faced, he stepped out onto the rain-soaked pavement and a wave of determination washed over him as he slammed the car door shut. He was here now and he would fix this—to his advantage. Whatever it took, he would get what he wanted—and he wanted his son.

He hadn't told Keira he was coming. He hadn't wanted to give her the opportunity to elude him. He wanted to surprise her—as she had surprised him. To allow her no time to mount any defences. If she was unprepared and vulnerable then surely that would aid him in his determination to get his rightful heir. Moving stealthily up the narrow path, he rapped a small bronze knocker fashioned in the shape of a lion's head and moments later the door was opened by a woman with tight, curly hair and a hard, lined face.

'Yes?' she said sharply. 'We don't buy from the doorstep.'

'Good afternoon,' he said. Forcing the pleasantry to his unwilling lips, he accompanied it with a polite smile. 'I'm not selling anything. I'd like to see Keira.'

'And you are?'

'My name is Matteo Valenti,' he said evenly. 'And I am her baby's father.'

The woman gasped, her eyes scanning him from head to toe, as if registering his cashmere coat and handmade shoes. Her eyes skated over his shoulder and she must have observed the shiny black car parked so incongruously among all the sedate family saloons. Was he imagining the look of calculation which had hardened her gimlet eyes? Probably not, he thought grimly.

'You?' she demanded.

'That's right,' he agreed, still in that same even voice which betrayed nothing of his growing irritation.

'I had no idea that...' She swallowed. 'I'll have to check if she'll see you.'

'No,' Matteo interrupted her, only just resisting the desire to step forward and jam his foot in the door, like a bailiff. 'I *will* see Keira—and my baby—and it's probably best if we do it with the minimum of fuss.' He glanced behind him where he could see the twitching of net curtains on the opposite side of the road and when he returned his gaze to the woman, his smile was bland. 'Don't you agree? For everyone's sake?'

The woman hesitated before nodding, as if she too had no desire for a scene on the doorstep. 'Very well. You'd better come in.' She cleared her throat. 'I'll let Keira know you're here.'

He was shown into a small room crammed with porcelain figurines but Matteo barely paid any attention to his surroundings. His eyes were trained on the door as it clicked open and he held his breath in anticipation—expelling it in a long sigh of disbelief and frustration when Keira finally walked in. Frustration because she was alone. And disbelief because he scarcely recognised her as the same woman whose bed he had shared almost a year ago—though that lack of recognition certainly didn't seem to be affecting the powerful jerk of his groin.

Gone was the short, spiky hair and in its place was a dark curtain of silk which hung glossily down to her shoulders. And her body. He swallowed. What the hell had happened to *that*? All the angular leanness of before had gone. Suddenly she had hips—as well as the hint of a belly and breasts. It made her look softer, he thought, until he reminded himself that a woman with any degree of softness wouldn't have done what she had done.

'Matteo,' she said, her voice sounding strained—and it was then he noticed the pallor and the faint circles which darkened the skin beneath her eyes. In those fathomless pools of deepest blue he could read the vulnerability he had wanted to see, yet he felt a sudden twist of something like compassion, until he remembered what she had done.

'The very same,' he agreed grimly. 'Pleased to see me?'

'I wasn't—' She was trying to smile but failing spectacularly. 'I wasn't expecting you. I mean, not like this. Not without any warning.'

'Really? What did you imagine was going to happen, Keira? That I would just accept the news you finally saw fit to tell me and wait for your next instruction?' He walked across the room to stare out of the window and saw that a group of small boys had gathered around his limousine. He turned around and met her eyes. 'Perhaps you were hoping you wouldn't have to see me at all. Were you hoping I would remain a shadowy figure in the background and become your convenient benefactor?'

'Of course I wasn't!'

'No?' He flared his nostrils. 'Then why *bother* telling me about my son? Why now after all these months of secrecy?'

Keira tried not to flinch beneath the accusing gaze which washed over her like a harsh ebony spotlight. It was difficult enough seeing him again and registering the infuriating fact that her body had automatically started to melt, without having to face his undiluted fury.

Remember the things he said to you, she reminded herself. But the memory of his wounding words seemed to have faded and all she could think was the fact that here stood Santino's father and that, oh, the apple didn't fall far from the tree.

For here was the adult version of the little baby she'd just rocked off to sleep before the doorbell had rung. Santino was the image of his father, with his golden olive skin and dark hair, and hadn't the midwife already commented on the fact that her son was going to grow up to be a heartbreaker? Keira swallowed. Just like Matteo.

She felt an uncomfortable rush of awareness because it wasn't easy to acknowledge the stir of her body, or the fact that her senses suddenly felt as if they'd been kicked into life. Matteo's hair and his eyes seemed even blacker than she remembered and never had his sensual lips appeared more kissable. Yet surely that was the last thing she should be thinking of right now. Her mind-set should be fixed on practicalities, not foolish yearnings. She felt disappointed in herself and wondered if nature was clever enough to make a woman desire the father of her child, no matter how contemptuously he was looking at her.

She found herself wishing he'd given her some kind of warning so she could at least have washed her hair and made a bit of effort with her appearance. Since having a baby she'd developed curves and she was shamefully aware that her pre-pregnancy jeans were straining at the hips and her baggy top was deeply unflattering. But the way she looked had been the last thing on her mind. She knew she needed new clothes but she'd been forced to wait, and not just because of a chronic shortage of funds.

Because how could she possibly go shopping for clothes with a tiny infant in tow? Asking her aunt to babysit hadn't been an option—not when she was constantly made aware of their generosity in providing a home for her and her illegitimate child, and how that same child had disrupted all their lives. The truth was she hadn't wanted to spend her precious pennies on new clothes when she could be buying stuff for Santino. Which was why she was wearing an unflattering outfit, which was probably making Matteo Valenti wonder what he'd ever seen in her. Measured against his made-to-measure sophistication, Keira felt like a scruffy wrongdoer who had just been dragged before an elegant high court judge.

She forced a polite smile to her lips. 'Would you like to sit down?'

'No, I don't want to *sit down*. I want an answer to my question. Why did you contact me to tell me that I was a father? Why now?'

She flushed right up to the roots of her hair. 'Because by law I have to register his birth and that brought everything to a head. I've realised I can't go on living like this. I thought I could but I was wrong. I'm very…grateful to my aunt for taking me in but it's too cramped. They don't really want me here and I can kind of see their point.' She met his eyes. 'And I don't want Santino growing up in this kind of atmosphere.'

Santino.

As she said the child's name Matteo felt a whisper of something he didn't recognise. Something completely outside his experience. He could feel it in the icing of his skin and sudden clench of his heart. 'Santino?' he repeated, wondering if he'd misheard her. He stared at her, his brow creased in a frown. 'You gave him an Italian name?'

'Yes.'

'Why?'

'Because when I looked at him—' her voice faltered as she scraped her fingers back through her hair and turned those big sapphire eyes on him '—I knew I could call him nothing else but an Italian name.'

'Even though you sought to deny him his heritage and kept his birth hidden from me?'

She swallowed. 'You made it very clear that you never wanted to see me again, Matteo.'

'I didn't know you were pregnant at the time,' he bit out.

'And neither did I!' she shot back.

'But you knew afterwards.'

'Yes.' How could she explain the sense of alienation she'd felt—not just from him, but from everyone? When everything had seemed so *unreal* and the world had suddenly looked like a very different place. The head of Luxury Limos had said he didn't think it was a good idea if she carried on driving—not when she looked as if she was about to throw up whenever the car went over a bump. And even though she hadn't been sick—not once—and even though Keira knew that by law she could demand to stay where she was, she didn't have the energy or the funds to investigate further. What was she going to do— take him to an industrial tribunal?

She'd been terrified her boss would find out who the father of her unborn child was—because having sex with your most prestigious client was definitely a sacking offence. He'd offered her a job back in the workshop, but she had no desire to slide underneath a car and get oil all over her hands, not when such a precious bundle was growing inside her. Eventually she'd accepted a mind-numbingly dull job behind the reception desk, becoming increasingly aware that on the kind of wages she was being paid, she'd never be able to afford childcare after the birth. She'd saved every penny she could and been as frugal as she knew how, but gradually all her funds were running out and now she was in real trouble.

'Yes, I knew,' she said slowly. 'Just like I knew I ought to tell you that you were going to be a father. But every time I picked up the phone to call you, something held me back. Can't you understand?'

'Frankly, no. I can't.'

She looked him straight in the eye. 'You think those cruel words you said to me last time we spoke wouldn't matter? That you could say what you liked and it wouldn't hurt, or have consequences?'

His voice grew hard. 'I haven't come here to argue the rights and wrongs of your secrecy. I've come to see my son.'

'He's sleeping.'

'I won't wake him.' His voice grew harsh. 'You've denied me all this time and you will deny me no longer. I want to see my son, Keira, and if I have to search every room in the house to find him, then that's exactly what I'm going to do.'

It was a demand Keira couldn't ignore and not just because she didn't doubt his threat to search the small house from top to bottom. She'd seen the brief tightening of his face when she'd mentioned his child and another wave of guilt had washed over her. Because she of all people knew what it was like to grow up without a father. She knew about the gaping hole it left—a hole which could never be filled. And yet she had sought to subject her own child to that.

'Come with me,' she said huskily.

He followed her up the narrow staircase and Keira was acutely aware of his presence behind her. You couldn't ignore him, even when you couldn't see him, she thought despairingly. She could detect the heat from his body and the subtle sandalwood which was all his and, stupidly, she remembered the way that scent had clung to her skin the morning after he'd made love to her. Her heart was thundering by the time they reached the box-room she shared with Santino and she held her breath as Matteo stood frozen for a moment before moving soundlessly towards the crib. His shoulders were stiff with tension as he reached it and he was silent for so long that she started to get nervous.

'Matteo?' she said.

Matteo didn't answer. Not then. He wasn't sure he trusted himself to speak because his thoughts were in such disarray. He looked down at the baby expecting to feel the instant bolt of love people talked about when they first set eyes on their own flesh and blood, but there was nothing. He stared down at the dark fringe of eyelashes which curved on the infant's olive-hued cheeks and the shock of black hair. Tiny hands were curled into two tiny fists and he found himself leaning forward to count all the fingers, nodding his head with satisfaction as he registered each one. He felt as if he were observing himself and his reaction from a distance and realised it was possession he felt, not love. The sense that this was someone who belonged to him in a way that nobody ever had before.

His son.

He swallowed.

His *son*.

He waited for a moment before turning to Keira and he saw her dark blue eyes widen, as if she'd read something in his face she would prefer not to have seen.

'So you played God with all our futures,' he observed softly. 'By keeping him from me.'

Her gaze became laced with defiance.

'You paid me for sex.'

'I did not *pay you for sex*,' he gritted out. 'I explained my motivation in my note. You spoke of a luxury you weren't used to and I thought I would make it possible. Was that so very wrong?'

'You know very well it was!' she burst out. 'Because offering me cash was insulting. Any man would know that.'

'Was that why you tried to sell your story to the journalist, because you felt "insulted"?'

'I did not *sell my story* to anyone,' she shot back. 'Can't you imagine what it was like? I'd had sex for the first time and woke to find you gone, leaving that wretched pile of money. I walked into a charity shop to get rid of it because it felt…well, it felt tainted, if you must know.'

He grew very still. 'You gave it away?'

'Yes, I gave it away. To a worthy cause—to children living in care. Not realising I was pregnant at the time and could have used the money myself. The journalist just happened to be in the shop and overheard—and naturally she was interested. She bought me a drink and I hadn't eaten anything all day and…' She shrugged. 'I guess I told her more than I meant to.'

Matteo's eyes narrowed. If her story was true it meant she hadn't tried to grab some seedy publicity from their brief liaison. *If it was true.* Yet even if it was—did it really change anything? He was here only because her back was up against the wall and she had nowhere else to turn. His gaze swept over the too-tight jeans and baggy jumper. And this was the mother of his child, he thought, his lips curving with distaste.

He opened his mouth to speak but Santino chose that moment to start to whimper and Keira bent over the crib to scoop him up, whispering her lips against his hair and rocking him in her arms until he had grown quiet again. She looked over his head, straight into Matteo's eyes. 'Would you...would you like to hold him?'

Matteo went very still. He knew he *should* want that, but although he thought it, he still couldn't *feel* it. There was nothing but an icy lump where his heart should have been and as he looked at his son he couldn't shift that strange air of detachment.

His lack of emotional empathy had never mattered to him before—only his frustrated lovers had complained about it and that had never been reason enough to change, or even *want* to change. But now he felt like someone on a beach who had inadvertently stepped onto quicksand. As if matters were spinning beyond his control.

And he needed to assert control, just as he always did.

Of course he would hold his son when he'd got his head round the fact that he actually *had* a son. But it would be in conditions favourable to them both—not in some tiny bedroom of a strange house while Keira stood studying him with those big blue eyes.

'Not now,' he said abruptly. 'There isn't time. You need to pack your things while I call ahead and prepare for your arrival in Italy.'

'What?'

'You heard me. He isn't staying here. And since a child needs a mother, then I guess you will have to come, too.'

'What are you talking about?' She rocked the child against her breast. 'I know it's not perfect here but I can't just walk out without making any plans. We can't just go to *Italy.*'

'You can't put out a call for help and then ignore help when it comes. You telephoned me and now you must accept the consequences,' he added grimly. 'You've already implied that the atmosphere here is intolerable so I'm offering you an alternative. The only sensible alternative.' He pulled a mobile phone from the pocket of his cashmere overcoat and began to scroll down the numbers. 'For a start, you need a nursery nurse to help you.'

'I don't *need* a nurse,' she contradicted fiercely. 'Women like me don't have nurses. They look after their babies themselves.'

'Have you looked in the mirror recently?'

It was an underhand blow to someone who was already feeling acutely sensitive and once again Keira flushed. 'I'm sorry I didn't have a chance to slap on a whole load of make-up and put on a party dress!'

He shook his head. 'That wasn't what I meant. You look as if you haven't had a decent night's sleep in weeks and I'm giving you the chance to get some rest.' He forced himself to be gentle with her, even though his instinct was always to push for exactly what he wanted. And yet strangely, he felt another wave of compassion as he looked into her pale face. 'Now, we can do this one of two ways. You can fight me or you can make the best of the situation and come willingly.' His mouth flattened. 'But if you choose the former, it will be fruitless because I want this, Keira. I want it very badly. And when I want something, I usually get it. Do you believe me?'

The mulish look which entered her eyes was there for only a second before she gave a reluctant nod. 'Yes,' she said grudgingly. 'I believe you.'

'Then pack what you need and I'll wait downstairs.' He turned away but was halted by the sound of her voice.

'And when we get there, what happens then, Matteo?' she whispered. 'To Santino?' There was a pause. 'To us?'

He didn't turn back. He didn't want to look at her right then, or tell her he didn't think there was an 'us'. 'I have no crystal ball,' he ground out. 'We'll just have to make it up as we go along. Now pack your things.'

He went downstairs, and, despite telling himself that this was nothing more than a problem which needed solving, he could do nothing about the sudden and inexplicable wrench of pain in his heart. But years of practice meant he had composed himself long before he reached the tiny hallway and his face was as hard as granite as he let himself out into the rainy English day.

CHAPTER SIX

GOLDEN SUNLIGHT DANCED on her closed eyelids and warmed her skin as Keira nestled back
into the comfortable lounger. The only sounds
she could hear were birdsong and the buzz of
bees and, in the far distance, the crowing of a
cock—even though it was the middle of the day.
Hard to believe she'd left behind a rain-washed
English autumn to arrive in a country where it
was still warm enough to sit outside in October. And even harder to believe that she was at
Matteo Valenti's Umbrian estate, with its acres
of olive groves, award-winning vineyards and
breathtaking views over mountains and lake. In
his private jet, he'd announced he was bringing
her here, to his holiday home, to 'acclimatise'
herself before he introduced her to his real life
in Rome. She hadn't been sure what he meant

by that but she'd been too exhausted to raise any objections. She'd been here a week and much of that time had been spent asleep, or making sure that Santino was content. It felt like being transplanted to a luxury spa cleverly hidden within a rustic setting—with countless people working quietly in the background to maintain the estate's smooth running.

At first she'd been too preoccupied with the practical elements of settling in with her baby to worry about the emotional repercussions of being there. She'd worried about the little things, like how Matteo would react when he discovered she wasn't feeding Santino herself. Whether he would judge her negatively, as the whole world seemed to do if a woman couldn't manage to breastfeed. Was that why, in a rare moment of candour, she'd found herself explaining how ill she'd been after the birth—which meant breastfeeding hadn't been possible? She thought she'd glimpsed a brief softening of the granite-like features before his rugged features resumed their usual implacable mask.

'It will be easier that way,' he'd said, with a shrug. 'Easier for the nursery nurse.'

How *cold* he could be, she thought. Even if he was right. Because despite her earlier resistance, she was now hugely appreciative of the nursery nurse they'd employed. The very day after they'd arrived, he had produced three candidates for her to interview—top-notch women who had graduated from Italy's finest training establishment and who all spoke fluent English. After asking them about a million questions—but more importantly watching to see how well they interacted with her baby—Keira had chosen Claudia, a serene woman in her mid-thirties whom she instinctively trusted. It meant Keira got all the best bits of being a mother—cuddling and bathing her adorable son and making goo-goo noises at him as she walked him around the huge estate—while Claudia took over the dreaded three o'clock morning feed.

Which meant she could catch up with the sleep she so badly needed. She'd felt like a complete zombie when she arrived—a fact not helped by the disorientating experience of being flown to Italy on Matteo's luxury jet then being picked up by the kind of limousine which only a year ago she would have been chauffeuring. The drive to his Umbrian property had passed in a blur and Keira remembered thinking that the only time emotion had entered Matteo's voice was when they drove through the ancient gates and he began to point out centuries-old landmarks, with an unmistakable sense of pride and affection.

She almost wished Santino had been a little older so he could have appreciated the silvery ripple of olive trees, heavy with fruit and ready for harvest, and the golden pomegranates which hung from the branches like Christmas baubles. She remembered being greeted by a homely housekeeper named Paola and the delicious hot bath she took once the baby had been settled.

There had been the blissful sensation of sliding between crisp, clean sheets and laying her head on a pillow of goose-down, followed by her first full night's sleep since before the birth. And that was pretty much how she'd spent the last seven days, feeling her vitality and strength returning with each hour that passed.

'You're smiling,' came a richly accented voice from above her as a shadow suddenly blotted out the sun.

Shielding her eyes with the edge of her hand, Keira peered up to see Matteo towering over her and her smile instantly felt as if it had become frozen. She could feel her heart picking up speed and the tug of silken hunger in the base of her belly and silently she cursed the instinctive re-action of her body. Because as her strength had returned, so too had her desire for Matteo—a man who she couldn't quite decide was her jailer or her saviour. Or both.

Their paths hadn't crossed much because he'd spent much of the time working in a distant part of the enormous farmhouse. It was as if he'd unconsciously marked out different territories for them, with clear demarcation lines which couldn't be crossed. But what she'd noted above all else was the fact that he'd kept away from the nursery, using the *excuse* that his son needed to settle in before getting used to too many new people. Because that was what it had sounded like. An excuse. A reason not to touch the son he had insisted should come here.

She'd seen him, of course. Glimpses in passing, which had unsettled her. Matteo looking brooding and muscular in faded denims and a shirt as he strode about the enormous estate, conversing in rapid Italian with his workers— or wearing a knockout charcoal suit just before driving to Rome for the day and returning long after she'd gone to bed.

Another image was burnt vividly into her mind, too. She'd overslept one morning and gone straight to the nursery to find Claudia cradling Santino by the window and telling him to watch

'Papa' going down the drive. *Papa*. It was a significant word. It emphasised Matteo's importance in their lives yet brought home how little she really knew about the cold-hearted billionaire. Yet that hadn't stopped her heart from missing a beat as he'd speeded out of the estate in his gleaming scarlet sports car, had it?

'It makes me realise how rarely I see you smile,' observed Matteo, still looking down at her as he stood silhouetted by the rich October sun.

'Maybe that's because we've hardly seen one another,' said Keira, flipping on the sunglasses which had been perched on top of her head, grateful for the way they kept her expression hidden. Not for the first time, she found it almost impossible to look at the man in front of her with any degree of impartiality, but she disguised it with a cool look. 'And you're a fine one to talk about smiling. You don't exactly go around the place grinning from ear to ear, do you?'

'Perhaps our forthcoming trip to Rome might

bring a smile to both our faces,' he suggested silkily.

Ah yes, the trip to Rome. Keira felt the anxious slam of her heart. She licked her lips. 'I've been meaning to talk to you about that. Do we really have to go?'

In a movement which distractingly emphasised the jut of his narrow hips, he leaned against the sun-baked wall of the farmhouse. 'We've agreed to this, Keira. You need to see the other side of my life, not just this rural idyll. And I'm mainly based in Rome.'

'And the difference is what?'

'It's a high-octane city and nothing like as relaxed as here. When I'm there I go to restaurants and theatres. I have friends there and get invited to parties—and as the mother of my baby, I will be taking you with me.'

She sat up on the lounger, anxiety making her heart thud even harder against her ribcage. 'Why bother? Why not just leave me somewhere in the background and concentrate on forming a relationship with your son?'

'I think we have to examine all the possibilities,' he said carefully. 'And number one on that list is to work out whether we could have some kind of life together.' He lifted his brows. 'It would certainly make things a whole lot easier.'

'And you're saying I'll let you down in my current state, is that it?'

He shrugged his broad shoulders with a carelessness which wasn't very convincing. 'I think we're both aware that you don't have a suitable wardrobe for that kind of lifestyle. You can't wear jeans all the time and Paola mentioned that you only seem to have one pair of boots.'

'So Paola's been spying on me, has she?' Keira questioned, her voice dipping with disappointment that the genial housekeeper seemed to have been taking her inventory.

'Don't be absurd. She was going to clean them for you and couldn't find any others you could wear in the meantime.'

Keira scrambled up off the lounger and stared into his hard and beautiful features. He really came from a totally different planet, didn't he? One which was doubtless inhabited by women who had boots in every colour of the rainbow and not just a rather scuffed brown pair she'd bought in the sales. 'So don't take me with you,' she said flippantly. 'Leave me behind while you go out to all your fancy places and I can stay home and look after Santino, wearing my solitary pair of boots.'

A flicker of a smile touched the corners of his lips, but just as quickly it was gone. 'That isn't an option, I'm afraid,' he said smoothly. 'You're going to have to meet people. Not just my friends and the people who work for me, but my father and stepmother at some point. And my stepbrother,' he finished, his mouth twisting before his gaze fixed her with its ebony blaze. 'The way you look at the moment means you won't fit in. Not anywhere,' he continued brutally. 'And there's the chance that people will talk about you if you behave like some kind of hermit, which won't make things easy for you. Apart from anything else, we need to learn more about each other.' He hesitated. 'We are parents, with a child and a future to consider. We need to discuss the options open to us and that won't be possible if we continue to be strangers to one another.'

'You haven't bothered coming near me since we got here,' she said quietly. 'You've been keeping your distance, haven't you?'

'Can you blame me? You were almost on your knees with exhaustion when you arrived.' He paused as his eyes swept over her again. 'But you look like a different person now.'

Keira was taken aback by the way her body responded to that slow scrutiny, wondering how he could make her feel so many different things, simply by looking at her. And if that was the case, shouldn't she be protecting herself from his persuasive power over her, instead of going on a falsely intimate trip to Rome?

'I told you. I don't want to leave the baby,' she said stubbornly.

'Is that what's known as playing your trump card?' he questioned softly. 'Making me out to be some cruel tyrant who's dragging you away from your child?'

'He's only little! Not that you'd know, of course.' She paused and lifted her chin. 'You've hardly gone near him.'

Matteo acknowledged the unmistakable challenge in her voice and he felt a sudden chill ice his skin, despite the warmth of the October day. How audacious of her to interrogate him about his behaviour when her own had hardly been exemplary. By her keeping Santino's existence secret he had been presented with a baby, instead of having time to get used to the idea that he was to become a father.

Yet her pointed remark about his lack of interaction struck home, because what she said was true. He *had* kept his distance from Santino, telling himself that these things could not be rushed and needed time. And she had no right to demand anything of him, he thought bitterly. He would do things according to *his* agenda, not hers.

'Rome isn't far,' he said coolly. 'It is exactly two hundred kilometres. And I have a car constantly on standby.'

'Funnily enough that's something I *do* remember—being at your beck and call!'

'Then you will know there's no problem,' he said drily. 'Particularly as my driver is solid and reliable and not given to taking off to remote areas of the countryside in adverse weather conditions.'

'Very funny,' she said.

'We can be back here in an hour and a half should the need arise. We'll leave here at ten tomorrow morning—and be back early the next day. Less than twenty-four hours in the eternal city.' He gave a faintly cynical laugh. 'Don't women usually go weak at the knees at the prospect of an unlimited budget to spend on clothes?'

'Some women, maybe,' she said. 'Not me.'

But Keira's stubbornness was more than her determination not to become a rich man's doll. She didn't *know* about fashion—and the thought of what she might be expected to wear scared her. Perhaps if she'd been less of a tomboy, she might have flicked through glossy magazines like other women her age. She might have had some idea of what did and didn't suit her and would now be feeling a degree of excitement instead of dread. Fear suddenly became defiance and she glared at him.

'You are the bossiest man I've ever met!' she declared, pushing a handful of hair over her shoulder.

'And you are the most difficult woman I've ever encountered,' he countered. 'A little *gratitude* might go down well now and again.'

What, gratitude for his high-handedness and for making her feel stuff she'd rather not feel? Keira shook her head in frustration as she tugged her T-shirt down over her straining jeans.

'I'll be ready at ten,' she said, and went off to find Santino.

She put the baby in his smart new buggy to take him for a walk around the estate, slowly becoming aware that the weather had changed. The air had grown heavy and sultry and heavy clouds were beginning to accumulate on the horizon, like gathering troops. When eventually they returned to the farmhouse, Santino took longer than usual to settle for his sleep and Keira was feeling out of sorts when Paola came to ask whether she would be joining Signor Valenti for dinner that evening.

It was the first time she'd received such an invitation and Keira hesitated for a moment before declining. Up until now, she'd eaten her supper alone or with Claudia and she saw no reason to change that routine. She was going to be stuck with Matteo in Rome when clearly they were going to have to address some of the issues confronting them. Why waste conversation during a stilted dinner she had no desire to eat, especially when the atmosphere felt so close and heavy?

Fanning her face with her hand, she showered before bed but her skin still felt clammy, even after she'd towelled herself dry. Peering up into the sky, she thought she saw a distant flash of lightning through the thick curtain of clouds. She closed the shutters and brushed her hair before climbing into bed, but sleep stubbornly eluded her. She wished the occasional growl of thunder would produce the threatened rain and break some of the tension in the atmosphere and was just drifting off into an uneasy sleep when her wish came true. A loud clap of thunder echoed through the room and made her sit bolt upright in bed. There was a loud whoosh and heavy rain began to hurl down outside her window and quickly she got up and crept into Santino's room but, to her surprise, the baby was sound asleep.

How did he manage to do that? she thought enviously—feeling even more wide awake than before. She sighed as she went back to bed and the minutes ticked by, and all she could think about was how grim she was going to look, with dark shadowed eyes and a pasty face. Another clap of thunder made her decide that a warm drink might help relax her. And wasn't there a whole stack of herb teas in the kitchen?

To the loud tattoo of drumming rain, she crept downstairs to the kitchen with its big, old-fashioned range and lines of shiny copper pots hanging in a row. She switched on some low lighting and not for the first time found herself wistfully thinking how *homely* it looked—and how it was unlike any place she had imagined the urbane Matteo Valenti would own.

She had just made herself a cup of camomile tea when she heard a sound behind her and she jumped, her heart hammering as loudly as the rain as she turned to see Matteo standing framed in the doorway. He was wearing nothing but a pair of faded denims, which were clinging almost indecently to his long and muscular thighs.

His mouth was unsmiling but there was a gleam in his coal-dark eyes, which made awareness drift uncomfortably over her skin and suddenly Keira began to shiver uncontrollably, her nipples tightening beneath her nightshirt.

CHAPTER SEVEN

THE WALLS SEEMED to close in on her and Keira was suddenly achingly conscious of being alone in the kitchen with a half-naked Matteo, while outside she could hear the rain howl down against the shuttered windows.

With a shaking hand she put her mug down, her eyes still irresistibly drawn to the faded jeans which hugged his long and muscular thighs. He must have pulled them on in a hurry because the top button was undone, displaying a line of dark hair which arrowed tantalisingly downwards. Soft light bathed his bare and gleaming torso, emphasising washboard abs and broad shoulders.

She realised with a start that she'd never seen his naked torso before—or at least hadn't really noticed it. She'd been so blown away when they'd been having sex that her eyes hadn't seemed able to focus on anything at all. But now she could see him in all his beauty—a dark and forbidding beauty, but beauty all the same. And despite all the *stuff* between them, despite the fact that they'd been snapping at each other like crocodiles this afternoon, she could feel herself responding to him, and there didn't seem to be a thing she could do about it.

Beneath her nightshirt her nipples were growing even tighter and her breasts were heavy. She could feel a warm melting tug at her groin and the sensation was so intense that she found herself shifting her weight uncomfortably from one bare foot to the other. She opened her mouth to say something, but no words came.

He stared at her, a strange and mocking half-smile at his lips, as if he knew exactly what was happening to her. 'What's the matter, Keira?' he queried silkily. 'Can't sleep?'

She struggled to find the correct response.

To behave as anyone else would in the circumstances.

Like a woman drinking herb tea and not wishing that he would put his hand between her legs to stop this terrible aching.

'No. I can't. This wretched storm is keeping me awake.' She forced a smile. 'And neither could you, obviously.'

'I heard someone moving around in the kitchen, so I came to investigate.' He stared down at her empty cup. 'Is the tea working?'

She thought about pretending but what was the point? 'Not really,' she admitted as another crash of thunder echoed through the room. 'I'm still wide awake and I'm probably going to stay that way until the storm dies down.'

There was a pause while Matteo's gaze drifted over her and he thought how pale she looked standing there with her nightshirt brushing against her bare thighs and hair spilling like dark silk over her shoulders. Bare-footed, she looked *tiny*—a tantalising mixture of vulnerability and promise—and it felt more potent than anything he'd ever experienced. She was trying to resist him, he knew that, yet the look in her eyes told him that inside she was aching as much as he was. He knew what he was going to do because he couldn't put it off any longer, and although the voice of his conscience was sounding loud in his ears, he took no notice of it. She needed to relax a little—for all their sakes.

'Maybe you should try a little distraction technique,' he said.

Her eyes narrowed. 'Doing what?'

'Come and look at the view from my study,' he suggested evenly. 'It's spectacular at the best of times, but during a storm it's unbelievable.'

Keira hesitated because it felt as if he were inviting her into the lion's lair, but surely anything would be better than standing there feeling totally out of her depth. What else was she going to do—go back to bed and lie there feeling sorry for herself? And they were leaving for Rome tomorrow. Perhaps she should drop her guard a little. Perhaps they should start trying to be friends.

'Sure,' she said, with a shrug. 'Why not?'

His study was in a different wing of the house, which hadn't featured in the guided tour he'd given her at the beginning of the week—an upstairs room sited at the far end of a vast, beamed sitting room. She followed him into the book-lined room, her introspection vanishing the instant she saw the light show taking place outside the window. Her lips fell open as she stood watching the sky blindingly illuminated by sheet lightning, which lit up the dark outlines of the surrounding mountains. Each bright flash was reflected in the surface of the distant lake, so that the dramatic effect of what she was seeing was doubled. 'It's…amazing,' she breathed.

'Isn't it?'

He had come to stand beside her—so close that he was almost touching and Keira held her breath, wanting him to touch her, *praying* for him to touch her. Did he guess that? Was that why he slid his arm around her shoulders, his fingers beginning to massage the tense and knotted muscles?

She looked up into the hard gleam of his eyes, startled by the dark look of hunger on his face.

'Shall we put a stop to all this right now, Keira?' he murmured. 'Because we both know that the damned storm has nothing to do with our inability to sleep. It's desire, isn't it? Two people lying in their lonely beds, just longing to reach out to one another.'

His hands had slipped to her upper arms, and as his hard-boned face swam in and out of focus Keira told herself to break away and escape to the sanctuary of her room. Yet her body was stubbornly refusing to obey. All she could seem to focus on were his lips and how good it felt to have him touching her like this. She'd never stood in a storm-lit room with a half-dressed man, completely naked beneath her frumpy nightshirt, and yet she knew exactly what was going to happen next. She could feel it. Smell it. She swayed. Could almost *taste* the desire which was bombarding her senses and making her pounding heart the only thing she could hear above the loud hammer of the rain.

'Isn't that so?' he continued, brushing hair away from her face as the pad of his thumb stroked its way over her trembling lips. 'You want me to kiss you, don't you, Keira? You want it really quite badly.'

Keira resented the arrogance of that swaggering statement—but not enough to make her deny the truth behind it. 'Yes,' she said. 'Yes, I do.'

Matteo tensed, her whispered assent sharpening his already keen hunger, and he pulled her against his body and crushed his mouth over hers. And, oh, she tasted good. Better than good. Better than he remembered—but maybe that was because her kiss had lingered in his memory far longer than it should have done. He tried to go slowly but his usual patience fled as his hands began to rediscover her small and compact body. Before she had been incredibly lean—he remembered narrow hips and the bony ladder of her ribcage. But now those bones had disappeared beneath a layer of new flesh, which was soft and tempting and just ripe for licking.

Her head tipped back as he rucked up her nightshirt, his hand burrowing beneath the bunched cotton until he had bared her breast. He bent his head to take one taut rosebud in between his lips and felt her fingers digging into his bare shoulders as he grazed the sensitive areola between his teeth. Already he felt as if he wanted to explode—as if he would die if he'd didn't quickly impale her. Was the fact that she'd borne his child the reason why he was feeling a desire which felt almost *primitive* in its intensity? Was that why his hands were trembling like this?

'Do you know how long I've been wanting to do this?' he husked, his fingers sliding down between her breasts and caressing their silken weight. 'Every second of every day.'

Her reply was a muffled gasp against his mouth. 'Is that why you've stayed away from me?'

'That's exactly why.' He let his fingertips trickle down over her belly and heard her catch her breath as they travelled further downwards. 'You needed to rest and I was trying to be a... *gentleman*,' he growled.

'And how does this qualify as being...*oh*!' Her words faded away as he slid his hand between her legs, brushing over the soft fuzz of hair to find the molten heat beneath.

'You were saying?' he breathed as he dampened his finger in the soft, wet folds before starting to stroke the little bud which was already so tight.

He heard her give a shaky swallow. 'Matteo, this is...is...'

He knew exactly what it was. It was arousing her to a state where she was going to come any second, and while it was turning him on to discover how close to the edge she was—it was also making his own frustration threaten to implode. With a necessary care which defied his hungry impatience, he eased the zip of his jeans down over his straining hardness—breathing a sigh of relief as his massive erection sprang free. The denim concertinaed around his ankles but he didn't care. He knew propriety dictated he should take them off, but he couldn't. He couldn't wait, not a second longer.

Impatiently he pushed her back against his desk, shoving aside his computer and paperwork with uncharacteristic haste. And the moment the moist tip of his penis touched her, she seemed to go wild, clawing eagerly at his back—and it took more concentration than he'd ever needed to force himself to pull back. Through the distracting fog of desire, he recalled the condom concealed in a drawer of his desk and by the time it was in place he felt as excited as a teenage boy as his hungry gaze skated over her.

Like a sacrifice she lay on the desk, her arms stretched indolently above her head as he leaned over to make that first thrust deep inside her.

And this time there was no pain or hesitation. This time there was nothing but a gasped cry of pleasure as he filled her. Greedily, he sank even deeper and then he rode her—and even the crash of something falling from the desk wasn't enough to put him off his stroke. Or maybe it was just another crash of thunder from the storm outside. Who cared? He rode her until she came, her frantic convulsions starting only fractionally before his own, so that they moved in perfect time before his ragged groan heralded the end and he slumped on top of her, her hands clasped around the sweat-sheened skin of his back.

He didn't say anything at first, unwilling to shatter the unfamiliar peace he felt as he listened to the quietening of his heart. He felt spent. As if she had milked him dry. As if he could have fallen asleep right there, despite the hardness of the wooden surface. He forced himself to open his eyes and to take stock of their surroundings. Imagine if they were discovered here in the morning by one of the cleaners, or by Paola—

already surprised that, not only had he brought a woman here, but he had a baby son.

A son he had barely seen.

Guilt formed itself into an icy-cold knot deep in his chest and was enough to dissolve his lethargy. Untwining himself from Keira's arms, he moved away from the desk, bending to pull up his jeans and zip them. Only then did he stare down at her, where she lay with her eyes closed amid the debris of his wrecked desk. Her cotton nightshirt was rucked right up to expose her beautiful breasts and her legs were bent with careless abandon. The enticing gleam between her open thighs was making him grow hard again but he fought the feeling—telling himself he needed to start taking control. He would learn about his son in time—he *would*—but for now his primary purpose was to ensure that Santino remained a part of his life, and for that to happen he needed Keira onside.

So couldn't their powerful sexual chemistry work in his favour—as effective a bargaining tool as his vast wealth? Couldn't he tantalise her with a taste of what could be hers, if only she was prepared to be reasonable? Because Keira Ryan was unpredictable. She was proud and stubborn, despite the fact that she'd been depending on other people's charity for most of her life, and he was by no means certain that she would accede to his wishes. So maybe it was time to remind her just who was calling the shots. He bent and lifted her into his arms, cradling her against his chest as her eyelashes fluttered open.

'What are you doing?' she questioned drowsily.

'Taking you back to bed.'

She yawned. 'Can't we just stay here?'

He gave an emphatic shake of his head. 'No.'

Keira closed her eyes again, wanting to capture this feeling for ever—a feeling which went much deeper than sexual satisfaction, incredible though that side of it had been. She had felt so close to Matteo when he'd been deep inside her. *Scarily* close—almost as if they were two parts of the same person. Had he felt that, too? Her heart gave a little leap of hope. Couldn't they somehow make this work despite every-thing which had happened? Couldn't they?

Resting her head against his warm chest, she let him carry her through the house to her own room, not pausing until he had pulled back the duvet and deposited her in the centre of the soft bed. Only then did her eyelids flutter open, her heart missing a beat as she took in his gleam-ing torso and powerful thighs. She stared up at him hopefully. Was he going to lose the jeans and climb in beside her, so she could snuggle up against him as she so desperately wanted to do and stroke her fingers through the ruffled beauty of his black hair?

She watched as his gaze swept over her, the hectic glitter of hunger in their ebony depths unmistakable. And she waited, because surely it should be *him* asking her permission to stay? She didn't know very much about bedroom etiquette, but instinct told her that. She recognised that she'd been a bit of a pushover back there, and it was time to show the Italian tycoon that he might need to work a little harder this time.

'So?' She looked at him with what she hoped was a welcoming smile.

'That's better. You don't smile nearly enough.' His finger traced the edges of her lips as he leaned over her. 'All the bad temper of this afternoon banished in the most pleasurable way possible.' He stroked an exploratory finger over the tightening nipple beneath her nightshirt. 'Was that what you needed all along, Keira?'

It took a few moments for his meaning to sink in and when it did, Keira could hardly believe her ears. A powerful wave of hurt crashed over her. Was that all it had been? Had he made love to her as a way of soothing her ruffled emotions and making her more *amenable*? As if he were some kind of *human sedative*? She wanted to bite down hard on her clenched fist. To demand how someone so cold-blooded could possibly live with himself. But she forced herself to remain silent because only that way could she cling onto what was left of her battered pride. Why give him the satisfaction of knowing he'd hurt her? If he was going to act so carelessly, then so would she. And why be so surprised by his callous behaviour when he hadn't shown one fraction of concern for his baby son. Matteo Valenti was nothing but a manipulative and cold-blooded *bastard*, she reminded herself.

Hauling the duvet up to her chin, she closed her eyes. 'I'm tired, Matteo,' she said. 'Would you mind turning off the light as you go?'

And then, deliberately manufacturing a loud yawn, she turned her back on him.

CHAPTER EIGHT

KEIRA DIDN'T SAY a word to Matteo next morning, not until they were halfway to Rome and his powerful car had covered many miles. The fierce storm had cleared the air and the day had dawned with a sky of clear, bright blue—but the atmosphere inside the car was heavy and fraught with tension. She was still feeling the painful tug of saying goodbye to Santino, though he'd been happily cradled in Claudia's arms when the dreaded moment had arrived. But as well as the prospect of missing her baby, Keira was still smarting from what had happened the night before.

She'd woken up with a start soon after dawn, wondering why her body felt so...

Slowly she had registered her lazy lethargy and the sweet aching between her legs.

So…*used.*

Yes, used, that was it. *Used.* Vivid images had flashed through her mind as she remembered what had happened while the storm raged outside. Matteo unzipping his jeans and pushing her onto his desk. Matteo rucking up her nightdress before thrusting into her and making her cry out with pleasure. It had hardly been the stuff of fairy tales, had it? So why not concentrate on the reality, rather than the dumb romantic version she'd talked herself into when she was lying quivering beneath his sweat-sheened body?

He had cold-bloodedly seduced her after days of acting as if she didn't exist. He had invited her to witness the storm from the best vantage point in the house and, although it had been the corniest request in the world, she had agreed. Trotting behind him like some kind of puppy dog, she'd had sex with him. Again. Keira closed her eyes in horror as she remembered the way she'd clawed at his bare back like some kind of wildcat. Did her inexperience explain the fierce hunger which had consumed her and made her unable to resist his advances? Or was it just that Matteo Valenti only had to touch her for her to come apart in his arms?

And now the trip to Rome, which she'd already been dreading, was going to be a whole lot worse. Bad enough being in the kind of car she'd lusted after during her days as a mechanic—and having it driven by *someone else*—without the knowledge of how smug Matteo must be feeling. Why, he hadn't even wanted to spend the night with her! He'd just deposited her in her bed like some unwanted package and behaved as if what had happened had been purely functional. Like somebody scratching an itch. Was that how it had been for him, she wondered bitterly? Had he seen her as a body rather than a person?

'So, are you going to spend the next twenty-four hours ignoring me?' Matteo's voice broke into her rebellious thoughts as they passed a signpost to a pretty-looking place called Civita Castellana.

Keira wanted to pretend she hadn't heard him but that was hardly the way forward, was it? She mightn't be happy with the current state of affairs, but that didn't mean she had to lie down and passively accept it. Unless she was planning on behaving like some sort of victim—allowing the powerful tycoon to pick her up and move her around at will, without her having any say in the matter. It was time she started asserting herself and stopped beating herself up. They'd had sex together as two consenting adults and surely that put them on some kind of equal footing.

So *ask* him.

Take some of the control back.

She turned her head to look at his profile, trying not to feel affected by that proud Roman nose and the strong curve of his shadowed jaw. His silk shirt was unbuttoned at the neck, offering a tantalising glimpse of olive skin, and he exuded a vitality which made him seem to glow with life. She could feel a trickle of awareness whispering over her body and it made her want to fidget on the plush leather car seat.

She wanted him to touch her all over again. And when he touched her she went to pieces.

Firmly pushing all erotic possibilities from her mind, she cleared her throat. 'So why this trip, Matteo?'

There was a pause. 'You know why. We've discussed this. We're going to buy you some pretty clothes to wear.'

His words were deeply patronising and she wondered if that had been his intention—reminding her that she fell way short of his ideal of what a woman should be. 'I'm not talking about your determination to change my appearance,' she said. 'I mean, why bring me to Italy in the first place? That's something we haven't even discussed. What's going to happen once you've waved your magic wand and turned me into someone different? Are you planning to return me to England in your fancy plane and make like this was all some kind of dream?'

His mouth hardened into a flat and implacable line. 'That isn't an option.'

'Then what *are* the options?' she questioned quietly.

Matteo put his foot down on the accelerator and felt the powerful engine respond. It was a reasonable question, though not one he particularly wanted to answer. But he couldn't keep on putting off a conversation they needed to have because he was wary of all the stuff it might throw up. 'We need to see whether we can make it work as a couple.'

'A *couple*?'

He saw her slap her palms down on her denim-covered thighs in a gesture of frustration.

'You mean, living in separate parts of the same house? How is that in any way what a *couple* would do?' She sucked in a breath. 'Why, we've barely *seen* one another—and when we have, it isn't as if we've done much talking!'

'That can be worked on,' he said carefully.

'Then let's start working on it right now. Couples aren't complete strangers to one another and we are. Or at least, you are. I told you a lot about my circumstances on the night we…' Her voice wavered as she corrected herself before growing quieter. 'On that night we spent together in Devon. But I don't know you, Matteo. I still don't really know anything about you.'

Matteo stared at the road ahead. Women always asked these kinds of questions and usually he cut them short. With a deceptively airy sense of finality, he'd make it clear that he wouldn't tolerate any further interrogation because he didn't want anyone trying to 'understand' him. But he recognised that Keira was different and their situation was different. She was the mother of his child and she'd given birth to his heir— not some socially ambitious woman itching to get his ring on her finger. He owed her this.

'What do you want to know?' he questioned.

She shrugged. 'All the usual stuff. About your parents. Whether or not you have any brothers or sisters. That kind of thing.'

'I have a father and a stepmother. No siblings,' he said, his voice growing automatically harsher and there wasn't a damned thing he could do to stop it. 'But I have a stepbrother who's married, with a small child.'

He could feel her eyes on him. 'So your parents are divorced?'

'No. My mother is dead.'

'Like mine,' she said thoughtfully.

He nodded but didn't say anything, his attention fixed on the road ahead, trying to concentrate on the traffic and not on the bleak landscape of loss.

'Tell me about your father,' she said. 'Do you get on well with him?'

Some of the tension left his body as he overtook a truck and he waited until he had finished the manoeuvre before answering. He wondered if he should give her the official version of his life, thus maintaining the myth that all was well. But if she stayed then she would soon discover the undercurrents which surged beneath the surface of the powerful Valenti clan.

'We aren't close, no. We see each other from time to time, more out of duty than anything else.'

'But you mentioned a stepmother?'

'You mean the latest stepmother?' he questioned cynically. 'Number four in a long line of women who were brought in to try to replace the wife he lost.'

'But…' She hesitated. 'None of them were able to do that?'

'That depends on your definition. I'm sure each of them provided him with the creature comforts most men need, though each marriage ended acrimoniously and at great financial cost to him. That's the way it goes, I guess.' His hands tightened around the steering wheel. 'But my mother would have been a hard act for any woman to follow—at least according to the people who knew her.'

'What was she like?' she prompted, and her

voice was as gentle as he'd ever imagined a voice could be.

Matteo didn't answer for a long time because this was something nobody ever really asked. A dead mother was just that. History. He couldn't remember anyone else who'd ever shown any interest in her short life. He could feel the tight squeeze of his heart. 'She was beautiful,' he said eventually. 'Both inside and out. She was training to be a doctor when she met my father—an only child from a very traditional Umbrian family who owned a great estate in the region.'

'The farmhouse where we've been staying?' she questioned slowly. 'Is that…?'

He nodded. 'Was where she grew up, *sì*.'

Keira nodded as slowly she began to understand. She gazed out of the window at the blue bowl of the sky. Did that explain his obvious love for the estate? she wondered. The last earthly link to his mum?

'Does your father know?' she questioned suddenly. 'About Santino?'

'Nobody knows,' he said harshly. 'And I won't let it be known until we've come to some kind of united decision about the future.'

'But a baby isn't really the kind of thing you can keep secret. Won't someone from the farm have told him? One of the staff?'

He shook his head. 'Discretion is an essential quality for all the people who work for me and their first loyalty is to me. Anyway, my father isn't interested in the estate, only as…'

'Only as what?' she prompted, her curiosity sharpened by the harsh note which had suddenly entered his voice.

'Nothing. It doesn't matter. And I think we've had enough questions for today, don't you?' he drawled. He lifted one hand from the steering wheel to point straight ahead. 'We're skirting Rome now and if you look over there you'll soon be able to see Lake Nemi.'

Her gaze followed the direction of his finger as she tried to concentrate. 'And that's where you live?'

'That's where I live,' he agreed.

They didn't say much for the rest of the journey, but at least Keira felt she knew a little more about him. And yet it was only a little. He had the air of the enigma about him. Something at the very core of him which was dark and unknowable and which seemed to keep her at arm's length. Behind that formidable and sexy exterior lay a damaged man, she realised—and something about his inner darkness made her heart go out to him. *Could* they make it as a couple? she wondered as they drove through a beautiful sheltered valley and she saw the silver gleam of the lake. Would she be a fool to want that?

But the stupid thing was that, yes, she did want that, because if Santino was to have any kind of security—the kind she'd always longed for— then it would work best if they *were* a couple. Her living with Matteo Valenti as his lover and mother to his son…would that be such a bad thing?

Her daydreaming was cut short by her first

sight of Matteo's villa and she began to wonder if she was crazy to ever imagine she would fit in here. Overlooking Lake Nemi, the apricot-coloured house was three storeys high, with high curved windows overlooking acres of beautifully tended gardens. And she soon discovered that inside were countless rooms, including a marble-floored dining room and a ballroom complete with a lavish hand-painted ceiling. It felt more like being shown round a museum than a house. Never had her coat felt more threadbare or the cuffs more frayed as it was plucked from her nerveless fingers by a stern-faced butler named Roberto, who seemed to regard her with complete indifference. Was he wondering why his powerful employer had brought such a scruffy woman to this palace of a place? Keira swallowed. Wasn't she wondering the same thing herself?

After ringing the farmhouse and being told by Paola that Santino was lying contentedly in his pram in the garden, Keira accepted the tiny cup of espresso offered by a maid in full uniform and sat down on a stiff and elegant chair to drink it. Trying to ignore the watchful darkness of Matteo's eyes, she found herself thinking about the relaxed comfort of the farmhouse and felt a pang as she thought about her son, wondering if he would be missing his mama. As she drank her coffee she found herself glancing around at the beautiful but cavernous room and suppressed a shiver, wondering how much it must cost to heat a place this size.

'Why do you live here?' she questioned suddenly, lifting her gaze to the dark figure of the man who stood beside the vast fireplace.

He narrowed his eyes. 'Why wouldn't I? It has a fresher climate than the city, particularly in the summer months when it can get very hot. And it's a valuable piece of real estate.'

'I don't doubt it.' She licked her lips. 'But it's *enormous* for just one person! Don't you rattle around in it?'

'I'm not a total hermit, Keira,' he said drily.

'Sometimes I work from here—and, of course, I entertain.'

The question sprang from her lips before she could stop it. 'And bring back loads of women, I expect?'

The look he shot her was mocking. 'Do you want me to create the illusion that I've been living a celibate life all these years?' he asked softly. 'If sexual jealousy was the reason behind your question?'

'It wasn't!' she denied, furious with herself for having asked it. Of *course* Matteo would have had hundreds of women streaming through these doors—and it wasn't as if he were her *boyfriend*, was it? Her cheeks grew red. He never had been. He was just a man who could make her melt with a single look, no matter how much she fought against it. A man who had impregnated her without meaning to. And now he was observing her with that sexy smile, as if he knew exactly what she was thinking. As if he was perfectly aware that beneath her drab, chain-store sweater her breasts were hungering to feel his mouth on them again. She could feel her cheeks growing warm as she watched him answer his mobile phone to speak in rapid Italian and when he'd terminated the call he turned to look at her, his hard black eyes scanning over her.

'The car is outside waiting to take you into the city centre,' he said. 'And the stylist will meet you there.'

'A stylist?' she echoed, her gaze flickering uncertainly to her scuffed brown boots.

'A very famous stylist who's going to take you shopping.' He shrugged. 'I thought you might need a little guidance.'

His condescension only intensified Keira's growing feelings of inadequacy and she glared at him. 'What, in case I opt for something which is deeply unsuitable?'

His voice was smooth. 'There is a different way of looking at it, Keira. I don't expect you've been given unlimited use of a credit card before, have you?'

Something in the way he said it was making Keira's blood boil. 'Funnily enough, no!'

'So what's the problem?'

'The problem is *you*! I bet you're just loving this,' she accused. 'Does flashing your wealth give you a feeling of power, Matteo?'

He raised his eyebrows. 'Actually, I was hoping it might give you a modicum of pleasure. So why don't you go upstairs and freshen up before the car takes you into the city?'

Keira put her empty cup down on a spindly gold-edged table and rose to her feet. 'Very well,' she said, forcing her stiff shoulders into a shrug.

'By the way,' he said as he gestured for her to precede him, 'I notice you didn't make any comment about my driving on the way here.'

'I thought it might be wise, in the circumstances.'

'But as a professional, you judged me favourably, I hope?'

She pursed her lips together. 'You were okay.

A little heavy on the clutch, perhaps—but it's a great car.'

She took a stupid and disproportionate pleasure from the answering humour which gleamed from his eyes before following him up a sweeping staircase into a sumptuous suite furnished in rich brocades and velvets, where he left her. Alone in the ballroom-sized bathroom, where water gushed from golden taps, Keira dragged the hairbrush through her hair, wondering what on earth the stylist was going to think about being presented with such unpromising raw material.

But the stylist was upbeat and friendly—even if the store on the Via dei Condotti was slightly terrifying. Keira had never been inside such an expensive shop before—although in her chauffeuring days she'd sat outside places like it often enough, waiting for her clients. A slim-hipped woman named Leola came forward to greet her, dressed in an immaculate cream dress accessorised with gleaming golden jewellery and high-heeled patent shoes. Although she looked as if she'd stepped straight off the catwalk, to her credit, she didn't seem at all fazed by Keira's appearance, as she led her around the shop and swished her fingertips over rail after rail of clothes.

In the chandelier-lit changing room, she whipped a tape measure around Keira's newly abundant curves. 'You have a fantastic figure,' she purred. 'Let's show it off a little more, shall we?'

'I'd rather not, if you don't mind,' said Keira quickly. 'I don't like to be stared at.'

Leola raised perfectly plucked black eyebrows by a centimetre. 'You are dating one of the city's most eligible bachelors,' she observed quietly. 'And Matteo will expect people to stare at you.'

Keira felt a shimmer of anxiety as she tugged a blue cashmere dress over her head and pulled on some navy-blue suede boots. What possible response could she make to that? What would the stunning Leola say if she explained that she and

Matteo weren't 'dating', but simply parents to a darling little boy? And even that wasn't really accurate, was it? You couldn't really describe a man as a parent when he regarded his newborn infant with the caution which an army expert might display towards an unexploded bomb.

Just go with the flow, she told herself. Be amenable and do what's suggested—and after you've been dressed up like a Christmas turkey, you can sit down with the Italian tycoon and talk seriously about the future.

She tried on hip-hugging skirts with filmy blouses, flirty little day dresses and sinuous evening gowns, and Keira was reeling by the time Leola had finished with her. She wanted to protest that there was no way she would wear most of these—that she and Matteo hadn't even discussed how long she would be staying—but Leola seemed to be acting on someone else's orders and it wasn't difficult to work out whose orders they might be.

'I will have new lingerie and more shoes sent

by courier to arrive later,' the stylist explained, 'since I understand you're returning to Umbria tomorrow. But you certainly have enough to be going on with. Might I suggest you wear the red dress this evening? Matteo was very specific about how good he thought you would look in vibrant colours. Oh, and a make-up artist will be visiting the house later this afternoon. She will also be able to fix your hair.'

Keira stared at the slippery gown of silk-satin which was being dangled from Leola's finger and shook her head. 'I can do my own hair,' she said defensively, wondering if dressing up in all this finery was what Matteo usually expected for dinner at home on a weekday evening. 'And I can't possibly wear that—it's much too revealing.'

'Yes, you can—and you must—because you look amazing in it,' said Leola firmly, before her voice softened a little. 'Matteo must care for you a great deal to go to so much trouble. And surely it would be unwise to displease him when he's gone to so much trouble.'

It was a candid remark which contained in it a trace of warning. It was one woman saying to another—don't look a gift horse in the mouth. But all it did was to increase Keira's sensation of someone playing dress-up. Of being moulded for a role in the billionaire's life which she wasn't sure she was capable of filling. Her heart was pounding nervously as she shook the stylist's hand and went outside to the waiting car.

And didn't she feel slightly ashamed at the ease with which she allowed the chauffeur to open the door for her as she slid onto the squishy comfort of the back seat? As if already she was turning into someone she didn't recognise.

CHAPTER NINE

THE CLOCK WAS striking seven and Matteo gave a click of impatience as he paced the drawing room, where an enormous fire crackled and burned. Where the hell *was* she? He didn't like to be kept waiting—not by anyone, and especially not by a woman who ought to have been bang on time and full of gratitude for his generosity towards her. He wondered how long it would have taken Keira to discover how much she liked trying on lavish clothes. Or how quickly she'd decided it was a turn-on when a man was prepared to buy you an entire new wardrobe, with no expense spared. He was just about to send Roberto upstairs to remind her of the time, when the door opened and there she stood, pale-faced and slightly uncertain.

Matteo's heart pounded hard in his chest because she looked… He shook his head slightly as if to clear his vision, but the image didn't alter. She looked *unrecognisable*. Light curls of glossy black tumbled over her narrow shoulders and, with mascara and eyeliner, her sapphire eyes looked enormous. Her lips were as red as her dress and he found himself wanting to kiss away her unfamiliar lipstick. But it was her body which commanded the most attention. *Santo cielo!* What a body! Scarlet silk clung to the creamy curve of her breasts, the material gliding in over the indentation of her waist, then flaring gently over her hips. Sheer stockings encased her legs and skyscraper heels meant she looked much taller than usual.

He swallowed because the transformation was exactly what he'd wanted—a woman on his arm who would turn heads for all the *right* reasons—and yet now he was left with intense frustration pulsing through his veins. He wanted to call their host and cancel and to take her straight to bed instead, but he was aware that such a move would be unwise. He had less than twenty-four hours to get Keira Ryan to agree to his plan— and that would not be achieved by putting lust before logic.

'You look…beautiful,' he said unsteadily, noticing how pink her cheeks had grown in response to his compliment, and he was reminded once again of her innocence and inexperience.

She tugged at the skirt of the dress as if trying to lengthen it. 'I feel a bit underdressed, to be honest.'

He shook his head. 'If that were the case then I certainly wouldn't let you leave the house.'

She raised her eyebrows. 'What, you mean you'd keep me here by force? Prisoner of the Italian tycoon?'

He smiled. 'I've always found persuasion to be far more effective than force. I assume Leola organised a suitable coat for you to wear?'

'A coat?' She stared at him blankly.

'It's November, Keira, and we're going to a

party in the city. It might be warmer than back in England, but you'll still need to wrap up.'

Keira's stomach did a flip. 'You didn't mention a party.'

'Didn't I? Well, I'm mentioning it now.'

She gave the dress another tug. 'Whose party is it?'

'An old friend of mine. Salvatore di Luca. It's his birthday—and it will be the perfect opportunity for you to meet people. It would be a pity for you not to have an audience when you look so very dazzling.' His gaze travelled over her and his voice thickened. 'So why not go and get your coat? The car's waiting.'

Keira felt nerves wash over her. She was tempted to tell him she'd rather stay home and eat a *panino* in front of the fire, instead of having to face a roomful of strangers—but she was afraid of coming over as some kind of social misfit. Was this some strange kind of interview to assess whether or not she would be up to the task of being Matteo's partner? To see if she was capable of making conversation with his wealthy friends, of getting through a whole evening without dropping a canapé down the front of her dress?

Her black velvet swing coat was lined with softest cashmere and Keira hugged it around herself as the driver opened the door of the waiting limousine, her heart missing a beat as Matteo slid onto the seat beside her. His potent masculinity was almost as distracting as the dark suit which fitted his muscular body to perfection and made him look like some kind of movie star on his way to an awards ceremony. 'You aren't driving, then?' she observed.

'Not tonight. I have a few calls I need to make.' His black eyes gleamed. 'After that I'm exclusively yours.'

The way he said it sent ripples of excitement whispering over her skin and she wondered if that had been deliberate. But there was apprehension too because Keira wasn't sure she would be able to cope with the full blaze of his undi-

vided attention. Not when he was being so…
nice to her.

She suspected he was on his best behaviour
because he wanted her to agree to his master-
plan—whenever he got around to unveiling it.
And although he hadn't shown any desire to parent their son, something told her that he saw
Santino as his possession, even if so far he had
exhibited no signs of love. Because of that, she
suspected he wouldn't let her go easily and the
stupid part was that she didn't want him to. She
was beginning to recognise that she was out
of her depth—and not just because he was a
billionaire hotelier and she a one-time car mechanic. She didn't have any experience of relationships and she didn't have a clue how to react
to him. Part of her wished she were still in the
driver's seat, negotiating the roads with a slick
professionalism she'd been proud of until she'd
ruined her career in the arms of the man who
sat beside her, his long legs stretched indolently
in front of him.

She forced herself to drag her eyes away from the taut tension of his thighs—and at least there was plenty to distract her as she gazed out of the window at the lights of the city and the stunning Roman architecture, which made her feel as if she'd fallen straight into the pages of a guide book.

Salvatore de Luca's apartment was in the centre of it all—a penthouse situated close to the Via del Corso and offering commanding views of the city centre. Keira was dimly aware of a maid taking her coat and a cocktail being pressed into her hand and lots of people milling around. To her horror she could see that every other woman was wearing elegant black and her own expensive scarlet dress made her feel like something which had fallen off the Christmas tree. And it wasn't just the colour. She wasn't used to displaying a hint of cleavage, or wearing a dress which came this high above the knee. She felt like an imposter—someone who'd been more at home with her hair hidden beneath that peaked hat, instead of cascading over her shoulders like this.

She saw a couple of the men give her glances which lingered more than they should have done—or was that just something Italian men did automatically? Certainly, Matteo seemed to be watching her closely as he introduced her to a dizzying array of friends and she couldn't deny the thrill it gave her to feel those dark eyes following her every move.

Keira did her best to chat animatedly, hugely grateful that nearly everybody spoke perfect English, but conversation wasn't easy. She was glaringly aware of not mentioning the one subject which was embedded deeply in her heart and that was Santino. She wondered when Matteo was planning to announce that he was a father and what would happen when he did. Did any of his friends have children? she wondered. This apartment certainly didn't look child-friendly and she couldn't imagine a toddler crawling around on these priceless rugs, with sticky fingers.

Escaping from the growing pitch of noise to the washroom, Keira took advantage of the relative calm and began to peep into some of the rooms on her way back to the party. Entering only those with open doors, she discovered a bewildering number of hand-painted salons which reminded her of Matteo's villa. His home wasn't exactly child-friendly either, was it?

The room she liked best was small and book-lined—not because she was the world's greatest reader but because it opened out onto a lovely balcony with tall green plants in pots and fabulous views over the glittering city. She stood there for a moment with her arms resting on the balustrade when she heard the clip-clop of heels enter the room behind her and she turned to see a tall redhead who she hadn't noticed before. Maybe she was a late arrival, because she certainly wasn't the kind of woman you would forget in a hurry. Her green gaze was searching rather than friendly and Keira had to concentrate very hard not to be fixated on the row of emeralds which gleamed at her slender throat and matched her eyes perfectly.

'So *you're* the woman who's been keeping Matteo off the scene,' the woman said, her soft Italian accent making her sound like someone who could have a very lucrative career in radio voice-overs.

Keira left the chilly balcony and stepped into the room. 'Hello, I'm Keira.' She smiled. 'And you are?'

'Donatella.' Her green eyes narrowed, as if she was surprised that Keira didn't already know this. 'Your dress is very beautiful.'

'Thank you.'

There was a pause as Donatella's gaze flickered over her. 'Everyone is curious to know how you've managed to snare Italy's most elusive bachelor.'

'He's not a rabbit!' joked Keira.

Either Donatella didn't get the joke or she'd decided it wasn't funny because she didn't smile. 'So when did you two first meet?'

Aware of the sudden race of her heart, Keira suddenly felt *intimidated*. As if she was being backed into a corner, only she didn't know why. 'Just under a year ago.'

'When, exactly?' probed the redhead.

Keira wasn't the most experienced person when it came to social etiquette, but even she could work out when somebody was crossing the line. 'Does it really matter?'

'I'm curious, that's all. It wouldn't happen to have been two nights before Christmas, would it?'

The date was burned so vividly on Keira's memory that the affirmation burst from her lips without her even thinking about it. 'Yes, it was,' she said. 'How on earth did you know that?'

'Because he was supposed to be meeting me that night,' said Donatella, with a wry smile. 'And then I got a call from his assistant to say his plane couldn't take off because of the snow.'

'That's true. The weather was terrible,' said Keira.

'And then, when he got back—nothing. Complete radio silence—even though the word was out that there was nobody else on the scene.' Donatella's green eyes narrowed thoughtfully. 'Interesting. You're not what I expected.'

Even though she hadn't eaten any of the canapés which had been doing the rounds, Keira suddenly felt sick. All she could think about was the fact that another woman had been waiting for Matteo while he'd been in bed with *her*. He must have had his assistant call Donatella while she'd been in the bath and then preceded to seduce *her*. Had it been a case of *any* woman would do as a recipient of all that hard hunger? A man who'd been intent on sex and was determined not to have his wishes thwarted? What if all that stuff about not finding her attractive had simply been the seasoned technique of an expert who'd recognised that he needed to get her to relax before leaping on her. She swallowed. Had he been imagining it was Donatella beneath him instead of her?

'Well, you know what they say…there's no accounting for taste.' From somewhere Keira dredged up a smile. 'Great meeting you, Donatella.'

But she was trembling by the time she located Matteo, surrounded by a group of men and women who were hanging onto his every word, and maybe he read something in her face because he instantly disengaged himself and came over to her side.

'Everything okay?' he questioned.

'Absolutely lovely,' she said brightly, for the benefit of the onlookers. 'But I'd like to go now, if you wouldn't mind. I'm awfully tired.'

His dark brows lifted. '*Certamente.* Come, let us slip away, *cara.*'

The practised ease with which the meaningless endearment fell from his lips made Donatella's words seem even more potent and in the car Keira sat as far away from him as possible, placing her finger on her lips and shaking her head when he tried to talk to her. She felt stupidly emotional and close to tears but there was no way she was going to break down in front of his driver. She knew better than most how domestic upsets could liven up a sometimes predictable job and that a chauffeur had a front-row seat to these kinds of drama. It wasn't until they were back in the villa, where a fire in the drawing room had obviously been kept banked for their return, that she turned to Matteo at last, trying to keep the edge of hysteria from her voice.

'I met Donatella,' she said.

'I wondered if you would. She arrived late.'

'I don't give a damn when she arrived!' She flung her sparkly scarlet clutch bag down onto a brocade sofa where it bounced against a tasselled cushion. 'She told me you were supposed to be meeting her the night we got stuck in the snow!'

'That much is true.'

She was so horrified by his easy agreement that Keira could barely choke out her next words. 'So you were in a sexual relationship with another woman when you seduced me?'

He shook his head. 'No, I was not. I'd been dating her for a few weeks, but it had never progressed beyond dinner and the occasional trip to the opera.'

'And you expect me to believe that?'

'Why wouldn't you believe it, Keira?'

'Because...' She sucked in a deep breath. 'Because you didn't strike me as the kind of man who would chastely court a woman like that.'

'Strangely enough, that's how I like to operate.'

'But not with me,' she said bitterly. 'Or maybe you just didn't think I was worth buying dinner for.'

Matteo tensed as he read the hurt and shame which clouded her sapphire eyes and was surprised how bad it made him feel. He knew he owed her an explanation but he sensed that this went deeper than anything he'd had to talk his way out of in the past, and part of him rebelled at having to lay his thoughts open. But he sensed there was no alternative. That despite the ease with which she had fallen into his arms, Keira Ryan was no pushover.

'Oh, you were worth it, all right,' he said softly. 'Just because we didn't do the conventional thing of having dinner doesn't change the fact that it was the most unforgettable night of my life.'

'Don't tell me lies!'

'It isn't a lie, Keira,' he said simply. 'It was amazing. We both know that.'

He saw her face working, as if she was struggling to contain her emotions.

'And then,' she said, on a gulp, 'when you got back—she says you didn't see her again.'

'Again, true.'

'Why not?' she demanded. 'There was nothing stopping you. Especially after you'd given me the heave-ho.'

If he was surprised by her persistence he didn't show it and Matteo felt conflicted about how far to go with his answer. Mightn't it be brutal to explain that he'd been so appalled at his recklessness that night that he'd decided he needed a break from women? If he told her that he'd never had a one-night stand before, because it went against everything he believed in, mightn't it hurt her more than was necessary? He didn't believe in love—not for him—but he believed in passion and, in his experience, it was always worth the wait. Deferred gratification increased the appetite and made seduction sweeter. And delaying his own pleasure reinforced his certainty that he was always in control.

Yet his usual fastidiousness had deserted him that snowy night when he'd found himself in bed with his petite driver, and it had affected him long after he'd returned to Italy. It wasn't an admission he particularly wanted to make but something told him it would work well in his favour if he did. What was it the Americans said? Ah, *sì*. It would buy him brownie points. 'I haven't had sex with anyone since the night I spent with you. Well, until last night,' he said.

Her eyes widened and the silence of the room

was broken only by the loud ticking of the clock before she blurted out a single word.

'*Why?*' she breathed.

He bent to throw an unnecessary log onto the already blazing fire before straightening up to face the dazed disbelief which had darkened her eyes. He had tried convincing himself it had been self-disgust which had made him retreat into his shell when he'd returned to Rome, but deep down he'd known that wasn't the whole story.

'Because, annoyingly, I couldn't seem to shift you from my mind,' he drawled. 'And before you start shaking your head like that and telling me I don't mean it, let me assure you I do.'

'But why?' she questioned. 'I mean, why me?'

He paused long enough to let her know that he'd asked himself the same question. 'Who knows the subtle alchemy behind these things?' He shrugged, his gaze roving over her as he drank in the creamy curves of her flesh. 'Maybe because you were different. Because you spoke to me in a way that people usually don't. Or maybe because you were a virgin and on some subliminal level I understood that and it appealed to me. Why are you looking at me that way, Keira? You think that kind of thing doesn't matter? That a man doesn't feel an incomparable thrill of pleasure to discover that he is the first and the only one? Then you are very wrong.'

Keira felt faint and sank down onto the brocade sofa, next to her discarded clutch bag. His words were shockingly old-fashioned but that didn't lessen their impact on her, did it? It didn't stop her from feeling incredibly *desired* as his black gaze skated over her body and hinted at the things he might like to do to her.

Did her lips open of their own accord or did he somehow orchestrate her reaction from his position by the fireplace—like some puppet master twitching invisible strings? Was that why a hard gleam suddenly entered his eyes as he walked towards her and pulled her to her feet.

'I think we're done with talking, don't you?'

he questioned unsteadily. 'Haven't I answered all your questions and told you everything you need to know?'

'Matteo, I—'

'I'm going to make love to you again,' he said, cutting right through her protest. 'Only this time it's going to be in a bed and it's going to be all night long. And please don't pretend you're outraged by the idea, when the look on your face says otherwise.'

'Or maybe you're just going to do it to pacify me?' she challenged. 'Like you did last night.'

'Last night we were in the middle of a howling storm and I wasn't really thinking straight, but today I am.'

And with that he lifted her up into his arms and swept her from the room and it occurred to Keira that no way would she have objected to such masterful treatment, even if he *had* given her the option. Because wasn't he making her feel like a woman who was completely desired—a woman for whom nothing but pleasure beckoned? Up the curving marble staircase he carried her, her ear pressed closely to his chest so she could hear the thundering of his heart. It felt like something from a film as he kicked the bedroom door shut behind them. Unreal. Just as the excitement coursing through her body felt unreal. Was it wrong to feel this rush of hungry pleasure as Matteo unzipped the scarlet dress and let it fall carelessly onto the silken rug? Or for her to gasp out words of encouragement from lips soon swollen by the pressure of his kiss?

Her bra swiftly followed and she gave a squeal of protesting pleasure as he hooked his fingers into the edges of her panties and ripped them apart and didn't that thrill her, too? Showing similar disregard for his own clothes, he tore them from his body like a man with the hounds of hell snapping at his ankles. But once they were both naked on the bed, he slowed things right down.

'These curves,' he said unevenly as his fingertips trickled over her breasts and hips.

'You don't like them?' she questioned breathlessly.

'Whatever gave you that idea? I seem to like you lean and I seem to like you rounded. Any way at all is okay with me, Keira.'

Slowly, he ran his fingertip from neck to belly before sliding it down between her thighs, nudging it lightly against her wet heat in a lazy and rhythmical movement. She shivered and had to stifle a frustrated moan as he moved his hand away. But then his mouth began to follow the same path as his fingers and Keira held her breath as she felt his lips acquainting themselves with the soft tangle of hair at her groin before he burrowed his head deep between her legs and made that first unbelievable flick of his tongue against her slick and heated flesh.

'Matteo!' she gasped, almost shooting off the bed with pleasure. 'What…what are you doing?'

He lifted his head and she saw pure devilry in his black eyes. 'I'm going to eat you, *cara mia,*' he purred, before bending his head to resume his task.

Keira let her head fall helplessly back against the pillow as he worked sweet magic with his tongue, loving the way he imprisoned her wriggling hips with the firm clamp of his hands. She came so quickly that it took her by surprise—as did the sudden way he moved over her to thrust deep inside her, while her body was still racked with those delicious spasms. She clung to his shoulders as he started a sweet, sure rhythm which set senses singing.

But suddenly his face hardened as he grew still inside her. 'How long do you think I can stop myself from coming?' he husked.

'Do you…?' She could barely get the words out when he was filling her like this. 'Do you *have* to stop yourself?'

'That depends. I do if you're going to have a second orgasm, which is my intention,' he murmured. 'In fact, I'm planning to make you come so often that you'll have lost count by the morning.'

'Oh, Matteo.' She closed her eyes as he levered himself to his knees and went even deeper.

She moaned as the finger moved between their joined bodies to alight on the tight nub between her legs and began to rub against her while he was deep inside her. The pleasure it gave her was almost too much to bear and it felt as if she were going to come apart at the seams. She gasped as pleasure and pressure combined in an unstoppable force. Until everything splintered around her. She heard him groan as his own body starting to convulse before eventually collapsing on top of her, his head resting on her shoulder and his shuddered breath hot and rapid against her neck.

His arms tightened around her waist and for countless seconds Keira felt as if she were floating on a cloud. Had he really told her he hadn't slept with anyone else because he hadn't been able to get her out of his mind? Yes, he had. With a sigh of satisfaction, she rested her cheek against his shoulder and he murmured something soft in Italian in response.

She lay there for a long time after he'd fallen asleep, thinking that sex could blind you to the truth. Or maybe lull you into such a stupefied state that you stopped seeking the truth. He'd commented on her curves and admired them with his hands, but he'd made no mention of *why* her body had undergone such a dramatic transformation. She bit her lip. Because she'd carried his son and given birth to him—a fact he seemed to find all too easy to forget.

And she thought how—despite the heart-stopping intimacy of what had just taken place—she still didn't know Matteo at all.

CHAPTER TEN

SHE HAD TO say something. She *had* to. She couldn't keep pretending nothing was wrong or that there weren't still a million questions buzzing around in her head which needed answering.

Keira turned her head to look at the face of the man who lay sleeping beside her. It was a very big bed, which was probably a good thing since Matteo Valenti's naked body was taking up most of it. Morning light flooded in from the two windows they hadn't bothered closing the shutters on before they'd tumbled into bed the night before. From here she could see the green of the landscape which spread far into the distance and, above it, the endless blue of the cloudless sky. It was the most perfect of mornings, following the most perfect of nights.

She hugged her arms around herself and gave

a wriggle of satisfaction. She'd never thought she could feel the way Matteo had made her feel. But the clock was ticking away and she needed to face reality. She couldn't keep pretending everything was wonderful just because they'd spent an amazing night together. He'd said he wanted to explore the possibility of them becoming a couple but there was more to being a couple than amazing sex. How could they keep ignoring the gaping hole at the centre of their relationship which neither of them had addressed? He for reasons unknown and she...

She turned her attention from the distraction of the view to the dark head which lay sleeping beside her. Was she too scared to ask him, was that it?

Because the most important thing was all out of kilter and the longer it went on, the worse it seemed. Matteo acted as if Santino didn't exist. *As if he didn't have a son.* To her certain knowledge, he'd never even cuddled him—why, he'd barely even asked after him.

It didn't matter how many boxes the Italian ticked—she could never subject Santino to a life in which he was overlooked. And trying to compensate for his father's lack of regard with her own fierce love wouldn't work. She'd grown up in a house where she had been regarded as an imposition and no way was she going to impose that on her darling son.

Which left her with two choices. She could carry on being an ostrich and ignore what was happening—or rather, what wasn't happening. Or she could address the subject when Matteo woke and make him talk about it. She wouldn't accuse him or judge him. Whatever he told her, she would try to understand—because something told her that was very important.

Quietly, she slipped from the bed and went to the bathroom and when she returned with brushed teeth and hair, Matteo was awake—his black gaze following her as she walked back towards the bed.

'Morning,' she said shyly.

'Is this the point where I ask whether you slept well and you lower your eyelids and say, *not really*?' he murmured.

Blushing like a schoolgirl, Keira slipped rapidly beneath the covers so that her naked body was no longer in the spotlight of that disturbingly erotic stare. It was all very well being uninhibited when the room was in darkness but the bright morning light was making her feel awfully vulnerable. Especially as she sensed that Matteo wasn't going to like what she had to say, no matter how carefully she asked the question. He drew her into his arms but she gave him only the briefest of kisses before pulling her lips away. Because he needed to hear this, and the sooner, the better.

'Matteo,' she said, rubbing the tip of her finger over the shadowed angle of his jaw.

His brows knitted together. 'Why does my heart sink when you say my name that way?' he questioned softly.

She swallowed. 'You know we have to go back to Umbria soon.'

'You think I'd forgotten? Which is why I suggest we don't waste any of the time we have left.'

He had begun to stroke a light thumb over one of her nipples and although it puckered obediently beneath his touch, Keira pushed his hand away. 'And we need to talk,' she said firmly.

'And that was why my heart sank,' he drawled, shifting his body to lie against the bank of pillows and fixing her with a hooded look. 'Why do women always want to talk instead of making love?'

'Usually because something needs to be said.' She pulled in a breath. 'I want to tell you about when I was growing up.'

The look on his face said it all. Wrong place; wrong time. 'I met your aunt,' he said impatiently. 'Over-strict guardian, small house, jealous cousin. I get it. You didn't have such a great time.'

Keira shook her head as uncomfortable thoughts

flooded into her mind. She needed to be completely honest, else how could she expect complete honesty in return? Yet what she was about to tell him wasn't easy. She'd never told anyone the full story. Even her aunt. Especially her aunt. 'I told you my mother wasn't married and that I didn't know my father. What I didn't tell you was that she didn't know him either.'

His gaze was watchful now. 'What are you talking about?'

Keira flushed to the roots of her hair because she could remember her mother's shame when she'd finally blurted out the story, no longer able to evade the curious questions of her young daughter. Would her mother be appalled if she knew that Keira was now repeating the sorry tale, to a man with a trace of steel running through his veins?

'My mother was a student nurse,' she said slowly, 'who came to London and found it was nothing like the rural farm she'd grown up on in Ireland. She was quite shy and very naïve but she had those Irish looks. You know, black hair and blue eyes—'

'Like yours?' he interrupted softly.

She shook her head. 'Oh, no. She was much prettier than me. Men were always asking her out but usually she preferred to stay in the nurses' home and watch something on TV, until one night she gave in and went to a party with a group of the other nurses. It was a pretty wild party and not her kind of thing at all. People were getting wasted and Mum decided she didn't want to stay.' She swallowed. 'But by then it was too late because someone had…had…'

'Someone had what, Keira?' he questioned as her words became strangled and his voice was suddenly so gentle that it made her want to cry.

'Somebody spiked her drink,' she breathed, the words catching like sand in her throat because even now, they still had the power to repulse her. 'She…she woke up alone in a strange bed with a pain between her legs, and soon after that she discovered she was pregnant with me.'

He gave a terse exclamation and she thought he was going to turn away in disgust but to her surprise he reached out to push away the lock of hair which had fallen over her flushed cheeks, before slipping his hand round her shoulder and pulling her against the warmth of his chest. *'Bastardo,'* he swore softly and then repeated it, for added emphasis.

She shook her head and could feel the taste of tears nudging at the back of her throat and at last she gave into them, in a way she'd never done before. 'She didn't know how many men had been near her,' she sobbed. 'She had to go to the clinic to check she hadn't been given some sort of disease and of course they offered her...' She swallowed away the tears because she saw from the tightening of his jaw that she didn't actually need to spell it out for him. 'But she didn't want that. She wanted me,' she said simply. 'There wasn't a moment of doubt about that.'

He waited until she had composed herself before he spoke again, until she had brushed the remaining tears away with the tips of her fingers.

'Why are you telling me all this, Keira?' he questioned softly. 'And why now?'

'Because I grew up without a father and for me there was no other option—but I don't want the same for my baby. For... Santino.' Her voice wavered as she looked into the hardness of his eyes and forced herself to continue, even though the look on his face would have intimidated stronger people than her. 'Matteo, you don't...you don't seem to feel anything for your son.' She sucked in a deep breath. 'Why, you've barely *touched* him. It's as if you can't bear to go near him and I want to try to understand why.'

Matteo released his hold on her and his body tensed because she had no right to interrogate him, and he didn't *have* to answer her intrusive question. He could tell her to mind her own damned business and that he would interact with his son when he was good and ready and not according to *her* timetable. Just because she wanted to spill out stuff about her own past, didn't mean he had to do the same, did it? But in the depths of her eyes he could read a deep compassion and something in him told him there could be no going forward unless she understood what had made him the man he was.

He could feel a bitter taste coating his throat. Maybe everyone kept stuff hidden away inside them—the stuff which was truly painful. Perhaps it was nature's way of trying to protect you from revisiting places which were too dark to contemplate. 'My mother died in childbirth,' he said suddenly.

There was a disbelieving pause as the words sank in and when they did, her eyes widened. 'Oh, Matteo. That's terrible,' she whispered.

Matteo instantly produced the self-protective clause which enabled him to bat off unwanted sympathy if people *did* find out. 'What is it they say?' He shrugged. 'That you can't miss what you've never had. And I've had thirty-four years to get used to it.'

Her muffled 'But…' suggested she was about to disagree with him, but then she seemed to change her mind and said nothing. Leaving him free to utter the next words from his set-piece statement. 'Maternal death is thankfully rare,' he bit out. 'My mother was just one of the unlucky ones.'

'I'm so sorry.'

'Yes,' he said. 'I think we've established that.' He chose his words carefully. 'I've never come into contact with babies before. To be honest, I've never even held one, but you're right—it isn't just inexperience which makes me wary.' His jaw tightened. 'It's guilt.'

'Guilt?' she echoed, in surprise.

He swallowed and the words took a long time in coming. 'People say they feel instant love for their own child but that didn't happen to me when I looked at Santino for the first time. Oh, I checked his fingers and his toes and was relieved that he was healthy, but I didn't *feel* anything.' He punched his fist against his heart and the words fell from his lips, heavy as stones. 'And I don't know if I ever can.'

Keira nodded as she tried to evaluate what he'd told her. It all made sense now. It explained why he'd thrown a complete wobbly when she'd kept her pregnancy quiet. What if history had grimly repeated itself and she'd died in childbirth as his mother had done? Nobody had known who the father of her baby was because she'd kept it secret. Wasn't it possible that Santino could have been adopted by her aunt and her cousin and grown up without knowing anything of his roots?

She felt another wrench as she met the pain in his eyes. What must it have been like for him—this powerful man who had missed out on so much? He had never experienced a mother's love. Never even felt her arms hugging him in those vital hours of bonding which followed birth. Who had cradled the tiny Matteo as the cold corpse of his mother was prepared for her silent journey to the grave, instead of a joyous homecoming with her newborn baby? No wonder he'd been so reluctant to get close to his little boy—he didn't know *how*.

'Didn't your father make up for the fact that you didn't have a mother?'

His mouth twisted and he gave a hollow laugh. 'People cope in their own way—or they don't. He left my care to a series of young nannies, most of whom he apparently slept with—so then they'd leave—or the new stepmother would fire them. But it didn't seem to matter how much sex he had or how many women he married, he never really got over my mother's death. It left a hole in his life which nothing could ever fill.'

Keira couldn't take her eyes away from his ravaged face. Had his father unconsciously blamed his infant son for the tragic demise of his beloved wife—would that explain why they weren't close? And had Matteo been angry with his father for trying to replace her? She wondered if those different stepmothers had blamed the boy for being an ever-present reminder of a woman they could never compete with.

And blame was the last thing Matteo needed, Keira realised. Not then and certainly not now. He needed understanding—and love—though she wasn't sure he wanted either. Reaching out, she laid her hand on his bunched and tensed biceps but the muscle remained hard and stone-like beneath her fingers. Undeterred, she began to massage her fingertips against the unyielding flesh.

'So what do we do next, now we've brought all our ghosts into the daylight?' she questioned slowly. 'Where do we go from here, Matteo?'

His gaze was steady as he rolled away from her touch, as if reminding her that this was a decision which needed to be made without the distraction of the senses. 'That depends. Where do you want to go from here?'

She recognised he was being open to negotiation and on some deeper level she suspected that this wasn't usual for him in relationships.

Because this *was* a relationship, she realised. Somehow it had grown despite their wariness and private pain and the unpromising beginning. It had the potential to grow even more—but only if she had the courage to give him the affection he needed, without making any demands of her own in return. She couldn't *demand* that he learn to love his son, she could only pray that he would. Just as she couldn't demand that he learn to love *her.* 'I'll go anywhere,' she whispered. 'As long as it's with Santino. And you.'

She leaned forward to kiss him and Matteo could never remember being kissed like that before. A kiss not fuelled by sexual hunger but filled with the promise of something he didn't recognise, something which started his senses humming. He murmured something in objection when she pulled back a little, her eyes of *profondo blu* looking dark and serious, but at least when she wasn't kissing him he was able to think straight. He didn't understand the way she made him feel, but maybe that didn't matter.

Because weren't the successes of life—and business—based on gut feeling as much as understanding? Hadn't he sometimes bought a hotel site even though others in the business had told him he was crazy—and turned it into a glittering success because deep down he'd known he was onto a winner? And wasn't it a bit like that now?

'I will learn to interact with my son,' he said.

'That's a start,' she said hesitantly.

The look on her face suggested that his answer had fallen short of the ideal—but he was damned if he was going to promise to love his son. Because what if he failed to deliver? What if the ice around his heart was so deep and so frozen that nothing could ever penetrate it? 'And I want to marry you,' he said suddenly.

Now the look on her face had changed. He saw surprise there and perhaps the faint glimmer of delight, which was quickly replaced by one of suspicion, as if perhaps she had misheard him.

'Marry me?' she echoed softly.

He nodded. 'So that Santino will have the security you never had, even if our relationship doesn't last,' he said, his voice cool but certain. 'And so that he will be protected by my fortune, which one day he will inherit. Doesn't that make perfect sense to you?'

He could see her blinking furiously, as if she was trying very hard to hold back the glitter of disappointed tears, but then she seemed to pull it all together and nodded.

'Yes, I think marriage is probably the most sensible option in the circumstances,' she said.

'So you will be my wife?'

'Yes, I'll be your wife. But I'm only doing this for Santino. To give him the legitimacy I never had. You do understand that, don't you, Matteo?'

She fixed him with a defiant look, as if she didn't really care—and for a split second it occurred to him that neither of them were being completely honest. 'Of course I understand, *cara mia*,' he said softly.

CHAPTER ELEVEN

KEIRA HEARD FOOTSTEPS behind her and turned from the mirror to see Claudia in a pretty flowery dress, instead of the soft blue uniform she usually wore when she was working.

'Is everything okay with Santino?' Keira asked the nursery nurse immediately, more out of habit than fear because she'd been cradling him not an hour earlier as she had dressed her baby son in preparation for his parents' forthcoming marriage.

Claudia smiled. 'He is well, *signorina*. His father is playing with him now. He says he is teaching him simple words of Italian, which he is certain he will remember when eventually he starts to speak.'

Keira smiled, turning back to her reflection and forcing herself to make a final adjustment to her hair, even though she kept telling herself that her bridal outfit was pretty irrelevant on what was going to be a purely functional wedding day. But Matteo's father and stepmother were going to be attending the brief ceremony, so she felt she had to make *some* sort of effort. And surely if she did her best it might lessen their inevitable disbelief that he was going to marry someone like her.

'What kind of wedding would you like?' Matteo had asked during that drive back from Rome after she'd agreed to be his wife.

Keira remembered hedging her bets. 'You first.'

She remembered his cynical laugh, too.

'Something small. Unfussy. I'm not a big fan of weddings.'

So of course Keira had agreed that small and unfussy would be perfect, though deep down that hadn't been what she'd wanted at all. Maybe there was a part of every woman which wanted the whole works—the fuss and flowers and clouds of confetti. Or maybe that was just her—because marriage had always been held up as the perfect ideal when she'd been growing up. There had been that photo adorning her aunt's sideboard—the bouquet-clutching image which had stared out at her over the years. She recalled visiting for Sunday tea when her mother was still alive, when attention would be drawn to Aunt Ida's white dress and stiff veil. 'Wouldn't you have loved a white wedding, Bridie?' Ida used to sigh, and Keira's mother would say she didn't care for pomp and ceremony.

And Keira had thought she was the same—until she'd agreed to marry Matteo and been surprised by the stupid ache in her heart as she realised she must play down a wedding which wasn't really a wedding. It was a legal contract for the benefit of their son—not something inspired by love or devotion or a burning desire to want to spend the rest of your life with just one person, so it didn't really count. At least, not on Matteo's part.

And hers?

She smoothed down her jacket and sighed. Because even more disturbing than her sudden yearning to wear a long white dress and carry a fragrant bouquet was the realisation that her feelings for Matteo had started to change. Was that because she understood him a little better now? Because he'd given her a glimpse of the vulnerability and loss which lay beneath the steely exterior he presented to the world? Maybe. She told herself not to have unrealistic expectations. Not to wish for things which were never going to happen, but concentrate on being a good partner. To give Matteo affection in quiet and unobtrusive ways, so that maybe the hard ice around his heart might melt a little and let her in.

He was doing his best to change, she knew that. In the busy days which followed their return from his Roman villa, he had meticulously paid his son all the attention which had been lacking before. Sometimes he would go to Santino if he woke in the night—silencing Keira's sleepy protests with a kiss. Occasionally, he gave the baby a bottle and, once, had even changed his nappy, even though he'd protested that this was one task surely better undertaken by women.

But as Keira had watched him perform these fatherly duties she had been unable to blind herself to the truth. That it *was* simply a performance and Matteo was just going through the motions. He was being a good father, just as he was a good lover—because he was a man who excelled in whatever he did. But it was duty which motivated him. His heart wasn't in it, that much was obvious. And as long as she accepted that, then she'd be fine.

She turned away from the mirror, wondering if there was anything she'd forgotten to do. Matteo's father, Massimo, and his wife, Luciana, had arrived only a short while ago because the traffic from Rome had been bad. Since they were due at the town hall at noon, there had been little opportunity for Keira to exchange more than a few words of greeting and introduce them to their new grandson. She'd been nervous—of course she had—she suspected it was always nerve-racking meeting prospective in-laws, and most people didn't have to do it on the morning of the wedding itself.

Massimo was a bear of a man, his build bulkier than Matteo's, though Keira could see a likeness around the jet-dark eyes. Her prospective step-mother-in-law, Luciana, was an elegant woman in her fifties, who had clearly embraced every-thing facial surgery had to offer, which had re-sulted in a disturbingly youthful appearance.

Keira picked up her clutch bag and went down-stairs, her heart pounding with an anxiety which seemed to be increasing by the second. Was that because she'd seen Luciana's unmistakable look of disbelief when they'd been introduced? Was she wondering how this little Englishwoman from nowhere had wrested a proposal of mar-riage from the Italian tycoon?

But the expression on Matteo's face made Keira's stomach melt as she walked into the hallway, where everyone was waiting. She saw his eyes darken and the edges of his lips curve into an unmistakable smile of appreciation as he took her cold hand in his and kissed it.

'Sei bella, mia cara,' he had murmured softly. *'Molta bella.'*

Keira told herself he was only saying it because such praise was expected of the prospective groom, but she couldn't deny the feeling of satisfaction which rippled down her spine in response. Because she *wanted* him to look at her and find her beautiful, of course she did. She wasn't stupid and knew she couldn't take his desire for granted. Someone like her was always going to have to work to maintain it. Leola the stylist had been dispatched from Rome with a selection of wedding outfits and Keira had chosen the one she felt was the most flattering but also the most *appropriate*. Steadfastly pushing away the more floaty white concoctions, she had opted for functional rather than fairy tale. The silvery-grey material of the dress and jacket reminded her of a frosty winter morning but there was no doubt that it suited her dark hair and colouring. Only the turquoise shoes and matching clutch bag provided a splash of colour—because she had refused all Leola's inducements to carry flowers.

At least Massimo Valenti seemed enchanted by his grandson. Keira travelled in one of the cars with him to the nearly town and watched as he spent the entire journey cooing at the baby in delight. It made her wonder why he hadn't been close to his own son—but there was no time for questions because they were drawing up outside the town hall where Matteo was waiting to introduce her to the interpreter, which Italian law demanded.

Twenty minutes later she emerged from the building as a married woman and Matteo was pulling her into his arms, his hands resting on either side of her waist—but even that light touch was enough to make her want to dissolve with lust and longing.

'So. How does it feel to be Signora Valenti?' he questioned silkily.

Her heart was pounding as she stared up into the molten darkness of his eyes. 'Ask me again next week,' she said breathlessly. 'It feels a little unreal right now.'

'Maybe this will help you accept the reality,' he said, *'mia sposa.'*

And there, beneath the fluttering Italian flag of the town hall, his lips came down to claim hers with a kiss which left her in no doubt that he would rather they were somewhere private, preferably naked and horizontal. It set off an answering hunger and reminded Keira of the slightly incredible fact that he couldn't seem to get enough of her. Didn't he demonstrate that every night when he covered her trembling body with his own? And wasn't that *enough*? she wondered as they drove back to the farmhouse together, her golden ring glinting as she fussed around with Santino's delicate shawl. Was it just her inherently cautious nature which made her wonder if her relationship with Matteo was as superficial as the icing sugar sprinkled over the top of the chocolate wedding cake which Paola had baked?

Yet when he carried her over the threshold, it felt real. And when she returned from putting Santino down for a nap, having removed the silvery-grey jacket to reveal the filmy chiffon dress beneath, Matteo had been waiting in the shadowed hallway for her.

Pulling her into a quiet alcove, he placed his palm over her hammering heart and she licked her lips as her nipple automatically hardened beneath his touch.

'Ever wish you could just wave a magic wand and make everyone disappear?' he drawled.

She shivered as the light stroking of her nipple increased. 'Isn't that a little…anti-social?'

'I'm feeling anti-social,' he grumbled, his lips brushing over the curve of her jaw before moving upwards to tease her now trembling lips. 'I want to be alone with my new wife.'

Keira kissed him back as his words set off another whisper of hope inside her and she wondered if it was wrong to allow herself to hope, on this, her wedding day.

'You were the man who once told me about the benefits of waiting,' she teased him. 'Won't this allow you to test out your theory?'

Matteo laughed as she pulled away from him, the prim twitch of her lips contradicting the hunger in her eyes, and he shook his head slightly, wondering what kind of spell she had cast over him. He was used to the wiles of women yet Keira used none of them. She wasn't deliberately provocative around him and didn't possess that air of vanity of someone who revelled in her sexual power over a man. On the contrary, in public she was almost demure—while in private she was red-hot. And that pleased him, too. She pleased him and unsettled him in equal measure. She left him wanting more—but more of *what*, he didn't know. She was like a drink you took when your throat was dry yet when you'd finished it, you found that your thirst was just as intense.

He stroked his fingers down over her belly, his gaze steady as they stood hidden by the shadows of the staircase. Hard to believe that a child had grown beneath its almost-flat curve. 'I want you to know you are an amazing mother,' he said suddenly. 'And that Santino is blessed indeed.'

He saw the surprise behind the sudden brightness in her eyes, her mouth working as she struggled to contain herself.

'Don't make me get all emotional, Matteo,' she whispered. 'I've got to go in there and make conversation with your father and stepmother and I'm not going to make a very good impression if I've been blubbing.'

But he disregarded her soft plea, knowing he needed to express something which had slowly become a certainty. He owed her that, at least. 'I shouldn't have taken you to Rome when I did and made you leave the baby behind,' he admitted slowly. 'No matter how good the childcare we had in place. I can see now that it was a big ask for a relatively new mother in a strange country.'

He saw her teeth working into her bottom lip and he thought she might be about to cry, when suddenly she smiled and it was like the bright summer sun blazing all over him with warmth and light, even though outside it was cold and wintry.

'Thank you,' she said, a little shakily. 'I love you for saying that.'

He stilled. 'Really?'

A look of horror crossed her face as she realised what she'd said. 'I didn't mean—'

'Didn't you?' he murmured. 'How very disappointing.'

Keira told herself he was only teasing as he led her into the salon, but she felt as if she were floating on air as she took a grizzling Santino from Massimo's bear-like arms and rocked him dreamily against her chest. Had Matteo really just admitted he'd been in the wrong by taking her to Rome and told her she was a good mother? It wasn't so much the admission itself, more the fact he was beginning to accept that each and every one of them got it wrong sometimes—and that felt like a major breakthrough.

And had she really just let her guard down enough to tell him she loved him? It hadn't been in a dramatic way or because she'd expected an instant reciprocal response. She'd said it affectionately and Matteo needed that, she reckoned. How many times had he been told he'd been loved when he was growing up? Too few, she suspected.

Still high from the impact of their conversation, Keira refused the glass of vintage champagne which was offered and accepted a glass of some bittersweet orange drink instead.

But unusually, Santino grizzled in her arms and she wondered if it was the excitement of the day which was making him so fractious.

Discreetly, she slipped away to the nursery to feed and change him before rocking him until he was sound asleep and carefully putting him in his crib.

She picked up the empty bottle and was just on her way out when she was startled by the sight of Luciana, who suddenly appeared at the nursery door in a waft of expensive scent. Keira wondered if she'd wandered into the wrong room or if she'd been hoping for a cuddle with Santino. But there was an odd smile on her new stepmother's face and, for some reason, whispers of trepidation began to slide over Keira's spine.

'Is everything okay, Luciana?' she questioned, hoping she sounded suitably deferential towards the older woman.

Luciana shrugged. 'That depends what you mean by *okay*. I was a little disappointed that my son and his family were not invited to the ceremony today.'

'Oh, well—you can see how it is.' Keira gave a nervous smile, because Matteo had hinted that there was no love lost between him and his step-brother, Emilio. 'We just wanted a very small wedding.'

'*Sì.*' Luciana picked up a silver-framed photo of Santino and began to study it. 'And naturally, it would have been very *difficult* for Emilio.'

'Difficult?'

Luciana put the photograph down. 'In the circumstances.'

Keira blinked. 'What circumstances?'

Elegantly plucked eyebrows were raised. 'Because of the clause in my husband's will, of course.'

Keira's heart began to pound as some nameless dread crept over her. 'What clause?'

'Surely Matteo has told you?' Luciana looked surprised. 'Though perhaps not. He has always been a man who gives very little away.' Her expression became sly. 'You are aware that this house belonged to Massimo's first wife?'

'To Matteo's mother?' questioned Keira stiffly. 'Yes, I knew that. It's where she was born and where she grew up. It's one of the reasons he loves it so much.'

Luciana shrugged. 'Ever since Matteo reached the age of eighteen, Massimo has generously allowed his son to use the estate as his own. To all intents and purposes, this *was* Matteo's home.' She paused. 'But a strange thing happens to men as they grow older. They want to leave something of themselves behind.' Her surgically enhanced eyes gleamed. 'I'm talking, of course, about continuing the Valenti name. I am already a grandmother. I understand these desires.'

Keira's head was spinning. 'I honestly don't understand what you're getting at, Luciana.'

'Ah, I can see you know nothing of this.' Luciana gave a hard smile. 'It's very simple. He loves this house for obvious reasons, but he does not *own* it. And Massimo told him he intended bequeathing the entire estate to his stepson, unless Matteo produced an heir of his own with the Valenti name.' She shrugged her bony shoulders. 'I wondered if he would be prepared to sacrifice his freedom for an heir, not least because he has always shown a certain…*disdain* for women. And yet here you are—a pretty little English girl who arrived with a baby in her arms and got a wedding ring for her troubles. The perfect solution to all Matteo's problems!'

'You're saying that…that Matteo would have lost this house unless he produced an heir?'

'That's exactly what I'm saying. His gain, my son's loss.' Luciana shrugged. *'C'est la vie.'*

Keira felt so shocked that for a moment her limbs felt as if they were completely weightless. With a shaking hand, she put the empty bottle down on a shelf and swallowed, trying to compose herself—and knowing that she had to get away from Luciana's toxic company before she did or said something she regretted. 'Please excuse me,' she said. 'But I must get back to the wedding party.'

Did she imagine the look of disappointment which flickered across Luciana's face, or did she just imagine it? It didn't matter. She was going to get through this day with her dignity intact. Matteo had married her to get his hands on this property, so let him enjoy his brief victory. What good would come of making a scene on her wedding day?

Somehow she got through the rest of the afternoon, meeting Matteo's questioning stare with a brittle smile across the dining table, while everyone except her tucked into the lavish wedding breakfast. Did he sense that all was not well, and was that the reason why his black gaze seemed fixed on her face?

She was relieved when finally Massimo and Luciana left—though her father-in-law gave her the most enormous hug, which brought an unexpected lump to her throat. Leaving Matteo to dismiss Paola and the rest of the staff, Keira hurried to tend to Santino, spending far longer than necessary as she settled her baby son for the night.

At last she left the nursery and went into the bedroom but her hands were clammy as she pulled off her wedding outfit and flung it over a chair. Spurred on by Leola, she had been planning on surprising Matteo with the shortest dress she'd ever worn. A bottom-skimming dress for his eyes and no one else's. She'd wanted to wear it in anticipation of the appreciative look on his face when he saw it and to hint at a final farewell to her residual tomboy. But now she tugged on a functional pair of jeans and a sweater because she couldn't bear the thought of dressing up—not when Matteo's motives for marrying her were making her feel so *ugly* inside.

Although she would have liked nothing better than to creep into bed on her own and pull the duvet over her head to blot out the world, she knew that wasn't an option. There was only one acceptable course of action which lay open to her, but she couldn't deny her feeling of dread as she walked into the room which overlooked the garden at the back of the house, where Matteo stood beside the fire, looking impossibly handsome in his charcoal wedding suit. Don't touch me, she prayed silently, even though her body desperately wanted him to do just that—and maybe something had alerted him to her conflicted mood because his eyes narrowed and he made no attempt to approach her.

His face was sombre as he regarded her. 'Something is wrong.'

It was a statement, not a question, but Keira didn't answer straight away. She allowed herself a few more seconds before everything changed for ever. A final few seconds where she could pretend they were newly-weds about to embark on a shared life together. 'You could say that. I had a very interesting conversation with Luciana earlier.' She inhaled deeply and then suddenly the words came spilling out, like corrosive acid leaking from a car battery. 'Why didn't you tell me you were only marrying me to get your hands on an inheritance?' she demanded. 'And that this house would only become yours if you produced a legitimate child? I would have understood, if only you'd had the guts to tell me.'

He didn't flinch. His gaze was hard and steady. 'Because the inheritance became irrelevant. I married you because I care for you and my son and because I want us to make a future together.'

Keira wanted to believe him. The child-woman who had yearned for a long white dress and big bouquet of flowers longed for it to be the truth. But she couldn't believe him—it was a stretch too far. Once she'd thought he sounded like someone reading from a script when he'd been addressing a subject which would make most people emotional—and he was doing it again now.

I care for you and my son.

He sounded like a robot intoning the correct response, not someone speaking from the heart. And his lack of emotion wasn't the point, was it? She'd known about that from the start. She'd known the reason he was made that way and, filled with hope and with trust, had been prepared to make allowances for it. She bit her lip. When all the time he'd been plotting away and using her as a pawn in his desire to get his hands on this estate.

'I understand that you're known as an elusive man who doesn't give anything away,' she accused shakily. 'But how many more people are going to come out of the woodwork and tell me things about you that I didn't know? Can you imagine how it made me feel to hear that from Luciana, Matteo? To know you'd been buttering me up to get me to marry you? I thought… I thought you were doing it for your son's future, when all the time it was because you didn't want to lose a piece of land you thought of as rightfully yours! You don't want a family—not really—you've just used me as some kind of incubator!'

'But there's a fundamental flaw in your argument,' he grated. 'If inheriting the estate meant so much to me, then why hadn't I fathered a child with someone else long before I met you?'

'Because I don't think you really like women,' she said slowly. 'Or maybe you just don't understand them. You never knew your mother and she died so tragically that it's inevitable you idealised her. She would have had flaws, just like we all do—only you never got to see them. No woman could ever have lived up to her and maybe that's one of the reasons why you never settled down.' She sucked in a deep breath. 'And then I came along and took the decision away from you. A stolen night, which was never meant to be any more, suddenly produced an heir. You didn't have to go through the whole tedious ritual of courting a woman you didn't care for in order to get yourself a child. Fate played right into your hands, didn't it, Matteo? Suddenly you had everything you needed, without any real effort on your part.'

His face blanched. 'You think I am so utterly ruthless?'

She shrugged. 'I don't know,' she said, and there was a crack in her voice. 'Maybe you do care—a little. Or as much as you ever can. But you're missing the point. I thought growing up without a father was difficult, but at least I knew where I stood. It may have been grim at times but it was honest and you haven't been honest with me.' She swallowed. 'It feels like I'm in the shadows of your life—like someone in the wings watching the action on stage. I see the way you are with the baby—and with me—and it comes over as a performance, not real. How could it be, when Santino and I were only ever a means to an end?'

Matteo flinched as he met the accusation in her eyes, because nobody had ever spoken quite so candidly to him. 'For someone so tiny, you certainly don't pull any punches, do you, Keira?'

'What's the point in pulling punches? All we have left is the truth,' she said wearily. 'You've got what you wanted, Matteo. We're married now and your son has been legitimised. You have continued the Valenti name and will therefore inherit the estate. You don't need me any more.'

Matteo felt his chest tighten and his instinct

was to tell her that she was right—and that he *didn't* need anyone. He'd spent his whole life not needing anyone because there had been nobody there to lean on, nobody to get close to—why change that pattern now? But some unknown emotion was nudging at his conscience as something deep inside him told him this was different.

'And what if I say I do need you?' he said hoarsely as he attempted to articulate the confusion of thoughts which were spinning around inside his head.

Her eyes widened, but he could see a wariness in their depths of *profondo blu*. 'You do?' she queried uncertainly.

The moment it took for her to ask the question was all Matteo needed to shift things into perspective, because he knew he mustn't offer her false promises or false hope. She deserved more than that. So stick to the facts, he urged himself grimly. You're good with facts. Allow her to consider all the advantages of remaining here, as his wife.

'Of course,' he said. 'And logistically it makes perfect sense.'

'Logistically?' she echoed, her voice a little faint.

'Sure.' He shrugged. 'If we're all living together under one roof as a family, it will be much better for Santino. Better than having a father who just jets in and sees him on high days and holidays.'

'There is that, of course,' she said woodenly.

'And I've married you now, Keira,' he said softly. 'I have given you the security of bearing my name and wearing my ring. Your future is assured. You don't need to worry about money ever again.'

'You think that's what it's all about?' she questioned, her voice trembling. 'Money?'

'Not all of it, no—but a big part of it. And we have plenty of other reasons to keep our marriage going.' He curved her a slow smile. 'What about the sexual chemistry which exists between us? That fact that you are the hottest woman I've ever had in my bed?'

She gasped as if she had been winded before staring at him—as if she were looking at someone she'd never seen before. 'You just don't get it, do you, Matteo? You list all the reasons I should stay with you and yet you haven't mentioned anything which really *matters*!'

He flinched with pain as he met the undiluted anger in her gaze, but at the same time a strange sense of relief washed over him as he realised that he no longer had to try. She was going and taking their child with him and he would just have to learn how to deal with that. And anyway, he thought grimly—why would he want to prolong a relationship when it could hurt like this? Hadn't he vowed never to let anyone hurt him, ever again?

'Okay, I get it. What do you want?'

With an effort he held up the palms of his hands, in silent submission, and the sudden wobble of her lips made him think she might be about to backtrack—maybe to soften the blows which she'd just rained on him, but all she said was, 'I'd like us to separate.'

He told himself it was better this way. Better to go back to the life he was used to and be the person he knew how to be, rather than chase after the glimmer of gold which Keira Ryan had brought shimmering into his life.

'Tell me what you want, in practical terms,' he said flatly.

He could see her throat constricting as she nodded.

'I'd like to return to London as soon as possible and to rent somewhere before I decide to buy,' she said, before sucking in a deep breath. 'But I want you to know that I'll take only what is necessary for our needs and you're not to worry. I don't intend to make a great hole in your wealth, Matteo.'

And even that got to him, because he couldn't even level the charge of greed against her. She wasn't interested in his money, he realised, and she never had been. She'd taken the cash he'd thoughtlessly left beside the bed and had given it away to charity. She'd fought like mad against him buying her a fancy wardrobe. She was a jewel of a woman, he realised—a bright and shining jewel. But it was too late for them. The cold, pinched look on her beautiful face told him that. So let her go, he told himself. Set her free. At least you can give her that.

'That can all be arranged,' he said. 'But in turn, I need your reassurance that I can continue to see my son.'

There was surprise on her face now and he wondered if secretly she had expected him to cut all ties with his own flesh and blood.

'Of course. You can see as much of Santino as you wish,' she said quietly. 'I will never deny you your son, Matteo, and I hope you will see him very often, because he...he needs you. You're his daddy.'

A lump rose in his throat as he moved away from the blaze of the fire.

'I'd like to say goodnight to him now,' he said and she nodded and made as if to follow him.

'Alone,' he gritted out.

But Matteo's heart was heavy as he walked towards the nursery—as if a dark stone had lodged itself deep inside his chest. The night light made the room appear soft and rosy and Matteo stared down at the sleeping child. He remembered the first time he had seen him. When he had counted his fingers and toes like someone learning basic mathematics, and had felt nothing.

But not this time.

This time he could barely make out any detail of his sleeping son, his vision was so blurred. Too late, his heart had cracked open and left room for emotion to come flooding in, powerfully and painfully. And Santino stirred as Matteo's tears fell like rain onto the delicate white shawl.

CHAPTER TWELVE

IT WAS RAINING by the time Keira got back from her walk and she had just let Charlie off his lead when she noticed the letter lying in the centre of the hall table, where Claudia must have left it. She pulled a face. Another one.

The envelope carried an Italian stamp and the airmail sticker seemed to wink at her. Quickly, she slid it into a drawer to lie on top of all the others, because she couldn't quite bring herself to throw them away. Her reluctance to dispose of the growing pile of correspondence was just about equal to her reluctance to read them, because they were from Matteo—she recognised his handwriting. And why would she wish to read them and risk making the hole in her heart even bigger? Why was he even *writing* to her when she'd told him it was better if all correspondence took place between their respective solicitors? Why had he arrogantly elected to take no notice?

Because she was fighting like crazy not to go under. Not to give into the tears which pricked at her eyes at night when she lay in bed missing the warm embrace of her estranged husband. She was determined to pour all her energies into being there for Santino—into being the best mother she possibly could—and she couldn't manage that if her heart stayed raw and aching from thinking about Matteo all the time.

She'd wondered whether his determination to keep in close contact with his son would have faded once she and Santino had left Umbria but to her surprise, it hadn't. He'd already paid two visits and they'd only been back in England a little over a fortnight. On both those occasions she had absented herself from the house, leaving Claudia in charge of the baby—Claudia who had been happy to accompany her from Umbria when Keira had made the emotional return to her homeland.

She supposed people might think it a form of cowardice that she couldn't bear the thought of confronting the man with whom she hadn't even shared a wedding night. But that was too bad. It didn't matter what anyone else thought, only what was right for her and her son. Sooner or later she hoped she'd be able to greet him with a genuine air of indifference but for now she didn't trust herself not to burst into noisy howls of sorrow and to tell him how much she was missing him.

With the money he'd settled on her, she was renting a house. A house with a garden and a front door which wasn't shared—the kind of house in Notting Hill where she used to drop off her prep-school charges when she was working at Luxury Limos. And she'd bought a dog, too. A scruffy little thing with a lopsided ear and the saddest eyes she'd ever seen. The staff at the rescue centre had told her he'd been badly beaten and was fearful and shy, but he had taken one look at Keira and hurled himself at her with a series of plaintive yelps. Charlie was the best thing to have happened to them since they'd returned to England and had reinforced her intention to give Santino a proper childhood. The kind she'd never had—with a dog and a mother who was always waiting for him when he got home from school.

Pulling off her rain-soaked coat, she went upstairs to the nursery where Claudia was just putting Santino down to sleep. The nursery nurse straightened up as Keira entered the room and she found herself wondering why Claudia's cheeks were so pink. Walking over to the crib, Keira stared down into the sleepy eyes of her son, her heart turning over with love.

'He looks happy,' she murmured as she leaned over to plant a soft kiss on his silken cheek.

'He should be!' said Claudia. 'After you took him out for such a long walk this morning.'

'Good thing I did. At least we missed the rain,'

said Keira, with an idle glance out of the window as she drew the curtains.

There was a pause. 'Would you mind if I went out earlier than planned?' asked Claudia.

'Of course I don't mind.' Keira smiled because she knew that Claudia had struck up a close friendship with a man she'd met at the Italian Embassy. 'Hot date?'

Claudia smiled as she put her forefinger over her lips and Keira was so preoccupied with tidying up the nursery that she barely registered the nursery nurse leaving the room, though she did hear the distant bang of the front door. She turned the light out and was just about to make her way downstairs when her mobile phone began to ring and she pulled it from the pocket of her jeans, frowning when she saw Matteo's name flashing up on the screen.

Fury began to bubble up inside her. She'd asked him not to write and he had ignored that. She'd asked him not to call her and he was ignoring that too! So why now, coming straight after yet another unwanted letter from him? She clicked the connection.

'This had better be urgent,' she said.

'It is.'

She frowned as she registered a curious echo-like quality to his voice. 'And?'

'I need to see you.'

She needed to see him too, but no good would come of it. Wouldn't it make her hunger for what she could never have and certainly didn't need—a man who had lured a woman into marriage just because he wanted to inherit a house? 'I thought we'd decided that wasn't a good idea.'

'No, Keira...*you* decided.'

Still that curious echo. Keira frowned. Shouldn't she just agree to see him once and get it over with? Steel her heart against her own foolish desires and listen to what he had to say? 'Very well,' she said. 'We'll put an appointment in the diary.'

'Now,' he bit out.

'What do you mean...*now*?'

'I want to see you now,' he growled.

'Matteo, you're in Italy and I'm in England and unless you've discovered the secret of teleportation, that's not going to happen.'

'I'm downstairs.'

She froze. '*What* did you say?'

'I'm downstairs.' The echo began to get louder. 'Coming up.'

Her heart slamming against her ribcage, Keira rushed from the nursery to see Matteo with his mobile phone held against his ear, making his way up the stairs towards her. His face was more serious than she'd ever seen it as he cut the connection and slid the phone into the pocket of his jeans.

'Hi,' he said, the casual greeting failing to hide the tension and the pain which were written across his ravaged features.

She wanted to do several things all at once. To drum her fists against his powerful chest, over and over again. And she wanted to pull his darkly handsome face to hers and kiss him until there was no breath left in her body.

'What are you doing here?' she demanded.

'I need to speak to you.'

'Did you have to go about it so dramatically? You scared me half to death!' She looked at him suspiciously. 'You don't have a key, do you?'

'I don't,' he agreed.

'So how did you get in?'

'Claudia let me in before she left.'

'Claudia let you in?' she repeated furiously. 'Why would she do something like that?'

'Because I asked her to.'

'And what you say goes, I suppose, because you're the one with the money,' she said contemptuously.

'No.' He sucked in a ragged breath. 'I'm the one with the broken heart.'

It was such an unbelievable thing for him to say that Keira assumed she'd misheard him, and she was too busy deciding that they needed to move out of Santino's earshot in case they woke him to pay very much attention to her husband's words. 'You'd better come with me,' she said.

Matteo followed the denim-covered sway of her bottom as they went downstairs, watching her long black ponytail swinging against her back with every determined stride she took. Her body language wasn't looking promising and neither was her attitude. But what had he expected—that she would squeal with delight when she saw him again? Welcome him into the embrace he had so missed—as if that whole great betrayal had never happened? His throat thickened. He had tried playing it slow and playing by her rules but he'd realised she would be prepared to push him away for ever if he let her.

And he couldn't afford to let her.

They reached a beautiful, high-ceilinged sitting room dominated by a tall Christmas tree, which glittered in front of one of the tall windows. Fragrant and green, it was covered with lights and tiny stars and on the top stood an angel with gossamer-fine wings. A heap of presents with ribbons and bows stood at the base of the giant conifer and Matteo thought it looked so homely. And yet he wasn't connected to any of it, was he? He was still the outsider. The motherless boy who had never really felt part of Christmas.

So what are you going to do about it, Valenti? he asked himself as she turned to face him and they stood looking at one another like two combatants.

'You wanted to talk,' she said, without preamble. 'So talk. Why did you sneak into my house like this?'

'You've been ignoring my letters.'

She nodded and the glossy black ponytail danced around her shoulders. 'I told you I wanted to keep all written communication between our respective solicitors.'

'You really think that my lawyer wants to hear that I love you?' he demanded, his breath a low hiss.

Her lips opened and he thought she might be about to gasp, before she closed them again firmly, like an oyster shell clamping tightly shut.

'And that I miss you more than I ever thought possible?' he continued heatedly. 'Or that my life feels empty without you?'

'Don't waste my time with your lies, Matteo.'

'They aren't lies,' he said unevenly. 'They're the truth.'

'I don't believe you.'

'I didn't think you would.' He sucked in a deep breath. 'Which is why I wrote you the letters.'

'The letters,' she repeated blankly.

'I know you got them, because I asked Claudia. What did you do with them, Keira—did you throw them away? Set light to them and watch them go up in flames?'

She shook her head. 'No. I didn't do that. I have them all.'

'Then, I wonder, could you possibly fetch them?'

Was it the word 'fetch' which brought Charlie bounding into the room, his tail wagging furiously and his once sad eyes bright and curious as he looked up at the strange man? Keira glared as she saw Matteo crouch down and offer his hand to the little dog, furious yet somehow un-surprised when the terrier edged cautiously to-wards him. The shock of seeing Matteo again had shaken her and weakened her defences, making her realise that she was still fundamen-tally shaky around him—and so she nodded her agreement to his bizarre request. At least leav-ing the room and his disturbing presence would give her the chance to compose herself and to quieten the fierce hammering of her heart.

Slowly she walked into the hallway to retrieve the pile of envelopes from the drawer and went back into the sitting room, holding them gingerly between her fingers, like an unexploded bomb. By now Charlie's tail was thrashing wildly, and as Matteo straightened up from stroking him the puppy gave a little whine of protest and she wondered how he had so quickly managed to charm the shy little dog. But the terrier had been discovered wriggling in a sack by the side of the road, she remembered, the only survivor among all his dead brothers and sisters. Charlie had also grown up without a mother, she thought—and a lump lodged in her throat.

'Here,' she croaked, holding the letters towards him.

'Don't you want to open them?' he said.

She shook her head. 'Not really.'

'Then maybe I'd better tell you what's in them,' he said, his eyes not leaving her face as he took them from her. 'They are all love letters. With the exception of one.'

He saw her eyes widen before dark lashes came shuttering down to cloak their sapphire hue with suspicion.

'What's that? A hate letter?' she quipped.

'I'm serious, Keira.'

'And so am I. Anyone can write down words on a piece of paper and not mean them.'

'Then how about I summarise them for you out loud?'

'No.'

But that one word was so whispered that he barely heard it and Matteo had no intention of heeding it anyway. 'Four words, actually,' he husked. 'I love you, Keira. So how about I say it again, just so there can be no misunderstanding? I love you, Keira, and I've been a fool. *Uno scemo!* I should have been honest with you from the start, but...' He inhaled deeply through his nostrils and then expelled the air on a shuddered breath. 'Keeping things locked away inside was the way I operated. The only way I knew. But believe me when I tell you that by the time I asked you to marry me, I wasn't thinking about the house any more. My mind was full of you. It still is. I can't stop thinking about you and I don't want to. So I'm asking you to give me another chance, Keira. To give *us* another chance. You, me and Santino. That's all.'

She didn't say anything for a moment and when she spoke she started shaking her head, as if what he was demanding of her was impossible.

'That's *all*?' she breathed. 'After everything

that's happened? You don't know what you're asking, Matteo.'

'Oh, but I do,' he demurred. 'I'm asking you to be my wife for real. With nothing but total honesty between us from now on, because I want that. I want that more than anything.' His voice lowered. 'But I realise it can only work if you love me too. Once, in a shadowed hallway after we had taken our wedding vows, you whispered to me that you did, but you may not have meant it.'

Keira clamped her lips together to try to contain the stupid tremble of emotion. Of course she had meant it. Every single word. The question was whether he did, too. Was it possible that he really loved her, or was this simply a means to an end—the manipulative declaration of a man determined to get his rightful heir back into his life? Or maybe just pride refusing to let a woman walk away from him.

Yet something was stubbornly refusing to allow her to accept the bleaker version of his reasons for coming here today. Was it the anguish she could see in his black eyes—so profound that even she, in her insecurity, didn't believe she was imagining it? She flicked the tip of her tongue over her mouth, wondering if it was too late for them, until she realised what the reality of that would mean. Matteo gone from her life and free to make another with someone else, while she would never be able to forget him.

And she wasn't going to allow that to happen. Because how could she ignore the burning inside her heart and the bright spark of hope which was beginning to flood through her veins?

'I've tried not to love you,' she admitted slowly. 'But it doesn't work. I think about you nearly all the time and I miss you. I love you, Matteo, and I will be your wife, but on one condition.'

His body grew very still. 'Anything,' he said. 'Name it.'

She had been about to ask him never knowingly to hurt her, but she realised that was all part of the package. That hurt and pain were the price you paid for love and you just had to pray they didn't rear their bitter heads too often in a lifetime. She knew also that if they wanted to go forward, then they had to leave the bitterness of the past behind. So instead of demanding the impossible, she touched her fingertips to his face, tracing them slowly down over his cheek until they came to rest on his beautiful lips.

'That you make love to me,' she said, her voice softened by tears of joy. 'And convince me this really is happening.'

His voice was unsteady. 'You mean, right now?'

She swallowed and nodded, rapidly wiping underneath her eyes with a bent finger. 'This very second,' she gulped.

Framing her face within the palms of his hands, he looked at her for one long moment before he spoke. 'To the woman who has given me everything, because without you I am nothing. *Ti amo, mia sposa.* My beautiful, beautiful wife,' he husked, and crushed his lips down hard on hers.

EPILOGUE

OUTSIDE THE WINDOW big white flakes floated down from the sky, adding to the dazzling carpet which had already covered the vast sweep of lawn. Keira gazed at it and gave a dreamy sigh. It was unusual for snow to settle in this part of Umbria and she thought she'd never seen anything quite so magical, or so beautiful. She smiled. Well, except maybe one other time...

Looking up from where she was crouched beside the Christmas tree where she'd just placed a couple of presents, she saw Matteo walk into the room—with snowflakes melting against his dark hair. He'd been outside, putting the finishing touches to a snowman, which would be the first thing Santino saw when he looked out of his window tomorrow morning. Their son's first real Christmas, Keira thought, because last year he'd been too young to realise what was going on and she...

Well, if she was being honest, she could hardly remember last Christmas herself. She and Matteo had been busy discovering each other all over again—and finding out that things were different from how they'd been before. They couldn't have been anything *but* different once the constraints of the past were lifted and they'd given themselves the freedom to say exactly what was on their minds. Or in their hearts.

Matteo had given her the option of living in London, Rome or Umbria—and she'd opted for the sprawling Umbrian estate which had once belonged to his mother's family. She figured it was healthier for Santino to grow up in the glorious Italian countryside, especially now that they had acquired a beautiful black cat named Luca who, against all odds, had become a devoted companion to Charlie the terrier.

But it was more than that. This estate was Matteo's link with his roots. It represented continuity and stability—something which had been lacking in both their lives until now. One day Santino might listen to the call of his forebears and decide he didn't want to be a businessman, like his daddy. He might want to grow up and farm the fertile acres of this beautiful place. A place which might so nearly have disappeared from the family.

Because Keira had discovered that the very first letter Matteo had sent during their separation contained estate agent details marketing the property. He'd put it up for sale to demonstrate that the house meant nothing, if he didn't have her. They had quickly aborted the prospective sale, despite the frantic bidding war which had been taking place at the time. And had decided to make the estate their permanent home.

'What are you smiling at?' questioned Matteo softly as he walked over to the Christmas tree and pulled her to her feet.

Her contented expression didn't change. 'Do I

need a reason?' She sighed. 'I'm just so happy, Matteo. Happier than I ever thought possible.'

'Well, isn't that a coincidence? Because I feel exactly the same way,' he said, his fingers beginning to massage her shoulders, their practised caress never failing to arouse her. 'Have I told you lately that I love you, Mrs Valenti?'

She pretended to frown. 'I think you might have mentioned it before you went out to build Santino's snowman. And just for the record, I love you, too. So very much.'

He bent his head and kissed her, deeply and passionately and it was some time before she broke off to graze her lips against the dark stubble of his angled jaw.

'Did you speak to your father?' she said.

'I did. And he's looking forward to Christmas lunch tomorrow. He says he'll be here soon after eleven and is bringing his new girlfriend.' His eyes gleamed down at her. 'And that we should prepare ourselves for what he calls a *significant* age gap.'

Keira giggled as she rested her head on Matteo's shoulder. Massimo had divorced Luciana in the spring and although Keira had tried to feel sad about it, she just couldn't. Not only had the older woman been a troublemaker—it transpired that she'd been unfaithful to her husband as well. And one night, soon after the decree nisi had come through and Matteo had been away on business, Keira and her father-in-law had dined together in Rome. He'd told her it wasn't a desire to manipulate which had made him threaten to disinherit Matteo if he didn't produce an heir— but concern that his son was becoming emotionally remote and would end up a rich and lonely old man.

'And then you stepped in and saved him and made him happy. Truly happy—and I cannot thank you enough for that, Keira,' he had whispered, his voice cracking a little. 'I know I wasn't a good father when he was growing up.' He had fallen silent for a moment and his eyes had grown reflective. 'I missed his mother so much and he…well, he looked so much like her, that sometimes it was painful to be around him.'

'Have you told him that, Massimo?' she had said quietly, pressing her hand over his across the table. 'Because I think you should.'

And he had. Keira closed her eyes, remembering the long overdue heart-to-heart between father and son, and the growing closeness of their relationship which had resulted.

Her mind flicked back to the present as Matteo began to caress her bottom, murmuring his appreciation that these days she almost always wore a dress. She liked wearing dresses, although she could still resurrect her inner tomboy when needed—and she suspected she was going to need to do that a lot if Santino played as much football as Matteo intended he should. 'Would you like part of your Christmas present tonight?' she whispered, snuggling up to him.

He pulled away to look at her and raised his eyebrows. 'Is that an offer I shouldn't refuse?'

'Put it this way—I'm wearing it underneath

this dress and I need you to unwrap it for me. Matteo!' She giggled as he began to lead her towards the bedroom. 'I didn't mean *now*—I meant later.'

'Too bad,' he murmured, not lessening his pace by a fraction. 'Because I have something for you which can't wait.'

Actually, that wasn't quite true—he had two things for her. The first was sitting in the garage wrapped in a giant red bow ready to be untied on Christmas morning. A neglected Ferrari 1948 Spider sports car which he'd tracked down with great difficulty and at considerable expense, because she'd once told him it was her dream to restore beautiful vintage cars—and Matteo was rather partial to making his wife's dreams come true.

The second gift was rather different and he didn't give it to her until after he'd dealt with her outrageous panty thong with its matching boned bodice, which he damaged beyond repair in his eagerness to unhook it. And once he had her naked, he was distracted for quite some time…

His throat thickened with unexpected emotion as he pulled the small box from his discarded trousers and flipped open the lid to reveal a flawless white solitaire which sparkled like a giant star against dark velvet.

'What's this?' she questioned breathlessly, from among the sheets which were rumpled around her.

He lifted her left hand and slid the solitaire in place above her wedding band. 'I never gave you an engagement ring, did I? And I didn't give you a dream wedding either. A civil ceremony in a town hall was never something we were going to enjoy telling our grandchildren about.' He lifted her hand to his lips and kissed her fingertips. 'So I wondered if you'd like to renew our vows in my favourite church in Rome. You could wear a big white dress and do it properly this time, and we could throw a party afterwards. Or not—whichever you prefer. What I'm asking is, would you like to marry me again, Keira Valenti?'

Keira opened her mouth to say that she didn't care about pomp or ceremony, but that wasn't quite true. And weren't she and Matteo all about the truth, these days? She thought about something else, too, something which had been niggling away at her for a while now. Because weddings could bring people together and heal old wounds, couldn't they? Motherhood had changed her. Softened her. She realised now that her aunt might have been strict when she was growing up, but she'd given an orphaned little girl the home she'd badly needed and had stopped her from being taken into care. And didn't she owe her aunt Ida a great deal for that? Wasn't it time to invite her and Shelley to Italy, to share in her good fortune and happiness and to introduce Santino to some of *her* roots?

She wound her arms around Matteo's neck and looked into his beautiful black eyes, her heart turning over with emotion. 'Yes, Matteo,' she said breathlessly. 'I'll be proud to marry you. To stand before our family and friends and say the thing I'll never tire of saying, which is that I love you—and I'll love you for the rest of my life.'

* * * * *

LET'S TALK
Romance

For exclusive extracts, competitions and special offers, find us online:

f facebook.com/millsandboon

◎ @millsandboonuk

🐦 @millsandboon

Or get in touch on 0844 844 1351*

For all the latest titles coming soon, visit millsandboon.co.uk/nextmonth

*Calls cost 7p per minute plus your phone company's price per minute access charge